ENDURING
Legacies

TIMBERLINE BOOKS

Stephen J. Leonard and Thomas J. Noel, editors

The Beast, Benjamin Barr Lindsey with Harvey J. O'Higgins

Colorado's Japanese Americans, Bill Hosokawa

Denver: An Archaeological History, Sarah M. Nelson, K. Lynn Berry, Richard F. Carrillo, Bonnie L. Clark, Lori E. Rhodes, and Dean Saitta

Dr. Charles David Spivak: A Jewish Immigrant and the American Tuberculosis Movement, Jeanne E. Abrams

Enduring Legacies: Ethnic Histories and Cultures of Colorado, edited by Arturo J. Aldama, Elisa Facio, Daryl Maeda, and Reiland Rabaka

The Gospel of Progressivism: Moral Reform and Labor War in Colorado, 1900–1930, R. Todd Laugen

Ores to Metals: The Rocky Mountain Smelting Industry, James E. Fell, Jr.

A Tenderfoot in Colorado, R. B. Townshend

The Trail of Gold and Silver: Mining in Colorado, 1859–2009, Duane A. Smith

ENDURING
Legacies

Ethnic Histories and Cultures of Colorado

EDITED BY
ARTURO ALDAMA

ELISA FACIO,
DARYL MAEDA,
AND
REILAND RABAKA,
ASSOCIATE EDITORS

UNIVERSITY PRESS OF COLORADO

© 2011 by the University Press of Colorado

Published by the University Press of Colorado
245 Century Circle, Suite 202
Louisville, Colorado 80027

All rights reserved

 The University Press of Colorado is a proud member of
the Association of University Presses.

The University Press of Colorado is a cooperative publishing enterprise supported, in part, by Adams State University, Colorado State University, Fort Lewis College, Metropolitan State University of Denver, University of Colorado, University of Northern Colorado, University of Wyoming, Utah State University, and Western Colorado University.

Library of Congress Cataloging-in-Publication Data

Enduring legacies : ethnic histories and cultures of Colorado / edited by Arturo J. Aldama . . . [et al.].
  p. cm. — (Timberline books)
  Includes bibliographical references and index.
  ISBN 978-1-60732-049-4 (hardcover : alk. paper) — ISBN 978-1-60732-050-0 (pbk. : alk. paper) — ISBN 978-1-60732-051-7 (e-book)
  1. Ethnohistory—Colorado. 2. Colorado—Ethnic relations—History. 3. Colorado—Population—History. 4. Hispanic Americans—Colorado—History. 5. Indians of North America—Colorado—History. 6. African Americans—Colorado—History. 7. Asian Americans—Colorado—History. I. Aldama, Arturo J., 1964–
  F785.A1E64 2011
  305.8009788—dc22

2010044293

Design by Daniel Pratt

The University Press of Colorado gratefully acknowledges subventions from the Eugene M. Kayden Fund and the Center for Studies of Ethnicity and Race in America (CSERA) at the University of Colorado at Boulder in partial support of the costs of production on this volume.

Contents

List of Figures | ix

Foreword | xi

Acknowledgments | xv

Editors' Introduction: Where Is the Color in the Colorado Borderlands? | 1
Arturo J. Aldama, Elisa Facio, Daryl Maeda, and Reiland Rabaka

PART I: EARLY STRUGGLES

1. Pictorial Narratives of San Luis, Colorado: Legacy, Place, and Politics | 23
   Suzanne P. MacAulay

2. Santiago and San Acacio, Foundational Legends of Conquest and Deliverance: New Mexico, 1599, and Colorado, 1853 | 35
   Enrique R. Lamadrid

3. Music of Colorado and New Mexico's Río Grande | 51
   Lorenzo A. Trujillo

4. Representations of Nineteenth-Century Chinese Prostitutes and Chinese Sexuality in the American West | 69
   William Wei

5. Religious Architecture in Colorado's San Luis Valley | 87
   Phillip Gallegos

6. Dearfield, Colorado: Black Farming Success in the Jim Crow Era | 101
   George H. Junne Jr., Osita Ofoaku, Rhonda Corman, and Rob Reinsvold

PART II: PRE-1960S COLORADO

7. Racism, Resistance, and Repression: The Creation of Denver Gangs, 1924–1950 | 121
   Robert J. Durán

8. The Influence of Marcus Mosiah and Amy Jacques Garvey: On the Rise of Garveyism in Colorado | 139
   Ronald J. Stephens

9. "A Quiet Campaign of Education": Equal Rights at the University of Colorado, 1930–1941 | 159
   David M. Hays

10. Journey to Boulder: The Japanese American Instructors at the Navy Japanese Language School, 1942–1946 | 175
    Jessica N. Arntson

11. "So They Say": Lieutenant Earl W. Mann's World War II *Colorado Statesman* Columns | 195
    William M. King

12. Latina Education and Life in Rural Southern Colorado, 1920–1945 | 219
    Bernadette Garcia-Galvez

PART III: CONTEMPORARY ISSUES

13. Recruitment, Rejection, and Reaction: Colorado Chicanos in the Twentieth Century | 239
    David A. Sandoval

14. "Ay Que Lindo es Colorado": Chicana Musical Performance from the Colorado Borderlands | 257
    Peter J. Garcia

15. When Geronimo Was Asked Who He Was, He Replied, I am an Apache | 273
    Helen Girón

16. Institutionalizing *Curanderismo* in Colorado's Community Mental Health System | 291
    Ramon Del Castillo

17. Finding Courage: The Story of the Struggle to Retire the Adams State "Indian" | **309**
    Matthew Jenkins

18. Pedagogical Practices of Liberation in Abelardo "Lalo" Delgado's Movement Poetry | **327**
    Miriam Bornstein-Gómez

19. (Re)constructing Chicana *Movimiento* Narratives at CU Boulder, 1968–1974 | **347**
    Elisa Facio

20. Running the Gauntlet: Francisco "Kiko" Martínez and the Colorado Martyrs | **365**
    Adriana Nieto

21. Toward a Critical Theory of the African American West | **379**
    Reiland Rabaka

    List of Contributors | **401**

    Index | **407**

Figures

1.1. *El Milagro de San Acacio,* embroidery by Josephine Lobato, 1992 | **26**
1.2. *La Sierra,* embroidery by Josephine Lobato, 1999 | **27**
3.1. Photo of Karen Trujillo-Guzman | **53**
3.2. A piece available from Southwest Musicians: Musical Traditions of Colorado and New Mexico | **55**
3.3. Photo of the Marcha de los Novios taken at the August 2, 1972, wedding of Suzanne Rael and Derrick Martinez in Arroyo Seco, New Mexico | **56**
3.4. *La Entriega de los Novios,* music score | **58**
3.5. An indita learned from Arsenio Cordova of El Prado, New Mexico | **61**
3.6. Photo of Mariachi Vargas | **64**
5.1. San Luis / Taos Valley | **89**
5.2. San Luis / Taos Valley capillas | **92**
5.3. San Acacio reconstruction | **94**
5.4. San Rafael | **95**
5.5. Santo Niño | **96**
15.1. Elicia (Martinez) Girón and Tiburcio Girón, circa 1940s | **280**
15.2. Elicia (Martinez) Girón, age around ten, circa mid-1920s | **281**
15.3. Francisco Girón, July 7, 1938, to October 3, 1969 | **282**

Foreword

Enduring Legacies: Ethnic Histories and Cultures of Colorado is a welcome addition to the University Press of Colorado's Timberline series, which features meritorious books relating to Colorado.

Since its inception in 1965, the University Press of Colorado, a cooperative effort sponsored by most of the state's public universities and colleges, has given special attention to books focusing on Colorado and the West. During the past two decades it has published more works relating to people of African, Asian, Hispanic, and Native American heritage. Many have been used as texts or supplementary reading in ethnic studies and regional history courses.

Among the press's titles covering African Americans are Robert B. Betts's *In Search of York: The Slave Who Went to the Pacific with Lewis and Clark* (revised edition, 2002), Monroe Lee Billington and Roger D. Hardaway's edited volume *African Americans on the Western Frontier* (2001), Monroe Lee Billington's *New Mexico's Buffalo Soldiers, 1866–1900* (1994), Angel David Nieves and Leslie M. Alexander's edited volume *"We Shall Independent Be": African American Place-Making and the Struggle to Claim Space in the United States* (2008), and Nicholas Patler's *Jim Crow and the Wilson Administration: Protesting Federal Segregation in the Early Twentieth Century* (2004).

Chinese Americans provide the focus for two press books: Benson Tong's *The Chinese Americans, Revised Edition* (2003) and Liping Zhu's *A Chinaman's*

Chance: The Chinese on the Rocky Mountain Mining Frontier (2000). The late Bill Hosokawa graced the press with three books: *Out of the Frying Pan: Reflections of a Japanese American* (1998), *Nisei: The Quiet Americans, Revised Edition* (2002), and *Colorado's Japanese Americans: From 1886 to the Present* (2005).

In addition to its titles on Central America, Mexico, and New Mexico, the press has published several books on Hispanos, including Vincent C. de Baca's edited collection *La Gente: Hispano History and Life in Colorado* (1998), which offers contributions from José Aguayo, Ramon Del Castillo, Aileen Lucero, Deborah Mora-Espinosa, George Rivera Jr., M. Edmund Vallejo, Ernesto Vigil, and others on topics such as migrant workers and Rodolfo "Corky" Gonzales, founder of Denver's Crusade for Justice. Richard Gould's *The Life and Times of Richard Castro: Bridging a Cultural Divide* (2007) treats another major Colorado leader. Virginia McConnell Simmons's *The San Luis Valley: Land of the Six-Armed Cross, Second Edition* (1999) includes material on early Hispano settlements in southern Colorado.

More than a dozen press books on Native Americans remain in print. *The Arapaho Language* (2008) by Andrew Cowell and Alonzo Moss Sr. provides a much-needed dictionary of an endangered tongue. Arapaho heritage is also preserved in *Tell Me, Grandmother: Traditions, Stories, and Cultures of Arapaho People* (2004) by Virginia Sutter.

John H. Monnett's *The Battle of Beecher Island and the Indian War of 1867–1869* (1992) chronicles the Cheyenne's waning years in Colorado. One of the press's most lavishly illustrated books, *Cheyenne Dog Soldiers: A Ledgerbook History of Coups and Combat* (1997) by Jean Afton, David Fridtjof Halaas, Andrew E. Masich, and Richard N. Ellis, also treats the Cheyenne. Virginia McConnell Simmons tells of the Utes, the state's most deeply rooted people, in *The Ute Indians of Utah, Colorado, and New Mexico* (2001).

Other press books on Native Americans include Donald Fixico's *The Invasion of Indian Country in the Twentieth Century: American Capitalism and Tribal Natural Resources* (1998), Andrew Gulliford's *Sacred Objects and Sacred Places: Preserving Tribal Traditions* (2000), Stan Hoig's *White Man's Paper Trail: Grand Councils and Treaty-Making on the Central Plains* (2008), and Brian Hosmer and Colleen O'Neill's edited volume *Native Pathways: American Indian Culture and Economic Development in the Twentieth Century* (2004).

Broader works that include chapters and other material on Colorado's ethnic groups include Carl Abbott, Stephen J. Leonard, and Thomas J. Noel's *Colorado: A History of the Centennial State, Fourth Edition* (2005), particularly chapters 3, 11, and 19; Stephen J. Leonard and Thomas J. Noel's *Denver: Mining*

Camp to Metropolis (1991), chapters 16, 26, and 27; and Stephen J. Leonard's *Lynching in Colorado, 1859–1919* (2002), chapter 6.

Obviously, thanks in part to the University Press of Colorado and its authors, Colorado history has become far more inclusive than it was thirty years ago, when even the best textbooks were just beginning to pay adequate attention to African Americans, Asian Americans, and Hispanos.

Enduring Legacies advances ethnic studies by presenting recent scholarship on these ethnic groups. It demonstrates that ethnic studies, once an emerging academic area, has reached adulthood and is poised to make even more substantial contributions to the world of scholarship. In keeping with their long commitment to serving Colorado, the University Press of Colorado and its Timberline series are proud to count *Enduring Legacies* among its contributions to our understanding of all peoples of our state and region.

STEPHEN J. LEONARD
COEDITOR OF THE TIMBERLINE SERIES

Acknowledgments

This book project began during Dr. Arturo J. Aldama's final year as the director of the Center for the Study of Ethnicity and Race in America (CSERA), as a way to pay tribute to ethnic studies scholarship about the Colorado borderlands.

On behalf of the editors of *Enduring Legacies*, we acknowledge the College of Arts and Sciences at the University of Colorado at Boulder for the Eugene M. Kayden Award for new book projects in 2009. We thank the Office of Diversity, Equity, and Community Engagement (ODECE), at the University of Colorado at Boulder, for financial support of CSERA, specifically Dr. Christine Yoshinaga-Itano.

We also thank the wonderful students in the Department of Ethnic Studies (DES) who have helped out with our book, in particular Marissa Chaney-Manriquez, for her research assistance to Dr. Elisa Facio, and Amber Camus and Tiya Trent, for providing fresh critical eyes on the entire book. Also, heartfelt thanks to DES staff member Sandra Lane, for helping to paginate and organize the book. And thanks to Dr. Kenneth Orona, a former DES faculty, for his expertise in Chicano history and culture in southern Colorado.

And a final thank you to those we would like to acknowledge most, the families and communities of color in Colorado, whose struggles and legacies we try to honor with this book.

ENDURING
Legacies

Arturo J. Aldama, Elisa Facio, Daryl Maeda, and Reiland Rabaka

Editors' Introduction: Where Is the Color in the Colorado Borderlands?

A rich mosaic of histories and cultures converges within the borderlands of Colorado. Situated on what was the northernmost boundary of Mexico prior to the U.S.-Mexico War of 1846–1848, the state of Colorado forms part of what many scholars call the U.S.-Mexico Borderlands—a zone in which collisions structured by forces of race, nation, class, gender, and sexuality inevitably lead to the transformation of cultures and the emergence of new identities.[1] The impetus for this volume of scholarship arises, first, out of a deep and profound respect for the struggles of communities of color to forge or maintain a cultural and political space in the Colorado portion of the borderlands. Second, it comes from the need to honor scholarship that strives to tell the stories of communities of color in Colorado. These communities consist of the original denizens—Utes, Cheyenne, Arapahoe, Kiowa, and Apaches—displaced and sometimes massacred by the Anglo-American empire and expansionism. (Unfortunately, despite our best efforts, this volume does not address Native communities.)[2] They also consist of Colorado's Mexican, Hispano, and Chicano families and their complex mestizo (fusion of Spanish and Indian) identities as revealed through ritual, song, architecture, food, and dance. The book is also driven by the need to tell the stories of the arrival of African

American miners, cowboys, and "freedom" seekers in the "free towns" of northern Colorado; the hard work of Chinese miners and businesspeople; the sexual violence Chinese women endured, forced to function as "exotic" spectacles in the businesses of burlesque and prostitution; and the ways Japanese American families resisted their structural criminalization and forced incarceration during World War II.

Despite Colorado's remarkable ethnic, cultural, and racial diversity, the state's dominant narrative—expressed in museums, murals, and history tours—often reflects an Anglo-centric perspective that begins with the 1859 Pike's Peak Gold Rush and the establishment of statehood in 1876.[3] For example, the historical museum at the Arvada Center for the Arts and Humanities features the restored 144-year-old Haines log house. The museum extols the history, virtues, and struggles of European wheat farmers but overshadows the history of the original indigenous communities and Mexican families. This exhibit reifies a Eurocentric history that marginalizes the Cheyenne Arapahoe and later Mexican families as insignificant actors in Colorado's history. Similarly, the heavily trafficked Garden of the Gods visitor center in Colorado Springs focuses on the area's geology and the "discovery" of what is now called Pikes Peak but relegates the legacies of Colorado's indigenous and Mexican peoples to a few photos and objects on the lower level. As these examples show, Colorado's diversity has yet to be fully integrated into public histories of the state.

Enduring Legacies aims to complicate the study of Colorado's past and present by adopting a borderlands perspective that emphasizes the multiplicity of peoples who have inhabited its territory, the diversity of cultures they have practiced, and the various ways they have contended with racism. In doing so, this volume draws on an extensive corpus of borderlands scholarship that highlights the intersections of race, nation, culture, and power in the contact zone between what is now the United States and Mexico. This literature has impacted studies of states like California, Texas, Arizona, and New Mexico but has yet to be extended to considerations of Colorado.

Borderlands scholarship has affected fields such as American studies, ethnic studies, history, anthropology, literary studies, and Chicana and Chicano studies. Foundational texts include Américo Paredes's *"With His Pistol In His Hand": A Border Ballad and Its Hero* (1970), which charts unequal power relations in turn-of-the-century Texas through the story of Gregorio Cortez; Hector Calderón, José Saldívar, and Ramón Saldívar's anthology, *Criticism in the Borderlands: Studies in Chicano Literature, Culture, and Ideology* (1991), which brings post-structural theory to bear on borderlands literary and cultural productions; and Gloria Anzaldúa's widely influential *Borderlands/Frontera: The New Mestiza* (2nd edition, 1999), which is grounded in her family's history of dispossession in southern Texas and her struggle for mixed racial, as well as cultural and sexual, identities. Key historical studies include Rodolfo Acuña's *Occupied America: A History of Chicanos* (2009), which spans the borderlands history of the Southwest from before the U.S.-Mexico War to the present; and Vicki L. Ruiz's *From Out of the Shadows: Mexican Women in the 20th Century* (1999), which examines women leaders of Mexican descent in social struggles for equality, labor, and justice.

While the majority of U.S. and Mexico borderland studies have focused primarily on Mexican American histories, struggles for identity, and cultural survival, *Enduring Legacies* not only expands the geographic space of scholarly attention but also provides a comparative venue for examining Asian Americans and African Americans in the U.S. and Mexico borderlands. Their experiences are distinct, yet they overlap with those of Chicanas and Chicanos in terms of immigration, racism, and self-determination—as seen with Chinese miners, Chinese women forced into prostitution in Denver, Japanese American farmers, and Africans Americans fleeing the violence of slavery and Jim Crow codes. In presenting narratives of experience in a comparative frame that complicates Eurocentric narratives of Colorado history, *Enduring Legacies* continues the comparative analysis Tomás Almaguer pioneered in his highly regarded history of California, *Racial Fault Lines: The Historical Origins of White Supremacy in California* (2nd edition, 2008). It also dialogues with the New Western History, inaugurated with Patty Limerick's award-winning study *The Legacy of Conquest: The Unbroken Past of the American West* (1987), which portrays the West as a colonized space characterized by inescapable interracial contact and conflict.

While a growing number of scholarly monographs discuss specific communities of color in Colorado—including Japanese American, Utes, and Chicanos—this volume is the first to bring together comparative scholarship on historical and contemporary issues that span groups including Chicanas and Chicanos, African Americans, and Asian Americans.[4] The combined essays in this volume examine the histories of struggle, survival, and resistance shared by diverse peoples. Methodologically, the selections in this volume weave a rich interdisciplinary tapestry that draws from historical studies, educational history, literature, ethnographies, archival work, architecture, cultural anthropology, visual studies, legal studies, policy studies, and ethnomusicology.

The history of struggle by communities of color in Colorado includes Hispano families attempting to maintain their land grants after Mexico ceded much of the state to the United States through the Treaty of Guadalupe-Hidalgo (1848). More recent highlights include the civil rights struggles of Rodolfo "Corky" Gonzalez and the Crusade for Justice's fight for youth rights, equal access to higher education, and voting rights and against poverty, segregation, and police brutality;[5] the ongoing work of Colorado's AIM (American Indian Movement) to protest the annual Columbus Day Parade in Denver, which is linked to the struggle for human rights for all indigenous peoples; the battles for political empowerment of African American communities, from the Garvey-influenced "free towns" in northern Colorado to the Black Panthers in Denver; and the movements for equality mounted by Chinese and Japanese Americans in Colorado.

Despite our best efforts to secure essays on the history of American Indian nations and communities in Colorado, we were unable to obtain any chapters on the state's original denizens. It is our strongest hope that in the future, comparative volumes on the Colorado borderlands will include a strong body of interdisciplinary scholarship on Colorado's Ute, Comanche, Apache, Cheyenne-Arapahoe, and Kiowa communities, as well as studies of the urban Indian cultural centers in Denver and the pan-Indian communities throughout the state.

The book comprises three chronologically divided parts: Early Struggles, Pre-1960s Colorado, and Contemporary Issues. These parts show how Colorado's racial, ethnic, and cultural histories changed broadly over time. However, it is also important to understand the uniqueness of Asian American, African American, and Chicana and Chicano experiences. Thus, the subject-area introductions that follow discuss each ethnic/racial group across all the historical periods that divide the book. Each introduction includes a brief overview of the historical legacies, population demographics, and contemporary issues of one ethnic/racial community in the Colorado borderlands and then discusses how each particular chapter fills a scholarly lacuna. Both the chronological and ethnic/racial perspectives are necessary to comprehend the complexity of the tapestry of voices and community histories that make up Colorado's diverse ethno-cultural landscape.

ASIAN AMERICANS IN THE COLORADO BORDERLANDS

Asian Americans have a long and varied history in Colorado, dating to the time before it became the Centennial State. They have played key roles in developing Colorado's industries and agriculture, and an examination of their experiences reveals much about the state and its racial politics. The first Asian arrival in Colorado, recorded in 1869, was an anonymous Chinese immigrant known only by the generic epithet "John Chinaman."[6] As historian William Wei speculates, "John" was likely drawn to the United States as part of the wave of Chinese immigrants who initially sought riches in California's Gold Rush and later found work constructing the railroads. More Chinese were drawn by dreams of finding gold in Colorado, and by 1880 the state was home to 612, who worked mainly as laborers, placer miners, and laundrymen.[7] Although the Territorial Legislature initially welcomed the Chinese as a source of cheap labor, White workers in Colorado—as in the rest of the West—displayed virulent racism toward them. Anti-Chinese incidents ranging from threats and expulsions to mob violence occurred throughout the state, fueled by the yellow journalism of *The Rocky Mountain News*. The violence culminated in the Denver Riot of 1880, in which a crowd of 3,000 rampaged through "Hop Alley"—as the city's Chinatown was pejoratively known by outsiders—leaving businesses ransacked and burned, many Chinese injured, and one dead.[8]

The earliest Japanese arrived in Colorado between 1886 and 1888, but the first large wave of Japanese immigrants from the Pacific Coast states arrived between 1903 and 1908. They worked most commonly as laborers, railroad workers, miners, farmhands, factory workers, and domestics.[9] The state's Japanese population increased from a scant 48 in 1900 to around 2,300 in 1910 according to official census figures, which probably represented an undercount.[10] Japanese Coloradoans soon made agriculture a mainstay of their ethnic economy, farming in the Arkansas Valley, in the San Luis Valley, in western Colorado, and on the Front Range in communities such as Brighton, Fort Lupton, and Greeley. In 1909 an estimated 3,000 Japanese Americans worked the fields of Colorado, many as laborers on sugar beet farms north and east of Denver.[11] An urban community coalesced in Denver, where "Little Tokyo" featured Japanese restaurants, merchandise stores, small businesses, a laundry, barbershops, and several hotels; the area was home to over 800 residents who lived among Mexicans, African Americans, and assorted immigrants.[12]

Like the Chinese before them, the Japanese in Colorado were scorned as the "yellow peril," subjected to violence, and excluded from union membership.[13] *The Rocky Mountain News* and *The Denver Post* ran anti-Japanese stories and editorials beginning in 1901, and by 1908 the Colorado State Federation of Labor had formed a Japanese and Korean Exclusion League.[14] During World War II, Colorado was home to thousands of Japanese Americans expelled from the West Coast. During a brief period in which Japanese Americans could "voluntarily" relocate, a number headed for Colorado. Despite widespread anti-Japanese sentiment, Governor Ralph L. Carr welcomed them, stating, "They are as loyal to American institutions as you and I."[15] From 1942 to 1945, a concentration camp located in southeastern Colorado, known as the Granada Relocation Center (nicknamed Camp Amache), imprisoned over 7,500 Japanese Americans behind barbed wires.

After World War II, Colorado's Asian American population increased dramatically and diversified considerably in terms of ethnicity. Filipinos, Koreans, and Asian Indians began arriving in large numbers after 1965 as a result of the federal Immigration Reforms of 1965, which encouraged the entry of professionals into the United States. Vietnamese, Cambodian, Hmong, and other Southeast Asians migrated after the end of the Vietnam War in 1975 and the passage of a series of refugee resettlement acts. By 1980 Colorado's Asian/Pacific Islander population stood at 34,257, which represented 1.2 percent of the state's population.[16] The most recent decennial census (2000) reported that 95,213 Asian Americans lived in Colorado, making up 2.2 percent of the state's population, with major ethnic groups including Asian Indians, Chinese, Filipinos, Japanese, Koreans, Vietnamese, and "Others" (see Table I.1). When multiracial Asian Americans were included, the population rose to 120,779 (2.8% of the state's population).[17]

Table I.1. Colorado's Asian Population, 2000

Ethnic Group	Population	Percentage of State's Population
Asian Indian	11,720	0.3
Chinese	15,658	0.4
Filipino	8,941	0.2
Japanese	11,571	0.3
Korean	16,395	0.4
Vietnamese	15,457	0.4
Other Asian 1	15,471	0.4
Total	95,213	2.2

Source: 2000 Census.

Asian Americans in Colorado currently tend to be clustered in the Greater Denver metropolitan area. The vast majority reside in Arapahoe, Denver, Jefferson, Adams, Boulder, and Douglas counties, with substantial populations also in El Paso and Larimer counties. Businesses and ethnic institutions—vital components of flourishing Asian American communities—are concentrated in Sakura Square and the Alameda/Federal area of Denver and in Aurora. The poverty rate among Asians in Colorado was 10.7 percent in 2000, compared with 18.4 percent for Hispanics, 14.7 percent for African Americans, and 7.4 percent for Whites—although it ranged as high as 18.8 percent among Cambodians and 14.0 percent for Hmong.[18] The state's Asian American population continues to grow rapidly, both in terms of raw numbers and proportionate to the state's total population. According to the most recent estimate by the United States Census Bureau (dated July 1, 2006), Asians in Colorado numbered around 156,035, representing approximately 3.3 percent of the state's population and 1 percent of the national Asian American population.[19] As their presence grows, Asian Americans will undoubtedly play an increasing role in Colorado's culture, politics, and economy.

Several chapters in this collection shed new light on Asian Americans in Colorado by focusing on the roles they have played, both in the popular imagination and in building the state. In "Representations of Nineteenth-Century Chinese Prostitutes and Chinese Sexuality in the American West," William Wei explores how mainstream antagonism toward Chinese immigrants was frequently expressed through depictions of aberrant Chinese sexuality, particularly by sensationalizing prostitution. Although Chinese were never numerous in Colorado, they were targets of hatred and violence, including the Denver Riot of 1880, which left Chinatown devastated and one Chinese American dead. Furthermore, they were the subjects of an extensive campaign of yellow journalism that portrayed them as exotic and lawless, representations that Wei shows continue to resonate in current cinema.

While Wei examines the racialization and sexualization of Asian Americans' bodies, Jessica Arntson's chapter, "Journey to Boulder," recounts the lost history of Japanese Americans who made vital contributions to building the state and its institutions. Arnotson examines the Japanese American instructors at the Navy Japanese Language School in Boulder, Colorado. During World War II, this remarkable group of individuals, although branded as less than American by their nation, nevertheless provided an invaluable service to the U.S. war effort. They and their families made concerted efforts to demonstrate their loyalty to the United States, and a public relations campaign conducted by university, military, and city officials smoothed initial resistance to their presence in Boulder. As Arntson shows, not only did the Japanese American language instructors aid the war effort by training interpreters, translators, and interrogators, but their efforts were highly influential in building U.S.-Japan understanding in the postwar years.

Arntson's focus on the University of Colorado pairs well with David M. Hays's essay, which shows that the struggle for equality had to be waged even in the putatively liberal college town of Boulder. His narrative of a civil rights campaign at the University of Colorado and the surrounding community highlights the complex alliance between Black, Japanese American, and Jewish students and their White allies, including students, faculty, and administrators. In examining this grassroots movement, Hays demonstrates that civil rights have long been more than simply a Black and White issue, that the American West was a complicated political terrain, and that movements for equality occurred long before the 1960s.

AFRICAN AMERICANS IN THE AMERICAN WEST

African Americans migrated to the West in the late nineteenth and early twentieth centuries because, according to historian Quintard Taylor, it represented their "last best hope" to escape racial oppression and economic exploitation in the South, the Northeast, and the Midwest.[20] Colorado was second only to California in terms of Black migration to the West during this pivotal period. Perhaps surprisingly, during and after the Civil War, African Americans were welcomed by the early White settlers of the free territory and, ultimately, the state of Colorado in ways Native Americans and Asian immigrants were not.[21] Our colleague and one of the contributors to this volume, William King, has elsewhere written that during this period "Whites viewed Blacks as superior to the Chinese and Native Americans who were believed to be heathens or savages because of the strange languages and unfamiliar cultures. Blacks were treated less harshly than either the Italian or Chinese populations."[22] Yet what African Americans found in the West was not *their* "American Dream" but rather a dream that was, in the weighted words of Langston Hughes, "deferred."[23] While none of the western states participated in slavery, each eventually developed its own brand of anti-Black racism.[24] As historian Roger Hardaway emphasizes, African Americans' efforts to integrate were often unwelcome, and they "usually settled together—in parts of existing cities, in all-Black towns, and in agricultural colonies."[25] Colorado proved not to be the "promised land" of freedom, but conditions in the state were still better than those in the East and the South.

According to the census data, no African Americans were residing in the territory of Colorado in 1850. The African American population grew from 46 of a total population of 34,277 in 1860 to 456 of a total population of 39,221 in 1870. Between 1870 and 1900, Colorado's African American population ballooned from 456 to 8,570.[26] Not all African Americans who immigrated to Colorado during the post-Reconstruction period settled in its two top urban areas, Denver and Pueblo. Because many were farmers, ranchers, and miners, they gravitated toward Colorado's high plains and parched prairies. At the turn of the twentieth century, 5,236 African Americans lived in cities, while 3,334 resided in rural areas.[27]

African Americans in Colorado enjoyed better educational and occupational opportunities than their counterparts in other parts of the country. Statistics on African American literacy levels indicate that Black children received an education comparable to that of White children in urban areas of Colorado after the turn of the twentieth century.[28] From their humble beginnings as cowboys and buffalo soldiers in the mid-nineteenth century, African Americans went on to engage in occupations ranging from farmers and field hands to entrepreneurs and entertainers, from doctors and lawyers to politicians and police officers. These opportunities led to a nearly twentyfold increase in the African American population in Colorado, from 8,570 in 1900 to 165,063 in 2000.[29] The booming businesses in the Denver metropolitan area and the military bases in Colorado Springs were major draws for African Americans coming to Colorado, who contributed to almost every major episode in African American history: from the Black Women's Club Movement and the Harlem Renaissance to the Civil Rights and Black Power movements.[30]

The chapters on Black experiences in this volume fill a scholarly void in African American studies, which has tended to focus chiefly on the South and on urban areas on the East and West coasts but rarely on the Rocky Mountain and Southwest regions.[31] In "Dearfield, Colorado," George Junne and his coauthors reconstruct the lost history of Colorado's premier Black settlement and explain why African Americans found the state attractive despite the presence of white supremacist organizations. Citing the impact of Booker T. Washington and Marcus Garvey on the settlement, Junne and colleagues suggest that Dearfield could potentially serve as a model for contemporary Black liberation, self-determination, and self-reliance. Like Junne and his coauthors, Ronald Stephens argues that Garveyism was an important presence in Colorado. In "The Influence of Marcus Mosiah and Amy Jacques Garvey on the Rise of Garveyism in Colorado," he highlights African Americans' search for a "homeland" in an American West that was also home to groups such as the Ku Klux Klan. Furthermore, he shows how Coloradoans reinvented Garveyism to make it address the particular needs of Blacks in the American West.

William King's "'So They Say': Lieutenant Earl W. Mann's World War II *Colorado Statesman* Columns" examines an underappreciated Black legislator (who served in the Colorado House of Representatives from 1943 to 1954), civic leader, and newspaper columnist. King shows that Mann's advocacy for African

Americans extended to other disenfranchised groups in Colorado, including Japanese Americans, as well as the physically and mentally challenged. While admitting that we may not agree with Mann's stances in every instance, King contends that he deserves wider recognition and critical reappraisal.

In "Toward a Critical Theory of the African American West," Reiland Rabaka provides a broad overview of the history, nature, and tasks of theory in African American (and the emerging Africana) studies. The express intent is to demonstrate that African American studies has matured to the point where it can shift (albeit not completely) from grand or macro-narratives preoccupied with the national African American experience to micro-narratives focused on regional or local African American experiences. Although more and more micro-narratives are being produced in African American studies, many of these works are marred by their often uncritical reliance on Eurocentric and white supremacist perspectives and theories. This chapter puts forward a critical theory of the African American West, which highlights the wide range and wide reach not simply of the African American experience in the West but also of the theories and research methods African American studies (among other) scholars and students employ to critically engage African Americans and their distinct history, culture, and contributions to the American West.

FROM HISPANOS TO CHICANAS AND CHICANOS

People of Mexican ancestry have occupied the Colorado borderlands since the seventeenth century. This chapter uses the terms "Hispano" and "Chicana/Chicano" to refer to people of Mexican ancestry. Families of Mexican origin called themselves Hispanos for hundreds of years; even today, many families in northern New Mexico and southern Colorado who have multi-generational lineages in the same area continue to use that terminology, as do many people who grew up prior to the 1960s. During the Civil Rights Movement of the 1960s, the term "Chicano" became a cultural and political proclamation used to denote ethnic pride, working-class consciousness, and a reference to the indigenous roots of Mexican ancestry.[32] The early Hispano settlers in what was northern New Mexico and is now southern Colorado were subjects first of the Spanish Crown and later of Mexico, after it gained independence in 1821. Between 1833 and 1843, the governor of New Mexico gave immense land grants that covered thousands of miles and are now entire counties in the state of Colorado to encourage families to move north, farm, herd their sheep, and continue the cultural and religious traditions of their ancestors. Some of the largest land grants include the Conejos, Sangre de Cristo, Baca, and Vigil, among others. Many Hispano families moved from the Taos area to the

San Luis area and created an agriculturally and culturally rich communal way of life. Anglo-Americans and even Canadians were also encouraged to settle these land grants, which covered 8 million acres in southern Colorado.[33]

A common saying among Chicanos who have multi-generational family histories in southern Colorado, New Mexico, and other parts of the Southwest (Texas, California, and Arizona) is "We did not cross the border. The border crossed us." Indeed, the Treaty of Guadalupe-Hidalgo, which formally ended the U.S.-Mexico War of 1846–1848, resulted in Mexico ceding its Northern Territories to the United States in exchange for $15 million. The treaty guaranteed that land rights, religious and cultural customs, and the Mexicans' Spanish language were to be respected and that the new Mexican Americans were to be afforded the full rights of U.S. citizenship and the protections of the United States Constitution. However, from the 1850s to the early 1900s, most Mexican-owned land in what is now the Southwest was lost to newly arrived Euro-American businessmen and families through litigation, force, coercion, sale, intermarriage, and squatters rights. Thus, as historian David Gutierrez argues, "[T]he ethnic Mexican population of the region was slowly but surely relegated to an inferior, caste-like status in the region's evolving social system."[34]

The Hispano population of what is now Colorado is difficult to determine with precision. In the seventeenth and eighteenth centuries, their numbers were small. However, the mid-nineteenth century experienced a huge population growth, particularly in the San Luis Valley. The authors of *Colorado: A History of the Centennial State* argue that "The Spanish-speaking population along the upper Rio Grande experienced a minor population explosion in the early nineteenth century. Perhaps 16,000–20,000 strong in the 1790s, they totaled nearly 60,000 by 1850."[35]

Since statehood, Hispanas and Hispanos have been the largest non-Anglo/Euro-American group in Colorado. The decennial U.S. census has proven to be an inconsistent measure of Hispano demographics (or "Hispanics," to use the U.S. Census Bureau's terminology), in part because Hispanics were counted as White until the 1940s. The 1940 census counted 92,549 Hispanic-origin residents; by 1970 their numbers had increased to 255,994 and by 1990 to 424,302. In 2000 there were 735,601 Hispanic or Latino residents in Colorado, almost 18 percent of the state's total population. Around 450,760 of these Latinos were of Mexican origin. In 2007 the Latino portion of Colorado's population increased to 19.5 percent. Colorado's demographics reflect the national numbers, as Latinos make up the largest group of residents of the United States after non-Hispanic Whites. The U.S. Census Bureau estimated on July 1, 2006, that 44.3 million residents of the United States were of Hispanic descent, representing 15 percent of the national population; 65 percent of these Latino residents were of Mexican origin. Colorado currently has the eighth-largest Hispanic population of any U.S. state.

Hispano culture reflects the racial and cultural *mestizaje* (mixture) or hybridity of Spanish colonial cultures, languages, and mores with indigenous (Pueblo, Apache, Navajo, and Ute, among others) customs in food, architecture, religious practices, clothing, and worldviews. Southern Colorado, especially the San Luis Valley, represents a core of the Hispano-Mexicano legacy in its architecture, ethnic makeup, food, language, customs, and rural lifestyle, even though many former residents have left this once thriving agricultural and cultural center for jobs in the cities. Several chapters in this book discuss the Hispano and mestizo legacies of the early period in terms of the visual arts, music, and architecture.

In "Pictorial Narratives of San Luis, Colorado: Legacy, Place and Politics," Suzanne P. MacAulay argues that contemporary visual and material culture reflects the historical legacies of Hispano communities in San Luis by examining how embroidery narratives and murals reflect a communal archive of the Mexican and mestiza/o (mixed race) denizens of San Luis. Her chapter considers how the layering of history, ancestral legacies, and cultural values is reflected in Hispano-Chicano public folk art practices.

Continuing Macaulay's discussion into the foundational myths of miracles in Santiago and San Acacio, folklorist Enrique Lamadrid discusses the history of mestizaje and conflict among the Utes, Pueblos, Spanish, and mixed race Hispanos in "Santiago and San Acacio, Foundational Legends of Conquest and Deliverance: New Mexico, 1599, and Colorado, 1853." The chapter "The Music of Colorado and New Mexico's Río Grande" by Lorenzo A. Trujillo, assistant dean of the Law School at the University of Colorado, Boulder, and a member of one of Colorado's best-known Chicano musical families, charts the historical legacy of music as a cultural text and its synchrony of historical identity and cultural survival. Trujillo provides a fascinating description of the historical evolution of Río Grande Chicano/Hispano music and dance in Colorado and New Mexico, dating from the medieval period (1100–1400) to the early 1900s and to contemporary Chicano musical practices of the Colorado borderlands. Architectural scholar Phillip Gallegos continues the discussion of cultural mixing in "Religious Architecture in Colorado's San Luis Valley." He argues that church architecture reveals mestizaje and shows how studying the material culture of buildings can provide a sense of the values, cultural legacies, and worldviews of the Mexican settlers who arrived in Colorado during the 1800s.

The next group of chapters addresses racial stratification, criminalization, exploitation, and resistance in rural and urban contexts. David Sandoval documents how Hispano communities struggled against race and class oppression in the early twentieth century, noting that racism toward Colorado's Mexican population and their relegation to harsh working conditions in the agricultural and railroad industries caused many Mexicans to question their racial ethnic heritage and identity. But in response to the psychic trauma of self-doubt or internalized racism, a number of *mutualista* societies (community self-help organizations) arose to protect the civil rights and cultural heritage of Mexican people.

"Latina Education and Life in Rural Southern Colorado, 1920–1945" by Bernadette Garcia Galvez recovers the voices of Hispanas (Chicanas, in more engaged and current nomenclature) in the historically and culturally important but overlooked Huerfano County. Her chapter looks at the ways race, class, and gender intersected to prevent women of Mexican or mestiza descent from taking full advantage of educational opportunities, regardless of their talent or motivation. By examining these women's sense of agency, Garcia provides witness to the testimony of mestiza lives that challenge offensive stereotypes of Mexican indolence and disdain toward education.

To address issues of racialization, urban segregation, police violence, and the pervasiveness of the Ku Klux Klan in Colorado politics and in Denver's daily life, Robert Durán's "Racism, Resistance, and Repression: The Creation of Denver Gangs, 1924–1950" provides a compelling look at the criminalization of Chicana/o youth. While much scholarship and attention has been paid to the 1942–1943 Zootsuit Riots and the criminalization of zootsuiters in California,[36] this is the first major chapter that discusses zootsuiters, *pachucos*, and *pachucas* in Colorado.

Helen Girón's autobiographical essay, "When Geronimo Was Asked Who He Was, He Replied, I am an Apache," reflects the confluence of indigenous and Chicana/Chicano peoples in Colorado's urban environs. Her Apache family's removal from the reservation and insertion into an urban assimilation program resulted in Girón growing up among Chicanas and Chicanos and developing a bimodal political consciousness with Chicana/o and urban Indian issues. While the intention of the 1953 Termination Act was to motivate Indian peoples— in her case the Apaches—to leave the reservation, assimilate into a White American culture, and live the "American Dream," Girón assimilated more readily into Chicana/o culture because of her skin color, shared issues of poverty, racism, and geographic proximity. As an Apache woman, she maintains and celebrates her Apache identity and challenges other Chicana/os to recognize their indigenous identities, which are sometimes subsumed by over-identification with Spanish and Hispano heritages.

Colorado gained national prominence for its central and defining role in the Chicano Civil Rights Movement in the 1960s–1970s. Through the multifaceted struggles of the Crusade for Justice, led by the charismatic Rodolfo "Corky" Gonzalez and his extended family and close friends, programs dedicated to implementing social justice in the educational system, labor, housing, health, and the arts were implemented to contribute to the political and cultural well-being of Chicanos and all oppressed peoples in Colorado.[37] For example, the Denver Youth Leadership Conference gathered young Chicanas and Chicanos from all over the United States to affirm their cultural values, histories, languages, and indigenous legacies in ways that mirrored Black Panther and the American Indian Movement's calls for education, self- and community empowerment, and community self-determination.

The next group of chapters examines histories, cultures, and politics in Colorado from the Civil Rights Era to the present. "(Re)constructing Chicana *Movimiento* Narratives at CU Boulder, 1968–1978" by Elisa Facio seeks to fill an important lacuna on Chicana political organizing by recovering the herstory of activism at CU Boulder. This chapter highlights the crucial and often overlooked roles Chicana students played in political and community leadership, paying particular attention to how Chicanas engaged in community struggles not only at the university but also in urban contexts, including the Crusade for Justice's Denver Youth Leadership Conference, and in rural contexts such as the land grant struggles in New Mexico and farmworker struggles throughout the Southwest. Similarly, Adriana Nieto's chapter resuscitates the historical memory of Chicano lawyer Francisco "Kiko" Martínez, who fought against police brutality and hate crimes and for free speech and prisoners' rights. Labeled an overzealous crusading attorney, he became the subject of racial intimidation and COINTELPRO-style tactics for his defense of the Chicano Movement in Colorado. Nieto argues that this important lawyer should be better recognized as a pioneer of Chicano activism.

Like frontline activists and grassroots organizers, social service agencies also sought to improve the physical and mental well-being of Coloradoans of color. Ramon Del Castillo's chapter considers how Southwest Denver Community Mental Health, a full-service agency directed by certified psychiatrists, decided to hire a prominent *curandera*, Diana Velazquez, to supplement its allopathic regimens with health *remedios* (remedies) grounded in the indigenous legacies of Chicana/o peoples.

Colorado is also a space/place of incredible cultural richness in terms of music, literature, theater, dance, and art. Several chapters in this volume pay tribute to particular musicians and poets and discuss how music can express Hispano-Chicano historical legacies in the state and how literary arts can intertwine with community-based struggles for civil rights and social justice. For example, "Pedagogical Practices of Liberation in Abelardo 'Lalo' Delgado's Movement Poetry" provides a conceptual framework of Chicano Movement Poetry by deploying Paulo Freire's concept of critical pedagogy. It considers how Lalo Delgado, one of Colorado's most prominent and beloved cultural workers, created a poetic discourse that exposed the impact of oppressive cultural forces on Chicanas and Chicanos in the Southwest.

Peter Garcia's *"Ay Que Lindo es Colorado"* is a case study of a popular Chicana singer, Michelle Lobato. Lobato's music resonates with the Chicana/Chicano cultural renaissance of the 1970s, wherein musicians, dancers, thespians, poets, and other artists committed to reclaiming the Spanish language and relearning and reinventing long-standing cultural traditions and the arts. Garcia looks at the ways Lobato's performances keep alive the musical legacies of the San Luis area and of Colorado's Hispano-Chicano community.

Matthew Jenkins's "Finding Courage: The Story of the Struggle to Retire the Adams State 'Indian'" looks at how people of all ethnic backgrounds formed a coalition to stop the deeply offensive practice of using an Indian mascot at Adams State College in Alamosa. His analysis considers how stereotyped Indians comprise a part of the meta-history of the West and how he, as a White male ally, appreciated the opportunity to step out of the privilege of apathy and listen to Colorado's Native and Chicana/Chicano voices. In this spirit, we encourage all members of U.S. society and residents of the state of Colorado—regardless of race, class, sexuality, and gender—to listen to the voices and stories of communities of color whose enduring legacies are intrinsic to the multifaceted character, history, and cultures of the Colorado borderlands.

CONCLUSION

The chapters in this book argue powerfully that any understanding of the borderlands of Colorado must necessarily take into consideration the histories, experiences, racializations, resistances, and cultural productions of African American, Asian American, and Chicana and Chicano communities. Furthermore, they suggest that these histories of race and resistance are ineluctably intertwined. Together, these chapters resuscitate the lost histories of people of color in Colorado, a state often wrongly thought of as exclusively White. Not only do they show how each group was racialized in particular ways, but they also examine the resistance Chicana/os, African Americans, and Asian Americans mounted against the racial structures they faced. Collectively, these histories and ongoing struggles make up the enduring legacies of Colorado. We thank all the scholars who responded to our call for essays, and we hope this volume will be the first of many to produce knowledge about communities of color in the Colorado borderlands.

NOTES

1. Key texts in U.S. and Mexico borderlands studies include R. Acuña, *Occupied America: A History of Chicanos*, 7th ed. (Englewood Cliffs, NJ: Prentice-Hall, 2009); Patricia Limerick, *The Legacy of Conquest: The Unbroken Past of the American West* (New York: W. W. Norton, 1987); Vicki Ruiz, *From Out of the Shadows: Mexican Women in Twentieth Century America* (New York: Oxford University Press, 1999); Jose David Saldívar, *Border Matters: Remapping American Cultural Studies* (Berkeley: University of California Press, 1997).

2. For readings, consider Peter Decker, *"The Utes Must Go!" American Expansion and the Removal of a People* (Golden, CO: Fulcrum, 2007); Virginia McConnell Simmons, *The Ute Indians of Utah, Colorado, and New Mexico* (Boulder: University Press of Colorado, 2001); Stan Hoig, *The Sand Creek Massacre* (Norman: University of Oklahoma Press, 1974); John Stands, *Cheyenne Memories* (New Haven: Yale University Press, 1998).

3. One notable exception is the Colorado Historical Society's important ongoing exhibit, *Tribal Paths: Colorado American Indians, 1500 to Today*.

4. In addition to the studies on American Indians in Colorado cited earlier, see Vincent C. De Baca, ed., *La Gente: Hispano History and Life in Colorado* (Denver: Colorado Historical Society, 1998) for an excellent collection of essays that chronicle Hispano-Chicano life in Colorado from the 1800s to the present. For key references in Asian American studies and African American studies in Colorado, see the remaining notes in this chapter.

5. See Ernesto B. Vigil, *The Crusade for Justice: Chicano Militancy and the Government's War on Dissent* (Madison: University of Wisconsin Press, 1999).

6. William Wei, "History and Memory: The Story of Denver's Chinatown," *Colorado Heritage* (Autumn 2002): 3.

7. Population figures from United States Census Office, *Statistics of the Population of the United States at the Tenth Census (July 1, 1880)* (Washington, DC: Government Printing Office, 1883), table V, "Population, by Race and by Counties: 1880, 1870, 1860," 382. Available at http://www2.census.gov/prod2/decennial/documents/1880a_v1-13.pdf. Accessed July 5, 2007. Occupations cited in Wei, "History and Memory," 8, and William Wei, "The Anti-Chinese Movement in Colorado: Interethnic Competition and Conflict on the Eve of Exclusion," in *Chinese America: History and Perspectives, 1995*, Marlon K. Hom, Him Mark Lai, et al., eds. (San Francisco: Chinese Historical Society of America, 1995), 181–182.

8. Wei, "Anti-Chinese Movement," 180–193.

9. Bill Hosokawa, *Colorado's Japanese Americans: From 1886 to the Present* (Boulder: University Press of Colorado, 2005), 22–27; Fumio Ozawa, *Japanese American Who's Who* (Denver: Colorado Times, 1954), quoted in Hosokawa, 28–29.

10. 1940 Census, Colorado, table 4, "Race, by Nativity and Sex, for the State: 1850 to 1940," 694.

11. Russell Endo, "Japanese of Colorado: A Sociohistoric Portrait," *Journal of Social and Behavioral Sciences* 31 (Fall 1985): 102. The discrepancy between the 1909 and 1910 figures can be chalked up to the difficulties of enumerating a non-English-speaking and partially migrant workforce.

12. John deYoung, "A Preliminary Survey of the Adjustment of Japanese Evacuees in Denver," (1943): 2–4, Bancroft Library, MSS 67/19c.

13. Carl Abbot, Stephen J. Leonard, and David McComb, *Colorado: A History of the Centennial State*, 3rd ed. (Niwot: University Press of Colorado, 1994), 211–213.

14. Endo, "Japanese of Colorado," 103.

15. Hosokawa, *Colorado's Japanese Americans*, 87.

16. United States Bureau of the Census, *1980 Census of Population*. Vol. 1: *Characteristics of the Population* (Washington, DC: Government Printing Office), table 194, "Nativity, Place of Birth, and Citizenship by Age, Race, and Spanish Origin: 1980," 7-7. Available at http://www2.census.gov/prod2/decennial/documents/1980a_coD-01.pdf. Accessed June 27, 2007.

17. American FactFinder. Available at http://factfinder.census.gov/servlet/QTTable?_bm=y&-geo_id=04000US08&-qr_name=DEC_2000_SF1_U_DP1&-ds_name=DEC_2000_SF1_U. Accessed June 27, 2007.

18. American FactFinder. Available at http://factfinder.census.gov/servlet/SAFFFactsCharIteration?_event=&geo_id=04000US08&_geoContext=01000US%7C04000US08&_street=&_county=&_cityTown=&_state=04000US08&_zip=&_lang=en&_sse=on&ActiveGeoDiv=&_useEV=&pctxt=fph&pgsl=040&_submenuId=factsheet_2&ds_name=DEC_2000_SAFF&_ci_nbr=029&qr_name=DEC_2000_SAFF_R1040&reg=DEC_2000_SAFF_R1040%3A029&_keyword=&_industry=. Accessed July 5, 2007.

19. Table 4, "Estimates of the Population by Race and Hispanic or Latino Origin for the United States and States: July 1, 2006 (SC-EST2006-04)" and table 5, "Estimates of the Population by Race Alone or in Combination and Hispanic or Latino Origin for the United States and States: July 1, 2006 (SC-EST2006-05)." Available at http://www.census/gov/popest/states/asrh/SC-EST2006-04.html. Accessed June 27, 2007.

20. Quintard Taylor, *In Search of the Racial Frontier: African Americans in the American West, 1528–1990* (New York: Norton, 1998), 17; see also Eugene H. Berwanger, *The West and Reconstruction* (Urbana: University of Illinois Press, 1981); Nell Irvin Painter, *Exodusters: Black Migration to Kansas after Reconstruction* (Lawrence: University Press of Kansas, 1986).

21. For further discussion, see M. Thomas Bailey, *Reconstruction in Indian Territory: A Study of Avarice, Discrimination, and Opportunism* (Port Washington, NY: Kennikat, 1972); James F. Brooks, ed., *Confounding the Color Line: The Indian-Black Experience in North America* (Lincoln: University of Nebraska Press, 2002); Arnoldo De León,

Racial Frontiers: Africans, Chinese, and Mexicans in Western America, 1848–1890 (Albuquerque: University of New Mexico Press, 2002); Jack D. Forbes, *Black Africans and Native Americans: Color, Race, and Caste in the Evolution of Red-Black Peoples* (New York: Oxford University Press, 1988); Jack D. Forbes, *Africans and Native Americans: The Language of Race and the Evolution of Red-Black Peoples* (Urbana: University of Illinois Press, 1993); Hosokawa, *Colorado's Japanese Americans*; Morgan Monceaux, *My Heroes, My People: African Americans and Native Americans in the West* (New York: Frances Foster Books, 1999); Jesse T. Moore Jr., "Seeking a New Life: Blacks in Post–Civil War Colorado," *Journal of Negro History* 78, 3 (1993): 166–187; Kenneth W. Porter, *The Black Seminoles: History of a Freedom-Seeking People* (Gainesville: University Press of Florida, 1996); Ronald Takaki, *Strangers from a Different Shore: A History of Asian Americans* (Boston: Little, Brown, 1998); Ronald Takaki, *Iron Cages: Race and Culture in 19th-Century America* (New York: Oxford University Press, 2000).

22. William King, *Going to Meet the Man: Denver's Last Legal Public Execution, 27 July 1886* (Niwot: University Press of Colorado, 1990), 6.

23. Langston Hughes, "Harlem," in *The Collected Poems of Langston Hughes*, Arnold Rampersad, ed. (New York: Knopf, 1996), 426.

24. For further discussion of anti-Black racism in the American West, see Eugene H. Berwanger, *The Frontier against Slavery: Western Anti-Negro Prejudice and the Slavery Extension Controversy* (Urbana: University of Illinois Press, 1967); Michael A. Morrison, *Slavery and the American West: The Eclipse of Manifest Destiny and the Coming of the Civil War* (Chapel Hill: University of North Carolina Press, 1997); Howard Dodson, *In Motion: The African American Migration Experience* (Washington, DC: National Geographic Publishing, 2004). For the key text on "American apartheid," see Douglas S. Massey and Nancy A. Denton, *American Apartheid: Segregation and the Making of the Underclass* (Cambridge: Harvard University Press, 1993).

25. Roger D. Hardaway, "African American Communities on the Western Frontier," in *Community in the American West*, Stephen Tchudi, ed. (Reno: University of Nevada Press, 1999), 131.

26. Census data extracted from *Historical Census Statistics on Population Totals by Race, 1790 to 1990, and by Hispanic Origin, 1970 to 1990, for the United States, Regions, Divisions, and States*, Campbell Gibson and Kay Jung, eds. (Washington, DC: Population Division, U.S. Census Bureau, 2002), Working Paper Series 56. Available at http://www.census.gov/population/www/documentation/twps0056.html. Accessed July 19, 2007.

27. *Twelfth Census of the United States, 1900* (Washington, DC: U.S. Government Printing Office, 1901), 1, part 1, LIX, cxxii.

28. Ibid., table XCVI, ccvi. For further discussion, see Janet Cornelius, "'We Slipped and Learned to Read': Slave Accounts of the Literacy Process, 1830–1865," *Phylon* 44, 3 (1983): 171–186; Robert F. Engs, "Historical Perspectives on the Problem of Black Literacy," *Educational Horizon* 66, 1 (1987): 13–17; Price V. Fishback and John H. Baskin, "Narrowing the Black-White Gap in Child Literacy in 1910: The Roles of School Inputs and Family Inputs," *Review of Economics and Statistics* 73, 4 (1991): 725–728; Anne R. Gere and Sarah R. Robbins, "Gendered Literacy in Black and White: Turn-of-the-Century African American and European American Club Women's

Printed Texts," *Signs* 21, 3 (1996): 643–678; Carl F. Kaestle, *Literacy in the United States: Readers and Reading Since 1880* (New Haven: Yale University Press, 1991); and Moore, "Seeking a New Life."

29. Census data extracted from *Historical Census Statistics on Population Totals by Race, 1790 to 1990*.

30. For example, see Sue Armitage, Theresa Banfield, and Sarah Jacobus, "Black Women and Their Communities in Colorado," *Frontiers: A Journal of Women's Studies* 2, 2 (1977): 45–51; Lynda F. Dickson, "The Early Club Movement among Black Women in Denver, 1890–1925" (PhD diss., University of Colorado at Boulder, 1982); Lynda F. Dickson, "Toward a Broader Angle of Vision in Uncovering Women's History: Black Women's Clubs Revisited," *Frontiers: A Journal of Women's Studies* 9, 2 (1987): 62–68; Lynda F. Dickson, "Lifting as We Climb: African American Women's Clubs in Denver, 1880–1925," *Essays in Colorado History* 13 (1992): 69–98; Elizabeth Jameson and Susan Armitage, eds., *Writing the Range: Race, Class, and Culture in the Women's West* (Norman: University of Oklahoma Press, 1997); Ira de Augustine Reid, *The Negro Population of Denver, Colorado: A Survey of Its Economic and Social Status* (Denver: Lincoln Press, 1929); James P. Thogmorton, "The Urban League of Denver: A Study in Techniques of Accommodation" (MA thesis, University of Denver, 1951); Matthew C. Whitaker, *Race Work: The Rise of Civil Rights in the Urban West* (Lincoln: University of Nebraska Press, 2007); Robert L. Zangrando, *The NAACP Crusade against Lynching, 1909–1950* (Philadelphia: Temple University Press, 1980).

31. Furthermore, Black/African American/Africana studies work has been overly focused on men and heterosexuality. For further discussion on the need to expand the foci, see Delores Aldridge, "Women in the Development of Africana Studies," in *The Handbook of Black Studies*, Molefi Asante and Maulana Karenga, eds. (Thousand Oaks, CA: Sage, 2006), 51–66; Delores Aldridge and Carlene Young, eds., *Out of the Revolution: An Africana Studies Anthology* (Lanham, MD: Lexington, 2000); Jacqueline Bobo and Claudine Michel, eds., *Black Studies: Current Issues, Enduring Questions* (Dubuque, IA: Kendall/Hunt, 2000); Jacqueline Bobo, Cynthia Hudley, and Claudine Michel, eds., *The Black Studies Reader* (New York: Routledge, 2004); David Ross Fryer, "African American Queer Studies," in *A Companion to African American Studies*, Lewis Gordon and Jane Anna Gordon, eds. (Malden, MA: Blackwell, 2006), 305–329; David Ross Fryer, "On the Possibilities of Posthumanism, or How to Think Queerly in an Antiblack World," in *Not Only the Master's Tools: African American Studies in Theory and Practice*, Lewis Gordon and Jane Anna Gordon, eds. (Boulder: Paradigm, 2006), 227–242; E. Patrick Johnson and Mae G. Henderson, *Black Queer Studies: A Critical Anthology* (Durham: Duke University Press, 2005); Manning Marable, ed., *The New Black Renaissance: The Souls Anthology of Critical African American Studies* (Boulder: Paradigm, 2005); Obioma Nnaemeka, ed., *Sisterhood, Feminisms, and Power: From Africa to the Diaspora* (Trenton, NJ: Africa World Press, 1998); Reiland Rabaka, "Africana Critical Theory of Contemporary Society: Ruminations on Radical Politics, Social Theory, and Africana Philosophy," in *The Handbook of Black Studies*, Molefi Asante and Maulana Karenga, eds. (Thousand Oaks, CA: Sage, 2006), 130–151; Reiland Rabaka, "The Souls of Black Radical Folk: W.E.B. Du Bois, Critical Social Theory, and the State of Africana Studies," *Journal of Black Studies* 36, 5 (2006): 732–763.

32. For a discussion of how the term "Chicano" came to be used through historical and social processes, see James Diego Vigil, *From Indians to Chicanos*, 2nd ed. (Long Grove, IL: Waveland, 1998); Rodolfo Acuña, *Occupied America: A History of Chicanos*, 6th ed. (New York: Longman, 2006).

33. For a historical overview of these land grant histories, see Vincent C. De Baca, "Introduction," in De Baca, *La Gente: Hispano History and Life in Colorado* (Denver: Colorado Historical Society, 1998), xi–xvii. Other sources on the land grants include Virginia McConnell Simmons, *The San Luis Valley: Land of the Six Armed Cross* (Boulder: Pruett, 1979), which actually reproduces the land grant maps; Richard L. Norstrand, *The Hispano Homeland* (Norman: University of Oklahoma Press, 1992).

34. David Gutierrez, *Walls and Mirrors: Mexicans, Mexican Immigrants and the Politics of Ethnicity* (Berkeley: University of California Press, 1995), 13. Other studies that look at the dispossession of Mexican-owned land, the imposition of new cultural styles, and agriculture methods that aid in the attempted erasure of the Hispano way of live include Sarah Deutsch, *No Separate Refuge: Culture, Class, and Gender on an Anglo-Hispanic Frontier in the American Southwest* (Oxford: Oxford University Press, 1987); John Chavez, *The Lost Land: The Chicano Image of the Southwest* (Albuquerque: University of New Mexico Press, 1984). Studies that examine the ways Mexicans who are now Mexican Americans became racialized in the Southwest in terms that Mexican culture and even skin color signals them as inferior, backward, immoral, violent, and savage include Arnoldo de Leon, *They Called Them Greasers: Anglo Attitudes towards Mexicans in Texas, 1821–1900* (Austin: University of Texas Press, 1983); Tomás Almaguer, *Racial Faultlines: The Historical Origins of White Supremacy in California* (Berkeley: University of California Press, 1994). It is of interest to see whether these same patterns of White supremacy existed in Colorado as well, especially given the historical parallels in terms of the Gold Rush and the Anglos' land grab of Mexican land grants seen in other states.

35. Carl Abbot, Stephen J. Leonard, and Tom Noel, *Colorado: A History of the Centennial State*, 4th ed. (Boulder: University Press of Colorado, 2005), 35.

36. See Mauricio Mazon, *The Zootsuit Riots: The Psychology of Symbolic Annihilation* (Austin: University of Texas Press, 1984).

37. For the best and most comprehensive study of the Crusade for Justice, see Vigil, *Crusade for Justice*.

PART I
Early Struggles

Suzanne P. MacAulay

Pictorial Narratives of San Luis, Colorado: Legacy, Place, and Politics

> So, anyway I created that [embroidery of *La Sierra*]. It was more of a contemporary kind of thing, but it was history. And I thought, "If I don't get this down . . . now that it's happening, somebody might not think of it as part of the historical documentation of the area."
>
> —JOSEPHINE LOBATO[1]

Traveling along State Highway 159 heading south to New Mexico, one passes through San Luis, locally acclaimed as the "Oldest Town in Colorado," founded in 1851. At one of the main intersections in this small community is a mural—somewhat faded but still evocative of the community's history and value system.[2] Its themes represent local perceptions of the area's legacy: the era of nomadic Indian tribes, a dynamic foreshortened view of the upper portion of the crucifix suspended in clouds from which Spanish conquistadors emerge, an allegorical rendering of the largesse of Mother Earth, and other panels depicting settlers, hunters, farmers, and scenes of adobe making. The mural's prominent position advertises a symbolically constructed glimpse of the community's belief system with respect to the primacy of Catholicism, ethnic heritage and pride, and a deep connectedness to the earth through hunting and agriculture. Among these various images, one of the most binding elements around which the San Luis community coheres is land—its constancy, its use, and the power exercised through its possession and maintenance. The links between the belief in land as a God-given birthright and the Spanish conquest of the region in the name of God and religion is apparent in the mural's iconic arrangement of conquistadors, Christ, and cultivation.

This chapter investigates the local sense of place and heritage in San Luis through a study of ethnicity and the ways cultural identity is conceived and constructed. By analyzing the processes of place making and identifying the forces of cultural politics active in San Luis, we ask how "understandings of locality, community and region are formed and lived [in this particular place]."[3] In addition, the notion of material culture as an objectification of cultural values and a group's aesthetic system is considered basic to this inquiry. This discussion argues for the importance of material objects in the formation of personal and collective identities and demonstrates how this operates in terms of the creative work of a particular San Luis artist, Josephine Lobato. Lobato creates embroidered narratives about Hispanic life in the San Luis Valley using an innovative style derived from a traditional Spanish colonial textile technique known as *colcha* embroidery. Colcha, in its modified contemporary version as a stitched pictorial narrative (visual storytelling) linked to a historical creative practice, becomes a means to explore issues of colonial legacy and ancestral rights. Its mode of creation also relies on reflexivity as a form of artistic and meditative feedback flowing between art and life's experiences. Thus an ethnographic examination of ethnicity and sense of place along with an art historical descriptive analysis take "culture" as the subject of investigation and work together to foreground a specific genre of artwork as critical to the interplay of aesthetic and socio-cultural interaction in San Luis.

San Luis is located in one of the most impoverished counties in Colorado, Costilla County. It is a place of contrast—rich in natural resources yet poor economically. It is also culturally distinct from other towns in the area. In recent years, when ethnic solidarity emerging in the face of historic Anglo dominance in this region has been invigorating self-esteem and community pride, the issues of land and birthright are crucial determinants of legitimacy. As broadcast through the imagery of the "civic" mural, in present-day San Luis the prevailing attitude identifies with a cultural legacy from Spain rather than Mexico. One year during the annual summer fiesta of Santana and Santiago, an older resident ardently informed me that San Luis townspeople label themselves as Spanish—not Latinos or Mexican Americans: "Somos españoles" (we are Spanish). The majority of San Luis residents use the terms "Hispano," "Hispanic," and "Spanish" interchangeably, with Hispanic the most frequent.

Thus community members' cultural and genealogical understanding of heritage (as publicly espoused to outsiders) honors the persistence of Spanish lineage apart from the vicissitudes of time and birthplace.

The anthropologist Clifford Geertz has written that ethnography is the discovery of a particular group's perception of "who they think they are; what they think they are doing; and to what end they think they are doing it." He goes on to say that the object of ethnography is to gain a familiarity with the "frames of meaning within which they enact their lives" (2000:16). A few of the discernible "frames of meaning" applicable to the ethos or worldview of San Luis residents are represented through the iconography and symbolism in Josephine Lobato's colcha embroideries. These pertain to the salient notions of legacy, ancestral and communal rights, ethnicity, and religious faith. Furthermore, Lobato's pictorial narratives provide a double-layered reading of human history and relationship in this community. One layer is concerned with the story and the recording of meaning. The other is more abstract and involves the synthesis of human action and interpretation viewed through the artist's creativity and imagination. Artifacts, such as colcha embroideries, are containers of human histories, collective memories, and political relations as much as they are cultural and aesthetic properties of the environment. These more intangible properties are subject to the same dynamism that acts as a vector of cultural identity helping to shape the lives and consciousness of individuals living in particular places.

Visualization of stories is a complex process of translating words and concepts into images accompanied by the subsequent transformation of lines of verbal narrative into a symbolic rendering of the suggestive, the evocative, and the poetic. Memory stories shared among the people of San Luis are artistically expressed through Josie Lobato's imagination. As pictorial narratives they become visual accounts of lives "lived." They are created out of remembrance, which is part of an ongoing collective enterprise belonging to the entire community that is never finished. Each time people from the San Luis area look at Lobato's colchas, they add their own reminiscences to the story lines, thus expanding the pieces' power and inclusiveness. Not everyone, however, shares the exact same memories or interprets them in the same way. Within a community such as San Luis, the similarity of memories is based more on resemblance than on replication. Individual memories differ but align with group interests in recalling certain experiences that resemble or resonate with each other. These reminiscences are part of the collective memory patterns of a group and are thus recognized for their significance and commonality.

26 PICTORIAL NARRATIVES OF SAN LUIS, COLORADO

1.1. *El Milagro de San Acacio,* embroidery by Josephine Lobato, 1992. Permission granted by Lobato.

One of Josie Lobato's early embroideries, *El Milagro de San Acacio* (1992), reveals how social memory and landscape implicate kin relations in light of a religious miracle. This folktale is widespread around the Southwest, but in this case it legitimates the founding of the San Acacio settlement near San Luis and the line of descent from the original settlers. Another colcha embroidery, *La Sierra* (1999), shows how memories of ancestral heritage, which are inscribed in the land, become the basis for upholding traditional, customary Spanish land rights in the face of outside wealth and power. The discussion that follows analyzes the imagery of these two pictorial narratives as representing native San Luis perceptions of the legacy and the right to not only be rooted in a certain place but to also be inseparable from that place.

El Milagro de San Acacio is inspired by a localized version of a folktale about the religious intervention and miraculous salvation of a mid–nineteenth-century settler community from being slaughtered by a band of Ute Indians. This settlement was eponymously named "San Acacio" in honor of the avenging patron saint. Enduring memories of these people's religious faith along with the names of individual families still residing in the San Luis area con-

1.2. *La Sierra*, embroidery by Josephine Lobato, 1999. Permission granted by author.

stitute a legacy of kinship located in an inimical, unfriendly landscape and nurtured through generations of descendants as a sacred inheritance.

La Sierra portrays a scene of a fairly recent political environmental protest staged in 1999 in the alpine meadows of a section of the traditional Spanish Land Grant, located in the mountains east of San Luis. The land grant was originally bestowed in the sixteenth century and was validated again in the nineteenth century when settlers were issued deeds to the land specifying rights for grazing and communal access to water, firewood, and timber. The people of San Luis view the history of the Spanish Land Grant as intertwined with issues of heritage and cultural autonomy that depend on the collective right to use resources (not necessarily "ownership" but the right to use). This arrangement is clearly stated in the 1863 Beaubien Deed, based on the original tenets of the Spanish Land Grant: "As such, everyone should exercise scrupulous care with the use of water without causing harm to their *vecinos* [neighbors] . . . nor to anyone; all of the inhabitants shall have the convenient arrangement, the enjoyment of the benefits of the pastures, the water, wood, and lumber, always being careful not to prejudice one another" (Sandoval 1985:22).

In 1960 a southern lumber baron named Jack Taylor privately purchased 77,750 acres belonging to this tract of land in the Sangre de Cristo Mountains. He enclosed the land and fenced it off, thus making it inaccessible to Spanish descendants in San Luis who had been using the land for over 100 years. After almost three decades in the court system, communal grazing rights were reestablished in 2003 by a U.S. Supreme Court decision. *La Sierra* not only represents one scene in a long period of disenfranchisement but also celebrates the potency of collective memories of ancestral rights embedded in the landscape. This factor of memory as a viable mode of establishing ancestral authority was decisive in the 2003 U.S. Supreme Court ruling, which upheld an earlier Colorado Supreme Court decision in favor of San Luis residents.[4]

One of the basic themes underscoring the artistic creation of *La Sierra* concerns the cultural, social, and lineal attachment to place where memory (i.e., individual and collective) is configured as both the agent and the subject of recall while art, expressed as pictorial narrative, is the cultural form or its material manifestation. Throughout the long process of resistance to private ownership of the land, the descendants of the San Luis settlers—the original grantees—claimed a certain degree of "moral authority" not based on wealth or power but substantiated by their continuous cultural practice of respect and identification with the land through a stewardship predicated on ancestral rights and customary use. Ortega y Gasset suggests a similar, but more poetically expressed, affinity between identity and place: "Show me the landscape in which you live and I will tell you who you are" (quoted in Lane 1988:64).

People commonly inscribe their presence on the landscape in enduring ways, such as the apportionment of space and the construction of the built environment. Whenever Josephine Lobato documents evidence of the effects of this manifesting presence in her embroidered scenes of historical moments and cultural enactments, she metaphorically transforms "space" into "place." In this way real environment becomes intelligible through visualization as an instance of place—a locus of happening—composed of actual and symbolic individual and group experiences.

Coupled with the cognitive is the kinetic. Memory is activated by stitching, and stitching is motivated by memory. Imagery spills out onto the embroidery fabric, with the visual evoking the narrative and the commemorative. Thus the rendering of the story in all its richness is determined not only by aesthetic choice and historical understanding but also by the dynamics of mnemonic processing catalyzed through the act of stitching. This is implied by another San Luis stitcher, Julia Valdez, when she says, "You express and you remember" ("you stitch and you remember"). In the San Luis style of colcha embroidery, we can see how art literally constructs and reconstructs history through remembrance (and also forgetting) as personal and collective forces are channeled into embroidery.

For Josie Lobato, her kinetic engagement with art making is also linked to the kinetic knowledge of place. Her pursuit of pictorial accuracy often compels her to walk the landscape around the hills outside San Luis that she is portraying in her embroidery. These solitary walks through the countryside are Josie's means of strengthening the connection to the spirit of her colcha and transmuting her work into a kind of "visual topography," a realm where pictorial narrative embodies symbolic experiences of place. In this way the creative process embraces both the aesthetic and the mobile. Furthermore, in her artwork, these places cannot be considered apart from Josie's subjective "interpreting consciousness" as she remembers, reimagines, and concretizes them through embroidery.

As a cultural commentator and artist-as-social-actor, Josephine Lobato renders her subjects from an inside-outside perspective. In Josie's artwork, she visually narrates the subject while memorializing her own connections to the theme of the stitcheries. She may not directly represent herself as the subject of her narratives, but the throes of creativity—the exhilaration and the anguish—implicate her as creator, interpreter, and participant.

The legend of *El Milagro de San Acacio* is a charter myth detailing the source of the ethical, moral, and familial underpinnings of the village of San Acacio (and, by extension, the San Luis Valley where the village is located). The story is a tale of bravery and exemplary spiritual devotion. It revolves around the courageous actions of an old man and his young grandson, both of whom figure prominently in local genealogies. According to Josie, "Everyone wants to claim descent from these heroic ancestors."[5]

Josie's version shows the dramatic moment when the most vulnerable settlers remaining in the unprotected village (women, children, and the elderly) are attacked by a band of Ute Indians while those who could protect them are away hunting or working in their gardens outside the settlement. In the center of the background, the villagers huddle together to pray fervently to their patron saint, San Acacio (Saint Acatius). Just as the marauding Indians reach the village, they suddenly stop "dead in their tracks," turn around, and rapidly flee. Puzzled but jubilant, the villagers attribute their salvation to a miracle—the intervention of their divine protector, San Acacio. Years later the same Indian who led the raid was ill and was being treated by a Hispanic *curandera* (healer) near the village of San Acacio. In answer to her questions about why his band fled so abruptly, he replied that they had seen a regiment of armed horsemen behind a fierce soldier emerge from the clouds.

Josie Lobato's recounting of this legend is enhanced by her personal connections and remembrances: "I've heard the legend ever since I was very small. The legend of San Acacio is . . . a fireside type of story which has been told over and over again." Referring to certain families tracing their lineage through the grandfather figure, she says, "Many names have been told me that this man. . . . But, of course, every family wants to claim him. . . . I've heard the Candelaria's kind of talk about him. I have heard the old man called Jacquez . . . There is a lot of history [from] generation to generation in that [Jacquez] family . . . almost everybody was related, so it depends on who is [telling] the story of the legend."[6] Josie's interpretation of this colorful communal legend illustrates the concept of cultural memory in operation, as it represents "the many shifting histories and shared memories that exist between a sanctioned narrative . . . and personal memory" (Hamilton 1994:20).

With *La Sierra* Josie Lobato adds "artist-as-witness" to her compound role of cultural commentator and artist-as-social-actor. She is wielding memories still active in the present as she observes, participates, and then translates what she sees into the visual imagery in her embroidery. As an aesthetic and cultural form, her composition is layered with sediments from the past, present, and future. Thus in *La Sierra*, Josie creates the *conditions of possibility* by informing the present with elements from the past while visually forecasting a more hopeful future.

Artistic allusions abound that refer to the pristine landscape of the original Spanish Land Grant, replete with abundant forests, water, and game. This mountainous land is known locally as *La Merced*, "the gift." However, since 1960, when Jack Taylor acquired over 77,000 acres of the area documented as the "Mountain Tract," the land has been riddled with logging roads and scarred by clear-cutting—all of which has affected the entire watershed of the region, from the denuded forests to the valleys. Josie describes the situation this way: "It [*La Merced*] was not too far from our place. I tried to label Culebra Creek and the ditches that are there to show that it was a watershed problem. That was one of the main reasons for the conflict."[7] A defendant in the recently settled court case *Lobato v. Taylor*, Gene Martinez, says, "That's what we inherited, a damaged mountain. Our forefathers always looked at the land like it was our mother. They would never abuse the land so it couldn't recover" (quoted in Curtin 2005:A-04).

The colcha embroidery *La Sierra* represents an event held to protest logging that occurred four years prior to 2003, when the U.S. Supreme Court upheld the Colorado Supreme Court's ruling that restored the rights of certain San Luis Valley families to resume wood gathering and grazing on land their ancestors were given to homestead over 150 years ago. The protagonists in *La Sierra* are the Valley Land Rights Council supported by two or three outsider college activists, one of whom has handcuffed himself to the underside of the truck in the lower right-hand corner. The protestor chained to the gate is Rocky Madrid, who lives in San Luis. Josie Lobato has sprinkled descriptive and didactic labels throughout her embroidery, naming Culebra Peak, a barricade erected when Jack Taylor set up residence, designated rivers and ditches—even a "pond" and Jack Taylor himself. On the left, the protestors shout "Stop logging." They are placed opposite Taylor on the right side, who died in 1988 but is shown shooting his gun. Artistic destiny has put him in the same frame with the descendants of the people he shot at and pistol-whipped for thirty years. Now they shout their grievances across time and space. Josie uses labels liberally because she says without them, "you wouldn't know what I was doing."[8]

Josie also includes her husband Gene's tract of land contiguous with the Taylor Ranch, which is located in the middle of the lower edge of the embroidery: "So I actually put a strip down below that says "Gene's Acres' 'cause our place is right there."[9] Many La Culebra ranchers whose land abutted the Mountain Tract testified in court that they were harassed by Taylor and the hired ranch hands of subsequent landowners. "Gene's Acres" symbolizes the geographically intertwined placement of these historical native landholdings relative to Taylor's boundaries, which were carved out of the original Spanish Land Grant. "Rio de Los Vigiles" (the river of the Vigil family) is another one of these signifying landmarks, located in the lower left corner.

The style Josie has chosen for this piece conveys a sense of an agitated, molten landscape crowned by a turbulent sky about to spill over onto the frontal picture plane. The impression is one of frenetic energy. Josie regards all these visual elements as "symbols": "I always say symbols because it [the embroidery] has a lot of symbols. The peak itself is a symbol . . . and the cloud over it because there was a cloud over the whole incident. The variegated sky tells you that it was conflict . . . constant conflict. . . . The elk were a symbol of the wildlife being trapped in all the logging."[10]

By using a continuous narrative device familiar from medieval manuscripts, where all elements are presented simultaneously within one framework irrespective of chronology, Josie creates a seamless, timeless moment in which angry memories of past transgressions meld with recent protest actions to supersede temporal and spatial constraints. In another sense, Josie Lobato has created an "intercultural" moment, with different factions colliding in a composition reflecting the eternal moments of an imagined "ethnographic present" where everything is possible at all times. In *La Sierra*, the muted disenfranchised voices of the past now shout clamorously in the present. Despite the fact that in 1999 Lou Pai, an Enron executive, owned the Taylor Ranch, Josie's inclusion of Jack Taylor's image represents his notoriety for violence but also symbolizes his callous legacy of private ownership brutally maintained by the owners who followed in his footsteps.

The enclosure of the Taylor ranchlands and the banning of Spanish descendants from lands they had always used in common disrupted area residents' memorialized connections to that place, *La Merced*, on the slopes of the Sangre de Cristo Mountains. The subsequent replacement memories that were narrated during the three decades of court cases recount loss, beatings, and humiliation. Virgil Sanchez recalls being threatened with a gun and called a "wetback" by Taylor. During a hearing, when Joe Gallegos described the pristine beauty of the mountain tract he remembered from his childhood, he was mocked by Taylor's lawyers, who claimed he was too young at the time to remember the "eerie, magical forests often draped in mist" (Frazier 2003:4A). Alternately, in the hearts of residents, memories of place (denied) intensified so that when the case was won, Valley Land Rights Council members and neighboring ranchers began to speak of creating a local stewardship based on sustainability of resources to "instill values of the land to a generation that have not been on it," as well as to teach cultural customs such as adobe making, peeling timber for *latillas* (ceiling components) and preparing green wood for corrals and gates (Frazier 2003:4A). Thus by drawing on cultural memories, descendants pave the way for a collective practice of caretaking and teaching an ecological, sustainable way of living.

The theme of *El Milagro de San Acacio* sanctions the right of the Hispanic villagers to settle in a particular landscape revealed through an act of divine intervention and interpreted as a sign from the heavens. This legend then establishes a code of religiosity and collective identity, which is embedded in cultural memory and inextricably bound to a distinct place existing over time. Residents of San Luis and San Acacio know this story and refer to it to emphasize their genealogical roles and connections to its primary characters.

La Sierra is governed by the trajectory of displacement in which a different agent of intervention—the court system—nullifies long-term acts of banishment. Although *La Sierra* depicts a definitive moment in time, as an artwork it commemorates a specific memory of one of many episodes leading to the court settlement in December 2003. San Luis residents regard this protest event as one element within an experiential continuum of ongoing resistance subject to shifts in different strategies of power on both sides of the conflict. Akhil Gupta and James Ferguson suggest that the experience of resistance over time "constructs and reconstructs the identity of subjects" (1997:19). This type of profound experience conditioned by struggle, which grounds identity in terms of place making (or place claiming), can also be transformative, as exemplified in San Luis residents' accounts of biographical connections to *La Merced* underscoring future commitments to conserve its natural resources.

These two pictorial narratives shift elusively and continually between levels of artistic intention and collective meaning. They are stories told to reify legacy and myth in *El Milagro* and to portray documentary evidence ultimately leading to justice in *La Sierra*. Through processes of conceptualization and execution, Josephine Lobato shows in her creative work that both the medium of colcha embroidery and the subject of "named" or contested places (e.g., San Acacio and *La Merced*) are complexly imagined and constructed cultural objects. Lobato uses colcha as an art form to express individual and collective memories that become the foundation for the myriad ways ethnicity and cultural identity are enacted and embedded in San Luis history, heritage, and landscape. After all the conflicts, losses, and gains, San Luis residents would probably relate to Ernest Hemingway's words: "We live by accidents of terrain. . . . And terrain is what remains in the dreaming part of our mind" (quoted in Kennedy 1993:11).

NOTES

1. Josephine Lobato, taped interview with author, Chama, Colorado, October 13, 2003.

2. Carlos Sandoval from Denver created this mural in 1988. He was a native of San Pablo, one of the villages around San Luis, and was inspired by Father Patrick Valdez, head of the local Sangre de Cristo parish, to return and create public artworks in San Luis during the late 1980s.

3. Refer to Gupta and Ferguson (1997:6–12).

4. In recent times the case was referred to as *Lobato v. Taylor*, with the lead name for the group of defendants associated with the Lobato family, which was Josie's husband, Eugene Lobato's, family.

5. Josephine Lobato, taped interview with author, Fort Garland, Colorado, July 20, 1990.

6. Ibid.

7. Lobato interview, 2003.

8. Josephine Lobato, taped interview with author, Chama, Colorado, August 1, 2006.

9. Lobato interview, 2003.

10. Lobato interview, 2006.

REFERENCES

Curtin, Dave. "Home Again, but It's Changed after 45 years: Heirs to a San Luis Valley Land Grant Return." *The Denver Post*, August 8, 2005, A-04.

Frazier, Deborah. "Land War Ends but New Battle Looms," *The Rocky Mountain News*, December 13, 2003, 4A.

Geertz, Clifford. *Available Light*. Princeton: Princeton University Press, 2000.

Gupta, Akhil, and James Ferguson, "Culture, Power, Place: Ethnography at the End of an Era." In *Culture, Power, Place*, Akhil Gupta and James Ferguson, eds. Durham: Duke University Press, 1997, 1–29.

Hamilton, Paula. "The Knife Edge: Debates about Memory and History." In *Memory and History in Twentieth-Century Australia*, Kate Darian-Smith and Paula Hamilton, eds. Oxford: Oxford University Press, 1994, 9–32.

Kennedy, J. G. *Imagining Paris: Exile, Writing, and American Identity*. New Haven: Yale University Press, 1993.

Lane, B. *Landscapes of the Sacred: Geography and Narrative in American Spirituality*. New York: Paulist, 1988.

Sandoval, Ron. "The San Luis Vega." In *La Cultura Constante de San Luis*, Randall Teeuwen, ed. San Luis, CO: San Luis Cultural and Commercial Center, 1985, 18–25.

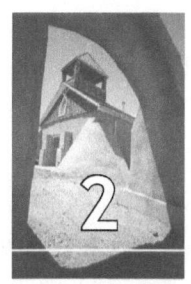

Enrique R. Lamadrid

Santiago and San Acacio, Foundational Legends of Conquest and Deliverance: New Mexico, 1599, and Colorado, 1853

When Spanish Mexican colonists invoked the warrior saint Santiago at the 1599 siege of Acoma Pueblo, slaughter ensued.[1] Two and a half centuries later, the Utes in the settlement of southern Colorado opposed their descendants. The miraculous intervention of San Acacio, a crucified warrior, led not to bloodshed but rather to an 1853 armistice. The fierce Santiago's sword, shield, and warhorse gave way to the compassionate San Acacio's cross and crown of thorns as Nuevo Mexicanos became indigenous to the Upper Río Grande.

In the bloody siege at the natural citadel of Acoma Pueblo in January 1599, Don Vicente de Zaldívar and a few score of soldier colonists from the expedition of Don Juan de Oñate miraculously prevailed against hundreds of desperate warriors defending their homes. Two hundred and fifty-four years later, in the spring of 1853 in San Acacio, a pioneer settlement in the San Luis Valley, descendants of the Spanish Mexican settlers of New Mexico faced an even more hopeless situation. As a sizable army of well-mounted and well-armed Muache Utes charged in battle formation toward the unarmed villagers, the warriors suddenly stopped in their tracks and rode away in retreat. In both situations, divine forces unseen by the Hispanos saved the day. When the dust settled, both the defeated and undefeated Indians reported seeing apparitions attributed to Santiago and the Virgin at Acoma and to San Acacio at the southern Colorado town that still bears his name. Time and time again, through the divine intervention of saints, the colonizing project was rescued, and the "people of God" were delivered.

The political and cultural strategies of Nuevo Mexicanos in their relations with Native Americans shifted over time from conflict and subjugation, as inscribed in a discourse of power, to respect and coexistence, as narrated in a discourse of survival and resistance. Hagiography and iconography also register this evolution. As we shall see, in the colored light of history, both events are narrated from the perspective of the victors rather than the vanquished. Spain's dominions in the sixteenth century were U.S. territory in the mid-nineteenth century, and the fortunes and stories of the people are ultimately tied to the powers that be.

FOUNDATIONAL MIRACLES

Whether sung, recounted, or read, foundational poetry—as in the epic—and foundational narrative—as in chronicle or legend—articulate a social and moral charter for emerging and evolving societies. Cultural tradition and identity are negotiated and endowed with value and prestige by tracing the group's origins back to a loftier, even supernatural vision of initial events (Bakhtin 1981:45). Thus are the foundational histories of Nuevo México linked to miracles through the hagiographic narrative practices so deeply rooted in the Iberian imagination (DeMarco 2000:163).

Saints assisted the colonists in defeat as well as victory. At the fall of Santa Fe in the great Pueblo Revolt of 1680, a statue of La Virgen del Rosario traveled south to El Paso with the refugees, then returned with the Reconquest in 1692–1693, for which she was credited and renamed "La Conquistadora" (Chávez 1974:177, 190–191). Across the Upper Río Grande region, there are many other stories of deliverance. At Isleta Pueblo, where Hispanos and their Pueblo allies defended the church in a siege, San José appeared and scared off the invaders' horses by hitting them with his staff. One of the attackers later identified him from a painting in the church (Robe 1980:520–521). At San Antonio and Tularosa, attacking Apaches perceived Matachines dancers at saints' fiestas as mystical soldiers and retreated in fear (Sharp 1936). The character of the people and their relations with Native Americans emerge clearly in all these stories. But we return to Acoma and San Acacio to consider the clearly foundational nature of both miracles.

MILAGRO DE ACOMA

The foundation of the new colony in 1598 is chronicled in Gaspar Pérez de Villagrá's Renaissance epic poem *Historia de la Nueva México* (1610). The heroic deeds of the Spanish Mexican colonists are sustained and facilitated by miracles of their patron saints. Their journey to New Mexico across the deserts of Chihuahua to the Río Grande are likened to another band of God's chosen people in their journey across the Sinai deserts to the River Jordan and the Promised Land. When impediments of nature are surmounted and human obstacles appear in the form of Native resistance, more militant spiritual resources are called upon.

In the midst of a battle, Santiago, the patron of the Spanish Reconquest, was invoked with war cries. In more than a dozen "well-documented cases" pertaining to the conquest of the Americas, he appeared in battle with a sword and a white horse (Meyers, Simmons, and Pierce ca. 1991:17). The enemies' heads began to roll, and the killing fields were washed with blood. After the January 1599 siege of Acoma Pueblo, the elderly Acoman warrior Chumpo questioned the Spanish chief Don Vicente de Zaldívar about the whereabouts of two unusual figures the Indians saw during the battle.

Buscan éstos, mis hijos, a vn Castilla	These sons of mine seek a Castilian
Que estando en la batalla anduvo siempre	Who, being in the battle, always rode
En vn blanco caballo suelto, y tiene	Upon a great white horse and has
La barba larga, cana y bien poblada	A great long beard, both white and thick,
Y calva la cabeza. Es alto y ciñe	And a bald head, is tall and wears
Vna terrible espada, ancha y fuerte,	A terrible and broad and mighty sword
Con que a todos por tierra nos ha puesto,	With which he has stricken us all to earth,
Valiente por extremo. Y, por extremo,	A man extremely valiant. And also
Vna bella donzella también buscan,	My people seek, as well, a beauteous maid,
Más hermosa que el Sol y más que el Cielo.	More beautiful than the sun or the heavens.
Preguntan dónde está y qué se han hecho.	They ask where they are, what they have done.
(PÉREZ DE VILLAGRÁ 1992:298–299)	(PÉREZ DE VILLAGRÁ 1992:174, ENGLISH TRANSLATION)

The astonished Spanish officer realized that none other than Santiago and the Virgin had come to their aid in the slaughter of 800 Acomans. Even with such fierce spiritual resolve, it was in the material realm and with the technological advantage of steel and gunpowder that the deadly work was carried out in what was deemed *una guerra justa*—a just war—the legal justification demanded by Spanish law for military actions such as the Battle of Acoma (Campa 1979:31).

MILAGRO DE SAN ACACIO

Although the kingdom of Nuevo México was initially founded through armed conquest and forced tribute, the 1680 Pueblo Revolt shattered imperial dreams forever. The survival of the colony depended on military alliance and cultural accommodation with the Pueblos forged in the eighteenth century during sporadic but constant warfare with nomadic Comanches, Apaches, Navajo, and Utes. Hispanos and Pueblos fought side by side in defense of their communities (M. Simmons 1977:77–106).

The Nuevo Mexicano pioneers who founded the first settlements in the San Luis Valley in the mid-nineteenth century were markedly distinct in spirit and cultural complexion from their conquistador forebears. The struggle for survival had tempered a way of life based on accommodation and cooperation with their neighbors. Despite the American invasion in 1846 and the hindrance of a legal system hostile to their interests, the new promised land (the last frontier) was settled in what was to become southern Colorado (Campa 1979:142–155; Nostrand 1992:82–88). After dwellings were raised from the earth and *acequias* were dug to water the fields, the human obstacle in this new landscape was confronted. The Muache Utes did not appreciate Hispano encroachment on their homeland. San Acacio, a crucified warrior saint whose intervention led not to bloodshed but rather to an armistice with the Utes who opposed the settlement of the San Luis Valley, miraculously mediated the conflict.[2]

Since no contemporaneous literary or documentary source exists for the milagro, the story is best recovered from the chain of oral performances that link it to the present. In a search for tellers of the milagro, my starting point was the 1853 church in San Acacio, the oldest church in Colorado. One September afternoon I contemplated the altar and took notes from an old newspaper article mounted in a frame on a post.

The oldest layer of the story is carved and engraved in the holy images of San Acacio behind the altar, which portray a crucified Roman centurion dressed in the black hat and blue uniform of a nineteenth-century Mexican dragoon. In Nuevo Mexicano folk theology, San Acacio and Santa Librada are the two crucified saints in the regional pantheon. Through their sacrifice, they share the redemptive power of the cross with Jesus himself (Steele 1994:48). In early Christian times, Acacio was one of a legion of Roman soldiers who converted to Christianity and were crucified on the slopes of Mount Ararat in Armenia. His valor and sacrifice were an inspiration to Crusaders, and his crown of thorns and other relics are still venerated in Cologne, Germany, and Prague, Czechoslovakia (Kelly and Rogers 1993:3). Since Rome considered the Reconquest of Spain a Holy Crusade, it is no mystery how his devotion spread to Spain and New Mexico.

The next artifact I examined was a narrative, the framed newspaper story mentioned earlier entitled "Miracle That Saved the People Is Early Legend," dated June 25, 1951, from the *Alamosa Courier*:

> Religion played an important role in the lives of early settlers with almost all of them devout Catholics. When it came to naming their towns, it was the custom to select their favorite saint and name the town after the saint. This was the case in many of the towns settled in the San Luis area. San Francisco, San Acacio, San Luis, San Pedro and others were all saints. This is the legend told by many of the old timers about San Acacio. It is called The Miracle That Saved The People. Indian attacks were always violent and sudden against early settlers whom the Indians hated for their trespassing [on] what the Red Men felt were their hunting grounds. Thus explorers and settlers were forced to take extreme precautions against attacks, usually in the form of two or three guards constantly watching for Indians. It was in the spring of 1853, only two years after San Luis had been settled, that the story, which developed into the legend, which is told below, happened.
>
> **EVERYTHING QUIET**
>
> Beautiful spring weather had turned the grass to a smooth green carpet with most of the men in the fields to work the crops and the boys of the town herding the settlement's small flocks of sheep. The women were serenely taking care of their usual household chores and caring for the small children. As was the custom, two or three men had remained on watch against Indian attacks and to give the alarm in the event one occurred. On this day it was the duty of Juan Vigil, Miguel Jáquez, and a young lad to guard the plaza. As they stood guard, the trio suddenly saw a black cloud of dust rising in the east and as they watched, it grew closer and larger. They could see that it was a great band of Indians rapidly approaching with an obvious intention of attacking the unprotected village. As they watched in horror, the skies darkened with clouds, and violent flashes of lightning speared through the heavens, one after another. Crashing peals of thunder rumbled through the air, but the Indians rushed forward.

PRAY FOR HELP

Seeing it was too late to send the boy to the fields for help from the men, since the Indians were almost upon them, Juan Vigil asked his two companions to join him in prayer to San Acacio. This saint had been particularly brave [and] had been sainted for his efforts in behalf of Christianity. So in the face of the onrushing Indians, the trio knelt in prayer, asking aid in their great distress and promising to build a church in San Acacio's honor if they were saved from the attack. The Indians were close enough now for one to see their fierce features and hear their yells. Suddenly, a strange look came on the face of the chief who was leading the band. He immediately turned and fled with great speed in the direction from which they had attacked, his tribe following him. The three men were much surprised, but were sure their saint had answered their prayers and had saved them. To express their gratitude, they called the women and children of the village and all offered a prayer of thanksgiving. In the fall of 1853 they started building the church as promised in their prayer to San Acacio. The building stills stands in the town today.

A close reading of other published sources reveals the author of the article as Luther E. Bean, a prominent educator and community historian based at Adams State College. In an interview with a retired San Acacio teacher whom Bean recruited and mentored during the teacher shortage caused by World War II, his unacknowledged sources became clear (Jáquez 1997). Dolores "Lula" Jáquez is one of the keepers and narrators of the Milagro de San Acacio who lives across the lane from the church. For a class project at Adams State with Bean during the war, she interviewed an elderly Navajo named Alejandro López, who told her a complete and lengthy version of the miracle story. She had heard fragments of it growing up in San Acacio, especially since both Juan Vigil and Miguel Jacques, mentioned in the article, are ancestors of hers and her husband's.[3]

Lula Jáquez's performance of the milagro, minus the literary embellishments, contains almost all of the features in the newspaper report, which was probably based on her college paper. The most notable difference is the credit given to the faith of the women of San Acacio for the miracle. It was the women who had stayed behind in the village, engrossed in child care and the annual adobe plastering of the houses:

It is said that the men would go to work in the fields, to sow, because that is all there was to do here. And some . . . had their animals. And the women stayed behind here, working on the houses, plastering with something like cement, but it was earth, yes, earth plaster. That is how they plastered their houses. And there were Indians all around and they hadn't made friends yet, they were only wanting to make mischief. (Jácquez 1997; author's translation)

When the band of attacking Indians was spotted, the men were outside the village walls working in the fields and with their flocks, too far away to answer the alarm. According to Lula's telling, the fervent prayers of the women brought the attackers to a halt:

> And they say that a dust cloud appeared raised by horses. I understand that it was from that direction that they came on horses, from the south, and it was the Indians. Navajos I think they were.[4] Well the Indians were coming on their horses, and the women came out very frightened, they were afraid. And their little ones were there and they wanted to protect their families. But the Indians were coming very close, and it is said that they [the women] said, "No, we can't do anything, we have to appeal to God." And they all kneeled and began praying. Well here they say that the Indians turned back. By and by they made friends with them. (Jácquez 1997; author's translation)

Later the Indians reported seeing a group of soldiers dressed in uniforms like San Acacio's, and they decided to halt the attack.

> And there they talked about what had happened . . . to them and why the Indians had retreated and gone back. There were other soldiers, they were going to get them and they were many more than the Indians that were coming. So they said that it was God who had saved them because of their prayers. . . . Everyone said that their parents had told them this story and then a man came, he was a Navajo, and he told it to me. And I wrote it [down]. His name was Alejandro López. He liked to read very much. He wrote it down for himself . . . and he told me that he had written what people had told him. And that is why I told it too there in Adams State. I think I talked to Mr. Bean about it. I wrote something on it, a report that I had to write for school, but I think that's the way I told it to them, the way that they had told it to me. (Jácquez 1997; author's translation)

Remarkable also in this schoolteacher's narrative are the numerous references to her education. Lula was embarrassed by her family's humble adobe house and its cloth ceilings when Bean visited to recruit her to Adams State College while the boys were away at war. Her research on community history is much appreciated, if unacknowledged by Bean, who validates local history and culture in his writings. For Lula Jáquez, a personal part of the miracle was that San Acacio helped her become a teacher, since his story gave her academic credibility and, ultimately, the credentials to teach.

Lula Jáquez's college project, Bean's 1951 newspaper article and subsequent 1962 book (Bean 1951, 1972a), and Lula's 1997 performance of the Milagro de San Acacio (Jácquez 1997) all attribute the miracle to God and the crucified warrior saint. Bean never speculates about what the Indians saw that caused them to retreat. Jáquez says it was the apparition of "other soldiers," more numerous than the Indians. In saying "other," her point of reference is the presence in the village of the soldier saint, San Acacio.

THE SEARCH FOR "PIONEERS": HISPANO VS. AMERICAN AGENCY

In the small city of San Luis, Colorado, outside the Costilla County Courthouse is a plaque dedicated to the "Pioneers" of the San Luis Valley on a generic monument with no indication or acknowledgment of the community's Hispano roots. Colorado was granted statehood in 1876, after the arrival of its Anglo-American founding fathers in the Gold Rush of 1859. In honor of Colorado's status as the "Centennial State," historic buildings have plaques, and ranches are celebrated.

The fact that Colorado's Spanish Mexican heritage predates everything else by several generations is not part of public official discourse, even in the southern part of the state. Finally, however, a mid–twentieth-century interest in regionalism emerged, spurred by surveys by the Farm Security Administration and the Works Progress Administration (Deutsch 1987:162–199). A series of articles on Hispanic contributions to Colorado history publicized little-known facts on early settlements, farming and irrigation, and place names (Cheetham 1928; Hafen 1932; V. Simmons 1979; Smith 1947). Important surveys of Hispano folklore followed in the 1980s (Everts 1986; Reyna 1980).

However, most historical accounts stop short of attributing any significant sense of agency to Colorado's Hispano pioneers. American historians link Colorado's Hispano settlement to the establishment of U.S. Army installations during the Ute wars, notably Fort Massachusetts, which was renamed Fort Garland (Hart 1974:46). Revisionist historians tell a different story. Greater numbers of Hispano settlers did come to southern Colorado after hostilities subsided, but many had arrived years before, fully prepared to coexist and even trade with the Utes. Frances Swadesh writes that "[t]he growth of trading partnerships with the Utes made it possible for settlers to petition for new grants and set up residence in areas remote from administrative, ecclesiastical, and military supervision" (quoted in Swadesh 1974:47). In the 1850s, when Anglo politicians proposed an "All Ute Removal" plan—with its genocidal implications—Hispanos actively opposed it (Swadesh 1974:77–78). According to Ute oral histories, when the plan was implemented many Muache families and individuals used their Spanish surnames to defy Indian agents, pass as "Mexicans," and remain in their homeland area—from the San Luis Valley east toward Walsenburg and north toward Denver (Naranjo and Luján 2000:11).

The foundational Milagro de San Acacio is rooted in this context of accommodation and coexistence with Indian people. The implications of the scholarly imposition of the *"leyenda negra"* (Black legend) stereotype of the conquering knight in shining armor must be challenged.[5] True, it does fit better with the hispanophile image of Hispanos as "Spanish Colonials" promoted by scholars and native elites alike in the first two-thirds of the twentieth century. But the days and the discourse of colonial glory are long gone. A question of cultural authority emerges when scholars working from outside a cultural tradition misread the process of cultural translation and misconstrue a tradition in their writings. The Milagro de San Acacio is a story that must be heard from its most authoritative source: the voice of its narrators.

EL MILAGRO DE SAN ACACIO: CULTURAL RECOVERY

A search for the authoritative keepers and tellers of the San Acacio legend led to the same Costilla County Courthouse with the generic "Pioneers" plaque and to County Assessor Maclovio Martínez, who was raised in San Acacio and is a cousin of Lula Jáquez. Just as Lula prefaced her performance with a brief genealogical introduction, he began by fully situating himself within the chain of oral transmission, thereby establishing his narrative authority (Martínez 1997):

> I was born in San Acacio . . . across the road from where the church is. That was the house of my grandfather, José Elías Argüello, but the people for some reason called him Moises. He never worked for anyone else, he always worked for himself. And there he had a good portion of land, and what is interesting is that the father of my grandfather was Tiwa, he was from Taos. And the people of San Acacio remember that he still used his blanket like the old ones in Taos. He had his braids he wore, and this was the father of my grandfather. He married here with a woman and they had an only son, my grandfather. And then my grandfather married a Córdova, the ones from there in San Acacio. And we always gathered to hear about what was going on. And I believe that in those gatherings the story of San Acacio was told and how San Acacio came to be the patron of that place. (Martínez 1997; author's translation)

Then Maclovio set the stage with a description of the village and the fact that it was built as a line of joined houses like a fort, for defensive purposes. With the stage set and the lines of his authority clear, the Milagro de San Acacio began:

> In the first days of the settlement of the village, the people already had their fields outside town, but their houses were always in the village because of the security there. And they said that on that particular day, the

women stayed in the village to do their chores, to wash wool, to wash as they did before, no? Because before they made mattresses of wool that they themselves sheared from their sheep, from the lambs that they had. . . . And then . . . all of a sudden on the rise that is toward the south, which is about half or three quarters of a mile from the town, the women saw that there were Utes there, those which we believe were the Utes, mounted on horseback, and they were coming very fast because there was a lot of dust where the horses kicked it up because they came running, galloping. And when they arrived, when they saw [the band of Utes], well, it was too late to warn the men that were out in the fields. Then they say that they wanted to hide, but they didn't know where, they were very confused, they didn't know what to do. Then one señor Vigil, I think that was the name, or Valdez, I don't remember well the name anymore . . . was one of the elders that were there. They say that he knelt down and told them, "Let us pray." And when they were praying, then they said, "Let us pray to San Acacio" who was a centurion, who was a soldier that died. (Martínez 1997; author's translation)

The now familiar elements of the legend are all there in unembellished language but rich in detail. The women are occupied with a typical spring chore, the washing of wool-stuffed mattresses, while the men are in the fields. The dust cloud raised causes them to spot the band of mounted Utes, and the patriarch Vigil leads the desperate prayers to San Acacio. Surrounded by a library of tomes in the office of the county assessor, Maclovio speculated that his ancestors must have learned of the obscure Roman saint from their reading: "It was probably him . . . because surely in one of those old books, those books of saints or something, they had read about that youth that had been a martyr in Turkey, I think. Very early it was, he was a Roman, yes, a Roman soldier. And then they started praying to him to intercede and save them or to warn the people to come and save us" (Martínez 1997; author's translation).

In an extensive aside, Maclovio explained in great detail how an old Ute woman separated from her band revealed the miracle to the people of San Acacio. He also refers to the *criados,* or Indian servants Hispano families kept, and their knowledge of Native languages:

But they tell that in those days the Utes passed by here on the way to their places, surely toward the San Luis Valley, toward Ignacio and all those places that were theirs, and further north also in Mesa Verde, in all those places where they had established their homes, no? And they did pass by, and sometimes when they did, the Indians, and we don't know why or what for, but sometimes they abandoned the old Utes, men and women would separate from the tribe because they probably couldn't follow them as fast as they were going and they decided they would end their life, no?

> But it was surely one of these things that happened near García or Costilla and all. And they found an old woman that was left behind, well, in the sage brush. She had stayed behind and they found her and brought her to their villages, and then there were many servants in the households of the people over there, many Indians, Utes and Navajos and Apaches probably as well, who were servants of the people in these parts. And the people understood, they were bilingual and knew the Indian and Spanish languages there. (Martínez 1997; author's translation)

Then Maclovio carefully addressed the central question of attribution of the miracle. Did San Acacio or Santiago deliver the people? Using rhetorical questions, reported speech, and speculative subjunctive constructions, he stated, then answered, the doubts. According to the Ute woman's report, the attackers saw a Spanish soldier on a white horse in the clouds, but the apparition was caused by the "magic" of San Acacio. The white horse may have been an attribute of Santiago, but the people decided that their deliverance was attributable to San Acacio. The prayers had been directed to the crucified centurion, not the Moorslayer, and they had been answered.

> And they communicated, and by these means I believe that this old woman told the people who understood the language what had happened at that instant when San Acacio was going to be attacked because when they came there was the image of a Spanish soldier, surely they saw it, on a white horse, in the clouds, and for that reason they thought that it was the magic of the people in San Acacio that had created this rescue for themselves, this champion for themselves, no? And that that's how it had happened, and that is why . . . this bunch of young men as they surely were . . . turned around and didn't arrive at the village because this image that they had seen in the sky had frightened them and they believed that it was some kind of magic and they left. And that more or less is the story of San Acacio. (Martínez 1997; author's translation)

In the continuing discussion, Maclovio implied that a conflation of attributes had been the cause of the doubts, and he settled those doubts. He also mentioned attributes of San Isidro that are ascribed to San Acacio. On his feast day the saint is taken out to bless the fields. Personal petitions are made for health and well-being, and an *alabado* (hymn of praise) to San Acacio is sung with the same tune as the hymn to San Isidro. Additional petitions were made for the protection of Hispano soldiers in World Wars I and II, Korea, and Vietnam—a request squarely within San Acacio's purview.

In his miracle, San Acacio may have sent an apparition that resembled Santiago, but not for the purpose of exterminating Indian foes; rather, he did so to pacify hostile relations and set the stage for communication and peace.

The saint serves as a cultural and political mediator for communication and coexistence, not for conquest and annihilation. The legend articulates a new sense of nationhood based on a discourse of survival and resistance, not one of power and subjugation.

CONCLUSION: "LA NACIÓNCITA DE LA SANGRE DE CRISTO"

The popular poet Cleofes Vigil, who was from San Cristóbal, New Mexico, not far south of San Acacio, christened the Hispano nation "La Nacióncita de la Sangre de Cristo" (Little Nation of the Blood of Christ)—a cultural community built on sacrifice, redemption, and perseverance. It is a hybrid, mestizo nation, named after the mountain range that traverses it and built on an indigenous sense of belonging, which he calls *"querencia"* according to the folk term. Mikhail Bakhtin defines this "natio," or sense of belonging, as a force more deeply rooted than conventional nationalism: "As for the 'nation,' it is both historically determined and general. As a term, it refers both to the modern nation-state and to something more ancient and nebulous—the 'natio'—a local community, domicile, family, condition of belonging. The distinction is often obscured by nationalists who seek to place their own country in an 'immemorial past' where its arbitrariness cannot be questioned" (1981:45).

The Milagro de San Acacio is not situated in a glorious immemorial past but instead in the difficult spring of 1853, when Hispano settlers made peace with their Ute neighbors and affirmed their tenuous presence in a new corner of their homeland, their querencia. Hispano narrators may insist that the miracle was verified by contemporary Ute accounts, namely the legendary accounts of the old Ute woman found wandering in the sage (Martínez 1997). But such corroboration seems wishful, since there appear to be no independent Ute oral historical accounts of what may have happened at San Acacio in 1853. What is known is that the Utes were comfortable enough with the Hispano presence that they frequently camped and traded in the area into the late 1860s. The Muache Utes loved the San Luis Valley so much that Bear Dances were held near San Acacio as late as 1868, when the ethnic cleansing and removals by the U.S. Army were finally complete (Naranjo and Luján 2000:11).

In his "Himno a la Nacióncita de la Sangre de Cristo," Cleofes Vigil sings the praises of querencia and the mestizo nation he calls *"la nueva raza,"* the new race.[6] Idyllic scenes of harmony, intercultural desire, and the abundance of the harvest prevail. Performed in the hybrid musical style of the nineteenth-century *"indita"* (Indian) ballads, a vocable refrain ends each stanza with a lyric invocation of indigenous roots. The new race that inhabits the New

Mexico–southern Colorado homeland is born of Spanish and Indian parents and imbued with the sacred notion that the land itself is the Holy Mother of us all:

Vinieron los españoles	The Spaniards came
de la España a esta tierra,	from Spain to this land,
donde hallaron sus querencias	where they found their heart's desire
hermosas indias morenas,	and beautiful dark Indian women,
jeyá, jeyá, jeyá, ja.	heya, heya, heya, ha.
Aquellas indias hermosas	Those beautiful Indian women
virtuosas y llenas de gracia,	virtuous and full of grace,
escogieron para esposas	were chosen as wives
donde nació linda raza,	and bore a new handsome race,
jeyá, jeyá, jeyá, ja.	heya, heya, heya, ha.
Raza buena y amorosa	A good and loving race
color bronce de mestizo,	bronze-colored people,
mezcla del indio del pueblo	mixture of the Pueblo Indian
donde salió un genízaro,	from whence came the janissary,
jeyá, jeyá, jeyá, ja.	heya, heya, heya, ha.
Con sus cantos penetrantes	With their penetrating song
y sus cuadros espirituales,	and spiritual paintings,
alaban la santa tierra	they praise the holy earth
que para todos es la madre,	a mother to us all,
jeyá, jeyá, jeyá, ja.	heya, heya, heya, ha.
Ya se oía en los campos	In the countryside that song
aquel canto aquella danza,	that dance could be heard,
retumbaba en la montaña	echoing in the mountains
que Sangre de Cristo llamaban,	they called the Blood of Christ,
jeyá, jeyá, jeyá, ja.	heya, heya, heya, ha.
Españoles y cumanches	Spaniards and Comanches
todos en armonía,	all in harmony,
se juntaban a cantar	would come together to sing
y a bailar con alegría,	and dance with gladness,
jeyá, jeyá, jeyá, ja.	heya, heya, heya, ha.
Comiendo elotes tostados	Eating roast corn
que la tierra producía,	that the earth produced,
machucando carne seca	pounding dried meat
de cíbolo que había,	from the buffalo,
jeyá, jeyá, jeyá, ja.	heya, heya, heya, ha.

(LAMADRID AND LOEFFLER 1994:37–38)

NOTES

1. Fieldwork in southern Colorado supported by the Southwest Hispanic Research Institute and the Center for Regional Studies at the University of New Mexico.

2. The U.S. Army campaigned against the Utes after hostilities broke out in December 1854 when Fort Pueblo was attacked by Chief Blanco, the leader of a band of Muache Utes and Jicarilla Apaches. The major battles of the 1855 campaign took place well north of San Acacio and on the other side of the Front Range in the Arkansas Valley (Meketa and Chacón 1986:98–104).

3. Jáquez and Jaques are the Spanish and Portuguese spellings, respectively, of the last name of Lula's husband's family. Her grandfather was Juan Vigil, a descendant of the Juan Vigil in the story.

4. Another difference is Jáquez's identification of the attacking Indians as Navajos. Historically, mostly Utes and Jicarilla Apaches frequented the San Luis Valley. All other references to the legend and the history of the valley mention the Utes as the most prominent tribe in the area.

5. With a cast of stereotypical characters such as cruel conquistadors, corrupt priests, lazy dons, and miscegenated, superstition-ridden masses, the *leyenda negra* was the Black legend about Spain and its empire propagated in England. Used over centuries for propaganda purposes, the legend has saturated folk and popular culture and is a perpetual source of images and ideas that fuel anti-Hispanic sentiment and racism among English-speaking peoples (Juderías y Loyot 1967).

6. Cleofes Vigil was honored in 1976 with the Smithsonian National Heritage Award as a mastersinger of *alabado* hymns and other traditional New Mexican music.

REFERENCES

Bakhtin, Mikhail. *The Dialogic Imagination,* Michael Holquist and Caryl Emerson, eds. Austin: University of Texas Press, 1981.

Bean, Luther E. *Land of the Blue Sky People: A Story of the San Luis Valley.* Alamosa, CO: Printed by Ye Olde Print Shoppe, 1972 [1962], 97–98.

———— [probable author]. "Miracle That Saved the People Is Early Legend." *The Alamosa Courier,* June 25, 1951.

Campa, Arthur L. *Hispanic Culture in the Southwest.* Norman: University of Oklahoma Press, 1979.

Chávez, Fran Angélico. *My Penitente Land: Reflection on Spanish New Mexico.* Santa Fe: Museum of New Mexico Press, 1974.

Cheetham, Francis T. "Early Settlements of Southern Colorado." *Colorado Magazine* 5 (1928): 1–8.

DeMarco, Barbara. "*Cantaron la victoria*: Spanish Literary Tradition and the 1680 Pueblo Revolt." In *Recovering the U.S. Hispanic Literary Heritage,* vol. 3, María Herrera-Sobek and Virginia Sánchez Korrol, eds. Houston: Arte Público Press, 2000, 163–172.

Deutsch, Sarah. *No Separate Refuge: Culture, Class, and Gender on an Anglo-Hispanic Frontier in the American Southwest, 1880–1940.* New York: Oxford University Press, 1987.

Everts, Dana. *Tradiciones del Valle: Folklore Collected in the San Luis Valley.* Alamosa, CO: Río Grande Arts Center, 1986.

Hafen, LeRoy R. "Colorado Cities—Their Founding and the Origin of Their Names." *Colorado Magazine* 9 (1932): 182.

Jáquez, Dolores. Personal interview with the author. San Acacio, CO, September 12, 1997.
Juderías y Loyot, Julián. *La Leyenda Negra: Estudios acerca del Concepto de España en el Extranjero*. Madrid: Editora Nacional, 1967 [1912].
Kelly, Sean, and Rosemary Rogers. *Saints Preserve Us! Everything You Need to Know about Every Saint You'll Ever Need*. New York: Random House, 1993.
Lamadrid, Enrique R., and Jack Loeffler. *Tesoros del Espíritu: A Portrait in Sound of Hispanic New Mexico*. Embudo, NM: Academia and El Norte, 1994.
Martínez, Maclovio. Personal interview with the author. San Luis, CO, September 12, 1997.
Meketa, Jacqueline D., and Rafael Chacón. *Legacy of Honor: The Life of Rafael Chacón, a Nineteenth-Century New Mexican*, Jacqueline D. Meketa, ed. Albuquerque: University of New Mexico Press, 1986.
Myers, Joan, Marc Simmons, and Donna Pierce. *Santiago: Saint of Two Worlds*. Albuquerque: University of New Mexico Press, 1991.
Naranjo, Alden B., and Mónica Luján. "Ute Creation Story." In *Ute Indian Arts and Culture: From Prehistory to the New Millennium*, William Wroth, ed. Colorado Springs: Taylor Museum, 2000, 7–19.
Nostrand, Richard L. *The Hispano Homeland*. Norman: University of Oklahoma Press, 1992.
Pérez de Villagrá, Gaspar. *Historia de la Nueva México, 1610*, trans. and ed. by Miguel Encinias, Alfred Rodríguez, and Joseph P. Sánchez. Albuquerque: University of New Mexico Press, 1992.
Reyna, José R. *Folklore Chicano del Valle de San Luis, Colorado*. San Antonio: Penca, 1980.
Robe, Stanley L. *Hispanic Legends from New Mexico: Narratives from the R. D. Jameson Collection*. Berkeley: University of California Press, 1980.
Sharp, D. D. 1936. "The San Antonio Fiesta." S-240 Folk Ways, file no. 5, drawer no. 5, folio no. 2, 5/23/36 cl-1700. Albuquerque: Works Progress Administration, New Mexico Federal Writers Project.
Simmons, Marc. *New Mexico: An Interpretive History*. Albuquerque: University of New Mexico Press, 1977.
Simmons, Virginia McConnell. *The San Luis Valley: Land of the Six-Armed Cross*. Boulder: Pruett, 1979.
Smith, Emilia Gallegos. "Reminiscences of Early San Luis." *Colorado Magazine* 24 (1947): 24–25.
Steele, Thomas J. *Santos and Saints: The Religious Folk Art of Hispanic New Mexico*. Santa Fe: Ancient City Press, 1994.
Swadesh, Frances. *Los Primeros Pobladores: Hispanic Americans of the Ute Frontier*. South Bend, IN: University of Notre Dame Press, 1974.

Lorenzo A. Trujillo

Music of Colorado and New Mexico's Río Grande

A JOURNEY IN TIME: PAST, PRESENT, FUTURE

Traditional Río Grande Chicano/Hispano[1] music and dance in Colorado and New Mexico are influenced by many cultures of the world. Indigenous peoples, European settlers, and recent Mexican and Latino immigrants have all created a unique expression in music and dance among Río Grande peoples. This chapter provides insight into the many influences in the traditions, old and new, that we hear and see. More important, it presents common themes of culture transmission through many generations. The music and dance of Hispano populations of Colorado and New Mexico have developed over the past 600-plus years. The evolution begins and moves through various hallmark periods in time: the medieval period (1100–1400), the conquest of Mexico (1500–1600), the early explorations into New Mexico and Colorado (1700–1800), the early 1900s into the last half of the 1900s, to today.

MEDIEVAL PERIOD–RENAISSANCE

Spain is a country of many influences: Celt-Iberians, Iberians, Greeks, Phoenicians, Carthaginians, Romans, Jews, Visigoths, Moors, and Arabs. From 711 until 1492, Spain was under the tremendous influence of the Moors and Arabs.

Moorish and Arabic influences are very evident today in the architecture, music, dance, and general culture of Spain as it has evolved into Hispano America. Ceramic tiles, the flair for clicking the heels in a flamenco-type rhythm, the syncopation of beats, and the sense of honor, pride, and the importance of the *caballo*[2] all bring to life the influence of the Moors and Arabs.

For example, the Moors and Arabs proudly represented their feelings in their songs and dance. An anonymous poem was written to Abenamar, the last Moorish king, as he left Spain in 1492, the beginning of the Renaissance. In the poem, a song about the great last king is sung: *"El día que tú naciste grandes señales había"* (The day you were born there were great signs). He sang of the great castles built by the Moors (*"Altos son y relucían"*). This sense of pride as represented in their songs and poetry remains today among the descendants of Spain who migrated to the United States in the 1500s and 1600s and is represented in the music and dance, which is so statuesque.

This cultural value of pride is developed even further in the legend and life story of "El Cid" (Rodrigo Díaz de Vivar, 1043–1099). El Cid was a knight whose fame has transcended centuries. Of particular importance today is a tradition described in the epic poem *El Cantar de Mío Cid*, written in approximately 1140.[3] The tradition described is one that is reenacted to this day in Colorado and New Mexico. It ties the sense of pride to the value of family honor. The tradition of *La Entriega* is the ceremony in which the parents and family of the bride and groom symbolically give the two away to each other and acknowledge that they are no longer the children of their parents but are one with each other.

The poetic structure of *El Cantar de Mío Cid* (Poema) is important to understand because this same structure is used in contemporary music and songs. The Poema was called a *cantar* (literally, "to sing") because it was sung by *juglares* (troubadours). The Poema of 3,730 verses of assonant rhyme (rhyme in the last accented vowel or any final vowel that may follow in the line but not of consonants), of variable syllables and hemistich metric (shortened line of metric patterns), tells a tale of the wedding of the daughters of El Cid.[4] This poetic structure, as it evolved, will be discussed later in this chapter as it developed in the song and poetry written for the entriega ceremony previously referred to and will be described herein.

In the second cantar of *Mío Cid*, we are told about a series of events that occurred at the wedding of the two daughters of El Cid. Two courtiers, the Princes of Carrión, wished to marry two daughters of El Cid, Doña Elvira and Doña Sol, who with their mother, Doña Ximena, were reunited with the hero (El Cid) in Valencia. The princes asked the king to arrange the marriage,

3.1. Photo of Karen Trujillo-Guzman. Permission granted by Trujillo-Guzman.

and it was agreed to by El Cid.[5] The wedding party, wearing elegant clothing, walked to be greeted by El Cid and Doña Ximena. They sat down on a magnificent *escaño* (bench with a back).[6] Then El Cid gave his two daughters to the young princes. As he did so, he told the princes to take them for their wives for the honor and good of the four of them.[7] They left the church and paraded on their horses to the place of the wedding reception. These elements of the wedding ceremony are replicated today in *La Entriega de los Novios*. The ceremony of giving of the newlyweds to each other, followed by a procession or parade, is explained next in its more modern version.

LA ENTRIEGA DE LOS NOVIOS

La Entriega de los Novios is the final part of the traditional wedding ceremony of the Hispano people of southern Colorado and northern New Mexico.[8] This ceremony, with the bonding of the bride and groom to each other and the parade or march of the wedding party, can be seen at traditional Hispano weddings today as in the past, since the 1100s. The wedding ceremony is usually held in a church. A contemporary rite of the ceremony is for the father to give the daughter to her future husband. This is the tradition in most church weddings, when the father walks his daughter to the altar and hands her over to the groom. La Entriega is similar, but it offers the newlyweds much more.

When El Cid gave his daughters away to his new sons-in law, a procession followed. At that time and because the members of the wedding party were royalty, they left the church in a procession mounted on stallions. Today, the bridal party leaves the church in decorated cars or limousines in a procession to the reception. Less today than twenty years ago, young men would decorate their cars (equivalent to the stallions of the Cid party) and parade them through town, honking their horns to announce the wedding and the bridal party. This still occurs in smaller rural towns of Colorado and New Mexico.

When the bridal party arrives at the reception, they are received by the guests and families of the newlyweds. This activity is similar to what was presented in the Poema, described earlier. The newlyweds enter the reception hall in a promenade. The *padrinos* (godparents and a special couple of honor)[9] lead the procession in weaving circles, bridges, and lines through the reception hall. The guests typically join in the procession to start the special celebration of the marriage. The procession is led by a traditional ensemble of guitar and violins (Figures 3.2, 3.3). In the 1100s the procession was probably led by the juglares playing the string instruments of that period—the viol, guitar-like and violin-like instruments.

Marcha De Los Novios

As played by Eva Nuáñez and Lorenzo A. Trujillo
Transcription by Lorenzo F. Trujillo and Lorenzo A. Trujillo

3.2. A recording of this piece is available from Southwest Musicians: Musical Traditions of Colorado and New Mexico, 4660 West 101 Place, Westminster, CO 80031.

As a result of contemporary immigration patterns and the proximity to Mexico, this ceremonial march is often done to the tune of the "Marcha de Zacatecas." The "Marcha de Zacatecas" is a contemporary piece of music composed in 1891 by Génaro Codina Fernández. This composition is more widely recognized by Mexican immigrants and their descendants as the marcha music—an interesting development because the "Marcha de Zacatecas" was composed as a march for soldiers going off to war. In 1910 it was the hymn of revolutionary groups, especially in the powerful Division of the North commanded by Francisco Villa. Even with the different music, the procession remains the same throughout the southwestern United States.

Even though La Entriega is discussed here as a historical celebration, the ceremony is very much a part of modern wedding celebrations. In contemporary celebrations, La Entriega de los Novios is presented at the end of the reception meal and before the dance. According to Enrique Lamadrid, in colonial times in Colorado and New Mexico, there were too few priests in rural areas. If a couple wanted to get married, La Entriega de los Novios served as the marriage ceremony.[10]

In the 1800s and early 1900s, La Entriega was done at the home of the bride's parents. The newlyweds knelt on a white sheet, surrounded by their

3.3. The photo of the Marcha de los Novios was taken at the August 2, 1972, wedding of Suzanne Rael and Derrick Martinez in Arroyo Seco, New Mexico. Permission granted by author.

godparents, parents, grandparents, and other family members. The singer sang the verses of advice and wisdom to the newlyweds and their guests. If a verse impressed a listener, he or she would drop money on the sheet on the floor. In the past, the money was collected and paid to the *cantador* (singer).[11] However, the custom has changed; the bridal couple now keeps the money, and sometimes the parents pay the singer who has composed special verses for the event.

The song is presented in a traditional *romance* (romance) poetic verse structure. The form presented earlier, from the time of El Cid, was in a free verse form with assonant rhyme on the last accented vowel. In the romance form, the versification is more structured and represents a higher level of sophistication and difficulty. Romance structure is composed in four-line stanzas with eight syllables in each line, with stress on the seventh syllable and assonance in alternate lines, and with rhyme occurring on the penultimate and final vowels in the second and fourth lines.[12] There are often thirty or more stanzas of advice, blessings, and farewells. Traditional singers have always composed many of their own verses, especially for a particular occasion. Legend has it that very good *cantantes* would improvise the verses simultaneously while singing. For example, here are two stanzas from La Entriega de los Novios, as sung by Eva Nuánez:

Esta mañana salieron	This morning they left
Cuatro rosas de la igl<u>e</u>si<u>a</u>	four roses from the church
El padrino y la madrina	the best man and the matron of honor
Y el princés con su princ<u>e</u>s<u>a</u>	the prince with his princess
Estos nuevos esposados	These newlyweds
Reciban las bend<u>i</u>ci<u>o</u>nes	receive the blessings
De sus padres y sus madres	from their fathers and mothers
Y también sus abuel<u>i</u>t<u>o</u>s	and from their grandparents.

(EVA NUANEZ [AUTHOR'S AUNT]; AUTHOR'S TRANSLATION)

The romance form is evident, as follows:

Es/ta/ ma/ña/na/ sa/lier/on
1 2   3 4 5   6 7   8   eight syllables

Rhyme occurs in the underlined syllables in the vowels in the second and fourth stanzas, as follows:

Cuatro rosas de la igl<u>e</u>si<u>a</u>	e and a
Y el princes con su princ<u>e</u>s<u>a</u>	e and a

    This traditional versification reappears in songs that songwriters are composing today. One of these songs is presented later in this chapter. Figure 3.4 provides the music Eva Nuánez uses when she sings La Entriega de los Novios. However, different cantadores will use different melodies, usually a waltz tempo.

    Verses like those sung in *El Cantar de Mío Cid* are still present in La Entriega. For example, in the Poema cited earlier the advice is "take them for your wives for the honor and good of the four of you."[13] In the La Entriega verses sung today, these same words often appear in the stanzas. It is notable that the same sage advice has been repeated throughout the centuries and still has meaning today.

    To further the understanding of how history remains alive in contemporary culture, the Spanish that was used in *El Cid* is used today in La Entriega, often in the parlance of old-time Río Grande people and the young who

La Entriega De Los Novios

As sung and played by Eva Nuánez and Lorenzo A. Trujillo
Transcription by Lorenzo F. Trujillo and Lorenzo A. Trujillo

___

3.4. *La Entriega de los Novios*, music score.

learned Spanish from their grandparents. The conjugation and use of *entriega* represents a linguistic archaism characteristic of the traditional Spanish used in Colorado and New Mexico. In ancient Spanish, examples of this conjugation are found in published works of the Middle Ages. For example, in *El Conde Lucanor* (1330), the text provides: *Et despues, fallamos homnes en el camino que nos dixieron que non era bien* (And after we encountered men on the road who told us that it was not good).[14] *Dixieron* (they told us) is an archaic verb conjugation and orthography of Spanish, a form not used in modern-day Spanish. The modern Spanish form is *dijieron*. This is like the use of the word "entriega." The modern Spanish form is *entrega*. Also, the Spanish language in the 1300s, which was Latin Vulgar (common Latin), provided the basis for the Spanish grammar first codified by Antonio de Nebrija under commission of the new king and queen of Spain—Fernando and Isabella.

The Poema and La Entriega de los Novios, through poetry and ceremony, provide insight into the fundamental values of Hispano culture that have survived for many centuries. These values translate into three categorical concepts represented by family honor, the woman, and a man's horse. The traditional role of the *caballero* (knight) was to protect and defend his lady's honor, especially from unscrupulous suitors like legendary Don Juan types, who would bring shame and scandal to the man, his honor, his family, and his lady. The caballero defended his lady's honor mounted on his trusty stallion—his caballo. The family honor, his horse, and his lady were the most important aspects of a caballero's life.

In *Don Quixote*, a passage tells of a custom of knights and their women that involves a lady's treasured scarf. When a lady had a fancy for a young knight she would give him her scarf, scented with her body perfume. In the epic of Don Quijote, the reader learns that Dulcinea gave him her scarf. He kept it close to his chest and would take it out to remember the knight's role and to defend the honor of his lady when he set about to fight dragons (well, windmills).

The scarf was given to a knight during or after a special dance of the scarves. That dance is performed today at traditional weddings and other festive occasions. It is called the *Valse de los Paños* (Waltz of the Scarves).[15] This dance was and is still done after the wedding march. It provides an opportunity for young people to meet each other and for a man to gain a lady's attention. The waltz was originally danced when ladies were tied up in corsets and wearing head gear with multiple scarves—as portrayed in medieval movies with knights and ladies in waiting. Once a lady gave a man her scarf, it was his responsibility to defend her honor from shame and other suitors. When anyone made an inappropriate advance to a lady or spread malicious rumors about her, it was understood as a challenge to the man's honor. Only through the shedding of blood could that honor be regained.

This music was originally played on a viol type of instrument and was danced in the courts of Spain. However, this dance and similar music came to the Río Grande area of the southwestern United States with the early settlers of Colorado and northern New Mexico and is now played on the violin, accompanied by guitar.

INDIGENOUS INFLUENCES

Native Americans have a history of using dance and music for celebrations and ceremony. They present their music with flutes, rattles, drums, and other native instruments. These instruments accompany native dancers as they dance in communion with their gods, to celebrate seasons, to imitate animals, and for other religious, courting, and ceremonial purposes.

Native American and Hispano music and dance merged into a form known as the *indita*. The indita represents the mixture of the two cultures. Adrian Treviño suggests that the indita form "may have originated with the *genízaros*, or Indians held captive by the Spanish."[16] Jack Loeffler believes the form originated because of a "convergent evolution, that is, it appeared wherever Spanish and Indian peoples maintained contact long enough for their music to begin to meld."[17] There is substantial research on the indita form and the songs that formed the style. John Donald Robb states that he thinks "the origin of the *indita* is as natural as the mixture of Spanish and Indian blood by intermarriage."[18] He further describes the indita "as unmistakably an Indian type of melody, but sung to a mixture of Indian syllables and Spanish words."[19] Whatever the origin, the music and dance came together to join the two cultures in the unique form of the people of the Río Grande del Norte.

An example of an indita composition is presented in Figure 3.5. The dance is a combination of percussive walking steps in a circle for Part A and a polkita for Part B.

EUROPEAN INFLUENCES OF THE 1800S

Many of the traditional dances and much of the music that survive today come from European courts. The music was and is still played on the violin and guitar. The European influence is witnessed in the music and dance but also in the legends about the many Stradivarius and other fine violins played by old-time traditional violinists in the Río Grande area.[20]

Most of the pieces that are popular dance tunes of the Río Grande music traditions come from the period 1864–1867. This was the time when the king of France sent the French emperor Archduke Maximilian and his wife, Carlota, to rule over Mexico. These pieces came to be known as the Spanish colonial-period dances of the Río Grande.

> Much of the music came to the New World from the salons of Paris, where cues of fashion were generated by the Empress Eugenie, wife of Napoleon III. The music worked its way northward from Mexico, where it melded with the traditions of *la gente* [the people], who claim it as their own and who play it to this day. This music came to be performed in the *salas*, or drawing rooms, of the well-to-do of northern New Mexico and southern Colorado.[21]

My grandmother often told me about the wonderful dances in the *salas*. She said her mother and grandmother would move all the furniture out of the

La Indita

Traditional as played and sung by Arsenio Cordova
Transcribed by Lorenzo F. Trujillo, Brenda Romero, and Lorenzo A. Trujillo

3.5. This indita was learned from Arsenio Cordova of El Prado, New Mexico. This melody is commonly used for the singing of Los Dias, a commemoration on January 1 of every year to honor the day of people named Manuel or Manuela, because January 1 is the celebration of the day of El Rey Emmanuel (The King Emanuel). For a detailed explanation of this celebration, see Angel Vigil, *Una Linda Raza: Cultural and Artistic Traditions of the Hispanic Southwest* (Golden, CO: Fulcrum, 1998), 53.

sala and sweep the floor clean. In the corner of the room they set a small table with their best chokecherry wine, which my great-grandfather made, and some *biscochitos* (cookies) and *empanaditas de calabaza* (pumpkin-filled turnovers) as refreshments for the guests. The *músicos* (musicians), including a violinist and a guitarist, would begin to play the old tunes and everyone would dance and visit, discussing politics, religion, and social matters. In my childhood, I remember the family clearing out the *comedor* (dining area) or the living room, and my aunt and her musicians would begin to play the music they learned from the elder músicos. Damián Archuleta of Taos, New Mexico (the violinist in the last scene of the movie *Milagro Beanfield War*), Victor Cárdenas of Ranchos de Taos, New Mexico, and Eva Nuánez of Denver were all great culture bearers who performed and passed on the music played today by younger violinists. This is how the music and dances were taught from one generation to another, without music but instead by ear and rote memorization.

These fiestas were called *fandangos* and were common throughout the Río Grande. Today, many families still have these parties but do not necessarily know their roots, origin, or the fact that they were called fandangos. A public fandango that occurs every year in Colorado is held at The Fort at the annual Tesoro Foundation Spanish Market in Morrison. Similar events are held for the fiesta days in San Luis, Colorado, Taos, New Mexico, and at the Las Golondrinas Ranch in northern New Mexico, among other villages throughout southern Colorado and northern New Mexico.

One of the popular dances at the fandango was *La Cuna* (the Cradle). *La Cuna* is a dance in which four dancers (two couples) make a baby cradle formation and rock it during the dance. The dance and music are in two parts. One part is a polkita jumping step danced with a partner. For the second part the two couples join hands and dance in a waltz-like ¾ step, while the four dancers make a window with their arms, dance under it, and resolve by making a basket cradle form with their arms, which they sway back and forth in a cradle-rocking manner. Dancers of Austrian traditional folk dances often join hands and weave in and out, making window box formations with their arms in the same manner as in La Cuna. This dance may have its origins in the traditional dances of Austria and have evolved during the period of Maximilian and Carlota.

Another popular dance that comes from the European tradition is the *chotís* (schottische). The Río Grande *gente* (people) often named dances or music pieces after a person, event, or animal. *El Vaquero* (the Cowboy), alternatively known as *El Vaquerito* (the Little Cowboy), is a schottische. The *chotís* or *chote* is a form of contra dance known in German as schottische. Some believe the dance is of French origin, conveying the French notion of what a Scottish two-step might be. There are many reports that the schottische was a dance popular in Mexico at the time of Maximilian and that it worked its way northward during that period.[22]

Waltzes and polkas were played and danced with great delight. The tunes and melodies followed similar two- or three-part patterns. Commonly known pieces included the "Valse Apasionado" (Passionate Waltz), "Polka Luz" (Polka of Light), "Chotis El Vaquero" (the Cowboy Schottische), and more.

CORRIDOS AND RANCHERAS

During the 1840s to 1900, the foundations were established for the music and dance that became the cowboy ballads and mariachi music of the 1900s through 2008. *Corridos* (ballads) developed in the romance form from medieval times and were sung by the juglares, as explained earlier. Corridos provided a story about famous people or an event in history. *Rancheras*, now known as Mexico's country music, tell the stories of personal loss, sadness, and pain. These genres of music became the basis for American cowboy songs that describe losing a wife, a dog, a truck, and the like.

A popular corrido written by a contemporary songwriter, Roberto Martínez of Albuquerque, New Mexico, tells of the 1967 raid on the courthouse in Tierra Amarilla, New Mexico, by the Alianza (Alliance) led by the Texas-born former preacher Reyes López Tijerina. This was one of the most significant events for late–twentieth-century Hispanos in New Mexico. The raid focused national attention on the ongoing controversy over Hispano land rights and the massive loss of common lands promised to be respected in the 1848 Treaty of Guadalupe-Hidalgo.

Añ/o de/se/sen/ta y/sie/te	In the year sixty-seven
Cinco de junio fue el día	the fifth of June was the day
Hubo una revolución	there was a revolution
Allá por tierra Amarilla.	Up there in Tierra Amarilla.

In this romance verse/song, eight syllables with rhyme occur in the second and fourth stanzas on the vowels "i" and "a." Also, much like the epic poems discussed earlier, an epic story is told about Reyes López Tijerina in this modern composition and song. This musical form and tradition had their origins in the Middle Ages and continue today.

MARIACHI MUSIC AND FOLKLÓRICO DANCE

Ethnomusicologists have given considerable thought to the origin of mariachi. Some studies have concluded that the word has an indigenous origin, and others claim a French etymology of the word. The origin of the term "mariachi" is less important than the genre of music that is uniquely Mexican. Mariachi music, in its purest form, is composed of the *son* (melody) and *jarabe* (a series of *sones*). For example, the "Jarabe Tapatío"[23] was originally a composition of nine sones. The earliest references to the son are in the records of the Inquisition. In 1739 the Inquisition prohibited the playing of certain sones "because [of] their being insolent and containing seditious expressions which are profane and disparaging and very injurious to the respect and honor of a certain ecclesiastical leader."[24] The Inquisition tribunal was the first to use the term "son" in 1766 in an attempt to prohibit the dance and the accompanying music. The music and dance that evolved were denounced as "licentious dance."

The first mariachi groups were composed of harps, violins, guitars, vihuelas, and a guitarrón (which supplanted the harp because it was too big, heavy, and cumbersome to carry). In around 1940, the trumpet was added to the ensemble (Figure 3.6).

3.6. Photo of Mariachi Vargas. Used by permission of Federico Torres.

The songs of the mariachi evolved from the ballads that preceded their evolution to what we know today as the mariachi form. The son and jarabe are unique music styles, but the songs of lost love and tales of valor have their origins in the earliest songs of the juglares.

1960S TO THE TWENTY-FIRST CENTURY

All of these foundations are listened to in the mariachi, Chicano, Tex-Mex, and Hispano music that is popular today. As a result of the Chicano movement, there was a renaissance of interest in the traditional music and dance that were evolving in Colorado and New Mexico. Organizations to study and promote traditional music and dance were created. Three of these organizations that have flourished and continue to develop are the Asociación Nacional de Grupos Folklóricos, Mariachi conferences, and Hilos Culturales.

In 1972 the Asociación Nacional de Grupos Folklóricos (National Association of Folkloric Groups; ANGF) was created by six university teachers of ethnic dance and music who foresaw a new awakening of interest in the old and evolving traditions of the people of the Río Grande, Mexico, and Spain. Susan Cashion of Stanford University, Ismael Valenzuela of the University of New Mexico, Herman and Patsy Martinez of Adams State College in Alamosa, Colorado, Benjamín Hernández of the University of California at Los Angeles, and Lorenzo Trujillo of the University of Colorado joined forces to create the ANGF. The first conference was held in 1974 in Albuquerque, New Mexico, hosted by Ismael Valenzuela. At the conference, interested youth studied the music and dances of Mexico and Spain. Subsequent conferences incorporated the music and dances of the Río Grande traditions. These conferences provided education and training and attracted enthusiasts from throughout the United States. The ANGF has evolved to host annual workshops and concerts throughout the United States and Mexico over the past thirty years.

Eventually, the mariachi movement developed and split from the ANGF conferences, establishing itself as a series of focused mariachi workshops and concerts. Mariachi conferences are now held in Tucson, Arizona; Albuquerque and Las Cruces, New Mexico; San Jose, Fresno, and San Diego, California; Wenache, Washington; and Denver, Colorado. In addition, many groups continue to initiate their own regional workshops and conferences. At these conferences, students study standardized versions of the mariachi repertoire and listen to masters of mariachi in lecture-demonstrations and concerts.

In 1999 a group of practitioners, including many of those who initiated the ANGF, met in Commerce City, Colorado, to create Hilos Culturales (Cultural Threads), an organization that focuses on supporting the teaching, preservation, and learning of traditional Río Grande music, dance, and related art forms. The organization has presented annual workshops and conferences teaching the early music and dance of the Upper Río Grande.

As these organizations work to preserve the past, the past is made present in the music passed on to our youth. For example, the Bracero Program was very much a part of U.S. immigration history and law. Its relevance is with us today as the United States struggles with issues of immigration. Some are considering the Bracero Program as a model to bring back to address American immigration issues. However, in the song described next, a worker explains his troubles when he came to America to work as a bracero.

A popular song that has meaning in current U.S. politics is "El Bracero"[25] (bracero means a strong armed man). The Bracero Program was started on August 4, 1942, as a response to the high demand for manual labor in the United States. "El Bracero" is a song about a Mexican laborer who knows some English but not much. He comes to the United States to earn money and finds himself in a language dilemma, something many contemporary migrants experience.

Here is my translation of the story told in the song: little brothers, if you are going to work in the United States, I would advise you to be very careful so that what happened to me because of my poor English will not happen to you. I went to the United States as a bracero to earn some money. I got off at the bus stop. I took out a cigarette, and I didn't have a match. I saw an American and asked him to give me a match. He said, "What did you say?" And I responded, "Juan José. That is my name." Then he asked me, why do I bother him? And I told him, "No, señor, I do not like Ford, and although I do not have a car, I like Chevrolet." So I asked him again for a match. He said, "I don't know." I told him, "I want a *mecha* to light this cigarette." Then he said, "Listen here, you big bad bozo." And I told him, "I am not a slobbering fool" (*baboso*). Then he said he was going to call the police, and he began to scream "I'll sue you." I hollered back "La suya," meaning "your mama." I had to take off running because police were chasing me. When they caught me, they took me before the judge, who asked "ten days or ten dollars?" Well, I figured what good luck I finally had, and so I told him to give me the ten dollars. I don't understand what happened, but they grabbed me by the arms and threw me in jail. After ninety days I returned home, and I don't ever want to speak English again.

In the Spanish verse of this song, a romance type of versification of eight syllables is used.

Her/man/i/tos/ de/ mi /ra/za
1   2   3 4   5   6   7 8

Si/ se/ van/ a /tra/ba/jar/ (*e paragógica*)[26]
1   2   3   4 5   6   7

En/ los/ es/ta/dos/ u/ni/dos
1   2   3 4   5   6 7 8

Yo/ les/ quie/ro/ a/con/se/jar
1   2   3   4   5   6   7   8

As new songs and music are created, the characteristics of archaic Spanish forms are still used as the foundation for new compositions. The new generation of composers of popular music will compose based on traditional styles but will reach out to create new forms using the same historical bases. For example, contemporary international singer and musician Lila Downs transcends borders, time periods, and cultures to create a new sound representing the world of music and reality while being grounded in the traditions discussed here.

Music and dance are representations of culture. Culture is a dynamic expression of the values of society at the levels of language, social structure, and worldview. Language, social structure, and worldview are represented through the symbols of music and dance. As a result, the music and dance of our ancestors will continue to thrive, although in various and different creative developing forms but, it is hoped, with the same underlying foundations.

NOTES

1. Chicano, Hispano, Latino, Mexican American, and Spanish American are all terms used by the descendants of the Spanish settlers of Colorado and New Mexico's Río Grande. The term of preference is often a reflection of the person's age and sociopolitical values and beliefs. Chicano is often used to recognize our Indian and Spanish heritage. Many Chicano activists do not like the term "Hispano" because they believe it places undue emphasis on the Spanish influence and not enough on Chicano indigenous roots. What people choose to call themselves is a personal choice.

2. Caballo = horse. In contemporary culture, what was once caballo is now a young man's car.

3. Anonymous, *Poema del Cid* (Buenos Aires: Editorial Losada, S.A., 1938 [1140]), 7–8.

4. Angel Del Río, *Historia de la Literatura Española*, Edición Revisada, vol. 1 (New York: Holt, Rinehart, and Winston, 1963).

5. Gullermo Díaz-Plaja, *A History of Spanish Literature* (New York: New York University Press, 1971), 6.

6. Anonymous, *Poema del Cid*, 159. "Escaño" was the term used to describe the bench. This type of seating was reserved for distinguished guests as opposed to a "banco," a bench without a back.

7. For a detailed study of the concept of honor, see Ramon A. Gutierrez, *When Jesus Came, the Corn Mothers Went Away: Marriage, Sexuality, and Power in New Mexico, 1500–1846* (Stanford: Stanford University Press, 1991).

8. For a detailed explanation of the La Entriega de los Novios ceremony, see Lorenzo A. Trujillo and Marie Oralia Trujillo, "La Entreiga de los Novios, Ayer y Hoy en Taos: Yesterday and Today in Taos County and Northern New Mexico," Taos County Historical Society (Spring 1995): 3–11.

9. Padrinos are friends or family members who become spiritually joined with the newlywed through the ceremony in a family-type relationship. They assume a similar status as godparents during a baptism. Also, as padrinos, they traditionally assume familial spiritual responsibility for the couple's future well-being, as would a parent.

10. Enrique R. Lamadrid, "Music Straight from the Heart," *New Mexico Magazine* (July 1988): 62.

11. "Cantador" is the term old-time singers and verse writers use to describe themselves. Modern Spanish uses the term "cantate."

12. See José Sanchez, "Spanish Versification," in *Nineteenth-Century Spanish Verse*, José Sanchez, ed. (New York: Appleton-Century-Crofts, 1949), xxv.

13. Ibid., x.

14. D. Juan Manuel, *El Conde Lucanor* (Madrid: Editorial Ebro, Novena Edición, 1965), 32.

15. The standard Spanish term for waltz is vals. However, in archaic Spanish an "e" is added to the end of the word in a linguistic device known as the "e paragógica."

16. Quoted in Jack Loeffler, *La Música de los Viejitos: Hispano Folk Music of the Rio Grande del Norte* (Albuquerque: University of New Mexico Press, 1999), 25.

17. Ibid.

18. John Donald Robb, *Hispanic Folk Music of New Mexico and the Southwest: A Self-Portrait of a People: Indita* (Norman: University of Oklahoma Press, 1980), 419.

19. Ibid.

20. Throughout the nineteenth and twentieth centuries, copies of fine violins in the styles of the famous violin makers of Cremona, Italy—like Stradivarius—were made by machine and sold with a famous maker label. The old-time musicians often claimed, and their families believed, they had one of the highly valuable instruments. However, these instruments were usually mere copies and of limited value. But because of the European values and famous names, the old timers assumed that their instruments, with their famous maker labels, had special value.

21. Loeffler, *La Música de los Viejitos*, 134.

22. Ibid., 159.

23. Jarabe Tapatio means a series of sones of the people of the Mexican state of Jalisco.

24. Mark Stephen Fogelquist, "Rhythm and Form in the Contemporary Son Jalisciense" (MA thesis, University of California, Los Angeles, 1975), 7–8.

25. A recording of this piece is available from CDBaby.com (*Southwest Musicians: Musical Traditions of Colorado and New Mexico*, Lorenzo Trujillo, artist). The original was written by Wello Rivas and recorded on the Unichappell Music, Inc., Dunbar music label.

26. In archaic Spanish, an "e" is added to the end of the world in a linguistic device known as the "e paragógica." In this situation it establishes the eight syllables in the verse.

William Wei

Representations of Nineteenth-Century Chinese Prostitutes and Chinese Sexuality in the American West

> The most symbolic figure of commodified human relations, relations based on flattery, illusion, immorality, and cash, is the prostitute.
> —IAN BURUMA AND AVISHAI MARGALIT[1]

Chinese sex slaves flee cruel bondage to marry their childhood sweethearts and live happily ever after in Fairplay, Colorado.* That is the gist of "A Chinese Romance," a news report in *The Daily Denver Tribune,* June 1, 1874, about the escape of a pair of sisters who had been forced into prostitution in Denver's Chinatown.[2] In many ways, the account is typical of the yellow journalism periodically published about the Chinese in America during the second half of the nineteenth century—sensationalistic, replete with violence between two Chinese clans and the intervention of local law enforcement agents. What makes this particular newspaper article different is that it is one of the few with Chinese women, albeit as exotic sex objects, at the center of the narrative. The women in question are two Chinese prostitutes, vulnerable and voiceless victims dependent on the Chinese men who exploit them sexually.

---

* The author thanks Daryl Maeda for his editorial comments and suggestions.

Arguably, the newspaper also exploits these women, since the story's purpose seems less to inform the public about their plight than to entertain the public at their expense.

While offering little information about, and even less insight into, the lives of the two Chinese prostitutes in Colorado, "A Chinese Romance" does reveal much about how the nineteenth-century public represented the sexuality of Chinese people in general and of Chinese women in particular. Indeed, as this chapter will discuss, this representation of Chinese women in Colorado was evident elsewhere in the American West. Euro-Americans perceived Chinese through the ideological prism of Orientalism, "a set of relations of power, a form of knowledge that inscribed upon people all kinds of meanings about ignorance, inferiority, sexuality, and most importantly, the desire for one set of people to dominate and control another."[3] Edward Said, the well-known critic of Orientalism, mistakenly said that Americans had neither a "deeply invested tradition" of, nor an "imaginative investment" in, Orientalism before World War II because their frontier was the American West rather than the Orient.[4] On the contrary, it was precisely because their frontier was the American West that Euro-Americans were invested in Orientalism, which they used to justify their conquest of the region.

As an unknown territory, the Wild West gave Euro-Americans license to fantasize about the Chinese they encountered there. Euro-Americans regarded them as inferior racial Others: irrational, aberrant, backward, crude, despotic, inferior, inauthentic, passive, feminine, and sexually perverse. These characteristics then "justified" Euro-American dominance. In the Euro-American mind, the Chinese and other Asians in the American West became especially identified with licentious sex. Enterprising madams installed "Mikado parlors" in their bordellos to stimulate sexual fantasies.[5] These lavishly decorated rooms were meant to convey a sense of the luxurious but decadent Orient, where every whim of the imagination could be satisfied.

The primary vehicle for promoting this Orientalist perspective was the popular press, which published lurid stories ascribing to the Chinese an array of attributes demeaning their intelligence and character. Chinese immigrant women were stereotyped as prostitutes. Although Chinese women in America actually included wives and daughters, students, workers, and others, the popular press made it nearly impossible for anyone but the wives of Chinese merchants to escape the stigma of prostitution. With its deleterious depictions, the popular press helped pave the way for the exclusion of almost all Chinese women and, later, almost all Chinese men from entering the country.

As this chapter will discuss, the portrayal of Chinese prostitutes in Colorado is emblematic of their treatment elsewhere in the country. This representation of Chinese prostitutes reveals much about common attitudes toward Chinese sexuality and the threat it seemed to pose to the dominant society. These distorted views would contribute to the passage of discriminatory miscegenation and immigration laws, along with other anti-Chinese rulings. Ironically, although these laws were eventually eliminated, the perceptions have persisted in modern cinema, shaping contemporary attitudes toward the Chinese and other Asians.

LOVE, CHINESE STYLE

The highly stylized story about Denver's Chinese American community, "A Chinese Romance," conveys little compassion for King Yow and King Yok, two orphaned sisters from Canton, or for their putative lovers, Loo Quong and Fong Lea.[6] As enslaved sex workers, the King sisters might have evoked sympathy rather than hilarity. But the reporter constructs the narrative in such a way as to provoke laughter at the "peculiar" Chinese, calling attention to their racial features and exotic customs. Loo and Fong, for example, are described as "tallow faced shaved headed lovers," and the brides wore "red bandana handkerchiefs" over their faces. Interspersed throughout the story are strange-sounding Chinese names riddled with typographical errors.[7] The reporter is unable to keep the names of the main characters straight, sometimes referring to the King sisters as King Uok and Ging Yow. There are also passing references to Chinese culture, as in the use of the subtitle "Shades of [Confucious]!" for no apparent reason other than that the venerable sage is a cultural artifact most westerners can recognize. The near-pun on "confusion" may even have been intended to mirror the turmoil the story actually describes.

Nothing is really known about King Yow and King Yok except what the reporter tells the reader; it is precisely their silence that conforms to what Edward Said considers "a widely influential model of the Oriental woman."[8] Said's most famous passage about women in *Orientalism* concerns Gustave Flaubert's encounter with Kuchuk Hanem, an Egyptian courtesan. Kuchuk Hanem is the archetype of the Oriental woman in that she "never spoke of herself . . . never represented her emotions, presence, or history. *He* [Flaubert] spoke for and represented her."[9] Furthermore, "Kuchuk is a disturbing symbol of fecundity, peculiarly Oriental in her luxuriant and seemingly unbounded sexuality."[10] Said found Flaubert's relationship to Kuchuk Hanem representative of the "pattern of relative strength between East and West, and the discourse about the Orient that it enabled."[11]

According to the newspaper article, the King sisters were victims of an international prostitution network that began in Canton, where they were involuntarily contracted to the Hok Yop Tea and Coolie Importing Company of San Francisco to serve as prostitutes for two years in Hop Alley, the name for Denver's Chinatown.[12] There, they were two of the fifteen Chinese women who worked in Wah Kee's house of prostitution on Wazee Street. When their contracts expired they demanded their freedom, only to be refused. Instead, Ah Fee, who operated the brothel and gambling house where they worked, abused them in a way that serves in the article as a type of Chinese torture: he "tied a cat to the girl's leg, and beat the girl about the room, causing the cat to scratch and bite the girl's legs in a manner most fearful."

This scene is so arresting that it bears further scrutiny. Ah Fee's use of the cat seems to convey a dual meaning. First, sadistic Chinese are experts in torture; they can transform the most innocuous items into instruments of pain. Euro-Americans are less adept, requiring specially designed devices. Later in the narrative there is a reference to Chinese "vengeance," which is presumably worse than the western variety. Second, cats, with their distinctive eyes, often symbolize Chinese, who are characterized as having sly, feline qualities.

Except for their initial resistance to continued bondage as sex slaves, the King sisters are primarily passive victims whose fates are determined by men, including their would-be saviors. Loo Quong and Fong Lea are King Yow and King Yok's "pig-tailed lovers," respectively. Nothing is really known about the two men except for their affiliation with the Sam Sing Company, a rival of Hok Yop. They are portrayed as effeminate, childlike individuals who compare unfavorably to the masculine, mature Euro-American men who later intervene to assist them.

According to the story, Loo and Fong supposedly knew the sisters when they were all children in the streets of Canton. After their childhood love for the two girls is "rekindled" in Denver, Loo and Fong seek to marry them and naively request that Ah Fee free the sisters. When Ah Fee rejects their demand, Loo and Fong burn down two of his houses, but to no avail: Ah Fee still refuses to release his human property. With the assistance of men from the Sam Sing clan and in the presence of a reporter from *The Denver Daily Tribune*, Loo and Fong abduct (actually rescue) the King sisters from Ah Fee's "vile den." Almost immediately, the plan goes awry and anarchy ensues. Describing the rescue, which resembles the Keystone Kops at a Chinese circus, the reporter recounts at least "twenty yelling and shrieking Chinese men and women" trying to prevent the escape of the two girls, who improbably turn "complete summersaults over the carriage doors landing flat upon their backs in the arms of their . . . lovers." There is "a perfect babel of confusion" as the carriage drives off with the Hok Yop men in hot pursuit. The seriousness of the situation is overshadowed by the circus-like antics of all those involved. It is the sort of scene for which the derogatory figure of speech "Chinese fire drill" was coined.

The denouement of "A Chinese Romance" involves the intervention of Euro-Americans, who represent the forces of law and order and occupy a dominant position of power in U.S. society. First, there is Judge Sayer, who presides over the civil ceremony in which the two Chinese prostitutes, described incongruously as "blushing brides," are married to their rescuers. Sayer is described as "generously [declining] to enact his legal perquisites of the first kisses upon the brides; both of whom stood patiently waiting and blushing." Here the reporter may be alluding to the general Euro-American belief that Chinese prostitutes were unclean. Indeed, it was said that Chinese prostitutes transmitted an especially loathsome strain of venereal disease. Actually, Chinese prostitutes were no more diseased than their non-Chinese counterparts; given their fewer numbers and mainly Chinese clientele, they were probably less of a health threat to mainstream society.

Next is City Attorney Patterson, who serves as the authorized attorney for the King sisters. When brothel owner Ah Fee discovers that they have escaped, he tries to prevent them from leaving town by leveling a charge of theft at King Yow, the older of the two sisters, accusing her of stealing $400. Patterson manages to defend the sisters successfully in court. Judge Whittier decides that the prosecution cannot sustain the charge and sets King Yow free. Meanwhile, at least twenty members of the Hok Yop clan harass the bridal party, threatening "the worst kind of Chinese vengeances." As a result, the party has to call in a detachment of police for protection.

With their problems resolved, the bridal party leaves Denver for Fairplay, Colorado, accompanied by forty members of the Sam Sing clan who work there as miners, never to be heard from again. With the sinful women redeemed through the sanctity of marriage, this may seem a fitting end to what in many ways is a morality play. But "A Chinese Romance" actually has something less than a Hollywood ending, with the happy couples riding off into the sunset to live happily ever after in a town with the fortuitous name Fairplay. Instead, it concludes with predictions of violence and allusions to the *boo how doy* (Chinese hatchet men) who work for the secret societies—"There will be some Celestial blood spilled here before long, as the Sam Sing men threaten to marry all of the Hok Yop women."[13] An even more pessimistic conclusion is to have the King sisters continue working as sex slaves, although for the Sam Sing clan. Euro-Americans believed that even if Chinese prostitutes got married, "their husbands usually ended up pimping them."[14]

The Orientalist perspective about Chinese in "A Chinese Romance" continued into the twentieth century. Complementing the popular press are influential cinematic narratives delivered in that unique and globally influential American art form—the Western. The Western serves a nationalistic purpose, justifying westward expansion and presenting the United States as an advanced civilization by depicting the Others as backward people who need to be subjugated. In Westerns, of course, the central Others are Native Americans. In those with Chinese and other Asians, they are usually presented as part of the background rather than as part of the plot. They have insignificant roles that are a mishmash of inaccurate images and well-worn clichés presented in a decontextualized fashion.[15] Chinese women usually have roles as either degraded prostitutes with the generic name "Chinese Mary" or sensual Chinese villainesses with designs on the White male protagonists. In either case, Chinese women are invariably cast as subordinate to the men in the film, White or Chinese.

Even the so-called anti-Western *McCabe & Mrs. Miller* (1971) contains a host of anti-Chinese stereotypes. Robert Altman's film is set in a Presbyterian Church located somewhere in the Pacific Northwest, although it could just as well be in any mining community on Colorado's Western Slope. *New York Times* film critic Vincent Canby describes the town as a "scenic mess of squalid shacks, bordered by an even more squalid ghetto for Chinese laborers," referred to in the film as "Chinkyville."[16] Throughout the film, the White men and women make derogatory remarks about Chinese people, revealing their racism as well as ignorance. The Chinese are held in such low esteem that upon her arrival in town, one of Mrs. Miller's White prostitutes tells her companions that she will not fornicate with Chinese men, an attitude that helps explain the importation of Chinese prostitutes. Ironically, one of the secondary characters is Masie, a Chinese prostitute in Mrs. Miller's brothel. Masie never utters a word during the entire film and seems to be there for the sole purpose of revealing the misconceptions White men of the period had about Chinese women—physical as well as cultural. White men foolishly pay to have sex with Chinese women, whom they believe have vaginas slanted like their eyes.

If Altman's intent was in part to critique White society's attitude toward the Chinese, he may have been a little too subtle. Although his film is more realistic about life on the American frontier than the standard Western is, it nevertheless perpetuates derogatory images, thereby reinforcing preexisting prejudices and affirming stereotypes. Having the film end with a scene of Mrs. Miller drifting off into a drug-induced haze in a Chinese opium den is a case in point.[17] Even though she possesses her own equipment and could just as easily have smoked the drug in her own room, Altman has her smoking it in a Chinese opium den, implicitly reminding viewers that the opium is intimately associated with Chinese and, by extension, Chinese with moral degeneracy. With these images, the modern Western—Altman's included—are nothing more than a powerful reiteration of nineteenth-century newspaper stories such as "A Chinese Romance."

"A Chinese Romance" is at least about real Chinese people. The King sisters are authentic historical figures whose lives are similar to those of other exploited Chinese sex workers in nineteenth-century Colorado. Almost all of their fellow Chinese prostitutes remain individually anonymous,[18] although they are publicly acknowledged as a group to be a danger to White men's health and morality.

A MENACE TO AMERICAN MANHOOD

During the second half of the nineteenth century, there was a serious disparity in the ratio of Chinese women to Chinese men in the United States, one that lasted more than a century. The conventional wisdom held that so few Chinese women immigrated to the United States because of Chinese culture: tradition dictated that a married Chinese woman would remain in China to care for her husband's parents. Another widely held explanation was that Chinese men working in America had a sojourner's mentality and were unwilling to bring or send for their wives because they themselves did not plan to stay long. But George Anthony Peffer's definitive study of Chinese female immigration to America argues persuasively that it was actually the racial hostility toward Chinese women that constituted the central barrier to their entry into the country, with the other reasons of only secondary importance.[19]

In any case, according to the 1880 national census, there were only 4,779 Chinese women in the United States, while there were as many as 100,686 Chinese men, or 4.5 percent women to 95.5 percent men. The gender ratio in Hop Alley was somewhat better. There were 29 Chinese women out of 238 Chinese in the city of Denver, or 12 percent women to 88 percent men. There would have been 31 Chinese women if the King sisters had remained in Denver.[20]

This imbalance in the gender ratio of the Chinese in America gave rise to so-called bachelor societies and the procurement of prostitutes to provide them with sexual services. The overwhelming majority of Chinese prostitutes came from the poorest stratum of the Guangdong Province peasantry. They were often mere teenagers whose destitute parents had sold them into sexual servitude. As orphans, the King sisters were clearly two of the most vulnerable people in Chinese society. According to the newspaper account, "a worthless loafer in Canton" called So Frane, whose relationship to the girls was unknown, arranged their contract as sex workers. Ah Fee, the owner of the gambling den and bagnio where they worked, paid $1,600 for them. The sisters had to pay off their $800 passage money and presumably their initial purchase price by working in the brothel for two years. While there, they were probably forced to provide sexual services to as many as ten men daily and were subjected to humiliation and abuse, including beatings. However, as deplorable as working in a Hop Alley brothel was, it was probably preferable to working in the womanless mining camps, where living conditions were known to be worse and the men more brutal. For sex workers in the mining camps, life was horrifically Hobbesian—nasty, brutish, and short. The average working life of a Chinese prostitute was brief, lasting about four to five years before venereal disease or illness resulting from mistreatment and neglect ended both her career and her existence.

The King sisters were worse off than their non-Chinese counterparts who worked in the red-light district adjacent to Hop Alley. According to Jan MacKell's study of prostitution in Colorado, White prostitutes were usually free agents who hoped—although mostly in vain—to "make money fast, marry well, and become socially acceptable."[21] By contrast, after what Lucie Cheng Hirata has called the period of free enterprise (ca. 1849–1854)—during which select Chinese prostitutes could exercise individual initiative and enterprise to make money and leave the trade[22]—most of them fell into the net of organized traffic in women and, because of their race, were exploited in ways their White counterparts never were. Euro-American men took advantage of the powerlessness of Chinese prostitutes to fulfill their sexual fantasies, forcing them to perform deviant sexual acts in pursuit of unconventional erotic gratification. Even young White boys paid for a ten-cent "lookee" to see whether Chinese women had slanted vaginas.[23]

Prior to the passage of the Page Act in 1875, the main moral complaint against the Chinese was the existence of Chinese prostitutes. Euro-Americans perceived Chinese prostitutes' sexuality as a peril to the purity and integrity of White America—especially youth—and blamed them for the country's opium problem, as both users and purveyors.[24] As far as Euro-Americans were concerned, opium and prostitution went together since the drug was deemed an aphrodisiac that caused the user to experience uncontrollable sexual desire leading to sexual promiscuity. From testimonies before state and congressional committees that investigated Chinese immigration in 1876, Sucheng Chan has concluded, "Chinese prostitutes were seen as potent instruments for the debasement of White manhood, health, morality, and family life. Thus, their continued presence was deemed a threat to White civilization."[25]

Accordingly, Chinese prostitutes became an implicitly important issue in national and local politics. In Colorado, they became intertwined with presidential politics.[26] During the 1880 presidential election in which James R. Garfield (Republican) faced Winfield S. Hancock (Democrat), Chinese immigrants figured as political scapegoats. Chinese laborers were condemned as an economic threat, competing with White workingmen for scarce jobs. Local Democrats railed against "Garfieldism," which was defined as pro-capitalist and consequently in favor of the importation of cheap Chinese labor. Actually, Garfield and Hancock were of like mind when it came to opposing Chinese immigration. Garfield favored the exclusion of Chinese laborers, considering them inferior to their White counterparts.

As part of the presidential campaign, the local Democratic Party sponsored a parade in Denver on the evening of October 30, 1880, with an anti-Chinese theme. Marchers carried placards proclaiming "Garfield may become a Mandarin but a President never." Other placards depicted him in the embrace of a Chinese woman, which in the public eye meant a Chinese prostitute. Such inflammatory displays aroused anti-Chinese feelings, and the following day, October 31, 1880, the populace rioted against the Chinese, totally destroying Hop Alley.[27] The mob destroyed Chinese businesses, looted Chinese homes, and injured many Chinese. Among the casualties was Look Young, who was beaten to death and lynched. He left behind a wife, father, and mother in China, who were totally dependent on him for support.

Ironically, the bronze plaque on display in the Lower Downtown (LoDo) Historic District, captioned "Hop Alley/Chinese Riot of 1880," was intended to commemorate the Chinese community, but the title inadvertently conveys the impression that it was the Chinese who rioted.[28] Perhaps to appeal to tourists visiting the LoDo area, the plaque also calls attention to the more exotic elements of the Chinese community, noting that people went there to visit opium dens where one could "hit the pipe" or "suck the bamboo." It also recalls the rumors about Hop Alley having "buildings . . . connected by tunnels and secret rooms accessible by trap doors," a mythical underworld of illicit activities. The plaque certainly expresses sympathy for the nameless Chinese residents who eked out an existence "amidst persecution, poverty, and wretched living conditions." At the same time, however, it especially recognizes "several white residents [who] showed remarkable courage in protecting the Chinese: Saloonkeeper James Veatch sheltered refugees, as did gambler Jim Moon and Madam Lizzie Preston,[29] whose girls armed themselves with champagne bottles and high heels to hold the mob at bay." The overall impression one gets of the Hop Alley residents is that they were helpless victims who needed to be protected by heroic Whites, even those mainstream society regarded as disreputable.[30]

Surprisingly, the Chinese in Denver remained to rebuild their community. From their original location on Wazee Street, they eventually spread out to different areas of LoDo. By 1940, most Chinese residents ended up on the periphery of LoDo in the area of Market and Twentieth streets, near the present Coors Field. The rebuilt Chinese community continued to be the subject of sensational press stories from an Orientalist perspective. Their segregated community was stigmatized as an unsavory place replete with gambling halls, opium dens, and brothels that contained exotic Chinese prostitutes. A particularly pernicious piece appeared in *The Denver Times* in December 1909. S. A. Meyer described Chinatown as

> a dark, narrow alley, a series of dingy entrances, cubbyholes, underground passages, dismal, all-smelling places . . . the much-discussed, much-feared rendezvous of the tongs. It is only at night that you can see the Mongol quarter of Denver awaken into exotic life. Its people come into being with the dark and disappear with the dawn. Its acrid odors sting the nostrils. Fiery, contemptuous, bland, serene, foul smelling, your Oriental maintains that indefinable barrier that had kept East and West apart since the centuries began.[31]

What Meyer describes is a nightmarish vision of hell on earth—a smelly, nocturnal realm of the damned. It is a shadow world where only bad things happen to those foolish enough to go there. Meyer's final insult is to blame the "Mongols" for maintaining a wall between themselves and the civilized world of the West. Meyer conveniently overlooks the hostile racial environment and the host of anti-Chinese laws that prevented Chinese from integrating into mainstream society.

Hop Alley was hardly alone: Chinatowns in general were perceived as mysterious and depraved places in both the nineteenth and twentieth centuries. In his 1974 movie *Chinatown*, Roman Polanski used the title as a metaphor for political and personal corruption. Murray Sperber, in his review of the film, observes that Polanski turned

> Chinatown—the place as well as the idea—into a symbol of human corruption, chaos, and immorality unimaginable to most straight Westerners. It is possibly even a symbol of early sexual mysteries, primal scenes, about

which, he suggests, it is best not to inquire.... And those people who see the world as inevitably corrupt and controlled by alien and dark forces will chant the movie's final line like a mantra, "Forget it . . . it's Chinatown."[32]

Given such an unfavorable reputation, it is hardly surprising that most Chinatowns in America declined and eventually disappeared.[33] Hop Alley became first an industrial area filled with factories and warehouses and now a gentrified neighborhood with upscale boutiques. All that remains of Denver's first Chinese community today is the bronze plaque for tourists to read and reflect upon.

EXCLUDING CHINESE WOMEN FIRST

To cleanse the country of Chinese, anti-Chinese forces in the nineteenth century were able to obtain the passage of immigration laws preventing most Chinese from entering the country and of anti-miscegenation laws in many states prohibiting Chinese from intermarrying with Whites. With the passage of these various laws, anti-Chinese forces believed they had successfully ended the economic rivalry and sexual threat Chinese men and women in America posed to Whites. They would no longer compete with White workers for jobs, no longer endanger the purity of the White race through intermarriage, and no longer found "corrupt" communities since they were denied the right to have families in America.

Indeed, the number of Chinese in America steadily declined. Anti-Chinese forces focused on Chinese women, who were central to the life of the Chinese community and its perpetuation. As an old Chinese working woman once remarked, women stand "with one hand grasping the generations that have gone before and with the other the generations to come."[34] Excluding Chinese women from the country meant breaking the link between generations, leading to the eventual extinction of Chinese American communities.

Even before the passage of the notorious Chinese Exclusion Act (May 6, 1882) that suspended Chinese immigration, anti-Chinese forces were able to obtain the passage of the Page Act (March 3, 1875) forbidding the "involuntary immigration" of laborers and the importation of women for the purpose of prostitution. In practice, the Page Law effectively restricted the entry of Chinese women in general. According to George Peffer, from 1876 to 1882, the number of Chinese women entering the country declined by 68 percent over the previous seven-year period.[35]

To further ensure that there was no permanent Chinese community in America, anti-Chinese elements also enacted anti-miscegenation laws to prevent Chinese men and women, and other Asians, from intermarrying with

Whites. Even in states with no anti-miscegenation laws, such as Colorado, intermarriage was still fraught with difficulties. Such was the case for Leo Latt Sing and Nellie Mershon, coworkers at the Beebe Hotel in Idaho Springs, who decided to get married in 1902.[36]

In *The Denver Times*, Sing was identified as a Mongolian or a "greasy-looking Chinaman" and described as "anything but handsome," with a "large nose and glassy eyes," making him look like "a god in the Chinese joss house."[37] Mershon, on the other hand, was described as a rather "good-looking white woman, with blue eyes and light hair . . . plump and prepossessing." Presumably fearing "racial mongrelization," some locals tried to prevent their marriage by hanging Sing until he nearly died and then ordering him to leave town.

The couple eloped to Denver, only to have Mershon's brother-in-law, Charles Thorpe, obtain a warrant to have them arrested for violating a nonexistent anti-miscegenation law. As Mershon observed to a newspaper reporter, "[Thorpe] says he thought there was a law preventing my marriage to Leo Sing, and he got the police officers to act first and find out afterward. There is no such law—nor does there seem to be one that might have protected me in the case. I have been a byword on the streets, and my personal affairs have been talked about all over the country."[38] Evidently, a Chinese man and a White woman getting married was sufficiently scandalous to warrant national attention.

Charles Thorpe also claimed that drugs had influenced Mershon. Mershon denied this, saying, "It is not true that he [Sing] gave me dope. He does not use it." Instead, Mershon claimed she fell in love with Sing because he "was good and kind to me." Furthermore, she said that Sing was "one of the truest gentlemen I ever saw, and much nicer than the majority of white men." Mershon may be forgiven for exaggerating her fiancé's personal qualities; he probably did compare favorably with her first husband, whom she had had to support for five years while he languished in a madhouse.[39] But given the hostile racial climate of the era, her remarks probably outraged White men near and far.

After being discharged from jail, Sing and Mershon tried to find a judge who would marry them. The second judge they tried, Justice Hynes, refused to even see the couple, let alone marry them. Having studied the state statutes, Justice Hynes had concluded that the "legislature never intended that people of the character of Chinese coolies should become assimilated into the American nation." Finally, they found a sympathetic judge. Justice William T. Printz "saw no reason to disregard the license duly made out and presented to him," so he married the couple without further delay. Afterward, a reporter paid Leo Latt Sing a backhanded compliment, saying:

> No Chinaman has ever been known to abuse the white woman he takes to wife.... An Irishman, an Italian, a German—men of almost any nationality figure in the police courts for brutality to the woman they made a drudge and buffet of, but never the Chinaman. John [John Chinaman was a derogatory ethnic name for Chinese] isn't lovely, but he is known to be devotion itself—if one cares for the devotion.[40]

Almost a century later, the devotion of a Chinese man to a White woman was one of the secondary themes in Maggie Greenwald's provocative film *The Ballad of Little Jo* (1993). According to the critic Roger Ebert, the film is about the "role-playing that allowed women and minorities to survive in the macho, racist West."[41] It is one of the rare films that deal with the forbidden miscegenation between Whites and Asians. Tinman, the film's Chinese character, has a sexual and de facto marital relationship with the central character, Little Jo Monaghan. Transgressing the mores of the period, they become lovers and soul mates.

As the tagline that opens the film says, "In the Wild West, a woman had only two choices: she could be a wife or a whore.... Josephine Monaghan chose to be a man." Masquerading as a man on the American frontier, Little Jo Monaghan rescues Tinman, whose real name is Wong Tian-ma, from being lynched by xenophobic White men. During the post–Civil War period, Tinman, a former railroad laborer looking for work, wanders into the mining town of Ruby City, where he is immediately set upon for no other reason than being Chinese. The fictional Ruby City could just as well have been Leadville, Colorado, where the citizens posted a sign saying "All Chinamen Will Be Shot." When a Chinese did have the temerity to enter the town, he was reportedly shorn of his queue, deprived of his blankets, and abandoned on a mountain in the midst of a snowstorm, where he presumably froze to death.[42]

The White men who are about to hang Tinman contend that he is seeking to steal a job that rightfully belongs to some White man; besides, as Little Jo's closest friend in town, Frank Badger, says, it is a well-known fact that Chinese are all "ravishers and opium smokers." But as the film progresses, it is clear that Tinman is the better man. His gentle manner stands in marked contrast to the boorishness of the main White male characters, all of whom are depicted as hard-drinking, rapacious frontiersmen prone to violence.

Even this feminist interpretation of the Old West, however, cannot resist the temptation to traffic in Orientalist stereotypes such as opium smoking. Tinman, played by Korean American actor David Chung, is portrayed as a recreational opium smoker who introduces the practice to Little Jo as a postcoital activity; affectionately, she repeats Frank Badger's earlier remark that the Chinese are "ravishers and opium smokers."

Also, Maggie Greenwald unwittingly stereotypes Tinman as an emasculated, feminized Chinese man by partnering him with a woman transgressively pretending to be a man. The role reversal places him in a subordinate position throughout the film as a "kept man," arguably even a Chinese prostitute. Since there are no Chinese women in the area, not even a female Chinese prostitute (although there are plenty of White prostitutes), his prospects of ever having a family, raising a child, and doing those things expected of Chinese men are nonexistent.

Even when Little Jo tires of pretending to be a man and tries to revert to a traditional feminine role by wearing a dress and baking a pie, it becomes painfully evident to them both that she can never be his wife and he can never be her husband. As a matter of necessity, both Little Jo and Tinman are outsiders who must maintain their roles as White master and Chinese servant rather than make their love public through the normal ritual of marriage. The failure to maintain this charade would have resulted in their deaths at the hands of White men.

As Chinese characters in American Westerns go, Tinman does comparatively well. He does get the "girl," after all. Although he and Little Jo can never have what was then considered a normal relationship between a man and a woman, they are still able to enjoy an enviable and enduring personal relationship in the hostile milieu of the American frontier. In a standard American Western, the best that could have been expected for him would have been marriage to a Chinese prostitute, as in "A Chinese Romance."

CONCLUDING COMMENTS

In nineteenth-century Colorado as well as elsewhere, Chinese prostitutes usually lived anonymous, short, oppressive lives of sexual exploitation. It was a grim existence from which there was usually no escape. In the world of the demimonde, they were at the bottom of the social hierarchy on the American frontier, ranking below White prostitutes, who had greater opportunities to leave the world's oldest profession to join mainstream society. They were also exploited politically as part of the larger anti-Chinese movement. As part of a racialized and gendered Orientalist discourse, Chinese prostitutes served as potent symbols for the exclusion of Chinese from the United States and were indeed the first to be excluded. Their sexuality was considered a threat to White men's morality and health, a canard that contributed significantly to White society's successful effort to cleanse the country of an entire racial group it considered inferior. Although Chinese women and men were once again allowed to enter the country in numbers more or less equal to those of other immigrants following the passage of the Immigration Law of 1965, portrayals of them in the cinema continued to conform to images first formed in the nineteenth century. As long as the Orientalist discourse that underlies them persists, these representations will continue into the indefinite future.

NOTES

1. Ian Buruma and Avishai Margalit, *Occidentalism: The West in the Eyes of Its Enemies* (New York: Penguin, 2004), 19.

2. Unless otherwise noted, references to "A Chinese Romance" are from a typed manuscript of "A Chinese Romance," *The Daily Denver Tribune*, June 1, 1874, in the file "Ethnic Groups—Chinese," Colorado Historical Society, Denver.

3. Henry Yu, "Edward Said, Dispeller of Delusions," *Amerasia Journal* 31, 1 (2005): 67–70.

4. Edward W. Said, *Orientalism* (New York: Vintage, 1979), 290.

5. Jan MacKell, *Brothels, Bordellos, and Bad Girls* (Albuquerque: University of New Mexico Press, 2004), 274n13, observes that in Cripple Creek and Silverton there were "Mikado parlor houses." MacKell is puzzled as to why the word was frequently used with respect to prostitution, since it referred to a Japanese emperor. She attributes the usage to the influential Gilbert and Sullivan opera of the same name, as well as a way to distinguish the parlor house as a place that was "a cut above the rest." I argue that the word used in the prostitution industry because it was a readily recognized Asian name whose actual meaning was less important than the fact that it was Oriental. As such, the name conveyed eroticism and sensuality, especially of a perverse sort.

6. In "A Chinese Romance," the reporter uses the standard Chinese naming convention of placing the surname first.

7. It is unclear whether the typographical errors in the typescript were in the original newspaper article.

8. Said, *Orientalism*, 6. Not incidentally, Said actually said very little directly about women, earning for himself the sobriquet "Accidental Feminist." Sondra Hale, "Edward Said—Accidental Feminist: Orientalism and Middle East Women's Studies," *Amerasia Journal* 31, 1 (2005): 1–5.

9. Said, *Orientalism*, 6 (original emphasis). Said considers Flaubert the archetypal Orientalist. For additional comments about Flaubert, see Edward W. Said, "On Flaubert," in *Orientalism: A Reader*, Alexander Lyon Macfie, ed. (New York: New York University Press, 2000), 108–110.

10. Said, *Orientalism*, 187.

11. Ibid., 6.

12. For information about Denver's Chinatown, see William Wei, "History and Memory: The Story of Denver's Chinatown," in *Western Voices: 125 Years of Colorado Writing*, Steve Grinstead and Ben Fogelberg, eds. (Golden, CO: Fulcrum, 2004), 373–391.

13. MacKell, *Brothels, Bordellos, and Bad Girls*, 195. This fact-filled study about prostitution in Colorado makes some questionable assertions in explaining how Chinese girls were deceived into becoming prostitutes. For example, MacKell mistakenly uses

the terms "mail-order brides," a contemporary social phenomenon, and "picture brides," a Japanese American phenomenon. She also says "tongs" means "pimps"; actually, tongs were organizations, including secret societies engaged in prostitution. She may have confused the word with the term *t'ang-tzu*, "brothel." For the most reliable information available about Chinese prostitution in America, see Benson Tong, *Unsubmissive Women: Chinese Prostitutes in Nineteenth-Century San Francisco* (Norman: University of Oklahoma Press, 1994).

14. MacKell, *Brothels, Bordellos, and Bad Girls*, 195.

15. There are, of course, exceptions, such as the "message" movie *Walk Like a Dragon* (1960) in which Chinese immigrant Cheng Lu (played by Japanese American actor James Shigeta) takes Chinese slave girl Kim Sung (played by Nobu McCarthy) away from good cowboy Linc Bartlett (played by Jack Lord). In his brief review of the movie, Bosley Crowther ("Screen: Sea Adventure: Under Ten Flags on New Double Bill," *The New York Times*, September 16, 1960, nytimes.com) notes that it was inevitable that Cheng Lu gets the girl since 1960 was "much too soon for integration," that is, racial miscegenation. Even as late as the 1960s, Whites feared genetic contamination, leading to inferior biracial offspring.

16. Vincent Canby, "The Screen: *McCabe and Mrs. Miller*: Miss Christie Portrays Prostitute in West, Beatty Is a Gambler in Altman's Film," *The New York Times*, June 25, 1971, nytimes.com.

17. Ibid.

18. Mainly because of Ruthanne Lum McCunn's biographical novel *Thousand Pieces of Gold*, first published in 1981, the best-known Chinese woman in nineteenth-century America is probably Polly Bemis (aka China Polly, Lalu Nathoy, and Gung Heung). A film of the same name was produced in 1991, starring Korean American actress Rosalind Chao as Bemis. Because so little information is available about Bemis, McCunn fictionalized her life. Whether Bemis was a prostitute is disputed. According to McCunn, George Bancroft thought she was a prostitute, but all the pioneers she contacted "insisted Polly had never worked as a prostitute, although they acknowledged that she may have been purchased by Hong King for that purpose." Ruthanne Lum McCunn, *Thousand Pieces of Gold* (Boston: Beacon, 2004), 316.

19. George Anthony Peffer, *If They Don't Bring Their Women Here: Chinese Female Immigration before Exclusion* (Urbana: University of Illinois Press, 1999).

20. Wei, "History and Memory."

21. MacKell, *Brothels, Bordellos, and Bad Girls*, 6. According to Lucie Cheng Hirata ("Free, Indentured, Enslaved: Chinese Prostitutes in Nineteenth-Century America," *Signs* 5, 1 [Autumn 1979]: 3–29), like their White counterparts Chinese prostitutes are able to leave their past behind after getting married. They are able to do this because the Chinese community "did not attach the same stigma to prostitution as whites did," and prostitutes "were usually accepted in [Chinese] working-class society" (Hirata, "Free, Indentured, Enslaved," 19).

22. Hirata, "Free, Indentured, Enslaved."

23. Sheridan Prasso (*The Asian Mystique* [New York: Public Affairs, 2005], 10) notes that the myth about Asian women having horizontal vaginas has persisted since the Korean War. Obviously, the myth was started much earlier.

24. A discussion of the opium problem and the Chinese can be found in Henry O. Whiteside, *Menace in the West: Colorado and the American Experience with Drugs, 1873–1963* (Denver: Colorado Historical Society, 1997).

25. Sucheng Chan, "The Exclusion of Chinese Women, 1870–1943," in *Entry Denied: Exclusion and the Chinese Community in America, 1882–1943*, Sucheng Chan, ed. (Philadelphia: Temple University Press, 1991), 138. According to Buruma and Margalit (*Occidentalism*, 127), in the non-Western world the West is viewed as the "main corruptor of sexual morality."

26. William Wei, "The Anti-Chinese Movement in Colorado: Inter-Ethnic Competition and Conflict on the Eve of Exclusion," in *Chinese America: History and Perspective 1995* (Brisbane, CA: Chinese Historical Society, 1995), 179–197.

27. Ibid. This study discusses the Denver race riot in detail.

28. This plaque is located on 20th Street between Market and Blake streets on the side of the building occupied by Sportsfan, a store that sells pro and college team apparel.

29. There is a passing mention of Lizzie Preston in MacKell, *Brothels, Bordellos, and Bad Girls*, 68, although her role in the Denver race riot is not discussed.

30. As one reviewer of an earlier draft of this chapter observed, among those who protected the Chinese during the riot were Dave Cook and the Colorado State Militia, which was associated with the Republican Party that liked cheap labor. They could have been included on the plaque, but that would have made it less sensational for tourists.

31. Quoted in Wei, "History and Memory," 377–378.

32. Murray Sperber, "*Chinatown* 'Do as Little as Possible' Polanski's Message and Manipulation," *Jump Cut: A Review of Contemporary Media* 3 (1974): 9–10.

33. The sociologist Rose Hum Lee predicted as much in her study, "The Growth and Decline of Chinese Communities in the Rocky Mountain Region" (PhD diss., University of Illinois, Champaign-Urbana, December 1947), reprinted by Arno Press in 1978, 345–351.

34. Ida Pruitt, *A Daughter of Han: The Autobiography of a Chinese Working Woman* (Stanford: Stanford University Press, 1945), 239.

35. George Anthony Peffer, "Forbidden Families: Emigration Experiences of Chinese Women under the Page Law, 1875–1882," *Journal of Ethnic History* (Fall 1986): 28–46. Also see Peffer's book-length study, *If They Don't Bring Their Women Here*.

36. Unless noted otherwise, information about Leo Latt Sing and Nellie Mershon is from these newspaper accounts: "Tried to Marry a Chinaman," *The Denver Times*, June 11, 1902; "Chinaman and the White Woman Are Freed in Court," *The Denver Times*, June 12, 1902; "Refused to Marry Chinaman," *The Denver Times*, June 13, 1902 (source of the quotation); "Sing Weds Mrs. Mershon," *The Denver Times*, June 15, 1902; and "She Is Finally Mrs. Sing," *The Times*, June 14, 1902. These articles refer to Sing using the standard western naming convention of placing the surname last.

37. "Joss house" refers to a Chinese place of religious worship.

38. "She Is Finally Mrs. Sing," *The Times*, June 14, 1902.

39. "Chinaman and the White Woman Are Freed in Court," *The Denver Times*, June 12, 1902.

40. "Sing Weds Mrs. Mershon," *The Denver Times*, June 15, 1902.
41. Roger Ebert, "The Ballad of Little Jo," *The Sun Times*, September 10, 1993.
42. Wei, "The Anti-Chinese Movement in Colorado."

Phillip Gallegos

Religious Architecture in Colorado's San Luis Valley

This chapter is the culmination of field research work cataloguing religious church architecture in southern Colorado's San Luis Valley. The building survey fieldwork reinforced the evidence of historical Hispanic roots in Colorado. What began as a cataloguing of small churches, or *capillas*, became a history of Hispanic migration settlement patterns, a history of the built environment, and a definition of physical spaces before the intervention of North Americans after the Mexican-American War. As Hispanics migrated north from Santa Fe and Taos in the early 1800s and 1900s, establishing settlements in Colorado, every small village built and established *placitas* (villages arranged around small plazas), *moradas* (locally organized, unconsecrated spaces for worship during important religious seasons, such as Easter and Christmas), and capillas. In many ways, the resultant history of built environment and architectural remnants reflects Hispanics' cultural, political, and social survival. The small village capillas were built to provide divine intervention during the settlement of the land. They also served as symbolic and religious invocations to counter difficult events, such as the aggressive intrusion of North American doctrines like Mormonism.

This chapter documents the building of churches parallel to Colorado's evolving social, political, and physical history. Fieldwork for this project was underwritten by the College of Fellows of the American Institute of Architects (AIA). The AIA supported the historical building survey of the religious architecture of Colorado's San Luis Valley. Fieldwork was divided along the western and eastern edges of the valley. The southern end of the valley within Colorado represents the earliest settlements by Spanish-speaking inhabitants. The San Luis Valley consists of Conejos County at the western edge of the valley and Costilla County at the eastern end. The survey's initial architectural purpose was to provide an accurate database of religious architecture, as it exists today. In the case of destroyed churches, an attempt at reconstruction in the form of a drawing was made, using records or field measurements as a guide.

PHYSICAL CONTEXT

The Spanish American churches of the San Luis Valley region rest in a high desert valley surrounded by mountains (Figure 5.1). Hispanic settlers arrived in Colorado in the mid-1800s. This migration north resulted first from Spanish and later Mexican governmental policy to settle the frontiers of their borders. The upper region of the Río Grande Valley in Colorado and New Mexico contains enclaves of Spanish-speaking settlements often isolated from eastern and western villages as well as the outside world. Separation between eastern and western settlements is an extension of the isolation imposed across the Río Grande Canyon in New Mexico and the river's extension in Colorado. Geographically, the entire valley straddles the present-day Colorado–New Mexico border. The valley is called San Luis on the Colorado side of the border and Taos in the New Mexico portion. When the southwestern United States shifted from Spanish and Mexican governance to U.S. governance, the Taos Valley became (and remains) an enclave physically isolated from many outside influences. As an isolated valley, a uniqueness remains in the San Luis/Taos region's people and architecture, which is clearly a continuation of the sixteenth-century conquest and settlement of Mexico, the northern frontiers, and present-day New Mexico–Colorado. The U-shape of the enclosing northern mountains provided both a physical terminus to the northern migration of settlements and a physical isolation of the San Luis Valley from North American settlers from the east.

HISTORICAL INTRODUCTION

The search for the Hispanic community's historical roots uncovers sources stretching from Mexico to Spanish settlements in southern Colorado. A continual movement of peoples, families, and genealogies is simultaneously

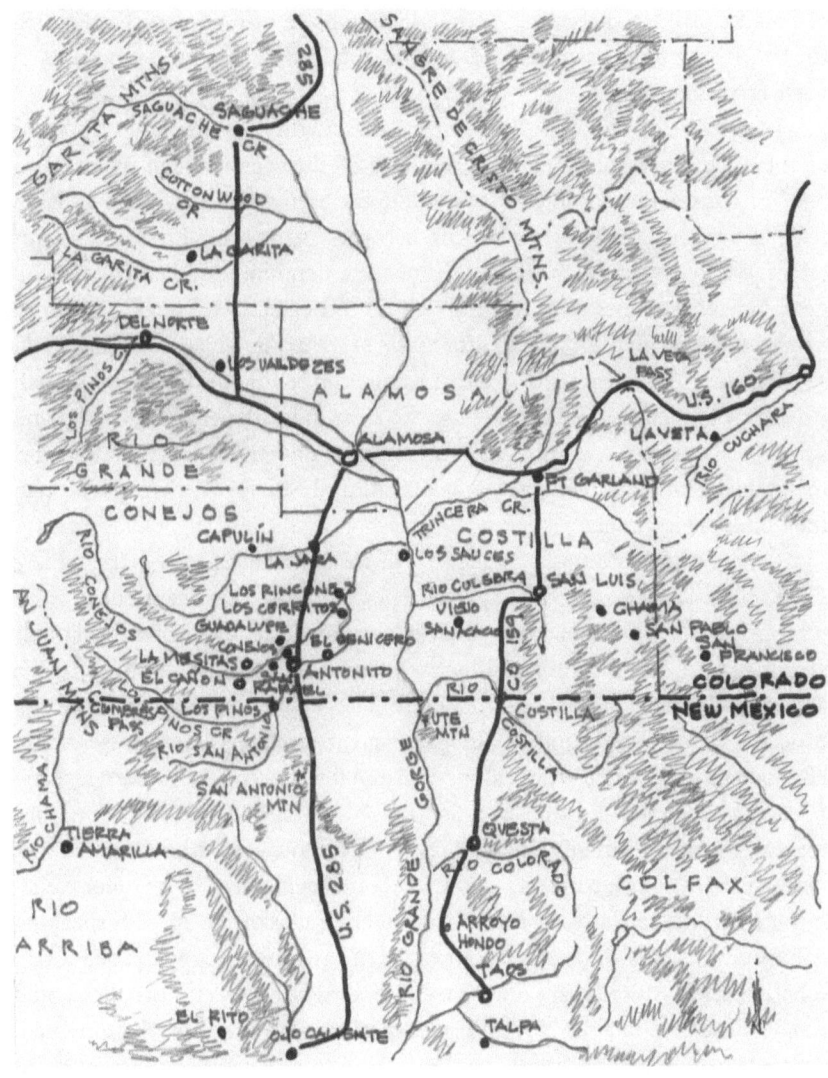

5.1. San Luis/Taos Valley.

recent and old in Colorado. The historical roots of some families and villages in southern Colorado predate the U.S. political incursion into the Southwest. The continual time line of migrations north from Mexico in the 1800s resulted in the founding of communities, some of which have been abandoned, and ignored the invisible shifting political melodrama of changes wrought by the Mexican-American War. In California, Arizona, Texas, and New Mexico, the routes of settlements can be physically traced and located as the seeds of present urbanized centers. As the meeting place of commerce and North American culture, Hispanics and Anglos engaged each other's societies in these communities.

In the case of Colorado's San Luis Valley, nature intervened in the form of the enclosing mountains on three sides of the region's high plains. As a result, a culture that settled in Colorado in the early 1800s survives on a large scale in the San Luis Valley by having become deeply rooted in the religious life of isolated villages. Survival has meant a continuity of language, manners, behavior, values, and religion. All of the values have been reinforced by the survival of the built environment of Hispanic villages. Villages and social institutions were built, grew, and sometimes disappeared before North American influences could be brought to bear in northern New Mexico and southern Colorado. A combination of seen and unseen environmental forces maintained and reinforced a physical and cultural base for Hispanics to sustain their built environment.

One of the most important legacies of a maintained culture is the artifact of religious architecture, which represents the most significant social institution. A study of the Hispanic built environment can begin with religious architecture, given the strong influence of the Catholic Church. In southern Colorado, Hispanic religious architecture is largely intact, along with the cultural life of the communities. Religion and its architectural representation have been paramount to cultural survival and the consequential lifestyle. New Mexico as a whole, and the Taos–San Luis Valley specifically, has a long history of mission churches and capillas, built by villages without the benefit of permanent clergy, convents, and consecrated cemeteries. In parallel, building also included the greatly misunderstood moradas of the Spanish-speaking community, largely in response to the lack of ordained clergy required for an official church. Moradas are not a part of this study, however, since they could not be located. While the New Mexico experience has been well documented, little has been recorded about the geographically isolated San Luis Valley on the Colorado side of the border.

EARLIER HISTORICAL ANTECEDENTS

The Hispanic influence in the San Luis Valley in general, and in the Conejos area in particular, has its roots in the sixteenth-century Spanish conquest of the Mexican Indian nations. Beginning with the 1519 capture of Tenochtitlan (Mexico City) by Hernán Cortes, Hispanic settlements spread increasingly northward. Settlements reached the line of the current U.S.-Mexican border at El Paso del Norte, and Spanish settlements pushed even further north into present-day New Mexico, with a series of mission churches being built for the Indian population. Spanish placitas were built and settled in a second wave following the Indian rebellions between 1680 and 1692. The settlements were encouraged with grants of land not only to counter hostile Indians but also to check French and American incursions into Spanish territory. Southern Colorado has its share of land grants, largely as a result of the infamous Trinchera Land Grant from the Mexican government in 1842. To the extent that the Spanish settlers' religious nature impelled them to construct churches or chapels, the chronology of church building documents the continual settlement movement northward. The series of churches built chronologically after the 1692 rebellion graphically depicts the movement north by Spanish settlers.

By 1833 the stage had been set for settlements to be extended into what is today the San Luis Valley in Colorado. At the southern end of the valley, a settlement had long been established at Taos, New Mexico (1706), and in the Ranchos de Taos, with a church built in 1780. The settlement of the Taos Valley was extended northward with the settlement and building of a church in Abiquiu, New Mexico, in 1754 and in El Rito, New Mexico (date unknown) (Figure 5.2).

COLORADO GEOGRAPHIC INFLUENCES

El Rito and Taos stand at the southernmost end of the naturally valley that extends northward. The valley provided access for settlers moving north on either side of the Río Grande. Since the valley is protected on three sides by mountains, these New Mexican settlements provided the only non-mountainous routes north. The ring of mountains, therefore, isolated the high plain that forms the valley floor from all directions except the south. The Río Grande, which divides the valley, is a deep gorge on the New Mexican side of the border with Colorado. The gorge inhibited east-west travel from a point sixty miles south of Taos to the Colorado border. While the Colorado side of the Río Grande is not a significant barrier to travel, the river still channeled settlements on the edges of the valley. Because of that reality, combined with the fact that the best farmland lies at the base of the mountains, the central portion of the valley remains largely uninhabited. The settlements in Colorado's present-day Conejos County, along the edge of the San Juan Mountains, are a natural extension of the Abiquiu–El Rito–Ojo Caliente region and are on the same side of the Río Grande. Likewise, the settlements in Colorado's present-day Costilla County, along the edge of the Sangre de Cristo Mountains, are a natural extension of the Taos-Picuris region of New Mexico.

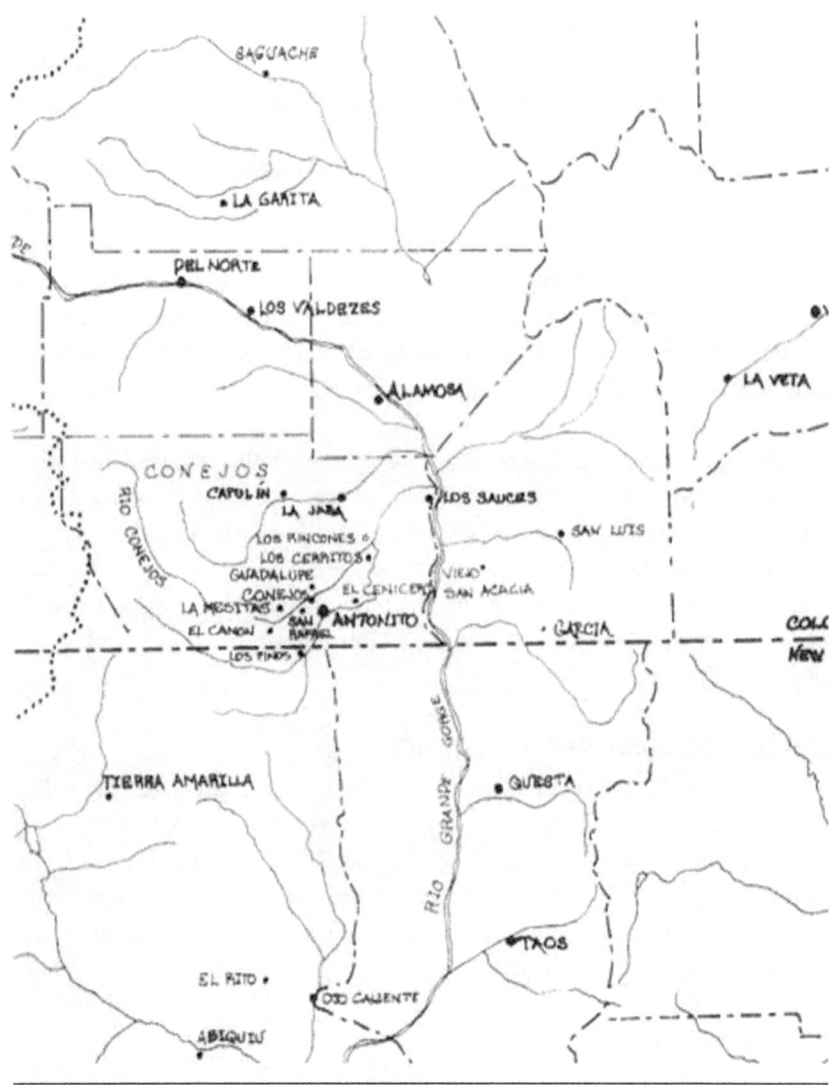

5.2. San Luis/Taos Valley capillas.

In the history of settlement in the Conejos area, the first record of Spanish presence on the Colorado side of the valley is that of Diego De Vargas in 1694, who traveled north during the Indian rebellions. Serious efforts at settlement did not begin until 1833, however. In that year, the Mexican government granted land to a group of settlers along the Conejos River. The settlement on the Conejos Land Grant was quickly abandoned because of the presence of hostile Indians. In 1843, forty-eight families made a second attempt to settle at the confluence of the Conejos and San Antonio rivers. That settlement, called San Francisco, was also abandoned. Finally, in 1846 a third attempt at settlement was made with a camp called San Margarita; it was also quickly abandoned.

In the summer of 1847, the stage had been set for the first successful Mexican settlement when Atanacio Trujillo and his son, Luis Rafael, came to the vicinity of Los Rincones in Colorado from El Rito, New Mexico. The summer encampment was successful enough to allow the two men to raise a crop and return to El Rito. In 1849 Atanacio and two brothers, Ignacio Francisco and Antonio, came north again and established a successful settlement in the Conejos region. As a parallel to the movement northward of placitas and capillas, the history of the Trujillo family is a rich legacy of a family seemingly always moving northward. Atanacio's grandfather was Mariano Trujillo, who lived in Abiquiu in the mid-1750s. His father was Jose María Trujillo, who was born in Abiquiu in 1784. Atanacio was born in 1801 in Ojo Caliente. After settling Conejos, he died in 1889 in a recorded settlement called Río de Costilla. The son who came north with him on the first encampment, Luis, was born in Abiquiu and died in 1908 in Conejos. Descendants of the family continue to live in the Conejos area.

In 1851 an additional fifty families from El Rito and Abiquiu, led by Jose Maria Jacques and Crescencio Valdez, came to the area and named a community settlement Guadalupe. By 1853 the bishop of the region, Bishop Lamy of Santa Fe, felt safe enough to visit Guadalupe and no doubt urged the construction of a church. In rapid order, villages or placitas were established and began to prosper in the entire region. Between 1854 and 1856 an adobe fort was built and became the community of Conejos. The first church, Iglesia de Nuestra Señora de Guadalupe, was built; it was dedicated in Conejos on June 10, 1856. Also in 1856, Paisaje, otherwise known as San Rafael, was founded. In 1857 Las Mesitas was established, followed by Capulin in 1858 and Los Sauces in 1863. It is said that by 1867, more than twenty-five placitas existed in the region, with about 6,000 residents. In short order, each community began to construct its own chapel or capilla.

The building traditions of the capillas in Conejos were a direct outgrowth of the adobe building style in New Mexico. In this regard, a church across the valley known as La Capilla de San Acacio is very illuminating. In the summer of 1989 it was undergoing renovation, and much of its structural wall and roof system was exposed. Built in about 1856, it was constructed of 18-inch-thick adobe walls. The current building has three generations of exterior plaster

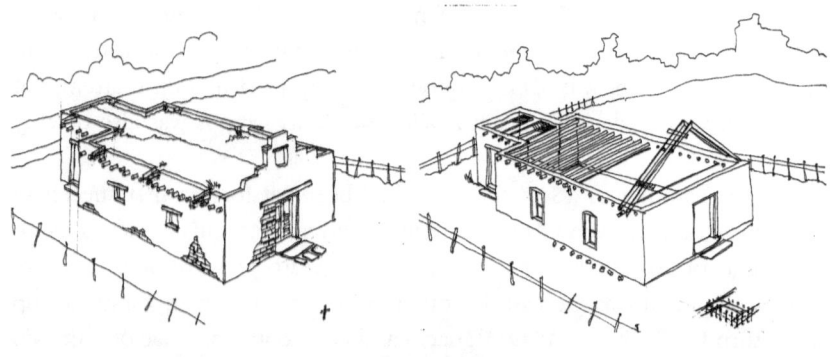

5.3. San Acacio reconstruction.

over the exposed adobe walls. When exposed, it revealed 14- to 16-inch wood *vigas* (round wood beams) that held the roof. The flat earthen and log roof was surely very difficult to keep watertight. Sometime around 1910, according to verbal history, the local priest, Father Garcia, had the vigas removed and replaced the flat, earthen roof typical of New Mexico churches with a system of pitched rafters and tie rods. The ceiling was then sloped and exposed. A cupola was placed on this pitched roof of wood and tin to hold a bell. Finally, in an attempt to slow the movement of water damage to the walls, concrete buttresses were added sometime around 1950 (Figure 5.3).

It is safe to assume that many of the capillas in the Conejos area were originally built with flat roofs. Once the movement began to modernize the structures with pitched roofs and cupolas for bells, however, all the churches were eventually altered. Those churches built after 1900, however, could well have been built with pitched roofs and metal roofing. As it happened, the same trend of changing rooflines was taking place in New Mexico. The history of the church in Abiquiu, Santo Tomas, is instructive in this regard. It also provides a key example for churches on the Colorado side of the border, since many inhabitants of Conejos came from the Abiquiu and El Rito areas.

The original church was built in 1754 with a flat, earthen roof. It burned in 1867 and was rebuilt by the residents. It is unclear if the church was rebuilt with a flat or a pitched roof, although there are indications that it may have had a flat roof as late as 1920, with a parapet front wall in the shape of a roof. However, a 1935 photograph clearly shows a church with a pitched, gabled roof and a cupola for a bell. In the 1960s the community restored the church roof to a flat system.

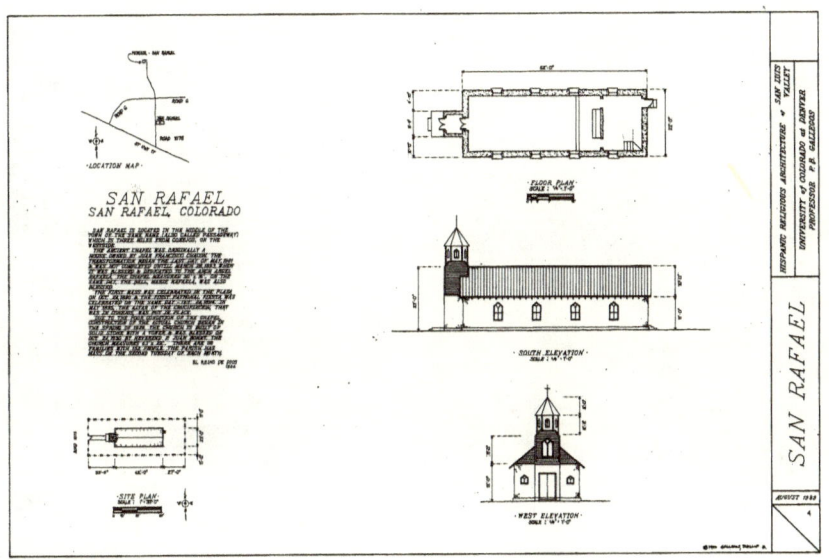

5.4. San Rafael.

Table: Churches Built in the Conejos Area, Chronological Order (illustrations, drawings, and histories from fieldwork)

1863	Iglesia de Nuestra Señora de Guadalupe, Conejos (first capilla constructed in 1855)
1879	Capilla de San Antonio de Padua, Los Sauces
1888	Capilla de San Augustine, Antonito
1891	Capilla de San Rafael, San Rafael (Paisaje)
1905	Capilla de San Luis Beltran, La Jara
1910	Capilla de Santo Nino, Espinosa
1912	Iglesia de San Jose, Capulin (first capilla constructed in 1878)
1912	Capilla de Inmaculada, Concepcion, Romeo
1927	Capilla de San Francisco, Cerritos (first capilla constructed at Rincones in 1879)
1927	Capilla de San Juan Nepomuceno, Ortiz
1932	Capilla de San Enrique y San Isidro, Las Mesitas (first capilla constructed in 1878)
1950	Capilla de Sagrada Familia, Lobatos (first capilla constructed in 1879; see reconstruction)
1950	Capilla de San Antonio de Padua, San Antonio (first capilla constructed in 1899; see reconstruction)

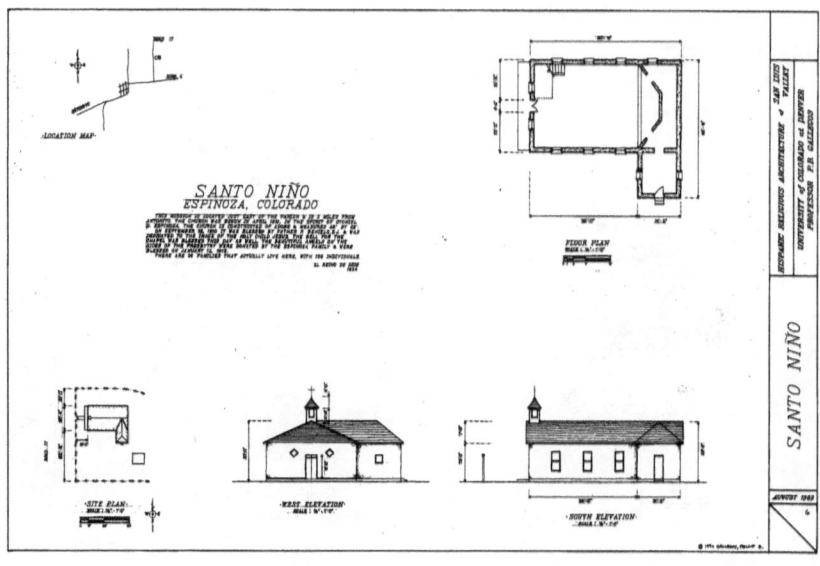

5.5. Santo Niño.

COMPILATION OF CONSECRATED CHURCHES, SAN LUIS VALLEY

The ancient chapel was originally a house owned by Juan Francisco Chacon. The transformation began the last day of May 1881 and was not completed until March 28, 1893, when it was blessed and dedicated to the archangel Rafaela. The chapel measured 50' × 16'. On the same day, the bell, Marie Rafaela, was also blessed. The first mass was celebrated in the plaza on October 24, 1890, and the first patronal fiesta was celebrated on the same day, October 24, 1894. In May 1895, the altar to the crucifixion that was in Conejos was put in place. Due to the poor condition of the chapel, construction of the actual church began in the spring of 1929. The church is built of solid stone with a tower and was blessed on October 24, 1930, by Reverend P. Juan Bonet. The church measures 63' × 22'. There are 38 families with 152 people. The parish has mass on the second Tuesday of each month.

("EL REINO DE DIOS," DIOCESE OF DENVER, 1934)

On September 18, 1910, it [Santo Niño] was blessed by Father P. Behiels, S.J. and was dedicated to the image of the Holy Child Jesus. The bell for the chapel was blessed this day as well. The beautiful angels on the sides of the presbytery were donated by the Espinoza family and were blessed on January 12, 1912. There are 36 families that live here with 158 individuals.

("EL REINO DE DIOS," DIOCESE OF DENVER, 1934)

SOME HISTORY OF CONEJOS COUNTY

The county of Conejos is one of the 17 counties that divided the State of Colorado in 1861. But at that time it was called Guadalupe County. In October 1842, a considerable part of the Conejos County was granted to Jose Marro, Antonio Martinez, J. Gallegos, and Celedon Valdez. But until 1854, Jose Maria Jaquez looked for an appropriate place and established a colony which is known today as Guadalupe. Located to the north of Conejos River, the county actually has 9803 inhabitants and occupies an area of 1252 square miles, being the lower half of the Valley. In 1855 a colony of Hispanic Americans of New Mexico settled definitely in Guadalupe. The first order of business was to build a jacal [mud and tree-limb construction easily built and quickly lost] of small proportions to pay tribute to Our Lady of Guadalupe, patron of the new village. The small jacal was built in 1856. This marked the beginning of the village Guadalupe, the oldest in the County. The Conejos River destroyed the jacal and village of Guadalupe by flooding. It was then that Bishop Lamy of Santa Fe (at that time he had jurisdiction over all of Colorado) gave his permission to begin construction of the first church south of the Conejos River. Because the settlers were poor, they could only build a lager jacal. It is known that the first mass celebrated in these parts was in 1856 in the primitive jacal by Rev. P Gabriel Ussel, then part of the Taos, Mexico parish. Many years later it ceased and became part of the Walsenburg parish. The official information on the oldest church in Colorado was found in the official books that have been saved up to the present day. The first official document states, "On this Sunday after Pentecost, Father Jose Miguel Vigil visited the jurisdiction of our Lady of Guadalupe in Conejos and administered the sacrament of confirmation. The parish of our Lady of Guadalupe was established June 10, 1857 by Bishop Lamy of Santa Fe. Father Montano was the first pastor. He began construction of the first church of Adobe in the original place. Father Miguel Vigil continued the construction and blessed the church on the feast day of our Lady of Guadalupe, December 12, 1863. During those years when Father Vigil was pastor, the first chapel[s] of Los Pinos and Los Rincones were built. Father Miguel Rolly was his successor from 1866 to December 1871. Father Salvadore Persone, S.J. and a brother arrived on February 1, 1872. Father Alejandro Leone, S.J. and another brother arrived. The parish in 1871 extended north 120 miles to Saguache, to the south 10 miles to Los Pinos, to the east 30 miles [to] Los Sauces, and to the west 7 miles to Las Mesitas. There were 25 villages: Guadalupe, Guadalupita, Las Mesitas, Canon, San Rafael, Codo, San Antonio, Los Pinos, Pura & Limpia, Isla, Cenicero, Rincones, Los Sauces, Cerritos, Fuertecitos, Brazo, Servilleta, Jara (today Capulin), Alamosa, Casillas, Lomas, Garita, Carnero, San Luis, and Saguache. In July of 1872, the first bishop of Colorado, Joseph Machebeuf, made his pastoral visit. He was impressed by the grand welcome he was given by all. The actual boundaries to the north, according to the Bishop on July 31, 1877 were the La Jara and Alamosa Rivers, and to the south (determined by the Bishop on January 24, 1882) was Tres Piedras N.M., to the west Cumbres station or the summit of the Conejos Mountains, and on the east by the Rio Grand River.

(FROM THE PUBLICATION "EL REINO DE DIOS: A LA PARROQUIA DE CONEJOS EN SUS BODAS DE DIAMANTE ANTONITO, COLORADO," LOCATED IN ANTONITO, CO, JUNE 1934)

CONCLUSION

In architectural terms, the churches of the Conejos settlement area in Colorado represent religious architecture of modest means. The churches are, however, direct descendants of the Taos, El Rito, Abiquiu, and Ojo Caliente peoples and environment of the mid-1800s. They represent the physical evidence of the continuation of Spanish and Mexican efforts to colonize the northern frontier. In 1776 a Franciscan priest named Fray Francisco Atanacio Dominguez created a stir among his superiors when he recorded and depicted the churches of New Mexico as little more than earthen warehouses. However, he had entered a frontier lifestyle driven by fear of attacks and necessities of survival. The churches that were built were important to the survival of the community and had no extensive superficial embellishments. An economy of means was required when they were constructed. They are a physical representation of the materials and labor skills available in an economy of scare means.

The most critical criteria guiding the design and construction of the churches in both the eighteenth and nineteenth centuries were the needs of fortification, adobe construction methods, and the minimum symbolism of a cupola and a bell. These were the design tools that helped form the church spaces, both internally and externally, in northern New Mexico and southern Colorado. The political bounder called a state line is not reflective of the region's unified cultural landscape. While the history of the New Mexico side of the political border has been widely explored, the Colorado side has been largely ignored. The churches represent a significant element necessary in the struggle to survive and prosper in a time of scarce means. Yet even though they were symbols of survival, many churches have been significantly altered, damaged, or abandoned—to be destroyed by nature.

In the colonization efforts on the northern frontiers, each placita seems to have been able to send forth a new group of settlers to establish the next new community link. As each community became entrenched enough to survive, the next settlement was also characterized by the construction of a capilla. The importance of the capilla is seen not just in religious terms but also in practical and political terms. For the placita, building a capilla indicated a sense of establishment that would allow for the repository of important religious documents, such as birth certificates. The priest visited, baptized, and recorded the inhabitants of a placita along with the next settlement to the north. This had great importance in establishing the legitimacy of the government and the colonizing people.

George H. Junne Jr., Osita Ofoaku, Rhonda Corman, and Rob Reinsvold

Dearfield, Colorado: Black Farming Success in the Jim Crow Era

EARLY BLACK MIGRATION TO COLORADO

The history of African Americans in the Dearfield, Colorado, area is intimately linked to early-nineteenth-century westward expeditions that cut through today's Weld County, Colorado. Dearfield was one of approximately fifteen all-Black communities planned for the state and was its most famous. The roots of settlements similar to Dearfield began during the Revolutionary War era when American Blacks hoped to build communities for themselves and their families—places where they could avoid racism and the accompanying segregation. The migration initiatives that led Blacks to Colorado lead to the history of the Dearfield community.

In 1820 President James Monroe sent Stephen H. Long to lead a group of men on a pioneering venture, known as "the Yellowstone Expedition," to explore the Louisiana Purchase's southwestern boundary. On Monday, July 3, 1820, the men reached the South Platte River basin. Long included this area in what he described as the "Great American Desert."[1] This geographical metaphor remains crucial to understanding the force of the human spirit that championed the Dearfield project, as well as its tragic collapse.

101

Jacob Dodson followed in the tradition of York, who traveled with Lewis and Clark, and other African Americans who pioneered the westward movement. Between 1833 and 1834, Dodson participated in the second excursion of the U.S. Army's Corp of Topographical Engineers to what is now the Trans-Mississippi West; he also participated in the scouting of the Great Salt Lake. John C. Frémont, commander of the exploration parties, described Dodson as "only eighteen, but strong and active, and nearly six feet [tall]. . . . He was of the good colored people of the district, born free, but with the feeling of belonging with a family and giving to it unchanging service."[2] All five of Frémont's expeditions went through Colorado.[3]

The 1849 Gold Rush sparked mining activity in the western frontier. Later gold discoveries in "Nevada, Colorado, Arizona, New Mexico, Montana, Idaho, Wyoming, and even South Dakota" caused westward migrations, which included Blacks.[4] The first known permanent African American settler in Colorado Territory (1859) was Lorzeno Boman, a runaway slave, successful miner, and inventor of a mining apparatus. Although many Blacks came to Colorado with hopes of finding employment as gold miners, they were rarely able to work in the trade because the larger Colorado companies were involved in quartz mining. However, they did find work in mining camps and towns springing up in the Pikes Peak area near Colorado Springs. One of Colorado's most famous Black citizens, former slave Clara Brown, rode eight weeks on a wagon train from St. Louis to Denver. At age fifty-five she arrived in Denver carrying her freedom papers.[5] Brown eventually went to Central City and ran a thriving laundry business. She used some of her wealth, which included mining investments, to finance Black wagon trains coming to Colorado.

Blacks who moved to Colorado after 1865 believed they would find less racial tension and more economic opportunities. Their perception of Colorado was allegedly valid to the extent that it was a better place for Blacks than states east of the Mississippi River, the Midwest, and the South. Furthermore, many Whites in Colorado had not experienced Reconstruction and "did not have a debt to settle with Blacks."[6] The 1860 census recorded 436 Blacks in Colorado; in 1880, it recorded 2,435 and in 1900, 8,570.[7] Most Blacks settled in the areas of Colorado Springs, Denver, and Pueblo.

When Colorado achieved statehood in 1867, Article IX, Section 8, of the new constitution stipulated that no "distinction or classification of pupils be made on account of color."[8] It would be approximately ninety years before integrated schools reached some of the states from which Colorado Blacks had emigrated. The time to test Colorado's seemingly progressive constitution, however, came with the establishment of the Bureau of Immigration in 1872.

Blacks throughout the United States received information from the bureau, encouraging them to immigrate to Colorado. Despite what many immigrants must have interpreted as an open invitation, questions still remained about encouraging Blacks to settle in the state. As evidenced by views expressed by opinion leaders, the White community's reactions were mixed, if not ambiguous. The most favorable reactions came from individuals who believed Blacks could contribute to the economic development of the state as unskilled laborers. Proponents of migration believed, however, that the influx of Blacks into Colorado should be controlled. For instance, former governor John Evans stated: "I think a limited number might be brought here with good results. This is a growing state, and as she grows, the demand for laborers increases. Quite a number could be accommodated here in Denver as house servants and stock trainers, and the like.... I think that a number of colored men could do well here, but they ought not be brought in indiscriminately."[9]

Denver mayor John Sopris echoed Evans's view: "a moderate immigration of Negroes into Colorado would rebound to our advantage as well as to theirs."[10] Opponents of Black migration raised the traditional questions regarding their ability to fit into a Eurocentric culture. Postmaster William N. Byers reflected: "I do not think it is well to encourage a large emigration of these people to Colorado. Some classes might be benefited by coming here. They might help fill the demand for house servants, and in some kinds of outdoor labor with advantage to themselves and their employers, but I do not think they will readily adapt themselves to the great labor tasks of this State."[11]

Interestingly, Horace Greeley, famous for his "Go West young man and grow up in the country" advice, was among those who adamantly opposed Black migration to Colorado. Although an abolitionist, he believed the West should be reserved for Whites. In contrast, prominent Colorado Black leaders such as barber Henry O. Wagoner did not accept the notion that Blacks should take a back seat to Whites in Colorado. He emphatically stated: "What immigration has done for the White man it can also do for the Black man."[12] In a similar vein, the Reverend Robert Seymour, pastor of the African Methodist Episcopal Church, suggested that the Black community in Colorado was able and willing to receive Black immigrants in spite of White opposition: "Why will not he [Governor Evans] and other philanthropic gentlemen organize a bureau and help them to get to our state, where the colored people stand ready to take care of them to the end of our resources? ... For the benefit of this great state let them come; aye, help them to come."[13]

The leader of Denver's Black community on legal rights issues was William Jefferson Hardin, a barber with White clientele and a strong connection to

White elites. Hardin served for several years as the unofficial spokesperson of Colorado Blacks. Hardin puzzled many Whites in Colorado Territory, though, because they knew the famous orator was an "octoroon," meaning he was one-eighth African American; he could have passed for a White person of Italian or French descent. Hardin aligned himself with the Black community, however, and fought vociferously for its rights on the local and national levels.[14] Others aided the cause of Black equality, including Wagoner; Edward Sanderlin, also a barber; and Barney Ford, a hotelier and restaurateur. These Black leaders eventually became important to White Republicans who courted their votes.[15]

Some Blacks who traveled from the former slave states of the South to Kansas with the Exoduster movement began to immigrate to Colorado, particularly to Denver. By the 1880s an Black community was evident on Blake and Larimer streets. By 1900 the Black population had increased to 4,000 and had its own newspapers and churches; after 1900 a significant pool of middle-class Blacks migrated to neighborhoods northeast of the original settlement.[16] Some of them would become involved in the Dearfield agricultural project.

During the 1860s and 1870s, Colorado began to change the negative images of agriculture on the dry plains by building extensive irrigation projects and establishing planned agriculture communities. Farmers were encouraged to take advantage of those incentives to make the territory a self-sustaining unit.[17] The creation of the Union Colony in 1869 was part of this effort. The first irrigation ditch the Union Colony completed in 1870 was the first in the United States constructed for the purpose of raising food.[18] An offshoot of the Union Colony project, Greeley would eventually draw farmers to eastern Colorado. It became a model for the farmers of Dearfield and other neighboring communities.[19] Great emphasis was placed on agriculture as the key to Black economic empowerment when Dearfield was in its planning stages. Statistics indicated that in 1890, 21.7 percent of Blacks in the United States were agricultural workers. The year 1900 saw a slight decrease to 20.6 percent. In 1910, 23.1 percent of all U.S. Blacks worked in agriculture.[20] Dearfield would have been an important addition to these statistics if it had been the success story envisaged by the Blacks who settled there.

DEARFIELD, COLORADO: A TWENTIETH-CENTURY BLACK SETTLEMENT

As reflected by the 1896 *Plessy* v. *Ferguson* Supreme Court ruling,[21] segregation was the preferred system of social organization for most White Americans at the turn of the twentieth century. Dearfield and similar community development projects grew from the determination of African Americans to survive in a society that insisted upon their exclusion from social, political, and economic life. Blacks wanted the opportunity to govern themselves, even if they had to live in a separate but equal society.

David Boyd's 1890 book, *A History: Greeley and the Union Colony of Colorado*, displayed the negative sentiments informing the actions of some Whites toward Blacks. He wrote that the best future for humanity rested on the total extinction of Native Americans "as a race."[22] Boyd would likely have been vehemently opposed to the idea of a community of Blacks living within thirty miles of his municipality twenty years later. Ironically, the book eloquently demonstrates the White hegemonic mind-set that drove Blacks to construct towns such as Dearfield. Even more ironic, Black communities emerged alongside similar White communities across the country. As William H. and Jane H. Pease noted in their article "Organized Negro Communities: A North American Experiment," both communities flourished at the same time, both were removed from the influences of traditional society, and both reflected the reform temperament of the Middle Period (1817–1858); notably, while many White communities were conceptualized as Utopian (socialist or communist) communities, the Black communities "ascribed to the traditional political, social, and economic tenets of the American Middle Class."[23] Dearfield demonstrated this reality.

Oliver Toussaint Jackson, the founder of Dearfield, was born on April 6, 1862, in Oxford, Ohio, the son of Hezekiah and Caroline Jackson, former slaves. They named him after Toussaint L'Ouverture, the maroon slave who successfully overthrew the French in Haiti in 1804. In 1887 O. T. Jackson moved from the Midwest to the Denver area where he worked as a caterer. In 1889 he married Sarah "Sadie" Cook; her brother was the famous composer Will Marion Cook.[24] In 1894 Jackson moved to Boulder, Colorado, and operated Stillman Café and Ice Cream Parlor on 13th Street between Pearl and Walnut streets; his house was at 2228 Pine Street. In 1898 he became a staff manager at the Chautauqua Dining Hall, supervising seventy people (and possibly holding the food concession). Jackson also owned and operated a restaurant at 55th and Arapahoe, where the Boulder Dinner Theatre is today; his restaurant was famous for its seafood.[25] By 1894 Jackson had made enough money to buy a farm outside Boulder, which he owned for sixteen years.

Boulder had a thriving and close-knit Black community in the early 1900s. Many lived in the Goss-Grove neighborhood between Canyon (formerly Water Street) and Goss streets and between 19th and 23rd streets. Many came from Mississippi and Tennessee, working at the Red Cross and in their own Pearl Street businesses. Black women worked as housekeepers, laundresses, nursemaids, and domestics; many of the men were porters, store clerks, and janitors. Black families boarded Black students because the University of Colorado did not allow them to live in dorms.[26]

Confusion exists about whether Jackson and his first wife divorced or if she died. Nevertheless, on July 14, 1905, he married Minerva J. Matlock, a schoolteacher from Missouri. His restaurant remained "a popular eating place for citizens of Boulder until it closed when the city voted dry in 1907."[27] In 1908 Jackson returned to Denver, where he began a twenty-year career as a messenger for Colorado governors. While he was working for Governor John F. Shafroth, Jackson decided to use his political connections to actualize his dream of starting an agricultural colony.[28] In 1909 he discovered that state lands offered few large tracts suitable for farming because most unoccupied areas were under lease for pasture. After considering three tracts of homestead land in Larimer, Elbert, and Weld counties, he selected a tract near Masters.[29] Jackson formed the Negro Townsite and Land Company in 1909 to obtain the Dearfield site.

The directorate of the town site included O. T. Jackson as president; J. B. Beckham, vice president; A. M. Ward, treasurer; and A. S. Newsom, secretary. In addition, committees were established to oversee aspects of the project such as finances, audits, roles of special agents, publicity, and applications. The pioneer group adopted the motto "When we build, let us think that we build forever." On June 8, 1910, O. T. Jackson resigned from the board, citing personal business reasons; on October 1, 1910, the directors and stockholders held a meeting to dissolve the organization.[30] Dearfield's geopolitical location posed peculiar challenges to Jackson and his supporters. In Colorado as elsewhere, African Americans were preoccupied with building up social networks and institutions that would serve as protective walls against the onslaught of racial oppression. The Dearfield project was consistent with this vision. Historian Sarah Deutsh summarizes the spirit of the time: "The efforts of minority groups in the West in this era [early twentieth century] often centered on the attempt to reserve a place apart where they could exercise control over their lives, society and surroundings."[31]

For the Dearfield project, the need for political and financial support against the need for outside political and economic support was critical. Many Blacks continued to view the Republican Party as the party of abolitionism at the turn of the twentieth century; the same Blacks regarded Democrats as conservatives and racists. This was particularly so in the southern and western states, where the Ku Klux Klan and other white supremacist organizations harassed, intimidated, and murdered African Americans during the early decades of the twentieth century and beyond. In Colorado, a senator, the governor, and Denver's mayor were Klan members, as were an estimated 5 percent of the state's 1 million residents. William Joseph Simmons, the man who revitalized the Klan in Georgia, came to Denver's Union Station in 1921 to initiate residents. This group, the Denver Doers Club, grew to become a powerful political order. Klan members focused mostly on Jews and Catholics, however, harassing them and boycotting their businesses. Denver's 17,000 Klan members sold cigars that had "CYANA" labels, meaning "Catholics, You Are Not Americans." The Klan did set off a bomb in the front yard of Walter Chapman, an African American mail carrier who had dared to buy a home at 2112 Gilpin, a White neighborhood; he was not injured.[32]

Consequently, while Jackson, a Democrat, was able to win the support of some White leaders, he lost the support of Denver's Black business community. Perhaps Jackson's choice reflected his inclination to adopt Booker T. Washington's strategy of pragmatic reliance on White patronage rather than his unabashed quest for personal glory. In the eyes of the Black business community, Jackson's association with White, Democratic leadership tainted the potential benefits of Dearfield as a model of Black self-help. Despite that major setback, Jackson forged ahead, using whatever support he could obtain from Denver officials as well as the presidents of Colorado State Teachers College and the State Agricultural College (University of Northern Colorado and Colorado State University, respectively).[33] In May 1910 Jackson filed a homestead entry on a tract of land outside Greeley. On February 4, 1914, he purchased forty acres of land in Dearfield for $400, and the community was officially born. Jackson selected that site for several reasons:

> There were large areas of government land available at nominal prices. The location was conveniently positioned in the valley of the Platte River, between the Burlington and Union Pacific railroads. In fact, the town site was about three miles north of the former and two miles from the latter. The presence of both railroads, with stations at frequent intervals, guaranteed acceptable transportation facilities during the entire year. Road transportation was good . . . and provided a reliable outlet by truck for more intensive crops raised in the district.[34]

Other advantages included a potential underground water source, fertile sandy loam soil, level terrain, and a view of the Rocky Mountains.[35] Jackson filed a desert claim, which is significant. Census figures from 1910 showed Weld County had a population of 39,177 and had 3,981 farms, each averaging

229.6 acres. The 1910 Desert Land Act allowed the homesteader more acreage than previously, 640 acres, but the homesteader had to irrigate the land within three years. Because of the prospect that land could be watered, a land rush occurred. Jackson was thus allegedly competing with other homesteaders.

The original site Jackson chose was in "Section 30-4N-61," where he built his house. Jackson purchased additional land from Robert F. Jackson, who had purchased said site from James G. Wright in 1872. Jackson lived in Dearfield with his wife, Minerva, his father-in-law, and George White, a boy from the State Home in Denver. A Denver friend, J. M. Thomas, who worked in a wrecking yard, was the next settler in Dearfield. Other individuals among the original pioneers of Dearfield include:

> J.N.B. Anderson, S. E. Bill, James F. Bruce, George Collier (father of Cornelius and Alfred), W. E. Danforth, Mrs. Clara B. Franklin, Lee Ford, Andrew S. Goodall, John J. Harrison, James Haskins, C. J. Hicks, Newton Hicks, J. M. Holley, J. H. Houston, Ernest Miller, Harvey Page (former postal worker), James W. Price, Walter Spates, Charles Stewart (veteran of the Civil War), Robert Thomas, J. A. Hazell, J. Mittie Williams and Joe Young. Dr. W. A. Jones, a native of Alabama and graduate of Tuskegee Institute, had one of the better homes and served as physician for the greater community regardless of color.[36]

Dr. Joseph H.P. Westbrook of Denver, a physician and one of the first settlers of Dearfield, gave the colony its name at the founding team's June 12, 1909, meeting, explaining that the area "will be very dear to us."[37] Born in Hernando, Mississippi, he graduated from Maharry Medical College in 1904 and moved to Denver in 1907, opening his Allen Drug Store in 1909. Westbrook served as assistant city physician, and for seventeen years he was on the staff of Denver General Hospital. A very light-skinned man who could pass for white, Westbrook actually infiltrated the Denver Ku Klux Klan and kept the Black community informed about its activities. A great supporter of Dearfield, he left the community in 1914.[38]

The first group of settlers who moved to Dearfield had many problems. Some of the early settlers were so poor they could not afford to ship their possessions from Denver, and they walked part of the distance. Among the members of this group, only two families could afford to erect a 12' by 14' building with a fence. The other five families had to live in tents or in holes they dug in a hillside. Sometimes the men had to work on other farms to earn spending money while the wives and children worked the land. Prejudice also existed against the first settlers; White residents treated Blackness as an indelible mark of inferiority. Also, the cattlemen in the area did not want fences crisscrossing the range. The Dearfield Black settlers seemed ill prepared for the challenges of creating an agricultural community in a desert-like environment. However, Bob Jackson cites an eloquent testimony to the settlers' unyielding courage and determination: "The winter of 1911–1912 was exceptionally severe. . . . Fuel was scarce and as there was no timber available on the bare prairie, they frequently carried wood on their heads from the valley of the Platte River— from three to seven miles. Three of their six horses died of starvation during the winter and the other three were weakened."[39]

Another critical problem, which manifested itself in later years, was that Dearfield had no water rights from the Platte River. The settlers also had no money to buy water rights from the Empire Ditch Company, owner of the Empire Reservoir about eight miles southeast of Dearfield. Irrigation depended on a small creek and on rainfall, which were actually adequate for the colony's first few years. Later, at the beginning of the twenty-first century, the annual precipitation—including snow and rain—ranged from 11.6 inches in Greeley (formerly the Union Colony) to 13.9 inches in the northeastern part of the county; the success of agriculture is connected to the irrigation system, which waters 393,000 acres.[40]

Western Farm Life interviewed O. T. Jackson for its May 1, 1915, issue. According to Jackson, the Dearfield project included forty farms, 160 acres each, with the town site embodying 140 acres. In his judgment, "[I]t took plenty of nerve for this small group of Negroes to go out upon the barren, sage-brush prairie and undertake, without means or capital, to force a living from the unyielding soil."[41] In its November 1921 issue, *The Weld County News* ran a headline that read "Weld County's Negro Colony." The article's first paragraph was a tribute to both O. T. Jackson's leadership and Dearfield's Black residents' determination to succeed: "Eleven years ago a lone colored man filed a homestead . . . about 30 miles southeast of Greeley. . . . Although there was not a real farm within miles . . . he selected his homestead with a view to making it into a farm, and from that little incident grew a colony of Negro farmers which ranks high among the 14 of its kind in the United States today."[42]

Some of the White farmers in the area assisted their Black neighbors and sometimes traded goods and services. By 1914 Dearfield was beginning to show signs of prosperity. That year residents also experienced the "Big Snow"; precipitation stayed on the ground until April 15 of the following year. The population grew to 111 in 1915, and residents filed for homesteading on 8,400 of the 20,000 available acres in Weld County. For the small group of Black farmers and their families, the ideals of self-reliance and self-pride appeared to be coming true. Dearfield was a community whose courage and creativity began to draw the attention of neighboring communities and state officials. An article in the September 28, 1916, issue of *The Greeley Tribune* noted Dearfield's second annual festival and carnival, where prominent men of Colorado, including Governor G. A. Carlson, were scheduled to speak.[43]

The value of Dearfield's holdings reflected prosperity. In 1910 the holdings were valued at $25,000, or $1.25 per acre; in 1917 the value of the land had reached $432,500, or $15 per acre.[44] Not only was this community promising to be a successful experiment in economic terms, but the amount of resources invested in the construction of a cultural entity was impressive. The community got a post office, and 1917 saw the first marketable crops, which included "potatoes, beans, corn, watermelon, cantaloupe, pumpkin, squash, onions, turnips, cabbage, tomatoes, oats, rye, alfalfa, and native hay."[45] By the end of 1918, Jackson noted that Dearfield residents could no longer work on area farms because they had to tend to their own.

A Dearfield schoolteacher, Odessa McCollough, began planning "for an Industrial Agricultural College[,] possibly a branch of some southern college."[46] Jackson was attempting to attract tourists and wealthy Blacks, the latter to establish a bank in Dearfield. An unnamed White philanthropist offered a "financial inducement" to build a sanitarium.[47] By 1920 Dearfield had a population of almost 200 people who worshipped on Sunday in two churches.[48] The hotel, restaurant, school, and other amenities signaled the residents' devotion to build a functional community; plans for a canning factory were in the works, too. *The Weld County News* praised Dearfield's efforts:

> There are within the limits of the colony a school and two churches, both patronized wholly by the colored people of the district and both adding materially to the educational and moral standards of the community. The remarkable influence which the independence and freedom have had upon the settlers is indicated by the fact that since the first filing within the colony there has been but one arrest for any offense of any magnitude and the offender in that instance was not legitimately a resident.[49]

In 1921 the land was valued at more than $750,000, livestock at more than $200,000, and annual production at nearly $125,000. After eleven years, the colony's total value stood at over $1 million. Following World War I, residents could afford automobiles. Ten settlers pooled their money to buy a thresher, paying for it with money they received from harvesting beans.[50]

In the early 1920s the future looked bright for Dearfield. But no one could have foreseen the devastating conditions that would take a thriving, promising venture and reduce it to a ghost town within a few short years.

In his 1926 book on agriculture in the state of Colorado, Alvin T. Steinel devoted space to Dearfield, describing the settlement and the achievements of Black farmers:

> These settlers have come from various occupations, some having been tenant farmers in the cotton districts of the South, others in employment as Pullman porters, or as family servants, or in other wage-earning work which gave them little opportunity for independence. On the farm they are at least self-supporting from the products of the soil and some are now quite well-to-do. . . . The colony has proved successful and permanent.[51]

In 1921 Blacks elsewhere faced race riots in Tulsa, Oklahoma; Knoxville, Tennessee; Springfield, Ohio; Chester, Pennsylvania; and in many other communities. Yet 1921 seemed to hold promise for many Blacks. Marcus Garvey's Universal Negro Improvement Association became a national organization, and the Republican National Convention declared that Blacks must be admitted to state and national conventions. The National Negro Baseball League began, and the all-Black musical *Shuffle Along* opened on Broadway. The first Black record label, Black Swan, began to record music. Black artists had their first large show at the New York Public Library, and Black University of Iowa football player Frederick "Duke" Slater won a First Team All-American award. Bessie Coleman became the first Black licensed aviator. No wonder *The Weld County News*, Weld County Whites, and Dearfield Blacks envisioned a rosy future for the community.

THE END OF THE DREAM

World War I created a demand for American agricultural products in Europe; farmers reaped big profits from livestock and crops. However, the trend was reversed at the end of the war in 1919. In the 1920s the price of wheat fell from $2 to $1 a bushel in the global market. Argentina, Canada, Australia, and Russia began supplying wheat and meat to Europe. Between 1919 and 1923, more than 400,000 American farmers lost their farms. Into the mid-1920s, however, Jackson and others remained optimistic about Dearfield. The State Board of Immigration printed a four-page brochure titled "Dearfield, Colorado: Township and Settlement." The publication gave the history and location of Dearfield, as well as a description of Weld County and the county's agricultural statistics. Besides the obvious confidence, the board praised the interracial cooperation it saw: "Attracted by the success, white farmers began moving into the territory to take advantage of the cheap lands offered for sale, and today there are both white and colored farmers working harmoniously together in the region, striving for the interdependence which successful farming brings to the people of both races."[52]

One Dearfield resident, Eunice Norris, seemed to agree with the board's view that the Dearfield area was relatively free from racial strife. She recalled that people got along because "they didn't have time for trouble. There was a spirit of helpfulness."[53] The situation seemed to be the opposite of conditions in other parts of the United States, with the ascension of the Ku Klux Klan and the increase in race riots.

With the coming of droughts in the 1930s, Weld County became part of the Dust Bowl.[54] The county was still doing well in 1930, however, as dust storms blew from Montana to Texas. In Colorado the mining industry took a nosedive, but farming made up for the losses. That year (1930), farm production in some Colorado counties increased 100 to 200 percent. Weld and El Paso counties led all other Colorado counties in dairying, and the state ranked first in the United States in sugar beet production. Wheat production in Weld County peaked at 202,996 acres. The U.S. Census reported that Weld County farms had 1,681 tractors, 820 farms had electricity, and 2,617 had telephones; the average annual income for a farm family was $400—but all of that was about to change. In 1931 farm mortgages rose to $9.2 billion nationwide as farmers tried to buy new equipment; farm prices dropped, and banks began foreclosing on mortgages. By 1932 almost 10 percent of America's farmers had lost their farms. In Colorado approximately 100 northeastern dry-land farming communities folded during the 1930s.[55]

By 1936 Dearfield was almost deserted. Jackson's plans to build a fifty-room tourist hotel, a soap factory, a college, and a bank never materialized. In 1939 O. T. Jackson made this statement to his co-pioneers, perhaps for the first time revealing his reluctant resolve to eventually move out of Dearfield: "Many of the pioneers still own their own land here and are living in hopes that someday they can return. We are sorry, but Mrs. Jackson and I will not be here when they return. . . . We have put in the best years of our lives trying to make this colony a success. We hope to be able to interest some of the younger people in taking up where we leave off."[56]

World War II sealed Dearfield's fate. The draft took men from all over the country, and after the war, many of those with skills and training did not return to farming communities. It is difficult to deduce whether Dearfield's Black residents would have abandoned their farms for big U.S. cities in the absence of the Depression and the Dust Bowl. However, the residents faced conditions that left them with few or no options. For instance, Blacks in Boulder, an hour-and-a-half trip from Dearfield, could not resist the attraction of the war economy. The Boulder Black community vanished and reappeared in California, where its former residents could make more money in a month than they had in the previous years.[57]

As residents left Dearfield, Jackson began to sell vacant houses for lumber. Jackson kept the lunchroom and filling station open until 1946. He promised George White, the man he raised from the state home, that he could have Dearfield at the end of his military service, but White's new wife was not interested. On April 4, 1946, an advertisement appeared in *The Greeley Tribune* offering the town site of Dearfield for sale.

The August 8, 1955, issue of *Empire Magazine*, a *Denver Post* Sunday supplement, published an article titled "Dearfield, Colorado: Population 1." The article recounted Dearfield's history and profiled the town's last resident, Jennie Jackson, a niece of O. T. Jackson. When O. T. Jackson became bedridden in 1943, Jennie Jackson left Chicago to care for him. She expressed surprise at the way the experiment ended: "I was shocked at what had happened to Dearfield. I had visited it before the depression, and Dearfield then was lively and growing. . . . Everyone believed in Dearfield. In 1943, everything was different. Almost all the people had gone. . . . Everyone said that Dearfield was done for, but Uncle never believed it. He always told me to hold on to the land that he left me in his will."[58]

O. T. Jackson died on February 18, 1948, at the Weld County Hospital in Greeley; he was eighty-six years old.[59] With Dearfield almost vacant, Jackson's demise marked the end of "the last major attempt at agricultural colonization on the high plains."[60] Dearfield's original hotel became Jennie Jackson's home, where she kept treasures belonging to her uncle; they included portraits of Booker T. Washington and former Colorado governors. She also had her uncle's Colorado State House desk.[61]

Although Miss Jackson inherited the land, she did not inherit Jackson's modest fortune. A few weeks before he died, a female relative from California visited him. Before she left, Jackson changed his will, leaving his money to the visitor. Jennie Jackson did not seem bitter about her uncle's decision;[62] an optimist like her uncle, she appeared more interested in reviving the Dearfield project. She told a reporter: "I have my home here and the land that Uncle Oliver left me. Right now people tell me I'm land poor. But someday it will be worth something, and our people will come back."[63] However, the future offered her little comfort. At that time, Jennie Jackson's nearest neighbors were Mr. and Mrs. Harry E. Nolds, who operated a gas station.[64] Harry Nolds and his wife sold the station to Ted Noller of South Dakota. Noller, his wife, and their two children operated the station and lived in the attached apartment.

Noller and family, Whites, became the only people living in the former all-Black colony with Jennie Jackson.

Empire Magazine ran a follow-up on Dearfield in 1969. The Colorado Highway Department had erected a green-and-white sign on Highway 34 across from the lunchroom and the gas station that said "Dearfield." Jackson's niece, Jennie Jackson, was eighty-five years old and living in Greeley's Weld County Nursing Home. According to *Empire Magazine*: "She still tries to get back to the colony to inspect her property whenever she can. But, as the years pass, the trip is getting more difficult."[65] Born on April 24, 1886, in Morris, Minnesota, Jennie Jackson died in Greeley at age eighty-six. She had moved to Greeley in 1953 to live with Ethel Carter, a cousin, and her husband, the Reverend H. C. Carter; the Carter's church was at 600 Fourth Avenue.[66] In 1986 Ethel Carter was living in a nursing home and owned most of land designated as Dearfield.[67]

In 1969 the gas station remained open, but "the man who runs that octane outpost is not a Dearfield native; he knows little about the hamlet's history—and cares less."[68] The *Empire Magazine* article noted a small rubber skeleton dangling from a beam inside the gas station with a hangman's noose around the neck. A sign tacked on the beam said the skeleton was "all that remains of Dearfield's last original settler." Commenting on the mockery of the hanging skeleton, reporter Cary Stiff said: "To those who know Dearfield's history, the joke is a cruel and ironic one, because the original settlers of the town were Black. . . . Solid, hard-working Black men, and Black women and children. Negroes who had just come to the high prairies voluntarily . . . hoping to escape from that very world where White men could mirthlessly joke about stringing up men of another color."[69]

In 1990 Lorrie Holmes operated the Dearfield store and was the town's only resident. She spent most of her life in Orchard, a town about ten miles away. She rented the building and began selling snacks such as pickles, Polish sausage, pickled pig's feet, and pickled eggs. Lorrie's Place opened on Father's Day, and the sixty-seven-year-old proprietor hoped for a community renaissance that did not occur.[70]

In February 1999 both *The Greeley Tribune* and *The Denver Post* reported that Colorado lieutenant governor Joe Rogers, the only African American in the United States to hold that title, had named Dearfield to "Colorado's Most Endangered Places" list. The Black American West Museum (BAWM) in Denver began working to preserve the home last occupied by O. T. Jackson's niece. As part of that effort, the museum purchased it and a second house. In addition, the BAWM hired a consulting firm to develop a plan to preserve

Dearfield. The museum wants to purchase the original 600 acres for open space, historic preservation, and restoration.[71] The Rushings, a White family, owned the Jackson house and were ready to raze it in the 1990s when they learned of its history; Ben Rushing is a Weld County sheriff's deputy. The BAWM purchased land in the area and swapped it for the house, which is now listed on the National Register (5WL.744). Another White person and retired Denver sheriff's deputy, Jerry Toler, purchased the store and made plans to reopen it; however, the state diverted a new section of Highway 34 away from the building, so the BAWM obtained ownership. Two African Americans, Donald Fachs and Ronald Oakley, owned the adjacent property that included the restaurant. According to Toler, they drove taxis in Denver and had plans to develop their acreage.[72] The BAWM has obtained ownership of that property as well.

The preservation plan came together when Colorado's General Assembly passed "An Act Concerning the Preservation of Historic Dearfield, and Making an Appropriation Therefor." The assembly approved the senate act on June 1, 2000. The accompanying appropriation was $250,000 for the fiscal year beginning July 1, 2000.[73] The act further stipulated that monies appropriated to the Department of Higher Education for the Dearfield preservation and the park would be distributed to the Black American West Museum in Denver.[74] The BAWM began working with Colorado Preservation Inc., a nonprofit organization that manages the project. The Architectural Preservation Institute at Colorado State University became the subcontractor for restoring the two buildings: the O. T. Jackson house and the Squire Brockman house. Brockman, a blacksmith and fiddler, was one of the last of Dearfield's residents to occupy the house.[75] In November 2000, the Dearfield preservation project officially began. The two standing houses in various stages of decay at the Dearfield site, though, belie the fact the town was once a vibrant Black community.

NOTES

1. Harlin M. Fuller and LeRoy R. Haffen, comps., *The Journal of Captain John R. Bell: Official Journalist for the Stephen H. Long Expedition of the Rocky Mountains, 1820* (Glendale, CA: Arthur H. Clark, 1957), 144.

2. John Charles Frémont, *Narratives of Exploration and Adventure*, Allan Neving, ed. (New York: Longmans, 1956), 185.

3. Stanley L. Welsh, *John Charles Frémont: Botanical Explorer*, Monographs in Systemic Botany from the Missouri Botanical Garden Series, Marshall R. Crosby, ed., vol. 66 (St. Louis: Missouri Botanical Garden Press, 1988), 172.

4. Monroe Lee Billington and Roger D. Hardaway, *African Americans on the Western Frontier* (Niwot: University Press of Colorado, 1998), 92–93.

5. William Loren Katz, *Black People Who Made the Old West* (Trenton, NJ: Africa World Press, 1992), 98–99.

6. Jesse T. Moore Jr., "Seeking a New Life: Blacks in Post–Civil War Colorado," *Journal of Negro History* 78 (Summer 1993): 184.

7. W. Sherman Savage. *Blacks in the West*, Contributions in Afro-American and African Studies 23 (Westport, CT: Greenwood, 1976), 19.

8. Ibid., 180.

9. Quoted in George H. Wayne, "Negro Migration and Colonization in Colorado—1870–1930," *Journal of the West* 15 (January 1976): 108.

10. Quoted in ibid.

11. Quoted in ibid., 109.

12. Quoted in ibid.

13. Quoted in ibid.

14. Billington and Hardaway, *African Americans on the Western Frontier*, 39.

15. Ibid., 38.

16. William Wyckoff, *Creating Colorado: The Making of a Western Landscape, 1860–1940* (New Haven: Yale University Press, 1999), 122–123.

17. Rick Scovill, "Dearfield, Colorado: A Forgotten History" (class paper, Department of History, University of Northern Colorado, Greeley, 1999), 4.

18. Bill Jackson, "Water," in *Raised in Weld*, magazine insert in *The Greeley Tribune*, September 2009, 20; Carol Rein Shwayder, ed., *Weld County—Old and New*, vol. 1, *Chronology of Weld County, Colorado—1836–1983* (Greeley, CO: Unicorn Ventures, 1983), A102.

19. Greeley grew out of the Union Colony concept of Horace Greeley, New York newspaper editor and abolitionist. Nathan C. Meeker, Greeley's agricultural editor at *The New York Tribune*, founded the Union Colony. Greeley publicized the Union Colony in his newspaper, and Meeker decided to settle on the Cache la Poudre in the South Platte Valley in 1869. He purchased 12,000 acres from the original settlers for $60,000 so he could settle his own colonists. Meeker also took provisional title to another 60,000 acres. In 1870 Meeker brought fifty colonists to the "rolling prairie covered with cactus and the short grama grass of the region," according to Workers of the Writers' Program of the Work Projects Administration in the State of Colorado, comp., *Colorado: A Guide to the Highest State* (New York: Hastings House, 1948), 162–163.

20. Monroe N. Work, *Negro Year Book: An Annual Encyclopedia of the Negro, 1916–1917* (Tuskegee, AL: Negro Year Book, n.d.), 296.

21. In *Plessy v. Ferguson*, the Supreme Court decided the United States could be "Separate but Equal." The ruling was not overturned until the 1954 case *Brown v. Board of Education, Topeka, Kansas*.

22. David Boyd, *A History: Greeley and the Union Colony of Colorado* (Greeley, CO: Greeley Tribune Press, 1890), 343–344.

23. William H. Pease and Jane H. Pease, "Organized Negro Communities: A North American Experiment," *Journal of Negro History* 47 (January 1962): 27.

24. Eileen Carlson, *A View of Orchard—Roots and All* (Boulder: Johnson, 1994), 7. Will Marion Cook was a composer, conductor, and violinist whose parents graduated from Oberlin College. Cook studied music in Berlin under the famous violinist Josef

Joachim; he returned to the United States and studied at the National Conservatory of Music in New York, where his composition teacher was Antonín Dvoák. Cook composed several musicals with Black themes, according to Eileen Southern, *The Music of Black Americans: A History* (New York: W. W. Norton, 1971), 268.

25. Linda Womack, *From the Grave: A Roadside Guide to Colorado's Pioneer Cemeteries* (Caldwell, ID: Caxton, 1999), 78–79.

26. Julie Marshall, "A Living History," *The Daily Camera* (Boulder), February 24, 2002, at http://www.buffzone.com/community/stories/24phist.html; Pascale Fried, "African Americans in Boulder County," Winter 2001, at http://www.co.boulder.co.us/openspace/resources/culhistory/african_amerbc.htm.

27. Carlson, *View of Orchard*, 7.

28. Andrew Harris, "Deerfield [sic], a Negro Ghost Town in Weld County, Colorado," *Negro History Bulletin* 27 (September 1963): 38.

29. *The Weld County News*, "Weld County's Negro Colony," Historical, Development and Harvest Edition (Greeley: Northern Colorado Digest, November 1921), 60.

30. Carlson, *View of Orchard*, 8.

31. Sarah Deutsh, "Landscape of Enclaves," in *Under an Open Sky: Rethinking America's Western Past*, William Cronon, George Miles, and Jay Gitlin, eds. (New York: W. W. Norton, 1992), 119.

32. Ibid.

33. Karen Waddell, "Dearfield . . . a Dream Deferred," *Colorado Heritage* (July 1988): 6.

34. Wayne, "Negro Migration and Colonization in Colorado," 113.

35. Norris, "Dearfield, Colorado," 127–128.

36. Carlson, *View of Orchard*, 7.

37. Ibid.

38. Bob Jackson, "Black Pioneers of Colorado Helped Build State," *The Rocky Mountain News*, May 15, 2005, at http://www.diac.com/~ekwall2/info/0221hist4.shtml.

39. Ibid.

40. Jackson, "Water."

41. Frederick P. Johnson, "Agricultural Negro Colony in Eastern Colorado," *Western Farm Life Magazine* (May 1, 1915): 5.

42. *The Weld County News*, "Weld County's Negro Colony," 60.

43. "Politicians at Negro Fair in Dearfield," *The Greeley Tribune-Republican*, September 28, 1916.

44. O. T. Jackson, Dearfield, Colorado, letter to W. J. Harsha, Kremling, Colorado, December 5, 1918. Hazel E. Johnson Collection, Denver Public Library.

45. Ibid.

46. *The Weld County News*, "Weld County's Negro Colony," 60.

47. Ibid.

48. Although claims exist that 700 people resided in Dearfield, the figure most likely comes from the population of the census tract. The actual number of Dearfield residents was more likely between 200 and 300.

49. *The Weld County News*, "Weld County's Negro Colony," 60.

50. Alvin T. Steinel, *History of Agriculture in Colorado, 1858–1926* (Fort Collins: State Agricultural College, 1926), 405.

51. Ibid.

52. Ibid. See also O. T. Jackson, Dearfield, Colorado, letter to W. J. Harsha, Kremling, Colorado, December 5, 1918. Hazel E. Johnson Collection, Denver Public Library.

53. Quoted in Katz, *Black Women of the Old West* (New York: Ethrac, 1995), 55.

54. Wayne, "Negro Migration and Colonization in Colorado," 116.

55. Shwayder, *Weld County—Old and New*, vol. 1, A137–A139.

56. Quoted in Carlson, *View of Orchard*, 10.

57. Deutsh, "Landscape of Enclaves," 123.

58. D. B. Strubel, "Dearfield, Colorado: Population 1," *Empire Magazine* [*The Denver Post*], August 8, 1955, 33.

59. Carlson, *View of Orchard*, 10.

60. Quintard Taylor, *In Search of the Racial Frontier: African Americans in the American West, 1528–1990* (New York: W. W. Norton, 1998), 153.

61. Ibid.

62. Carlson, *View of Orchard*, 10.

63. Quoted in Taylor, *In Search of the Racial Frontier*, 153

64. Carlson, *View of Orchard*, 10.

65. Cary Stiff, "The Dream of Dearfield: Black Colorado II," *Empire Magazine* [*The Denver Post*], November 2, 1969, 47–48.

66. Carlson, *View of Orchard*, 10.

67. Andrea Koutonen, "A Dream That Lived for a While," *The Fence Post: Your Local Farm and Ranch Magazine*, January 20, 1986, 3.

68. Stiff, "The Dream of Dearfield: Black Colorado II," 47–48.

69. Ibid.

70. Katie Kerwin, "1-Woman Business Carries This Town: Former Community Reduced to Outpost," *The Rocky Mountain News*, December 17, 1990, 10.

71. Jared Fiel, "Dearfield Legacy," *The Greeley Tribune*, February 6, 1999; Joanne Ditmer, "5 Locales 'Endangered,'" *The Denver Post*, February 6, 1999.

72. T. R. Witcher, "Woe, Pioneers: A Whole New Crop of Problems Is Sprouting in a Historic Black Farming Settlement," *Denver Westword*, May 1, 1997.

73. Colorado Senate, Concerning the Preservation of Historic Dearfield, and Making an Appropriation Therefor: An Act, Senate Bill 00-170 (approved June 1, 2000).

74. Ibid.

75. Coleman Cornelius, "Broken Dream Dusted Off," *The Denver Post*, December 24, 2000, 1(B).

PART II
Pre-1960s Colorado

Robert J. Durán

Racism, Resistance, and Repression: The Creation of Denver Gangs, 1924-1950

This chapter provides a historical overview of Mexican American gangs and gang enforcement in Denver, Colorado. The contemporary fascination with gangs in Denver has continued to generate media and public appeal, but little is reported about their origination. Looking to the past allows an opportunity to analyze decision making by public officials and how they responded to a perceived minority group threat. To carry out the research for this chapter, I gathered an extensive number of newspaper clippings and primary documents. In addition, I conducted five years of ethnographic research (2001–2006) to report on the gang experience for my dissertation at the University of Colorado. Jennifer Earl and colleagues (2004:76) reported that newspaper data "facilitate longitudinal research, and make quantitative research on social movements more viable." During this period, newspapers and official statistics were filtered through the eyes of the dominant group and thus offered a glimpse of their understanding of the situation. My goal is to reexamine this dominant viewpoint by incorporating the previously silenced voice of Denver's Mexican American community.

DENVER'S GANG HISTORY AND CONTROL OF THE KU KLUX KLAN

Before the creation of Mexican American gangs in Denver, another group had a major influence. World War I ended, and the general ideology was pro-

Protestant and anti-Black, Catholic, foreigner, and Jew. These anti-sentiments were based on assumptions that certain groups of people caused crime and lacked patriotic allegiance. People of Mexican descent constituted a small percentage of the population (possibly as few as 1,390 residents),[1] but they endured the dominant population's dislike of Catholics and foreigners. Denver's new residents did not acknowledge the families of Mexican descent who had lived in the state of Colorado longer than the people who considered themselves citizens and the rightful heirs to the area. The Ku Klux Klan emerged as a political powerhouse, yielding community pressure for law and order and resisting demographic and cultural changes (Davis 1963; Goldberg 1981). As Robert Alan Goldberg (1981:12) reported, "The Denver klavern was the largest and most influential member of the Colorado Klan federation."

The Klan reached the height of its influence in the winter of 1924–1925. In 1924 the Denver Klan had grown to an estimated 17,000 members, with a total of 50,000 members in the state of Colorado (Davis 1963; Goldberg 1981). It controlled every aspect of city and state government: attorneys, city appointments, the governor, the House of Representatives, judges, police, senators, and school boards (Davis 1963; Goldberg 1981; Ku Klux Klan Collection 1920s). The Klan's symbol was the American flag. Klan members constituted the majority in the Republican Party and operated in a secret society with handshakes, symbols, and covert words to maintain a community stronghold (Davis 1963). A backlash arose against the Denver Klan when national attention on the group increased, largely because of its bigotry in the South. This opposition coincided with internal disputes among Klan leaders, an opposing Republican faction, and an outcry from two excluded groups: Catholics and Jews. Nevertheless, the law-and-order beliefs that formed the Klan lingered and were demonstrated in countless future encounters with people of Mexican descent.

Mexican Americans faced an ambiguous racial status in Colorado, even with a greater numerical and historical presence in southern portions of the state. Many moved from rural communities in New Mexico and southern Colorado to work in Denver's surrounding sugar beet fields harvesting the crops. Mexican Americans were racially labeled White, yet they regularly faced systematic discrimination (Delgado and Stefancic 1999; Dorsett and McCarthy 1986; Leonard and Noel 1991). In 1930 an estimated 7,000 residents of Mexican descent remained in Denver, despite Anglo hostility (Dorsett and McCarthy 1986). The Denver Commission on Human Relations (1947) reported that Blacks, Mexicans, and Japanese were denied service at restaurants and hotels, relegated to work the most menial jobs, and forced to live in the poorest housing. Signs in several Colorado cities proclaimed that Mexicans were not allowed (Delgado and Stefancic 1999).

In April 1936 Colorado governor Edwin Johnson declared martial law and utilized the National Guard to escort 100,000 Mexicans out of the state (Dorsett and McCarthy 1986). Governor Johnson placed the National Guard at Colorado's southern border to make sure Mexicans did not reenter (Meier and Ribera 1996). They stopped and searched all automobiles, buses, and trains that attempted to enter southern Colorado ("Armed Forces Acting under Martial Law," *Rocky Mountain News* [RMN] 1936). *The Englewood Monitor* proposed building concentration camps for those who refused to go (Leonard and Noel 1991). The Catholic Workers Protective Alliance, led by Spanish-surnamed individuals, protested the governor's actions and notified him that only those convicted of a felony could be legally removed by force ("Deportation Plans Protested," *The Denver Post* [DP], April 4, 1936). The National Guard's presence along the border was eventually declared unconstitutional, but nativistic fears remained.

Linking the behavior of people of Mexican descent with crime became a common tool used to enhance opposition and gain support from otherwise non-racist individuals. According to Hans von Hentig's Colorado Crime Survey (1940), the correctional facility for the state of Colorado in Cañon City had an overrepresentation of people of color. The rate of Whites incarcerated per 100,000 was 233.0, Mexicans 497.4, and "Negroes" 735.9. Thus Mexicans were more than twice as likely and Blacks more than three times as likely as Whites to be incarcerated. Despite reports of low crime in Denver during 1936 by *The Rocky Mountain News* ("Vigilance Holds Crime at Low Ebb"), with the majority of arrests being for drunkenness, youth delinquency patterns may have been different. In 1938 the Youth Survey Committee (YSC) of the Adult Education Council of Denver conducted a study on "The Youth Problem in Denver." The YSC looked at issues facing youths sixteen to twenty-one years of age. They reported that the area along the Platte River contained the highest rates of delinquency (33 percent and over) and unemployment (29 percent and over). According to the U.S. Census, the majority of the city's people of Mexican descent lived in this area (United States Census 1940). Black neighborhoods had the city's second-highest rates of delinquency and unemployment. White neighborhoods were reported to have less delinquency (11 percent and under) and lower unemployment (10 percent and under). The YSC concluded, "The high degree of concentration of the youth problem in certain areas of the city suggests the necessity for a program, geared to the attainments of the youth concerned, which will focus attention upon the needs of those areas"

(Adult Education Council of Denver 1938:8). At the time, Denver administrators refused to devote increased resources to combat these economic inequalities or racial and ethnic disparities. This lack of attention to exploring possible solutions had far-reaching consequences.

ZOOT SUIT RIOTS AND THE ORIGINATION OF DENVER'S SPANISH-SURNAMED[2] GANGS

James Patrick Walsh (1995) has argued that White gangs arose in Denver prior to Latino groups. He cited an 1889 *Denver Times* newspaper account and a judge's statement in 1904 that described gangs and gang fights. Walsh reported that the major difference between White gangs in the early 1900s and the developing Latino gangs involved the connection to culture and ethnicity that incited widespread fear among the general public. The growth of the Latino population was intertwined with city neglect, racism, and urban decay, creating ripe conditions for gang development. The Mexican population increased to 4 percent of the population (12,345) in 1940, double the percentage in the 1930s (Carmichael 1941). The population growth remained concentrated along the Platte River within four primary neighborhoods (11, 12, 16, and 22; see Appendix A: Denver 1940 Map).

The poor living conditions and lack of political power mirrored the colonial situation. Frantz Fanon (1963) described the colonial world as cut in two: the zone where the natives lived was well built, easy going, and clean, and people had plenty to eat; the colonized lived in a place of poverty, ill fame, evil repute, and high density. The Mexican barrio housing structures lacked central heating, refrigeration, and indoor plumbing. F. L. Carmichael (1941) reported that nine of every ten Spanish American families lived in substandard housing, compared with 23.9 percent of all Denver residents. Mexican Americans entered the 1940s with many Anglo officials and administrators elected during the Klan years in control.

World War II, much like World War I, had increased U.S. patriotism as well as hostility toward perceived foreigners. On December 19, 1942, the first article about a potential Mexican American gang hit Denver's major newspaper, *The Rocky Mountain News* ("Hoodlums Watched by Police"). A Denver Police captain issued orders to his officers to "keep close check on activities of flashily dressed youths" in the vicinity of Denver amusement resorts. Reportedly, the numbers of flashily dressed youth were increasing. The captain was quoted as saying that the majority of these youth had "no malicious intent"; however, there had been instances of burglaries, gas tanks siphoned, and purses snatched. The captain believed these crimes were caused by a group of youths called "zoot-suit commandos." Two days later a more negative account splashed across the headlines: "Zoot Suit Gang: Companion Unmasks Youth, Five Arrested" (*RMN*, April 21, 1942). The police sergeant reported that a sixteen-year-old girl had been held captive by four boys while another youth dragged a seventeen-year-old girl down an alley, where she was repeatedly attacked.[3] Authorities attributed the assault to "wartime pressure on youthful morals" (*RMN*, April 21, 1942).

In June 1943 the Zoot Suit Riots occurred in East Los Angeles. *The Rocky Mountain News* ("Mexicans Warned off Streets in L.A.," June 8, 1943) reported five nights of rioting between well-organized gangs, whose members wore baggy pants, and military soldiers and sailors. The zoot-suited gangsters were reported to have attacked two navy wives along with beating numerous sailors. The sailors responded with a military maneuver called "pantsing," in which sailors stripped the juveniles of their pants and left them in their underwear.

Most scholarly accounts of this event describe a moral panic that swept the area, which was more violent and destructive than "pantsing" (Escobar 1999; McWilliams 1990; Obregón Pagán 2003). As Edward Escobar (1999:234) argued, "The Zoot Suit Riots resulted from the public hysteria over the alleged Mexican American crime wave and from the anti-Mexican campaign conducted by public officials and the press." He described servicemen attacking Mexican Americans while police officers stood by. Eduardo Obregón Pagán (2003) reported that ninety-eight civilians were arrested and a similar number reported serious injuries, whereas eighteen servicemen reported serious injuries and only two were arrested. The terror servicemen waged against the Latino community was considered by many, including Eleanor Roosevelt, to constitute a race riot.

Following the Zoot Suit Riots, newspaper headlines reported that the Denver Police Department had received increasing reports of California zoot suiters relocating to the city ("No Coast Zoot Suiters Can Alight in Denver," *RMN*, June 19, 1943). The police emphasized that *local* zoot suiters had not received community complaints, but outsiders would be watched carefully because "[t]he zoot suit apparently has become a sort of insignia for the hoodlum and that element will not be tolerated here." Zoot suiters were uncommon except in the Five Points district, an area with a high concentration of Blacks and Latinos. Their criminal activities were limited to drunkenness and vagrancy. On August 31, 1943, Denver had its first media allegation that zoot suiters from California were in the local area. *The Rocky Mountain News* reported, "The shadow of violent death moved forward yesterday to darken further a series of abductions, slugging and terrorization of Denver women by a hoodlum gang of zoot-suitists who styled themselves, The Order of the Wolf" ("Wolf Order Zootists Sought in Auto Death"). The Order of the Wolf hailed from Los Angeles, and its members traveled in a car that had hit a nineteen-year-old Denver resident who later died. The Order of the Wolf had also allegedly abducted three women.

A "Report on the Delinquency Situation in Denver" by Judge Philip B. Gilliam (1943) noted that a few years earlier, 40 percent of the boys appearing in Juvenile Court had been Spanish American. In 1942 the number decreased to 35 percent. During the first three months of 1943 the number decreased even further, to 24 percent. The decline in juvenile delinquency did not last long, however, as 1943 ended with the highest figures in a decade. Much of this increase included 331 girls brought before the Juvenile Court, or 32.8 percent of all cases before the court that year ("Juvenile Hall: A Division of Denver's Famous Juvenile Court," 1959). These percentages reflect an overrepresentation of Mexicans at six to ten times higher than their percentages of the population.

In the spring of 1944, one year after the Los Angeles Zoot Suit Riots, reports of people wearing zoot suits in Denver became more frequent. On May 5, thirty people wearing zoot suits were arrested for fighting and charged with loitering. Three Lowry Air Force Base soldiers reported that they were attacked by a "group of nine zoot-clad youths." A *Rocky Mountain News* reporter became curious about zoot suiters and drove to 18th and Curtis, where he saw forty zoot suiters hanging out at 1:00 in the morning taunting cars ("Outbreaks of Violence," May 8, 1944). The following day, city officials requested more police patrols along the areas bounded by 14th, 20th, Curtis, and Larimer streets ("High Officials Probe City's Zoot Flareup," *RMN*, May 9, 1944). These streets bordered the growing Latino neighborhoods adjacent to the downtown district.

City officials wanted dance and age curfews enforced, along with charges for loitering, following an assault on two women by a group of thirty youths that included several girls ("Warrants for Arrest of 19 Accused Zooters Are Issued in Denver," *RMN*, May 13, 1944). The Denver City Council reported that zoot suit hoodlumism in downtown Denver had recently subsided because of vigorous police action but added that legislation could prevent future violence ("Curfew Revision Planned," *RMN*, May 10, 1944). City council members agreed that targeting hoodlum behavior required changing the age of those affected by the city's 10:00 P.M. curfew law from fourteen to seventeen. They formed a committee composed of residents and members of city organizations who were notified any time zoot suiters were picked up for loitering, so they could meet with their parents to discuss how to correct the youths' behavior or pursue the possibility of charging the parents for failing to supervise their children. Although not always stated directly, all of these policies targeted youths of color.

The Rocky Mountain News (May 9, 1944) exacerbated the panic with such headlines as "A Terrible Denver Tragedy": "GANGS OF YOUTHS, 16 to 18 years old, wandering the downtown streets, beating up women, assaulting soldiers, dragging spectators from movie houses, kicking them and pulling their hair! . . . It is the pathetic picture of certain unhappy members of minority groups venting their fury in a blind, confused way on innocent persons." The reporter argued that the city's punishments needed to be harsher and more strictly enforced. He mentioned briefly the need for city officials, private individuals, and "elements of the minority groups" to have greater understanding because punishment alone is not the solution.

In response to the gang reports, the May 11, 1944, issue of *The Rocky Mountain News* described the police and city officials waging a "war on gangs" ("Sentences up to $300 or 90 Days Given"). The war on gangs included fines and ninety-day jail sentences for people charged with vagrancy, in an attempt to curb "outbreaks of hoodlumism on Denver streets." Within several days more than fifty "gang members" had been arrested for vagrancy, which means "wandering" or walking around a city. Walsh's (1995) research on Denver's early gangs included interviews with numerous people who described the use and abuse of this law. One woman interviewed described being put in jail for seven days simply for being in a park. According to Walsh (1995), the Denver Police Department's Annual Report data indicated that 31 percent of all those arrested for vagrancy between 1945 and 1954 were Latino. During that time, Latinos represented only 4 to 10 percent of the city's population. By 1972 vagrancy laws designed to control "undesirables" were found to violate the Eighth Amendment's prohibition against cruel and unusual punishment, but in the mid-1940s these laws were used regularly.

A May 1944 *Rocky Mountain News* headline reported that warrants had been issued for nineteen zoot suiters for allegedly assaulting two young women ("Warrants for Arrest of 19 Accused Zooters," May 13, 1944). Fourteen arrests were made the following day. The demographics of those arrested were somewhat surprising: six were young women. They wore the zoot suit counterpart: blue jean overalls and jumpers decorated with embroidered names and designs ("8 Youths, 6 Girls Are Arrested," *RMN*, May 14, 1944). In the early 1940s, the newspaper and police regularly alleged that zoot suiters were attacking young women, but actual numbers were never provided. The early gangs often included women members or auxiliaries, and it is possible that the crimes remained gender-specific. Public fears were enhanced because a greater number of men were away from home during World War II, and women were perceived as vulnerable. The local media regularly played on community fears with unsupported or fictional evidence to mobilize support for racially and ethnically biased policies.

The increased legislation and police patrols coincided with Regis College holding a four-day seminar on Spanish Americans in October 1944. More than forty delegates from six states discussed issues such as prejudice, inadequate education, and employment discrimination ("Problems of Spanish-Americans Will Be Studied," *RMN*, October 8, 1944; "Urge Community Councils to Aid Spanish-Americans," *RMN*, October 18, 1944). A letter to the editor (*RMN*, May 23, 1944) explained that "They're Neighbors, Too":

> While on an international basis we may be quite friendly with our neighbors South of the border, too many people in Denver have no friendly regard at all, not the barest of courteous treatment, toward these people of Spanish descent living in their midst. . . . It is not surprising that such intolerable racial discrimination should result in juvenile outbreaks such as have occurred recently. . . . It does no good to claim, as some do, that these people should not live in such conditions, as long as discriminatory employment practices bar them from improving themselves economically. . . . One wonders what these young fighting men of Uncle Sam, the older brothers, undoubtably [sic], of some of these "hoodlums," would have to say on this subject. And those that will never return—what have we to say to them?

Two additional letters to the editor agreed with this sentiment: "This good neighbor policy must begin at home. . . . All of the human race is born the same way and dies the same way—so why all the feeling of superiority" ("Wonders Whether Denver Will Wake Up," *RMN*, May 29, 1944). The number of Latinos fighting in World War II created greater confusion for locals who recognized that Germany's discrimination against Jews needed to be addressed in this country: "When you read the many Spanish names on our casualty list how do you feel about cafes with 'White Trade Only' signs where the families of those men are barred" ("Giving a Lesson in Tolerance," *RMN*, April 8, 1945). Several other people wrote letters to the editor questioning the Anglo- and Spanish-surnamed double standard.

Despite the fact that several Whites opposed an unequal double standard, racial disturbances persisted. On March 11, 1945, at least eight people in military uniform were among sixty-five youths picked up by police for invading a community center and beating "Spanish-speaking" youths. The names of the Anglo youths were taken, and they were released without charges. Mexican American citizens were outraged that the Klan-elected mayor Benjamin Stapleton and the Denver Police Department were not providing protection for them. People of Mexican descent were upset that their children were dealt with more harshly than Whites. Walsh (1995:124) found that all of the fifteen people he interviewed expressed animosity toward the police: "The police were assigned the task of 'controlling' this threatening culture of young people and forcing upon them a set of prescribed social boundaries. The police department was not a protective unit in these communities as much as it was a force of repression and surveillance."

Walsh's interviewees described beatings by police and an overwhelming show of force when Latinos were apprehended. District Attorney James T. Burke corroborated Latinos' negative experience with the police. He accused Mayor Stapleton and the chief of police of "doing nothing to weed misfits out of the police department" (Lusky 1946). Burke argued, "The policemen committed crimes [ranging] from murder to petty larceny," and neither of these officials did anything about that behavior. A grand jury investigated charges of police brutality and indicted three officers: one had stolen linen, another beat two Latinos with a billy club, and the third officer had obtained money under false pretenses ("Grand Jury Returns Indictments," *RMN* 1946, month and day unknown). James Fresques, a city council member, presented evidence that Latinos were treated badly by police (Burke 1946). The majority of the police force was White, with only one Latino and two Blacks. The police department refused to change its aggressive practices against Latinos, and no person or law could make it do so. A district judge upheld the police chief's refusal to answer questions about the death of a Spanish-surnamed man, along with other cases of police brutality (Lehman 1947). The Latino community lacked the political power and sufficient support from the Anglo community to push for changes in the way minority groups were treated.

In 1947 Mayor James Quigg Newton succeeded the previous Klan-supported mayor. Newton honored a pledge to establish a task force on human relations in an attempt to end discrimination and to reach out to the minority community (Delgado and Stefancic 1999). The eleven-member Denver Commission on Human Relations (DCHR) reported "a linked spiral: job discrimination means that minorities earn less; their lower income drives them to poor housing areas; prejudice keeps them there; the neighborhoods become full to overflowing; facilities break down; the inhabitants try to escape but run 'into a wall of prejudice'" (Delgado and Stefancic 1999:38). (The DCHR found the cost of prejudice staggering and described it as an "expensive luxury." The DCHR developed the first documentation of racism in Denver.[4]

Although government and public interest in problems in Denver began to increase, gang feuds reported in *The Rocky Mountain News* grew in severity from 1946 to 1948. Gang activities resulted in wars between East and West Side neighborhoods ("Two Youths Wounded in East Side Gang War," *RMN*, April 8, 1946). The use of guns increased, and more Latinos were being shot or arrested for carrying weapons. Juvenile Court judge Gilliam thought the rise in the use of weapons was influenced by the movie *City across the River* based on the book *Amboy Dukes*, which dealt with juvenile gangs in New York (Lusky 1949b). Several of the people interviewed by Walsh (1995) corroborated these theories of origination by describing how they had learned to make zip guns from watching the movie.

Sam Lusky, a writer for the *Rocky Mountain News*, described his version of gang members in a report titled "Rich and Poor Kids Alike Want to Be 'Tough Guys'" (1949c). He viewed the rising popularity of this lifestyle with disdain:

> They're suckers. Fall guys for somebody else. Or just Chumps. Deep down they know it. But they shove it farther and farther back into their consciousness, and block it out with more swaggering and strong-arming. They think they look hard to the cops . . . [but] these juveniles look silly. . . . These gangs recognize only one law—force. They beef about discrimination and unfairness. Sure there's discrimination. It's rotten and unfortunate. But, even where it doesn't exist these gangs pretend it does.

Lusky reported that the police preferred to use their billy clubs to help gang members understand, and the officers resented the "current straight-down-the-middle attitude of the Piloce [sic] Department and the city administration."[5] Near the end of 1949 Lusky (1949a) found sympathy for his aggressive stance; a Denver judge issued a three-point ultimatum: work, go to school, or go to jail. The youths before him had been charged with vagrancy and some with illegal possession of firearms. The judge saw no reason for these youths "being idle, staying up all night, and sleeping all day" (Lusky 1949a). Perceived gang members received very oppositional press coverage that pushed for Mexicans to be punished until an unachievable goal of conformity was achieved.

On the other hand, Walsh (1995:1) vividly captured the Latino worldview of the time. Latinos were growing up in the midst of White racism, external opposition from law enforcement, and increasing legislation to control their perceived misbehavior. In addition to the external opposition, Latino youth faced a rising threat from rival gang members. Gangs took on the image of being more organized by using gang names, whereas before they had been primarily groups of boys known by their leaders' names (Ernesto Vigil 2004 interview with the author). The names of male gangs in 1949 included the Aces, Dukes, Heads, Lefties, and Lincoln Park Brothers.[6] There were three girl gangs: Jeans, Proxies, and Sisters. Walsh quoted Jack Chavez on his experience in this complex and troubling social environment:

> You walked with pride. People had walks. We called them Pachuco walks. It was a strut. It was a real strut. It was designed to put fear in the enemy, whoever the enemy happened to be. The enemy could be the guy two or three blocks over; or if you went downtown on sixteenth street, not knowing what the White element happened to be. That created fear. So you strutted down the street scared to death. You didn't know what the Anglo element happened to be. So it was a matter of strutting down the street saying, "Hey, I can conquer the world." (1995:1)

The increasing population of Latinos and the style of clothes some of their children wore when they made the transition from a rural to an urban way of living led to public fear of difference. Walsh (1995:30) stated that "these youth rejected the rural, passive values of their parents at the same time in which they were themselves rejected and barred from true citizenship in their new urban surrounding." Latino youth faced many challenges. They organized to confront discrimination and urban decay, but these groups were beginning to pose a threat to Latinos' overall safety in Denver.

During the 1940s the Latino population in Denver doubled, to 24,950 people (Dorsett and McCarthy 1986). Another estimate placed the population between 40,000 and 45,000, or 10 percent of the city's population (National Committee against Discrimination in Housing 1951). The 1950s included a gang fight, in which two youths were stabbed. A member of the Aces ended up in critical condition. *The Rocky Mountain News* reported that residents in the lower east side neighborhood said youthful gangs were on the prowl (Zuckerman 1950). Ernesto Vigil, Denver's Chicano historian, described the early 1950s as filled with high racial and ethnic tension:

> [M]y neighborhood became the first significant one that had people of Mexican descent and there were fights and rivalries. Some of it was gang rivalries but a lot of it was neighborhood and ethnic violence. Our neighborhood [was] becoming increasingly Chicano and Globeville being heavily white ethnics and usually southern Europeans first and second generation, and it was working class. In retrospect, I didn't see it at that time, they [the residents] were really concerned into proving their own Americanism. . . . They used to call Globeville the United Nations neighborhood because you had all kinds of first and second generation immigrant families and I think

their status was threatened in their eyes by competing Mexican laborers[,] and one of the first things they did, immigrant communities in acculturating, it became as racist as the U.S. is, and so Mexicans were good people to look down upon and it would help them to feel superior and reinforce their own ideas about their status[,] but Mexicans were typically victimized. I remember families that would try and move in[to] the neighborhood, the Globeville neighborhood, and people would throw Molotov [cocktails] on their front porch. . . . So my recollection of the gang Los Santos was primarily about their fights with the young men from Globeville. . . . Part of that was an ethnic fad for the youth in the community. I also think in terms of the racial conflicts that existed[,] part of it was self-protection. In particular, I remember in elementary school when we would want to go swim it was dangerous to go to the Globeville neighborhood[,] and they had a much bigger and better swimming pool . . . the only time that we would go was when there would be a big number of us because if we went individually there was a good chance that you would get beaten up. . . . [W]hat those guys on Globeville would do is they would contaminate the pool. They would throw in gasoline, oil, because they didn't want Mexicans to use it[,] so they would throw that type of stuff in the pool and it would shut it down for everybody[,] but that was a way of sending a hint that we weren't wanted so I think it should be stated as a supposition[;] clearly I never asked these older guys, I was too little, but I got the strong impression that one strong motive for them to join the gang was protection against the white gangs that existed and they were very aggressive, very violent, and very racist. (Zuckerman 1950)

Vigil recalled the harshness of growing up during these times. The media and community officials blamed Latinos for their circumstances. Juvenile Court judge Gilliam took proactive steps to decrease gang feuds. He became an honorary member of the Heads gang in an attempt to help the forty to fifty members "reform" ("Gilliam Joins Hoodlum Gang," *RMN*, March 12, 1950). *The Denver Post* labeled the Heads "one of Denver's most notorious hoodlum gangs" ("Hoodlum Gang Here Joins Side of Law," *DP*, March 11, 1949). However, the youths told Gilliam that they would become good citizens. More than half of the members had been expelled from school, their crimes ranging from assault to car stripping. The gang members started to try to keep each other out of trouble. Gilliam loaned three of them money to buy bicycles so they could get to work ("Gilliam Joins Hoodlum Gang," *RMN*, March 12, 1950).

A *Rocky Mountain News* writer (Castel 1950) found hope in Gilliam's attempt to support the reformation of the Heads. However, he criticized Father Flanagan, who claimed, "There is no such thing as a bad boy." Castel responded, "I think there are no bad babies, but I am plumb sure that there are bad boys. . . . You have to realize that some boys (and girls and men and women) are rotten and there is nothing that will help them. But you must be a pessimist of the worst sort to condemn them as a whole." He emphasized that many famous Americans had overcome their environments to succeed, but it was much harder to be an honest person when one faced dismal living conditions. Castel's support for the Heads gang's reformation and Judge Gilliam's role, despite negative public opinion, signaled additional controls counter to the favored punitive approach when dealing with the Latino community.

Although Judge Gilliam gave the Heads a way out of the gang life and a path into the conventional middle-class Anglo worldview, fellow youths in the barrio responded with ridicule. Heads gang members were taunted by various gangs as "sissy" and "Junior policeman" for their attempt to reform. This led the Heads to second-guess Judge Gilliam's plan. Thirty-five Heads members were arrested for fighting or preparing to fight. Judge Gilliam urged the Heads to stay the course for change (Gaskie 1950). Gilliam conceded to the media that he had strong feelings that adult communists were "masterminding the epidemic of juvenile gang warfare sweeping the country" (Kelly 1950). The consensus across the nation, according to Judge Gilliam, was that adults were guiding these new gangs, helping them to last longer and causing more trouble for the police. Gang fears began shifting from attacks on women to affiliations with communists worldwide who were attempting to change the United States. This concern initiated a trend that was repeated consistently through the enforcement of gang activity: linking them with the major fears of the time.

In May 1950 police and the news media portrayed girl gang members as "more vicious than the boys" because they continued to fight until someone was severely injured. Reportedly, young women gang members were "waging a war among themselves." The young women gangs went by the names Heads (auxiliary to the male Heads gang), KC's, Legs, and Sisters ("Girl Gangs in Denver," *RMN*, May 4, 1950). At the end of the year, *The Denver Post* published a special section entitled "Girl Gangs: A Civic Problem. They flaunt authority and fight among themselves for the sake of excitement" (Little 1950). The reporter wrote, "Emily was an attractive, dark-haired girl with one very ungirlsh talent: She could punch like a pugilist." The reporter interviewed a female Denver probation officer who said, "When boys get to fighting they quit when somebody gets the worst of it. Not the girls, though. They fight like animals. They're fearless. They just seem to like to fight." Juvenile authorities reported that the young women carried knives, and they were surprised that none of the fights had ended with a fatality. The girls reportedly came from homes with delinquent parents or from broken families and often from blighted living conditions. They were described as lonely girls seeking companionship because they lacked fathers or father figures. A psychiatrist reported that "girl gangs" often engaged in sexual promiscuity to show that they were not afraid. The year 1950 had the second-highest percentage (35.2) of girl court cases and hearings in a decade, slightly less than 1943 (35.3) ("Juvenile Hall: A Division of Denver's Famous Juvenile Court," 1959). However, in 1943 delinquency among young women was mentioned only briefly. Newspaper articles in 1950 portrayed young Latina women negatively, as animals, and they were framed in patriarchal definitions of women's roles.

CONCLUSION

Denver's early history was racially hostile in both behavior and ideology. The data indicate that the Zoot-Suit Riot in Los Angeles increased attention on people of Mexican descent in Denver, as well as on their clothing. The fear of zoot-suiters relocating to Denver caused city officials to begin labeling Latinos as gang members. It was not until the late 1940s that gangs of Mexican descent began giving themselves names, often devised from neighborhood friends or movies.

People of Mexican descent thought Denver was unwelcoming because they were forced into the worst housing and jobs. They were under-protected by the police. The Ku Klux Klan attitude persisted in the denial of equal rights to Latinos, who were perceived as inferior and foreign. Police had free rein to harass and abuse people of Mexican descent; if law enforcement agents' behavior was perceived as illegal, the law was changed to make it legal by imposing a curfew and punishing loitering and vagrancy.

A small percentage of people of Mexican descent, both men and women, responded to their feelings of unwelcomeness and lack of integration into Denver society by wearing fancy clothes (zoot suits) and hanging out together. The clothes one wears and the groups with which one associates are non-criminal behaviors. Nevertheless, these pachucos/as became symbols of resistance. Latino/a gangs originated in the face of racial hostility, police neglect, police abuse, and victimization. Over time and with governmental pressure, Latinos were no longer able to maintain gangs primarily for ethnic support. The new enemies became Latinos/as from other parts of town suffering similar oppressive circumstances. The Ku Klux Klan in Denver applauded its improved divide-and-conquer tactic.

APPENDIX A: DENVER 1940 MAP, WITH LATINO NEIGHBORHOODS HIGHLIGHTED

Source: United States Census 1940. Population and Housing. Denver, Colorado

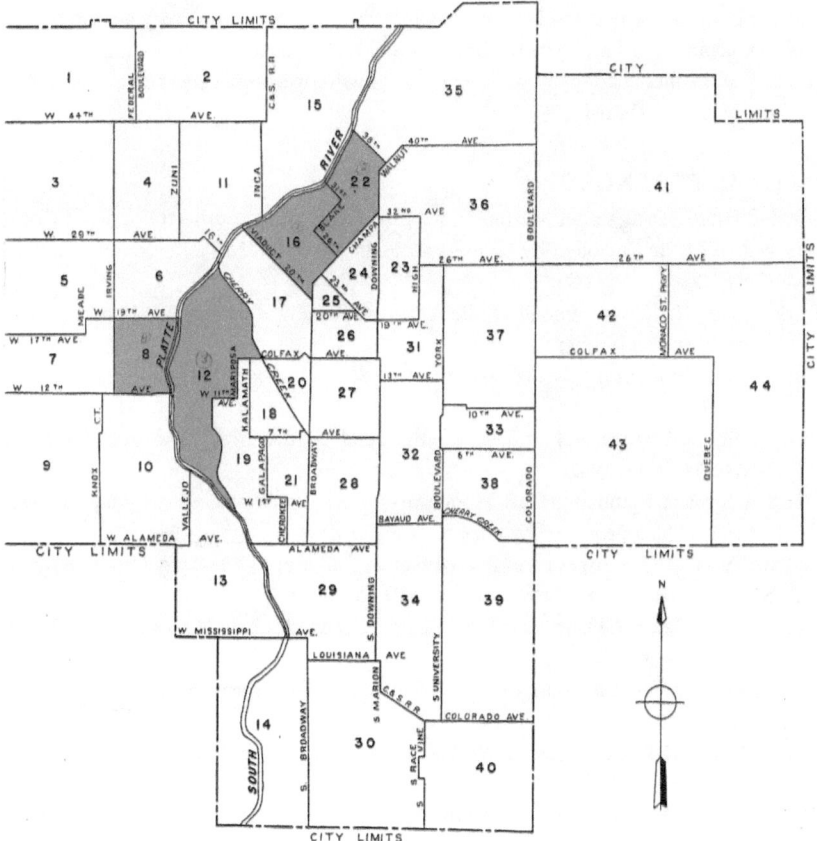

NOTES

1. Walsh (1995) cites the WPA Writer's Program, 1936–1946. In Western History Collection, LAC 3, Community Relations, Denver Public Library, Denver, CO.

2. From the 1930s into the 1960s, people of Mexican descent in Denver were called Spanish surnamed or Spanish American.

3. For the sake of retaining words used in the past, I use "girl" and "boy," which were used by the media and in official reports.

4. In 1947 it was also found that Judge Gilliam's court lacked minority representation. "Gilliam's Court Target of Race Prejudice Report," *Rocky Mountain News*, November 23, 1947. The report estimated that Denver's population was 471,000, which included 30,000 Spanish Americans, 16,500 Jews, 15,000 Negroes, and 2,500 Japanese Americans.

5. Lusky also reported that the ways of joining a gang included being battered and beaten; thus, gang "jump-ins" were occurring in 1949 (Lusky 1949c).

6. Walsh quotes Haymoe (pseudonym), who says: "The Dukes had Curtis park sewed up. That was their territory. The Heads boundary was around 28th and Arapahoe to about 21st street, and Larimer to Champa. The Hoods' territory was up by the ballpark around 23rd and Stout. The Aces had their territory down around the Bottoms. The Brothers had their territory around Lawrence street center on the Westside by Cherry Creek" (Walsh 1995:70).

PRIMARY REFERENCES

"Armed Force Acting under Martial Law to Stop All: Entire Southern Border of Colorado Will Be Patrolled by Soldiers to Halt Aliens, Needy." *The Rocky Mountain News*, 1936.

Burke, James T. "Grand Jury Probe Background Reviewed by District Attorney." *The Denver Post*, September 8, 1946.

Castel, Jack. "Encourage These Boys to Succeed." *The Rocky Mountain News*, March 31, 1950.

"City Officials, Groups Seek to Avert Youth Racial Disturbances." *The Rocky Mountain News*, March 11, 1945.

"Curfew Revision Planned to Curb Hoodlums." *The Rocky Mountain News*, May 10, 1944.

"Deportation Plans Protested by Group." *The Denver Post*, April 4, 1936.

"8 Youths, 6 Girls Are Arrested as Part of Gang of Zooters." *The Rocky Mountain News*, May 14, 1944.

Gaskie, Jack. "Judge Gilliam Lays Down Law to Teenage Gang He Joined." *The Rocky Mountain News*, March 30, 1950.

"Gilliam Joins Hoodlum Gang to Help Them Out." *The Rocky Mountain News*, March 12, 1950.

"Gilliam's Court Target of Race Prejudice Reports." *The Rocky Mountain News*, November 23, 1947.

"Girl Gangs in Denver Wage Worse Battles Than Boys, Police Say." *The Rocky Mountain News*, May 4, 1950.

"Giving a Lesson in Tolerance." *The Rocky Mountain News*, April 8, 1945.

"Grand Jury Returns Indictments on Three Denver Police Officers." *The Rocky Mountain News*, 1946.

"High Officials Probe City's Zoot Flareup." *The Rocky Mountain News*, May 9, 1944.

"Hoodlum Gang Here Joins Side of Law." *The Denver Post*, March 11, 1949.

"Hoodlums Watched by Police." *The Rocky Mountain News*, December 19, 1942.

"Juvenile Hall: A Division of Denver's Famous Juvenile Court." Denver Juvenile Court, 1959.

Kelly, George V. "Adult Reds Guiding Kid Gangs, Belief of Denver Judge." *The Rocky Mountain News*, May 9, 1950.

Lehman, Edward II. "Steele Upholds Hanebuth Refusal to Answer Grand Jury Questions." *The Rocky Mountain News*, January 11, 1947.

Little, Charles. "Girl Gangs: A Civic Problem." *The Denver Post*, December 10, 1950.

Lusky, Sam. "Gang Kids Get Choice: Work, School or Jail." *The Rocky Mountain News*, October 26, 1949a.

———. "Kids Form Gangs, Send Juvenile Crime Rate Soaring." *The Rocky Mountain News*, October 23, 1949b.

———. "Kirschwing Charges Burke Never Asked for Help as Political Dispute Breaks over Police Probe." *The Rocky Mountain News*, August 12, 1946.

———. "Rich and Poor Kids Alike Want to Be 'Tough Guys.'" *The Rocky Mountain News*, October 24, 1949c.

"Mexicans Warned off Streets in L.A. as Zoot Rioting Overwhelms Police." *The Rocky Mountain News*, June 8, 1943.

"No Coast Zoot Suiters Can Alight in Denver." *The Rocky Mountain News*, June 19, 1943.

"Outbreaks of Violence; 7 Are Held." *The Rocky Mountain News*, May 8, 1944.

"Problems of Spanish-Americans Will Be Studied at Regis Seminar." *The Rocky Mountain News*, October 8, 1944.

"Sentences up to $300 or 90 Days Given 11 Youths in War on Gangs." *The Rocky Mountain News*, May 11, 1944.

"A Terrible Denver Tragedy." *The Rocky Mountain News*, May 9, 1944.

"They're Neighbors, Too." *The Rocky Mountain News*, May 23, 1944.

"Two Youths Wounded in East Side Gang War." *The Rocky Mountain News*, April 8, 1946.

"Urge Community Councils to Aid Spanish-Americans." *The Rocky Mountain News*, October 18, 1944.

"Vigilance Holds Crime at Low Ebb in Denver: 28 Men Patrol Downtown with Bulk of Arrests for Drunkenness." *The Rocky Mountain News*, October 23, 1936.

"Warrants for Arrest of 19 Accused Zooters Are Issued in Denver." *The Rocky Mountain News*, May 13, 1944.

"Wolf Order Zootists Sought in Auto Death." *The Rocky Mountain News*, August 31, 1943.

"Wonders Whether Denver Will Wake Up and Act." *The Rocky Mountain News*, May 29, 1945.

"Youthful Gang, the Heads, Tell Judge Gilliam, 'We'll Go Straight.'" *The Rocky Mountain News*, March 15, 1950.

"Zoot Suit Gang: Companion Unmasks Youth, Five Arrested." *The Rocky Mountain News*, December 21, 1942.

Zuckerman, Leo. "Teen Gang Wary Flares Again; 2 Boys Stabbed." *The Rocky Mountain News*, January 23, 1950.

SECONDARY REFERENCES

Adult Education Council of Denver. "The Youth Problem in Denver." *A Report by the Youth Survey Committee of the Adult Education Council of Denver*, 14, 2, July 1938. In Colorado Clipping Collection, Reference Department, Denver Public Library, Denver, CO.

Carmichael, F. L. *Housing in Denver*. Published by the City and County of Denver, 1941. In Western History Department, Denver Public Library, Denver, CO.

Davis, James Harlan. *Ku Klux Klan Interviews*. 1963. In Western History/Genealogy Department, Denver Public Library, Denver, CO.

Delgado, Richard, and Jean Stefancic. "Home-Grown Racism: Colorado's Historic Embrace—and Denial—of Equal Opportunity in Higher Education." *University of Colorado Law Review* 70 (1999): 1–92. Working Paper 1, Latino/a Research and Policy Center, University of Colorado at Denver.

Denver Commission on Human Relations. *A Report on Minorities in Denver, with Recommendations by the Mayor's Interim Survey Committee on Human Resources.* Denver: Denver Commission on Human Relations, 1947. In Box 1, Western History/Genealogy Department, Denver Public Library, Denver, CO.

Department of Commerce, Bureau of the Census. *6th Census of the United States 1940: Population and Housing Statistics for Census Tracts, Denver, CO.* Washington, DC: Government Printing Office, 1940.

Dorsett, Lyle, and Michael McCarthy. *The Queen City: A History of Denver.* Boulder: Pruett, 1986.

Earl, Jennifer, Andrew Martin, John O. McCarthy, and Sarah A. Soule. "The Use of Newspaper Data in the Study of Collective Action." *Annual Review of Sociology* 30 (2004): 65–80.

Escobar, Edward J. *Race, Police, and the Making of a Political Identity: Mexican Americans and the Los Angeles Police Department 1900–1945.* Los Angeles: University of California Press, 1999.

Fanon, Frantz. *The Wretched of the Earth.* New York: Grove, 1963.

Gilliam, Philip B. *Report on the Delinquency Situation in Denver: From January 1, 1943 to September 1, 1943.* Juvenile Court, Denver, CO, 1943.

———. "Juvenile Court Hearings." 1960 [1943].

Goldberg, Robert Alan. *Hooded Empire: The Ku Klux Klan in Denver.* Urbana: University of Illinois Press, 1981.

———. Papers, 1975. In Western History Collection, WH649, Denver Public Library, Denver, CO.

Hentig, Hans von. "The Colorado Crime Survey," April 1, 1940. In Archives, University of Colorado–Boulder.

Ku Klux Klan Collection, 1920s. In Western History Collection, Denver Public Library, Denver, CO.

Leonard, Stephen J., and Thomas J. Noel. *Denver: Mining Camp to Metropolis.* Niwot: University Press of Colorado, 1991.

McWilliams, Carey. *North from Mexico: The Spanish-Speaking People of the United States.* Westport, CT: Praeger, 1990 [1948].

Meier, Matt S., and Feliciano Ribera. *Mexican Americans/American Mexicans: From Conquistadors to Chicanos.* New York: Hill and Wang, 1996.

National Committee against Discrimination in Housing Report, March 1951. In Western History Collection, Denver Public Library, Denver, CO.

Obregón Pagán, Eduardo. *Murder at the Sleepy Lagoon: Zoot Suits, Race, and Riot in Wartime L.A.* Chapel Hill: University of North Carolina Press, 2003.

Walsh, James Patrick. "Young and Latino in a Cold War Barrio: Survival, the Search for Identity, and the Formation of Street Gangs in Denver, 1945–1955." Master's thesis, University of Colorado at Denver, 1995.

Ronald J. Stephens

The Influence of Marcus Mosiah and Amy Jacques Garvey: On the Rise of Garveyism in Colorado

During the second decade of the twentieth century, the Universal Negro Improvement Association and African Communities League (UNIA-ACL)[1] experienced extraordinary growth in its promotion of chartered chapters and divisions in local communities in nearly every region of the United States.[2] In the Rocky Mountain region of the West, a small yet distinguishable number of citizen-activists in Colorado Springs and Denver participated in this effort. Garveyites who resided on St. Vrain Street in Colorado Springs, who were also members of the Peoples Methodist Episcopal Church, and those on Welton Street in the Five Points Neighborhood of Denver engaged with the movement as political and religious activists. This occurred following the 1922 and 1924 organizational tours of Marcus Garvey and Amy Jacques, who succeeded in attracting and capturing the attention, imagination, and spirit of racial consciousness and activism among Black Coloradoans.[3] The Garveys came to the state to increase UNIA-ACL membership in these communities, two years after the 1920 UNIA-ACL International Convention. Their goal was to rally people in these communities to fight for a free and redeemed Africa and to fight collectively for their citizenship and economic and social rights. This call for racial pride, solidarity, and self-determination also came as a response to a wave of racism and discrimination that had swept through the state, dominated by the racial politics of Colorado's chapters of the Ku Klux Khan. A close reading of Denver UNIA-ACL Division Number 118 reports published in *The Negro World* (the official organ of the UNIA-ACL), *The Colorado Statesman,* and *The Denver Star,* as well as the activities of Colorado Springs Division Number 508 published in *The Colorado Springs Gazette* from January 1921 to the mid-1930s, reveal some astonishing results.[4]

This chapter examines the phenomenal rise of Garveyism in the Black neighborhoods of Colorado Springs and Denver at the height of Garvey's popularity and as he was confronted with legal troubles and out on bail. The chapter explores the grassroots political and religious activism of Black men, women, and children who were successful in building close-knit communities and religious institutions in Colorado Springs and Denver and who unapologetically embraced the Garveys' prophetic messages of racial pride, self-reliance, and African redemption. The local and regional activism of the two Colorado divisions was also reinforced through themes in public addresses by the Garveys.

Because the activities of these two divisions illustrate how the couple's travels to the state influenced the rise of the divisions,[5] this chapter warrants scholarly attention for three major reasons. First, there is a need to consider the gender aspect of the UNIA-ACL, which illustrates how the activism of Amy Jacques before, during, and after she legally became Amy Jacques Garvey was as important as that of Marcus Garvey. This is critically important in light of the fact that previous studies of Garvey and Garveyism have often overlooked the contributions of women like Amy Jacques Garvey and others.[6] Second, the subject deserves attention because despite the threat of Garvey's imprisonment, the couple boldly traveled to the Rocky Mountain region of the West to increase UNIA-ACL membership and to promote and ensure Black political representation through the success of the UNIA-ACL's African Political Union. A third reason this topic deserves attention involves the mobilization initiatives of two small groups of Black citizen-activists who pooled their resources in Colorado Springs and Denver to achieve the organizational objectives of the UNIA-ACL at the micro-level.[7] Through an exploration of the reasons behind Black Denver's campaign to encourage Black migration to the state, the popularity of the Garvey Movement in relation to the activities of the two divisions should shed greater light on the significance of Garveyism and the UNIA-ACL in Colorado.

After Reconstruction and during the first two decades of the twentieth century, a combination of social factors had influenced wave after small wave of former slaves and free Black families to migrate to Colorado; these social forces gave rise to Garveyism and the UNIA.[8] The first of these factors involves the southern Black collective response to white supremacy, which was to escape racial discrimination and Jim Crow segregation practices in the South. A second set of factors concerns Black men and women's search for meaningful entrepreneurial and employment opportunities; a third set of factors concerns their search for better schools for their children and housing for their families. It has been noted that "between 1850 and 1860 California's Black population increased from 962 to 4,086."[9] During the movement west to California, a number of pioneering Black families found Colorado an appealing location to resettle, and in the years following the Civil War, "black servants from the South [migrated to the state] with their masters."[10] One example was Frank J. Loper, who was born in Mississippi on the plantation of Confederate president Jefferson Davis. Loper migrated to Colorado Springs in 1886 when his overseer left Mississippi.[11] By the early 1920s other Black families, workers, and professionals had relocated to Denver, Colorado Springs, and the Pikes Peak area, which was known as a place where they could find rest and relaxation, as well as an escape from the Jim Crow segregation and racial discrimination in the South.[12] In an editorial published in *The Colorado Statesman* on July 17, 1920, the editor's motivation for encouraging a Black exodus to Colorado was to "note with extreme satisfaction and pride that countless numbers of prominent, well-to-do colored citizens in many of the Southern states are leaving the Southland and migrating to the North and West because of the vicious and inhuman conditions that prevail in the South" (p. 4). Describing Blacks enduring "untold barbarities," not to mention "unspeakable treatment," the editorial continued:

> No justice in the courts, poor housing conditions for the Negro laborers, peonage, lack of protection to the Negro under the laws of the South—all these things and many more are breaking the back of the camel and he is becoming restless and dissatisfied, and hence the Great Exodus. Government statistics report that upwards of 300,000 Negroes have left the South in the past four years and settled in the North and West. These immigrants are composed of all classes—the poor, the well-to-do, the professional man, the common laborer and the bad, along with the good.[13]

The editorial also noted reasons these families should consider Colorado:

> To the sturdy farmer, the honest laborer and the educated professional man, we invite you to Colorado, whose sunny, health-giving and cheerful climate will renew your vigor and strength, and whose laws will throw around you and your family the same protection that is afforded to all

citizens, regardless of race or color. Colorado is famous for many things. Her climate is ideal, superb; her scenery is unequalled; she is noted for her mining industry and her agricultural interests are taking first rank; stock raising is also forging to the front. Then with thousands of acres of vacant land [a]waiting you, why not try Colorado?[14]

For established Black farmers and professional men and women who were leaving the South, the *Statesman*'s editorial essentially painted a picture of an oasis in the West, highlighting the profitable advantages of acquiring land as well as the state's beauty. The editorial framed these advantages in comparative terms as a means to entice hardworking and respectable business leaders, workers, and homeowners to take notice of the profits they could earn from their investments:

> The present indications this year for the production of corn and wheat in Colorado show that the crops will be the greatest in the history of the state. The Colorado Crop Reporting Service estimates a crop of 24,498,000 bushels of wheat, compared with 17,645,000 last year; 15,203,000 bushels of corn, compared with 11,205,000 bushels last year. The production of potatoes for this year is estimated at 13,072,000 bushels, compared with 11,040,000 bushels last year. So we see that there is an increase each year both in crops and in the acreage. The Colorado Statesman advises and urges the settlement of honest, upright, sturdy and industrious farmers from the South into Colorado.[15]

As Denver's population increased, African American professionals and their families discovered other reasons to relocate to the city that had the largest Black population in the state, as well as to the St. Vrain neighborhood in Colorado Springs. By the early 1920s Black professionals in the Colorado Springs area either owned various businesses or were employed in limited middle- and working-class occupations. For example, John Stokes Holley wrote that "James McCottery [who] was believed to be the city's first Black butcher" during the 1920s was a meat cutter "at James Thomason's grocery on East Cucharras across the street north of the courthouse, a grocery operation which McCottery himself financed."[16] Other Black-owned businesses included two weekly newspapers in Colorado Springs. *The Enterprise* was founded and edited by P. S. Simpson, and *The Colorado Springs Sun* was edited by Z. M. Booker, with W. H. Duncan as city editor. With the departure of Dr. R. S. Grant in 1919, the only Black physician in Colorado Springs was Dr. Isaac Edward Moore, who migrated from St. Louis, Missouri, "opened a practice from his home at 317 West Monument Street in 1921,"[17] and "announced the opening of his Lincoln Sanatorium for Colored People in a two and a half story red brick house in the 300 block of West Williamette,"[18] a sanatorium with provisions for ten patients. There were also the Sadler brothers, well-known builders and remodelers of homes, and Ed Beckwith, known as an expert caterer. Black men were also successful as farmers and ranchers.[19]

Colorado Springs was also known as a city of churches and schools. At first, there were no religious structures in town for African Americans. That soon changed as four brothers from the Carter family, known as the African Methodist Episcopal (A.M.E.) Congregation, pulled resources together and began construction on donated property obtained through the Colorado Springs Company on Pueblo Avenue and South Weber Street. Dorothy Bass Spann remembered that "[t]he building, which followed, eventually became Payne Chapel A.M.E. Church."[20] Other churches, such as the Peoples Methodist Episcopal Church, soon followed.

As early as March 1903, a small group of former slaves and children of former slaves, who had been meeting, praying, and planning for over a year, began constructing a new church at the corner of North Oak and East St. Vrain streets. In 1904 the new church hired its first minister, the Reverend C. W. Holmes, who served the congregation from March 1903 to August 1905. Because of the nature of their jobs, many members of the church had to work on Sunday mornings and were unable to attend the morning service. An afternoon service was established to better serve the majority of members. The leading charter member of the church was Frank J. Loper, who was also a member of the church's trustee board and first building committee. Through Loper's activism, the participation of the new pastor, and the membership, Peoples was extremely active in supporting numerous civic affairs and community events.[21] The church also served as headquarters of Colorado Springs UNIA Division Number 508 from 1921 to the mid-1930s.

Concurrent with these developments in Colorado Springs, African American migrants were also rushing to Denver "to find work and their fortune in silver and gold. Denver seemed to be the perfect place to begin a new life."[22] As African Americans escaped "the oppression and racism of the Post Civil War South [many] found work laying track for the railroad companies."[23] Denver's Black population had grown more rapidly than the city's population as a whole during the 1870s and 1880s, increasing to 3,045 in 1890.[24] By 1890 "Denver had a population of 106,713."[25] Segregation was also in full effect in Denver, which confined African American citizens principally to portions of Lower Downtown (LoDo) and to the Five Points neighborhood.[26]

Initially, the demographic character of the Five Points area was "white with a large German, Irish, and Jewish population. The community was named in

1881 for the five-way intersection of Welton Street, 27th Avenue, Washington Street, and 26th Street. The Curtis Park district, which is within the Five Points area, was considered the most elegant streetcar suburb of Denver in the 1880s."[27] By 1893, though, after the "wealthy moved on to more prominent neighborhoods such as Capitol Hill to the south, Black Americans began moving into the area in significant numbers by Denver's standards. Prior to the 1890s, the Denver African American population had been scattered throughout the city, but as Denver's overall population grew, the area known as Five Points became the heart of the African American community."[28]

As Denver's small African American community continued to grow during the early twentieth century, the Five Points area played an important role in shaping African American social, political, and economic history and identity. The 1920 U.S. Census indicated a total of 6,075 African American residents in Denver, an increase of 649, or 12 percent, since 1910. The continued Black migration from the South created a political, economic, and cultural base for businesses in the Five Points area. Black and White businesses thrived as Denver witnessed an increase in the number of attorneys, physicians, surgeons, and embalmers who had migrated to the city. This resulted in the establishment of Douglass' Undertaking, the Rossonian Hotel, and the White-owned Atlas Drug Store.[29] Denver was also home to two Black-owned newspapers, *The Colorado Statesman* and *The Denver Star*. Both papers "encouraged change" through the efforts of their editors, who supported and promoted "civil rights" issues. For example, Joseph D. Rivers, editor of *The Colorado Statesman* and a close friend of Booker T. Washington, "used his newspaper to encourage blacks to come west to invest in real estate and establish businesses."[30]

Essentially, Welton Street from 22nd to 29th streets served as the "main street of Denver's Black community by the mid-1920s."[31] The Welton Street business district in Five Points during the 1920s not only "attracted a variety of businesses such as restaurants, tailors, real estate agencies, saloons, pool halls, doctors, dentists, and a branch of the American Woodmen Insurance Company,"[32] it also served as an important resource site for residents. R. Laurie Simmons and Thomas H. Simmons explained the diverse ways business and social arrangements were actualized:

> Local businessmen served as role models for neighborhood children and their enterprises symbolized success and stability. Often these local businessmen became leaders within the community and were granted added status among their peers. Local business establishments became meeting places for the entire community, where issues of relevance to the neighborhood were discussed. In addition, the owners of businesses in the district

aided their neighbors by extending credit and helped many survive and recover from hard times.[33]

The social purpose that businesses served held the neighborhood together. The most enduring institution responsible for cementing the community, however, was the church.

Churches in the Five Points neighborhood played a pivotal role in the lives of community residents. Serving as "a kind of settlement house and social club," Black churches offered incoming migrants and permanent residents a place they could call home away from home.[34] As was the case elsewhere in the country, Black churches functioned as houses of worship, providing both members and visitors with opportunities for Christian fellowship, meaningful sermons from their distinguished pastors and invited guest speakers such as UNIA-ACL and NAACP officials, and sacred and secular sites for community networking. Shorter African Methodist Episcopal (A.M.E.) Church, for example, was the first African American church established in Colorado. Organized in Denver in 1868 by Bishop Thomas M.D. Ward, a pioneer of African Methodism in the West, Shorter A.M.E., with its rich history in the community, fulfilled multiple needs of Black residents in the Five Points area. As in other Black communities throughout the country, a number of similar and different religious denominations developed, calling for other churches to be built. The Scott Methodist congregation, which traces its roots to 1904, was established as Denver's only United Methodist denomination to serve Blacks at the time. Scott Methodist purchased the building that originally belonged to the Christ Church congregation at 22nd and Ogden streets.

Racial residential segregation was pervasive in Denver. So was the Ku Klux Klan. Born alongside D. W. Griffith's film *The Birth of a Nation*, the Klan in Denver, which was organized during the early 1920s, functioned as a

> Blow against outsiders who were pushing their way into positions formerly held by native-born citizens. Jews and African Americans with a modicum of self-respect were bad enough. Roman Catholics were worse—they represented the spearhead of a conspiracy against the Puritan civilization that had made the country great. At the same time, the average Klan member worried about the peace of his community and the honor of his daughter.[35]

Fear of change and cultural difference was the driving force that inspired the Klan. The changing demographic face of residential life and, to some extent, of employment dynamics in Denver accelerated racial and religious tensions in the city:

In its first year Denver's Klan followed the national pattern, mixing petty violence and harassment with conviviality. For Friday night entertainment, Klan members routed auto caravans through the Jewish neighborhood on West Colfax, honking their horns and shouting insults. The local NAACP suffered Klan threats, and at least one African-American who allegedly failed to observe the code of interracial contact was driven out of town.[36]

Klan participation in Denver during the 1920s, according to these historians and Laura Mauck, was "at an all time high" as around "fifty thousand Coloradans" were members, "making [the state] second only to Indiana" in the number of Klan members. Some elected officials were Klan members, such as "Colorado's Governor Clarence Morley," who served the state from 1925 to 1927; Denver's Mayor Benjamin Stapleton, who served the city from 1923 to 1931; and Denver's chief of police.[37] Mauck added, "Communities surrounding Five Points formed Neighborhood Improvement Associations which created covenants that banned residents from selling their homes or property to non-whites."[38] The political climate in Colorado during the Progressive Era left African Americans with no choice but to create internal opportunities, which developed as a result of the influence of a series of progressive New Negro thinkers such as Garvey, W.E.B. Du Bois, and James Weldon Johnson, all of whom were connected to the Five Points area. Garvey and his organization, the UNIA-ACL, offered an abundance of hope to millions of Africans worldwide.

The Garvey Movement illustrated how collective and individual confidence, faith, and pride can achieve African redemption. Marcus and Amy Jacques Garvey's thundering voices were not only spellbinding, persuasive, and inspiring; they were also pragmatic in constructing and promoting a human civilization based on racial equality. Garvey's slogan "Africa for the Africans" at home and abroad situated the African predicament on the same continuum with other global liberation movements struggling in a white supremacist world. But the aims and objectives of the organization did not become widely known until shortly after the opening of the first International Convention of the UNIA-ACL on August 1, 1920,[39] which outlined the purpose of electing a Black world leader of 12 million people in the United States and a provisional president of Africa.[40]

Garvey's untimely demise came as a result of his conviction for using the mail to defraud investors in connection with the sale of stock for the Black Star Steamship Line. Although Garvey was convicted and out on bail from 1922 to 1925, he and Amy Jacques helped increase UNIA-ACL membership in both

Denver and Colorado Springs and to promote the UNIA-ACL's newly formed African Political Union, an initiative that enabled members of Black communities to promote and elect fair-minded White political candidates running for office. Interestingly, the spread of Garveyism in Colorado did not materialize until Black Coloradoans read published accounts of the UNIA-ACL's 1920 International Convention in *The Colorado Statesman* and members in Denver and Colorado Springs joined the Garvey Movement. During the strategic meetings of the Denver division, key UNIA-ACL officials were invited to the Mile High City. In 1921, for example, the secretary general of the parent body of the UNIA-ACL, James D. Brooks, traveled to the city at the invitation of Denver Division Number 118. Hewetson Watson, a reporter for *The Colorado Statesman,* served as the local president, and Edward C. Davis, also a writer for the paper, served as secretary. Both men were instrumental in persuading Brooks to come to Denver.[41]

Targeting the Five Points neighborhood during the last week of February and the first two weeks of March 1921, Brooks delivered a series of well-received public addresses before large audiences at several of Denver's Black churches and community halls. Speaking first at the Peoples' Methodist Presbyterian Church, Brooks discussed the Black Star Steamship Company, the Negro Construction Loan, and the redemption of Africa. Nearly 300 persons were present at these events, despite the fact that revival services were being held in two of the city's leading churches. Brooks "swayed the audience with his powerful appeals for race solidarity, race maintenance," and participation in the good life, proving again "the intelligence and spirit permeating the Negro of today, who is making a determined stand for real Liberty, Justice and a place in the recognition of the world for his contribution to civilization and the propagation of that democracy which knows no bounds."[42] Brooks's impressive statements included this one: "Every race has answered the racial call quicker and earlier than ours. Our cause is not against the white man but [rather against] Negroes who have not measured [up] and even when given the vision refuse to accept. The white man prepares to live while we prepare to die, even though we are aware that death is inevitable."[43] Members of various churches and organizations who were in attendance applauded these addresses. Brooks spoke at Fern Hall, St. Stephen's Baptist Church at Thirty-Second Avenue and Lafayette Street, Central Baptist Church, and Campbell A.M.E. Chapel. At the next division meeting a 100 percent increase in the membership was reported, as were subscriptions fulfilling nearly two-thirds of the division's quota in the Black Star Line Steamship Company and the Liberian Construction Loan.

As the Denver division membership continued to increase, emphasis was placed on the youth in the Five Points community, who were "energized by the electrifying influence and spirit of the movement. Fathers, mothers, grandparents realized that parental control and training in the home was essential to having a sound mind in a sound body."[44] This emphasis on preparing young and adults "for life's battle(s) [and] the shouldering of responsibility" was designed to help achieve and accomplish goals toward the redemption of Africa. With news of the addition of the *Phyllis Wheatley* to the Black Star fleet, the Denver division credited the New York headquarters for "having a ship large enough to accommodate nearly 2,000 passengers and all the equipment for modern traveling."[45] Members were encouraged to participate in a fundraiser called the "Dollar Drive" to help furnish equipment for the *Phyllis Wheatley*, with an exhibition of photographs of the ship to entice support. Division leaders noted that the ship would be capable of carrying 4,500 tons of cargo and a large number of passengers. A spirit of pride and joy seemed "to illuminate every countenance over this addition" because the ship implied power and a return to Africa.

In planning for the Second International Convention of the UNIA-ACL, division members were motivated and inspired during the July 5, 1921, meeting held at the Mason's new hall. Local president Hewetson Watson was elected the division's delegate to the upcoming August 1–31 convention. The division's membership continued to grow, and the president and other key officers of the division doubled their efforts to reach the 200-member mark. "KEEP UP THE SPIRIT" was the new slogan for the Denver division.[46]

Based on early references to the Denver division's activities published in *The Colorado Statesman*, the division may have been organized at least one year prior to the Colorado Springs division. According to an oral history interview with Richard Walker of Peoples, whose parents were members and officers of the Colorado Springs division, and to a letter written by J. B. Yearwood, assistant secretary general of the parent body, the Colorado Spring Division was not organized until 1922.[47] In the letter, addressed to the Reverend G. Sterling Sawyers of Peoples Methodist Episcopal Church and dated January 12, 1922, Yearwood acknowledged "receipt for the sum of $32.50" as the required payment "of charter for the Colorado Springs Division." Yearwood's letter extends to Reverend Sawyers, the division's president, and "the members of the Colorado Springs Division a hearty welcome," stating:

> We have to congratulate you on your appointment as the Chief Executive officers of the Division, and are sure that you will bring to your duties the tact and patience and ability which your responsible office demands. We

are glad to be able to inform you that the Association is advancing by leaps and bounds. Every week sees new Divisions added and our membership increased by thousands throughout the world.

It is the aim of this Association to bring into its fold every community of Negroes in the world, and we trust that Colorado Springs will so work that it will be a shining example to the people of the State of Colorado, and thereby help the rapid growth of the work in that State.

Charter and supplies are being mailed to you tomorrow, and we trust they will arrive in good condition. We are enclosing instructions for your guidance in making out reports. Please see that these instructions are carefully studied by your Secretaries, as it is of the utter importance that they arrive here in a clear and concise manner.[48]

In the months that followed this letter, other written exchanges occurred among Yearwood, Reverend Sawyers, and S. Leon Hughes, secretary of the Colorado Springs division. The topics of these exchanges ranged from requests for buttons, news releases of two postponements of Garvey's trial, and payments of new membership dues. In addition, during the planning for Garvey's visit to a meeting of the Colorado Springs division, Garvey wrote a letter to Reverend Sawyers on May 2, 1922, informing him that Garvey would be visiting the area to "speak in the interest of our [the UNIA-ACL's] spring and summer drive for new members, and for stirring up interest in the Association."[49] Garvey's letter details the specific provisions needed for the meeting:

You are, therefore, asked to arrange immediately for this meeting in a Church or Hall for the night. You will please get as many of your members as can sing and recite to take part in the concerted program. You will also ask strangers to help in the program to make it a success. Please do not offer to pay anyone to sing or recite so as to keep down expenses.

You will also try to get one or two local speakers to help us to make the program interesting. We would like a big crowd to attend these meetings. Please go ahead and make all arrangements and get your circulars printed, and boost the meeting. Admission is 50 cents.

After expenses are paid, one half of the net proceeds go to the Parent Body, and one half to your Division. We shall accept no excuse from you, but that you and the other Officers will co-operate immediately for this meeting, and make it a success.

Prepare lodgings for two ladies, and two gentlemen; the two ladies together, and the two gentlemen in separate rooms in the same building.

With very best wishes, I have the honor to be your obedient servant.[50]

Garvey arrived in Colorado Springs on May 23, 1922, along with Amy Jacques, his private secretary; Lillian Willis, orator; and Charles Zampty, auditor general.[51] Speaking before what Holley identified as a large interracial audience that evening in Perkins Hall on the Colorado College campus, Garvey began his address in classic Black nationalist UNIA-ACL form as the crowd greeted him and listened spellbound: "America is the white man's country. We are constantly reminded of the fact, and it is indisputable. Africa is for the Negro, and it is there that we must make our future homes. Throughout the world are towering monuments to the accomplishments of the white man. The Negro must accomplish something noteworthy to win the respect of the world and then he will be ready to make for himself a nation in his God-given land."[52]

Cited as one of the most forceful talks ever heard in Perkins Hall by *The Colorado Springs Gazette*, Garvey's speech "expressed [the] aim(s) of the association to unite the 400,000,000 Negroes of the world together into one organization, and to emigrate with them to their native and rightful home in Africa."[53] Garvey, the article continued, had been called the second Booker T. Washington and had done more toward realizing Washington's dreams "than the great thinker himself."[54] Capturing the audience's imagination, Garvey stated:

> We must establish a government and ourselves build an empire. I admit the manifold difficulties that would be entailed in the undertaking. But it can be done. It must reflect the nationality of the people as do the nations of France, Germany, Italy and other countries. Negroes are scattered all over the earth. They have become accustomed to the ways and customs of other lands, but there is not one that we can call our own. Africa is the only land on the face of the earth that we can claim as ours. The Negro must set out and accomplish something to win the respect of the world. I do not preach the hatred of races. Instead, I would lavish praise upon the white man. But the Negro must for obvious reasons find another land in which to live.[55]

Garvey scorned the idea that Africa had no opportunities for the Black race, noting that it is the richest continent in the world. He continued: "Its rich mineral deposits, huge and wealth-abounding forests of mahogany and other valuable species of timer, and various other natural resources were named. As long as the Negro waits and attains no goal, so long then will he continue to be slave and servant. The great part of the blame for his condition rests with himself. Let him make good."[56]

Pointing out that the total population of North America had jumped from 100 pilgrims to 90 million Americans within 300 years, Garvey argued that, at that rate, within the next 100 years the country would be overcrowded. Stating that there would be no room for the 400 million African descendants, Garvey emphasized: "it is our own negligence that has placed us in this state. Let us arise morally and mentally and gain [the] respect of all."[57]

Following the address, a reception was held at the home of Lonnie C. Bassett.[58] Garvey and his staff of UNIA-ACL officials then traveled to Denver, where the next day he delivered two addresses on behalf of the Denver division. Garvey left Denver the afternoon of the 25th, greatly disappointing those unable to hear him speak on May 24. Willis remained in Denver for a week to continue meeting with the division. Based on reports, she won the "division's heart and soul with her graciousness, and answered questions pleasantly and patiently."[59] Filled with an ethical conviction to promote racial pride and self-determination, two months before their second visit to Colorado (October 5–14, 1924) Garvey professed: "I was in jail last August. I am ready to go back to jail or [to] hell for the principles of the Universal Negro Improvement Association. Some men . . . make a big noise about jail. Every time they write about the UNIA they say Marcus Garvey was sentenced to jail, and so on." Quoting himself in an entry in the FBI files, Garvey continued, "Now, Mr. Newspaperman, let jail go to hell. You can tell the whole world that Marcus Garvey does not give a damn about jail when it comes to the emancipation of 400,000,000 Negroes."[60]

Amy Jacques may have been invisible as a convention speaker during the UNIA-ACL International Convention in 1922, as Ula Yvette Taylor has observed, but that does not mean she was not active as an UNIA official. Taylor also claims:

> As the organization grew, so did the public role of Amy Jacques Garvey. One month after her marriage in 1922, the annual UNIA August convention (marking the date of slave emancipation in the British colonies) took place in Harlem. Unlike Amy Ashwood, who had had a visible role at the previous conventions, often reciting the poetry of Paul Laurence Dunbar, Jacques Garvey was still working behind the scenes, never once sharing the limelight with her husband. Yet the issues raised at this meeting provide a sense of the concerns that were escalating when Jacques became Garvey's wife.[61]

Contrary to Taylor's observation that Amy Jacques only became visible "one month after her marriage" in July 1922, the tenets of Jacques's activism in UNIA-ACL affairs had already been developed; she was being trained to lead while serving as Garvey's private secretary and as his fiancée. Garvey recognized and respected her intellectual skills before their marriage, and although it may have appeared that she was invisible because of her personal relationship with him, one cannot assume that she was, in fact, invisible and did not perform as an individual. Women such as Amy Jacques, Henrietta Vinton Davis, and Madame Maymie Leona Turpeau de Mena—as their own persons and as

UNIA-ACL leaders—were active nationally both prior to and after Garvey's imprisonment, speaking in cities such as New York, Philadelphia, Chicago, Cleveland, Detroit, Gary, Colorado Springs, and Denver. Thus, just because Amy Jacques Garvey was not given the platform to speak during the 1922 convention does not mean Garvey did not value her and that he did not offer her the training she needed to be a successful international UNIA-ACL official.

The personal leadership training Garvey provided to Amy Jacques elevated her position as chief spokeswoman following the 1922 convention. Their personal relationship may have dictated that she take a back seat until after Garvey's indictment. During the couple's second organizational tour of Colorado, for example, both Marcus and Amy delivered persuasive public addresses. Marcus Garvey spoke in Denver on October 5, 1924,[62] and Amy delivered a speech during the Colorado Springs division meeting at Peoples Methodist Episcopal Church the evening of October 13, 1924. The couple traveled to Denver and Colorado Springs to attend enthusiastic meetings of both divisions. Katie Fenner, recording secretary of the Denver division, described Garvey as persuasive in impressing "upon the minds of his listeners the importance of organization and unity" and reported that active "members and well-wishers of the division enjoyed the visit of the President-General and his wife, Mrs. Amy Jacques Garvey," as they "pledged to work with new energy for the uplift of Negroes everywhere."[63] The two speeches Garvey delivered on October 5, 1924, were the last two he gave in the Five Points community.[64] Garvey spoke before two large gatherings, one in the afternoon and one during the evening.

Taylor was correct when she observed that as a spokeswoman for the UNIA-ACL, Amy Jacques Garvey, like other UNIA women of rank, "brought hope to discouraged Black people."[65] At the Colorado Springs division meeting, Amy charmed a large and appreciative audience with a "clear and concise, and yet forceful presentation of her message."[66] Amy's well-attended public address "set forth anew the aims and objects of the organization, as she [was] repeatedly interrupted by hearty applause."[67] The stirring message was communicated in typical "Garvey fashion," showcasing Amy Jacques's intellect and unique rhetorical skills. The local division, "which had been practically inactive for some time, had taken on new life, due primarily to the message of Mrs. Garvey to this city."[68] Amy Jacques's challenge was to support Garvey while at the same time communicating what Taylor favored as "a sense of self" in "a public space with feminine characteristics."[69] The Colorado invitation to the couple had been extended individually, and the gender dynamics that ensued after Amy's presentation were commented upon in *The Negro World*. In a letter to the editor of *The Negro World*, Anna Underwood of Fayetteville, North Carolina, had this to say about Amy's elegant speech in Colorado Springs:

> Kindly allow me space in your paper as a devoted subscriber. When I read of the wonderful address that Mrs. Garvey made at Colorado Springs appealing for more race pride it made my heart leap for joy to know that we have two women that have the stamina to make a fight for their people in the person of Mrs. Garvey and Lady Henrietta Davis.
>
> The fight is on. Will the greater activity of women in all the affairs of life bring the woman['s] mind to the level of the man['s] mind or the man['s] mind to the level of the woman['s] mind? Well, she will attend to that; we need not be afraid. Usually she has figured things just about right, and she doesn't always play Pandora either. The man['s] mind and the woman['s] mind will continue very much as they are now, except the woman will enlarge her mental horizon, and the mind of man will meet and accommodate itself to the change. Socially, racially and otherwise conditions will be better in the proportion to her activities.[70]

Amy Jacques's presentation thus raised awareness not only among her immediate audience but also among those who read the women's section of the newspaper and the editorial page.

CONCLUSION

This chapter has illustrated how the macro-level activism of the UNIA-ACL influenced local political and religious activism among a small group of Black residents in Colorado and how group and individual confidence, faith, and pride worked to their advantage in achieving African redemption. It also demonstrated that the Garveys were not only spellbinding, persuasive, and inspiring but also pragmatic in constructing a human civilization based on racial equality. The Garveys were successful in organizing and inspiring the masses and as leaders and visionary thinkers in liberating the mind-set of the Black population in Colorado and in rallying those Blacks to resist white supremacy and racial discrimination, dominance, and oppression. Central to the couple's plans and vision to uplift hundreds of thousands of people of African descent, living on the African continent and scattered throughout the African diaspora, was their activism, which essentially prompted the existence of the UNIA-ACL in two historic Black communities in Colorado.

NOTES

1. This chapter builds on my earlier essay, "Methodological Considerations for Micro Studies of UNIA Divisions: Some Notes Calling on an Ethno-Historical Analysis," *Journal of Black Studies* (November 2008): 2, 38, 281–315.

2. See E. D. Cronon, *Black Moses: The Story of Marcus Garvey and the Universal Negro Improvement Association* (Madison: University of Wisconsin Press, 1955); Robert A. Hill (ed.), *The Marcus Garvey and the Universal Negro Improvement Association Papers*, vol. 4: *September 1921–September 1922* (Los Angeles: University of California Press, 1985); Tony Martin, *Race First: The Ideological and Organizational Struggles of Marcus Garvey and the Universal Negro Improvement Association* (Dover, MA; Majority Press, 1976); Theodore G. Vincent, *Black Power and the Garvey Movement* (Berkeley: Ramparts, 1971); Amy Jacques Garvey, *The Philosophy and Opinions of Marcus Garvey. Or, Africa for the Africans. New Preface by Tony Martin* (New York: Random House, 1974); John Henrik Clarke (ed.), *Marcus Garvey and the Vision of Africa* (New York: Random House, 1974); Judith Stein, *The World of Marcus Garvey: Race and Class in Modern Society* (Baton Rouge: Louisiana State University, 1986); Randall K. Burkett, *Garveyism as a Religious Movement: The Institutionalization of a Black Civil Religion* (Metuchen, NJ: Scarecrow Press and the American Theological Library Association, 1978).

3. The Colorado Springs UNIA-ACL Division Number 508 was chartered in 1922, and Peoples Methodist Episcopal Church was designated as its Liberty Hall. The Denver UNIA-ACL Division Number 118 was chartered in 1921. During Marcus's two organizational tours of the state, Amy Jacques traveled with Garvey. During the 1922 tour, she was recognized as Garvey's private secretary. During the 1924 tour, however, Amy spoke in Colorado Springs. The only source that visually documents Marcus Garvey and Amy Jacques's presence in Colorado Springs is Lerone Bennett Jr., "The Ghost of Marcus Garvey: Interviews with Crusader's Two Wives," *Ebony* (March 1960): 53–56. In a caption of a photograph of Marcus and Amy "enjoy[ing] sights at Cheyenne Canyon in Colorado Springs" in 1922, Bennett acknowledges Amy Jacques as Garvey's second wife. However, Marcus and Amy were not married until two months after the May 1922 visit to Colorado Springs. According to an article originally published in *The Afro-American-Baltimore* and later in *The Colorado Statesman* with the headline "Marcus Garvey Marries Here," published August 5, 1922: "Marcus Garvey and Miss Amy E. Jacques were married Thursday morning [August 3, 1922] at the residence of Rev. J.R.L. Diggs, 713 Mosher street [in Baltimore, Maryland], and left immediately for New York City.... The first Mrs. Garvey secured a divorce last winter."

4. *The Colorado Statesman*, founded by Joseph D. Rivers, began publishing information about the Denver division's activities as early as January 1921, following an article it published in 1920 announcing the 1920 UNIA-ACL International Convention. The Colorado Historical Society and the Library of Congress are the only repositories that own the newspaper on microfilm. The holdings of the Colorado Historical Society, which was responsible for microfilming the newspaper, cover the period October 29, 1904, up to 1954, with some gaps. I reviewed issues of *The Colorado Statesman* from 1920 to 1930 in the Denver Public Library's Western History/Genealogy Department in 2007. *The Denver Star* also published weekly announcements of the division's activities; however, limited microfilmed copies of this newspaper are available. *The Negro World* published reports about the Denver division's activities. *The Negro World*, the official organ of the Universal Negro Improvement Association, published its first issue in 1920 and ceased publication in 1933. The newspaper was published in New York throughout the duration of its existence. As for the Colorado

Springs division, an article that first appeared in *The Colorado Springs Gazette* on May 24, 1922, and was reprinted in the newspaper on May 31, 1992, with the headline "Black Leader Made Plea for Unity" documents Garvey's visit to the city, calling for Black self-determination. I also combed through issues of *The Colorado Springs Gazette*, from 1920 to 1925. See Colorado Springs, Gazette Printing Co., 1887–1946, in the Western History Department, Denver Public Library, Denver, CO, for additional information about the division.

5. John Stokes Holley, *The Invisible People of the Pikes Peak Region: An Afro-American Chronicle* (Colorado Springs: Friends of the Colorado Springs Pioneer Museum, 1990). Holley's book only recaptures the essence of *The Colorado Springs Gazette* article about Garvey's 1922 speech, as well as a few additional details about some members of the Colorado Springs division. Holley does not discuss the staff representatives traveling with Garvey, much less details about the Denver division.

6. This point is made clear in Debra White Gray"s *Too Heavy a Load: Black Women in Defense of Themselves, 1894–1994* (New York: Norton, 1999).

7. With the exception of Holley's work, researchers over the past forty-plus years have instead been documenting the achievements and contributions of pioneering Black men and women in the West (i.e., Arizona, California, New Mexico, Oregon, and Utah), showcasing the many heroic deeds and horrific battles African American mountain men, miners, buffalo soldiers, and cowboys performed and endured. See Andrew K. Black, "Comparative Mortality between African-American and White Troops in the Union Army," *Journal of Black History* 79 (Fall 1994): 317–333; William H. Leckie, *Buffalo Soldiers: A Narrative of the Black Cavalry in the West* (Norman: University of Oklahoma Press, 1967); Theodore D. Harris (ed.), *Negro Frontiersman: The Western Memoirs of Henry O. Flipper, First Negro Graduate of West Point* (El Paso: Texas Western College Press, 1963); William Loren Katz, *The Black West: A Documentary and Pictorial History of the African American Role in the Westward Expansion of the United States*, rev. ed. (New York: Harlem Moon, 2005); Paul W. Stewart, *The Black Cowboys* (Broomfield, CO: Phillips, 1986); LaVere Anderson, *Saddles and Sabers: Black Men in the Old West* (Champaign: Garrard, 1975); Philip Durham and Everett L. Jones, *The Negro Cowboys* (Lincoln: University of Nebraska Press, 1965). Moreover, only a few works explore the Black presence in the Rocky Mountain region in the early twentieth century. For example, in Moya B. Hansen, "Try Being a Black Woman! Jobs in Denver, 1900–1970," in *African American Women Confront the West, 1600–2000*, Quintard Taylor and Shirley Ann Wilson Moore, eds. (Norman: University of Oklahoma Press, 2003), 207–227, and William Loren Katz, *Black Women of the Old West: Illustrated with Archival Photographs and Prints* (New York: Atheneum, 1995), the early occupations of Black women who lived in Denver from 1900 to the mid-1970s and played pioneering roles in the region are investigated.

8. The Black historian John Hope Franklin, in his pioneering work *From Slavery to Freedom* (New York: Vintage Books, 1969), discusses these early migration patterns.

9. See *Black Settlers of the Pikes Peak Region, 1850–1899*, 6. This was a special publication of the Negro Historical Association of Colorado Springs (NHACS), published in 1986. Lu Lu Pollard, a pioneering lay historian, spearheaded this project, having first published "He Fought and Died for Freedom, A Study in American Negro History,"

in *The Colorado Voice* for Black History Month in 1949. Pollard served as the founding president of NHACS.

10. Pollard, *Black Settlers of the Pikes Peak Region, 1850–1899*, 7.

11. Frank Loper was a well-respected citizen of the Colorado Springs area. He published the first Black newspaper in the area, along with James Booker and W. E. King. For more information, see "Sun Illuminated Truth; Newspaper One of First Black-Owned Businesses in Springs," *The Colorado Springs Gazette*, February 25, 2001, section 1, 2; "Profile of Frank Loper," *The Colorado Springs Gazette*, February 8, 1998, section 1, 2; "Obituary of Frank Loper," *The Colorado Springs Gazette*, November 10, 1937, 5; "Appointed Senate Page in Denver Legislature, *The Colorado Springs Gazette*, January 4, 1935, 12. See also Holley, *Invisible People of the Pikes Peak Region*, 131–134, which also provides a photograph of Loper.

12. Dorothy Bass Spann as told to Inez Hunt, in *Black Pioneers: A History of a Pioneer Family in Colorado Springs* (Colorado Springs: Little London Press, 1978).

13. Editorial, *The Colorado Statesman*, July 17, 1920, 4.

14. Ibid.

15. Ibid.

16. Pollard, *Black Settlers of the Pikes Peak Region, 1850–1899*, 8–9.

17. Holley, *Invisible People of the Pikes Peak Region*, 105.

18. Ibid.

19. Pollard, *Black Settlers of the Pikes Peak Region, 1850–1899*, 9.

20. Spann, *Black Pioneers*, 8.

21. Interview with Marcus Greene, historian for Peoples United Methodist Episcopal Church, Colorado Springs, CO, February 28, 2007. Greene also shared an early roster he developed with the names of the church's pastors and charter members.

22. Laura M. Mauck, *Five Points Neighborhood of Denver* (Chicago: Arcadia, 2001), 7.

23. Ibid., 8.

24. Ibid.

25. Ibid.

26. "Denver Neighborhood History Project, 1993–94: Five Points Neighborhood," prepared for the City and County of Denver, Denver Landmark Preservation Commission and Office of Planning and Community Development, 200 West 14th Avenue, Denver, CO, by R. Laurie Simmons, M.A., and Thomas H. Simmons, M.A., Front Range Research Associates, Inc., 3635 West 46th Avenue, Denver, CO.

27. Ibid., 24.

28. Mauck, *Five Points Neighborhood of Denver*, 8.

29. Simmons and Simmons, "Denver Neighborhood History Project, 1993–94," 25, 37–38.

30. Ibid., 55.

31. Ibid., 23–24.

32. Ibid., 47.

33. Ibid., 54.

34. Ibid., 29–35.

35. Carl Abbott, Stephen J. Leonard, and David McComb, *Colorado: A History of the Centennial State*, 3rd ed. (Niwot: University Press of Colorado, 1994), 45–46.

36. Ibid., 283–284.

37. Mauck, *Five Points Neighborhood of Denver*, 68–70.

38. Ibid., 68.

39. "Negroes in New York Elect President of Africa: Convention Will Also Select Leader of Blacks throughout World, over 12,000,000 in U.S.," *The Colorado Statesman*, August 14, 1920, 1.

40. In Robert Hill's 1924 chronology, *The Marcus Garvey and the Universal Negro Improvement Association Papers*, he outlines organizational tours Garvey embarked on to "promote sale of Black Cross Navigation and Trading Company stock; travels to Detroit, Raleigh, North Carolina, Denver, and Ogden, Utah [and Oakland and San Francisco, CA]," lvii.

41. According to a series of articles published in *The Colorado Statesman* from February 21 to March 26, 1921, Brooks spoke at the Peoples Presbyterian Church, Scott M.E. Church, Fern Hall, St. Stephen's Church, Central Baptist Church, and Campbell Church. As a result, the division's drive for UNIA members resulted in 200 new members. In addition, $500 in shares for the Steamship and Construction Loan fund were collected.

42. Edward C. Davis, "The Garvey Movement Invades the Middle West. Denver Division No. 118 Increases Its Membership 100 Percent: Hon. James D. Brooks, Sec.-General UNIA and ACL Arouses Negroes to Race Consciousness and Betterment of Economic Conditions—Heweston Watson, President of Division, Determines on Opening up Avenues for Our People and a Free and Redeemed Africa," *The Colorado Statesman*, March 19, 1921, 4. Davis was not only a reporter for the *Statesman*; he was also secretary of the Denver division.

43. Ibid.

44. Ibid.

45. Hon. James D. Brooks on "The Garvey Movement," *The Colorado Statesman*, March 2, 1921, 5.

46. Virgie Cole, "Universal Negro Improvement Association Elects Delegate to Convention," *The Colorado Statesman*, July 9, 1921, 1.

47. Richard Walker is an elder of the Peoples United Methodist Episcopal Church in Colorado Springs. The interview with him was conducted in March 2007 at his home.

48. Letter to G. Sterling Sawyer, 601 E. St. Vrain Street, Colorado Springs, CO, from J. B. Yearwood, assistant secretary general, January 12, 1922, private collection of Richard Walker. The letter was typed on UNIA-ACL letterhead.

49. Letter to Reverend Sawyer from Marcus M. Garvey, May 2, 1922, private collection of Richard Walker.

50. Ibid.

51. Charles Zampty was one of the elder members of the Detroit division of the UNIA-ACL, and Garvey considered him a close ally.

52. "Greatest Republic in Africa Dream of Negro Educator," *The Colorado Springs Gazette*, May 24, 1922, 5.

53. Ibid.

54. This is the first time Garvey was referred to as "the second Booker T. Washington." In other reports, it is widely acknowledged that Garvey admired and was influenced by Washington.

55. "Greatest Republic in Africa Dream of Negro Educator," *The Colorado Springs Gazette,* May 24, 1922, 5.

56. Ibid.

57. Ibid.

58. Lonnie C. Bassett was perhaps one of the most active members of the Colorado Springs division of the UNIA-ACL. He lived a block from Peoples Methodist Episcopal Church and published several reports on the division's business in both *The Negro World* and *The Colorado Springs Gazette.* Bassett received his education through his own effort. He worked as a doorman at the Broadmoor Hotel, according to an article published in *The Colorado Springs Gazette,* January 21, 1923, 6.

59. "Mrs. Garvey's Address at Colorado Springs," *The Negro World,* November 15, 1924, 12. Zampty also did good work while he was in Denver, auditing the division's books and giving instructions on how they must be kept to avoid complications in the future.

60. "Special Report," Marcus Garvey: Federal Bureau of Investigation File, Wilmington, DE, Scholarly Resources, made available on microfilm in 1979, as reported by agent Joseph G. Tucker, August 9, 1924.

61. Ula Yvette Taylor, *The Veiled Garvey: The Life and Times of Amy Jacques Garvey* (Chapel Hill: University of North Carolina Press, 2002), 42.

62. Garvey spoke at Fern Hall, Sunday, October 5, at 3 P.M. and again at 8 P.M. The announcement was published twice in *The Colorado Statesman* three weeks prior to his arrival. An ad in the *Statesman* entitled "Look Who Is Coming," September 27, 1924, 5, generated positive feedback.

63. Katie Fenner, "News and Views of UNIA Divisions," *The Negro World,* Denver Division No. 118, November 15, 1924.

64. After leaving Denver, Garvey eventually arrived in Detroit before being summoned to New York.

65. Taylor, *The Veiled Garvey,* 45.

66. Lonnie C. Bassett, "Mrs. Amy Jacques Garvey Charms Big Audience with Wonderful Address at Colorado Springs," *The Negro World,* October 25, 1924, 3.

67. Ibid.

68. Ibid.

69. Taylor, *The Veiled Garvey,* 55.

70. Anna Underwood, "Mrs. Garvey's Address at Colorado Springs," *The Negro World,* November 15, 1924, 12.

David M. Hays

"A Quiet Campaign of Education": Equal Rights at the University of Colorado, 1930-1941

Immediately prior to World War II, the University of Colorado (CU) began a campaign against racial, ethnic, and religious discrimination that predated the normally cited beginning of the Civil Rights Movement. This movement connected with minority students on campus, but its primary force was drawn from White progressives. Faculty, such as history chair Carl Eckhardt, and student groups, such as the American Student Union (ASU), played important roles in the struggle. By initiating this antidiscrimination movement, the university administration shifted from a detached stance to an active role in off-campus social problems.

The beginning of the Civil Rights Movement in the United States is often dated to *Brown v. Board of Education* in 1954. There appears to be a preference for eastern origins and solutions to social problems, with their expected movement West. More important is a prevailing belief that the civil rights question was a Black-White affair, defined and elaborated by its southern expressions and battles. Settling for *Brown* as a start point also betrays the tendency to seek top-down causes for the movement. Convincing arguments have been given recently for somewhat earlier western, grassroots antecedents. However, the propensity to define the civil rights campaign by only its minority-led struggles continues, along with top-down, East-West, and South-centered approaches. An examination of the records of the University of Colorado reaffirms the earlier origins of the Civil Rights Movement that only some historians have suggested. Although these records do include reports or policies from other institutions, there is no indication that CU's efforts spread from any other institution or region. Instead, the civil rights efforts at CU appear to have sprung from a multiethnic, local racial grassroots impetus.[1]

The University of Colorado seems an unlikely site for sources of a campaign for minority rights, given its tiny minority populations. While the state's Hispanic and immigrant inhabitants were more numerous than the number of minorities at CU, they were mostly of the industrial or agricultural working class and sent few of their children to the state university. Universities, too, particularly in the Rocky Mountain West, do not appear to be promising locations in which to seek the grassroots origins of early–twentieth-century liberalism. But appearances can be deceiving.[2]

On the CU campus, requests to apply democratic principles to minority questions appear as early as 1900. If in the West minorities did not need to be present to be loathed or feared, they also were not required to be numerous for their rights to become a question of abiding importance. Some civil rights historians have located the "seedtime of the modern Civil Rights Movement" in the 1930s and World War II. While universities and colleges have rarely been included as sowers of such grain, there is ample evidence that higher education institutions provided fertile ground for civil rights activism. The University of Colorado provides one case of a university confronting the question of minority rights in a segregated society.[3]

The University of Colorado never installed or maintained an official system of ethnic or racial segregation with regard to employment, enrollment, or the provision of goods, services, or privileges. On the contrary, the university establishment rang with the exultant post–Civil War ethos of freedom and equality. The Colorado State Constitution forbade that "any distinction or classification of pupils be made on account of race or color" in a public educational institution.[4] Statutes of the University of Colorado overtly and continually referred to this constitutional requirement. Nevertheless, both the university and the surrounding Boulder community manifested a de facto segregation of students by race that peaked in the 1920s and 1930s. University officials either reflected, or had to operate within the context of, a local and state community that often exhibited racist and ethnocentric attitudes. University officials and student leaders who sought change found they had to move cautiously while traditional views held sway.[5]

The university found itself in a difficult position. On one hand, it was bound by law and regulation to allow minority attendance and to educate without prejudice. In addition, the principles of in loco parentis required the university to act in the place of parents to protect student welfare. On the other hand, students, faculty, and administrators were not encouraged to address any inequality they were commanded to observe or to protect the welfare of students they were bound to protect. For many decades, this contradiction went unnoticed by students and campus authorities, so ingrained were the practices of racial separation and white supremacy. Passive egalitarianism appears to have coexisted with campus and local customs of segregation. Nevertheless, early sparks of idealism in university publications gradually gave way to glimmers of student activism in the 1930s. As George Norlin's presidency came to a close in 1938, student concerns—previously confined to antifascism, peace, and social justice—began to extend to civil rights for minorities, or what today are regarded as racialized ethnic communities.[6]

By the end of the nineteenth century, Boulder's mine, mill, and industrial economy was beginning to shift to a white-collar marketplace. With the loss of blue-collar jobs, the Black population—almost 2 percent of the city's population in 1910—fell to 4 hundredths of a percent in 1940, even as the White population doubled. The reduction of Boulder's Black population may have led to its marginalization both on and off campus.[7]

A Colorado version of Jim Crow developed unchallenged between 1910 and the 1930s, regulating social, economic, and personal interaction in Boulder as well as at the University of Colorado. As with other universities, minorities were absent or severely underrepresented on the CU faculty during the first half of the twentieth century. On- and off-campus publications often featured racial and ethnic stereotypes in advertising and cartoons. In attacking Harvard University's refusal to allow a Black student into its freshman dormitories (which also excluded Jews) in 1923, a student editorialist had to admit, "Equality before the law has been attained to a fair degree, but people are far from ready to embrace their own ideals in other ways."[8]

The "other ways" included segregated housing and restaurants and various informal color restrictions. By the 1930s Boulder Blacks were segregated into a small area north of campus, barred from all but a very select number of restaurants and shops, and limited to a small number of balcony seats at city theaters. Such discrimination was outlawed by Colorado after 1895, but violations went unnoticed and unenforced in Boulder. On campus during the 1930s, some faculty members and deans refused admittance, declined assistance, or denied facilities to Black undergraduates and graduate students.

Some professors ridiculed their African American students in class. Jim Crow in Boulder was entrenched but undiscussed before 1938. Before progress could be made in minority civil rights, Whites would have to uncover and confront the contrast between their ideals and segregation. At the same time, minority students had to develop faith in White allies and patrons, as well as the self-confidence with which to address what they believed was majority White racism.[9]

It was not as if students and faculty were unaware of minority problems in America. Forums and speakers on the evils of racism and anti-Semitism were fairly common on campus, especially after 1930. Black performers regularly visited CU, often calling on President Norlin during their stay. Faculty members, such as sociology professor W. S. Bernard, sponsored speakers and discussed racism in class. However, students normally focused on international or national ills rather than local ones. Moreover, Greek life and with it the Associated Students of the University of Colorado (ASUC, the student union) seemed preoccupied with the campus social calendar, leaving political concerns and liberal causes to the "Barbs," or Barbarians, as the Greeks liked to refer to independent students. The Barbs considered themselves less advantaged and more socially conscious than the affluent Greeks. Fraternities and sororities practiced "overt and explicit discrimination" against ethnic and racial minorities. In reaction to perceived elitism within the Greek system, as well as to national and international events, liberal Barbs organized challenges to the racial and ethnic status quo.[10]

Both the Cosmopolitan (Cosmo) Club and the ASU had established antidiscrimination committees by 1938. On February 16, 1938, a joint session on racial and ethnic discrimination featured presentations by Professor Bernard and three Black speakers from Denver. Bernard spoke on anti-Asian discrimination. Harold Brown, a statistician from a Black fraternal order in Denver, John A. Waller, an African American from the Bureau of Land Reclamation, and Harry E. Polk, a Black with the Social Security Administration, all spoke on contributions made by African American culture, various aspects of discrimination, and strategies for combating racism. Chair Ruth Inabu asked the audience to work with the Japanese American Citizens League to assist Japanese residents in gaining citizenship. The audience included twenty Blacks from Boulder and Denver; faculty, students, and members of the community; White liberals from the ASU and the Cosmo Club; Japanese Americans, and other nationalities and ethnicities—around fifty people in all. Strikingly, after the meeting they broke into small groups and went to Hill cafés as a demonstration against Boulder's unwritten color bar. It was the first time Blacks had been served in Hill restaurants in decades. However, to be served in small, accompanied interracial groups was not the same as equal treatment. But if discriminatory practices continued unaffected, these students were affected, and they began to mobilize against policies of racial bigotry.[11]

In November 1938, events in Germany heightened on-campus sensitivity to bigotry. That month *The Boulder Daily Camera* featured daily front-page stories highlighting the brutalization, disenfranchisement, and systematic looting of Jews in Germany. After President Norlin and CU faculty protested the persecution, the Cosmo Club divided into five groups to study international and domestic political and social problems. The ASU, led by Clinton E. Jencks, condemned German persecution of Jews and requested a trade embargo. However, in discussions of Nazi anti-Semitism, ASU members agreed that they could not fully denounce Germany "without first looking into a somewhat similar situation here." Jencks summarized the color bar on the Hill to the *Silver and Gold* and claimed that "a great number of white people resent this discrimination but do not say anything about it." Believing that nothing would be done about the situation without agitation, the ASU planned to survey large numbers of students and Boulder residents to verify its belief that segregation was not supported by either students or the community.[12]

A small committee from the ASU, led by White senior Donald E. Boothroyd, approached Professor Carl Eckhardt, historian of modern Europe and long-term chair of the History Department, with their plan to poll the city and the student body regarding racial segregation. The students believed a poll demonstrating Boulder and campus support for desegregation might prove an effective tool with which to convince merchants to drop their color bar.[13]

Professor Eckhardt advised the students to leave the matter to him and brought the ASU plan before the December 8, 1938, meeting of the Faculty Senate. The faculty response was not enthusiastic. Many professors might have surmised that neither Boulder nor the student body would answer as the ASU anticipated. A vote denouncing segregation, with accompanying publicity, might have been embarrassing and problematic for minority rights, but a city and student vote endorsing segregation might have far worse consequences. It was fortunate that the faculty members acted as they did. *Fortune Magazine*'s first national opinion poll, taken in 1939, would show that a meager 19 percent of northeastern respondents favored allowing Blacks "to live wherever they wanted to live." Only 12 percent of midwestern respondents supported such residential desegregation.[14]

At the Faculty Senate meeting, Professor Eckhardt questioned the wisdom of raising the issue publicly, convinced that such a course could cement discrimination. Law School dean Robert L. Stearns wondered whether the university ought to take on social problems, suggesting that the ASUC should handle the issue. Professor Earl Swisher cited the success that attended the efforts at Harvard University and the University of California on behalf of equal rights for all students.[15] Graduate School dean O. C. Lester believed that provoking the community and the students on this matter would worsen conditions. Professor Joseph Cohen motioned that a committee be formed to study the issue, determine the extent of campus and community discrimination, and report on possible solutions. The Faculty Senate formed a committee with Eckhardt as chair and Stearns and Swisher as members, echoing Eckhardt's desire that the investigation be conducted with all possible discretion.

The committee's February 9, 1939, report, issued just two months later, was both a statistical measurement of minority attendance at CU and a mapping of racial and ethnocentric behavior in 1939.[16] Statistically, twenty-three students were enrolled as Europeans; however, with no more than four of any one nationality, none were counted as "minorities." Four Chinese students were in attendance, and "only one of the four is an American citizen."[17] They were also not counted as a group, since none expressed feelings of discrimination or problems arising from their nationality or religion.[18] Three groups were determined, by numbers and treatment, to justify consideration by the Senate committee: Jews, Japanese Americans, and Blacks.

There were at least eighty-six Jewish students counted and perhaps as many as twice that number attending CU in 1938. Practically all of them were U.S. citizens. Seventeen Japanese American students were attending the university, all of whom were citizens and fourteen of whom were Colorado residents. The ten Black students were all citizens, seven from Colorado. Hence, virtually all students under consideration were American citizens, since no other nationals appeared in sufficient numbers or complained of discriminatory treatment. Perhaps in 1938, few international students could complain of the Colorado version of the virulent racism abroad in Europe and Asia. Interestingly, although Hispanic students numbered more than fifteen and as many as twenty-three, they did not present themselves as an aggrieved minority group.[19]

The minority students the committee interviewed enthusiastically complimented the university, its faculty, and its student body: "All testified to almost universally fair and friendly treatment by other students and praised the general atmosphere of classroom and campus." Members of each minority group seemed intent on cooperating with the faculty, wanted to cooperate with other minority groups, and were "anxious to know what their attitude should be." This obliging behavior is exactly what should have been expected from such small groups of ethnic and racial minorities in a largely White university at the height of Colorado Jim Crow. The ack of initial grievances and a shortage of student funds, along with the pressing nature of a rather comprehensive subject, required the committee to delay investigating the university and concentrate on off-campus problems.[20]

Complaints, while difficult to elicit, finally came forth.[21] Jews protested that there was no "Jewish problem on the campus." They did, however, cite exclusion from at least one honorary society. Mainly, they expressed a wish for better knowledge of Jewish culture and tradition on campus, more support for persecuted Jews in foreign countries, more Jewish speakers, and perhaps a multicultural organization to discuss these issues.[22] Female Japanese students complained that they were frequently refused housing on the grounds that White females would object, an eventuality the Japanese women had yet to encounter. They believed increased tension over the Sino-Japanese war had aggravated anti-Japanese discrimination in Boulder, despite the fact that these women were American citizens.

Black students fared far worse, and the committee recognized their situation as the most pressing. Blacks had to go to Denver to get haircuts, as they were barred from Boulder barbershops. Black student teachers could not practice-teach in Boulder and had to do so at Denver University. African American students were not accepted at the Boulder-Colorado Sanitarium. Blacks were not served in the nearby Hill cafés and restaurants, although some would allow Blacks in their kitchens. This color bar affected Black women more than Black men, since many Black males found kitchen and custodial work in boardinghouses, fraternities, and sororities on the Hill. Although Black students could normally purchase goods on the Hill, summertime brought stricter exclusion from restaurants and shops.[23]

This summer hardening of segregation was caused by two contributing factors. The first was that the Summer Session brought a fivefold increase in the number of southern Black students on campus, from ten to more than fifty. At the same time, the Colorado Chautauqua (formerly the Texas-Colorado Chautauqua) brought numbers of White southern and Texas families to their cottages higher up on the Hill. These southern visitors frequently patronized Hill establishments. Greenmans, Owens, Casa Grande, Quine's Drugs, the Sunken Gardens, and other stores believed their White customers, especially the summer Texans, avoid integrated establishments. Ruth Cave Flowers (BA 1924), a longtime Black resident of Boulder, recalled Black residents referring to Boulder as "Little Oklahoma and Little Texas" because of the influence of

Chautauqua's southern visitors. In reality, southerners made up a tiny percentage of both the permanent population of Boulder and the CU student body. Nevertheless, the summer influx of Texans clearly had a disproportionate sway in the minds of the Boulder business community, especially given the larger numbers of Blacks attending Summer Session.[24]

The specter of southern racism was again raised as an excuse to explain why the Boulder-Colorado Sanitarium discouraged admittance of Black students. While stating that all university students were admitted, Harry Carlson, director of men's physical education at the university, wrote to Professor Eckhardt that "the Sanitarium is faced with a rather difficult problem arising from the fact that many of its patients are from the South and have a prejudice against mixing socially with colored people." Under university pressure, the sanitarium allowed that it would admit Blacks, but it would house them in private cottages and feed them separately from Whites.[25]

Last and perhaps most serious, the report confirmed an intensifying practice that was at least two decades old—segregated housing. By 1939 the only "Negro" boardinghouses were on Goss Street, a neighborhood several blocks north of campus, to which an ever greater percentage of Boulder Blacks were relegated. They could not take advantage of the wider choice of housing, locations, and rents available to White students. Black students found themselves in cramped, aging houses, where at times they were made to pay higher prices for room and board than those charged elsewhere in the city: "Since the Negro students are not free to move to other boarding and rooming houses these students feel that they are being exploited by their own people and that they must simply endure their condition."[26]

Contrary to campus idealism and progressivism between 1900 and 1938, ethnic and racial minorities found themselves increasingly segregated in housing, services, and social activities. In 1910, C. Wilson Smith's photo album proudly showed a fellow student and boarder at 1061 14th Street, on the Hill, Lingoh Wang from China. In 1938 a Black student had to ask inquiring professors "if he could go to tea dances or other all-University functions, [adding] that he had been afraid to try and that there was no social life among the small Negro group." A Black pastor and CU graduate student added, "It was very difficult to explain to his people why they could not go to the same places that other Americans and Christians could."[27]

The 1938 faculty investigation would launch, by fits and starts, a thirty-year period of desegregation. The effort would require continual reexamination of segregation within both the university and the Boulder community. This civil rights endeavor would demand a sweeping reevaluation of the university's position within the larger community. The first phase of this thirty-year effort was about to begin.[28]

At the February 9, 1939, meeting of the Faculty Senate, Eckhardt's committee presented a fourteen-page report of its findings and recommendations. After initial misgivings, the committee had come to realize that the problems needed a thorough examination in light of federal and state laws and regulations. They stated that such laws must be applied both on and off campus to "preserve democracy with reference to minority rights." So while the committee may have been influenced by the prevailing belief in "Americanism," the Law School dean had made clear the possible cost of ignoring both the Colorado State Constitution and the Colorado Revised Statutes on the matter of discrimination, citing specific articles and sections. While measures needed to be taken to ensure equality on campus, the committee believed it should also inform the "townsmen" of the law. Not convinced that the outside community would support the plan, the committee suspected that it would need to develop policies should "hearty cooperation of extra-mural groups fail to materialize."[29]

Since minority housing seemed the most pressing concern, the committee recommended that the University Housing Committee investigate rooming houses to determine which would accommodate minority students. The University Housing Committee's job was to direct *all* student patrons to off-campus housing; "in consideration thereof the operators should be made aware of the need of cooperating in all respects." If campus officials failed to gain cooperation from the townspeople, then the university should look into creating International Houses and an on-campus barbershop. International Houses could provide room and board for minority students in an integrated setting.

The Ethnic Minorities Committee asked for a place on campus for minority students to eat and for lockers in which they could store lunches to reduce the necessity to return to "the negro section of the city" for lunch. At the same time, the committee suggested that minority students be made aware of their legal right to be served in Hill and downtown restaurants, soda fountains, shops, and theaters. The report urged university officials to inform the owners of Hill restaurants and soda fountains about the law concerning equal access to public services. Failing compliance, the committee suggested the university contemplate establishing a restaurant and soda fountain for student use. The ASUC agreed to undertake the task of investigating the Hill soda fountains and restaurants. As had happened in the Faculty Senate committee, the student government had undergone a change of heart regarding racial issues and was now firmly behind the faculty initiative.

The committee clearly expected the Boulder community to react with emotions ranging from reluctance to obstruction, so it included in its strategy the tactic of campus embargo. If the community would not serve minorities, then the university would do so, severely reducing all student patronage of off-campus restaurants. Since Boulder businesses depended on student patronage, this tactic promised results.

The report was well received by both President George Norlin and the Faculty Senate, which voted to accept the report and charged the committee to continue its investigations and to report as the situation warranted. The committee met with the ASUC to consider areas of student government cooperation. Professor Eckhardt seemed gratified to report to President Norlin that "Mr. Boothroyd, the prime mover concerning the Negro minority problem, has read the report and is enthusiastic over it." Norlin, satisfied with the direction of the committee's work, suggested that the report be made public, "since it [was] a very temperate statement of the situation."[30]

Diplomacy and discussion with off-campus entities did not always fail. In the months that followed, an accommodation was reached with Boulder Public School officials that allowed Black education students to practice-teach in a Boulder school. Interestingly, the obliging supervisor of teaching was "a Southerner by birth and background."[31]

The housing problem was far more delicate. The city attorney assured campus officials that no city zoning ordinances forbade Black residence on the Hill. However, there were too few Black female students to require outfitting and chaperoning a house for Black women. The summer housing situation was deemed "thoroughly unsatisfactory." Housing for fifty Black students for the Summer Session would have to await further efforts.

The ASUC formed a Committee on Minorities and, with Faculty Senate approval, sent a letter to businesses on the Hill, citing incidents of discrimination against Black, Japanese, Chinese, and Jewish students. The letter exhorted the businesses to end their discrimination and extend the same privileges to all students of the university irrespective of race and color. Investigations of conditions on the Hill followed the business owners' response.[32]

On campus, the university was not quite as blameless as obliging minority students had depicted. Honorary societies and clubs were investigated for exclusionary membership requirements. Even when clubs included minority members, like the debate team, intercollegiate competition imposed limits on meets in which Black team members could or could not compete. Most of the Athletic Department's intercollegiate teams barred African American participation to appease league teams from segregated schools and to "protect" Black players from the insults and restrictions imposed by away games. Although the residence halls were open to Black students, hall officials often attempted to discourage or redirect Black applicants to the Goss-Grove neighborhood. When forced to accept Black freshmen, they juggled room assignments to ensure that "embarrassments" did not result from White student complaints about shared bathrooms. Harry Groves, an African American and a freshman in 1939, was encouraged to take housing in Goss-Grove but after appealing to the president was allowed entrance to the men's dormitory. White CU students, staff, and faculty were more racist than depicted by minority assurances.[33]

In 1940 recently appointed president Robert L. Stearns alerted the *Silver and Gold* to a resolution of the American Legion at the organization's September 1939 national meeting declaring that racial, religious, and political intolerance was un-American and a threat to democracy: "The world today suffers as never before from the prejudices and intolerant attitudes of group against group, whether racial or otherwise. It is time that careful stock be taken of the essence of these views and a realization of the fact that they are superficial, undemocratic, and distinctly un-American."[34]

President Stearns had made the leap from university laissez faire to university militant on the basis of legal and constitutional necessity, to which he was adding the ideals of Americanism. As president, Stearns offered room in the President's House to all Black performers who came to CU and were denied rooms in local hotels. He also frequently befriended African American students and addressed their grievances. In Stearns, Professors Swisher and Eckhardt had an informed and powerful ally who could be counted on to press the issue "without unnecessarily antagonizing the personalities involved."[35]

While long-term faculty could be counted on for consistency, no such assumption could be made about the constantly circulating students. Although Clinton Jencks and many of the activists who had initiated the desegregation effort had graduated in 1939, enough remained to ensure that the cause was not dropped. The ASU and the Cosmo Club continued their ambitious plan to address discrimination by focusing on what could be done to save democracy at home while it was being lost overseas. In the spring of 1940, the American Student Union prodded the ASUC on its lack of progress on the minority issue, making racial discrimination its chief focus. By proposing and attending a joint meeting with the Cosmo Club and church groups that discussed establishing an International House for foreign and Black students, Boothroyd "built a fire under the ASUC."[36]

Quietly, the regents, Presidents Norlin and Stearns, and the faculty had been moving to address the question of discrimination in Hill restaurants. In the spring of 1938, the regents had agreed to fund the building of a kitchen in the Memorial Building. So in 1940 President Stearns saw to it that impoverished students and minorities could eat at the new on-campus café/cafeteria in the Memorial Building. Hill restaurant owners signed a petition protesting the cafeteria, but they were partially mollified when they discovered the scale of the facility and that some users would require proof of financial need.[37]

In September 1941 Harry Groves and other minority and liberal White students were delegated to select and repair suitable men's and women's International Houses. Unfortunately, this effort to create an integrated experience for all ethnicities and Whites ended with the beginning of World War II.[38]

Meanwhile, watchful minority students had been noting the civil rights efforts and statements of Jencks, Boothroyd, Donald Irish, Stanford Calderwood, and other liberal White students. The continued faculty commitment on the issue had also not escaped their attention. With the movement being made by the university in minority housing, dining facilities, and various other desegregation efforts, hopes began to rise across ethnic lines. Lucille Hawkins and Harry Groves had already applied for housing in the residence halls, provoking meetings and correspondence in high places but ultimately gaining special approval. They continued to press for their rights. In February 1941 student speakers discussed racial matters in the chapel. Three years later others began to rouse themselves on their own behalf. One Black student remembered attending a meeting in 1942 at which Congress on Racial Equality (CORE) representative James Farmer carefully described methods of nonviolent protest.[39]

Within three years of the time the ASU approached Professor Eckhardt, many strides had been taken. The university had shifted from passive to active egalitarianism, both on and off campus. Temporary solutions had been found to segregated practice-teaching, segregationist leanings at the sanitarium, the color bar practiced by Hill merchants, and segregated off-campus housing. Most of these successes had been achieved with considerable cooperation and consensus on campus, little concerted opposition from "extramural groups," and, perhaps most helpfully, very little negative press. The quiet phase of this "education" on civil rights was about to come to a close. The noisy phase would begin during World War II.

NOTES

1. Steven F. Lawson, "Freedom Then, Freedom Now: The Historiography of the Civil Rights Movement," *American Historical Review* 96, 2 (1991): 456–471; Quintard

Taylor, *In Search of the Racial Frontier: African Americans in the American West, 1528–1990* (New York: W. W. Norton, 1998), 278–310.

2. Robert M. Tank, "Mobility and Occupational Structure on the Late Nineteenth-Century Urban Frontier: The Case of Denver, Colorado," *Pacific Historical Review* 47, 2 (1978): 189–216; Robert L. Brunton, "The Negroes of Boulder, Colorado: A Community Analysis of an Ethnic Minority Group" (M.A. thesis, University of Colorado, 1948); James A. Atkins, *Human Relations in Colorado, 1858–1959* (Denver: Colorado Department of Education, 1961).

3. David R. Roediger, *The Wages of Whiteness: Race and the Making of the American Working Class* (New York: Verso, 1991), 3–5; Robert Paul Cohen, *When the Old Left Was Young: Student Radicals and America's First Mass Student Movement, 1929–1941* (New York: Oxford University Press, 1993); Merl E. Reed, *Seedtime for the Modern Civil Rights Movement: The President's Committee on Fair Employment Practice, 1941–1946* (Baton Rouge: Louisiana State University Press, 1991).

4. Article IX, Sec. 8, Colorado State Constitution, *The General Statutes of the State of Colorado* (Denver: Times Steam Printing and Publishing House, 1883), 57.

5. See *Statutes of the University of Colorado*, 1926, 95; Laws of the Regents of the University of Colorado [revised 1942], 110, Archives, University of Colorado at Boulder Libraries; Stephen J. Leonard and Thomas J. Noel, *Denver: Mining Camp to Metropolis* (Niwot: University Press of Colorado, 1990), 366–387; Taylor, *In Search of the Racial Frontier*, 202–204, 217, 223–224, 227, 229, 231, 236.

6. Richard M. Dalfuime, "The 'Forgotten Years' of the Negro Revolution," *Journal of American History* 55, 1 (June 1968): 92–106; August Meier and Elliott Rudwick, "The Origins of Nonviolent Direct Action Protest: A Note on Historical Discontinuities," in August Meier and Elliott Rudwick, *Along the Color Line: Explorations in the Black Experience* (Chicago: University of Illinois Press, 1976), 307–404.

7. Brunton, "Negroes of Boulder," 16–18, 56–62; Don Corson, "The Black Community in Boulder, Colorado," unpublished paper, 1996, Archives, University of Colorado at Boulder Libraries; see also note 13.

8. J. S. Schey, "The Negro Question of Today," *Silver and Gold*, February 25, 1902, 1–5; "This Problem of Race," *Silver and Gold*, October 28, 1922, 2; "Negro Race Problems Discussed in Boulder," *Silver and Gold*, June 29, 1923, 1–5; "Coon, Coon, Coon, as Sung by the Intercollegiate Athletic Association," *Silver and Gold*, October 12, 1905, 21–22; "Ethnic Stereotype Images," *Silver and Gold*, May 26, 1924, 2–6; *University of Colorado Dodo*, November 1921, xiv, October 1923, 21, April 1929, frontispiece, November 1931, 11, December 1931, 5, November 1933, back cover, January 1935, 6; "Harvard's Racial Attitude," *Silver and Gold*, January 12, 1923, 2 (source of the quotation); "Jim Crow at Harvard: 1923," *New England Quarterly* 44, 4 (1971): 627–634; Thomas D. Clark, *Indiana University, Midwestern Pioneer: In Mid Passage*, vol. 2 (Bloomington: Indiana University Press, 1973), 135–139.

9. Cohen, *When the Old Left Was Young*, 206–209; Tony Ray (African American from Boulder, CO), telephone interview with author, May 27, 1998; Black Local History, audiotape 56, Archives, University of Colorado at Boulder Libraries (AUCBL); "Sho' Nuff: A Special Dinner before the Prom, the Casa Grande," *Silver and Gold*, January 27, 1939, 3; *Mills' Annotated Statutes of the State of Colorado* (Denver: Mills, 1897),

139, sec. 1; Revised Statutes of Colorado, 1908 (Denver: Smith-Brooks, 1908), sec. 609; Colorado Statutes Annotated (Denver: Bradford-Robinson, 1936–1952), ch. 35, sec. 1, 6.

10. "Hayes Sings Tonight in Only State Appearance: Negro Tenor at Top in Rendition of Spirituals," *Silver and Gold*, November 3, 1936, 1; "Cosmopolitan Club Will Introduce First of Program Series," *Silver and Gold*, October 1, 1937, 3; "Students Warned against Fascism: Stevens Addresses American Student Union Wednesday," *Silver and Gold*, November 19, 1937, 1; "Race Problems: Negro Spirituals, Poetry Included in Program," *Silver and Gold*, May 24, 1938, 1; "Colored Soprano Will be Featured by Artist Series Tonight," *Silver and Gold*, November 9, 1938, 1; Clinton E. Jencks, telephone interview with author, July 1, 1998.

11. "Negroes and White Students 'Go Coking' Together at University Hill Restaurants to Break Down Reported Discrimination," *The Boulder Daily Camera*, February 17, 1938, 1. The next day the ASU attempted to demonstrate against the racism implicit in the call for an anti-Japanese boycott; see "Shivering CU Students See Anti-Japanese Meeting Turned into Farce after Lecture," *The Boulder Daily Camera*, February 18, 1938, 1; Ruth Chiyeko Inabu (BA 1940), treasurer of Delta Sigma Rho, Phi Gamma Mu, president of Women's Forensic Society, American Student Union, secretary of the Cosmo Club, president of the Peace Council, Klinger Oration winner, Delta Sigma Rho Extemporaneous Speech winner, BA; Minute Book, 1937–1949, Cosmopolitan Club Collection, book 1, AUCBL.

12. "Nazi Persecution Condemned by CU Professors," *The Boulder Daily Camera*, November 26, 1938, 1; "CU Law Faculty Protests against Nazi Persecution," *The Boulder Daily Camera*, December 2, 1938, 1; "Cosmo Club Plans Division to Study Problems," *Silver and Gold*, November 18, 1938, 4 (source of the quotation); "Student Union Asks America to Cut off Trade with Germany," *The Boulder Daily Camera*, November 30, 1938, 5; "ASU Will Study Racial Discrimination," *Silver and Gold*, December 2, 1938, 1–2; Clinton E. Jencks, BA 1939, ASU president, Adelphi, Phi Epsilon Phi, Phi Gamma Mu, see the *Coloradan*, 1938, 72, catalogued at AUCBL; Jencks interview.

13. Richard Polenberg, *One Nation Divisible: Class, Race, and Ethnicity in the United States since 1938* (New York: Viking, 1980), 22–45. Boothroyd's plan and the Faculty Senate's response are from Minutes, Senate of the University of Colorado, December 8, 1938, 149–150, Faculty Senate Papers, Box 1, AUCBL; Cohen, *When the Old Left Was Young*, 209–225.

14. Stephen Thernstrom and Abigail Thernstrom, *America in Black and White: One Nation, Indivisible* (New York: Simon and Schuster, 1997), 51–68.

15. Faculty Senate Papers, Senate Committee on Minorities, 1939, C. C. Eckhardt Collection, 1–17, AUCBL [hereafter Eckhardt Collection]. It is unclear what Professor Swisher meant by this. Harvard did not seem to have addressed its discriminatory residence hall practices prior to 1940, and its administration seemed unlikely promoters of off-campus desegregation; see Seymour Martin Lipset and David Riesman, *Education and Politics at Harvard* (New York: McGraw-Hill, 1975), 142–145, and Richard Norton Smith, *The Harvard Half Century: The Making of a University to a Nation* (New York: Simon and Schuster, 1986), 85–89. At the University of California at Berkeley in 1937, liberal students in the ASUC had ignored university administration resistance and

objections to address discriminatory off-campus housing practices through boycotts and petitions, along with endorsing non-discriminating landlords; see Verne A. Stadtman, *The University of California, 1868–1968* (New York: McGraw-Hill, 1970), 291–293.

16. The discussion that follows is from the Senate Committee Report on the Minority Problem at the University of Colorado, Minutes of the Senate, 1924–1939, appendix between pp. 156 and 157.

17. The casual lumping of foreign nationals with citizens of all minority ethnicities appears throughout this report.

18. "Three Chinese Come Here for Graduate Work because CU is 'Friendly' School," *The Boulder Daily Camera*, September 27, 1938, 1.

19. Spanish surnames are not easily separated from Italian surnames, of which there were many more in attendance: *University of Colorado Directory, 1938–1939* (Boulder: University of Colorado, 1938); Carey McWilliams, *North from Mexico: The Spanish-Speaking People of the United States* (Philadelphia: J. B. Lippincott, 1949 [ca. 1948]).

20. See Senate Committee Report on the Minority Problem, 7.

21. The following discussion is drawn from "Complaints of the Minorities," in ibid., 9.

22. The University of Colorado may have been somewhat less anti-Semitic than was common in universities at the time; Cohen, *When the Old Left Was Young*, 264, 268, 272–273.

23. Senate Committee Report on the Minority Problem, 10–11.

24. Ethnic Minority Commission, Eckhardt Collection, 1–19; "Ruth Cave Flowers Oral History" and Ruth C. Flowers, "Speech at Boulder High School," both in Carnegie Branch Library for Local History, Boulder, CO; Ray interview.

25. Harry Carlson to C. C. Eckhardt, March 27, 1939, Eckhardt Collection, 1–17.

26. Corson, "Black Community in Boulder," appendix B; Senate Committee Report on the Minority Problem, 10–11; Senate Committee on Minorities, Eckhardt Collection, 1–17.

27. Lipset and Riesman, *Education and Politics at Harvard*, 157–178; Stadtman, *University of California*, 281–301; Patricia Sullivan, *Days of Hope: Race and Democracy in the New Deal Era* (Chapel Hill: University of North Carolina Press, 1996), 72–73, 80–83; C. Wilson Smith Scrapbook, 1906–1910, University of Colorado Scrapbooks, Box 3, AUCBL; *Boulder City Directory* (Boulder: Frank V. Kirk, 1908), 178; Senate Committee Report on the Minority Problem, 10 (source of the quotations).

28. While students at Harvard University, the University of California at Berkeley, and other schools had attempted to address these issues previously, further research must be conducted to determine the degree to which the University of Colorado was exceptional in its administration efforts to desegregate itself and its outside community. However, a survey of sixty-seven large coeducational universities by the Social Relations Committee of the Student Body of the University of Wisconsin in 1946 found that 50 percent of the surveyed institutions reported having active programs to diminish prejudice and discrimination: "Race Discrimination Survey Conducted by the University of Wisconsin," *Silver and Gold*, June 18, 1946, 3.

29. Senate Committee Report on the Minority Problem; the following paragraphs are drawn from a draft version of the same report, p. 12.

30. C. C. Eckhardt to George Norlin, February 23, 1939, and George Norlin to C. C. Eckhardt, February 25, 1939, both in President's Office Papers, I-56-1, AUCBL.

31. Senate Committee on Minorities, April 13, 1939, C. C. Eckhardt Collection, 1–17, AUCBL. The elementary school opened to Black student-teachers first; Harry E. Groves was the first Black student-teacher at Boulder High School. Harry E. Groves, telephone interview with author, June 12, 1998.

32. President's Office Papers, I-56-1; "Committeemen Ask for No Racial Discrimination," *Silver and Gold*, October 6, 1939, 6.

33. Anne Byrd Kennon to George Lucille Hawkins, August 16, 1939, and Anne Byrd Kennon to George Norlin, August 17, 1939, both in President's Office Papers, I-56-1, AUCBL; Harry Edward Groves from Manitou Springs, CO, Kappa Delta Pi, Phi Delta Kappa, and Phi Beta Kappa, also in Adelphi, Honors Union, Window, Cosmo Club president, Debate, Religious Interest Committee, manager of the International Cooperative House for Men, BA cum laude in English literature, 1943, *Coloradan*, 1943, v. 45 (Boulder: ASUC, 1943), 7, 65, 77, 154, 225, 256; Harry E. Groves to David Hays, June 2, 1998, in author's possession.

34. Robert L. Stearns to *Silver and Gold*, February 20, 1940, President's Office Papers, I-26-6, AUCBL: published in *Silver and Gold*, February 23, 1940, 2.

35. C. C. Eckhardt to Mrs. Jerome C. Smiley, May 1, 1944, Eckhardt Papers, 1–16; Groves interview; Ray interview; Stearns to Eckhardt, September 13, 1939, President's Office Papers, I-26-6, AUCBL.

36. University of Colorado, "Programs of Commencement Exercises," 1931–1941, AUCBL; "ASU Plans Wide-Spread Year Program," *Silver and Gold*, October 10, 1939, 1; "ASU Outlines Year's Plans," *Silver and Gold*, October 17, 1939, 2; "ASU Presses ASUC on Minority Question," *Silver and Gold*, February 2, 1940, 1 (source of quotation); "Action on Minority Problem Raised," *Silver and Gold*, March 8, 1940, 1; "Committee on Minority Discrimination," *Silver and Gold*, March 8, 1940, 1; "Minorities Meet at 4," *Silver and Gold*, April 23, 1940, 1.

37. Regents Minutes, January 15, 1937–December 8, 1939, 115, AUCBL; "Book Store, Fees, and Cafeteria Undergo Study," *Silver and Gold*, April 30, 1940, 1; "Regents, Restaurant Men Talk Cafeteria," *Silver and Gold*, May 10, 1940, 1; "Regents Approve Student Cafeteria Plan," *Silver and Gold*, October 29, 1940, 1; "Coke Bar and Low Cost Eating Plan Awaits Only President's Final Word," *Silver and Gold*, January 17, 1941, 1; "Co-Op Adds Members to Fill Roll, Plans Concessions to Minorities," *Silver and Gold*, February 11, 1941, 1. A "coking date" referred to taking a date for sodas.

38. Harry E. Groves to David Hays, June 2, 1998; "Racial Minorities Find Housing in New International Cooperative Houses," *Silver and Gold*, September 25, 1941, 1; Student and Faculty Directory, University of Colorado, 1938–1943, AUCBL; Vivian Marinoff, "Harmony Reigns among Races Here," *Silver and Gold*, January 13, 1942, 2.

39. "Chapel to Hear First Student Speakers, Singh, Stroud and Roark Talk on Race—Aid Sunday," *Silver and Gold*, February 14, 1941, 1; "Negro Show Will Be Thursday Evening," *Silver and Gold*, April 22, 1941, 1; Groves interview; Dolores Hale Findley, telephone interview with author, October 14, 1998.

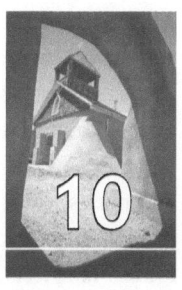

Jessica N. Arntson

Journey to Boulder: The Japanese American Instructors at the Navy Japanese Language School (1942-1946)

In April 1942, Joe Sano wrote a letter to his wife, Miya, who was being held at Tanforan Assembly Center in San Francisco with his elderly mother. Like 120,000 other Japanese Americans, the Sanos had been forcibly evicted from their home by Executive Order 9066 and imprisoned behind barbed wires. However, Joe had been secretly whisked away by Naval Intelligence officers and was only now allowed to explain his whereabouts to his wife. He had been brought to Boulder, Colorado, to teach the Japanese language to naval officers and was settling into his new environment. Joe promised Miya that when she joined him she would like Boulder, which he described as having a church or a bank on every corner.[1] Despite the idyllic setting Joe painted for Miya, the disruption caused by the evacuation, the dispersion of her family to unknown destinations, and their lives at the assembly center had strained them both. White Americans, affirmed by their government's policies, blamed Japanese Americans for Pearl Harbor and the war with Japan, and overnight all Americans of Japanese descent became suspected of betrayal. Would the Boulder community act any differently?

Over 150 Japanese Americans served as instructors at the University of Colorado–housed Navy Japanese Language School (JLS) during World War II.

Although evicted from their homes on the West Coast and imprisoned in concentration camps, they journeyed to Boulder to make vital contributions to the war effort by training interpreters, translators, and interrogators. The JLS instructors trained over 1,100 men and women officers to be proficient in the Japanese language and in the process altered their students' lives, career paths, and biases toward the Japanese people. In the Pacific theater, officers of the JLS fought restrictive protocols and contested their superiors' orders to lobby for humane treatment of Japanese prisoners of war. When they returned from their wartime posts, the former students of the JLS instructors went on to establish and nurture Japanese studies programs throughout the country to train new generations of scholars to understand the Japanese language, people, culture, economy, and history.

The experiences of the JLS instructors and their families present a compelling perspective on both the Internment and Japanese American participation in the war effort.[2] Their struggles in Boulder offer a glimpse of the hardships and racism Japanese Americans endured during World War II from neighbors and the media who labeled them the "enemy" even as they helped the United States win the war. The evacuation and Internment of West Coast Japanese Americans based "loyalty" and "disloyalty" on race. "[B]eing Japanese was anti-American," wrote Tomi Kaizawa Knaefler.[3] "War work" emerged as a way for Japanese Americans to prove their loyalty, get out of the camps, and resume their lives in society. Teaching Japanese to naval officers was one of a handful of opportunities available to a qualified few.

The hurricane of the evacuation and relocation of 120,000 persons of Japanese ancestry living on the West Coast following the declaration of war against the Japanese in December 1942 not only disrupted but also dissected families by separating and shipping members to Internment camps throughout the western states. President Franklin Delano Roosevelt determined the Internment to be a "military necessity" in Executive Order 9066 and designated the West Coast a "zone of combat" where the presence of Japanese Americans would confuse U.S. Army forces because of their resemblance to the enemy. Officials decided that all Japanese Americans, including women, children, and the elderly, were "potential enemies" who would turn against the United States if put to the test.[4]

The division in charge of the evacuation and Internment, the War Relocation Authorities (WRA), initially herded Japanese Americans into temporary housing or assembly centers, such as the one in which Miya Sano and her mother were living, after systematically evacuating neighborhoods on the West Coast. Japanese Americans were usually placed in fairgrounds or on racetracks. Families often slept in stables recently vacated by horses until they were transported inland to the permanent camps.

Overlooking "the paradoxes created by . . . outside labor recruitment,"[5] war relocation officials and branches of the military began actively recruiting Japanese Americans from assembly centers and Internment camps as farmhands in furlough work and as soldiers, interpreters, and language instructors. Over 33,000 Nisei, or American citizens of Japanese ancestry, served in the U.S. military. The selection and motivations of the JLS instructors serve as one example of minority war participation during World War II. In addition, in interviews with the instructors and their families, the opposition to war work by other Japanese Americans emerged as an additional challenge confronting those who joined in the war effort during the Internment and World War II. The motivations that compelled the instructors to join the JLS reveal that war participation was ambivalent, contested terrain.

Japanese American war participation, like that of other minorities such as African Americans and Navajo "code talkers," has only recently emerged as a topic within both Internment historiography and World War II history.[6] One reason it has taken so long to examine the full story of war participation is the absence of documents to verify their involvement in the war effort. When World War II military intelligence documents were declassified in 1972, the U.S. Navy, the U.S. Marine Corps, and many U.S. Army units had destroyed records of Japanese Americans in the army's Military Intelligence Service (MIS) attached to their outfits.[7] Furthermore, the division responsible for intelligence oversight of the JLS, the Twelfth Naval District of San Francisco, either failed to report to the flag secretary once the language school moved to Boulder or threw away the personnel files.[8] In addition, the U.S. Naval Intelligence Service did not keep or deliberately destroyed the personnel records of the JLS instructors.[9] This explanation, however, overlooks the underlying fact that the navy preferred to ignore the instructors' efforts until their advocates and former students insisted on their recognition.[10]

Because no documents reveal the instructors' perceptions of their experiences in the military as teachers of the "enemy's language" to naval officers while their families and friends remained interned in camps scattered throughout the United States, oral history has proved invaluable in the study of the JLS instructors. The more than 150 Japanese and Japanese American Issei (Japanese nationals who emigrated to the United States), Kibei (Americans of Japanese ancestry who returned to Japan for a portion of their education), and Nisei instructors at the Navy Japanese Language School have never been the central focus of a study of Japanese American war participation during World War II.[11]

THE JLS AS WAR WORK

Before the United States entered World War II, Japanese Americans were working in all branches of the military for the country's defense. The army enlisted approximately 3,500 Nisei before Pearl Harbor, but the attack caused the army to alter its policy.[12] The Selective Service System had reclassified Nisei soldiers as "4C," or "aliens not eligible for military service."[13] However, on February 1, 1943, President Roosevelt reversed this decision and announced that volunteer units of exclusively Japanese American soldiers would be accepted from the Internment camps housing persons of Japanese ancestry who had been living on the West Coast.[14] Prior to Roosevelt's decision, however, the future JLS instructors had already left the assembly centers and Internment camps to make their way to Boulder and their new roles as Japanese language instructors.

The evacuation, Internment, and recruitment of the JLS instructors are intertwined with their experiences as Japanese language instructors in the navy in Boulder. The memory of these events cannot be separated. In addition, the instructors' move to Boulder less than a year after Pearl Harbor, as new members of a small community that had no population of Japanese ancestry to speak of, also reveals the state of war hysteria within which the history of the JLS unfolds. Through interviews with surviving instructors and their families, the experiences and legacy of the JLS instructors emerge.

War participation by interned Japanese Americans had opponents both within the government and in the camps, among the Japanese Americans themselves. In addition, motives to participate were more complicated than simply the desire to prove loyalty to a nation despite its unlawful imprisonment of its citizens. Motivations to join the war effort varied enormously depending on the instructor's views of Internment, patriotism, and freedom. The debate over participation in the war effort spread throughout the Internment camps and divided their communities. Nisei internees resented the military's policy of banning Japanese Americans from enlisting in its ranks. Further, internees were aware that Nisei had been kicked out of the military after Pearl Harbor.

The strongest argument against signing up, however, lay in the obviously inconsistent policies of the WRA. Mass evacuation of *all* Japanese Americans from the West Coast was based on the argument that "loyal" and "disloyal" Japanese Americans could not be distinguished in the limited time available.[15] For the military to contradict itself and state that there was in fact a way to determine "loyalty" exposed the government's hypocrisy and racist underpinnings.

Loyalist groups such as the Japanese American Citizens League (JACL) insisted that despite this hypocrisy, the "opportunity" to fight and die for one's country must be utilized as a way to defend the birthrights of the Nisei against further erosion.[16] JACL leaders believed that volunteering for the armed forces would promote resettlement from the camps. More important, JACL members were looking to the future—to postwar society in which a record of having fought for the country, it was believed, would enable Nisei to win full citizenship rights and deter discrimination against Japanese Americans. To volunteer for the war effort was to volunteer for a new order in American society, one in which Japanese Americans would find better, more humane conditions.

Although loyalty played into the decisions of some Japanese Americans who volunteered to help in the war effort, motives varied within the ranks of the JLS instructors. Volunteers made decisions on a more intimate level that concerned family, environment, and economics. Although many instructors agreed with the JACL and saw the JLS as a way to prove their loyalty, not all responded out of patriotism, yet they furthered the war effort just the same.

Regardless of their motives for joining the JLS, future instructors were caught in the conflict about war work among Japanese Americans. When the call to teach Japanese to naval officers came to the Topaz Relocation Center in Utah, Koshi Suzuki had already established a Japanese language school for the children in the camp. To the dismay of his friends and students, Suzuki, a Japanese language instructor by profession, signed up for the JLS position immediately. His daughter, Takako Ishizaki, remembers, "[T]he parents of his students of his Japanese school [in the camp] said that he was deserting them and would work for the U.S. Navy when he was a Japanese."[17] Suzuki, however, withstood the opposition for his own reasons. Takako was seventeen at the time, and she said, "(My father) figured this was the only way I could get to college; and he ha[d] two other children."[18] Takako said her father "felt ... that teaching was his job, and the more people he could teach Japanese he would be accomplishing his dream."[19] His children entered schools in Boulder, and his daughter graduated from the University of Colorado in 1946.

James Otagiri and his family experienced similar opposition from internees while also at the Topaz Relocation Center. His daughter, Katherine Otagiri, remembers the criticism James and his wife, Chiyoko, experienced from "super-patriots" who saw his leaving the camp to teach U.S. naval officers as doing "traitor's work."[20] Despite fellow internees' beliefs that James was "helping the enemy," James went to Boulder because he was a pragmatist; according to his daughter, "it was his entrée into society."[21] James wanted to return to society and become productive again, so he accepted the instructorship at the JLS and helped to end the war.

Kozo Fujii sought to do something about the Immigration Act that prevented him from becoming a U.S. citizen:[22] "This was one of the reasons I taught at the U.S. Navy Language School . . . [to] serve the U.S. government and become eligible for naturalization."[23] Fujii's hopes of becoming a U.S. citizen compelled him to accept the JLS instructorship as an avenue to something that eluded him because of his ancestry.

Before the war, few white-collar professions were open to persons of Japanese descent in the United States, and during the war the few avenues that had been open were closed off. After graduating from top universities, many JLS instructors were relegated to service jobs and manual labor. Takeo Okamoto graduated from Berkeley with honors and worked as a shoe product salesman.[24] Ernest Kenichi Yamada also graduated from Berkeley (1923) and worked as a gardener.[25] The JLS instructors had few choices for employment outside of manual labor despite their education. Those who had been doctors before the war were forbidden to practice medicine after Pearl Harbor.[26] The stark contrast between the work at the JLS and the work available to most Japanese Americans was expressed by former instructor James Otagiri in a letter to a friend after Otagiri's arrival in Boulder: "Most of the Japanese are doing menial work, including manual labor and working in garages. . . . [N]ot too many earn good wages. . . . Even before the war, Japanese were shunned from certain professions and that still applies to many jobs now. But that can't be helped. In general, white-collar jobs are still not opened to Japanese."[27]

The selection and motivations of the JLS instructors, combined with the criticism they faced within Japanese American communities, present a complex image of Japanese American war participation.

RECEPTION IN BOULDER: HOSTILITY, AMBIVALENCE, AND ACCEPTANCE AWAIT

In late July 1942, some of the wives of instructors at the U.S. Navy Japanese Language School left the Tanforan Assembly Center in San Francisco, where the WRA had been holding them for four months. Escorted by armed guards, they boarded a train to join their husbands in the inland western United States. The drawn curtains on the train prevented Miya Sano, Vickie Yumoto, and Kathleen Kazuko Okamoto from seeing anyone and from being seen as they left the "evacuation zone" on the West Coast. U.S. Army guards escorted the JLS group from Tanforan, not to prevent them from doing any harm but instead to protect the group from any harm they might encounter as a result of war hysteria directed at Japanese Americans, misunderstood as the "enemy" because of their ancestry.

Some children of JLS instructors vividly remember this journey. Edwin Yamada, the son of former instructor Ernest Kenichi Yamada, related: "We were herded aboard these trains and all the shades were pulled. We couldn't look out and we would go through the day and night. We would pull the shade up whenever the train went uphill and I would peek out[,] and the local ranchers and the local people would be standing along the railroad tracks with rifles."[28] As if heading into enemy territory, the families of the JLS instructors rode on in fear and confusion.

Their arrival in Boulder, Colorado, marked the end of a long journey for the instructors and their families. They went from evacuation to forced Internment to release back into society. Despite the breathtaking views of the Rocky Mountains and relatively good relations between Whites and Japanese in the state, anti-Japanese sentiment experienced a resurgence during the West Coast evacuation as Coloradoans reacted negatively to Japanese resettlement in their state. Farm and labor organizations, civic and nativist groups, city councils, and other politicians drowned out those who spoke against injustices to Japanese Americans, such as Colorado governor Ralph Carr.[29] The climate of war hysteria the JLS instructors entered provoked a need for Boulder leaders to "sell the community" on the idea of the necessity of the school and its instructors for the war effort. Their new roles as Japanese language instructors in the military set the JLS instructors apart from other Japanese Americans in Colorado and placed them in an ambivalent position in the community. Their experiences and caution exercised in their new environment informed the predicament of all relocated and "free" Japanese Americans living in a situation of war hysteria.

Prior to 1942, the city of Boulder had very few Japanese Americans among its population. During the four years the Japanese language school was in Boulder, the community experienced an unprecedented influx of Japanese Americans as a result of the JLS. The University of Colorado also experienced an increase in enrollment of Japanese American students; the school was one of only a handful of institutions bordering the evacuation zone that accepted evacuees into its program.

War authorities appealed to governors and attorneys general for their support for a smooth relocation of Japanese Americans to their cities and towns. Opinions varied but tended to fall along the lines of "complete and bitter animosity toward any purchase of land or settlement of Japanese communities in their state."[30] The governor of Utah, Herbert B. Maw, insisted that his state could not protect incoming Japanese Americans from hostility and that protests were bound to occur. When the possibility of using Japanese to help relieve the serious labor shortage arose as a result of the draft, however, S. J. Boyer of the Utah State Farm Bureau supported the idea. "We don't love the

Japanese," Boyer said, "but we intend to work them, if possible."[31] Japanese American war participation became a selling point for the government to use Japanese Americans for various purposes.

Initially, opinions in Colorado toward Japanese Americans were divided. In a special report on the Japanese situation in Colorado, the attitude of Coloradoans reflected the national mistrust of Japanese Americans: "Most people feel that the Japanese are very untrustworthy and that they look out solely for their own interests. They feel that while they have caused no trouble as yet, they will do so if the opportunity presents itself."[32] The Japanese situation in Colorado became a subject of political controversy in 1942 when Governor Carr announced to the nation that Colorado would care for at least 3,500 evacuees if the need arose.[33] Carr's sympathetic attitude brought enormous criticism down on his head, as constituents drew a harder line than their governor regarding the idea of caring for incoming Japanese Americans. Many would not tolerate California Japanese as next-door neighbors, according to the special report, and the "public generally have a healthy hatred of all things Japanese."[34] Like most of the nation during the war, Coloradoans made no distinction between native-born American citizens of Japanese ancestry and Japanese nationals, the subjects of an imperial regime. The JLS instructors, although recruited to help America win the war, descended on a potentially hostile community.

The Denver Post launched a vicious campaign against internees at Heart Mountain Relocation Center in Wyoming and other Japanese. In an exposé of camp life, the *Post* published a produce order for internees at Heart Mountain, revealing that "4,000 pounds of bananas and 2,000 pounds of frozen peaches, as well as many other delicacies" were ordered for consumption in the camp. The exposé "went to the U.S. Senate military affairs committee and one Senator went on to tell the committee that according to his estimates, over seventy percent of internees are disloyal and that all Japanese in the Heart Mountain Camp are housed better than seventy five percent of the people of Wyoming, and have plenty of meat, canned goods, fresh vegetables, fruit, butter, cream, [and] milk."[35] This anti-Japanese campaign led to an attempt by the Colorado legislature in 1944 to pass a constitutional amendment prohibiting Japanese aliens from owning land.[36] The measure passed the Colorado House of Representatives by a vote of 48 to 15 but narrowly failed in the Colorado Senate by a vote of 12 to 15.[37] The environment into which the Japanese American instructors descended seemed rife with resentment and war hysteria.

Despite the obstacles that life in Colorado might have posed, their assimilation was surprisingly smooth in that all of the factors that contributed to a hostile attitude toward the instructors ultimately did not hamper them and their families from finding relative comfort in Boulder. Considering the hostile environment in which Japanese Americans were accustomed to living, the environment of the school and the community, according to a daughter of a JLS instructor, made it seem "like the war was a million miles away."[38] With camp life a recent memory, Boulder seemed to awaken the instructors and their families from a long, confusing nightmare.

What enabled the instructors and their families to have a good and safe life while surrounded by war hysteria, racism, and discrimination? Why was Boulder different from the rest of the United States, which did not see Japanese Americans as citizens of the same country? Only forty miles away in Denver, Japanese Americans were passively enduring a hate campaign led by *The Denver Post* and leading officials. How was the reception of the JLS instructors managed so successfully?

In an effort to understand the impact of various degrees of association on multiracial relations, in 1950 Paul Irish interviewed university leaders, Boulder residents, and former JLS instructors. His conclusions about the reasons for the relatively smooth assimilation of JLS instructors into the Boulder community during the war portray a successful campaign by university and civic leaders to gain acceptance and support. Boulder residents were not forewarned that the JLS was moving to Boulder because the navy considered the program a "secret weapon."[39] However, when the school began operations, officials of the University of Colorado and the U.S. Navy mobilized public agencies such as the Boulder City Council and the city's newspaper, *The Boulder Daily Camera*, into selling the community on the benefits of housing the school and its instructors.

University personnel appeared before community organizations and presented the case for the language school.[40] University of Colorado president Robert L. Stearns was interested first and foremost in the university's image and external relations.[41] Stearns sought to sell the community on the idea of the JLS and the new Japanese American instructors by appealing to residents' patriotism for the war effort. Like saving scrap metal and knitting socks for soldiers, the language school became Boulder's "war industry" and the tolerance exercised by residents a form of war participation. In a full-page advertisement published in *The Daily Camera*, Boulder citizens were solicited to make the necessary effort and help house the language school instructors: "The United States Navy asks Boulder to meet the most important quota Boulder has ever been asked to meet . . . and immediately."[42] The response was impressive, and Boulder's own war industry was soon well under way.

In an independent gesture, the university newspaper, the *Silver and Gold*, and its student writers backed the new instructors and relocated Japanese Americans in general. In retaliation to the *Post*'s hate campaign against the Japanese, university students responded: "Now that the *Denver Post* has embraced Hitler's doctrines of race and Aryan superiority, now that the *Post* has converted this war from a battle of principles or even of nations into a battle of peoples, now that the *Post* has declared war on the Japanese Americans in our cities and internment camps, it's about time we college students registered our protests against such fascist techniques in our midst."[43]

President Stearns took great care to ensure a positive reception of the JLS instructors, and his jurisdiction undoubtedly included the *Silver and Gold*. However, the strong show of support from university students reflected an unmitigated resistance to the war hysteria and a constituency supportive of the JLS instructors and their families.

The instructors and their families keenly felt the care university and naval officials took to create a positive image of the language school and its Japanese American instructors. Mikio Suzuki, son of former instructor Koshi Suzuki, was eleven when he left the Topaz Relocation Center to join his father in Boulder: "When I came to Boulder I didn't really know what to expect but everybody was very, very nice to me. To the best of my knowledge I didn't run into any prejudice. There were a few incidents here and there but not by any of my friends. I thought that Boulder was a very good place for a child to grow up in and it was kind of sad when we had to leave."[44] Mikio's memories echo those of many instructors and their families upon arriving in Boulder.

Basing his conclusions on interviews conducted with the instructors, civic leaders, and Caucasian residents, Paul Irish argues that the Japanese instructors were received well considering the war hysteria. Successful efforts to sell the community by using official navy and university endorsement of the instructors and gaining the support of local leaders and media were the major contributors to this success. His conclusion, however, does not attribute part of the success of the assimilation to the actions of the instructors and their families.

Japanese Americans participated actively in the attempt to allay fears about their presence in Boulder. As their husbands toiled at the university twelve to fourteen hours a day, the instructors' wives performed two tasks: doing war work in the community as good publicity for the school and working as teachers' aides at the JLS alongside their husbands. As part of the effort to sell the community on the usefulness and integrity of its new Japanese American residents, President Stearns mobilized the instructors' wives to go out into the community to perform war work. Miya Sano became the first JLS nurse's aide at Boulder Community Hospital.⁴⁵ University administrators also approached Vickie Yumoto to do war work; she volunteered for the Women's Auxiliary board, rolled bandages, and knitted khaki-colored shirts and socks.⁴⁶ JLS wives were also organized to present aspects of Japanese culture, such as the tea ceremony, to the community. Miya Sano organized and participated in a Japanese tea ceremony at a local Presbyterian Church that was attended by community members.⁴⁷

In addition to working in the community, the language skills of wives of JLS instructors were also utilized at the school. Because there were too few native speakers for navy officers to practice listening to, Chiyoko Otagiri, Kathleen Kazuko Okamoto, and other wives of instructors read Japanese books aloud in Japanese for the students to hear. They received a salary for their efforts. Whether in the community or at the language school, the wives of JLS instructors played an integral role in selling the community and in the success of the language program.

In addition to civic engagement, Japanese Americans also engaged in constant self-censorship and self-monitoring to avoid potential difficulties. Many instructors remember the care they took to keep a low profile. "Our neighbors did nothing to harm us but I remember how careful we were," said Martha Imai.⁴⁸ Martin Hirabayashi, too, maintained a careful attitude: "Our contacts with the community were most enjoyable, though we were cautious to be sure that we would not cause any social problems."⁴⁹ The reserve the Japanese American instructors exercised was instrumental in their reasonably smooth assimilation into the Boulder community.

Despite the best efforts of both community leaders and Japanese Americans, incidents of discrimination did occur. Martha Imai remembered her family's arrival in Boulder: "When we had just arrived in Boulder, we had heard and was [sic] warned against going to a certain restaurant in downtown Boulder—for they resented our presence and would not serve us. Their signs on the window read, 'No Japs Are Allowed.' These conditions were very hurtful and humiliating."⁵⁰

Instructors interviewed were well aware of the potential problems that might occur in their new community and took pains to avoid conflict. Although the Japanese American instructors at the JLS received special endorsement from the U.S. government and the university, the reality for "unprotected" Japanese Americans was always within view. While the Boulder City Council supported the school and its instructors, it did not support Japanese Americans as a whole. On August 4, 1942, the council moved to adopt a program that restricted Japanese Americans from settling in Boulder. In addition, it established a cap on the total number of Japanese Americans in Boulder, not to exceed seventy-five.[51] This policy also prevented many family members of JLS instructors from joining them in Boulder because most were not American citizens.[52]

Stearns urged the instructors to form a Committee for Public Relations to attend to incidents needing "special attention." The committee instructed all members of the Japanese faculty to be certain that their actions provoked no community or neighborhood animosity. In a congenial gesture, the committee officially expressed appreciation to the community by thanking the citizens for welcoming the instructors to Boulder and for making their residence there "possible and comfortable."[53]

Receiving the new instructors cordially required a leap of faith for many Boulder residents and for some proved more difficult than sending their own son to war: "[S]trangely, one of the hardest things to take, it being a small town after all, was the installing of a Japanese family next door."[54] In an article in *The Kansas Magazine* in 1944, Boulderite Margaret Henderson described her experiences as an ambivalent neighbor of a Japanese American JLS instructor and his family. At first, she hid her severe reaction from her new neighbors and "a sort of friendliness grew, but a friendliness founded only on a common garden interest . . . a quaint friendship that began and ended at the back door."[55]

By a remarkable coincidence, Margaret's soldier son was saved in the Pacific by a former JLS graduate and his Japanese language skills. The ensign who saved her son's life told him about the JLS and the "faculty that are teaching their native language to their fellow-Americans [and] are doing one of the finest, most important, and bravest things of this whole war."[56] After hearing this unbelievable story from her son, Margaret resolved to take her friendship with her neighbors a step further, and she invited them into her home. Margaret was not convinced of the need to be sincerely cordial to her Asian neighbors until their relationship was placed within the context of the war effort. Her war responsibility was to tolerate the naturally intolerable presence of her new neighbors.

Miya Sano vividly remembered an incident that occurred while she was volunteering as a nurse's aide in the Boulder hospital. She was looking after patients and seeing to their comfort when one female patient was shocked by Miya's presence (or ethnicity) and screamed that Miya had come to kill her. Miya recalled, "I was good enough to come and help. I wasn't getting paid or anything like that; I was just helping out."[57]

New JLS instructors were also apprehensive about their reception in the classroom. Allen Okamoto described his parents' misgivings about the new environment:

> When my father first was assigned here, he and my mother were very apprehensive about coming. Japan was at war with the United States and he was going to be teaching the Navy personnel, coming into a situation in the middle of America; he didn't really know what to expect. My father retells the story that the first day of class, when he entered the room, the students stood at attention and he said from that moment on, he knew that things were going to be okay.[58]

Irish mentions unpleasant episodes Japanese Americans experienced in the Boulder community, told to him by Japanese Americans residing in Boulder in 1950, including a barbershop whose owner refused to serve Japanese customers and real estate companies that refused to sell property to Japanese.[59] These incidents affected the JLS instructors and make problematic the conclusion that their assimilation into the Boulder community was entirely smooth. Further, the influence of the reserve the instructors exercised also prevents a fully positive assessment of their reception. Although the majority of Japanese Americans Irish interviewed felt they were treated cordially by merchants, students, and townsfolk, isolated incidents of individuals acting against Japanese Americans attest to the wartime climate of racism that could be quelled yet not erased by the wartime effort.

CONCLUSION

Life in Boulder, Colorado, provided a respite for the instructors and their families, weary from enduring the hardest of times. The Rocky Mountains seemed to shelter them from the hate to which they had grown accustomed. Yet even in this small town, with its churches and banks on every corner, the instructors could not avoid the racism and mistrust beneath the friendly surface. The protection their war work afforded and their understanding of their predicament enabled the JLS instructors and their families to find some balance between comfort and caution. The JLS instructors' success in Boulder is attested to not by the exceptional nature of the community; rather, it was in part a result of the integrity and patience of those who comprised Boulder's "war industry." War hysteria had caused Japanese Americans to police themselves and to avoid the attention and possible hostility of their neighbors.

Regardless of their ambivalence, the JLS instructors performed their roles so effectively and connected with the students so profoundly that the school excelled beyond the intent of the program and impacted future generations, who seldom realize that the current university program in Asian studies was started by a JLS graduate. The success of the JLS program's ability to foster understanding between the United States and Japan has far outlived the controversy within both the government and Japanese American communities regarding war participation and the paradox of war work. Over fifty years later, the efforts of the JLS instructors have transcended the politics that gave birth to their roles in the war effort. If World War II inextricably linked the fates of the United States and Japan, then the efforts of the JLS instructors ensured that the tools to nurture the relationship were at hand.

For many historians of the Internment, Japanese American achievements in the war won the nation's respect and directly led to its formal apology in a congressional bill signed by President Ronald Reagan in 1988, which forever lifted the stigma of disloyalty that hung as a cloud over Japanese Americans. California state representative Charles H. Wilson, during a 1963 congressional tribute to Japanese Americans who participated in the war effort, declared, "I think we can say with truth that it was the Japanese American fighting men that proved to our government of that day the loyalty and patriotism of the Nisei."[60] Japanese Americans did not have to cross the ocean to find their own battlefields raging in towns and cities throughout the United States. Despite their struggles outside the school, the JLS instructors performed their duties and in the process deeply impacted their students and inspired them to see the Japanese and Japanese Americans as human beings first.

The JLS not only revolutionized language education in the United States and Japanese language programs across the country through its curriculum, but it also sent forth Japanese language officers who, with their newly acquired proficiency and affection for their Japanese American instructors, conducted themselves valiantly in the Pacific theater and beyond. The "Boulder Boys" as they came to be called, with their appreciation for the Japanese people gained at the JLS, pressed for civil treatment of Japanese prisoners of war while on the battlefield. They also attempted to save Japanese soldiers and civilians at Okinawa and Iwo Jima by convincing them to surrender. A JLS soldier received an award for rescuing a Japanese unit from starvation as a result of bureaucratic neglect.[61] Still close to their instructors and their experiences in Boulder, JLS alumni acquired a sensitivity to and admiration for the Japanese people that followed them into war and impacted their decisions.

The furthest-reaching legacy, however, involves what the students did at home after returning from their wartime duties. Many returned to graduate school with the intent to make Japan and Japanese culture their professions. Donald Keene (1942), Edward Seidensticker (1942), Helen Craig McCullough

(1944), Thomas C. Smith (1943), and Roy Andrew Miller (1946) became internationally renowned scholars of Japanese literature, history, and linguistics.[62] These former JLS students "not only demystified Japan, they dispelled the vicious negative stereotypes of Japan by giving Americans an image based on a deep knowledge of Japanese language and culture," according to David Arase, a professor of politics at Pomona College and son of former JLS instructor Noboru Arase.[63] Donald Keene, an alum and a professor of Japanese literature at Columbia University, spoke of the impact the JLS had on his life: "My whole life was changed by my experience in learning Japanese . . . my whole way of looking at the world would have been different [without that experience]. Japan has been the most important factor in my life. . . . [M]y past was nothing; it has disappeared completely, so powerful was this experience and so memorable were the people I met."[64]

The experiences at the JLS altered the life directions of many of its students. The JLS instructors nurtured their students' interest in the Japanese language and culture and sent them out to bridge peace between Japan and the United States and to foster understanding through Asian studies programs throughout the country. The JLS created a place for Japanese studies on American campuses through its generation of linguists who returned after the war and established leading academic programs to train succeeding generations of aspiring Japan scholars. One former student wrote of this transmission of empathy through his study of Japanese at the JLS: "It is my personal belief that it is next to impossible for anyone to learn a foreign language without unconsciously developing sympathy for and understanding of the peoples who speak that language. This is a conviction that comes from my own experience."[65]

The legacy of the Japanese language instructors at the Navy Japanese Language School under the most adverse conditions lives on in their students, in the programs they inspired, and in future generations of Japan scholars, ensuring that such "war work" will never be needed again.

Few people in Colorado know about the Navy Japanese Language School and its temporary residence at the University of Colorado at Boulder during World War II. In addition, the achievements of their students overshadowed the JLS instructors and their contribution to the war effort and education about Japan in the United States. After the war ended, the majority of instructors returned to their previous homes on the West Coast and began to pick up the pieces of their lives in an environment that was openly hostile toward anything Japanese. Miya and Joe Sano decided to stay in Boulder to raise their three children and send them to the University of Colorado. Joe has since passed away, but Miya is in her nineties and still lives in Boulder. At the university, a plaque has been installed in memory of the students and instructors at the JLS, and the university archives houses the school's collection. Scholars visit the archives to research the school, but little information can be found about the instructors. With quiet dignity, the efforts of the JLS instructors still foster an understanding of and sympathy for the Japanese in Asian studies programs throughout the United States. Few people know about the Navy Japanese Language School and its instructors, but everyone who studies the language or culture of Japan still feels their impact today.

NOTES

1. Miya Sano, interview with author, Boulder, CO, 2001; Jessica N. Arntson, "Journey to Boulder: The Japanese American Instructors of the Navy Japanese Language School" (MA thesis, University of Colorado, 2003), transcript, appendix A, 86–161 (all transcripts of interviews by the author are found in appendix A of this thesis).

2. *The Pacific War and Peace: Americans of Japanese Ancestry in Military Intelligence Service, 1941–1952* (San Francisco: National Japanese American Historical Society, 1991), introduction. Other Japanese Americans who participated in the war effort include those who saw action in combat, such as the highly decorated all-Nisei volunteer regiments of the 442nd Regimental Combat Team, the 100th Infantry Battalion, and the 522nd Field Artillery Battalion. In addition, many Japanese Americans served during World War II in intelligence duties, utilizing their language skills in the Pacific theater as soldiers in the army's MIS.

3. Tomi Kaizawa Knaefler, *Our House Divided* (Honolulu: University of Hawaii Press, 1991), 17.

4. Roger Daniels, *America's Concentration Camps* (New York: Garland, 1989), vol. 4.

5. War Relocation Authority, *Project Director's Weekly Report*, James G. Lindley, project director, Granada, CO, October 31, 1942, Japanese American Evacuation and Relocation Survey Collection, Archives, Norlin Library, University of Colorado at Boulder, n.p.

6. Code talkers were Navajo members of the Marine Corps division in the Asian-Pacific theater who coded and decoded messages in their native language (modified for code purposes) almost instantaneously as "human code machines." The actions of the 420 code talkers were instrumental in the Pacific theater and transformed code breaking into a tactical maneuver. See Bruce Watson, "Navajo Code Talkers: A Few Good Men," *Smithsonian* 24, 5 (August 1993): 35.

7. *The Pacific War and Peace*, 11.

8. Monty Montgomery to Captain Roger Pineau, Pineau Collection, Archives, Norlin Library, University of Colorado at Boulder.

9. Monty Montgomery, *Saying Goodbye: A Memoir of Two Fathers* (New York: Alfred A. Knopf, 1989), 128–133.

10. The surviving instructors and their families were recognized for the first time in an official ceremony held by the U.S. Navy and Pomona College's Pacific Basin Institute on November 2, 2002.

11. During the Internment of over 120,000 people of Japanese ancestry from the West Coast, no distinction was made between Japanese American citizens and "aliens," or non-citizens. See Ronald Takaki, *Strangers from a Different Shore: A History of Japanese Americans* (Boston: Little, Brown, 1989), 391.

12. Robert A. Wilson and Bill Hosokawa, *East to America* (New York: William Morrow, 1980), 235.

13. Bill Hosokawa, *Nisei: The Quiet Americans* (New York: William Morrow, 1969), 360.

14. Masako Duus, *Unlikely Liberators* (Honolulu: University of Hawaii Press, 1987), 58.

15. Hosokawa, *Nisei: The Quiet Americans*, 360.

16. Ibid.

17. Takako Ishizaki, interview with author, Boulder, CO, June 7, 2002.

18. Ibid.

19. Takako Ishizaki, unpublished biography of Koshi Suzuki, JLS Instructors Collection, Archives, Norlin Library, University of Colorado at Boulder.

20. Katherine Otagiri to author, September 12, 2002, JLS Instructors Collection, Archives, Norlin Library, University of Colorado at Boulder.

21. Ibid.

22. Wilson and Hosokawa, *East to America*, 283. Also known as the National Origins Act, the Immigration Act forbade immigration by aliens "ineligible for citizenship," such as all Issei, or aliens living in the United States. Issei remained ineligible for U.S. citizenship until 1952, when the U.S. Congress passed the Walter-McCarran Act and lifted the ban on Japanese immigration, thereby allowing Issei to become naturalized citizens.

23. Kozo Fuji to William Hudson, January 16, 1989, Pineau Collection, Archives, Norlin Library, University of Colorado at Boulder.

24. Allen Okamoto, interview with author, Boulder, CO, June 7, 2002.

25. Edwin Yamada, interview with author, Boulder, CO, June 6, 2002.

26. Kaya Kitagawa to author, November 2, 2002, JLS Instructors Collection, Archives, Norlin Library, University of Colorado at Boulder.

27. James Otagiri to Mr. Asano, March 22, 1943, JLS Instructors Collection, Archives, Norlin Library, University of Colorado at Boulder.

28. Yamada interview.

29. Russell Endo, "Japanese of Colorado: A Sociohistorical Portrait," *Journal of Social and Behavioral Sciences* 31 (1985): 105.

30. Daniels, *America's Concentration Camps*, vols. 4 and 6, n.p.

31. Quoted in ibid.

32. Ibid., "Special Report on the Japanese Situation in Colorado, April 20, 1942," vol. 4, n.p.

33. *The Rocky Mountain News*, March 1, 1942, 1.

34. Daniels, *America's Concentration Camps*, vol. 4, n.p.

35. Cited in ibid.

36. Articles in *The Denver Post*: "Petition to Bar Jap Aliens from Colorado Land Filed," February 17, 1944, 32; "New Drive Started to Bar Jap Aliens," February 10, 1944, 1; "Granada Nips Cannot Vote in Colorado," March 19, 1944; "Anti-Japanese Petition Filed with 8,000 Names to Spare," March 7, 1944; "Letters Commend Denver Post for Stand on Japs in America," April 11, 1943; "Jap Camps Spread Hate for U.S., Says Chandler," April 21, 1943; "Supreme Court Votes to Bar Japs from Voting," May 2, 1943, 1.

37. Endo, "Japanese of Colorado," 105.

38. Marion Shikamura Osborne, interview with author, May 28, 2002.

39. Paul Donald Irish, "Reactions of Residents of Boulder, Colorado to the Introduction of Japanese into the Community" (MA thesis, University of Colorado at Boulder, 1950).

40. Ibid., 164.

41. Frederick S. Allen, *The University of Colorado, 1876–1976: A Centennial Publication of the University of Colorado* (New York: Harcourt Brace Jovanovich, 1976), 118.

42. Paid advertisement, *The Boulder Daily Camera*, November 14, 1942.

43. Editorial, *Silver and Gold,* April 27, 1943, 2. (Other editorials concerning the *Post's* coverage of Japanese Americans can be found in these issues: April 30, May 7, May 18, and June 30, 1943).

44. Mikio Suzuki, interview with author, June 17, 2002.

45. Sano interview.

46. Vickie Yumoto, interview with author, September 25, 2001.

47. Sano interview.

48. Martha Imai, telephone interview with author, October 15, 2001.

49. Martin Hirabayashi to author, September 13, 2001, JLS Instructors Collection, Archives, Norlin Library, University of Colorado at Boulder.

50. Imai interview.

51. The program stated that "1) any Japanese Americans who wished to move to Boulder had to have the approval of the Commandant of the Twelfth Naval District to leave the restricted areas, 2) had to submit evidence of self-support or employment in Boulder for a year in advance, 3) had to [be] approved by a Council committee, 4) had to make the total number of Japanese Americans residing in Boulder not greater than seventy-five individuals and 5) had to be American citizens." Boulder City Council Minutes, August 4, 1942, Carnegie Library, Boulder, CO.

52. The policy adopted by the Boulder City Council restricted JLS instructors from sending for their parents; however, it did not entirely prevent all instructors from bringing relatives to Boulder. Okamoto interview.

53. *The Boulder Daily Camera*, August 18, 1943, 5.

54. Margaret Henderson, "Sharper than the Sword," *The Kansas Magazine* (1944): 17.

55. Ibid., 20.

56. Ibid.

57. Sano interview.

58. Okamoto interview.

59. Irish, "Reactions of Residents," 164–165.

60. Quoted in Wilson and Hosokawa, *East to America*, 244.

61. Lt. J.G. Paul Desjardins, JLS class of 1943, JLS Collection, Archives, Norlin Library, University of Colorado at Boulder.

62. Other JLS graduates who went into Asian studies include, but are not limited to, William T. DeBary (1943), University of Chicago; Frank Gibney (1943), Pacific Basin Institute, Pomona College; Soloman Levine (1943), University of Michigan; Roger Pineau (1943), Massachusetts Institute of Technology; Robert Scalapino (1943), University of California at Berkeley; Donald Willis (1943), University of Colorado at Boulder; Ivan Morris (1944), Columbia University; Francis Hilary Conroy (1944), University of Pennsylvania; and Sidney Brown (1945), University of Oklahoma.

63. Teresa Watanabe, "Boulder Boys Shape Japan-US Relations," *The Coloradoan*, February 2001, 13.

64. Speech given at the Bridge to the Rising Sun Pomona Conference, April 2000, Pomona, CA.

65. Edward L. Hart (JLS 1943), "The Need Beyond Reason," *Charles E. Merrill Monograph Series* 10 (Provo, UT: Brigham Young University, 1976), 80.

William M. King

"So They Say": Lieutenant Earl W. Mann's World War II *Colorado Statesman* Columns

> Nothing discloses real character like the use of POWER. It is easy for the weak to be gentle. Most people can bear adversity. But if you want to know what a man really is, give him POWER. This is the supreme test.
>
> It is both interesting and enlightening to take note of the acts of various public officials; their reaction to matters affecting their constituency, and their analysis of these issues. Our country is sorely in need of men—not politicians, but men of character whose vision cannot be destructed by the petty occurrences of life.[1]

This chapter is about race, politics, and war in Colorado. Its principal source material is the series of columns written by Earl W. Mann, the third African American to serve in the Colorado State Legislature, following his election to that body in the fall of 1942.[2] These columns—almost 300 in all[3]—appeared weekly, with an occasional republication, in *The Colorado Statesman* between September 1, 1939, and September 2, 1945. *The Colorado Statesman* is one of Denver's oldest Black newspapers, founded in 1894 by Joseph D.D. Rivers with the assistance of Edwin H. Hackley. The columns, more illustrative than exhaustive of those available, begin with the German attack on Poland, continue with the beginning of war in Europe, and go on through the Japanese signing the "Instruments of Surrender" on the deck of the USS *Missouri* in Tokyo Bay, ending the conflict. Several of Mann's prewar offerings are included to create context and to establish a baseline against which to relate his later writings with his earlier writings. Around 11 million Americans were in uniform during this period, over 1 million of them African Americans who saw most of their service (except for a few small "test groups" near the end of the war and those serving on U.S. Navy ships) in segregated units, subject to discriminatory treatment from the military and civilian sectors of the society.

More often than not, the genesis for a column was an event Mann had witnessed or heard about, an article or book he had read, a letter he received,[4] a conversation he had with another person—Black or White—or simply something that struck his fancy and which he wrote about to illustrate and illuminate a larger issue he believed was important. This is particularly the case when the subject of a column, in any of the three periods identified in this chapter, addressed what might be called international or foreign affairs. The second- and third-period columns discussed here have been divided into two groups—those published before the attack on Pearl Harbor that initiated official American involvement in the war and those published thereafter, beginning with "David and Goliath," which appeared in the *Statesman* on December 12, 1941.

A recurrent theme in the second-period group is Mann's repeated contention that America's deep and abiding commitment to the preservation of white supremacy in its treatment of Blacks and other peoples of color was a far greater threat to the continuance of democracy than were Hitler and his counterparts, regardless of what the Axis powers (principally Germany, Japan, and Italy) might do. At the same time, however, he does not hesitate to exploit the excesses of the National Socialists to make the point that their racial policies and practices are different from those of the United States only in their brazenness and mass application, suggesting along the way, in both the prewar and wartime columns, that they might have learned some of their techniques by observing how the United States treated its Negro population.

In the third-period columns, Mann's apparent objective was to illuminate the observations made by Arthur Marwick and Gerald D. Nash, noted later, respecting the strains total war places on extant social institutions and the extra resources that must be brought in to deal with those strains. Further, he writes about what he sees as the consequences that might follow from newly created opportunities that were not there before the onset of the crisis—both for the institutions in question and the people who were called to duty after the war concluded.

Upon reflection, it seems clear that Mann's intended audience was neither Black nor White per se but was rather whoever he believed would take his words, chew and digest them, and act on them to reconcile the conflicts that inhibited the spread of democracy in the United States—a nation he believed talked a good game but did not always follow through on its intentions. In addition, his writings appear to have been motivated by his belief that he had a duty to the society to share with it the wisdom of his experience. Yes, he was bedeviled, as is evident in a number of these columns, by caste and class issues. However, he sees himself as a community leader who abhors facile solutions to complex problems because that is not the way the world works. He is, then, not a stereotypical Republican;[5] in not so being, he makes it easier for us to understand and appreciate the limitations inherent in all simplistic labeling. Before turning to the three sets of columns, it seems prudent to provide biographical information on Earl W. Mann and to briefly describe a few of the several contexts within which he wrote.

EARL WASHINGTON MANN: BIOGRAPHICAL OVERVIEW

Earl Washington Mann was born on a farm in Lyons, Clinton County, Iowa, on June 8, 1886. He was the son of Washington Mann of Virginia and Ida Robinson of Georgia. According to his obituary published in *The Denver Post*,[6] Mann "was a direct uncle of the world's greatest tenor singer, Roland Hayes, Mr. Mann being the brother of Mr. Hayes' mother," Fanny. With her husband, William, both former slaves, Fanny resided in Curryville, Georgia, at the time of Hayes's birth.[7]

Additional details about his life appear in a column titled "Passing Show," published on August 12, 1938, one week after Mann announced his first run for the state legislature. However, this column is more a candidate biography than his regular columns that began in 1937 and will be used to supplement his obituary to flesh out salient aspects of Mann's life.

In this column he writes that he came to Denver in 1919 as a patient at Fitzsimons Hospital, to which he would return several times over the course of his life,[8] "because he was disabled from exposure to [chlorine] gas while in action in France" during World War I.[9] He was honorably discharged from the army later that year. His intention was to enter the state university at Champaign, Illinois, to study mechanical engineering. He returned to Denver as a permanent resident in March 1920.[10]

Earl Mann graduated from Lyons High School in Iowa, completed a year of business college, and at age twenty moved to "Chicago to further his training in stationary engineering." He worked on automobiles for five years and then entered Lane Technical School to take "a course in engineering." Subsequently, he worked at the Lafayette Hotel in Clinton and at the Peter Van Schaack Drug firm back in Chicago. In 1914 Mann moved back to Champaign to enter the auto mechanic business. When the call came for men to enlist after the U.S. entry into World War I in 1917, he responded; completion of the officer's course at Fort Des Moines, Iowa, resulted in his commission as a first lieutenant prior to assignment to the 366th Infantry.[11] Mann was proud of his commission, and for the rest of his life he used that title rather than the standard male honorific "Mr."

From 1922 to 1925 after his return to Denver, he read the law in the office of Attorney Samuel E. Carey, for whom a local Black bar association was named after he died. He writes that he had to quit because the intensity of his studies adversely affected his health. Still, he learned enough to secure a posting as a deputy U.S. marshal, which lasted for more than a year before a recurrence of his lung problems forced a return to Fitzsimons for further treatment.[12] He also served as a court bailiff, something he refers to in a later column describing his fitness for public office.

On April 29, 1926, in the parsonage of Shorter A.M.E. Church, he married Grace Wills, who had arrived in Denver from St. Paul, Minnesota, in 1925. She died on October 10, 1974,[13] and was interred beside her husband at Fort Logan National Cemetery south of the city. They had no children.

In 1933 Mann secured a position in the Denver City Water Department,[14] and in 1938 he announced his first run for the Colorado State Legislature.[15] He did not win in the general election that November, as most African Americans whose support he sought were voting Democratic by that time, but he did place in the Republican primary election with largely White support. In 1940 there was a similar result.[16] In 1942, with significant political support from the Adolph Coors family, Mann was elected to the Colorado State Assembly. He was the third Black legislator to serve the citizens of Denver in the House of Representatives. His tenure totaled five terms, from 1943 to 1948 and 1951 to 1954.

While in the legislature, Mann focused primarily on very technical and specific bills in the areas of municipal and county affairs. Isetta Crawford Rawls writes that his most significant contribution was assisting the "passage of the Fair Employment Practices Act and defeat of a bill forbidding Japanese people to own land in Colorado."[17] It was as a columnist and civic leader,[18] however, that Earl W. Mann was best known to citizens of Denver. Early on, probably in 1919, he made friends with Joseph D.D. Rivers, the editor and publisher of *The Colorado Statesman*.[19]

Rivers was born in Lovettsville, Virginia, in 1856. Following his graduation from Hampton Institute in 1882 with honors, where he was a student and disciple of Booker T. Washington,[20] he moved first to Philadelphia and then to Denver in 1885, where he remained until his death from pneumonia on January 17, 1937. He married Richie Smith in 1893 and, like Mann, was a member of Shorter A.M.E. Church. Following Rivers's death, the *Statesman* was run briefly by George W. Davis, the assistant managing editor. Davis died on September 23, 1937, and was succeeded by Paul Hicks, the promotions manager. Hicks, along with E. V. Dorsey, the advertising manager, ran the paper until Dorsey took over in 1940 as owner and editor.[21] The *Statesman* ceased publication in either 1961 or 1962.[22] Throughout its long run of eighty-plus years, the *Statesman* covered the doings of middle-class Black Denver while reprinting materials from papers in other communities.

Editorially, the paper could be very moralistic in tone, especially when describing the behavior of less privileged Negroes that the middle classes saw as injurious to the image and social health of Black Denver at large. Financially, the *Statesman* was supported primarily through subscription revenue and advertisements placed mostly by local Black businesses and, frequently, White establishments large and small that sought an entrée into the Black community. During the Depression the paper shrank in size somewhat but did not suspend publication.

In the two years immediately prior to the U.S. entry into World War II, Black attitudes toward the upcoming conflict might best be summarized by saying that many African Americans saw what was going on in Europe as a "white man's war" that had nothing to do with them. Their concern was with realizing democracy at home, meaning being treated as equals in their struggles to secure respect, education, employment, housing, and health care that would improve the quality of their lives.[23] As for their view of the Japanese, at least since the Russo-Japanese War of 1905 Blacks had tended to see them as exemplars; after all, the Japanese were also colored people who had defeated Whites in combat.[24]

Following the attack on the Pearl Harbor Naval Base in Hawaii on Sunday morning, December 7, 1941, and the subsequent declaration of war by the United States on the Empire of Japan on December 8, 1941, Black Americans evinced an attitude shift. *The Pittsburgh Courier*, followed by *The Chicago Defender*, made clear in February 1942 that this would be a two-front war—against the Axis powers overseas and against prejudice and discrimination at home.[25] These two axes, victory abroad and victory at home, form a framework for an examination and assessment of the columns authored by Mann.

Under the first axis, he wrote about the military experiences of Black troops—recruiting, segregation, officer attitudes, training, promotions, awards, race relations, military justice, and enemy propaganda[26]—that might be used to lessen the morale of the Negro soldier. Under the second he addressed employment opportunities created by the crisis and the struggles Blacks had to undergo to find and keep jobs in the face of resistance by White workers who felt their security was threatened by the presence of Negroes on the shop floor. Housing, too, was a problem in rapidly expanding communities, like Denver, affected by the war. The presence of men and women in uniform, with less than servile attitudes, also brought trouble with the locals, not the least of which were disturbances in Detroit, Michigan, and New York City in 1943.[27]

Arthur Marwick, in his book *War and Social Change in the Twentieth Century*, writes that total war "is a supreme test of existing institutions, forcing reorganization in the interests of greater efficiency"[28] and requiring, at the same time, the involvement of previously dispossessed groups to meet the growing manpower needs of the crisis situation. Gerald D. Nash, in *The American West Transformed: The Impact of the Second World War*, adds that this gave "a decided impetus to [the] diminution of racial and ethnic prejudices on the part of a majority of Americans."[29] Moreover, it imbued African Americans and other racial and cultural groups, specifically in the West where their numbers were smaller, with heightened self-confidence and self-consciousness that led them to take a more active part in the pursuit of equal rights because of the realization that they were needed, that they were important.[30] The war also altered in some unpredictable ways "the economic, social, political and cultural life of Afro-Americans."[31] This happened because World War II was an event whose significance for Black people was comparable only to the War between the States, 1861–1865, which brought them freedom from bondage. It did not diminish the racial problems in American society, but it did provide a platform for them to protest their second-class citizenship as peoples of African descent in their struggle to be treated as equals.

In 1940, a little less than two years before formal U.S. entry into the war, Black Denver was a community of 7,800 men, women, and children; that number almost doubled by 1950. The Black community was essentially an isolated, segregated enclave centered in the Five Points area of the city (the intersection of 26th Avenue, Washington, Welton, Glenarm, and 27th streets). Negro patrons experienced proscribed service in the "better" restaurants, something they began to protest as early as the 1920s—a legacy inspired in part by the formation of an NAACP chapter in 1915 and by the Universal

Negro Improvement Association, which also had a strong presence in the city.[32] Movie theaters (the exception was the Roxy in the Five Points area) required them to sit in the balcony.

The area's resident population—including the four doctors, three dentists, five lawyers, and four druggists who made up part of its professional class—was composed mainly of small business owners, unskilled laborers, domestics, railroad porters, and employees of the U.S. Postal Service. The public utility companies, gas, electric, telephone, and streetcar services (there was no segregation in cars or buses) employed few Black workers. There were no Blacks on the police force at the time, although one Negro unit in the fire department had a long and glorious history. While the public hospital accepted Negro patients and did allow Black MDs to practice, the private hospitals tended to be totally White and provided very limited opportunities for the training of Black nurses.

Entertainment throughout much of the war was restricted to the clubs, hotels, and lounges on Welton Street and 26th Avenue, churches and local social organizations, and the colored branches of the YMCA and the YWCA. Even Black troops stationed at Lowry Field[33] and other bases along the Front Range—from Cheyenne, Wyoming, to Colorado Springs, Colorado, in increasing numbers after 1942—were not exempt from harassment. Although the U.S.O. at 1417 California Street was "open," most Negro soldiers went to the one at 2563 Glenarm Place, one block east of Welton, as a way of mitigating probable harassment from both military and civilian authorities.[34] While some modest opportunities opened up as a result of increased employment early in the war effort, they did not come without a struggle.[35]

Historically, Denver's Black population had formed numerous clubs and societies; however, these were mostly social in character. While instances of political work are reported here and there throughout the record, in particular the election of John T. Gunnell and Joseph H. Stuart to the Colorado State Legislature in the closing years of the nineteenth century,[36] there does not seem to be a tradition of sustained political activity in the Black community aimed at altering the balance of power in the city to improve life chances for its citizens of color, similar to efforts that occurred in other parts of the West.[37]

EARL W. MANN, THE COLUMNIST

When reading his writings, one acquires respect for the man and the extent to which he kept returning to the idea of character, those mental and moral qualities that are unique to each person. Mann saw a strong moral character as a fundamentally important element in guiding one's verbal and physical behavior. This was especially true when he wrote of human relations and the conflicts they generated in the light of America's seeming inability, perhaps even lack of will, to reconcile contradictions that grew from the heterogeneity of its population and the mono-cultural character of its priorities.[38]

Mann was a person of strong opinions who was not afraid to raise questions that often arose from the way he saw the world. He viewed himself as an American first, and he expected to be treated as an equal. He was not solely a representative of a group he often took to task for not supporting its own organizations or pressing its case for inclusion strongly enough. This tended to give his columns a conservative cast, reflecting his Victorian biases.

Mann believed African Americans in Denver were lethargic and content to let sleeping dogs lie. Their ethos seemed to be "if we do not call undue attention to ourselves, then nothing too bad will befall us." This attitude probably grew out of their realization that they were few in number,[39] held mostly menial jobs, and felt relatively powerless to alter either the conditions of their existence or their position in society. Accordingly, they exhibited more of an accommodationist posture rather than having to be sorry for exhibiting a kind of misinterpreted boldness that might endanger their meager accomplishments.[40]

Mann was both a public scold, in the ways he wrote about U.S. society's less than stellar attempts to abide by the truths it had put on paper, and in some ways not unlike the nineteenth-century "self-made" man Frederick Douglass. After his escape from slavery, Douglass became an orator, a newspaper publisher, and a crusader for human rights, among other things.

THE PREWAR COLUMNS

Mann's first column was an open letter to his comrades published in *The Colorado Statesman*[41] shortly after taking over as the new commander of Wallace Simpson Post No. 29 of the American Legion.[42] Contained herein are many of the themes that reappear in his later writings, beginning as a regular series of columns in 1937. Mann writes that his comrades must divest themselves of their apathy "and join hands with . . . a determined purpose to combat, in an intelligent, well organized, and Christian manner, all issues that must ultimately affect [them] and those dear to [them]." In short, he is making the case for being proactive before it is too late to address crucial issues effectively. Contrast this with what he writes in his first regular column.

Mann begins this untitled column, which appeared on March 6, 1937, by describing the actions of one Frank Bailey (colored) who shot up the office of the Denver County Public Welfare Bureau, killing three persons and wounding several others.[43] He does not condone Bailey's actions; however, society is not without responsibility here. A system that so demoralizes a man's soul through frequent rejections because of his color, he writes, might justify Bailey's belief that he was not wanted, that he was not desired, thereby occasioning the reported actions. If only those in charge had exhibited "a little more of the milk of human kindness," perhaps this tragedy could have been avoided.

In subsequent columns, Mann writes that society should honor its creed and rise above the failings of its constituent members. On July 10, 1937, he writes that no "trait in mankind is more destructive than that of insincerity, or hypocrisy. The individual who simulates virtue or piety for the purpose of winning approbation or favor, feigning to be other or better than he is[,] has been one of the greatest drawbacks to civilization's program of social uplift."

His August 20, 1937, response to the appointment of Hugo Black, a former senator from Alabama and a Democrat, to the U.S. Supreme Court reveals his ideological biases more clearly. Mann writes that it is "indeed regrettable that the economic and social security of a struggling people must be pawned to assure a partisan solidarity." He concludes the editorial first by asking his readers whether "the vicious and inhuman practices of the South [will] conquer the North, or will the spirit of those hardy Northerners who sacrificed their all to make and maintain America 'free and civilized' arise again, and diffuse the spirit and letter of Christian fellowship throughout this 'un-Christianized' land" and second by writing that the realization of human rights in the United States will require a critical consciousness to appreciate how "war, famine, pestilence, calamities, poverty and death recognize no 'class, race or color' in their claim." Accordingly, he hopes Justice Black will be able to "detach himself from unsound traditions, teachings, and philosophies, and by his decisions uphold the dignity of the world's greatest tribunal, the U.S. Supreme Court."

On September 3, 1937, Mann observes, in anticipation of a question that will be raised by the actions of African Americans after 1939, that the loyalty of Black people "to the institutions that have made both State and Nation cannot be disputed." In short, Black people must be included in the government, in power-sharing positions, so that democracy in America becomes more than a myth.

With the coming of a new year, Mann asks in a page 1 column whether America is destined "To Be Stamped by the Curse of Depravity," of the type he had described in earlier columns but revisited here.[44] His concern was with two topics: the southern "claim that if Negroes did not seek social equality all would be well" and the fact that the anti-lynching bill, supposedly intended to protect individuals, actually represented another case of federal intrusion into states rights. Not only was the term "social equality . . . both a misnomer and fallacious," it was also clear that "the hue of the skin [did] not stamp one as being another's social equal."[45] Moreover, while the savagery of those who felt threatened by Black people seeking treatment as equals needed to be punished, this was something best done locally. As long as these people were not held accountable, "additional hatred [might] some day . . . burst forth in various forms of violence, neither could the larger society continue to escape a charge of complicity that further eroded whatever moral standard the nation pretended to embrace."[46]

On April 22, 1938,[47] Earl Mann's column acquired the name "So They Say," by which it was known from that date until the paper ceased publication. In the April 22 column, which followed Easter Sunday (April 18), he writes, "There can be no security for the rich, nor advancement for the poor, as long as man refuses to adhere to the fundamentals of Christian fellowship." He wonders here, also, about the "many persons coming to this so-called land of the free, and home of the brave, to escape oppression abroad, [who] become most intolerant in their social views after a brief sojourn here." This raises the question of whether there is something in America's air, water, or soil that makes it "a breeding place for bigotry in all of its nauseating forms."

Having announced his candidacy for public office in August, Mann writes in a column published on September 2, 1938,[48] that one question that seems to be asked again and again is "what will the Negro do," as if Negroes are some strange alien "Other" incapable of being understood. Black people's increasing departure from the Republican Party probably generated this question, especially in light of the forthcoming election. After several weeks of repeated columns and columns that dealt with topics covered earlier, the column of May 26, 1939,[49] is of particular interest.

The second half of the column addresses a recent decision handed down by the Colorado State Supreme Court to the effect that "Negroes must be permitted to vote, irrespective of State Legislation to the contrary." Commending the members of the court, Mann writes that White Americans cannot sustain their claims of superiority by erecting barriers and obstacles to artificially stay their competition. Indeed, he concludes, if the country is to continue believing it is a "melting pot," equality of opportunity cannot be compromised in any way, shape, or form.

"So They Say": Columns Published Prior to U.S. Involvement in the Conflict

The column "Negroes Conceded Most Loyal of Americans," published on September 1, 1939, describes Mann's encounter a few days earlier with a gentleman of wealth. This person evidently spoke movingly of the manner in which Negroes had volunteered for service in World War I, demonstrating loyalty to country irrespective of how they had been persecuted—sometimes even in their uniforms—and what solace he felt knowing they would do the same again should the need arise. Mann heard him out and responded almost wistfully, "Thanks, my friend, but could that we depend upon you and yours also." Asked to explain, Mann noted "the lack of recognition of the noble qualities possessed by the Negro, in times of peace" and went on to list a number of incidents in Trinidad and Boulder, Colorado, in which Black folks—including some former servicemen—had been denied food and lodging because of their color. Chastened, the man shook hands and moved on. In parting, Mann commented, "The American dollar may rightfully be referred to as filthy lucre, but [it is] never so unclean as to fail to transcend righteousness."[50]

On September 15, 1939, Mann quoted Justice Louis D. Brandeis of the U.S. Supreme Court: "In establishing the equal right of every person to development, it becomes clear that equal opportunity for all involves this necessary limitation: 'Each man may develop himself so far, but only so far, as his doing so will not interfere with the exercise of a "like right" by all others.' America has believed that each race has something of a peculiar value which it can contribute to the attainment of those high ideals for which it is striving."[51]

From his columns, it is evident that Mann is a minimalist when it comes to government doing things for people and society. He is decidedly in favor of equality of opportunity in keeping with the economic rationales of capitalism and business development, for these items, after all, constitute the activity centers around which social evolution proceeds. This belief can be seen in an editorial titled "Hamburgers," published on April 19, 1940, in which he compares the "Dole" to settling for ground beef when what you really desire is steak. Only by reinvigorating private industry can we increase the income of everyone so that those who wish will have the resources they need to purchase the finer things of life. This is very different from being limited by a kind of federal paternalism that ensures survival but little more.[52]

Returning to a place he visited frequently in his weekly missives, in a column that appeared on May 10, 1940, Mann asked, "What evidence have Negroes given that they want to improve the conditions of their lives?" It is not that prejudice and discrimination are not everyday facts of life for colored people, and if they are, so what. The real issue is, what are they going to do in spite of this reality? For where there is a will, there is a way. Without organization and mobilization within our own communities, he writes, "many of the evils of a civic nature, of which we so loudly wail, are of our own contribution, for as long as we make no organized effort to benefit ourselves, just so long will we remain ghosts of the past." A crisis was coming, Mann told his readers. He even intimated how they might take advantage of it and the stress it would put on all U.S. social institutions. Negroes must accept where they were and what they were and struggle from there to effect a true democracy for each person and for all people.[53]

Mann writes in a column titled "The Curriculum of Hate," published on May 17, 1940, of additional contrasts between the activities of Hitler and those of Whites in the United States. The roots of bigotry, he argues, arise in "proportion to the encouragement, by followers, in the wrongful commission of small offenses against others, [enabling] . . . greater commissions [that follow]." In contrast, "Americanism was, and is, a question of spirit, conviction and purpose, not color or accident of birth." In brief, Hitler alone was not responsible for the depredation of peoples' rights in Germany and elsewhere. He had help, if only in the Burkean notion that "all that is required for evil to triumph is for good men to do nothing."[54]

As the time of America's involvement in World War II drew closer, Mann turned more often in his columns to the U.S. military's reluctance to enlist men of color, believing, as it had before, that White men could do the job alone. This was seen especially in the April 11, 1941, column "Negro Troops." Mann wanted a reduction in the restrictions imposed on Black people in uniform at Fort Warren in Cheyenne, Wyoming, and at Lowry Field in Denver "because of the contributions they are making[,] having been called to defend their country in a time of crisis."[55] Here he also contests the myth of the cowardly Negro soldier. How anyone who has to fight a two-front war because of the color of his skin can be considered a coward escapes him in light of the historical record.

In summarizing this section of the essay, Mann did not directly address the war in Europe extensively prior to the official U.S. entry into the global conflict. He did write, however, about the social consequences for Black people in particular and society in general of the Depression and the buildup to the war, both locally and nationally. Mann also spoke about the conflicts and contradictions that had long been part of the societal fabric and the resultant disparities in housing, employment, schooling, the administration of justice, and health care. Whenever something particularly egregious caught his fancy, his feelings shone through his writing—sometimes bitter, sometimes sardonic, sometimes sad, and sometimes amazed that the United States, with all its faults, was still up and running. What follows next is more of the same but also different, moderated by the lens of "total war."

After U.S. Involvement in the War

Five days after it occurred, in a column titled "David and Goliath" published on December 12, 1941, Mann addressed the Japanese attack on the U.S. Naval Base at Pearl Harbor, Hawaii. He relates the attack to the continuing prejudice and discrimination in the United States. He writes that the observant watcher of the American scene might easily conclude that there was some doubt about "the presence of wide spread patriotism" in the country at large, that this "knowledge [might even have] encouraged little David to strike Goliath. Who knows?" What is clear, however, is that "[r]eal patriotism must incorporate a willingness to understand the basic principles of a Democracy and contribute to its glorification." Indeed, there is some irony in Japan's attack on the navy, the most tradition-bound of the U.S. military services, "whose attitude has been both un-American, and un-Democratic" in its personnel policies. Perhaps this war, he concludes, "will thaw some of the asinine customs and traditions that have no place in America, as immense pressure is sometimes required to remove immense pressure, especially when [the] system of caste is stronger than the basic laws of the nation."[56]

A companion editorial in the same issue of the *Statesman* tells readers that the "strength of a democracy is a moral strength." The United States is now involved in a monumental struggle to "preserve our Democracy," and it is both "dangerous and stupid . . . to continue the sabotage, a morale sabotage, of one-tenth of our population. How this [struggle] is reconciled will tell us much about the country and whether the political victory won by the South at the conclusion of the Civil War and Reconstruction will be sustained at the end of World War II."[57]

What is especially interesting about the closing portion of this essay, which is unsigned but sounds very much like other editorials and columns authored by Mann, is that it presages the "Double V" campaign that will be announced in *The Pittsburgh Courier* in February 1942. Even more interesting is the fact that the essay's final sentence, "Discrimination Does Not Pay the Whites Who Practice It," is capitalized throughout, much like similar passages in many of Mann's other columns.

In columns published on January 9, 1942, "Tarzan the Ape Man," and January 16, 1942, "Tenacity of Purpose," Mann again makes clear that he has no doubt about who will win the war. But what must also happen is that White men must be "taught to get along with law abiding Negroes [and] it may be that this great carnage will convince him that skin pigmentation does not stamp the brand of quality upon either race or individual."[58] Clearly, the war was a chance for Black people to make significant gains, provided they took advantage of the needs of the crisis to press for inclusion in defense industries and the military and by organizing their resources in a timely and efficient manner.

In a column titled "Hitler or the Japs?" published on April 17, 1942, Mann informed his readers of increased agitation toward Japanese residents in Colorado and wondered whether "all of this clap-trap about the yellow peril is but a strategic piece of race mongering, designed to divert the attention of the gullible American public from the activities of that monster of monsters, Herr Adolf." It is unfortunate, he writes, that "of all the civilized peoples of the globe[,] [Americans] entertain a fear, bordering upon hysteria, of the vision of 'Yellow' dominion." Indeed, "America suffers a most peculiar racial and color complex, which is more damaging as a figment than can be any social production that might arise to dispute the popular acceptation that the color of the skin determines 'GREATNESS.'" One way to counter this fear, he concluded, was for the oppressed to organize and employ the power of the ballot to their best advantage; otherwise, they risked yielding their destiny to the forces of ignorance that also flourish in the U.S. democracy.[59]

The topic of war propaganda is addressed in "Eternal Vigilance: The Price of Liberty" on June 12, 1942, following the U.S. naval victories in the Battles of the Coral Sea (May 7–8) and Midway Island (June 3–6). Mann reviews the costs of war in terms of lives lost, persons injured—some permanently disabled—and resources expended "to a degree beyond our comprehension to grasp, in relation to its future influence, and which will lower our American standard of living." Because the war was likely to last for some time, Americans could not permit themselves to be victimized by those who would pit "white against black, Gentile against Jew, Protestant against Catholic, and labor against capital." The question was whether we would allow "Americans [to] fall for Hitler's propaganda?" To give readers examples of the kind of misinformation they would have to fight to sustain the struggle for unity and not defeat themselves from within, as their enemies desired, he then examines some of the "latest releases by Fascist minded white persons [that] have reached this column."[60]

The author of the "tommyrot" he received claimed that "[t]he true spirit of [the] U.S.A. is to unite all of the White people under one White Man's

Flag, and deny all Orientals and Negroes any power to dictate, own or rule any part of a White Man's Country, but to be satisfied to be in a White Man's Country and receive his blessing." The tragedy of this kind of propaganda, Mann contends, was that too many White people and even some Black people would read it, agree with it, and do everything in their power to preserve those policies and practices of prejudice and discrimination that further dissension, requiring vigilance and "a keen interpretation of the forces working to promote additional disharmony in America."

In "Local Observations," published on August 18, 1942, Mann writes about having "listened to one of our tycoons, in his discussion of the Negro, and the Negro problem, in America. Just what are we to do about the Negro, he asked?" As he sought to calm this man's fears, which appeared to have sprung from uncertainty about Blacks' loyalties during the current crisis, Mann reassured him that the "Negro is 'definitely' an American, and . . . the 'most trustworthy' of the so-called non-assimilable peoples."[61]

Less than a month later, in "All Out for Victory," which was intended to spark interest in the upcoming election, Mann mentions being "repeatedly twitted by many white friends for continuous[ly] dealing with the race problem." Mann believes this focus is necessary because "the problem or issue of race occupies a position upon the stage second only to that of the drama of war." He then highlights two incidents in Denver: a Black dentist not allowed to engage in clinical practice at one of the city's largest and most prestigious hospitals and Black women workers at another local hospital who were refused service at a soda fountain across the street, even though the proprietor was a minister "PREACHING THE DOCTRINES OF CHRISTIAN FELLOWSHIP." These instances give a lie to the prattle and cant about equality of opportunity, the supposed bedrock of life in the United States. Indeed, he concludes, there were so many of these kinds of incidents that he doubted "any political party will become a cure-all for the [world's] greatest cancer, racial prejudice. Our only hope for peaceful relations between peoples lies in the extension of an educational program along the lines of equitable adjustments."[62]

In "What Type Leadership," published January 1, 1943, Mann addresses two related questions, one dealing with local affairs and the other with international affairs. The first describes the arrival at Lowry Field "of an outstanding young Negro officer, a Second Lieutenant of the Air Corps." How would White people respond to the man's presence? His own experience, and that of others in World War I, "disproved allegations that Negroes would not follow Negro commissioned and non-commissioned officers upon the battle field, as Negro outfits under such leadership covered themselves with glory."[63] The second issue first appeared in a 1942 column and concerned the Negro's place in the postwar world and how that world might be very different from the prewar world.

Mann addresses this issue again in "Our Country," published on July 16, 1943. What, he asks his readers, might we learn between now and the end of the war, which cannot be that far off? Postwar planning "will call for the soberest judgment and counsel the most conservative action. It will not be a time to fire the imagination, but rather to discover, in calm reason, the way to truth, and justice, and right, and an avoidance of intolerances [that] lead to war. And when we discover these truths, to follow them with fidelity and courage, without fear, hesitation, or weakness." The nation, he believed, must commit to a "new life and purpose . . . or there will be weakness and decay." The country "can no longer confine itself to the narrow limits that have governed it in the past. Black men must be assured of freedom along with white men, or this nation will go as other tyrannical nations have gone."[64]

Three columns—"The Negro at War," published September 8, 1943, "Education Needs," published November 27, 1943, and "The Immutable Law of Progress," published December 11, 1943—address the impact of the war on African Americans. Mann writes that of the 3 million Negro draftees, fewer than 100 were indicted for Selective Service Act violations. Some gains had been made in the defense industries, and he hopes they will not erode once the conflict ends. New curriculum content would be needed to accelerate the demise of racial misunderstandings he believes had been one of the causes of the war.[65]

Two columns, "Who's Winning the War," published March 11, 1944, and "Aiding the Enemy," published June 10, 1944, four days after the Allied invasion of Europe, address different aspects of the same question: the continuing mistreatment of peoples of color to preserve the myth of a White nation. In the first of these columns, he also writes about attempts to change the Colorado State Constitution to "prohibit peoples of dark hue[,] now fighting to preserve this grand state, from real property ownership."[66] In the second, he writes, the war has shown "that we, like our Germanic adversaries, have a touch of the same disease, i.e., distorted racial beliefs," and that these beliefs have cost us in terms of our ability to effect a united front against our enemies. Without economic freedom, political freedom means little: "As long as a large element of our nation subscribe[s] to the theory of especial rights based upon skin pigmentation[,] just so long will chaos reign."[67] As 1944 came to a close and the war seemed all but finished, Mann turned more and more in his columns to the domestic scene, including his reelection to the state legislature in

November. He reported on changes he saw locally and shared with his readers items of importance to Black people in other parts of the country.

On January 13, 1945, Mann addresses postwar educational needs. Technical training, while important, he writes, is less important than placing greater emphasis on improving human relations to eradicate the cancer of racism, to catalyze a longer-lasting peace.[68] This could not be done efficaciously, Mann argues in a column on April 28, 1945, as long as public officials continue to "arrogate unto [themselves] authority at conflict with our laws." The race riots that erupted in New York, Detroit, and Los Angeles in 1943 could have been prevented had these officials not been permitted to "differentiate between their employees upon the basis of race and color. . . . The sowing of seeds of racial discrimination is a dangerous practice, and lest we forget, internal disintegration has crumbled more nations than has invasion by armed adversaries."[69]

In a column titled "V-E Day," published on May 12, 1945, five days after the cessation of hostilities in Europe, Mann reflects on Armistice Day, November 11, 1918. He finds it "difficult to entertain any warm and ardent anticipation of the universal love and peace between people and nations, as long as the germ of racial hatreds and distinctions graduating [the] rights of peoples is so subtly nurtured and cultivated."[70]

Finally, there is the column titled "'Interesting Happenings': A Blunder by Columbus," published on August 18, 1945, nine days after the atomic bombing of Nagasaki and four days after the Japanese capitulated. Mann writes here that as we celebrate the defeat of Japan with great enthusiasm, we must also remember that the United States faces a moral challenge unlike any other since the signing of the Declaration of Independence—namely, the difficulty we have defining who is an American and how Americans who differ from other Americans will be treated.[71]

What exactly does the nation believe? And how is what it believes made manifest in the real world? "Does [it] believe in the ennobling of the individual, and the brotherhood of man? [For throughout] the five years of this bloody global conflict too numerous have been incidents, damnably cruel, reflecting 'yet' racial bigotry and intolerance. Especially has this been true in the South, where Negro soldiers and WACS, in the uniform of their country[,] have been subjected to the most humiliating indignities."

How will the leaders of the 1 million occupation troops be selected, and who will select them?[72] What kind of message will they carry with them when they arrive in the defeated lands? In what ways will their conduct, especially as contrasted with what we do in Europe and what we do in Asia, influence our tenure on the world stage as exemplars to be emulated? "America stands, today, upon the threshold of opportunity. Whether she will prove herself truly democratic, capable of wholesome pattern weaving, or conversely a social fester from which may flow a pollution which may again engulf the entire world remains to be seen." History, he writes, provides many examples from which to choose.

NOTES

1. *The Colorado Statesman*, February 18, 1938, 1, col. 1. Mann speaks here about Alva B. Adams and Edwin C. Johnson, both Democrats who voted to close debate on an anti-lynching bill that was a chief topic of concern for Black people generally and the NAACP specifically.

2. I first became aware of these writings while researching the history of Denver's Black community coeval with the city's founding in 1858.

3. Sometimes a particular subject was the thrust of the entire column. Often he addressed several topics, tying them together at the end. I have had access to all of the columns except when there was a missing issue of the paper on the microfilm or the image itself was so badly damaged that it was unreadable.

4. Mann was a prolific correspondent with a wide range of persons and parties, as letters he received that are contained in his papers make clear. Unfortunately, he does not appear to have kept copies of letters he sent that would provide additional insight into his thinking about the issues that initiated the replies he received.

5. While there were Black Democrats from the nineteenth century onward, African Americas as a group did not shift from the party of Lincoln until the early 1930s. Mann is clear, in describing himself, that he began his political life as a Republican and expected to remain one until he died.

6. May 12, 1969, 54.

7. *New Georgia Encyclopedia*, www.georgiaencyclopedia.org/nge/Article.jsp?id=h–1671.

8. His hospitalizations are periodically reported in the "locals" column of the *Statesman*, especially throughout the 1920s.

9. Mann's papers are housed in the Blair-Caldwell African American Research Library. This branch of the Denver Public Library was dedicated on April 26, 2003, and is located on Welton Street, the longtime main thoroughfare of Black Denver. Hereafter cited as Mann Papers.

10. The "society" column of November 1, 1919, reports that Mann "has returned with his wife to their home." The same column dated March 6, 1920, marks his return, noting that he "has decided to cast his lot on the side of the Westerner and make Denver his permanent home."

11. See, for example, Bill Douglas, "Wartime Illusions and Disillusionment: Camp Dodge and Racial Stereotyping, 1917–1918," *Annals of Iowa* 57, 2 (Spring 1998): 111–134.

12. It is of interest that Mann talks about being permanently disabled from his war injuries and that medical experts believed he was not long for this world.

13. *The Denver Post*, October 10, 1974, 55.

14. According to his obituary published in the *Post*, he began as an inspector and retired "as a senior clerk in the services department in 1956."

15. *The Colorado Statesman*, August 5, 1938, 1, col. 5: "The friends of Lt. Earl W. Mann are pleased to learn that he is preparing to run for the lower house of the Legislature this coming election, on the Republican ticket."

16. A news report published on September 13, 1940, in *The Colorado Statesman* noted that Mann garnered 17,447 votes in the primary, making him eighth in a field of fifteen nominated.

17. Isetta Crawford Rawls, "The Negro in Early Colorado" (unpublished undergraduate paper, University of Colorado at Boulder, 1968), in author's possession.

18. On page 5 of the December 25, 1920, issue of the *Statesman* is a short description of a program conducted at the "colored" YMCA, with which Mann had become associated shortly after his return to Denver earlier that year. The program featured ten-minute talks by Major Thos Campbell, president of the Denver Colored Civic Association; Geo. W. Gross, president of the local branch of the NAACP; and Lt. Earl Mann, "president of the newly organized Protective league."

19. In a memorial to the "Passing of Joseph D.D. Rivers," published on January 23, 1937, Mann provides information regarding the connection between Rivers and himself, indicating that the late editor was a close friend. Further, he says, he (Mann) had "been intimately associated with [Rivers] in his journalistic work," in some instances publishing unsigned editorials in the years before his "So They Say" columns began to appear on a regular basis.

20. Materials provided by the archives department at Hampton University show that Rivers was one of Washington's students from 1879 to 1881. In 1883 he "was a steward in a hotel in Philadelphia, 'getting along splendidly.'" He relocated to Denver "'to better' his 'condition,' and was 'cordially received by both white and colored.'" The alumni notes also indicate without a specific date that Rivers dealt in real estate for a two-year period and spent time "studying law in Judge Dixon's office."

21. An appendix to a Federal Bureau of Investigation report, "Survey of Racial Conditions in the United States," composed in 1942 from notes taken by the Denver Field Division and provided by a colleague in the National Archives, includes a brief discussion of the *Statesman*, which is "published by E. V. Dorsey, weekly on Fridays and is devoted almost exclusively to racial matters. It is believed that as a rule, the Statesman treats racial matters more tolerantly than other Negro newspapers. However, every item of indicated discrimination is featured in the paper" (357).

22. It is difficult to be more accurate here because after 1954, the Colorado Historical Society stopped receiving the paper regularly.

23. A broad selection of opinions can be found in Herbert Aptheker (ed.), *A Documentary History of the Negro People in the United States*, vol. 3: *1933–1945* (New York: Citadel, 1974), 372–591. A decidedly more radical selection can be found in Fred Stanton (ed.), *Fighting Racism in World War II* (New York: Monad, 1980), 28–143. Particular care should be taken in reading the selections in this collection. Also see Christopher Z. Hobson, "Invisible Man and African American Radicalism in World War II," *African American Review* 39, 3 (2005): 355–376.

24. See, for example, two pieces by Ernest Allen Jr., "When Japan Was 'Champion of the Darker Races': Satokata Takahashi and the Flowering of Black Messianic Nationalism," *Black Scholar* 24, 1 (Winter 1994): 23–46, and "'Waiting for Tojo': The Pro-Japan Vigil of Black Missourians, 1932–1943," *Gateway Heritage* 16, 2 (Fall 1995): 38–55.

25. The *Defender*'s headline added reportage of a lynching in Missouri that was even more poignant in terms of the message to be conveyed to those in positions of power. See Dominic J. Capeci Jr., "The Lynching of Cleo Wright: Federal Protection of Constitutional Rights during World War II," *Journal of American History* 72, 4 (March 1986): 859–887. For more general pieces, see Neil A. Wynn, "Black Attitudes towards Participation in the American War Effort, 1941–1945," *Afro-American Studies* 3 (1972): 13–19; Jinx Coleman Broussard and John Maxwell Hamilton, "Covering a Two-Front War: Three African American Correspondents during World War II," *American Journalism* 22, 3 (2005): 33–54; two articles by Earnest L. Perry Jr., "It's Time to Force a Change: The African-American Press' Campaign for a True Democracy during World War II," *Journalism History* 28, 2 (2002): 85–95, and "A Common Purpose: The Negro Newspaper Publishers Association's Fight for Equality during World War II," *American Journalism* 19, 2 (Spring 2002): 31–43. More focused articles include Caryl A. Cooper, "The Chicago *Defender*: Filling in the Gaps for the Office of Civilian Defense, 1941–1945," *Western Journal of Black Studies* 23, 2 (1999): 111–118; Beth Bailey and David Farber, "The 'Double-V' Campaign in World War II Hawaii: African Americans, Racial Ideology and Federal Power," *Journal of Social History* 26, 4 (1993): 817–843.

26. As a particular case in point, see Sato Masaharu and Barak Kushner, "'Negro Propaganda Operations': Japan's Short-Wave Broadcasts for World War II Black Americans," *Historical Journal of Film, Radio and Television* 19, 1 (March 1999): 5–21.

27. For a general overview of the war and its consequences for the home front, see John Hope Franklin and Alfred A. Moss Jr., *From Slavery to Freedom; A History of African Americans*, 8th ed. (New York: McGraw-Hill, 2000), 475–504. More focused works include Mary Penick Motley, *The Invisible Soldiers: The Experience of the Black Soldier in World War II* (Detroit: Wayne State University Press, 1975); Neil A. Wynn, *The Afro-American and the Second World War*, rev. ed. (New York: Holmes and Meier, 1993). Information on Detroit and Harlem and the ways they differed from other instances of racial violence in U.S. history can be found in Richard Hofstader and Michael Wallace (eds.), *American Violence: A Documentary History* (New York: Alfred A. Knopf, 1970).

28. Arthur Marwick, *War and Social Change in the Twentieth Century* (New York: St. Martin's, 1974), 7.

29. Gerald D. Nash, *The American West Transformed: The Impact of the Second World War* (Bloomington: Indiana University Press, 1985), 88.

30. See, for example, Mario Barrera, *Race and Class in the Southwest: A Theory of Racial Inequality* (Notre Dame, IN: Notre Dame University Press, 1979), esp. 104–156.

31. Neil A. Wynn, *The Afro-American and the Second World War* (New York: Holmes and Meier, 1975), 1. Additional information on the postwar period can be found in Rayford W. Logan, *The Negro and the Post-War, a Primer* (Washington, DC: Minorities Publishers, 1945); Harvard Sitkoff, *The Struggle for Black Equality, 1954–1980* (New York: Hill and Wang, 1981); John Higham (ed.), *Civil Rights and Social Wrongs: Black-*

White Relations since World War II (University Park: Pennsylvania State University Press, 1997); Carol Anderson, *Eyes Off the Prize: The United Nations and the African American Struggle for Human Rights, 1944–1955* (New York: Cambridge University Press, 2003). More narrowly focused articles include Lawrence B. DeGraaf, "Significant Steps on an Arduous Path: The Impact of World War II on Discrimination against African Americans in the West," *Journal of the West* 35, 1 (1996): 24–33; Bruce Fehn, "'The Only Hope We Had': United Packinghouse Workers Local 46 and the Struggle for Racial Equality in Waterloo, Iowa, 1948–1960," *Annals of Iowa* 54, 3 (1995): 185–216; Wendy Plotkin, "'Hemmed In': The Struggle against Racial Restrictive Covenants and Deed Restrictions in Post–World War II Chicago," *Journal of the Illinois State Historical Society* 94, 1 (2001): 39–69; Eileen Boris, "'You Wouldn't Want One of 'em Dancing with Your Wife': Racialized Bodies on the Job in World War II," *American Quarterly* 50, 1 (1998): 77–108.

32. See Chapter 8 in this volume by Ronald J. Stephens.

33. In actuality, there were two Lowrys. Lowry One was reserved for White U.S. Army Air Force personnel, while Lowry Two was specifically designated for Negro personnel. The latter could go to the former, but they could not partake of entertainments there. The late William Greenwood told me this in a conversation in 1977.

34. James Rose Harvey, "Negroes in Colorado" (unpublished master's thesis, University of Denver, 1941), 54–97; Mark Hanna Watkins, "Racial Situation in Denver," *Crisis* 52, 5 (May 1945): 139–140. Also see Lionel Dean Lyles, "An Historical-Urban Geographical Analysis of Black Neighborhood Development in Denver, 1860–1970" (unpublished PhD diss., University of Colorado, 1977), 68–136; Lyle W. Dorsett, *The Queen City: A History of Denver* (Boulder: Pruett, 1977), 187–248.

35. See Leroy R. Hafen, *Colorado and Its People*, vol. 1 (New York: Lewis Historical Publishing, 1948), 587–625. Also see Denver Regional Association, "Employment Trends in Relation to the Post War Economy of the Denver Area" (Denver: University of Denver Government Center, October 1943).

36. Gunnell, the first African American to serve in the Colorado State Legislature, was elected in 1880 and served one term. Joseph H. Stuart, the second African American to serve, was elected in 1894. Ida DePriest, founder of the Colored Women's Republican Club in 1894— the first year women were allowed to vote in Colorado— and Black suffragist Elizabeth Easley were instrumental in his election. Stuart's claim to fame was the passage of a civil rights law in 1895 that outlawed discrimination in public accommodations on the basis of race, creed, or color. Although the law provided for fines, imprisonment, and monetary damages for violations and was the basis for lawsuits in the days ahead, it lacked the necessary enforcement machinery that would have made it more effective than it was. See Lael Montgomery Wanebo, "Black Political Leaders in Colorado, 1865–1900" (unpublished undergraduate paper, University of Colorado at Boulder, summer 1977), in author's possession.

37. See, for example, a general history of Blacks in the West by Quintard Taylor, *In Search of the Racial Frontier: African Americans in the American West, 1528–1990* (New York: Norton, 1998).

38. Mann had very definite ideas about the sources and development of one's character. His writings convey a special intensity whenever he makes reference to

the objectives of Christian teaching and its potential for establishing a kind of amity among the world's different peoples. The importance of religion, especially Christianity, for Mann seems apparent in his having saved a certificate from the First Congregational Church of Lyons, Iowa, given to him on March 9, 1902. The certificate recognizes one and one-half years "of faithful service in the Junior Society of Christian Endeavor [and notes that he] is recommended to proceed to the Intermediate Society." The certificate's presence when so many other items detailing the story of his life are missing from the materials he donated to the library augurs for this interpretation in light of his other church activities.

39. Even today, in the early twenty-first century, the percentage of Black people in the city's total population is not appreciably different than it was at the beginning of the twentieth century.

40. See, for example, Harmon Mothershead, "Negro Rights in Colorado Territory," *Colorado Magazine* 40, 3 (July 1963): 212–223; and two articles by Eugene H. Berwanger, "Reconstruction on the Frontier: The Equal Rights Struggle in Colorado, 1865–1867," *Pacific Historical Review* 44, 3 (August 1975): 313–329, and "William J. Hardin: Colorado Spokesman for Racial Justice, 1863–1873," *Colorado Magazine* 52, 1 (Winter 1975): 52–65. Also see William M. King, *Going to Meet a Man: Denver's Last Legal Public Execution, 27 July 1886* (Niwot: University Press of Colorado, 1990), 7. This topic will be explored more fully in William M. King, "Speaking Out for Self: The Black Struggle for the Right to Vote in Territorial Colorado, 1861–1867," in progress.

41. This column appeared on March 28, 1925 (4, col. 2), and was titled "An Open Letter to Comrads [sic] of Wallace Simpson Post No. 29," shortly after he became commander. The regularity of Mann's appearance—initially on the editorial page, sometimes signed and sometimes not—may have been catalyzed by the death of the paper's editor, Joseph D.D. Rivers, on January 17, 1937, and the subsequent illness of George W. Davis, the assistant manager who took over for Rivers temporarily. On page 1 of the April 3, 1937, issue, in the lower right-hand corner is an advertisement directed to the paper's readers listing several writers, including Earl Mann. This notice continued for another several months before it disappeared, by which time Mann was a regular contributor to *The Colorado Statesman*.

42. This post (colored) was named for a sailor in the United States Navy who was a crewman on the destroyer *Jacob Jones*, sunk by a German submarine off the Irish coast on December 6, 1917. His obituary is in the *Statesman* on page 5 of the December 15, 1917, issue.

43. *The Colorado Statesman*, March 6, 1937, 1, cols. 1–2. A recapitulation of the events begins on the same page in column 3.

44. Ibid., January 21, 1938, 1, col. 4.

45. This observation is very similar to the remarks of John S. Rock in a speech titled "I Will Sink or Swim with My Race," delivered at a March 5, 1858, commemoration of the Boston Massacre. The address can be found in Philip S. Foner (ed.), *The Voice of Black America: Major Speeches by Negroes in the United States, 1797–1971* (New York: Simon and Schuster, 1972), 203–207.

46. In a column published in the *Statesman* on April 1, 1938, 1, col. 5, Mann writes that "[r]acial bigotry and intolerance is as great a menace under a Lilly white program

in America as it is under a Nazi, fascist, or other guise in Europe. When political parties fail to develop an order in which 'all' people, irrespective of class[,] race[,] or station can enjoy a commensurate share of our [world's] material productions[,] they have failed to discharge their purpose and functions."

47. Ibid., April 22, 1938, 2, col. 1.

48. Ibid., September 2, 1938, 2, col. 1.

49. Ibid., May 26, 1939, 2, col. 5. Whenever Mann wishes to emphasize a particular point, he capitalizes the entire sentence or section that contains that point.

50. Ibid., September 1, 1939, 1, col. 1.

51. Ibid., September 15, 1939, 2, col. 1.

52. Ibid., April 19, 1940, 1, col. 1.

53. Ibid., May 10, 1940, 1 col. 1.

54. Ibid., May 17, 1940, 1, col. 1.

55. Ibid., April 11, 1941, 1, col. 1. In one of his columns, Mann talks about one group of troops throwing bricks through the barrack windows of another group of troops without specifying which group did what. Still, I have reason to believe, based on an interview with the late William Greenwood, who worked at the base and described a riot that took place in the spring of 1942 or 1943—he was not sure, and I have not been able to find supporting documentation of such an incident—that there was a fair amount of tension between the two groups, who were there for technical training and had brought a number of prejudices with them from their home states.

56. *The Colorado Statesman*, December 12, 1941, 1, col. 1.

57. Ibid., 2, col. 1.

58. Ibid., January 9, 1942, 1, col. 2 (source of the quotation); January 16, 1942, 1, col. 1.

59. Ibid., April 17, 1942, 4, col. 4. It is important to remember that Colorado would shortly become the site of one of the "relocation" camps to which Americans of Japanese ancestry would be sent, having been designated "potential enemy aliens." See Peter McQuilkin Mitchell, "Japanese Relocation in Colorado, 1942–1945" (unpublished MA thesis, University of Colorado at Boulder, 1960). For an extended treatment of race issues and their influence on the conduct of combat operations, see John W. Dower, *War without Mercy: Race and Power in the Pacific War* (New York: Pantheon, 1986).

60. *The Colorado Statesman*, June 12, 1942, 1, col. 1.

61. Ibid., August 18, 1942, 1, col. 1.

62. Ibid., September 9, 1942, 1, col. 1.

63. Ibid., January 1, 1943, 1, col. 1.

64. Ibid., July 16, 1943, 6, col. 5.

65. Ibid., September 8, November 27, and December 11, 1943, all on 6, col. 5.

66. Of the intended change, Mann writes: "It is the Japs now. It can be the Negroes next." This is when he authored a piece of legislation that halted this particular proscription, discussed earlier in this chapter.

67. *The Colorado Statesman*, March 11, 1944, 1, col. 1; June 10, 1944, 6, col. 5.

68. Ibid., January 13, 1945, 1, col. 6.

69. Ibid., April 28, 1945, 1, col. 6.

70. Ibid., May 12, 1945, 4, col. 5.
71. Ibid., August 18, 1945, 1, col. 6.
72. See, for example, Timothy L. Schroer, *Recasting Race after World War II: Germans and African Americans in American-Occupied Germany* (Boulder: University Press of Colorado, 2007).

Bernadette Garcia-Galvez

Latina Education and Life in Rural Southern Colorado, 1920-1945

This chapter explores how women of mestiza ancestry experienced the education system in Huerfano County, Colorado, between the years 1920 and 1945.[1] In addition to gaining an understanding of education, other goals of the study were to document the existence of people in the area and to challenge generalized stereotypes about mestiza/o peoples by exploring layers of identity. Documenting the participants' voices is significant, as I learned during research efforts when I discovered that the communities in question are largely absent from the state's published history and from legal documentation in the state archives.

Huerfano County is an area of approximately 1,592 square miles in the south-central region of the state.[2] Three towns/areas in particular are discussed in this chapter: Turkey Creek, Farisita, and Gardner.[3]

It is widely known that since the earliest documentation of peoples in the Southwest, travelers and "settlers" in the Texas, New Mexico, Arizona, and Colorado areas viewed the people they encountered as lazy, unmotivated, and backward (Getz 1997). These assumptions about the peoples of the area may have led to the idea that their histories were not worth recording. It is also the practice of colonization to erase the histories of the colonized as a way to assert power over those people, to erase that which came before to rewrite the history of the area for the benefit of the people in power.[4]

It is apparent from the numbers of students enrolled (see Table 12.1) that the majority of students with Spanish surnames attended schools in outlying areas and not in the area's largest settlement, Gardner.[5] The reasons for this are unclear, as there are no complete pupil census records to compare with the enrollment data. What is clear is that the number of school-age children with Spanish surnames who lived in the area was much larger than the number of students with Spanish surnames who attended school.[6] We can see this by comparing the enrollment records for most years with the pupil census records from the two years that were available (see Table 12.2).

Table 12.1. Huerfano County Enrollment Statistics

	1924	1926	1927	1929	1931	1934	1935	1936	1937	1938	1939	1940	1941
Gardner													
Total pupils	25	30	30	36	32	51	45	45	51	54	67	13	47
Pupils with Spanish surname	2	0	0	5	0	4	3	5	7	12	20	3	16
Talpa / Farisita													
Total pupils	—	—	50	—	40	34	30	37	15	39	28	—	16
Pupils with Spanish surname	—	—	49	—	38	34	28	36	14	37	28	—	16
Turkey Creek / Birmingham													
Total pupils	—	37	—	—	—	48	42	35	37	15	29	—	31
Pupils with Spanish surname	—	32	—	—	—	39	36	29	30	15	23	—	28

Source: Huerfano County Enrollment Lists

Table 12.2. Census of School-Age Youth

Gardner	1932	1933
Youth	112	131
Spanish surname	59	60
Talpa / Farisita	1932	1933
Youth	—	—
Spanish surname	—	—
Turkey Creek / Birmingham	1932	1933
Youth	98	87
Spanish surname	75	70

Source: Huerfano County Enrollment Lists

THE WOMEN

Miquela Salazar (nee Valdez), born in 1928 in Talpa.[7] One of three sisters and three brothers from her father's second marriage, Miquela was the youngest girl in the family. She started school in Farisita at the two-room schoolhouse that taught primary through eighth grades and was there through fourth grade. When her eldest sister started high school, she and her siblings were moved to the Catholic school in Gardner, where Miquela went to school until eighth grade. She was sent to an all-girl Catholic boarding high school in Yankton, South Dakota, called Mount Marty. Miquela remained at Mount Marty until her junior year, when she dropped out to go back home and help her family.

Jewel "Jay" Musso (nee Medina), born in 1938 in Turkey Creek, the eleventh of twelve siblings. Jay's family moved from Huerfano County to Pueblo following the harvesting season seeking work in beet, onion, and other fields in the area. Jay began school in Pueblo. She started third grade in the one-room schoolhouse in Turkey Creek, which taught primary through eighth grades. She went to school there through fifth grade. Her family continued to move from Turkey Creek to Pueblo throughout her years at school. Jay graduated from high school in Pueblo and then went to work at the Colorado State Hospital. A supervisor offered her a scholarship to attend college, and she earned a bachelor's degree in mental health from the University of Southern Colorado in Pueblo.

Marilyn Hostetler (nee Medina), born in 1930 in the mining town of Sunnyside. She is Jay's sister and was the ninth of twelve siblings. Marilyn started school at Sunnyside. She moved to the Farisita School for first through third grades and finished fourth through eighth grades at the Sunnyside School. Marilyn's family had moved to Turkey Creek and Farisita, but she was sent to live with her grandmother in Sunnyside. Marilyn went to high school in Walsenburg at Huerfano High School, the nearest high school to Sunnyside, but she quit after her sophomore year to begin working. Marilyn earned her GED years later and was successful in the one semester of college she attended.

Pabla Lovato (nee Cruz), born in 1928 in Pass Creek. Pabla went to school in a one-room schoolhouse called Rand School from primary through eighth grades. The school changed locations several times, moving in the area between Gardner and Pass Creek. Pabla went to Gardner High School. She graduated as valedictorian and was awarded a scholarship. She attended the University of Northern Colorado in Greeley, where she earned a bachelor's degree in chemistry.

Cora Coca (nee Martinez), born in 1932 in Turkey Creek. Cora started school in Clover, a settlement west of Turkey Creek. Cora attended primary school in Clover. After her father died, she and her mother and siblings moved in with her grandmother. She began attending school in Maes Creek. Her eldest brother began high school in Gardner, so her mother moved the family to Gardner where she attended school for one year. Her family then moved back to Turkey Creek, and she attended Paloma School in Turkey Creek. Between school years, her family moved to Avondale to follow the harvest seasons; during those times she attended school in Pueblo. Cora left school in the fifth grade.

Natividad Aguirre (nee Vallejos), born in 1910 in Gardner as one of twelve children. Her brothers attended public school in Gardner, but her father insisted that his girls be educated in a Catholic school. There was initially no Catholic school in Gardner when they were of school age, so her mother and the girls moved to Walsenburg during the school months so the girls could attend St. Mary's School. Natividad went to St. Mary's until she was thirteen, then she was sent to Atchison, Kansas, to attend a convent school. Natividad spent one term in Atchison. By that time there was a Catholic school in Gardner, St. George's, so she finished school there. She graduated from eighth grade when she was eighteen. There was no Catholic high school in Gardner, so Natividad did not have the opportunity to attend high school.

Magdalena Valdez (nee Valdez), born in 1923 in Gardner. Magdalena is the sister of Miquela Salazar and was the eldest child in their family. She went to school in Farisita until eighth grade. Magdalena began high school in Gardner. After she had successfully completed ninth grade at Gardner High School, Magdalena's mother became ill. Magdalena quit school to take care of her mother and to help run the family farm.

Ruth Mondragon (nee Martinez), born in 1930 in Turkey Creek. Ruth began school in Maes Creek. Her family moved from Turkey Creek to Gardner and then to Avondale during her years in school. She attended five schools in the seven years she was in school—Maes Creek, St. George's, Paloma, Pueblo, and Farisita—often more than one school in a given school year. Ruth quit school in seventh grade to take care of her mother and to work to make money for the family.

LAYERS OF IDENTITY

Education, as the women in the study experienced it, was much more than their interactions with teachers and peers in the classroom. Their stories reveal that family and community played an active part in the way they experienced education. Their class status and gender affected the ways they were regarded by teachers, the expectations placed on them in the classroom, and whether they were allowed to continue to go to school. This is apparent through statements like one from Ruth, who explains that "because we didn't have a dad, everybody mistreated us" (Mondragon 2003). She is aware of the way a family that was not traditional was regarded in her community and how that regard crossed over into the classroom. Through her stories, we learn that her family was also very poor. In addition, her native language, Spanish, also played a significant role in her experiences. From the perspective of Ruth's interactions in the classroom, it may seem that she was simply an unruly child—she admits to getting in trouble and being stubborn. However, when one considers her class and family status, a different perspective comes to light. It is impossible to isolate race[8] or ethnicity or even class or gender as single reasons for the ways these women were treated and for their experiences both in school and in the greater community.

Each of the women in the study had expectations placed on her based on her class, gender, and ethnicity. In Natividad's case, her gender affected where she went to school. Her father would only allow his girls to be educated in Catholic schools. Since there was no Catholic high school in the area, Natividad did not have the chance to attend high school. Natividad's family was less poverty stricken than many families in the Talpa/Gardner area. They owned land on which they grew alfalfa to feed their livestock and to sell, as well as acreage for orchards and gardens for their own sustenance. They made enough income so they could hire ranch hands. This meant the women of the family were not required to help run the family ranch, so they could be gone for long intervals. Also, her father earned enough money to be able to rent a house in Walsenburg for them to live in during the school term. If her family had not had the resources to enable her and her sisters to attend St. Mary's in Walsenburg, Natividad would not have been able to attend school until she was thirteen, the year a Catholic school opened in Gardner.

Likewise, Pabla came from a family that had land and livestock: "My dad sold apple trees around the area and he had three orchards himself. We even had meat when they butchered once in awhile" (Lovato 2003). Since her family had sufficient land and resources, Pabla was not required to contribute to running the farm or earning income for her family.

In contrast to Natividad's and Pabla's experiences, most of the women in the study were from families that relied on the children to help either run the household/farm or earn income to support the family. Responsibilities at home constituted a leading reason the women left school. For instance,

Magdalena and Ruth were required to quit school when their mothers became ill: "I quit school to take care of my mom. I had to feed the stock and milk the cows and we had pigs and chickens" (Valdez 2003). This was expected of them because they were girls, but it was also dependent on their birth order. Each was the eldest girl still at home.[9] While family responsibility depended on the child's gender, class also played a large part in the necessity to quit school. If the family had possessed sufficient financial resources to hire a nurse, it would not have been the eldest girl's responsibility to become caretaker. Ruth and Magdalena not only cared for their mothers, but they also took their mothers' places in earning money for the family and running the household.

Race and ethnicity combined with gender and class in determining how the women were treated in and out of the classroom. Natividad remembers, "[It] was like the English-speaking people had more. Of course, [they] had the right of way to everything. We were always put aside. They were first in everything. They called us Mexicans, treated us differently" (Aguirre 2003). Natividad is reluctant to acknowledge that the mistreatment they received from the community was based on race; as she talks about it, she uses language references.

Racism in the classroom was sometimes manifested by students being singled out because of particular physical characteristics. Ruth and Cora relate instances in which a particular teacher mistreated Ruth. They agree that the teacher did not like Ruth because of her hair. Ruth was petite and dark, and her hair had a tight curl. As Ruth relates: "One of the teachers didn't like my hair. That Miss Rodriguez. She used to write *monos* [cartoon characters] on the blackboard and say they were me, and everybody used to laugh at me" (Mondragon 2003). Her sister Cora confirmed the story:

> Ruth had curly hair, and when she was small her hair would dry and wheet [makes a motion as if all the hair flew up around her head]. Mrs. Rodriguez wanted to get mad at Ruth because she wanted her to go neat to school. She grabbed Ruth by the hair and banged her head against the desk over and over! She was so mad. When her hair was wet it was all nice and straight. I guess mom didn't have nothing or the time to make sure to put oil or something [on it] to make it [straight] . . . I don't know. (Coca 2003)

The internalization of the racism they experienced is clear in the fact that neither Ruth nor Cora blames Mrs. Rodriguez. Cora goes as far as to suggest that their mother did not groom Ruth well enough—as if their physical characteristics should be hidden or manipulated so as not to incite anger.

It seems as though the women's relatives were aware of the dangers their daughters faced because of their gender, ethnicity, and class. Several of the women remembered stories they were told by aunts and grandmothers that emphasized the need to remain vigilant:

> My grandmother was a great storyteller. She told us about this one time she was home alone and this man came. She was sweeping the yard and this guy walked up to her and said, is your husband home? When she said it, she knew she oughtn't have: no, he's away. Well, will he be back pretty soon? No, not 'til tomorrow. And he said, okay, I'll be back. She watched and he left [and] he went as far as the creek, but he never came out on the other side. She knew he was going to come back when it got dark. So she waited for my mother to come from school, and they left for the neighbors to spend the night there. In the morning, when they got back to the house, he had broken in. He had taken apples and other stuff from the house, but he would have raped her. I'm sure he would've. She would get scared when she told the story, and we'd get scared [hearing it]. (Lovato 2003)

Several of the women told accounts of their own physical and sexual attacks and the need to learn how to fight, take care of each other, and remain vigilant.

> We had to fight like that all our lives because everybody was always after us. Even those old men that lived up there that thought they were so good. So we learned how to fight. And we helped each other. We had to fight. They were mean to us, those people. One time we had to walk down to Farisita to get the mail. There were three or four men in a car and they tried to put us in a car. We got away. (Mondragon 2003)

> He [her mother's second husband] was way older than my mom. And there was a lot of pressure from her mom after her first husband, Alfredo, died. So she remarried this Sanchez, but he was worse than my dad. My mom's mom had Mother, Aunt Lupita, and Aunt Rose. Mother said he was always touching them inappropriately. I guess my Grandma didn't believe the girls or something. That was the reason they all got married so young and left the house. (Musso 2003)

These stories bring to light some of the realities girls were experiencing. Ruth mentioned earlier that she and her sisters were mistreated because they did not have a father. Ruth was a target for attack by community members and even her teacher, not only because she was a girl but also because her family was one of the poorest in the area. They were dark people, and their family was not traditional in the eyes of the community. In reading her stories, we learn that there were layers of her identity that contributed to the way people in the community and teachers and peers at school treated her. This is a similar trend with all the women in this study.

It is important to examine these layers of discrimination to better understand each woman's experiences throughout her education. We cannot understand scholastic achievement simply by looking at the curriculum taught or by blindly considering a student's performance in class and on exams. The realm of the classroom is not immune from being swayed by the currents of the community in which it operates. It is clear from these women's stories that their experiences with teachers, peers, administrators, and the wider community were affected by the social roles they were born into, which further contributed to their achievements in the school setting. When the reality of the situations the women in this study faced is taken into consideration, it is easier to recognize that it is inaccurate to generalize about their experiences or reactions just because they were the same gender or categorized by official records and history texts as being of the same race. Likewise, we learn that there were layers of each woman's identity that affected her everyday life, the choices she made, and whether she had choices in the first place.

THE ROLE OF FAMILY

Story after story in response to pointed questions about schooling segued into stories about family or community life. It was often necessary to attempt to bring the focus back on education, as the women's stories also explored family and community. One example was the interview with Natividad Aguirre. Natividad was asked where she went to school. She explained that her brothers went to public schools, but she never did. Natividad segued into a description of how she initially began to learn English—which was not in a classroom: "I remember when we came to school here in Walsenburg. We didn't know one word in English. I used to run from my house to the drugstore just to listen to people speak English. I would go on and on saying those words they would say. That's how I started learning English, just talking like they did" (Aguirre 2003). It is clear that Natividad's education was happening in her daily interactions with the community in which she lived. She was well aware that to function in the community she would need to learn English, and she did not wait to be in a classroom to begin to learn it.

Sometimes the women's discussions about family took another direction. Some of the women answered very reservedly when asked pointed questions about school, yet they became excited when talking about their siblings or their community. Marilyn Hostetler is a good example of this tendency. Her conversation was animated and plentiful throughout; however, she continually changed the subject to her siblings—mostly referring to the brothers she grew up with. She answered questions about school succinctly, yet as she talked about her brothers and her mother, her conversation grew more dynamic and detailed.

The movement away from talking about school could have happened for several reasons. One may be that school was not significant in the women's lives. It is apparent that survival took precedence over getting an education—not out of a lack of motivation or interest but out of necessity. Distance also played a large part in whether children went to school. "My sister Manuela, she never, ever went to school. I think because the school, you know where the Farisita school was? Well, that was the only school there. We lived way, way on the other side [of town]. There was no transportation" (Aguirre 2003). Families often intervened when they were unable to send their children to school, with literate family members sharing their skills with others. According to Natividad, "[Manuela] definitely knew how to read and write Spanish, but my father taught her. I remember in the wintertime he used to put us all together at a table and teach us in Spanish. I knew the A-B-Cs and a few words when I started school. He taught my mother how to read and write. My mother only went to school one year for about three months up in Chama" (Aguirre 2003).

When thinking about school and revisiting their time in the classroom, the women often allowed their school-day memories to blur into memories of their family, both past and present. Whether they unconsciously segued into talking about family members or purposefully changed the subject, family clearly played, and continues to play, an important role in their education and experiences in the classroom and in the community.

LANGUAGE

All the women interviewed spoke Spanish as their first language. There were similarities and differences in the way teachers treated them as a result. The most frequently discussed reaction from teachers was the punishing and ridicule of students who did not speak English. All of the women talked about their native language, and most included Spanish words in their conversations.

Based on the women's stories, the reactions by teachers and administrators to students' use of Spanish were most often negative:

> [I] didn't know a word of English, and they didn't want us to speak Spanish even on the playground. We had a teacher that she didn't know Spanish and I didn't know English, and she wanted me to read something. It was a fiasco.... She'd get mad at me and she'd slam a ruler on the desk! And she'd hit me and I couldn't make out the word *but*, B-U-T. (Valdez 2003)

> Oh, they [the teachers] were mean. If they heard you speaking Spanish they would wash your mouth out with soap. And we didn't know nothing about English growing up. We never went noplace. We went to visit neighbors or

relatives . . . they were all talking Spanish. When the kids started going to public school, my kids, they told me, why didn't I talk to them in Spanish? They didn't know how to speak it. Whoever it was from the high school [who asked why they didn't speak Spanish], I told him, first, you brainwash a person to speak English and not Spanish, and now you want for me to turn around and do it for the kids? Forget it! If they want to talk English they can do it or Spanish or whatever they want. They are on their own. I'm not gonna talk it. Well, you should, you're their parent. I'm the parent, and that's what I'm doing. And it was up to the kids to learn it. By the time we finished school, we were talking English. But another thing that was to make you break the habit of [speaking] Spanish, they [the teachers] got mean. I guess I got mad more when they came out and tell me that I should talk Spanish to my kids now. And really, we don't even talk the right Spanish. Some teacher in high school for Renee [one of her children], he said, it's better you don't try to help Renee with her Spanish 'cause it's way different. You'll just get her confused. We came up with a raw deal. They tell me to talk in Spanish . . . ha! Forget it! Talk in English. Forget it! I'll talk what I want to talk. (Coca 2003)

In every instance, Cora is being judged for her use of her first language. In all cases, the people doing the blaming do not necessarily speak the language; nor do they have the cultural capital to understand the social and educational implications of being bilingual or experiencing an educational setting when you cannot understand what the teachers are saying.

On a few occasions, the women in the study spoke about teachers who had taught them English without being cruel or belittling them. Several of the women spoke about a particular teacher:

Jeanette wasn't Spanish, she was Arabian, but her mother and dad knew Spanish. They learned it because they were among the Spanish people. So she knew Spanish and never gave us hell about it. She would say, we have to speak English today. And this is the way you [learn it]. . . . And we picked it up fast because everyone was saying what they could, and before we knew it we wanted to. (Hostetler 2003)

Miquela remembered the same teacher and how different she was in her approach to teaching the children to speak English: "We'd get punished if we spoke in Spanish while we were in school. Not Jeanette Faris though. She would tell us how to say words in English if she'd hear us say them in Spanish. She wouldn't punish us" (Salazar 2003).

Women who had older siblings who attended school well before they did had different experiences with English: "I spoke English and Spanish because I was one of the younger ones, so by the time I came along the other kids had gone to school already" (Lovato 2003). Pabla had a chance to practice her English skills with her siblings before going to school. As such, she did not have to contend with feelings of isolation or punishment when she initially entered formal education.

All the women seemed to have accepted early on that they had to learn English: "They never said why, just that we couldn't speak in Spanish. And I think now that maybe it was so we could learn the English language. 'Cause the country was run by white people, so if you didn't learn to speak English, you couldn't survive" (Salazar 2003). In most cases, they learned English at school or from older cousins and siblings. They did not appear to resent having to learn English, but they did seem frustrated at being expected not to speak their native language: "My mom didn't like that we were punished for speaking Spanish. She didn't like it. She spoke Spanish to us at home. She never spoke English" (Salazar 2003). Cora was particularly vehement when she talked about her daughter's high school teacher telling her she did not speak Spanish correctly. What is clear from these interviews is that as a result of being punished and berated because of their use of the Spanish language, these women were reluctant to teach their children to speak Spanish and in some cases purposefully did not do so: "In most southwestern school systems, educators believed that Mexican American children needed to be segregated until they learned English and became Americanized" (Donato 1999). This was far from the reality for the women in this study. Since the schools in Talpa, Gardner, and Turkey Creek were one- or two-room schoolhouses, there was neither the space nor the teacher resources to separate students. Students were expected to learn English by being immersed in it and by being punished for speaking Spanish. Several of the women reported that when they could not understand the assignments, they were held back until they could complete the coursework for a particular grade level. As a result, some native Spanish speakers were older than many of their peers at the same grade level:

> We didn't know one word in English. I was eighteen years old when I finished the eighth grade. That's how behind we were because of that [not knowing English]. I must have been about eight or nine years old when I started at St. Mary's. They would try to give us some work, but what could we do? . . . The children that were already like in the second grade we were starting in kindergarten, just learning to draw or learning A-B-Cs. (Aguirre 2003)

Natividad explains that pupils who did not speak English were given simpler work regardless of their age, so when she was nine years old she spent much of her school time drawing pictures or tracing the alphabet. The stories the women shared about language made it clear that language had a significant impact on how each of them experienced school. The effects of the punishment the women experienced as girls affected not only their progress in school but also the way they viewed themselves and their positions in the classroom and the community.

THE IMPORTANCE OF EDUCATION

After reading these women's stories, it might appear that no importance was placed on education. Historically, many have assumed that Latinas/os are "dull, devoid of reason, incapable of self government, and unwilling to improve themselves" (Getz 1997:2). As one reads deeper into the women's experiences, however, it is easy to recognize the significance placed on education: "Once we learned English it was easier for us. I liked school. I liked arithmetic and spelling" (Valdez 2003). Regardless of the level they achieved, most of the women said they enjoyed school: "I was a pesty student. I thought that when I went [to] the first [grade] I would come back home and know how to read. The teacher had all the letters across [the blackboard] and she had a yardstick. And she'd point and you had to make the sound for months and months. Come on, I want to learn to read" (Lovato 2003).

Even those who did not love going to school talked about their love of learning new things and having new experiences. It is apparent that all the women shared a love of learning, whether through formal or informal education.

Three of the eight women in this study attended college, and two of the three graduated. Many of the women did not make it past grade school, however, and only half went to high school. The reasons for not finishing school included having to quit to care for family members, moving as the family moved, and quitting because school was a bad place to be. Nevertheless, all of the women in the study remarked about the importance of education as a means to improve one's opportunities in life. Not only did they talk about it, but I saw that importance reflected in many ways. During the interview with Ruth, she was taking care of her great-grandson because her granddaughter was at the library doing research for her master's degree. She talked with great pride about her granddaughter. Most of the women had pictures of their children, grandchildren, nieces, and nephews in caps and gowns on their walls and shelves. Many spoke of their children and how they made sure to provide the opportunities they could for them with the resources they had. Jay talked about her success in school and how she was able to provide for her children: "College was fun in a way. And it was hard because I had the kids and I was working. And a house to take care of and a husband to put up with. But you know that I graduated with a 3.7 [grade point average]. When my children were born, each one had a bank account, and I always let them know that it was for their college. And they both used it after they got out of high school" (Musso 2003).

The acknowledgment of the importance of education was clear throughout all the interviews. Pabla talked about how well her grandsons were doing in high school. Miquela spoke with pride about how she had taught herself to read and write Spanish since they could not learn it at school: "I [learned] to read and write in Spanish because I had to write to my mother. And she would write to me too, so I had to read her letters. When she had business in Walsenburg, I had to go with her and translate for her. So I learned to read and write in Spanish" (Salazar 2003). Natividad was proud that her father was self-educated and reflected on how important education was to her and her husband: "My husband wanted everybody to be educated. And he only went up to the eighth grade, but he was a very smart man, my husband was. And when our nephew graduated my husband told him, I'll pay for your college" (Aguirre 2003). Regardless of the level each woman reached in her educational career, there is a clear regard for the significance of education throughout the stories.

To fully understand education in the 1920s, 1930s, and 1940s in Huerfano County, it is imperative to understand how the community and the students viewed education. The prevalent stereotype in historical accounts of mestiza/o peoples in this region is that they are unmotivated and uninterested. The stories of these women, however, refute those stereotypes. An understanding that education was held in esteem by both students and their families forces us to look at possible alternatives to explain school performance, aside from assuming that people either succeeded or failed in school because of hereditary predisposition.

CULTURAL SURVIVAL

While I feel it is necessary to discuss challenges these women faced as they lived and were educated in Huerfano County, I do not intend to present them as victims. The stories are predominantly stories of survival. As we hear the stories, especially as the women talk about their parents and grandparents, we learn that the tradition of survival is strong in their families. We learn from Ruth, Cora, and Pabla about how their families worked together to survive abject poverty and hunger. We learn that Ruth and Cora's mother was able to successfully keep her children after her husband died and the family threatened to take them from her: "My dad passed away when I was about six, so Mom had to raise six kids. She didn't have no education, so she did farm work. My aunt wanted her to put us in an orphanage. They brought some people that were going to take us. She put up a fight for us. She fought for us" (Coca 2003). Her strength was passed on to her children, as they all did what they could to remain together. In this way, their mother was able to keep her children and raise them in their community, maintaining their culture and heritage. Pabla tells us that school was not unbearable because all the children were native Spanish speakers, and they helped each other survive: "The ethnic problem was a problem. Very bad. When I was little, in school it wasn't so bad because we were mostly Spanish in the grammar school. We could be with each other and help one another get through" (Lovato 2003). In these stories, we learn how family and community contributed to everyday survival.

Amid the difficulties of survival, we learn of joy. All the women interviewed talked about the importance of community. Miquela shared a story about community socials and picnics:

> In the basket social, all the women that went had to take a basket with a lunch in it and then the men had to buy the baskets. The man that would buy the lunch would get to eat with whoever the basket belonged to. I always remember I was only about ten or eleven years old, and my mother made a basket for her three girls. Carl Gomez bought mine and he was old already compared to me, and I wouldn't eat with him. (Salazar 2003)

Many talked about communities sometimes gathering just to gather. The strength these women received and passed on is apparent by their participation in the study. Most of the women initially expressed trepidation at participating because they could not believe their lives were worth recording into history. The fact that the women showed courage in sharing their stories is in itself a success. They were often candid about things that were uncomfortable to talk about, especially sexual exploitation or sex in general.

THE IMPORTANCE OF DOCUMENTING A POPULATION RENDERED INVISIBLE BY HISTORY

It is important to understand the experiences of the generation of the women in this study to gain a better understanding of why the educational system and the social structure of the area as a whole are the way they are today. While some argue that history should remain in the past, I believe we need to understand the history of a region to gain better insight as to why things are the way they are in the present. According to Howard Zinn, "What we learn about the past does not give us absolute truth about the present, but it may cause us to look deeper than the glib statements made by political leaders and the 'experts' quoted in the press" (Zinn 2000:658). This is important especially in the realm of school reform. The people who create legislation that affects the education of students in the United States would do well to understand the historical context of different regions of the state. We could learn from the experiences of native Spanish speakers from our grandmothers' generation about their struggles in English-only schools. We could learn that mestiza/o people were far from lazy or unmotivated but instead had obstacles placed before them by their communities and the social structures of the area that affected their success in school. We could learn about historical practices of discrimination and how they carry on into the present to ensure success for some and failure for others.

By examining official historical documentation as it exists in the Colorado State Archives and the office of the Huerfano County School District Administration, it is impossible to obtain a complete picture of what education was like for the entire population of the county. Therefore, it is impossible to learn how the history of the region contributes to the present successes and failures of school-age children without including the voices of those who experienced the education system.

NOTES

1. For the purposes of this chapter, I refer to the ethnicity of the women involved as mestiza. I understand mestiza to be the mixture of Spanish, indigenous, and Mexican ancestries. However, none of the women referred to themselves this way. I use this word interchangeably with Latina, understanding that it carries the same connotation. My use of the terms "Latina" and "mestiza" to describe the women is in no way meant to imply that they embody exact ethnic or ancestral backgrounds. These women are from various, mixed ancestries.

2. Specific regions of the county are included in most histories published about southern Colorado. The largest town, Walsenburg, is the best known. West/northwest of Walsenburg are small towns spread across the valleys and mountains. It is an area of Huerfano County that consists of scattered houses and small, irrigated plots of land, on which today mostly alfalfa is grown and small herds of cattle are raised. There are settlements such as Gardner, where small homes, trailers, and community buildings create a larger town. Other "towns," such as Farisita, consist of scattered ranches, often separated by several miles.

3. Turkey Creek was known as Trujillo Creek in the earliest memories of some of the people in the area. Farisita was known as Talpa. Turkey Creek eventually became known as Birmingham. The names of locations in Huerfano County have changed to reflect the people who moved in after the United States took the land from Mexico. The Spanish names for places were likely given by the Mexicans and Spaniards who moved into the land while it was still inhabited by indigenous peoples.

4. While I do not discuss colonization in detail in this chapter, a good reference for discussion of this issue is *Europe and the People without History* by Eric Wolf. Prejudice and colonization may not completely explain the lack of documentation about rural populations, however. Poor record keeping and losses during the storage of records are problems with documenting the history of many rural locations in both Colorado and the United States. The consolidation of the numerous school districts in the county into one school district began in the late 1940s. Also, prior to consolidation, each of the schools in Huerfano County was, for the most part, considered its own district within the county. Once consolidation took place, documentation may have been lost while transporting the records to the central administration building in Walsenburg.

5. The only pupil census records located in the Colorado State Archives for Huerfano County were for Walsenburg. Similarly, there were teacher registers and yearbooks for Walsenburg only. Superintendents' annual reports were available for the entire county, although the majority of the pages were incomplete or empty. From the reports it appears that each school was considered its own district, and there were as many as fifty-two districts in Huerfano County before consolidation. Each district could have more than one school. The only information given about pupils in these reports is their grade levels. I was able to find limited information about Huerfano County, specifically focusing mostly on Walsenburg, at the Colorado State Archives in Denver and the Huerfano County Re-1 School District offices in Walsenburg. This information was gathered from superintendents' annual reports. Much of the published information available about Huerfano County focuses solely on the larger towns. Information about the small surrounding towns is sparse and often inaccurate. Finding written documentation about the school districts in western Huerfano County in the time period of this study proved difficult. At the Colorado State Archives in Denver, the only town that included census information was Walsenburg. Superintendent reports from Huerfano County dating from 1911–1945 were incomplete. The numbers of students reported were drastically different than the numbers reported in the enrollment lists at the Huerfano County School District Administration offices (see Table 12.3). Information found in the archives supported the information shared by the women in this study, including the names of schools, their locations, and the names of teachers.

Table 12.3. Data from the Superintendent's Annual Reports vs. Enrollment Records (SAR data not recorded for Turkey Creek)

	1924		1926		1927		1929		1934		1935	
	ER	SAR	ER	SAR	ER	SAR	ER	SAR	ER	SAR	ER	SAR
Gardner	—	25	107	30	97	30	112	36	102	51	111	45
Talpa/Farisita	—	—	131	37	116	50	126	—	110	34	115	30

Source: Huerfano County Superintendent Annual Reports

6. The Spanish surname does not give complete insight into the pupils' race and ethnicity. It does, however, give an idea of possible numbers of students with European ancestry and those with Mexican and/or indigenous ancestry.

7. All eight women interviewed for this study were born in the area and completed at least part of their schooling in Huerfano County school districts. Several criteria went into the selection of the women. They had to have been born in Huerfano County. The women's families also had to be from Huerfano County at least one generation past. The women had to have attended school in Huerfano County for at least part of their lives.

8. Race had little to do with the way they labeled themselves, as they all referred to themselves as "Spanish" regardless of their ancestry. The labeling of oneself as Spanish—or, more precisely, aligning one's ancestry with European blood as opposed to indigenous or Mexican blood—is a practice that has been explored by many Latino intellectuals, such as F. Arturo Rosales (1996). The debate over the development of and the reasons behind the creation of a "fantasy heritage" is not discussed in this chapter. What is apparent, however, is that all the women were aware of how Mexicans and Indians were considered in their communities and in their travels.

9. Ruth was not the eldest, but the eldest was married and gone from the house when their mother became ill.

REFERENCES

Aguirre, Natividad [pseud.]. Interview with author. Tape recording. Walsenburg, CO, March 27, 2003.

Coca, Cora [pseud.]. Interview with author. Tape recording. Farasita, CO, March 26, 2003.

Colorado State Archives. Huerfano County Superintendent Annual Reports, 1921–1945. Denver.

Donato, Ruben. "Hispano Education and the Implications of Autonomy: Four School Systems in Southern Colorado, 1920–1963." *Harvard Educational Review* 69, 2 (1999): 117–149.

Getz, Lynne Marie. *Schools of Their Own: The Education of Hispanos in New Mexico, 1850–1940*. Albuquerque: University of New Mexico Press, 1997.

Hostetler, Marylin [pseud.]. Interview with author. Tape recording. Pueblo, CO, March 6, 2003.

Huerfano County Superintendent Annual Enrollment Lists, 1928–1941. Huerfano School District Re-1 Administrative Offices, Walsenburg, CO.

Lovato, Pabla [pseud.]. Interview with author. Tape recording. Walsenburg, CO, March 26, 2003.

Mondragon, Ruth [pseud]. Interview with author. Tape recording. Pueblo, CO, March 27, 2003.

Musso, Jewel [pseud.]. Interview with author. Tape recording. Pueblo, CO, March 1, 2003.

Rosales, F. Arturo. *"Fantasy Heritage" Reexamined; Race and Class in the Writings of the Bandini Family Authors and Other Californios, 1828–1965*. Recovering the U.S. Hispanic Literary Heritage, vol. 2, Erlinda Gonzales-Berry and Chuck Tatum, eds., 81–104. Houston: Arte Público, 1996.

Salazar, Miquela [pseud.]. Interview with author. Tape recording. Fowler, CO, February 8, 2003.

Valdez, Magdalena [pseud.]. Interview with author. Tape recording. Walsenburg, CO, March 27, 2003.

Wolf, Eric. *Europe and the People without History*. Berkeley: University of California Press, 1982.

Zinn, Howard. *A People's History of the United States: 1492–Present*. New York: Perennial, 2000.

PART III
Contemporary Issues

David A. Sandoval

Recruitment, Rejection, and Reaction: Colorado Chicanos in the Twentieth Century

The twentieth century has often been called the American century, and U.S. dominance and prominence undoubtedly grew during that century. The industrial transformation of the United States as it began to displace Native Americans from their lands and tie the nation together with railroads undoubtedly created an industrial giant. But along with the captains of industry came the crew. The people who worked daily in those factories and fields provided the blood and sweat essential for the development of a country. Those immigrants began to come in larger and larger numbers throughout the late nineteenth century because of the need for workers. While Irish Americans built the initial transcontinental railroad from the east and Asian Americans from the west, Mexican workers who built over 80 percent of the railroads throughout the West constructed the bulk of the railroads. In agriculture, the majority of field hands were and still are Mexican American workers. Built on a base of conquered Mexicans, more and more migrants came into the United States, and they encountered a system that placed them at the bottom of the social scale.

The positivist government of Porfirio Díaz (1876–1911), which had encouraged economic development by foreigners like William Jackson Palmer and the Colorado-based mining entrepreneurs the Guggenheims, was in serious trouble by 1910 (Brenner 1942; Meyer, Sherman, and Deeds 2003). Precursors of revolution in Mexico often operated in the United States between 1900 and 1910, and while they were often persecuted by Díaz's police—even in the United States—they remained influential in political organizing among mining organizations and laborers affiliated with the Industrial Workers of the World (IWW) and the Western Federation of Miners. New Mexicans as well as Mexicans had been attracted to Colorado by the development of agribusiness and employment opportunities.

But while the economic pull was significant in migrations from farms to villages and subsequently to cities, the push of the Mexican Revolution (1910–1940) would change the character and culture of Mexicans in the Pikes Peak region, as it did throughout the borderlands (Galarza 1964).

The twentieth century heralded an intensive mass immigration and emigration of Mexicans and Chicanos who maintained different political perspectives than their predecessors. The diffused Spanish caste system and, to an extent, anti-Spanish orientation of the Mexican Revolution spurred a Mexican nationalism that affected the resident Manito population who had experienced the turmoil vicariously. The U.S. media's pronounced anti-Mexican bias also polarized the minority community. In response to economic interest propaganda and perceived levels of acceptability, many Colorado communities responded by differentiating themselves from the more vulnerable "newcomers."[1] A manifestation of the level of disassociation with the term "Mexican" can be perceived in the use of the term "Spanish American" to identify such Mexican Indian foods such as tortillas, chili, and beans.[2]

While these sociological and political phenomena continue in certain respects today, throughout the twentieth century some organizations continued to reflect the precepts of José Vasconcelos and identified themselves as Mexican organizations. Fraternal organizations known in Spanish as Sociedades Mutualistas flourished and provided benefits to Chicanos that were otherwise difficult to obtain, such as burial insurance. José Vasconcelos, as secretary of education, had promoted a new concept called "La Raza Cósmica," through which he asserted that the contemporary citizen of Mexico was the product of an amalgamation of diverse peoples from throughout the world that had produced a new race. He took the evolutionary arguments of the day and asserted that the new whole was greater than the sum of all its parts. He was able to attack the pro-European and White attitudes expressed by Porfirio Díaz's dictatorial government. Díaz had kept a staffer responsible for making him appear White while, in fact he was a mestizo. The reaction to Díaz also led to a reaction to the remnants of the Spanish caste system.

Furthermore, these fraternal organizations were consistent in their desire to preserve their culture through the celebration of traditional holidays, and they encouraged cultural preservation. The *mutualista* organization founded on June 3, 1922 (Ignacio Zaragoza in Pueblo), proclaimed itself "la unica 'mexicana' en la verdadera accepcion de la palabra" (the only "Mexican" in the true acceptance of that word). The group also identified itself as concerned with "PROTECCIÓN" (protection) and with maintaining traditions.[3] Mutualista organizations were particularly conscious of their national origins, and poetic contributions to pamphlets indicated as much.

The ensuing decades following the beginning of the Mexican Revolution in 1910 witnessed continual attacks against Mexicans, who were migrating to the United States in great numbers. Persons in California in 1914, concerned about and frightened by massive Mexican migration, called it the "Brown Scare," and nativism continued to manifest itself throughout the century. As more and more Mexican nationals came into the United States, more and more discriminatory actions were lodged against the resident ethnic group. Whenever the need for labor increased, protests against Mexicans decreased and additional labor was brought in. The classic example occurred in the 1930s during the Great Depression, when a policy of repatriation was followed and Mexicans were deported. In the 1940s, when the American military drained over 15 million men away from the U.S. labor force, a program involving Mexican workers called the Bracero Program went into effect.

Throughout the first half of the twentieth century, the label "Mexican" began to carry even more cultural baggage than a simple description of citizenship. It was used as a pejorative term. The mutualista organizations of the 1920s, which wanted to protect "Mexican" people, became bi-label organizations in the 1930s; "Spanish Americans" had their own organizations, and "Mexican Americans" had theirs. One obvious reason for the avoidance of the label "Mexican," aside from its almost universally negative connotations among English speakers, was the Repatriation of 1930–1940. In Texas, English speakers referred to Mexicans as "Mesicans" and "Meskins," much as Negroes were called "Nigras." As U.S. social agencies defined citizenship by cultural traits during Repatriation, it would seem that affected peoples would have become more cognizant of labels attached to them by government and social agencies. County governments were responsible for the implementation policies, and they often ignored the definition of citizenship in the United States Constitution and applied cultural standards instead. As such, every Mexican American was pressed to have Anglo-American friends who could testify that he or she was a citizen. At that, about 50,000 Mexican Americans were deported from their country.

In summary, from 1886 to 1940, Chicanos were perceived as a different type of person; they were segregated and treated as farm laborers. With few exceptions, newspapers, monographs, and articles ignored them; unless they became involved with Anglos, they were completely ignored. While the United States had legal segregation policies stemming from the 1896 Supreme Court decision *Plessy v. Ferguson*, the issue of how Mexicans were categorized in racial terms was addressed with the declaration that they were members of the "white" race. While efforts were made in California to define them as members of the "Indian" or "red" race, they were unsuccessful. If this population was defined as a different race, then different accommodations would have to be made, as the court case had said the "separate but equal" accommodations did not violate the requirement of equal treatment of citizens. For American Blacks, segregation provided an opportunity to build a middle class because Black teachers and administrators were needed for Black schools. But by defining Mexicans as members of the White race, distinctive provisions would not have to be made, and discrimination could continue.

The political strength of Colorado Chicano legislators did result in a few appointments, but they were significantly disproportionate to the numbers of Chicanos. European immigration was encouraged to provide labor during Colorado's expanding industrialization, and the most mundane details of Anglo life were worthy of comment in local papers, but Chicanos were systematically excluded.

Beyond political dominance and limited acceptance, terminology can change extensively as economics and education change. Thus terminology can be used as an index to the changing conditions and to an individual's class status. Even among immigrants from Mexico, a distinction within the group occurred; the "more highly educated distinguished themselves from lower-income, and usually more recent, immigrants by employing the term 'Spanish-American,' which, they felt, had connotations of higher social class" (Spicer and Thompson 1972:23).

The evolutionary development of the Colorado Chicano protest movement is so complex, controversial, and contemporary that the wish for a definitive history may never be realized. While some scholars have written about Chicano protest movements, organizations in Colorado have often been treated in a cursory, superficial, and inaccurate fashion.[4] A blatant inconsistency becomes apparent when one realizes that Colorado organizations have been significant in national affairs. Rodolfo Acuña perhaps best stated the obvious need for a collective history when he speculated wishfully about the need for Chicanos to wear battle ribbons and negate cautious distrust among Chicano activists.⁵ Beyond negating the consistent reinvention of the wheel, the history of Chicano activist organizations would contribute to a fuller understanding of a reactive nature to the dominant society.

While numerous organizations have reacted to the dominant society and to issues relative to demographic and socio-political status, several constants can be identified in spite of a rural-to-urban shift in population demography. Land grants and the desire to preserve culture are two such issues. Through the incident in 1936 when Governor Big Ed Johnson made a declaration of martial law to keep Mexicans out of the state of Colorado and the development of the New Hispano Party in the early 1960s, one can see political party patterns emerge.⁶

By 1930 efforts were being made in Colorado to reconcile "Mexican" organizations with those identified by the euphemism "Spanish American." Common cause and, most important, a realization that the dominant society did not differentiate between the two motivated the formation of a statewide organization called the Alianza Hispano America. Colorado governor Billy Adams was an honorary member of Barelas Lodge Number 180 in Denver. Since most mutualista organizations were primarily oriented to preserving Mexican culture as well as providing for social needs, the attempt to incorporate the Manito and the duplication of *logias* (lodges) in small towns is particularly interesting. In Trinidad and Walsenburg there were two distinct mutualista organizations, one for Mexicans and one for Spanish Americans.

By 1930 Chicano organizations were attempting to go beyond the recognition of cultural events and trying to influence legislation and protect the civil rights of Colorado Chicanos. Most important, organizational recognition that cultural preservation was a political issue now became apparent. Unlike the mutualista organization in Santa Barbara, California, Colorado mutualista organizations incorporated native-born Mejicanos. In 1968 one such organization in La Garita, Colorado (Sociedad Proteccion Mutualista de Trabajadores Unidos), paid burial insurance for the Espinosa family, which traces its origins prior to the 1846 conquest of New Mexico.⁷

While organizations in other areas, such as the Orden de Hijos de America (Acuna 1981; Cuellar 1974; McWilliams 1968), were advocating assimilation as a desirable goal and emphasizing political allegiance to the United States, Colorado organizations were concerned with cultural preservation and were beginning to function as protest entities against attempts at assimilation. To be sure, some individuals promoted assimilation, but statewide organizational efforts were not oriented toward that goal.

The 1930s witnessed renewed nativistic attacks on Chicanos. Repatriation, combined with anti-Mexico and anti-Cardenas sentiments, kindled the establishment of organizations in response to those attacks. Lázaro Cárdenas was elected president of Mexico in 1934. During his term in office he nationalized the oil industry, which put him at odds with nations such as the United States and Great Britain. While he was able to provide payment for those companies, he was widely criticized for his socialist policies. He welcomed back Mexicans returned through U.S. Repatriation policies, but he was still considered an enemy of both the oil industry and U.S. corporate interests.

The inability or the desire not to differentiate between members of the community by the press, politicians, and influence peddlers led to a continuation of intra-ethnic conflict and a diffusion of collective political power. Some may have believed that identification with Europe would protect them from anti-Mexican sentiment and rationalized that position through the "fantasy heritage" (Alvarez 1976). Events in 1936, however, should have quickly dispelled that notion. While all citizens suffered the misfortunes of the Great Depression, Chicanos also encountered thinly disguised racism cloaked as nativism and protectionism. Furthermore, they suffered the most of any Americans during the Great Depression (Gonzales 1999).

A story reported in *The Pueblo Chieftain* in February 1936 focused on a murdered author who had written an article about the Penitentes. Replete with innuendo, the reporter provided color for his story by describing the group's members as maniacs: "Authorities immediately began an investigation partly centered on the theory [that] members of the sect may have taken primitive vengeance on the stranger who attempted to probe their religious secrets."[8]

For over a week after the confessed murderer admitted that money was the motive, articles continued to refer to the Penitentes as a "torture cult," a weird cult that imposed the death penalty on anyone caught taking pictures of its dwelling or its acts. Sensationalistic journalism flourished as northern Mew Mexico was described as wild country barely under the control of the police.[9] The Pueblo paper was widely circulated in southern Colorado. In a recapitulation of 1936 chronology, the *Chieftain* referred to numerous incidents in which Chicanos were involved but did not mention the period April 18 to April 30 when Governor Ed Johnson declared Colorado's southern border under marital law and sent the National Guard to patrol against the entrance of Chicanos.[10] The ethnic unity displayed in 1930 had been openly shattered by 1936. A national and local effort was being made to organize Chicanos under the rubric "Spanish American Alliance." The purpose was stated to be the "building up of good relationships and better citizenships."[11] In Pueblo the group called itself American Citizens of Spanish Descent.

The Colorado border was manned by the National Guard in 1936. Massive deportations occurred beyond Mexican nationals, as Colorado's borders were also protected from New Mexican Manitos. Governor Johnson stated that he would distinguish between nationals and citizens according to how much money they had. Nativism and racism led to pronounced antagonism against the Mexican and Mexican American communities in the 1930s. While the policies of Repatriation led to deportations from Colorado, as they did throughout the borderlands (Hoffman 1974), Governor Johnson's declaration of martial law along the southern border exacerbated both inter- and intra-ethnic relationships. National Guardsmen, Highway Patrolmen, and peace officers were sent to patrol the 360-mile border against a "threatened invasion" of aliens and indigent persons. William L. Petriken, chairman of the board of the Great Western Sugar Company, responded to the choking off of Mexican American and Mexican national laborers: "We'll employ all the beet sugar labor available in Colorado and after that—well, if he [the governor] doesn't want beets grown in Colorado, that's that."[12]

Governor Johnson's private war against Chicanos and Mexicans had been preceded by his 1935 position of wanting them removed to concentration camps. A 1936 proclamation by the governor was based on theories of economic competition with local labor and the fact that these people were becoming public charges. Asked how border guards and troopers would distinguish "between aliens and persons of Mexican or Spanish origin who are citizens of the United States," Johnson responded: "We're going to count their money. Our main object is to head off destitute people from other states who will come here, perhaps work in the beet fields for a few weeks, and go on relief. If we catch a few aliens among them, so much the better, but the big thing is to keep out those who will become public charges."[13]

The proclamation that heralded this extreme solution to the "Mexican" problem read:

> The entering of aliens and indigent persons into this state in such large numbers constitutes an invasion that will create, encourage, and cause a condition of lawlessness and inevitably tend to discontent and unrest among the citizens of this state generally, and particularly along the southern border thereof, and will lead to social disorder and disturbances among our people, more particularly because the existing economic depression has rendered it impossible for large numbers of our citizens to find employment or to procure means of subsistence other than thru public and private charity.[14]

Armed with pistols and clubs, guardsmen were stationed in camps near Trinidad, Alamosa, Durango, and Cortez.

The first prisoners detained in Colorado were nineteen "Spanish Americans" apprehended near Monument. Governor Johnson believed these sugar beet workers, as well as another group arrested in Denver, had crossed into Colorado before troops were stationed along the border. In 1936 Governor Ed Johnson declared martial law along the Colorado and New Mexico border; the center of activity was Alamosa. An editorial in *The Alamosa Daily Courier* on May 16, 1936, provides a glimpse of the way Chicanos were viewed in the region: "There can be no justification of the importation of foreigners to work in the sugar beet fields of Colorado. There is enough Spanish-American labor in the state now to take care of the beet fields. . . . Nothing could be more incongruous than to bring several thousand Mexican laborers into a section while thousands of Spanish-speaking American citizens are drawing wages from the public fund."

The Pueblo Chieftain contained even more bilious and derogatory comments. Throughout April, newspapers across the state initially supported Johnson's "private war," but by the end of April the war was declared to be over as a result of labor shortages and New Mexico governor Clyde Tingley's adamant opposition, as well as threats of an economic boycott at Raton Pass. *The Alamosa Daily Courier* reported "that many Spanish Americans on the relief rolls are reluctant to take work in the beet fields." During February and March, several editorials were published concerning the employment of "Aliens" and "Mexicans."[15] In expressing support for not employing these persons, the *Chieftain* reported that Spanish Americans had protested the employment of Mexicans. The editor wrote a patronizing vignette about the "many other worthwhile Spanish Americans," like the character depicted in the editorial. The polemic protest maintained that alien Mexicans were deriving government benefits and that "Spanish-Americans are among the loyal patriotic citizens who are also interested in seeing that American citizens are given consideration first."[16] At about the same time, Governor Johnson began to charge that citizens of Colorado were suffering because of a financial drain caused by "alien Mexicans."

The neophyte American Citizens of Spanish Descent attempted to establish credibility by expressing support for Governor Johnson's position and for actions by city and county officials.[17] On April 19, headlines proclaimed that "Guardsmen [Were] to Keep Aliens Out of the State." A one-mile strip was declared under martial law, and Adjutant General Neil W. Kimball ordered fifty guardsmen to the border immediately. State troopers would assist the guardsmen, and promises were made that other borders would also be placed under martial law. The proclamation was to extend for an undetermined duration. By April 20 the Colorado–New Mexico border was being patrolled, protest groups were characterized as communist organizations, and the number of guardsmen had doubled. Apparently, the policy of permitting assignment by choice did not pose a manpower problem. Governor Johnson's real goal became apparent when he responded to the question of how Colorado would distinguish aliens from Chicanos, discussed earlier. The governor's position had been challenged by some organizations from the beginning, but he received support from some women's clubs and labor organizations. Some corporations denied the claims of exploitation and asserted that jobs would go unfilled.

Numerous articles attempted to portray job seekers as parasitical and as a means by which corporations were denying Coloradoans job opportunities. Cultural differences were emphasized under headlines such as "State's Troopers Halt Parasite Parade."[18] Every Chicano in Colorado became suspect, and constant reports of suspicious persons who appeared to look like Mexicans were reported in Monument, Denver, and numerous rural communities.

Local police authorities and "courtesy patrolmen" began to help in the attempt to stop the "aliens." The first detainees were Roman Ruiz and a family of eight from Crystal City, Texas. When Chicanos wanted to pass through Colorado on their way to jobs in adjacent states, they were informed that they could not do so.[19] One report from Kiowa County along the Oklahoma border reported the capture of a group of seven adults and six children, "composed of Mexicans."[20] On April 23, however, Governor Johnson's grand scheme, previously announced to be of indeterminate duration, ran into the problem presented by Governor Clyde Tingley of New Mexico.

Colorado officials had been crossing into New Mexico because it was feared that New Mexicans were not only crossing as individuals but were preparing to make a large-scale assault on the border. Governor Tingley's position was stated succinctly: "New Mexico does not object to Governor Johnson's private war so long as it is conducted in Colorado."[21] By this time the entire state was being patrolled to round up "out-of-state persons" who were in Colorado. Many New Mexican organizations protested Johnson's actions and began an economic boycott of Colorado products.

Governor Tingley threatened a statewide boycott of Colorado products. He was quoted as saying, "We'll stop every truck bringing shipments into New Mexico and force truckers to unload New Mexico bound shipments before they enter the state."[22] The next day, articles in *The Pueblo Chieftain* began to emphasize that jobs were going unfilled and blamed Johnson's actions. The editorial pages had emphasized earlier that Los Angeles had been un-American in attempting to stop indigents, but the paper had reversed its position to support

Governor Johnson. Tingley's pronouncement caused the *Chieftain*'s editor to propose a compromise: to possibly allow faithful *contrastistas* (contractors) to bring in some workers.[23] Discussion of the impact of a labor shortage began to fill the paper, and the need to patrol the Kansas border pointed to new complications.[24]

The blockade was lifted on April 30, as Governor Tingley's position, corporation pressure, and the exasperating task of enforcement continued to accelerate dissension against Governor Johnson's private war. Once again the *Chieftain*'s editor equivocated, proclaiming that discontinuing the blockade was a wise decision. Furthermore, according to the editor, the action had served a useful purpose. He qualified that statement somewhat, however, stating that "[r]efusing entry to this state to American citizens was a questionable act, although it was of some use at the moment."[25]

American Citizens of Spanish Descent reversed its support for the governor on April 27. The group opposed the use of marital law because the affected persons were of Spanish descent.[26] Even though this political organization made noises for a short time, it quickly became defunct. The members had personalized civil rights issues and had narrowly identified their issues, even to the degree of supporting discriminatory treatment of Mexicans. They were attempting to influence a power structure that did not differentiate between Chicanos. Whereas mutualista leader "Frank" Carpio was financing the support of a convicted murderer and Frank Aguilar and mutualistas were not visibly opposed to Governor Johnson's private war, they nevertheless continued to cater to a broad constituent group.[27]

Two significant points become apparent through Big Ed's war. The "fantasy heritage" could be used to divide Chicanos, and by personalizing an organization, strategy, and purpose, their political influence could be diffused. Americans of Spanish Descent attempted to pragmatically accommodate itself to the power structure on behalf of Colorado Chicanos and lost influence with the general population as well as the power structure as a result. Moreover, the attempt to differentiate themselves from other Chicanos had pitted members of the group against other Chicanos. That lesson had not been wasted; it would be employed many times in the future.

While circumstances and issues had changed thirty years later, the group, which preferred to identify with Spain rather than Mexico, had become somewhat more sophisticated. The tactic employed was to identify a term that could be used to accommodate all Chicanos yet emphasize the population's Spanish nature. The most articulate spokesperson for the new "Hispano" voice was sociologist Dr. Daniel T. Valdes, who in 1962 was instrumental in publishing a newspaper called *El Tiempo*. Political independence was asserted, even though it was apparent that the Democratic Party was the target of the Hispanos. Headlines such as "McNichols Defeat Would Be Victory for Hispanos" (October 11, 1962) maintained that the defeat of the Democratic candidate for governor would result in more equitable treatment of Hispanos. Polemic statements concerning the use of the term "Hispano" were also presented. The "fantasy heritage" demanded a spokesperson and a distortion of history. In this regard, Dr. Valdes found Tom Pino to be useful.[28] According to Marilyn Monteneqro, "In a tortuous argument purporting to prove that 'Hispanos' are white, Valdes and Pino seem to prove that not only are those of European ancestry white but also [that] those with Indian and Black antecedents who share a Spanish culture are also white" (1976: 19).

By 1966 Tom Pino and Dan Valdes had started another newspaper, *La Voz del Nuevo Hispano*.[29] This newspaper, less blatantly partisan than *El Tiempo*, included poetry and short stories concerned with civil rights issues. The editors' intent was apparent, however. They wanted to develop an ethnic political party, and the "New Hispano Party" was to be the vehicle. Individuals who did not want to participate were called "Uncle Toms," and the obvious strategy was to attack the Democratic Party.[30]

While asserting independence as a political party, the New Hispano leadership tried to capitalize on established Democratic partisan leaders such as Rodolfo "Corky" Gonzales. At the 1966 state convention in Pueblo, Dan Valdes was to be the keynote speaker, but Corky Gonzales was also invited to speak because he was fairly prominent in the Democratic Party. A Catholic newspaper, *The Southern Colorado Register*, called the formation of an ethnic political party a "tragedy." The editor, J. H. Kane, wrote that "[t]he Spanish surnamed people, instead of forming a new party, need to work to establish effective bargaining units within the Democratic and Republican parties, as Rudolph (Corky) Gonzales had urged."[31]

The New Hispano effort was not without critics. Political activists such as Manuel Diaz commented: "It is no crime to be inexperienced, but to enter an area of human endeavor without regard for what is happening currently, for what has happened in the past, and for whomever may at the moment be in a position of recognized leadership is to demonstrate contempt and utter disregard for what beneficial and positive projects may be in the making or in the process of being carried out." Diaz pointed to the New Hispano Party's major weakness by pointing out that the attempt to unify was in reality a thinly disguised attempt to pursue individual interests, a specific ideology, and a uniform philosophy.[32]

Despite efforts by Chicano leaders to diffuse the Chicano independent party, the New Hispano Party selected a slate of candidates in September 1966. Levi Martinez, a Pueblo attorney, was the candidate for governor and Tom Pino the candidate for lieutenant governor. By this time, Corky Gonzales had broken from the traditional power structure and formed the Crusade for Justice. Nevertheless, he opposed the new political party and maintained that he would favor independent action "if we could become victors instead of casualties." The Crusade for Justice was identified as a militant activist group, yet Gonzales advocated endorsing candidates by their abilities and not because they had a Spanish name.[33]

By the end of September 1966 the New Hispano Party was facing internal dissension and outside organized barriers. Delfino J. Mata withdrew his candidacy for the Colorado House of Representatives under the banner of the New Hispano Party and was appointed the Republican candidate for the same position. Other candidates broke publicly with the standard, and some were challenged by Chicanos within the Democratic Party.[34] The party further weakened itself as a credible alternative by endorsing Democratic candidates, including one individual who was not even a candidate. Other Chicano organizations such as the G.I. Forum discounted this political effort.[35]

The New Hispano Party suffered from the same problems as Americans of Spanish Descent. They both attempted to influence political parties through pragmatic politics. Not only did they ignore other organizations, but they asserted themselves as proselyte groups. The essence of a heterogeneous population was to be treated as a homogeneous group, and the standard chosen was not José Vasconcelos's concept of La Raza Cósmica but instead that of the Spanish caste system. The effect of the actual votes was minimal, and the Democratic Party probably gave the groups more credence than they deserved. The Democratic Party addressed the concerns of Colorado Chicanos, and much of the material was intended to weaken the possible impact of the new Hispanos.[36]

The New Hispano Party was a coalition of self-proclaimed leaders who used a general level of ignorance to apply pressure politics and were able, through their publishers, to proclaim positions without a constituent base. This effort was perhaps the most blatant attempt to influence politics made by any demagogic group. New Hispanos' characterizations of those who disagreed with them as Uncle Toms and sellouts would eventually work against them. Their obvious lack of a consistent ideology and their intense solicitation of publicity often provoked a public display of dissension and poor taste—all in the name of the Chicano population. Several of these self-proclaimed leaders later founded *La Luz* magazine, in which the emphasis on Spanish purity was also very strong. This group was highly successful with "paper organizations" but relied on the validity of its professional positions for leadership and influence.

Rodolfo "Corky" Gonzales and the Crusade for Justice went on to found the second Chicano political party in Colorado, La Raza Unida. However, the lessons of the New Hispano Party were lost on the José Ángel Gutíerrez wing of the party; in the aftermath of their manipulations of the 1972 national convention, La Raza Unida went into a decline. Gonzales had learned from the New Hispano Party that pressure politics, endorsement of other parties' candidates, and intra-ethnic conflict compounded by the "fantasy heritage" would prove fatal. However, the Texas experience had not included those lessons, and those were the issues that divided the national party.

The Civil Rights Movement of the 1960s and 1970s was fed by population growth, as well as the increased educational level and commitment of Chicanos who served in the Armed Forces during World War II, Korea, and Vietnam. Nevertheless, new labels and political definitions have been added to the U.S. lexicon. Of course, the government's responses have been based in part on groups that have been identifiable. While one has to admire the dedication and commitment brought to the struggle for the realization of civil and human rights during the 1960s and 1970s, one must also respect and admire the base of that movement, which had its origins in the 1940s and 1950s. The beginning has to be 1940, when Chicanos became an urban people. The 1940 U.S. Census indicated that Chicanos were no longer predominantly a rural population but that they had become an urban people, and it marks the date when cultural orientation was affected by an urban reality. The values of a rural people, such as fatalism, were not productive in an urban setting.

The major event of the 1940s was World War II, and Chicanos served in the U.S. military with great distinction, in both segregated and integrated units (Morin 1963). While problems continued at home, such as the Zoot Suit Riots (Mazon 1995), distinguished service in the military resulted in benefits, such as the G.I. Bill and home ownership. The creation of a middle class followed, as more and more veterans pursued a college education and, for the first time in U.S. history, real changes were made by a college-educated generation. As these veterans came home from fighting the racist policies of Nazi Germany, they were not inclined to accept racist policies on the home front. They began to organize into political groups such as the G.I. Forum to obtain their civil and human rights.

Beginning at an increased level in 1960, Chicanos began to assert national political influence through the political process. Viva Kennedy clubs from the 1960 election have continued in nature, and Chicanos have organized along ethnic lines to oppose or support various candidates and issues. Since 1960, labels have been extremely important in power politics. Inherent within labels have been political ideologies. Political differences between formerly mutually acceptable labels have been accentuated, and some continue to use labels for their singular profit or influence.

Mexicans were recruited to develop the U.S. economy, but as that economy fluctuated, they were rejected. They reacted to that rejection in a variety of ways. They turned against themselves and blamed themselves for their woes. They were deported, then, when economic demand required it, they were brought back. Programs such as the Bracero Act brought them in and magnetized the border; if they were turned down by the program, they simply came in illegally. In 1954, during the height of the Bracero Program, Operation Wetback was conducted to drive them back to Mexico.

Although decades have passed, the pattern has remained—recruitment, rejection, and reaction. In 1986 a new immigration law was passed, and in 2007 Congress rejected a new immigration law because the various interest groups could not come to grips with the need for Mexican labor and the desire to regulate that labor through law. It has been estimated that over 12 million illegal immigrants are currently in the country. However, a notable difference can be observed in more recent debate, which is that undocumented workers and their allies have taken to the streets to demand equity and fairness. The reaction has taken a new turn. Instead of blaming the victims for their illness, the victims are now blaming the system and seeking to correct it.

NOTES

1. The social circumstances that have polarized the Chicano community have been addressed by a variety of writers. I attempted to synthesize them in Sandoval 1982.

2. Manuel Diaz, interview with author, Pueblo, CO, December 1982.

3. Pamphlet published by Comision Honorifica Mexican and edited by Daniel Recivas, September 1925.

4. The literature concerning Chicano political organizations is extensive. Journal articles usually focus on the Texas and California experience. However, some writers, such as F. Chris Garcia, Frances Swadesh, and Clark Knowlton, do focus on New Mexico and southern Colorado. Richard Santillan's *La Raza Unida* (1973) is a good example of the distortion of Colorado Chicano political organizations. His section on the Colorado La Raza Unida is filled with errors. Other works concerned with La Raza Unida in California, such as Munoz and Barrera (1982), refer to the Colorado experience as if

it were tied solely to California, Texas, or both. One major consideration for the ideology and direction of La Raza Unida in Colorado was the nature of the New Hispano Party and, essentially, the evolutionary nature of Colorado protest organizations.

5. Conversations with Rodolfo Acuña, summer 1974.

6. The list of Colorado Chicano organizations is extensive. When those with a national affiliation are added, it becomes even more extensive. One of these groups is the Congress of Hispanic Educators, founded in Vail, Colorado, in 1968 by Denver Public School teachers. The name was a compromise that used the acronym CHE with the conservative position of "Hispano." Others include the CDC (Chicano Democratic Caucus, a state coalition of Chicanos), MEChA (Movimiento Estudiantil Chicanos de Aztlan), CUFA (Chicanos United for Action), and UMAS (United Mexican American Students). Organizations that are concerned with land rights should include the Land Rights Council, Chama, CO.

7. Juan Espinosa, interview with the author, Pueblo, CO, January 1983; Camarrillo (1979).

8. *The Pueblo Chieftain*: "Author of Article about 'Penitentes' Is Found Murdered," February 6, 1 (source of the quotation); "Boy Confesses He Killed Magazine Writer for Cash," February 7; "Slayer of Author Held for Trial on Murder Complaint," February 8; "Writer and Murder Brings Torture Cult to Light," February 11; "Slayer of Author Given Life Term," February 18, 1936.

9. *The Pueblo Chieftain*: "Author of Article about 'Penitentes' Is Found Murdered," February 6; "Boy Confesses He Killed Magazine Writer for Cash," February 7; "Slayer of Author Held for Trial on Murder Complaint," February 8; "Writer and Murder Brings Torture Cult to Light," February 11; "Slayer of Author Given Life Term," February 18, 1936.

10. "A Last Look at 1936," *Pueblo Star Journal and Sunday Chieftain*, January 3, 1937.

11. *The Pueblo Chieftain*: "Spanish-Americans Organize to Cement Public Confidence," February 17, 2; "Spanish-American Alliance to Seek Members in Valley," February 28, 5; "Spanish-Americans Will Meet Tonight," February 29, 1936.

12. "Guardsmen Move to Posts in Boulder," *The Pueblo Chieftain*, April 20, 1936, 2.

13. "Johnson Calls in Guardsmen," *The Pueblo Chieftain*, April 19, 1936, 1–2.

14. Ibid., 2.

15. *The Alamosa Daily Courier*, February 5, March 15, 1936.

16. "Leader of Pueblo Mexicans Denies They Overran WPA," *The Pueblo Chieftain*, February 5, 1936.

17. "State's Troopers Halt Parasite Parade," *The Pueblo Chieftain*, March 1, 1936.

18. *The Pueblo Chieftain*: "Guardsmen Move to Posts on Border: Prepare to Block Entry to State of Laborers, Aliens," April 20; "Governor Johnson and the Home Town Folks," April 21; "Johnson Calls on Guardsmen to Keep Aliens Out of State: State's Southern Border Is Put under Martial Law to Block Imported Labor," April 28, 1936.

19. *The Pueblo Chieftain*: "Governor Johnson and the Home Town Folks," April 21; "State's Troopers Halt Parasite Parade," April 21; "Great Western Company to Stop 'Raiding' Valley Beet Help," April 28, 1936.

20. "Troops Usher 350 Indigent out of State; Johnson to Keep National Guardsmen on Colorado Side," *The Pueblo Chieftain*, April 22, 1936.

21. *The Pueblo Chieftain*: "Guardsmen Stop 14 Penniless, Jobless Men en Route Here," April 22; "Border Patrol in San Luis Valley," April 22; "Lamar Guardsmen on Border Patrol," April 24, 1936.

22. "Tingley Threatens Colorado Boycott," *The Pueblo Chieftain*, April 24, 1936.

23. *The Pueblo Chieftain*: "Governor Johnson and the Home Town Folks," editorial, April 21; "New Mexico Should Be Fair and Consistent," editorial, April 25; "Detail of Highway Patrol Joins State Troopers at Border," April 25, 1936.

24. *The Pueblo Chieftain*: "Railroad Track Jobs Go Unfilled Following Border Ban on Indigents," April 25; "Border Blockade Causes Valley Labor Shortage," April 26, "Laborers 'Running' Colorado Blockade," April 26, 1936

25. *The Pueblo Chieftain*: "Ed Johnson Acts Wisely," editorial; "Border Blockade Lifted to Fill Labor Shortage," both April 30, 1936.

26. *The Pueblo Chieftain*: "Spanish Citizens Protest Blockade of State Border," April 27; "Vigilantes Warn Valley Mexicans," May 1, 1936.

27. *The Pueblo Star Journal and Sunday Chieftain*: "Aguilar Has Until Friday to Enter New Trial Plea," January 17, 1937.

28. *El Tiempo*, October 11, 1962, publishers Dan T. Valdes and Ruben C. Valdez.

29. *La Voz de Nuevo Hispano* 1, no. 2, September 13, 1966.

30. Ibid.

31. *The Southern Colorado Register*, September 23, 1966.

32. Manuel Diaz, unpublished position paper for COPE, 1966.

33. *The Rocky Mountain News*, September 19, 1966.

34. *The Pueblo Chieftain*: Ray Dangel, "Political Pot Boils: Objections Filed to Petitions for Three Nominees," September 29, 1; Ray Dangel, "Hispano Movement Will Grow, Say Backers at Meeting," November 1, 1966, 1.

35. Al Hernandez of G.I. Forum, Letters to the Editor, "Splinter Party, *The Pueblo Chieftain*, September 29, 1966.

36. "La Verdad," Democratic Party pamphlet. Includes Spanish text and emphasizes involvement by Chicanos.

REFERENCES

Acuna, Rodolfo. *Occupied America: A History of Chicanos*, 2nd ed. New York: Harper and Row, 1981.

Alvarez, Rodolfo. "The Psycho-Historical and Socioeconomic Development of the Chicano Community in the United States." In *Chicanos: Social and Psychological Perspectives*, C.A. Hernandez, Marsha Haug, and Nathaniel Wagner, eds. St. Louis: C. V. Mosby, 1976, 38–61.

Brenner, Anita. *The Wind That Swept Mexico*. Austin: University of Texas Press, 1942.

Camarrilo, Alberto. *Chicanos in a Changing Society*. Cambridge: Harvard University Press, 1979.

Cuellar, Alfredo. "Perspective on Politics." In *La Causa Politica*, F. Chris Garcia, ed. South Bend, IN: University of Notre Dame Press, 1974, 36–52.

Galarza, Ernesto. *Merchants of Labor: The Mexican Bracero Story.* Charlotte, NC: McNally and Loftin, 1964.
Gonzales, Manuel G. *Mexicanos: A History of Mexicans in the United States.* Bloomington: Indiana University Press, 1999.
Hoffman, Abraham. *Unwanted Mexican Americans in the Great Depression: Repatriation Pressures, 1929–1939.* Tucson: University of Arizona Press, 1974.
Mazon, Mauricio. *The Zoot-Suit Riots: The Psychology of Symbolic Annihilation.* Austin: University of Texas Press, 1995.
McWilliams, Carey. *North from Mexico.* New York: Greenwood, 1968.
Meyer, Michael C., William L. Sherman, and Susan M. Deeds. *The Course of Mexican History,* 7th ed. Oxford: Oxford University Press, 2003.
Monteneqro, Marilyn. *Chicanos and Mexican-Americans: Ethnic Self-Identification and Attitudinal Differences.* San Francisco: R and E Research Associates, 1976.
Morin, Raul. *Among the Valiant: Mexican-Americans in WW II and Korea.* Alhambra, CA: Borden, 1963.
Munoz, Carlos, and Mario Barrera. "La Raza Unida Party and the Chicano Student Movement in California." *Social Science Journal* 19, 2 (April 1982): 101–119.
Sandoval, David A. "What Do I Call Them? The Chicano Experience." *Colorado Association for Chicano Research Review* 3, 25 (September 1982): 3–25. Anthony Cortese, ed.
Santillan, Richard. *La Raza Unida.* Los Angeles: Tlaquelo, 1973.
Spicer, Edward H., and Raymond H. Thompson, eds. *Plural Society in the Southwest.* New York: Interbook, 1972.

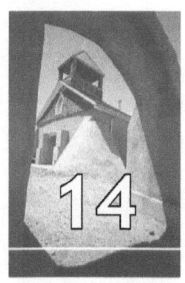

Peter J. Garcia

"Ay Que Lindo es Colorado": Chicana Musical Performance from the Colorado Borderlands

> Yo no soy de Colorado
> Soy un Nuevo Mexicano
> Pero vengo a cantarles yo
> Esta cancion que yo compuse
> Para ustedes mis amigos
> Mis amigos de Colorado!
> "Ay Que Lindo es Colorado."
> —ROBERTO GRIEGO

It is a busy Friday night at Señor Manuel's Mexican restaurant in Colorado Springs. The delicious smells, spicy dishes, and colorful *ambiente* are served along with the musical sounds of a well-known Chicana solo singer performing popular Mexican and New Mexican songs while accompanying herself on guitar. This local singer is an indigenous *trovadora* (troubadour) named Michelle Lobato, and her amazing story reflects Colorado's enduring Chicana musical legacy. Colorado's troubadour singers are legendary, dating back to the region's dynamic Spanish colonial period, turbulent Mexican era, and U.S. territorial days. In the early twentieth century, infamous trovadores were typically male, and they served as local *decímeros* (*decima* composers), *corridistas* (traveling minstrel ballad singers), *rezadores* (prayer leaders), and *cantantes* (singers) singing the traditional songs of Spain, Mexico, northern New Mexico, and southern Colorado while at the same time informing the public of important newsworthy events through their ballad singing. Today's trovadores are modern bards, social commentators, and popular singers who in some ways resemble the folk singers of the 1960s in the United States.

Southern Colorado has long maintained a strong ethnic heritage and has had an ongoing musical interaction with northern New Mexico since at least the 1850s. This important organic cultural interaction remains vibrant and dynamic today. Nuevo Mexicano native popular Chicano singer/songwriter Roberto Griego illustrates this point with the verse at the start of the chapter from his 1985 *exito* (hit) "Ay Que Lindo es Colorado." This lyrical local *cancion* (song) is an unofficial Chicano[1] anthem that hails many of Colorado's local place names and Mexican people. Among Chicano communities throughout the Southwest borderlands, Colorado holds a special status. Because Nuevo Mexicano musicians have transcended cultural borders since before the Civil Rights Movement, their local indigenous regional music remains popular throughout many parts of the borderlands. In this chapter, I consider more critically the local grounded aesthetics throughout southern Colorado in relation to diasporic articulations of race, class, generation, and gender within the greater Latina/o musical culture.

Today, the Chicana/o, Latina/o, Mexicana/o, and Hispana/o music of southern Colorado musicians expresses their own "grounded aesthetics,"[2] original styles,[3] eclectic sounds, and organic performances to express their homeland attachment, political struggles, passion and emotions, and unique socio-historical experiences. Colorado shares a similar traditional musical culture with Nuevo Mexico, including melancholy *alabado* (a para-liturgical unaccompanied chant lamenting Christ's suffering and death) singing throughout Semana Santa (Holy Week observances), *auto sacramentales* (Christian liturgical mystery, nativity, and musical folk plays and ritual dances) such as *Las Posadas* (the Inn) and *Los Pastores*, (the Shepherds), and a strong and dynamic *música de los viejitos* (music of the people).[4] New Mexico's popular Chicano musicians, singers, and *orquestas* (dance bands) also maintain a very strong fan base in Colorado and express an aesthetic influence on the regional *onda* (scene). Greater diasporic Latino, Mexican, and Latin American popular and folk musics and musicians are enormously popular throughout Colorado today; as social demographics continue to change, further interest in Latin popular musics is increasing throughout the United States.[5]

MICHELLE LOBATO: *LA NUEVA MESTIZA CANTANTE DE COLORADO*

Michelle Lobato is a singer from southern Colorado who enjoys musical fame throughout the state. She performs local indigenous Nuevo Mexicano, Greater Mexican, and Latin American popular folk,[6] regional (local), and traditional[7] musics. She is a mestiza singer who maintains a strong organic link to the Southwest borderlands. Well-known primarily in southern Colorado and New Mexico, Lobato has cultivated professional relations with Chicano regional musicians, especially Albuquerque's Lorenzo and Roberto Martínez. However, she has also forged her own unique musical style, local audience, and performance aesthetic expressing her Latina identity as a Colorado Mexicana native with long-standing ancestral roots in the region. Her musical highlights include several recordings and concerts throughout the state and New Mexico, Greater Mexico, and Latin America. She has long been a children's liturgist at Corpus Christi Catholic School in Colorado Springs and works for the Performing Arts for Youth Organization, where she does presentations on Latin American music for elementary through high school students throughout the state.

In high school Michelle Lobato was crowned the 1981 Colorado State Fair Fiesta queen and used her public identity to speak out against social injustice, poverty, and the importance of local spirituality. She also served as a "cultural ambassadoress" to Puebla, Mexico, in 1982, introducing Greater Mexican audiences to local Nuevo Mexicano musics from Colorado. The following year Lobato formed her own mariachi ensemble and was invited to perform at the Smithsonian Institution's annual Festival of American Folklife in Washington, DC, in 1985 and again in 1992. Lobato also records and promotes children's songs in Spanish and English and has recorded original spiritual music and hymns with renowned Catholic liturgical composer Jaime Cortez in California. In 1988 Lobato made her first solo recording of Mexican folk songs and ballads, titled *Palomita Mensajera*, and soon after she recorded a collection of spiritual music titled *Jesus Amor de Mi Vida*. Several of the composer's original alabanzas and hymns are published in *¡Aclama, Tierra Entera! Sing All You Lands*, a collection of bilingual psalms and other devotional songs by many leading U.S. Chicano and Latino Catholic composers. Regarding her Catholic faith and spirituality, Lobato explains:

> In my experience, the Catholic Church has made great strides in promoting equality and opening the doors of ethnic diversity. My work in the church reflects that practice. I have been blessed to work with some of the most talented and intelligent leaders in the Catholic community over the past

decade. People of many races and backgrounds have dedicated their [lives] to welcoming the *immigrantes* of Mexico and all Latin Americans as they come to this country to make a new life. The church has been very vocal in speaking out in favor of social justice and humanity toward those who come to this country to find a better life for themselves and their families. Our liturgical celebrations reflect that more and more every day through the music and Spanish language/bilingual celebrations. The church offers sacramental classes, catechesis, and many social ministries to the Mexican/Latino community. My part in that is contributing new scripture-based songs in the Spanish language to be used in liturgical celebrations [Masses] and to help educate and train more Spanish-speaking people to become leaders of ministry. Again, we still have a long way to go. One of our challenges is that we are working very hard to make the various Latino cultural gifts an integral part of church life, not just tokenism. (Lobato 2007)

Until recently, Lobato directed El Mariachi Tigre at Colorado College, and she is currently director of liturgical music at St. Francis of Assisi parish in Colorado Springs. One of the most memorable highlights of her musical career was her performance at the 1993 World Youth Day. In a recent interview at her home in Colorado Springs, she described the invitation:

[The invitation was] another miracle that fell from the sky. I was invited to sing for a wedding in Denver, and afterward the priest approached me and was very complementary. He gave me his business card and explained that he was on the World Youth Day Committee. A few weeks later I received a call from World Youth Day headquarters in Washington, DC, and was asked to sing with a mariachi for a morning *serenata* [serenade] in honor of the Feast of the Assumption. A few weeks later, after not having found mariachis available to play, I regretfully told them I wouldn't be able to provide the music they requested. The priest told me to put a group together and that would be fine. We prepared about six hymns, including "Las Mañanitas a la Virgen." When we finished our serenata, they asked me to sing more alabanzas. I began singing songs that spontaneously came to mind, including a song I composed, "Felicidad." I dedicated this song to the crowd and especially to our beloved [now late] Pope John Paul II. When we finished, we were escorted to a VIP section right in front of the sanctuary. As the pope processed up the aisle, the crowds began to push us up against the fence. So to protect my eight-month-old baby, Elena, I handed her to my husband, Jim. It was at that moment that the pope saw her. He came straight over to us (Secret Service scurrying about) and took Elena from Jim's arms. Pope John Paul II held her up, gazing into her eyes, then kissed her forehead and blessed her. Seeing the pope hold my child was even more special than singing that day. This was one of the most special moments in my life. (Lobato 2007)

THE DECOLONIAL IMAGINARY

Traditional and folk Nuevo Mexicana/o and Colorado music developed by uniquely incorporating indigenous Native American influences from local southwestern, neighboring plains, and northern Mexican tribes along with the Andalusian, Basque, Sephardic, Moorish, and other trans-national Afro, Arab, Jewish, and Gypsy music and cultural influences already present in Spanish and Mexican musics. Beginning in the nineteenth century, Mexican national, international Latin, Anglo-American, and Afro American musics joined the mix, so by the end of the twentieth century Colorado was seen as an important cultural crossroads for various international, commercial, and mass-mediated Latino popular musical styles and genres.

The long-standing Mexicana/o and Hispana/o descendants living in southern Colorado throughout the San Luis Valley represent the greater region's oldest indigenous "Indo-Hispano"[8] (mestizo) populations in North America. Their ancestors settled the frontier of New Spain in 1598, mixing with the indigenous Native American populations and brought into the United States following the 1846 war, invasion, and ongoing occupation of northern Mexico. Like neighboring south Tejas and northern Nuevo Mexico, Colorado's indigenous Hispanic and Native American residents remain marginal within the capitalist democracy. In fact, cartographers and demographers see much of the Greater Southwest borderlands as an interesting liminal Third World enclave within the U.S. imperialist social hierarchy. As in other conquered places throughout the United States, locals in Colorado and New Mexico lost the right to be educated in their own language and in general became second-class citizens. The Spanish-speaking Colorado Chicana/os who survived following the U.S. invasion, occupation, land theft, and political interference led to the development of a distinct, although often misunderstood, Indo-Hispano music culture, language, cuisine, architecture, and spirituality that are in serious danger of becoming extinct as a result of U.S. globalization, gentrification, linguistic terrorism, and corporate hegemony in the region. Michelle Lobato is a strong advocate who encourages bilingualism and promotes the Spanish language through her musical performances, compositions, teaching, and recordings. She explains:

> The young people preparing for and entering the workforce are very aware of the importance of speaking at least two languages. My son, Jimmy, told me recently that speaking Spanish goes without saying. Spanish should be required at a high school level and [should] begin even earlier. The challenge now is to learn more than English and Spanish. We are a very diverse country. It appalls and shocks me to hear about oppression and racism in

this day and age. It's about more than being "bilingual." It's about understanding the multifaceted beauty of all people. Language is only one aspect of who we are. Being Latino encompasses many cultural traditions. I am grateful to those who stand up and point out the beauty of Latino culture. The people that are here from south of the border are here to make a living, and we can't forget how much the United States has benefited from the exploitation of our neighbors. (Lobato 2007)

I refer to Michelle Lobato as Hispana because this is the term she most frequently uses in reference to her own ethnic group and identity. However, I regard her as a Chicana because of her commitment to social justice, the Spanish language, improved arts and music education, immigration rights, and land grant struggles. She explains:

I grew up in Pueblo, Colorado, a relatively small town populated by various minority groups and many Anglo-Americans. I know there was still much prejudice toward Hispanic people even in the 1980s but much less than was experienced by my father's generation. And certainly the identity "Chicano" was looked upon with great negativity, even within the Latino culture. It had a very militant connotation. I, at that time, never understood the mission or cause. Like myself, I think part of this thought process on the part of the mainstream was due to ignorance. Many (not all) didn't understand or try to know our culture or regard us as equals. I can now appreciate the efforts of the political activists of the 1960s who fought for equality. If not for their courage and struggles, we might still be subject to the racism and oppression of our parents and grandparents. Even my older brothers and sisters remember being mentored differently than their "white" friends. My siblings have achieved great things in life because of the encouragement of supportive parents and family. Our culture taught us to believe in ourselves. (Lobato 2007)

Today, a new class of Indo-Hispanas/os, or new mestizos, has emerged. These people call themselves Latinas/os and Mexicanas/os (Spanish-acculturated mestizos and mestizas). Some Latinas/os intermarried with U.S. Whites (Anglo-Americans) after the era of Americanization (1848). However, as the social demographics continue to change in Colorado, many Hispanas/os are intermarrying with Greater Mexican, Latina/o, and various *razas* from throughout the world. The term "mestizo" in the Spanish *casta* system was basically the mixture of White with Native American and implies a browning or darkening in overly simplistic terms.

COLORADO'S NEW MESTIZO/AS

Since the 1980s, Latina subjectivity has remained a leading innovative paradigm in Chicana/o literature and cultural studies. In her classic *Borderlands/*

La Frontera: The New Mestiza, the late writer Gloria Anzaldúa meditates on the experience of straddling cultural, psychological, sexual, and spiritual boundaries. A leading Chicana poet and lesbian by choice, born on the Texas side of the Río Grande, Anzaldúa explains: "[B]eing a writer feels very much like being a Chicana or being queer—a lot of squirming, coming up against all sorts of walls. Or its opposite: nothing definite or defined, a boundless, floating state of limbo. . . . Living in a state of psychic unrest, in a Borderland, is what makes poets write and artists create" (1987:94–95). According to anthropologist Renato Rosaldo, "This personal struggle with contradictions, this juggling of one's identities, like the crossing of genetic streams, yields hybrid vigor. It also fosters tolerance for contradictions and ambiguity and an acceptance of the negative shadow in one's subconscious" (1993 [1989]:216).

For Rosaldo, Gloria Anzaldúa has developed and transformed the figure at the crossroads in a manner that celebrates the potential of borders to open new forms of human understanding (Rosaldo 1993:216). Anzaldúa explains: "Where the *mestiza* stands is where phenomena tend to collide. It is where the possibility of uniting all that is separate occurs. . . . [The result] is a new consciousness—a new *mestiza*—and though it is a source of intense pain, its energy comes from continual creative motion that keeps breaking down the unitary aspect of each new paradigm. . . . Because the future depends on the straddling of two or more cultures" (1987:101–102).

For Anzaldúa, the new mestiza epitomizes the modern struggle with opposites because of her mixed race and culture and her feminist confrontation with sexism. This new mestiza (a person of mixed ancestry), she says, copes by developing a tolerance for contradictions and ambiguity. Rosaldo further explains that the new mestiza learns to be Indian in Mexican culture, to be Mexican from an Anglo point of view. She learns to juggle cultures. She has a plural personality, she operates in a pluralistic mode—nothing is thrust out, the good, the bad, and the ugly, nothing rejected, nothing abandoned. Not only does she sustain contradictions, she turns the ambivalence into something else (1993:216). Rosaldo explains:

> In making herself into a complex persona, Anzaldúa incorporates Mexican, Indian, and Anglo elements at the same time that she discards the homophobia and patriarchy of Chicano culture. In rejecting the classic "authenticity" of cultural purity, she seeks out the many-stranded possibilities of the Borderlands. By sorting through and weaving together its overlapping strands, Anzaldúa's identity becomes stronger, diffused. She argues that because Mexicanos have for so long practiced the art of cultural blending, "we" now stand in a position to become leaders in developing new forms of polyglot cultural creativity. In her view, the rear guard will become the vanguard. (1993:216)

The political activism, cultural renaissance, and social justice movements of the 1960s civil rights struggles came together for la raza with the emergence of el movimiento Chicano. Michelle Lobato was born and raised in Pueblo during the 1960s, and her musical career began at Corwin Middle and South High schools. She experienced firsthand the Chicano community's struggles as the United States transformed the former Mexican borderlands into a homogeneous monoculture. However, as increasing Mexican American working-class and ethnic "immigrant" communities became further segregated into the lowest economic *barrios*, Anglo-American suburbia, strip malls, and shopping centers continued to sprawl across colorful Colorado. Likewise, the conservative evangelical Christian movement, unfortunately, developed a strong presence in Colorado Springs. With the emergence of Dr. James Dobson's Focus on the Family and the development of several evangelical Christian churches, an intolerant, racist, homophobic neo-conservative stronghold grew to dominate much of southern Colorado's cultural life. This development has also been disastrous for local Hispana/o musical life and the Spanish language.

Following evangelical preacher Ted Haggard's resignation as pastor of the New Life Church after he admitted to soliciting prostitute Mike Jones for gay sex and methamphetamines, this unfortunate conservative backlash has been central in the historical erasure of the region's Hispana/o presence and in the undoing of the political gains and social accomplishments realized during el movimiento Chicano, such as the affirmative action and bilingual education that developed out of the Crusade for Justice and the Denver Youth Leadership Conference. Lobato's "musical ministry," as she recalls, began as a form of community service and spiritual activism, leading Spanish language choirs and working with Chicano priests in makeshift barrio churches set up temporarily in school gymnasiums, Boys' Clubs, and other civic spaces that provide social aid and human relief to Mexican immigrants and homeless populations. These spaces have been increasing throughout southern Colorado as the political economy has been transformed and much of the land dispossessed by Anglos. She describes her early work:

> I was eighteen representing the State Fair Fiesta Committee when Father Ralph Woodward in Pueblo, a political activist working with homeless people recruiting and bringing them into the church, asked me to help him minister. He loved the poor Mexican people and encouraged them to take pride in their language and culture. He worked as an evangelist ministering to the poor barrios in the late 1970s and throughout the 1980s. He encouraged me to be part of a parish mission in the housing project section in Pueblo called Sangre de Cristo. He would give Mass in the Boys' Club on the basketball court. He brought his own altar and vessels, vestments every

weekend, and he searched for local musicians including Lou Amella, an Italian accordionist, and Mel Romero, a guitarist and singer. Mel Romero actually taught me how to lead a choir and play at Mass. We didn't even have hymnals, and we sang the music that everyone knew. We used handwritten copies of hymns like "Bendito Sea Dios," "Adios Reina del Cielo," and "De Colores." (Lobato 2007)

Throughout high school, Lobato led choirs in working-class Chicano parishes, joined school choirs, and played violin in the youth orchestra. She continued her musical studies and performances throughout her university years. Lobato acknowledged the significant musical influence of her grandparents:

> My grandmother, Delfina Manzanares, was a great lover of music and a musician in her own right. She played a little piano and guitar and loved to sing. I think her favorite tune was "La Marcha de Los Novios," a much loved and anticipated custom at all family weddings. In a way, Grandma Delfina was responsible for my music formation. She taught me how to play my first guitar chords and gave me my first guitar. My grandfather, Manuel de Jesus Manzanares, also loved music. However, his musical expression came through the sacred. He didn't sing secular songs, though he loved to listen to folk music of the Southwest and mariachis. Grandpa Manuel loved to sing himnos, alabados, and was frequently asked to sing "La Entrega de Los Novios." He also led rosarios and said *"las gracias"* [a simple eulogy of the deceased and a few words of thanks to those in attendance]. He always added his profound and thought-provoking words of inspiration about how we live our lives and impact the world through our actions. Then he would end with a hymn such as "Si al Cielo Quieres Ir." My *abuelo* was also a devoted member of La Fraternidad de Nuestro Padre Jesus Nazareno. He belonged to la morada in El Puerto, near Walsenburg, Colorado. Our family attended every year during Holy Week. There, we sang traditional himnos like "Bendito Sea Dios" and we listened to the chant of the brotherhood singing alabados. (Lobato 2007)

I regard Michelle Lobato not only as an organic intellectual, artist, and cultural activist from the Colorado borderlands but also as a new mestiza troubadour who blends the best of the indigenous (Native American), Hispana/o (Colorado Mexican), and dominant (Anglo-American) cultures using her mixed regional Spanish language and musical performance to reconnect with broader raza communities (native, mestizo, trans-national, and immigrant). Her trans-national musical recordings, performances, aesthetics, and interests reflect her travels and interactions with various Latin American, Mexican, Latina/o, and Chicana/o artists over her lifespan. In addition to her love of classic Mexican and Latin American folk and popular songs, she equally loves performing Colorado's indigenous música de los viejitos and explains that it is not difficult to point out the many similarities between Colorado's indigenous Mexican folk songs and *bailes* (dances) and Greater Latin American traditional musics and dances.

Once during a vocal master class at Colorado College, Lobato described "Las Mañanitas" to students as a musical treasure when one considers the poetic lyrics and metaphors throughout the text. She believes it is the lyrical melody and simple harmonies that make the words so meaningful and flattering to the intended listener who is being celebrated in song. Musically, "the tuneful melody and poetry make it very emotional and moving to la raza who very much identify with it" (Lobato 2007). It is one of the most important songs in the Chicano musical repertoire because of its social and ritual affiliations.

Michelle Lobato has a powerful vocal quality that is intensely lyrical and soothing yet also passionate and dynamic. Her sound evokes intense emotional memories, grief, joy, and nostalgia among her adoring fans and devoted listeners. Her musical expression and lyrical interpretation make her live performances and recordings truly evocative of the broad range of human emotions and passion that inspired the classic songs. Lobato explains:

> I believe the music is a way of living and comes from our soul and innermost being. This is where our passion is, and it is not only expressed through the lyrical text but also in the singing style and of course the ensemble or instrumental accompaniment and musical arrangement. The message of the song is expressed through a passionate beautiful voice, although there are a variety of crude and raspy sounds used at just the right moments because the lyrics require a different register or range of the voice. The accompaniment and the way you perform a song [are] equally important. (Lobato 2007)

ROCKY MOUNTAIN ECHOES: MILE-HIGH CHICANO POETICS AND LYRICAL EXPRESSION

While some analysts are comfortable lumping White American musical styles in English with similar ethnic expressive genres to form a larger national heritage, Anzaldúa disagrees: "I grew up feeling ambivalent about our music. Country-western and rock-and-roll had more status" (1990:83). She explains, "In the 50s and 60s, for the slightly educated and (Americanized) or *agringado* Chicanos, there existed a sense of shame at being caught listening to our music" (Anzaldúa 1990:83). Despite this feeling, Mexican Americans from previous generations still listened to their music, and Michelle Lobato grew up listening to popular American music at the same time she enjoyed her parent's rancheras, boleros, corridos, and huapangos. She explains:

I was never a fan of rock and roll or that kind of thing. I was exposed to country Western music because my mother enjoyed the stars and I grew to like it. Since I could play guitar and sing, she encouraged me to sing cowboy ballads and some country Western tunes. I don't recall when I first discovered mariachi music, but [I] immediately fell in love with it. Before that, at an early age I was already interested in the regional folk and traditional musics that are heard throughout various parts of Latin America including Central and South America, Mexico, and the Caribbean. I was also interested in the *folklorico* music, especially the musical instruments, dances, and song types. As a teenager I joined an organization called Associacion Nacional de Grupos Folkloricos. Actually, the person who opened doors for me and encouraged my musical interests was a local man named Herman Martinez. He was a longtime friend of my father and he was well regarded by my parents. He and his wife, Patricia, invited me to various *folklorista* musical events, and this is where I first met Lorenzo Martinez. I began studying in Mexico and Central America. They held conferences throughout the Spanish-speaking world, and they even had one in Alamosa [Colorado]. Wherever they were held, I would travel to several of these conferences, and these were some of my earliest exposure[s] to Latin American folk and traditional musics and regional dances throughout the hemisphere. (Lobato 2007)

I first heard about Michelle Lobato in 1999, shortly after I arrived at Colorado College.[9] As I began exploring the local onda throughout southern Colorado, many locals pointed me in the direction of St. Mary's Cathedral in Colorado Springs where Lobato still performs regularly. I made it to a High Mass and was impressed with the vocal prowess of this local Hispana singer. I was surprised to encounter her again later that year at a Hilos de Oro conference on la música de los viejitos at Adams State College in Alamosa, where she was one of the featured guest artists.[10] She also played violin and performed with Los Reyes de Albuquerque, which also performs the older regional viejitos music. Lobato admits that violinist Lorenzo Martinez has been very influential in her musical development:

In my youth, I tended to be mostly interested in the folk music of southern Colorado and northern New Mexico and later fell in love with Mexican popular musics. The music continues to be performed by members of my extended family, and I developed a passion for the style very early on. First I taught myself how to play by listening to the recordings of Los Reyes de Albuquerque. Lorenzo Martinez struck a chord inside me, and I still really enjoy playing regional Hispano folk and traditional musics. I learned by ear and eventually developed a unique style of my own, different from Lorenzo's interpretation. Fortunately, about five years later I was invited to Adams State College and met Lorenzo and began taking music lessons with him. He is a wonderful teacher, easy to follow and very patient. I later brought him to Colorado to give a performance at a liturgical conference. He is very rooted in oral tradition, although he does read music. He is a musical genius but is also musically versatile and plays various styles. He doesn't depend on the written page. He can hear it and figure it out. (Lobato 2007)

ROCKY MOUNTAIN MUSICAL PEAKS

In 1998 Michelle Lobato recorded *Con Sabor a Latino America*,[11] a wonderful collection of classic popular songs from Latin America, Greater Mexico, and Colorado. I regard this brilliant recording as Lobato's most polished musical accomplishment to date. Her wonderfully entertaining live weekend musical performances at Mexican restaurants and her Sunday *misas* celebrated regularly at local parishes must be included among her many talents. *Con Sabor a Latino America* includes twelve classic and timeless songs, most composed during the "golden age" of Latin American and Mexican popular music from the 1940s and 1950s. Most of these memorable and beloved compositions continue to be rerecorded and performed in concerts by Latino artists throughout the world. "La Golondrina" is the oldest song on the CD, composed in 1862 by Narciso Seradell Sevilla. This song is a favorite of expatriate Mexicans, who, like the wandering swallow in the song, shed a tear when they think of their homeland far away. It is often requested at the funerals of Mexican Americans. Lobato's upbeat lyrical interpretation expresses the somber poetic text and evokes strong emotions and nostalgia in the melodic lyricism. Lobato's guitar accompaniment adds to the text painting with rhythmic *rasgueos* (prolonged "scratched" strums) and *apagónes* ("slaps") that muffle the strings, creating a percussive sound typical of *música romantica*. Her recording also features Leonel Cazares on *requinto* and additional musicians on Latin percussion and guitar, but her arrangement is original and her voice and lyrical interpretation first-rate.

Con Sabor a Latino America also features one of Lobato's original compositions titled "Si Tu Quisieras Amarme." In a published interview and recording review with journalist and music critic Yvette Padilla, Lobato explained, "I wrote that song because there are so many Spanish-speaking people in the United States and I wanted something on the CD from here" (1999:12). Other songs include "No Importa Que Tus Ojos," an Argentine tango performed more like a bolero, and an original rendition of "Yo Vendo Unos Ojos Negros." Ernesto Lecuono's 1948 classic huapango "La Malagueña" is performed in a familiar *trio norteño* style. Her popular ranchera-corrido "La Calandria" features lively *gritos* (shouts) and an upbeat "polka" dance tempo.

Consuelo Velázquez (1916?–2005) was a female Mexican songwriter who composed the classic bolero "Bésame Mucho." Lobato recalls her own musical experiences with and memories of "Bésame Mucho":

> "Bésame Mucho" is known all over Latin America, as well as [in] many other parts of the world. I discovered this as a teenager when I traveled to Mexico as the ambassador of the Pueblo/Puebla Sister City Exchange Program. There were many occasions when this romantic love song would be requested by people from various parts of the world. Each time, "Bésame Mucho" seems to evoke much emotion. It speaks of a passion that reaches to the depths of the heart. Each time I sing this song it brings tears, smiles, and embraces [among] those being serenaded. Others relate to its poetry and how it connects us. (Lobato 2007)

Alvaro Carrillo was one of the second-generation Mexican bolero writers in the late 1950s. His "Sabor a Mi" (composed in 1967) in general enjoyed popularity among Mexicans on either side of the border, especially during the heyday of the legendary Trío Los Panchos. Michelle Lobato treats "Sabor a Mi" with her own stylistic and lyrical interpretation and delivers an emotional and heartfelt rendition that brings out the nostalgic and powerful emotional impact of this classic bolero. The popular "En mi Viejo San Juan" was composed by Puerto Rican composer Noel Estrada and is one of the most sentimental and nostalgic boleros ever written. Many Puerto Ricans, especially those who live far away from the island—which is basically more than half of the entire population—consider this bolero a second national anthem. The city of San Juan adopted the song as its official city anthem. "En mi Viejo San Juan" is considered a classic and has been performed by popular Latina/o artists including Vikki Carr, Marco Antonio Muñiz, Rafael Cortijo, Ismael Rivera, Pedro Rivera Toledo, Celia Cruz, and Rocío Dúrcal.

Other Spanish language favorites include Yucatan songwriter Luis Demetrio's (1931–) 1958 classic "La Puerta" and Guadalajara composer Gabriel Ruiz's (1908–1999) 1948 "Amor, Amor, Amor." Lobato took "extra care in making sure the language and music were just right," and her recording is a testimony to her trans-national musical travels, experiences, and artistic interaction with Latin American singers, musicians, and composers.

Lobato is one of Colorado's organic musical treasures. She regards Colorado as her homeland, explaining:

> Colorado is a beautiful place to live and a wonderful place to grow up. I grew up in Pueblo, and it's a close-knit community that supports its children and native residents. Pueblo has a reputation for being friendly and hospitable, and I regard myself as a typical southern Colorado Hispana,

my parents are friendly and the community is too. I'm very spiritual, and I practice the Catholic faith that is intertwined with my culture and ancestral beliefs and customs. I always try to remain anchored in my family, faith, and place and I do this best with music, which allows me to communicate my inner ability to sing and express myself. I have had a very positive life experience through the expression of, and by teaching others about, this beautiful Mexican American *cultura*. It is because of the musical gifts God has bestowed upon me. People in general are very receptive to various musical experiences, and musica Mexicana/Latina is a wonderful tool to break down walls and open doors of diversity. (Lobato 2007)

NOTES

1. The ethnic and political label "Chicano" must be considered in its unique historical context because it refers to a personal commitment to social justice and political issues that were brought to public attention and scrutiny during the 1960s civil rights struggles. Roberto Griego refers to himself as a Chicano and as a Nuevo Mexicano (New Mexican) and is regarded as a musical activist throughout New Mexico and Colorado who sings about the entire region, people, culture, and their political struggles.

2. Paul Willis (2005) proposes the term "grounded aesthetics" to refer to the creative element in a process whereby meanings are attributed to symbols and practices and where symbols and practices are selected, reselected, highlighted, and recomposed to resonate further appropriated and particularized meanings.

3. Style generally refers to a complex or combination of musical characteristics and aesthetic traits in the melody, harmony, rhythm, ensemble, lyricism, performance, or form and treatment of materials (interpretation, accompaniment, composition, and arrangement) of a given musical performance or group of works.

4. New Mexican and Colorado Mexican or Hispano folk and traditional musics consist of familiar local vocal genres including ballad forms: romances, *relaciones, inditas, cuandos,* and *corridos;* songs (*canciones*); ceremonial music: *mañanitas, entriegas, posadas, marcha de novios;* religious hymns: *alabados, alabanzas;* and dance music: *varsoniana, valse,* polka, *chotís, raspa,* and mazurka. See Loeffler, Loeffler, and Lamadrid (1999) and Montaño (2001) for a more detailed analysis of the various genres, artists, and performances of the local Nuevo Mexicano and Colorado onda.

5. "The term 'Popular' in particular has heralded heated debate because it is not always necessarily clear what we're looking at when we look to popular culture. Its definitions are historically contingent and therefore frequently incongruous. It draws from the connotations of 'folk culture' often evoked to conceptualize the cultural practices and forms (for instance, the folksongs of an oral tradition, dance, and material culture) circulating in pre-industrial and pre-urban societies and is notoriously irreverent of the boundaries meant to distinguish mass-produced culture from more 'organic' or ostensibly 'rooted' culture. For these reasons, it is worth taking the time to elaborate on the development of these words' interconnected meanings" (Guins and Zaragoza Cruz 2005:4).

6. "Folk culture, derived from the German word *volk* for 'people,' 'common people,' or 'the masses,' signals a form of culture thought to originate from the elusive cat-

egory 'the people.' It is often regarded as culture *made of* or *of* 'the people' and, for this reason, has been thought to serve the needs and interests of its producers. Critics of mass-produced culture . . . predictably champion (and mourn the posited loss of) folk culture of an imagined pre-industrial epoch as a homogenous, more 'authentic' and 'organic' experience in contradistinction to capitalist society. With this maneuver, they simultaneously idealize folk culture of earlier epochs, and place it in opposition to the supposed 'cultural decline' of the interwar period" (Guins and Zaragoza Cruz 2005:5). However, among diasporic raza communities throughout Latin America, Mexico, and the United States, the terms "folklorico" and "popular" are interchangeable and are similar in meaning but not necessarily or entirely synonymous.

7. "Tradition is a vital element in culture, but it has little to do with the mere persistence of old forms. It has much more to do with the way elements have been linked together or articulated. These arrangements in a national-popular culture have no fixed or inscribed position, and certainly no meaning which is carried along, so to speak, in the stream of historical tradition, unchanged. Not only can the elements of 'tradition' be rearranged, so that they articulate with different practices and positions and take on a new meaning and relevance, [but] it is also often the case that cultural struggle arises in its sharpest form just at the point where different, opposed traditions meet, intersect. They seek to detach a cultural form from its implantation in one tradition, and to give it a new cultural resonance or accent. Traditions are not fixed forever: certainly not as separate 'ways of life' but as 'ways of struggle' constantly intersect: the pertinent cultural struggles arise at the points of intersection" (Hall 2005:70).

8. Legendary civil rights land grant activist Reyes Lopes Tijerina first used and popularized the term "Indo-Hispano" with the Alianza Federales de Pueblos Libres during the 1960s land grant struggle in northern New Mexico. "Chicano" was also applied to the land grant struggle by Greater Civil Rights Movement activists and recognized the indigenous ancestry of Nuevo Mexico's Hispanos, who for decades following the arrival of the Anglo-Americans typically denied their Native American ancestry and heritage, emphasizing instead the Spanish and Iberian elements seen here as another symptom of neocolonialism.

9. The Colorado College Office of Minority Student Life sponsored the research for this chapter. I thank Rochelle Mason for her continuing support of my professional research and teaching and in her role as co-founder and current director of El Mariachi Tigre. I am also grateful to Victor Nelson-Sisneros, Mike Edmonds, Michael Grace, and Victoria Levine for their ongoing encouragement and support since 1999.

10. Denver's renowned Trujillo family, led by violinist Lorenzo Trujillo and his aunt and violinist Eva Nuanez, also performed the New Mexican Spanish colonial folk dances, along with northern New Mexican composer and performer Cipriano Vigil and his family. The various musicos compared the regional particularities among the dance repertoires and performances and explained the music's ritual and social contexts.

11. *Con Sabor a Latino America* is available in Pueblo at Music Man's CDs and Tapes and the Union Trading Company.

REFERENCES

Anzaldúa, Gloria. *Borderlands/La Frontera: The New Mestiza.* San Francisco: Aunt Lute, 1987.

———. *Making Face, Making Soul/Haciendo Caras: Creative and Critical Perspectives by Women of Color.* San Francisco: Aunt Lute, 1990.

Guins, Raiford, and Omayra Cruz (eds.). *Popular Culture: A Reader.* London: Sage, 2005.

Hall, Stuart. "Notes on Deconstructing 'The Popular.'" In *Popular Culture: A Reader,* Raiford Guins and Omayra Zaragoza Cruz, eds. London: Sage, 2005, 64–71.

Lobato, Michelle. Interview with author. Colorado Springs, CO, 2007.

Loeffler, Jack, Katherine Loeffler, and Enrique Lamadrid. *La Musica de los Viejitos: Hispano Folk Music of the Río Grande del Norte.* Albuquerque: University of New Mexico Press, 1999.

Montaño, Mary. *Tradiciones Nuevomexicanas: Hispano Arts and Culture of New Mexico.* Albuquerque: University of New Mexico Press, 2001.

Padilla, Yvette S. "Michelle Lobato's New CD Offers Latin American Flavor," *The Pueblo Chieftain,* February 12, 1999, 12, 52.

Peña, Manuel. *The Texas-Mexican Conjunto: History of a Working Class Music.* Austin: University of Texas Press, 1985.

Rosaldo, Renato. *Truth and Culture: The Remaking of Social Analysis.* Boston: Beacon, 1993 [1989].

Willis, Paul. "Symbolic Creativity." In *Popular Culture: A Reader,* Raiford Guins and Omayra Zaragoza Cruz, eds. Thousand Oaks, CA: Sage, 2005, 241–248.

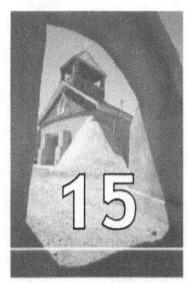

Helen Girón

When Geronimo Was Asked Who He Was, He Replied, I am an Apache

I was born in Trinidad, Colorado, in the 1950s, a decade when American society's zealous homogeneous policies began to take hold all over the country. These policies took place within the context of the greatest prosperity Americans had enjoyed, with the end of World War II, when the United States rose to the top of the world. By the 1950s, along with prosperity came the oppressive societal definition of who is an American. As an Apache woman, my journey toward self-identity begins within this climate.[1]

The definition of an American included the ideal physical appearance of having blue eyes and blonde hair, along with specific gender roles and class status. I did not fit into this definition of an American, and I can honestly state that neither did millions of other Americans.[2] White women especially suffered when their gender role was redefined—a definition that encapsulated all American women's gender role, including mine, until the 1960s with the insurgence of the Women's Movement.

White women were also forced back into the home, after their brief breath of freedom working for the war effort. Their homes represented another aspect of oppression for White women when they were built in isolated areas in the ever-growing popular suburban design of Levittown.[3] The isolation of homemaking and the breaking up of extended families took the greatest toll on these women's transition to suburban life.[4] Even though for most White women prosperity came in the form of oppression in their redefined roles of the 1950s, they did partake in "the belief that hard work would enable a person to rise in society and that their children would do better in life than the parents. The United States was indeed the land of opportunity."[5]

The United States did indeed represent the land of opportunity for White women and the White race; however, the same could not be said for Native Americans. The prosperity enjoyed by Whites did not trickle down to them, even though Native Americans were forced to live under the same societal and political pressures in the 1950s. In addition to the 1950s being a time of homogeneous identity policies for White women, my birth also coincided with the U.S. policy to terminate Native Americans' identity and replace it with the identity of an "American." This was how the U.S. government decided to solve the "Indian Problem."[6]

The Termination Act became official on August 1, 1953. With the stroke of a pen, the identities of millions of Native Americans were wiped out. Many Native Americans protested this act. An Apache's statement from the San Carlos Reservation encapsulates the condemnation of the Termination Act by many nations of Natives: "Today some people in Congress and the Department of the Interior would destroy our people with laws which divide us, endanger our property, and violate the provisions of our sacred treaties.... We will not let that happen."[7]

Unfortunately, it did happen in the midst of the homogeneous 1950s, when women's roles were redefined and Native Americans' identities erased. Thus, my birth became a symbol of this social and political environment. I would live in the margins of White society, forced to begin an odyssey in reclaiming what was taken from me the day of my birth—my identity.[8]

I have always known that I am Apache; I even knew it before I was born.[9] The first time my identity was challenged was when I entered public school. I remember running home one day from kindergarten, my eyes filled with tears and my heart broken because my classmates had taunted me, called me a savage, and then spit on me. Once at home, I searched for my father. He saw the tears in my eyes and asked what was wrong. My reply came in the form of a question. I asked him, if he knew they were not going to like me because I was an Apache, then why did he not have me as a White person? Tenderness came to his eyes. He hugged me and said, "You are an Apache, and you will have to fight to be one." Although this event took place almost fifty years ago,

I have never forgotten the profoundness of my father's words and ever since have fought in many different ways to live up to his reply.

Therefore, part of my identity was to resist the imposed identities of the women's role in American society and the racist stereotypes about Native Americans. Professor Luis Torres states in the video *La Raza de Colorado: La Historia* (2005) that "Chicana/o history is really about resistance in the past 500 years."[10] The form of my resistance would be different from that of my ancestors, but it would still be RESISTANCE.

I derive my courage to resist from my ancestors' stories of determination to be who they are—Apaches. There are many stories of determination and courage in the Apache oral tradition, but I will write just a few here.[11] These stories illuminate the resistance among the Apache to assimilate into colonial cultures, whether under Spanish or American colonizers.

First, I begin with the heroic story of a young Apache girl who was about twelve or thirteen when she was captured in the Nuevo Casas Grandes, Mexico. The title of the article about the young girl in *The Denver Post* read, "Apache History Goes beyond Geronimo."[12] The townspeople called this young girl "la nina bronca—the wild girl."[13] The community of Nuevo Casas Grandes lined up to see this Apache, selling food and creating a circus-like atmosphere. Guillermo Damiani Bassi stated in the article that "[w]e all grew up with rumors that Apaches still were hiding up in the Sierra, so what do we do when we actually find one? We treat her like an animal."[14] Meanwhile, the young Apache girl would not talk or eat. She curled herself in a ball with her back turned to the townspeople. She remained in that position until she starved herself to death. Death in the eyes of this young Apache was the only way she could return to her beloved Apache ways of life.[15] This story demonstrates sheer determination and resistance against capture into another's culture.

Another story demonstrating the same kind of determination and courage is the story of Dilchthe, a middle-aged grandmother who was captured and sold into slavery in the mid-1860s. Dilchthe belonged to the Warm Springs clan and was captured by Sonoran mercenaries in Esqueda, Mexico.[16] She was sold to a hacienda in Baja California.[17] Dilchthe was more than a thousand miles away from her homeland, but this did not deter her and other Apache women from making plans to escape back to their families. Once they executed their plan, the Apache women traveled by night and slept through the day. They were able to gather some provisions before their escape, but when these supplies were gone, the women survived by eating insects and desert plants. Mexican women along the way also aided them.

These women's escape became an embarrassment for search parties, who could not find women escapees led by a grandmother and on foot, with no map or food. On the border between Arizona and Mexico is "where [Dilchthe] was found by her son-in-law. Both were so overjoyed that they embraced, momentarily forgetting the Apache custom of avoidance [of contact] between a man and his mother-in-law."[18]

Many scholars have written about the Apaches' ability to hide so well in the surrounding environment that it seemed they were invisible; this was certainly true in this story of the escape of these Apache women.[19] This was also true in the story of Ma-si, who surrendered with Geronimo in September 1886.[20] The surrender of Geronimo marked an end to Apache wars for the Americans; however, as reflected in the first story told earlier, his capture did not end the Apache wars. Geronimo and his tribe of thirty-seven men, women, and children were to be taken to Florida, where they were to be imprisoned. Ma-si, who could not leave his homeland, decided to escape. He seized an opportunity and with the aid of an Apache woman escaped out a window. After he slipped out of the window he "dropped to the ground, and crawled into the weeds, where he [lay] in deathlike silence."[21] When he had the chance, Ma-si began his 1,500-mile trek back to his homeland.[22] Ma-si, just as in the story of the young Apache girl and Dilchthe, was determined not to have his identity taken away, and as an Apache he would have resisted any effort to do so.[23] I take my courage and determination against any efforts of assimilation into American society from these courageous stories of my ancestors.

However, the question must be raised as to what happens to Apaches or any other indigenous people who do try to assimilate and live in the White man's world. Assimilation did not work for the Cherokee Nation, as proven by the Trail of Tears, and it certainly would not work for some Apaches.[24] The story of Apache Kid showed many Apaches what assimilation meant and that it did not prevent betrayal by the U.S. government. Apache Kid from a very young age immersed himself in the White man's world by working in saloons, cleaning stables, or doing any other work he could find.[25] By the time he was a teenager he understood the White culture and language as well as his own. Apache Kid also became one of the best trackers in Arizona Territory, and the U.S. Army soon recruited him to help track down Apaches the government considered hostile. History had proven that neither the Mexican government nor the Americans could effectively track down Apaches, not even a grandmother; but Apache Kid could track, and he used his tracking skills to help the U.S. government:

> When [Apache Kid] picked up the trail of a runaway, his Apache instinct carries him with the swiftness of a bloodhound. No broken twig, misplaced rock, or bit of clothing that a fugitive might have lost in the brush along the trail escaped his detection. At the end of the trail he invariably found his fleeing Apache brother. If the overtaken fugitive resisted too much, he was shot. Scarcely past the age of eighteen, this Apache scout already had killed more than twenty of his own people. A white man had trained him, and the training was thorough.[26]

It is clear from this quote that Apache Kid had found a place in the White man's world, even to the point where he felt no guilt over killing other Apaches. He also participated in tracking down Geronimo and his band in the Sierra Madres with Al Sieber, the White man who trained him.[27] On the day Geronimo and his band were loaded onto a train to be taken to the prison in Florida, Sieber wondered what Apache Kid was thinking as he watched the train pull off. He did know that Apache Kid "was at a tender, plastic age and could easily be moulded. His fate hung in the balance. He was destined to become famous among the Apaches."[28]

Al Sieber was correct in stating that the Apache Kid could be easily molded, and he would become famous among the Apaches—but not for the reason Sieber predicted. After a misunderstanding in which Sieber was shot, not by Apache Kid but by another Apache who was standing near the Kid, Sieber turned on him. He accused Apache Kid of shooting him in the leg, leaving him with a limp for the rest of his life. Apache Kid was found guilty and sent to prison. As in the case of Ma-si he managed to escape, and until the day he died he was one of the most feared bandits in Arizona and Northern Mexico. Apache Kid did become famous for his terror tactics against the Mexican government and the Americans, making him loved among the Apaches—actions molded out of Sieber's betrayal.

Apache Kid would go down in history along with the names of other social bandits, such as Tiburcio Vasquez, Joaquin Murrieta, Jesse James, and others. The last quarter of the nineteenth century, according to some historians, was a time when "[c]ivilization was struggling with Marauding Apaches, and White and Mexican outlaws."[29] Apache Kid was a product of his time, and he was never captured. There is still debate over how he died; some say the Mexican soldiers killed him, while others say he died peacefully of old age.[30]

One can see from these stories that the last quarter of the nineteenth century and the first quarter of the twentieth century were turbulent times for Apaches. Both of my parents were born during this time. My father was born in 1894 in San Pablo, New Mexico, only eight years after the surrender of

Geronimo and four years after the end of the Indian Wars.[31] My mother was born in Las Vegas, New Mexico, in 1916, four years after New Mexico became a state. THEY WERE APACHES. I can now proudly state that for them. However, it would take another generation and almost 100 years to be able to state this.

Over the past ten to fifteen years, my siblings and I have been piecing together the history of our parents. As part of this task, my brother and I went on a genealogical expedition in New Mexico. We extensively researched any available archives such as churches, museums, and government resources. We also explored nearby cemeteries.[32] People in the area who are interested in the history they represent care for these cemeteries. One day while we were exploring, we were approached by one of the caretakers. We thought he was going to run us off, but instead he asked our last name. We said Girón, and he told us his father knew the Girón family. We made an appointment to meet with this man's father the next day.[33] From the story about the Girón family this elder told us, we were able to piece together the earlier part of our father's life. It was amazing that this man's recollection about the Girón family coincided with the knowledge we had about our father's later life. What an experience.[34]

He told us that the Girón family moved to Trinidad, Colorado, in the early 1900s in search of work in the railroads and coalmines.[35] He was not sure if they ever reached their destination, but I reassured him that they had, telling him that I was born in Trinidad. It turned out that the Girón family—Apaches—paralleled the diasporic movements of Chicana/os and Mexicana/os in the late nineteenth and early twentieth centuries.[36]

The end of the Mexican-American War in 1848 marked the beginning of the Mexican diaspora. Mexicans "were literally forced to leave their homeland to become strangers in alien lands."[37] This forced relocation had already taken place for many Native nations in the Southwest, including the Apaches, except that these Natives became aliens on their own land. Some Apache *genizaros*, who found safety and something of an identity among the Mexicans, followed their movements into the White man's world.[38]

For the Girón family, it began with seeking work. In the first decade of the twentieth century, thousands of Mexicans migrated to southern Colorado in search of work in the coalmines; among them were members of my family. Rodolfo Acuña, in his book *Occupied America,* describes the changes that occurred in southern Colorado when this migration took place: "The growth of coal mining in southern Colorado literally changed the landscape of Mexican pueblos there. Their plazas greatly resembled those in northern New Mexico in their social and economic function [in which] mining camps surrounded the villages."³⁹ It was when over 11,000 Mexicans migrated to southern Colorado and then became outnumbered by European immigrants that the landscape in this region changed. Moreover, as always happens when White people move into a region, racism against Mexicans/Mexicanos/Chicanos began to run rampant in southern Colorado. Susan B. Anthony even contributed her racist view of the situation in southern Colorado when she referred to Mexican as "greasers."⁴⁰ There would be no unity among mine workers until the advent of the coal strikes.

My mother repeated stories my father had told her about his participation in the coal strikes in Trinidad.⁴¹ What struck me the most about her stories was how united the coalminers were in fighting for a union. The mines were owned by John D. Rockefeller Jr., one of the richest men in America. The miners had to be united if they wanted to win. Their meetings were held in complete secrecy and in different topographical areas, such as arroyos. The tactics they employed against the coalmine companies were also held in complete secrecy.

She told me that these coalminers meant business and if they had to defend their right to make a decent living in a dangerous job by using violence, they would do so. In 1914 Mother Jones came to help organize the miners in Trinidad. She was considered the most dangerous woman in the United States, and as she stepped off the train in Trinidad she was arrested.⁴² She was then taken to Denver. When she was released there, she returned to Trinidad and was rearrested, leading to a protest by other women. During the protest some women were injured. The incident became a moral victory for the women and the miners.⁴³

After the Ludlow Massacre on April 20, 1914, the miners went into a rage.⁴⁴ My mother relayed stories of miners confronting federal troops and guards from the mine with bats, guns, rocks, and other weapons.⁴⁵ The violence used against the miners, as demonstrated at Ludlow, produced a profound commitment to the interests of the working man, such as my father. My father's participation in organizing a union in Trinidad led him to admonish his children to follow one of his few rules: NEVER CROSS A PICKET LINE. To this day, I have never crossed a picket line and I have helped organize many unions, including the United Farm Workers in the 1970s.⁴⁶

My parents were married in 1935 in Trinidad (Figures 15.1, 15.2). There was a twenty-year disparity in their ages. There is a gap in my father's whereabouts before he married my mother. We do know that he served in World War I in 1918. He was shot in France and was awarded the Purple Heart. My mother pulled out that medal and flag at every opportunity and told us of my father's participation in the war.

15.1. Elicia (Martinez) Girón and Tiburcio Girón, circa 1940s.

Like many Chicano/Mexican men, my father fought for what he considered his country. These young men wanted to prove their loyalty and to "prove their U.S. citizenship."[47] My older brothers, Jose Dolores Girón (Lolo) and Francisco Girón, followed in my father's footsteps by fighting in World War II and the Korean War. However, the sacrifices my father and brothers made in these wars did not lead to a better life for the family.

By the time I was born in 1952, my family had worked as farmworkers for many years. Acuna discusses how the Great Depression transformed farm work into factories in the fields.[48] My family labored among many Chicanos/Mexicans/Mexicanos during the 1950s to put food on the tables of Americans enjoying the American Dream in suburbia.[49]

The American belief that hard work would enable a person to rise in the ranks of society or that children would do better than their parents did not apply to the Americans toiling in the fields. Eddie Montour reflects on his memories of his parents' work in the fields. He states that his parents were proud of their work because it was an honest job. As he put it, they would work from "can't see in the morning to can't see at night."[50] This was same for my family, especially my father. We began work early in the morning, before the sun came up, and then the children were sent to school.[51] My father would continue his workday at Colorado Fuel and Iron (CF&I).[52] The family would not see him until the sun went down. This pattern continued until his death in 1962.

The American Dream was a lie for this generation, especially the belief that if you worked hard you would succeed. Despite the fact that this lie was ingrained in all Americans, some began to challenge its validity. I have always been proud of my older brothers' and sisters' involvement in the Pachuco Movement, in which young people began to create a space for their identity—an identity separate from that of an American, one that challenged the validity of white supremacy.

These young people were considered the first "Barrio Warriors," refusing to be silent and invisible.[53] It was not the right time for them to speak out, but this movement sparked the movements of the 1960s and 1970s among

15.2. Elicia (Martinez) Girón, age around ten, circa mid-1920s.

Chicana/os and Native Americans. Therefore, the oppressive homogeneous decade of the 1950s proved to be the breeding ground for the resistance demonstrated in the Civil Rights Movement, in which Chicana/os, Mexican Americans, Native Americans, African Americans, women, and others would define themselves.

The Civil Rights Movement provided the social space for my family to reclaim its identity as Apaches. The Girón family's journey parallels Paula Gunn Allen's remarks in *Off the Reservation*, which refers to her life and work as a "journey-in-between, a road [leading to] . . . where [she] was going [because she knew] where [she] was from."[54] This quote parallels my family's journey in-between, immersed in the culture of Chicana/os while never losing their Apache identity. Moreover, my family members knew where they were going, which was toward FREEDOM, because they knew where they were from.

However, freedom proved elusive for our family. First and most important was the problematic definition of Native Americans in the 1960s, a definition that continues to this day. Ever since the passage of the General Allotment Act in 1887, "the descendants of indigenous Americans had to define themselves by reference to federal laws and institutions for Indians."[55] One of the methods for defining Native Americans is based on the registration of a reservation, which, in turn, is based on the amount of Native American blood the residents possess.[56] Now, even Apaches denied their Apache identity.[57]

This did not deter me because, as Patricia Penn Hilden quotes in her book *When Nickels Were Indians*, "she was the maker of the song she sang."[58] My song has always been about freedom, and I do not need any Apache nation or the U.S. government to tell me who I am because I had strong and determined parents who gave me my identity. It tickles me when someone remarks that I look like a Chicana or a Mexicana, not understanding what my family has been through. I reply, NO CHICANAS AND MEXICANAS LOOK LIKE ME. This is the most appropriate answer, since few people have a strong historical understanding of the Southwest. I realize now that my parents gave me that history and helped me create the song I now sing.

It was their teachings that gave me the strength and courage to engage in the fights of the Civil Rights Movement. I first supported the Women's Rights Movement because it helped me escape the oppressive definition of what a

15.3. Francisco Girón, July 7, 1938, to October 3, 1969.

woman should be; for this I am eternally grateful and I, too, burned my bra. As a woman, I also believed in equal rights for women, but it has been hard for me to submit to the oppressive woman's role. I was raised in the Apache culture where men and women are treated as equals.[59] It has been difficult for me to live in a man's world.

On the other hand, the Chicana/o Rights Movement opened up the social space for identities other than White. Hence, in the late 1960s many of my family members and I joined this movement for equality, justice, an equal education, and an end to racism. My mother encouraged our participation, as if it was also her chance to undo the many injustices she had suffered. She used to tell me before I went to a demonstration or protest to "go out and kick those police's asses." I would remind her that the police were scary, with their guns and military garb. It *was* scary to have the police at every demonstration and protest, but I went anyway. I did understand my mother's feelings, and every hand gesture and scream of "CHICANA/O POWER" was imbued with my own liberation. Even though I am not Chicana, these words resonated with me. But two defining moments in the movement ensured that I would continue to fight for justice forever.[60]

The first was the death of my brother Frank in the Vietnam War on October 3, 1969 (Figure 15.3). After joining the Marines and fighting in Korea in the early 1950s, he became a lifer in the army.[61] By 1969 he was in the Special Forces, the group that goes into a war situation first. I protested this war, along with millions of others, because I wanted my brother to return home safely. It was not a secret that the Vietnam War was racially unjust and that men of color were killed in disproportionate numbers. It was considered a poor man's war, and poor men fought in the front lines.[62] I can understand my brother's motives in trying to prove himself to society and certainly his loyalty to his country and family. Here is a poem I wrote thirty years after he was killed:

> 30 Years
> For Francisco Girón
>
> 30 Years
> from that day
> in 1969,
> when the creator took you away.
>
> I miss you,
> and

wonder every day
what it would be like
if your path was to stay.

I love you,
and
there still is pain
every time
at
the mention of your name.

That war,
what a silly game!
It counted only for those
Who gained.

My Brother,
whose name is scratched on a wall.
I say,
on the day of your fall,
torn at the hearts of us all.

Brother you sacrificed
your life,
To give your sister,
the right to yell
BRING MY BROTHER HOME!

It was you
who made it right,
in the streets for me to fight.
And fight, I did!
Never, Never, to Quit.

Still, even with every scream for justice,
and even jail,
you never returned.
I feel now that I failed.

The 30 years has not made a difference,
the pain hidden deeper,
so no one can see.
I have accepted and respected your decisions
because you died in that shameful war
so I could be free.

  The other event was the murder of my *primo hermano* (first cousin) Luis "Junior" Martinez in 1973.[63] Luis was killed by the Denver Police Department. They shot him in the back. Luis was part of the Crusade for Justice (Crusade), having become a member when he was a teenager. In 1973 the American Indian Movement was involved in the takeover of Wounded Knee. The police thought the Crusade was helping the Native Americans with food and other supplies, so they were constantly harassing Crusade members.

On March 17, 1973, the police were supposedly responding to complaints of a wild party at the Crusade building. When they arrived, they began to harass everyone at the party and accused them of having a bomb. Luis confronted the police. While he was walking away from one of the police cars, he was shot.[64] Many in the community felt Luis was killed because of the connection between the Crusade and the American Indian Movement. This may be true, but it is ironic that a person of Apache heritage died in the resistance movement of Chicana/os and Native Americans. I found out years later that my cousin wanted to be buried in the Sierra Madres in northern New Mexico. I was told he had always felt a spiritual connection to that land. I wondered if he knew that this was the very land from which his ancestors came.[65] I also knew when I heard this that my cousin was at peace. QUE VIVA LUIS "JR" MARTINEZ.

The years after my cousin's death were turbulent for both the Chicana/o and American Indian movements. I did my part in both movements. I joined the United Farm Workers Union and worked for five dollars a week. I remained there for about a year. I had fun going into Safeway and crushing grapes or going into fast-food restaurants and pouring salt on the lettuce during the grape and lettuce boycotts. What was not fun was going to jail or being harassed on the picket line. I remember times on a picket line when we would call for help from other organizations because we were being shoved down and hit. The United Farm Workers might have been a nonviolent organization, but some other organizations were not. One thing I can say for certain about these turbulent times is that people were truly united.[66]

I am not sure when this kind of unity will happen again, but I do know it was the oppression of Apaches and being born in the oppressive 1950s that made me the warrior I became in the 1960s and since. Both my parents would be proud. After all, they produced the maker of the song I sing. I now know the reason I studied history—to take the stories of Apaches and many others out of the margins of American history and place them where they belong, which is in the American story.

NOTES

1. The history of Apaches, especially the historical actions of spiritual leaders like Geronimo, must be seen through the lens of colonialism—first by the Spanish, then the Mexican government, and finally the U.S. government. In fact, Apache history is

unique in that during the Apache wars this nation of Natives fought three colonizers in an attempt to maintain their ways of life. However, unfortunately, the Apache wars have been described through the eyes of the colonizers and not as the Apaches viewed them. A prolific amount of scholarship provides a more well-rounded account of the Apache wars, including firsthand accounts. See Britton Davis, *The Truth about Geronimo* (New Haven: Yale University Press, 1929); Eve Ball, *Indeh: An Apache Odyssey* (Norman: University of Oklahoma Press, 1980); David Roberts, *Once They Move Like the Wind* (New York: Touchstone Books, 1994); Angie Debo, *Geronimo* (Norman: University of Oklahoma Press, 1976); Edward Spicer, *Cycles of Conquest: The Impact of Spain, Mexico, and the United States on the Indians of the Southwest, 1533–1960* (Tucson: University of Arizona Press, 1962); and the most important work by anthropologist Jack Forbes, *Apache, Navaho, and Spaniard* (Norman: University of Oklahoma Press, 1960). This is by no means an exhaustive list of scholarship on the Apache wars, but it will give insight into the Apaches' perspective on these wars.

2. The psychology behind this American definition caused me to invent an imagery friend, Nancy, who did have blonde hair and blue eyes. Looking back on it now, I think Nancy was my defense against the racism I encountered when I entered the public school system.

3. Levittown was the original design of suburban living in the 1940s and 1950s. Suburban living had existed earlier, but not to the extent of the Levittown design. See James Patterson, *Grand Expectations: The United States, 1945–1974* (New York: Oxford University Press, 1996), 73.

4. An Irish woman once told me about her grandmother's experience with suburban living. Her grandmother could not adjust to the isolation and to the fact that she could not see her family, leading her to attempt suicide.

5. Patterson, *Grand Expectations*, 65.

6. Part of the "Indian Problem" was the fact that the Native Americans' lands were coveted by Americans. Another part was the lack of complete assimilation into American life. See James Rawls, *Chief Red Fox Is Dead: A History of Native Americans since 1945* (New York: Harcourt Brace College Publishers, 1996), 44.

7. After over two decades of resistance to the Termination Act, it was finally overturned during the Nixon administration in the 1970s. Ibid., 42.

8. My birth certificate indicates that I was born a White woman. There have been moves by some, including myself, to correct this error.

9. This belief of knowing who you are stems from the Apache Medicine Wheel, which dictates how one walks on his or her journey through life. I have never known anything else.

10. I am paraphrasing Professor Torres's statement here, but I agree that the Chicana/os' history is about resistance, as it has been for many other indigenous groups.

11. Many of these stories have now been written about and documented.

12. Paul Salopek, "Apache History Goes beyond Geronimo," *The Denver Post*, September 6, 1997, second A section, 21 and 22.

13. Ibid., 21.

14. Bassi is referring to the Sierra Madres in northern Mexico. Ibid.

15. My mother told me many stories about Apaches starving themselves when they wanted to escape life or various situations. It was a way they chose as part of the journey to the "Happy Place"—the Apaches' version of heaven.

16. These mercenaries were men from the United States or Mexico who were drawn into finding Apaches for their scalps, which paid handsomely. This practice continued well into the twentieth century.

17. Apache slavery begins with contact by the Spanish, as early as 1593, because of their resistance to colonization. All indigenous slaves' faces were tattooed to indicate who their master was. Alan Knight, in *Mexico: The Colonial Era* (Cambridge: Cambridge University Press, 2002), states that slaves had so many tattoos it was hard to see who the original owner had been. This practice continued because some sources refer to the tattooing of Apaches' foreheads under the U.S. government for the purpose of handing out rations.

18. Joseph Jastrzembski, "Treacherous Towns in Mexico: Chiricahua Apache Personal Narratives of Horror," *Western Folklore* 54, 3 (July 1995): 175.

19. During the years in which the Spanish, the Mexican government, and the Americans were tracking down Apaches, they seemed to be invisible. These Natives' ability to hide so well stems from a deep, intimate relationship with the environment. The art of hiding can be traced back to the culture of Teotihuacan beginning in 100 AD. I remember as a small girl my father putting my siblings and me on a large tract of land filled with tall weeds. He would say that the last one to find everyone else was the best at hiding. I would usually win. I did not understand then that my father was teaching his children the art of hiding, teaching them stillness, patience, perseverance, and how to become part of the environment. To this day, I appreciate these qualities.

20. Geronimo was a Bedonkohe Apache whose birth name was Goyakla, One Who Yawns. He was given the name Geronimo by Mexican soldiers who feared him.

21. Jess G. Hayes, *Apache Vengeance: The True Story of Apache Kid* (Albuquerque: University of New Mexico Press, 1954), 9.

22. Ma-si was never captured again, and some say he died of old age. But before his death he hooked up with Apache Kid and was considered a bandit by the U.S. and Mexican governments.

23. Geronimo and the rest of the Apaches, including Lozen, the second documented Native woman held as a prisoner of war, never forgot they were Apaches. They surrendered only when the United States promised to one day return them to Apache land. When Geronimo died in 1909, the Americans still feared him even in death and refused to allow his body to be returned to his homeland for burial. He is buried in Oklahoma.

24. The Cherokee made every effort to assimilate, creating a constitution and even adopting slavery (not the kind of chattel slavery used in the South). However, when gold was found on their land, they were moved to Oklahoma for their own protection, so the story goes. The move to Oklahoma is referred to as the Trail of Tears, which took place in 1832.

25. Apache Kid's real name was Haskay-bay-nay-ntay, meaning he was tall and brave and would come to a mysterious end. His Apache name was too difficult for the

White people he worked for to pronounce, so they just called him the Apache Kid. He was born in Globe, Arizona, in 1868. Hayes, *Apache Vengeance*, 4.

26. Ibid.

27. Al Sieber was also considered the best tracker in Arizona Territory, even though he was White; however, he could not track Geronimo and his band without the aid of Apache Kid.

28. Hayes, *Apache Vengeance*, 5.

29. I am not sure how this author is defining civilization. Is he saying that betrayal was part of the White man's civilization or that it was uncivilized to seek out justice the way Apache Kid did? See William Sparks, *The Apache Kid: A Bear Fight and Other True Stories of the Old West* (Los Angeles: Skeleton, 1926), 5.

30. Knowing the effectiveness of the Mexican and U.S. armies, I would go with the belief that he died peacefully of old age.

31. Geronimo surrendered on September 4, 1886. Many historians considered the end of the Indian Wars to be 1890, even though it has been documented that Native Americans continued to fight, as in Chipas, Mexico.

32. Cemeteries are considered primary documents and a great source for historical research.

33. We taped this meeting and included it in the family archives.

34. This trip turned out to be the most magical research effort the family has ever made. We saw and experienced signs as if our parents were guiding us. It truly was a spiritual experience.

35. Before the Girón family moved, this man said they lived on a mesa away from the rest of the town. Living on a mesa is indicative of the Apache ways of life because it allowed them to see in all directions from a high point. This was part of protecting the clan. Furthermore, every townsperson wanted to tell us their stories about taking in Apache children because their parents were running away from soldiers and for other reasons.

36. My mother once told me that she considered Chicanos and Mexicanos just another indigenous group, and there are many incidents of Mexicans aiding Apaches. Therefore, it was not unusual for my parents to feel comfortable among these indigenous people.

37. Rodolfo Acuña, *Occupied America: A History of Chicanos*, 5th ed. (New York: Pearson and Longman, 2004), 93.

38. Acuña uses the term "genizaros" to describe de-tribalized Native Americans. For some Apaches, giving up their freedom (a cherished aspect) to live on a reservation was impossible; therefore, many lived among Mexicans.

39. Acuña, *Occupied America*, 93. The description of the pueblos in southern Colorado would have been another reason the Girón family felt comfortable there, since it was similar to the Apache ways of life.

40. Susan B. Anthony belonged to the Women's Suffragist Movement. However, her only interest was White women's right to vote; she never took on issues of race. See ibid., 95.

41. She often commented that I reminded her of my father because of my participation in the Civil Rights Movement.

42. Mother Jones, who was Irish, was eighty-three years old when she stepped off that train. Unlike Susan B. Anthony, she understood the importance of unity within the working class, regardless of a person's color. See M. Edmund Vallejo, "Recollections of the Colorado Coal Strike, 1913–1914," in *La Gente: Hispano History and Life in Colorado,* Vincent C. de Baca, ed. (Denver: Colorado Historical Society, 1998), 94.

43. My mother never mentioned my father knowing of this incident, but we do know that he was in Trinidad during this time. Mother Jones is one of my favorite historical icons. I especially like her statement "pray for the dead, but fight like hell for the living."

44. The victims of the Ludlow Massacre were mostly Chicanas and their children.

45. Peace did not come to the region until the advent of the Rockefeller Plan in 1915; however, the union was not recognized until the 1930s.

46. I recently joined a teachers' union, and I was so proud to sign the union card. This was the first time in my life I had the opportunity to join a union; all other times I played a supportive role.

47. My mother told me many times that my dad fought in World War I to receive U.S. citizenship. However, his military records indicate that he was determined to be White. This statement could be true, since the Indian Citizenship Act did not pass until 1924. Our family is still researching this issue. Also see Acuña, *Occupied America,* 180.

48. My mother often showed a $500 bill she kept in an old tobacco bag pinned to her bra. She had lived through the Great Depression and was always cautious about saving in case a depression happened again. Also see ibid., 272.

49. When I see depictions of White suburbia, where the children are riding bikes and enjoying their youth, it brings out resentment in me because I was toiling in the fields to feed them. Child labor laws (I use the term loosely) did not really take effect in Colorado until the 1960s. I feel that children who toiled in the fields should be awarded early retirement.

50. Public Broadcasting System (producer), *La Raza de Colorado: La Historia* (videotape) (Denver: PBS Video, 2005).

51. My parents encouraged us to go to school, even if it meant less pay from farm work.

52. The CF&I was owned by the Rockefeller family and is located in Pueblo, CO.

53. Lalo Delgado refers to "Barrio Warriors" in *La Raza de Colorado: La Historia* (videotape).

54. Paula Gunn Allen, *Off the Reservation: Reflection on Boundary-Busting, Border-Crossing, and Loose Canons* (Boston: Beacon, 1998), 191.

55. Alexandra Harmon, *Indians in the Making: Ethnic Relations and Indian Identities around Puget Sound* (Los Angeles: University of California Press, 1995), 160.

56. Since my parents resisted the reservation system, they may not have been registered. We are still researching this issue. The idea of blood quantum is really a European tradition. Prior to the General Allotment Act, most indigenous peoples' concern was to preserve the culture, an idea that was prevalent in my family.

57. I am astounded at how Apaches now agree with the same government that oppressed them.

58. Patricia Penn Hilden, *When Nickels Were Indians: An Urban Mixed-Blood Story* (Washington, DC: Smithsonian Institution Press, 1995), 3.

59. My parents did not make a distinction between boys and girls. All their children were taught the same things: how to cook, work, chop wood, fix cars, and shoot a gun. I am not sure why my father taught me how to shoot a gun; maybe he was preparing me. The most important thing we were taught as children was not to be afraid of a challenge.

60. When I say forever, I mean forever because just as I was born to resist, so will my children and their children, and so on.

61. Frank taught his siblings a lot of things he learned in the army, like how to fold a parachute, train dogs, shine shoes, and perform a cadence he learned. I still sometimes repeat the cadence, I can shine shoes so well that I can see myself reflected in them, and I know how to train a dog, but I never had the need to fold a parachute.

62. This is described very well in the video *La Raza de Colorado: El Movimiento*.

63. In many indigenous cultures, the relationship between first cousins is a close one.

64. This was the story told to me by Luis's family members; however, over the years I have heard many different versions of what happened that night. None of these stories change the fact that my cousin was killed.

65. Because my cousin Luis's father and my mother were half-brother and sister, our part of the family was always considered the Indians. In those years, many claimed no Indian heritage, especially Apache, because it was not safe to do so. I was happy that my cousin joined the Chicano Movement because it gave him a sense of his indigenous self.

66. When I say this to people, they think I am romanticizing the movement. The only thing I can say is that our unity in those days was magical. To this day, I have never felt anything like it.

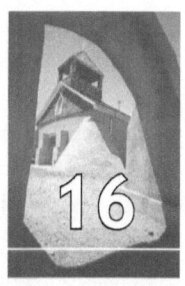

Ramon Del Castillo

Institutionalizing *Curanderismo* in Colorado's Community Mental Health System

This chapter chronicles the accounts of three individuals involved in the process of institutionalizing *curanderismo* in Colorado's community mental health system. Curanderismo is "a holistic approach to physical, psychosocial, and spiritual conditions used . . . by contemporary Chicanos despite the predominance of 'modern medical science'" (Lucero 1981:1). *Curanderos/as* traditionally practice "underground," outside of mainstream health and mental health systems. The implementation of curanderismo at Centro de las Familias, a unique specialty team later transformed into a specialty clinic under the auspices of Southwest Denver Community Mental Health Center, was an unprecedented introduction of a curandera into a publicly funded mental health system. Originally presented as a dissertation in the Graduate School of Public Affairs at the University of Colorado at Denver, this chapter describes the philosophy of curanderismo along with the management and policy challenges associated with an institutionalization process. Utilizing qualitative research, the author describes theoretical aspects and the efficacy of curanderismo, with a critique and synthesis of effective management practices utilized during the program's institutionalization in a community mental health system.

One of the interviewees, Diana Velazquez, was the curandera who practiced holistic healing at the clinic and later became its manager. Dr. Ernesto Alvarado, Diana's apprentice, also managed the clinic for several years and was responsible for initiating this program. The third person interviewed, Dr. Paul Polak, was the executive director of Southwest Denver Community Mental Health Center when curanderismo was introduced into the mental health system and was ultimately responsible for providing the leadership for its institutionalization. This chapter describes some of the lessons learned when radical approaches are introduced to mainstream psychiatric care during an institutionalization process.

DIANA VELAZQUEZ

The process of becoming a curandero/a begins with a revelation, a vision, or a dream (Foster 1953; Madsen 1964a; Romano 1965). Diana Guevera Velazquez's role in life began with the sounds of her crying in the womb. Dr. James Jaramillo has written, "Legend has it that if a child cries in the womb, she will be given the 'Don/Dona' and become a *curandera*" (quoted in Perrone, Stockel, and Kruger 1989:92). Velazquez was born in Lockhart, Texas, on March 11, 1939. At the age of eight, she began training to enhance her *don* (gift), accompanying her Grandmother Chona, a respected healer, throughout the community. With her own inherent abilities and her grandmother's counseling, mentoring, and guidance, Diana began to perform healing rituals with *barrio* women. She explained, "When I was eight, my mother would say, so and so is sick. Get what you need and go take care of them. I went. I picked up what I needed: the herbs, the eggs, the lemon, the charcoal, and I went and said, 'Chona told me to come.' They said okay, and I did what I was supposed to do. I did everything I was supposed to. And she did get well" (Velazquez 1993).

Don Herman "Chito" Velazquez was a Yaqui Indian and well-known curandero in Sonora, Mexico. The Velazquez family had a tradition of curanderismo; however, a generation had passed with no signs that a healer existed among that particular generation. It was Cecilio, the eldest son's, cultural duty to find a curandera to bring to the family to continue the cycle of curanderismo. He was sent on a mission to do this and found Diana. Through a traditional marriage contract, Diana was promised in marriage to Cecilio Velazquez at the young age of twelve. At age fifteen, Diana and Cecilio were married. Her mentoring began with Don Chito. While in the Yaqui Indian village, she was a *partera* (midwife) and nurse and was mentored by a general practitioner from the community. She treated Indian patients during this time. Velazquez delivered 612 babies and cared for expectant mothers during their pregnancies.

The teachings of Don Chito were centered on the philosophy of curanderismo passed down from Yaqui ancestors who had lived in Mexico for many generations. Lessons were designed to enhance the development of Velazquez's power as a healer. She recalls an important lesson in trusting oneself: "I had asked [Don Chito] for a solution to a problem. . . . He asked me to look for the solution to the problem I had. After sorting through the amber and the ashes [he had instructed me to bring to him] it finally came to me. . . . I did not find the solution outside. He was teaching me that I did not need a crystal ball . . . I had to trust what I already knew, that I had to trust myself" (Velazquez 1993).

In 1962 the Velazquez family returned to San Antonio, Texas, where Diana practiced curanderismo until age thirty-five, working in an underground networking system. Curanderismo had not been accepted by the American Medical Association; its practice was confined to Mexican barrios, and clients were referred by word of mouth.

Velazquez earned her "credentials" from the community as her healing practices became known as worthy of acclaim. Credentials earned by a curandero/a come from his or her reputation and an informal training curriculum within the culture. A curandera's reputation flourishes because of work accomplished, in contrast to modern society where one cannot practice medicine until he or she is certificated as a result of theoretical competence (Kurts and Chalfant 1984:144).

In 1972 Velazquez moved to Denver, Colorado. Clinically diagnosed with cancer and depression in 1973, she sought therapy—ironically, from a modern psychiatric counseling center. This was her first encounter with Centro de las Familias, a specialty clinic under the auspices of Southwest Denver Community Mental Health Center. Velazquez recollects her displeasure with the lack of compassion shown and the clinic's sterile ambience.

Coincidentally, Centro was in the process of hiring a secretary. Velazquez applied for the job and joined the staff. During a psychiatric case consultation, team leader Dr. Ernesto Alvarado inquired about her abilities as a healer. According to Velazquez, "The team was staffing families admitted into the clinic. In one particular case, the assigned mental health therapist shared feedback about intervention mental health strategies. My role was to take notes. However, I felt compelled to intervene" (1993). When Velazquez finished her assessment, the team leader asked how she knew what to do. She replied, "I am a curandera. I have been working with our people for a long time" (Velazquez 1997).

During this time period, government funds were available for creative and innovative mental health programs. Alvarado applied for funds to implement curanderismo as a specialized treatment modality. Following a training regimen in modern psychiatry, Velazquez grasped many of the concepts of community mental health and incorporated them into a well-rounded approach to healing referred to as ethno-psychiatry. Velazquez began to practice curanderismo at Centro de las Familias. Through word of mouth, the community came to know of her presence. She recalls one of her most vivid experiences with what she terms a "hexed" client:

> [We went] over the case history with the consultant. I listened to it.... I finally got to see the child.... I had a set of beads.... I took the beads and swept her with them, and we prayed the Our Father. [When] we finished the prayer I said to her, "Now I want you to move this finger" ... and very slowly she did it. I wheeled her out and the doctors said, "Is there anything that you are going to be able to tell us about her so we can help her? Is there anything you are going to be able to do to help us?" And I said, "Well, I think so." And I said, "Lisa, would you shake hands with your doctor?" So she extended one of her hands ... and then she waved with the other one. Velazquez states that this was her "first miracle." (Velazquez 1993)

The professional staff had mixed emotions about the experience. Some were in awe, others were dubious, and some were angry. Word that a healer had performed a miracle permeated the local psychiatric community.

Cultural Diagnostics and Treatment Methods

Velazquez utilizes cultural diagnostics to diagnose a client's disorders and needs. One example of cultural diagnostics is *trisia*, defined as "a [depression] that goes not only from the body but into your soul." Western psychologists and psychiatrists call it melancholia, except that it manifests itself in the spirit and the soul as well. Velazquez adds, "Trisia means that down to the very core of your soul there is this sadness.... I see this in a lot of men exhibiting it through bad luck, or they come in exhibiting symptoms of what you might call a hex" (1993). Velazquez treats men with these types of psychological and spiritual problems using cultural rituals, prayer, and empowerment. She believes she is a vessel, given power to heal by God and then to transmit energy and healing back into her clients. Her healing methods are laden with Chicano cultural values. Velazquez's insight and ability to "know" a client moves quickly to diagnosis and treatment. She builds respect with clients and psychologically uses a blend of common sense and various methods that are culturally responsive.

Mal de ojo, or evil eye, is another common occurrence in the Mexican American community. It is generally associated with children and is believed to have a supernatural or magical origin. Mal de ojo is another diagnostic

(Kiev 1968; Madsen 1964a; Rubel 1978). Certain people are believed to possess "a very strong or hot vision capable of harming another person. [If] a person happens to desire or admire a[nother] person, a supernatural force is projected onto that person, who then becomes ill" (Lucero 1981:36). Noted researcher Ari Kiev suggests that mal de ojo "is an expression of guilt and anxiety being projected onto another person (usually a stranger)" (Kiev 1968:1067). Treatment for mal de ojo is a simple touch by the person projecting the energy.

As a holistic healer, Velazquez believes God provides the tools for healing, including modern physicians, nurses, and other types of healers. Velazquez refers clients who have specific diseases she cannot treat to doctors. She deals with a person's spiritual aspects, a practice not used by psychiatrists. Religious figures from various denominations have contacted her about parishioners who were *embrujado/a* (bewitched). Velazquez has responded by doing consultative services through the community mental health center, building relationships with religious people, psychologists, and psychiatrists in the process.

Velazquez is familiar with Talcott Parsons's concept of "affective neutrality," the notion that doctors remain affectively neutral from their clients. She embellishes it with culturally responsive techniques. She is involved in her clients' personal spiritual lives, attending religious rites and rituals with them. This provides entrance into a family structure that is generally private and highly valued. Anyone admitted into "business of the family" has to be a special person; *familia* is central to Mexican American culture. Family allegiance, loyalty, and obligation are primary values adhered to in this cultural system.

By merging Western views of physician-client relationships with a culturally specific role determined by Indian, Mexicano, and Chicano cultures, Velazquez allows patients to have their cultural expectations of what a "doctor" does fulfilled while also meeting culturally specific expectations. She described one instance when a client refused to take psychiatric medication because she was "not *loca*" (crazy). Velazquez blended rituals and psychiatric medication into a tea as a *remedio* (remedy). Some of the client's delusional and paranoid thinking vanished.

The practice of curanderismo was met with mixed reactions from the psychiatric community. Many local psychiatrists have explored this concept; others remain firmly within their traditional boundaries as Western systems healers. Even former staff members at Centro de las Familias have given curanderismo mixed reviews. Recalls Velazquez, "A social worker presented a case of a woman who believed she was hexed and commented, 'Well, maybe if I wear a long black robe and get some feathers, and make some noises, she'll think she got well.' . . . I confronted the person. I told the person that this was nothing to laugh about. . . . This was a turning point in my life" (1993).

The Colorado State Division of Mental Health has sanctioned curanderismo as a viable form of transcultural psychiatry. The remedios Velazquez prescribes for clients, as well as her treatment plans, are approved by the staff psychiatrist. The psychiatrist's blessing allows the community's psychiatric needs to be met without violating any codes of medical or psychiatric treatment.

Management Philosophy

Velazquez became clinical supervisor and manager of Centro in 1993. She is well versed in aspects of community mental health and their relevant applications. She works with psychiatrists and staff interested in ethno-psychiatry. She has never been formally trained as a public administrator. "I am a curandera," she says. "I live the life of a curandera. I use my intuition in dealing with people, no matter who they are" (Velazquez 1997). Velazquez feels one must be spiritually attuned, qualified, and able to understand the philosophy of curanderismo at an administrative level to implement a successful program.

Velazquez learned aspects of management through her longevity at Centro under the supervision of a variety of executive directors and managers. After nineteen years of employment, Velazquez sees culture as the foundation for Centro de las Familias: "I think if the manager did not have a good cultural face, the clinic would die." She advocates a democratic style of management: "I don't make unilateral decisions unless it's absolutely necessary. What I try to do is work it so my staff feels that they have participated." Velazquez notes that clients participate in planning processes at the clinic: "They're very much a part of the clinic." She incorporates linguistic cultural competency into the clinic's philosophy so employees can effectively communicate with clients. Values such as *personalismo* and familia are utilized. She states, "Every time a new client or a new patient is admitted, I come out and I meet them and I greet them. . . . I speak to them in their own language" (Velazquez 1997).

The clinic's ambience is also culturally relevant to the clientele. While psychiatric settings are generally mundane and institutional, Velazquez describes Centro de las Familias as "a small clinic that looks very much like a home. . . . All of the psychiatrists talk to the people that come in" (1997).

Hiring Culturally Sensitive Staff

Because mental health workers have traditionally been trained in Western systems approaches, therapists are not familiar with alternative systems. This poses challenges for Velazquez. As she stated, "[T]here is a lot of fear around what I can and cannot do." Culturally competent therapists are lacking in mental health systems, so Velazquez seeks out the most qualified persons willing to work in a nontraditional setting. Many non-Latinos have worked at Centro de las Familias. Velazquez expects therapists to show a willingness to learn and an understanding of cross-cultural psychology. She explained, "I look for a person that is not looking for a story[book] clinical model. . . . [Y]ou can be Anglo, but you do need to know if you don't have the awareness, you need to be open and learn" (Velazquez 1997).

TREATMENT CONSIDERATIONS

Psychological evaluations are administered to all clients who enter the mental health system utilizing a Western systems approach. According to Velazquez, there are times when a curandero/a will use cultural diagnostics specific to disorders only a curandero/a can diagnose and treat, suggesting that there has to be a negotiation process wherein the psychiatrist pays deference to the curandero/a. For this to occur without resistance, the curandero/a and the psychiatrist must have a healthy and respectful working relationship. There is a definite learning curve wherein a psychiatrist's must be willing to learn about curanderismo. The curandero/a must also be willing to venture into a different approach to healing.

From a legal perspective, only psychiatrists are qualified and sanctioned to write medication prescriptions for mental health clients. There are times when the curandero/a must also prescribe remedios. A psychiatrist must approve a prescription when natural medicine is prescribed with culturally specific rituals. On other occasions, a mix of traditional psychiatric medication in combination with a ritual is used to obtain optimum results. Understanding, sensitivity, willingness, and agreement by both psychiatrist and curandero/a must be present for this to occur. Trust between the two healers is critical at this stage of the treatment process. As Velazquez stated, such trust led to a "psychiatric setting [in which it was] understood what they [patients] were talking about. And although the psychiatrists would not say, 'Yes, you do have a hex' . . . what is important [is] . . . you're able to say 'look, this means nothing to me but it means something to that person, go ahead and do it'" (1997).

DR. PAUL POLAK

Dr. Paul Polak attended medical school in London, England, followed by a residency in psychiatry at the University of Colorado Medical Center. A national movement to implement community mental health programs throughout the country existed, and Polak grabbed the opportunity to apply for the directorship of Southwest Denver Community Mental Health Center. Polak recalls, "The board at Southwest Mental Health . . . hired and fired the executive director of the mental health system. Since southwest Denver had a significant proportion (28%) of Spanish-speaking population . . . [o]ne of the things was how [to] make mental health services relevant to the Spanish-speaking population in southwest Denver." Centro de las Familias was the first specialty mental health clinic Polak started. His subsequent exposure to curanderismo was, he says, largely "luck, and jumping on the opportunity that presented itself to us" (Polak 1997).

According to Polak, "[I]t was not difficult to hire Diana Velazquez." The mental health system worked with her to accentuate her skill level so she could be classified within its personnel system. Velazquez was already seen as a "highbred curandera." "To some extent," says Polak, "it's a question of having already a structure which could take advantage of people's human experience in addition to formal clinical skills." The curanderismo program did not always enjoy overwhelming support. According to Polak, "There were several problems. . . . There are a lot of curanderas that are not very competent. There are some quacks who are curanderas, and Diana was a very top-notch person." There were also barriers that Velazquez, the first curandera to be hired by a formal mental health institution, had to overcome. Recalls Polak, "[Diana's] peer group saw her as a traitor to her culture and to the other curanderas. She had sort of betrayed them and joined the enemy. . . . Within the mental health system people regarded the curandera with a certain amount of suspicion." Polak asserts that mental health practitioners trained in Western systems approaches to mental health treatment do not always accept carte blanche anything perceived as outside that type of training. As he stated, "[A] lot of them [Western systems practitioners] said, 'That's a quaint practice, that's traditional.' A lot of people in the mental health system regard a curandera as a witch doctor, as a superstition, as basically ripping people off with superstitious gobbledygook" (Polak 1997).

As a pioneer in his own right, Polak had to deal with an enormous amount of criticism. His innovative approaches to treatment were often seen as "kooky." He was instrumental in developing the "alternative home setting," private homes where mentally ill people were admitted for treatment rather than being sent to institutional settings such as psychiatric wards. He built grassroots approaches with community support for this innovation. The mental health board generally approved his innovations. For Polak, introducing curanderismo into the mental health field was an innovative change occurring at a time when mental health centers were open to radical innovation.

According to Polak, when the formal implementation of culturally specific specialty services and curanderismo began, many Spanish-speaking people who wanted the same services as their Anglo counterparts were offended. But, he says, there was never an inclination to force specialty services onto the population: "We didn't want to force people to use a Chicano cultural mental health specialty service just because they were Spanish-speaking or came from the Chicano culture. We wanted to give them the options" (Polak 1997).

Input from residents was critical in developing specialized mental health services that would meet their specific cultural needs. Polak organized a communication campaign to hear and incorporate the community's voice. This boundary-spanning activity was instrumental in building relationships with the community's formal and informal leaders. Polak established a community advisory council that oversaw operations at Centro de las Familias. There were other issues he had to contend with as well. Once he fired a Chicano who had not followed a directive, resulting in conflict within the mostly Chicano advisory council. Polak was accused of being a racist. He describes this experience as "part of the process." He explains, "You have to be ready to wade through the controversy. . . . We did a lot of things that were offensive to some people. . . . You need to be straight up and say this is why you need it" (Polak 1997).

Organizational Barriers

For Velazquez to gain legitimacy, Southwest Denver Community Mental Health Center established a training program for staff members lacking "credentials." This provided clinicians with knowledge about community mental health systems. Western systems practitioners were challenged to learn about curanderismo. Various healers, including Velazquez, facilitated cross-cultural training seminars in which both types of healers could compare notes on each other's systems. Says Polak, "There was a training process to learn things about being a clinician. . . . The mental health staff taught Diana about the mental health system and how . . . the social systems work. Diana taught the mental health staff about curanderismo" (1997).

The controversy surrounding curanderismo was never fully resolved. Some clinicians chose to believe that curanderismo was superstitious. Others embraced it as one healing method within a continuum of healing methods and appreciated Velazquez and her contributions to the mental health field. She provided workshops at the medical school. According to Polak, many of the psychiatrists "really liked her. She gave lectures; you know, part of the training of medical students is to be aware of cultural things. She quickly built up quite a following" (1997).

The state mental health system supported Centro de las Familias and, according to Polak, once Velazquez and curanderismo had gained some level of legitimacy, professionals came to visit with her. He stated, "Legislators, professional people at a very high level, in addition to the people who were coming from Southwest Denver, came in. . . . That surprised me" (Polak 1997).

THE POLITICS OF INNOVATION

Polak understands the important role politics play in building support for any new program. He also feels hard evidence was needed to convince the critics that he and his staff knew what they were doing. He revealed, "I think that it's possible [to convince people] . . . if you can give good reasons why it works. . . . There was a lot of resistance to the idea of treating people in homes instead of hospitals. . . . But you can build plenty of support by explaining this and showing evidence" (Polak 1997). There was never any formal resistance to curanderismo by state-level bureaucrats. Polak developed strategies for how to introduce radical ideas in a non-radical manner. His style is clinically and politically astute. Communication with high-level officials seems to have offset any negative feedback. Once the legislature is aware of an innovation, it is easier for them to deal with any conflict that might arise. Polak feels "there are problems with all of the things that are not traditional that you introduce" (1997). He insists that community involvement and being able to talk to anyone about innovation and defend it allows for more general acceptance of the innovation.

MANAGEMENT STYLE

Polak does not see himself as a program innovator. As a pragmatist, he solves problems with things that work: "All of my life I've tried to define problems and find practical solutions." He adds, "I pushed it through the obvious. . . . You know, if a lot of people believe in curanderismo and see it as helpful, then why not provide it? What I have problems with is providing services . . . and having someone kill themselves because they were incompetently handled" (Polak 1997).

From a management standpoint, Polak believes clients are best served when they assist in the development of their own programming. He believes in utilizing the voice of the community, sometimes as experts. Today, as the CEO of International Development Enterprize, he practices this style of management. He shared, "We now work with peasants in Asia . . . but they don't talk to the one-acre farmers. . . . The experts say that they're superstitious and stupid. . . . But when you actually go and talk to them and see why they turned down the experts' solutions, they're right and the experts are wrong. . . . Then people say we are innovative. Well, is that innovative, or is it just stupid not to talk to the people" (Polak 1997).

Managerially, Polak says that "in some ways, I haven't been trained. I had no training in economic development either." Still, his style of management includes theories such as decentralization in an organization. He believes decentralization allowed strong community ties to be built in southwest Denver to deal with controversy. However, if needed, there was room at the top to deal with controversies; he did not "try to micro-manage everything" (Polak 1997).

Relative to decentralization, Polak asserts that key to success in an organization is for top-level management to be involved in program innovation; once political issues have been resolved, innovation should be turned over to the staff. He also feels day-to-day situations should be taken care of at the lower levels of the organization. He explained, "You only handle the things that can't be handled at the local level. I think this is effective management. And it's just not for mental health. Effective decentralization is a major issue in management of large corporations as well." According to Polak, Western culture is "far too focused on specialization practices and philosophies, and specialists lose track of the picture and the problem" (1997). He intimated that for innovation to work, systems have to be open and accessible. Open systems approaches open doors for a community to build trust with employees in the organization.

In terms of curanderismo, Polak does not believe any one management style works all of the time. It appears that a number of significant variables converged at the same time, allowing for curanderismo to be introduced into the system at Southwest Denver Community Mental Health Center. According to Polak, "[We had] a personnel system based on output rather than degree . . . we already had community support. We had support from the mental health establishment. There was a specialty service . . . curanderismo, [with] a niche, and there was a management structure that it fit into. . . . We had a structure that could run interference and a pretty active community board" (1997).

Polak believes in the power of communicating with everyone, including "ordinary people, about an innovation." The success of curanderismo also depended on building a healthy relationship with Velazquez. This strengthened their ability to work on a professional level on something both controversial and needed. Says Polak, "Diana and I have a very good relationship . . . she read me about like who I was. . . . [M]ost people didn't, and we liked each other. She knew that if she got into hot water or if there was a problem that I would back the establishment of curanderismo" (1997). Polak feels that through communication and dialogue, anything can be resolved. It was essential for

Diana Velazquez and Paul Polak to build a relationship because curanderismo utilizes power (*poder*) at all levels. Curanderas know power can be a vicious animal; however, harnessing it can also be a valuable tool for accomplishing tasks.

DR. ERNESTO ALVARADO

The year was 1975, and community mental health was a relatively new phenomenon in American society. The deinstitutionalization movement was operative, and specialized programming such as Centro de las Familias was in demand. Dr. Ernesto Alvarado's first experience with curanderismo occurred when he was the director of Centro de las Familias. Alvarado traces its roots to a "Native American, Chicano, Hispanic mental health theme." The clinic's goal was to develop and implement programs that could deal with the specialized mental health needs of Latino cultures. Cross-cultural knowledge was the cornerstone of the clinic, and curanderismo was critical as a specialty service.

Alvarado submitted a proposal to central administration requesting that curanderismo be implemented at Centro de las Familias. He argued that curanderismo "could be incorporated into a modern clinic" (Alvarado, August 30, 1977). Alvarado had already encountered Diana Velazquez. She had volunteered to present in-service training modules to the center's staff. Alvarado believed curanderismo could be utilized in a publicly funded mental health center as an innovation and sent his proposal to Washington, DC. He recalls Dr. Paul Polak giving him permission but also remembers Polak stating, "Go ahead, but it's your butt. If there are problems, well, you're the supervisor, so you'll have to answer for them" (Alvarado, August 30, 1997).

Within a few weeks of the program's wheels being set in motion, referrals began to come in to the clinic. The professional community swamped Velazquez with requests, surprisingly. Clientele from various ethnic and racial groups were requesting services. According to Alvarado, historically, patients enter clinics and do not necessarily expect cultural treatment: "You see, the choices for so long had been only Western European–trained psychotherapists who use treatments that don't work. . . . Research shows that 90 percent of ethnic people do not do well with community mental health. So whatever training is happening in modern schools, it's not effective with minority communities" (August 30, 1997).

Alvarado feels Western healing and curanderismo can be complimentary, with limitations. The sanctioning of processes by the central administration is critical when incorporating programs like curanderismo into a formal institutional setting. At times, there are commonsense approaches to dealing with clients who are experiencing severe stress or depression, but Western systems healers are not trained in cross-cultural psychology and are often unable to assist the client or address the symptomatology. In Alvarado's view, Velazquez brought both elements to the clinical setting: "Diana was the person who was able to do both. She had the backing of the mental health system for hospitalization. . . . To have someone in a psychotic episode . . . you needed to provide some controls . . . plus medication. You have to have the backing of the mental health center. The new cultural therapist has to be wise enough to recognize people's feelings and desires and incorporate them [into] the best treatment practice around" (Alvarado, August 30, 1997). With Velazquez, the integration of curanderismo and a Western systems approach in which culture was used as a vehicle had begun.

Organizational Barriers

At a time of significant cutbacks in community mental health, alternative methods to healing had become more accepted. But it was still difficult to expand services when cutbacks were occurring. Alvarado recalls, "How can you expand when you're cutting back our community service? Availability of traditional healers was slim pickings. Our saving grace was Diana's ability to work within a defined system of mental health" (August 30, 1997).

For curanderismo to be accepted as another method of healing, the curandera had to possess basic skills, as well as an ability to work successfully in treating mental health clients. Velazquez possessed many of these skills, including knowledge of working with individuals, an understanding of group therapy, and an ability to communicate with people in their native tongue. When she began formal practice, she was generally given clients who had already been seen by psychiatrists, psychologists, or both, who had been unsuccessful in providing effective treatment. This established her legitimacy as a curandera in particular and the legitimacy of curanderismo in general. According to Alvarado,

> [Staff] would have to ask themselves, why was she successful and we weren't? They were very interested when we came back and did case presentations on their own clients who were now functional. So they couldn't argue that it was not a successful treatment. The psychiatrists couldn't raise an argument. If she had failed, they could have said, "She's ineffective. We knew she was going to be bogus." But when she was effective with their clientele and they saw the difference, they'd have to back off and say, "we'd better look and see what she has done." They really didn't have an argument. (August 30, 1997)

Alvarado assisted Velazquez in writing treatment plans that incorporated curanderismo into the process while simultaneously respecting Western systems approaches. The addition of "a new dimension" to treatment planning set a tone of respect between Western systems approaches and curanderismo. This was one of many building blocks that eventually resulted in the effectiveness of curanderismo.

From a local perspective, there were problems in implementing curanderismo. Within the community, there were other types of healers who had created an unfavorable attitude toward curanderismo. This led to strict supervision of curanderismo, particularly when dealing with community residents. As Alvarado stated, "I have run across a lot of charlatans in the Denver area. I know that I had to come and clean up some of their messes. So I believe that it [curanderismo] should be supervised to a certain extent. The profit motive will drive people to do a lot of unethical things" (August 30, 1997).

According to Alvarado, another local problem arose. The heaviest conflict occurred within the first three months of the implementation process. Alvarado became a boundary spanner for the organization, visiting with naysayers and the charlatans who were giving a bad name to curanderismo. The demand for services and client satisfaction were key ingredients as curanderismo developed legitimacy within the field at a time when its success was questionable. Alvarado recalled, "It was the only treatment that they [some patients] had ever received that would make them feel better." Support evolved around the city, and curanderismo was eventually fully accepted within the institution. An initial problem involved "resolving the healer's belief system of no pay for service." Alvarado explained, "Some healers, not all . . . it varies tribally, but many healers believe that you don't accept money for your service. So one of the other problems was, how do we get this person reimbursed for their services? . . . That was resolved because the individual didn't take money directly; they were paid by a system" (August 30, 1997). According to Alvarado, use of the word "client" implies a paid relationship, but curanderismo was set up so the cost of services did not involve the curandera receiving money directly. The contradiction between the notion of charging for services and the curandera's unwillingness to accept payment was resolved; for example, the money was given to charities.

Alvarado attributes much of curanderismo's administrative success to an extremely "functional leader" able and willing to deal with controversy, although that leader had internal support. Centro de las Familias was a very productive team, with its own production and expectations placed on the staff. Effective treatment added to the acceptance of the team. Alvarado states, "[The team] was the highest producing unit in the mental health center" (August 27, 1997). Accountability was always expected for any new team members who came onboard. Therapists from other ethnic groups also joined the team, transforming what had been an all-Latino staff into a multicultural clinic.

Management Techniques

Alvarado had many years of experience in direct clinical supervision before coming to Centro de las Familias. One of his strongest assets was his ability to converse professionally in the nomenclatures of both psychiatry and curanderismo. This helped him deal with many issues associated with introducing curanderismo into a formal mental health setting. He was able to form a strong team and use an educational approach to deal with the differences in training team members brought to the table. Alvarado feels this allowed him to build a positive reputation within the community.

To be an effective manager, Alvarado feels one has to be able to document one's effectiveness. A strong monitoring process is important to avoid criticism from those who do not understand alternative systems of healing. Client satisfaction is equally important in managing this type of system. He stated, "Client satisfaction is actually a very, very weak measure of an effect with what's used in mental health.... Like any system that advocated developing our workers, you need a system that supports folk healers, allows them to train, allows them to move on, allows them to share their talents with others in the field" (Alvarado, August 27, 1997).

CONCLUSION

The accounts reported in this chapter clearly demonstrate that innovation can be controversial, forcing managers to challenge the status quo and not shy away from their vision. Innovation involves risk taking and conflict, with controversial issues not always fully resolved. Effective leaders are able to communicate with resistors satisfied with maintaining the status quo. Effective conflict management reduces stress on an organization. Resistance to, or a lack of awareness of, an innovation challenges managers to develop strategies to change perceptions and attitudes. Education and awareness are key to increasing knowledge, leading to more acceptance of an innovation. In-service training modules can be effectively utilized to provide cross-cultural awareness and training to staff members and key players, both internally and externally.

Another critical aspect of innovation is building support both internally and externally by creating boundary spanners, those who step out of their original defined spaces. Dialogue and outreach into the community are also important strategies in building a working relationship with community residents and solidifying relationships, especially when community support is needed. Enveloping the Chicano community was important in providing effective services for Centro de las Familias; thus, Paul Polak structured a community advisory council that acted as a support system and information feeder during the innovation process. He encouraged the staff at Centro de las Familias to develop relationships with community residents.

Support from decision makers such as the board of directors and advisory committees was crucial to the organization's success. This interactive process required managers to be skilled in areas such as conflict resolution and facilitation. Polak worked effectively with board members in sustaining the relationships necessary to achieve innovation. He also made political inroads with state decision makers. Addressing innovation at all levels of the structure was important, from state bureaucrats to informal leaders in the community.

Decentralization as a management strategy empowered the organization's staff. Polak delegated authority to the level at which he felt it was needed and would be most effective. He was aware that the reins to implement curanderismo needed to be held at the local level. Delegating major responsibility to Centro de las Familias not only legitimized curanderismo but also placed Polak on the map as a leader in the community. His trust in Dr. Alvarado's culturally competent abilities and authority was a significant strategy for the program's eventual success. A Chicano was leading the charge.

The accounts also suggest that innovation invites further innovation, and the introduction of new ideas during times of social change makes acceptance easier. Community mental health as an innovation provided avenues for the introduction of other new elements into the system. Unfamiliarity and associated challenges of the field attracted nontraditional psychiatrists, who were imperative to the success of community mental health. Polak's innovation in designing a personnel system "based on output rather than degrees" provided a legitimate means for incorporating indigenous healers into the system. The development, implementation, and nurturance of specialty clinics also served as a catalyst for innovative programming such as curanderismo.

Cultural competency, defined as "a set of congruent behaviors, attitudes, and policies that come together in a system, agency or amongst professionals and enable that system, agency or those professionals to work efficiently in cross cultural situations" (Cross, Isaacs, and Bazron 1992 [1989]:iv), was an essential building block. A major challenge was how to incorporate cultural competency into the organization while simultaneously reducing or avoiding cultural conflict. Cultural sensitivity and competency training were strong forces needed during this innovation experience as cultural awareness and sensitivity became vehicles used across the organization.

At a time when Western psychiatry was the dominant paradigm, the organization ventured out beyond that paradigm. Support for specialized programming relevant to cultural groups was developed and offered throughout the initiation and implementation of curanderismo and other programs. Polak showed an awareness of and sensitivity to the complex cultural issues involved.

Centro de las Familias's philosophy of utilizing culture in the healing process was instrumental in making curanderismo successful. The clinic's ambience was created based on the cultural needs of the community. Clients felt somebody understood them within their respective cultural contexts. The use of the Spanish language and the colloquial vernacular by treatment therapists was an important communication mechanism in treatment processes. A philosophy of cultural respect was created in which clients were treated with respect and dignity.

The accounts suggest that the staff members' ethnicity was less important than their cultural sensitivity. An understanding of curanderismo by therapists on the specialty team was not expected when they joined the staff, but sensitivity to and an understanding of curanderismo became an important variable in the clinic's success. It was less important for therapists to believe in the art of curanderismo than it was for them to support it as a viable method of healing. Team managers hired personnel willing to gain an understanding of curanderismo.

Whenever a new element is introduced into an entrenched system, anxiety surfaces among all individuals involved. It was necessary for the curandera to feel that her work would be respected and understood, but she also had to be willing to conform to a certain degree to the rules and regulations of the dominant paradigm. In turn, others who were used to the Western mental health system, particularly managers and high-level administrators, had to be supportive and flexible. Finding a balancing point at which the healer did not feel compromised and the system remained legitimate was crucial as both systems interacted to form a synthesis that allowed clients to receive optimum treatment results.

REFERENCES

Alvarado, Ernesto. Interviews with the author. Tape recordings. Denver, CO, August 27 and 30, 1997.

Cross, Terry L., R. Mareasa Isaacs, and R. Bazron. *Towards a Culturally Competent System of Care: A Monograph on Effective Services for Minority Children Who Are Severely Emotionally Disturbed.* Washington, DC: Georgetown University Child Development Center for Children's Mental Health, 1992 (reprint; initially printed in 1989).

Foster, George. M. "Relationships between Spanish and Spanish-American Folk Medicine." *Journal of American Folklore* 66 (1953): 201–217.

Kiev, Ari. *Curanderismo: Mexican-American Folk Psychiatry.* New York: Free Press, 1968.

Kurtz, Richard A., and H. Paul Chalfant. *The Sociology of Medicine and Illness.* Boston: Allyn and Bacon, 1984.

Lucero, Aileen. *A Profile of a Curandera and Her Curandera-Treated Clients: The Southwest Denver Community Mental Health Center.* Pullman: Washington State University, Department of Sociology, 1981.

Madsen, W. *Mexican-Americans of South Texas,* 2nd ed. New York: Holt, Rinehart, and Winston, 1964a.

———. "Value Conflicts and Folk Psychotherapy." In *Magic, Faith and Healing,* A. Kiev, ed. New York: Free Press, 1964b, 420–444.

Perrone, Bobette, H. Henrietta Stockel, and Victoria Kruger. *Medicine Women: Curanderas and Women Doctors.* Norman: University of Oklahoma Press, 1989.

Polak, Paul. Interview with author. Tape recording. Denver, CO, September 1, 1997.

Romano, O. I. "Charismatic Medicine, Folk-Healing, and Folk Sainthood." *American Anthropologist* 67 (1965): 1151–1173.

Rubel, Arthur J. "The Epidemiology of a Folk Illness: Susto in Hispanic America." In *Hispanic Culture and Health Care: Fact, Fiction, and Folklore,* Ricardo Arguijo Martinez, ed. St. Louis: C. V. Mosby, 1978, 75–91.

Velazquez, Diana. Interviews with the author. Tape recordings. Denver, CO, July 23, 1993, and June 30, 1997.

Matthew Jenkins

Finding Courage: The Story of the Struggle to Retire the Adams State "Indian"

This is a story about the end of the "Indian" mascot at Adams State College (ASC) in Alamosa, Colorado, and what it reveals about race, materiality, and coalition politics. It is a story of struggle, pain, loss, and, finally, victory. It is a story about a small college that had an "Indian" as its mascot and how a coalition of students protested that "Indian." The students who protested the "Indian" at Adams State encountered racism during their struggle. Some mascot supporters went so far as to physically threaten coalition members with violence and to vandalize their property. Some coalition members had difficulty getting their degrees, and others dropped out of ASC altogether. All coalition members lost friendships. Significantly, angry students frequently attacked young Native women and young Chicana women who were thought to be Native.[1] Yet in the face of such adversity, coalition members put everything they had on the line to see the "Indian" retired. They organized sit-ins, protests, and educational forums and spoke with pride and power.

Adams State is a small college located in the high, beautiful San Luis Valley of southern Colorado. The earliest recollection by a former student of the use of the "Indian" as the school's mascot comes from 1927.[2] Unlike the University of Illinois, Adams State did not have a specific origin story for its mascot.³ It seems to have emerged in various forms during the six-year period 1925–1931.⁴ Adams State College officially retired the "Indian" in 1995 when President James Gilmore created a committee that moved quickly to do so.⁵ Since then, the Adams State Grizzlies have joined the list of universities and colleges that have recently retired their mascots, including the University of Southern Colorado, St. John's University, the University of Miami (Ohio), Simpson College, and the University of Tennessee in Chattanooga.⁶

In his autobiographical memoir *The Names*, N. Scott Momaday (Kiowa) writes that "memory begins to qualify the imagination, to give it another formation, one that is peculiar to the self."⁷ The memories of the coalition have become a centerpiece of my methodology. Although I have a substantial collection of primary documents from the coalition, ethnographic interviews also serve as an important tool to help remember those events, which shaped us in dramatic ways. Yet a gap exists between my primary documents and my ethnographic interviews. It is an interstitial space that I can only explain as a product of colonialism, oppression, and resistance. It is a postcolonial space where narrative becomes the methodology of the oppressed.⁸ Homi Bhabba writes that the "theorist releases offending memories from their captivity."⁹ I hope this chapter helps release the offending memories of the "Indian" at Adams State.

The Coalition for the Respect of Indigenous Peoples was formed in the fall of 1992 by a group of students from diverse backgrounds who met to share their concerns over ASC's "Indian" mascot. The strongest presence in the coalition was that of Chicana/o and Native American students; however, a small group of Anglo students was active as well. The formation of the coalition came from our desire to see the "Indian" mascot retired. I hope to reveal the untold story of the experiences those students had as they embarked on a journey into new arenas of power, politics and protest, and self-determination.

When discussing the use of "Indian" mascots, many people often ask, "what's the big deal? It's just a mascot." In response, in 1992 the coalition emphasized that it is horrible massacres like Sand Creek that allow "Indian" mascots to be possible today. The Adams State "Indian," like all "Indian" mascots, must be understood in historical and social contexts. Therefore, the coalition urged the ASC community to understand that the combination of U.S. colonial history and the underrepresentation of Native students, faculty, and staff at Adams State made the use and performance of the "Indian" racist and particularly offensive, harmful, and discriminatory to Native students.

MATERIALITY: REMEMBERING THE MATERIAL CULTURE OF THE ADAMS STATE "INDIAN"

In this section I focus on the material forms of the Adams State "Indian" as they embodied a localized material culture at ASC. In so doing, I seek to stress the cultural process of the Adams State "Indian" mascot and its subsequent protection of imperial identities. The materiality of the Adams State "Indian" should be understood as dialectic between representation and embodiment, or as C. Richard King and Charles Fruehling Springwood argue, between "invented icons and embodied actors."[10] Therefore, this section is framed by basic questions about the "Indian" and materiality, as well as important questions about the experiences of Native students at Adams State. In what ways was the "Indian" emblematic of racism and colonization? Why are the material manifestations of the Adams State "Indian" important? How did the variation of such representations affect the embodied experiences of Native students at Adams State?

The formation of American national identity is a narrative that has evoked an imagined Indian-ness to preserve its own claim to power and wealth while simultaneously disguising the legacy and ongoing processes of colonization (postcoloniality). Moreover, American material inventions of Indian-ness are so ubiquitous in contemporary American life that they are almost invisible. In his innovative text *Playing Indian*, Phillip Deloria revisits the legendary Boston Tea Party and locates the first "Indian" imaginings of Anglo-America. He writes, "[A]s they first imagined and then performed Indianness together on the docks of Boston, the Tea Party Indians gave material form to identities that were witnessed and made real."[11] Deloria skillfully shows that since that terrible moment on the Boston docks, Anglo-Americans (and, more recently, non-Indians in general) have been "playing Indian" to fashion American national identities and narratives.

Importantly, the conceptual framework of playing Indian is a fundamental part of the larger and more complex representational system of Indian-ness. As King and Springwood write in their introduction to *Team Spirits*: "We begin to see that no single Native American mascot can fully be understood in any context that fails to engage the historical relationships uniting all Native American mascots. These Indian icons are signs, and as signs, the cultural work they do is accomplished only within the larger representational system to which they belong."[12]

This is a vast system that has produced myriad material forms throughout American history. Americans are used to seeing "Indians" as spectacle in one form or another, from the Boston Tea Party, to the nineteenth-century practice of ethnographic display, to contemporary American cinema and sporting events. Significantly, this notion of the spectacle of Indian-ness is juxtaposed by the absence of Native Americans in the contemporary experiences of most Americans.

In *Playing Indian*, Deloria writes that "more interesting are the faux Mohawks slinking home down Boston alleyways on a chill December night. Their feathers, blankets, headdresses, and war paint point to the fact that images of Indianness have often been translated into material forms."[13] The "Indian" at Adams State maintained a variety of material forms, from a performative dancing body to a logo-centric "Indian" head seen on T-shirts and football helmets. Adams State constructed an imagined "Indian" body that was at times fragmented but that always "moved ideas from brains to bodies, from the realm of abstraction to the physical world of concrete experience. There, identity was not so much imagined as it was performed, materialized through one's body and through the witness and recognition of others."[14] Thus I consider the corporeal representation of "Indian" body texts as they dehumanized Native students at ASC through a material process of performance and witness.

At Adams State the material construction of the "Indian" was a practice of community formation through a dehumanization ironically masked as a system of "honoring." The "Indian" at Adams State was constructed as a spectacle to ratify a certain non-Indian identity that had as its counterpart a complicity in the imperial rendering of the immediate colonial past in Colorado, of which Sand Creek is an example. According to King and Springwood in *Race and Spectacle in College Sport*, they do not "find that spectacles make people forgetful as much as they encourage them to remember particular events from specific standpoints. . . . [C]learly then, sports spectacles, rather than refusing the past, rework it, edit it, and reconstruct it. To make present and to materialize particular (racialized) histories, they make absent and dematerialize specific (racial) struggles and structures."[15]

Few people think of things like Sand Creek when they see "Indian" mascots dance. But during the years of the coalition, that is exactly what I was thinking about. I was haunted by the "Indian," for it recalled a version of Sand Creek I had been consciously trying to unlearn and divest myself from. For most participant spectators, the Adams State "Indian" was part of a seamless meta-history of the "West." But for anyone engaged with the history of consciousness, it was another interruption in the trajectory of progress and social change. It was hard not to feel like you were crazy for making those connections when everyone around you seemed to revel in the material performance.

For Native students at Adams State, the materiality of the "Indian" invaded almost every part of their collegiate lives. Imagine the daily litany of T-shirts, bumper stickers, coffee mugs, and baseball caps, even dish towels. Certainly, the material culture of the Adams State "Indian" was a bizarre blend of the mass-produced and the momentarily performative.[16] As stated earlier, the Adams State "Indian" was most often materialized as a body text. Significantly, this "Indian" body text was repeatedly fragmented. Phil Castillo was a student athlete at Adams State during the years 1990–1993. He remembers how, in contrast to the Anglo girl on a horse at football games, the "Indian" mascot was often a hyper-masculinized caricature of an "Indian": "There were also many caricatures in the buildings of the athletic facilities that I thought were ridiculous. In the weight room, for instance, they had an overgrown steroid-using Indian with the biggest muscles around to show its dominance. They also had an Indian head in the gym as well."[17]

Castillo represented a predicament for ASC's athletic programs. The construction and maintenance of the Adams State "Indian" rested upon one principal assumption—the absence of Indians. Yet here was a young man from Acoma who had just won a national championship in cross-country. His presence as a student athlete signaled the postcolonial contradiction between "Indians" as invented icons and embodied actors and Indians as actual people.[18]

> Being an athlete at Adams State I think was the hardest thing to do, while fighting the mascot issue, because I was known by many of the other athletes on campus. And I used the national spotlight as my biggest defense in getting the word out to the public about my issues. When something this big happens on a campus, the administrators there will try to put out the fire as soon as possible. But . . . my national attention in running and becoming an NCAA champion only added much fuel [to the fire] we already had started. I think that was the single biggest wedge, when I went on national TV to speak out about the mascot issue.[19]

Phil Castillo's story is important in understanding the painful and discriminatory contradictions Native students face when they attend colleges and universities that maintain "Indian" mascots. Phil's presence as an *actual* Indian on TV was a powerful moment for the coalition and the fight against the "Indian" at Adams State, not only because it gave the college unwanted national attention but because it showed that the mascot issue was about living, breathing, real people and not just constructs. The construction and maintenance of the "Indian" at Adams State proliferated a material culture that infiltrated the daily lives of all who attended the college. While this material culture solidified imperial identities through the spectacle and performance of Indian-ness, it accomplished this by dehumanizing Native students attending the college. Many who opposed the mascot change at ASC consistently called upon "tradition" as a reason to continue the life of the "Indian." I argue that the real tradition at Adams State was racism and the mockery of Native American culture.[20] This tradition had a materiality to it, one that relied on racist notions of Native American ethnicity on display in clothing, murals, logos, and especially performance. All of these material forms relied heavily on the imperialist construction of an imagined "Indian" body that was repeatedly fragmented and always dehumanizing.

MESTIZAJE: IDENTITY AND POSTCOLONIAL POLITICAL STRATEGY

Since the beginning of this project, I have been collecting primary documents regarding the Adams State "Indian" and, more specifically, the Coalition for the Respect of Indigenous Peoples. One of those documents is a petition that circulated in the spring of 1994 asking for the signatures of students willing to participate in a nonviolent takeover of the College Center building (Student Union) at Adams State. The takeover was planned in response to President William M. Fulkerson's two-year moratorium on the mascot issue.[21] As I read the names, I remember people willing to risk everything. By attempting a takeover of the College Center, we knew we faced expulsion, and some of us were only weeks away from graduating. I begin by mentioning the names on that petition because they signal one of the exceptional elements of the struggle to retire the "Indian" at Adams State: the contribution of Chicana/o students. In this section I focus on the activism of Chicana/o students in the coalition and ask: what was their role in the coalition? What specific strategies were successful against the "Indian?" How did the coalition's emergent voice result in a challenge to subjectivity at Adams State? The coalition had many strategies, but its identity proved most effective.

The Adams State "Indian" mascot was challenged by students at two major moments, one in the mid-1970s and the final challenge beginning in 1992. In both cases, one of the major forces at work was the voice of Chicana/o students at Adams State. This makes Adams State unique within the national context of college student protests against Native American mascots. My specific focus is on the 1992–1995 period leading up to the official change and the Coalition for the Respect of Indigenous Peoples. However, the Chicana/o student protests in the 1970s were undoubtedly a factor in the change. For Chicana/o students in the 1990s, just the knowledge that there had been protests earlier in the school's history gave them tremendous hope and a sense of history that is vital to transformation. Coalition member Adriana Nieto remembers attending a panel discussion in 1992 about Columbus Day at which Rogelio Briones, an Adams State alumnus and teacher at the local high school in San Luis, Colorado, raised the mascot issue: "That's where Rogelio, and maybe some other people, [brought up the fact] that in the 70s the Chicano student group back then, UMAS [United Mexican American Students], started a movement to change the mascot. . . . And he challenged us, as the new, young generation of activists, to do something about the mascot. Our getting together was a direct result of that challenge, at least in my mind."[22]

Rogelio's challenge at the Columbus Day forum was an important catalyst for the formation of the Coalition for the Respect of Indigenous Peoples. Members of the initial coalition came together from two student groups on campus—the Chicana/o student group, Estudiantes Unidos, and the Native American student group, Native Unity. Estudiantes Unidos members could not agree on the mascot issue and neither could the members of Native Unity, so the students from both groups who wanted to see the mascot changed came together to form the coalition, with the specific agenda of retiring the "Indian." Phil Castillo recalls the importance of Chicana/o students in the mascot struggle: "Without the Hispanic group at Adams, we couldn't have done this in any aspect. . . . And it also gave other non-Indian students on campus an opportunity to look more objectively at the issue as well. So it was great to have all our non-Indian students right there in the trenches as well."[23]

Chicana/o student activism was vibrant at Adams State throughout most of the Chicano Movement and thereafter. The height of mascot protests at ASC during this period came in 1977. Since the Chicano Movement, Chicana/o student articulations of *mestizaje* at Adams State have made them a powerful presence in the struggle to retire the "Indian."[24] Postcolonial coalition politics were an indispensable feature of the drive to retire the "Indian" at ASC. Furthermore, the coalition's multicultural membership challenged the conservative racial politics of the campus and the administration. In addition to the coalition's transformational politic, the large numbers of Chicana/o members, combined with their forthright articulations of mestizaje, resulted in a challenge to subjectivity at Adams State. As Native and Chicana/o students formed an alliance at Adams State, they became speaking subjects who urged the students, faculty, staff, and administration to "notice race" in terms other than Black and White.[25]

The year 1992 was deemed "The Year of Indigenous People" as people of color across the nation protested the quincentenary Columbus Day celebrations.

It was also the year of the Rodney King verdict and subsequent Los Angeles rebellions, as well as the "end" of the Persian Gulf War. For Chicana/os who were coming to consciousness, identification with their indigenous roots was important in forming political strategies against the English-only Proposition 187 in California and other contemporary manifestations of neocolonialism. Chicana/o students at Adams State had articulated a political consciousness rooted in the acknowledgment of indigenous ancestry since at least 1977. Within this historical and political context, the coalition was formed from Estudiantes Unidos and Native Unity. The majority of coalition members, however, were Chicana/o students who strongly identified with their indigenous heritage. Their alliance with Native students resulted in a challenge to subjectivity at Adams State because Native students were no longer isolated regarding the mascot issue. The conscious choice of the term "indigenous" expanded the base of political action and forced the Adams State community to reconsider its "Indian." Suddenly, there were more real people as opposed to constructs.

Walter Roybal was born and raised in the San Luis Valley near Blanca, Colorado. An active member of the coalition, he currently works as an admissions counselor at Adams State. I asked Walter to remember his position on mestizaje and the coalition:

> The thing is that with our culture there is no ideal term for identity or whatever. I don't necessarily like the term "Hispanic," however I don't completely identify with the word "Chicano" either, but I think being Mexican is one of the ways that identifies [us] the best. So I know that my roots come from the Native American[s] as well as the Spaniard[s] coming in. With this issue, it kind of brought awareness to me to be able to relate to the Native American struggle and the fact that our mascot at the time was something that was degrading to us as a mestizo people.[26]

Walter's position is exemplary of many Chicana/o coalition members. Although there was never total agreement among Chicana/o-, "Hispanic-," Mexican-, or Spanish-identified people on the issue of self-naming, those who did belong to any of these groups and were active in the coalition agreed that the use of the "Indian" was offensive not only to Native Americans but also to many Chicana/os.[27]

Adriana Nieto was co-president of Estudiantes Unidos in 1992, as well as vice president of Colorado's statewide Chicana/o student network. She never finished her BA at Adams State because of her passionate involvement in the struggle to retire the "Indian." I asked her to talk about her participation in the coalition. According to Adriana:

Coming into consciousness as a young Chicana/Mexicana, I was embracing the idea that I was indigenous, that I was affected by colonial legacies of racism. So with the mascot issue it was easy to put my full efforts into getting rid of it because I could ideologically claim it offended me as a mestiza. But then I realized I didn't feel the same pain immediately felt by Native students like Phil and Tomasina [Grey]. I didn't fully understand what a Native-identified person was feeling. But I could understand the mascot as a manifestation of colonialism and racism. I know what those feel like regardless of being a Mexicana. So as an individual who wanted to struggle against the forces of colonialism, it was an obligation to fight against the use of the mascot. As the president of Estudiantes Unidos, I thought we should officially support the change as well, and we articulated that through a recognition of our historical and cultural links to Native Americans.[28]

Both Walter and Adriana articulated a common identity as indigenous and a commitment to protest the "Indian." Notions of mestizaje were prevalent at Adams State throughout the Chicano Movement and obviously carried through to the 1990s. Many insightful approaches to and discussions of mestizaje by "borderlands" feminists such as Gloria Anzaldúa, Ana Castillo, Chéla Sandoval, Emma Pérez, Sonia Saldívar-Hull, and others influenced Chicana/o students at ASC. These complex and articulate discussions of mestizaje were manifested at Adams State in 1992 with the formation of the Coalition for the Respect of Indigenous Peoples.

Members of the coalition understood race as one of the primary operating structures that defined our experiences at Adams State College. The mascot issue seemed like the place to begin for all of us. Those of us who were non-Native also understood that the racism apparent in the use of the "Indian" mascot was nothing compared to the racism Native students were about to encounter as they organized against the "Indian." Thus it was incumbent upon every antiracist subject to stand beside Native students on the mascot issue. Through the deployment of mestizaje, the Coalition for the Respect of Indigenous Peoples became a postcolonial political strategy that insisted on "polymodal forms of poetics, ethics, identities, and politics, not only for Chicana/os but for any constituency resisting the old and new hierarchies of the coming millennium."[29] We challenged ourselves to develop a political strategy that encompassed the broad range of our experiences. The result was a postcolonial political strategy that dealt with race and the "Indian" according to our contemporary experiences and the conditions in which we lived.

In the epilogue to the revised edition of their landmark text *Racial Formation in the United States*, Michael Omi and Howard Winant write that at the turn of the twenty-first century it is bankrupt to continue to talk about race in Black-and-White binaries. They discuss the 1992 Rodney King verdict and the Los Angeles rebellion and assert that our models for analyzing race are outdated and have no value in understanding the conditions we live in presently.[30] The political alliance between Native and Chicana/o students at Adams State addressed this same issue in the immediacy of post–Rodney King 1992 and The Year of Indigenous People. The Coalition for the Respect of Indigenous Peoples without doubt urged the Adams State community to "notice race" on campus.

As the coalition formed from Native, Chicana/o, and Anglo students, each group retained its own understanding and reading of the offensive nature and inherent racism of the "Indian" mascot, all the while grounding the discourse of the coalition within the centrality of Native people as embodied actors, not invented icons. Mestizaje emerged as perhaps the most powerful method of struggle against the "Indian," and it was particularly successful within the social and historical contexts of the San Luis Valley, the Chicana/o Movement, and Adams State College. The coalition also developed a political strategy that answered the call of postcoloniality by responding to the distinctive context of 1992.

Perhaps the most inspiring element of the coalition's experience was the multicultural political process. Anglo people rarely "notice race" in American society, and if they do, they usually do not notice themselves as racialized. Furthermore, Anglo people most often conduct their racial consciousness in terms of binary relationships. For Anglos in the coalition, there was a special opportunity to listen to and learn about Native and Chicana/o students and to experience the political process of indigenous people fighting racism and colonization. This required those Anglo students to listen and to consciously critique their privilege and subjectivity on campus because "between knowledge and power, there is room for knowledge-without-power."[31] All the members of the coalition benefited from struggling alongside one another, from learning to speak "near by" rather than "for" or "about," and from the lesson that positive change can happen even in the face of tremendous adversity.[32]

MEMORY: THE STORY OF THE COALITION FOR THE RESPECT OF INDIGENOUS PEOPLES

I have had almost ten years to think about the story of the coalition. Indeed, I could focus on many momentous events: the surprise arrival of Dennis Banks and the Walk across America to free Leonard Peltier, the sit-ins in the president's office, the planned and deserted takeover of the Student Union building, students from the University of Illinois driving all the way to Alamosa to join our homecoming protest, Phil Castillo going on national television and denouncing the "Indian." But those events are not what is most important about the coalition. Instead, I want to share some of the memories of four key members: Tomasina Grey (Dineh), Phil Castillo (Acoma), Adriana Nieto (Chicana/Mexicana), and Walter Roybal (Chicano/Mexicano). Why are these memories important in understanding the Coalition for the Respect of Indigenous Peoples and its fight against the Adams State "Indian"? I consider *memory* a way of bearing witness because I want to remind readers of the pain and discrimination coalition members experienced and fought against at Adams State College.[33] Yet I believe many of us are finally dealing with this pain in positive ways. I learned that in my interviews with these four courageous people.

This is a story of remembrances that begins and ends in fragments. My efforts to tell it are motivated by a desire not to forge these fragments into a whole but rather to release them. Most of these memories are painful. All of them are precious. In *Claiming Breath*, Diane Glancy (Cherokee) writes: "I don't have to make it up with the imagination. Just think of the relationships."[34] I have thought about the relationships and believe that memory has something important to do with history because it becomes a tool for survival. Yet these memories are often fragmented and thus grow to be more active in the imagination than in the consciousness. For example, in *The Decolonial Imaginary*, Emma Pérez writes: "The decolonial imaginary embodies the buried desires of the unconscious, living and breathing in between that which is colonialist and that which is colonized. Within that interstitial space, desire rubs against colonial repressions to construct resistant, oppositional, transformative, diasporic subjectivities that erupt and move into decolonial desires."[35]

While I cannot speak for everyone in the coalition, I feel that my own memories and experiences of the "Indian" at Adams State have become part of a personal decolonial imaginary. I think that during the years of the coalition, our desire rubbed against colonial repression (the "Indian" mascot) and constructed resistant, oppositional, transformative, diasporic subjectivities that erupted and moved into decolonial desires (the formation of the coalition). Put more simply, while it is important that the mascot was changed, I think it is particularly significant that the students in the coalition found a voice and spoke from the heart.

During my conversation with Walter Roybal, I found that many students at Adams State College today are not aware that the school used to have the "Indian" as its mascot or that students struggled to retire it.[36] What, then, becomes of our experience in the coalition? Tomasina Grey told me that she "lives with it every day."[37] Tomasina came to Adams State in 1992 from the checkerboard area of the Dineh Nation near Crownpoint, New Mexico. She told me that after high school her parents said she was welcome to go to college or stay at home if she wanted, but if she stayed she would have to get a job. She got a job working at Taco Bell. One day at Taco Bell was all it took, and she was off to college at Adams State. Tomasina remembered:

> So we went to the homecoming parade, and all of a sudden coming down the road is this White girl on a horse. Practically wearing a bikini as I recall, and she had that colorful war bonnet. And I was just standing there. I was completely ashamed of who I was at that moment. And I thought, "Oh my God, this is not how, this is not me." It kind of made me feel like, at the time I remember, it kind of made me feel like questioning my own identity.[38]

That encounter with the "Indian" at the homecoming parade in 1992 was the beginning of Tomasina's fight against the "Indian" and of her participation in the coalition. Tomasina was one of the coalition's most articulate and devoted members. Today, when she remembers those years, she is just as articulate and devoted, perhaps more so. She never finished her degree at Adams State. Currently, she is finishing her BA at the University of New Mexico, and she then plans to apply to the graduate program in Native American studies at Arizona State.

Phil Castillo came to Adams State in 1990 from Acoma Pueblo, where he was born and raised. Phil was a highly recruited distance runner and chose Adams State because of its excellent running program and its head coach, Dr. Joe Vigil:

> Upon arriving at ASC I still had no idea what the mascot was there, nor did I care too much. . . . My first encounter with the mascot in action was when my mother came to Adams' annual Parents' Day celebration, held each year to give the parents an up-close view of college life for their kids there. We attended a football game that day, and that's when we saw with our own eyes the embarrassing display of Adams State's mascot. It was that day back in 1990 that I realized I had to do something about this. Of course, my mother was also upset, [and] we left . . . immediately at the start of the game.[39]

Phil Castillo went on to win an individual cross-country national championship as well as a perfect score team championship in 1992. As a member of the coalition, he also developed into a dynamic speaker. Since Adams State, Phil continues to run and train as part of the Army Athletes Program. He is also active in WINGS, an organization devoted to Native American distance runners. Phil remembered:

> I also got a lot of flack from my teammates for drawing attention to the team. But I was on a mission, and I felt strong enough about it that I was going to pursue it to the end. In the very beginning, I didn't get a lot of support from my teammates. In fact, they frowned upon the fact of what I was doing. When we would host rallies on campus, the majority of my teammates that would show up were my Hispanic teammates. I felt like my Anglo teammates didn't want nothing to do with my issues. And I never made or gave anyone a hard time about it because I always understood the consequences of our actions. My coach at first didn't support my decision either and was pressured by the administrators to get me to stop my actions. Coach Vigil never approached me about quitting this venture; therefore, he was also tarnished, I think, by the administration. It wasn't until about the fourth year, I think, that he finally came out publicly and gave me his 100 percent support for what I was doing. I think Coach Vigil was one of the most brilliant professors/coaches at Adams State, but because of his support for me, in the end it . . . proved to be his downfall from Adams State. He knew the administration would try to make his life difficult, so he left in 1993 from coaching Adams running. That was my senior year of college, and I felt so bad for his leaving the team that I also quit the team, giving up my senior year of running at Adams State. Coach Vigil is my mentor, and when he walked out in 1993 I followed him, just like I always did when I first met him in 1989.[40]

Early in its practice, the coalition organized educational forums that were open to the public. There would be an open microphone, and students could express their feelings about the "Indian" mascot. The idea was to educate people on the issue, so a lot of Native students took the initiative to read from written statements or just talk about how and why they were offended by the mascot. The forums were very difficult because a lot of angry students, ignorant of racial issues, would come and expect Native students to "explain" the pain the mascot caused them. Tomasina recalled her experiences at the forums: "And I remember being at some of those meetings. It was like, no offense to you, but it was like all these white people [were saying] 'oh what's the problem with it?' I think that a lot of shame came from the fact that it was portraying me as a woman in a negative way. And to top it all off, and you add the layers, it added [to] the fact that I was a Native person."[41]

Even though these forums were successful in garnering support for the change, they also became treacherous for Native students. After one forum at which Tomasina spoke, mascot supporters broke the windows in her truck. In spite of this, Tomasina continued to fight against the "Indian."

Adriana Nieto came to Adams State in 1990 from Denver. Like Tomasina, Adriana endured threats of physical violence, as well as confrontations with Anglo students and even on occasion with administration members. The coalition began the educational forums in 1992. By 1994 they had deteriorated into battlegrounds over the mascot issue. During those two years, Adriana had been putting everything she had into the coalition, and between those efforts and the racism she faced on campus, she was failing her classes. While going over the manuscripts I have collected from the coalition, I came across a photocopy of a "Letter to the ASC Community" from President William M. Fulkerson Jr., written in the spring of 1994. In the letter he called for a two-year moratorium on the mascot issue because he was retiring and felt it would be unfair to expect an interim president to make the decision about what to do. President Fulkerson claimed no one had come to his office to express their desire to retire the mascot. Adriana, however, remembers differently: "No, I remember talking to him because his big fat neck was hanging out of his collar that was too tight. I remember, and he turned bright red and was pounding on the desk."[42]

The letter from President Fulkerson, as well as the deterioration of the forums, moved the coalition to take more radical action. As a result, the group began holding daily sit-ins at the president's office.

Adriana dropped out of Adams State at the end of the spring semester of 1994. Today, she holds an MA in Latin American studies from the University of New Mexico and earned her PhD from the Iliff School of Theology at the University of Denver in 2009.

When I talked with Walter Roybal about those volatile times at Adams State, he reminded me that it was always very hard for him because he was from the San Luis Valley and had family there. He felt he had to pick and choose his battles carefully because he needed to be responsible to the people he cared about. Even so, he fought hard against the "Indian" at Adams State. I understand now that having people like Walter involved helped give the coalition additional credibility with the community. According to Walter,

> But I look back at that time, and I think that it was a real necessity for the time at Adams State, a real necessity at the time for my own personal life as well as some of my friends that were involved. Being on campus and being able to be represented on campus and not to stand for letting this happen on our campus, disrespect toward our own people, toward Native Americans. The whole idea of changing the mascot had to do with being offensive to a group of people. It wasn't a project that was set forth to diminish what the history of Adams State was, what the accomplishments were of the athletes, what the tradition was in the past of Adams State, or to demean any of the athletic programs or anything like that.[43]

Today, Walter works as an admissions counselor for Adams State and travels all over the Southwest on recruiting trips. When I went to Alamosa to interview Walter, I had not been to the campus in a long time. I still had a lot of mixed feelings about Adams State. Talking with Walter and seeing how comfortable and happy he was made me realize that the story of the coalition is a victory story. The "Indian" is gone, and we can all feel good about that.

In all my conversations with these four coalition members, I asked everyone if there was something they especially wanted to share or wanted people to know about them and their fight against the "Indian." I was particularly moved by Tomasina's response because even after all the research and writing I had been doing about the coalition, she reminded me of just how important our work was and why we should feel good about the "Indian" being gone. She said:

> I want to be a better person. And I want the generations behind me to have a better life. And in order for that to happen I need to do my part now. I felt like I was honoring my grandparents. Not just my immediate grandparents but my ancestors before. All these stories that were told to me, all these things that were passed down to me, all the way back down to my basics, like as far as my grandmother telling me the story about where I got my fingerprints, things like that. To me it felt like I was honoring that. I think I would like them to know maybe a few things. First, that never having [had] the advantage of money or having the advantage of stocks and bonds or anything like that, a trust fund, that for me the mascot issue was always a very personal issue simply because my riches [are] in my identity. And that it's a near and dear to my heart kind of issue. That there is really no personal benefit whatsoever, other than the fact that I'm standing up for justice. It's like women being battered. You come to a certain point of being battered that you can't take that battering anymore. You have to step out of it and make the change.[44]

In my collection of manuscripts from the coalition is a copy of the ASC student paper, *The South Coloradan*, which has a letter to the editor from the coalition tucked away in a corner. I remember that we had written a longer, more thorough letter but were told that in the interest of space, the paper would need to shorten our letter. It did not matter. I would like to end with that letter to the editor because even though the "Indian" is gone and it is more than ten years later, we still feel the same way:

> Dear Editor: The Coalition for the Respect of Indigenous Peoples was formed on Thursday. We as the Indigenous people of Adams State College have taken the initiative to change the "Indian" mascot. We believe the use of the "Indian" as the ASC mascot is very offensive to Indigenous people.

We came to this institution to get an education, not to be made fun of. The use of the mascot today is ignorant to the true identity of the Native American. We feel this way because it clouds the true image and culture of the Native American.

Sincerely,

The Coalition for the Respect of Indigenous Peoples.[45]

I would like to thank all those who fought against the "Indian" at Adams State for being who they are, absolutely and completely. I would especially like to thank the Native students who took such tremendous risks and entered into such traumatic spaces with their hearts in their hands. At Adams State College, the Coalition for the Respect of Indigenous Peoples demanded that the ASC community accept Indians "as full participants in and members of [the] world human cultural society." That was at the heart of the struggle at Adams State. Doing it took a lot of courage. In November 1995, Adams State College finally fulfilled that responsibility.

NOTES

1. Adriana Nieto, video conversation with the author, Albuquerque, NM, March 2003.
2. *ASC Arrow* (Alamosa) 8, no. 2, November 1995.
3. Ibid.
4. Ibid.
5. Ibid.
6. C. Richard King and Charles Fruehling Springwood, *Team Spirits: The Native American Mascots Controversy* (Lincoln: University of Nebraska Press, 2001), 4.
7. N. Scott Momaday, *The Names* (New York: Harper, 1976), 9.
8. Chéla Sandoval, *Methodology of the Oppressed* (Minneapolis: University of Minnesota Press, 2000).
9. Homi Bhabba, *The Location of Culture* (London: Routledge, 1994), 63.
10. King and Springwood, *Team Spirits*, 2.
11. Phillip J. Deloria, *Playing Indian* (New Haven: Yale University Press, 1998), 7.
12. King and Springwood, *Team Spirits*, 6.
13. Deloria, *Playing Indian*, 6.
14. Ibid., 184.
15. C. Richard King and Charles Fruehling Springwood, *Beyond the Cheers: Race and Spectacle in College Sport* (Lincoln: University of Nebraska Press, 2001), 26.
16. Adams State appears to have had a tradition of fluidity in the maintenance and expression of its "Indian." The mass-produced products one could buy at the bookstore seemed to change designs depending on the current styles that were hot on the market. The momentarily performative "Indian," like the Anglo girl on a horse, was subject to change depending on the current athletic director, president, or football coach. This is strikingly different from places like Illinois and Florida State, where a

strict sense of material "tradition" is central to their racism, and this difference may have allowed more space for change at Adams State.

17. Phil Castillo, e-mail correspondence with the author, Albuquerque, NM, March 2003.

18. King and Springwood, *Team Spirits*, 2.

19. Castillo e-mail, March 2003.

20. Walter Roybal, video conversation with the author, Alamosa, CO, March 2003.

21. William M. Fulkerson Jr., letter to the ASC community, March 8, 1994, manuscript collection of the author.

22. Nieto video conversation, March 2003.

23. Castillo e-mail, March 2003.

24. Mestizaje is the acknowledgment of European and indigenous roots and has a long academic and political tradition, from José Vasconselos to Chéla Sandoval.

25. Michael Omi and Howard Winant, *Racial Formation in the United States: From the 1960s to the 1990s* (New York: Routledge, 1994), 159.

26. Roybal video conversation, March 2003.

27. Nieto video conversation, March 2003.

28. Ibid.

29. Chéla Sandoval, "Mestizaje as Method: Feminists of Color Challenge the Canon," in *Living Chicana Theory*, Carla Trujillo, ed. (Berkeley: Third World Woman Press, 1998), 352.

30. Omi and Winant, *Racial Formation in the United States*, 158.

31. Trinh T. Minh-ha, *Woman, Native, Other: Writing Postcoloniality and Feminism* (Bloomington: Indiana University Press, 1989), 40.

32. Ibid.

33. Gloria Bird, "Breaking the Silence: Writing as Witness," in *Speaking for the Generations: Native Writers on Writing*, Simon Ortiz, ed. (Tucson: University of Arizona Press, 1998), 18.

34. Diane Glancy, *Claiming Breath* (Lincoln: University of Nebraska Press, 1991), 4.

35. Emma Pérez, *The Decolonial Imaginary: Writing Chicanas into History* (Bloomington: Indiana University Press, 1999), 352.

36. Roybal video conversation March 2003.

37. Tomasina Grey, video conversation with the author, Albuquerque, NM, March 2003.

38. Ibid.

39. Castillo e-mail, March 2003.

40. Ibid.

41. Grey video conversation, March 2003.

42. Nieto video conversation, March 2003.

43. Roybal video conversation, March 2003.

44. Grey video conversation, March 2003.

45. *The South Coloradan* (Alamosa), November 12, 1992.

Miriam Bornstein-Gómez

Pedagogical Practices of Liberation in Abelardo "Lalo" Delgado's Movement Poetry

This study draws on the work of Brazilian philosopher Paulo Freire as a conceptual framework for Chicano Movement Poetry in Colorado, particularly that of Abelardo Barrientos Delgado, affectionately known to many as "Lalo." A principal objective is to engage Delgado's poetry, the historical specificity of the word, and a particular political and cultural practice within the context of and in dialogue with Freire's work in critical pedagogy.

Delgado (1931–2004) achieved recognition for his contribution to Chicano Movement Poetry in many forms, particularly as a recipient of the Tonatiuh-Quinto Sol Award for literature in 1977 and as Denver's first Poet Laureate in 2004. Poet, writer, community organizer, educator, social worker, teacher, and administrator are among the various roles he played as part of his extensive civil rights work. Delgado gained notoriety as a writer after moving to Denver, Colorado, in the 1960s. By the time of his death "Lalo" had produced fourteen books, starting with *Chicano: 25 Pieces of a Chicano Mind* in 1969. Taking the publication of Chicano works into his own hands, he founded Barrio Publications, which published several collections of his poetry and fiction written in English and Spanish. Much of his poetry, fiction, and essays has appeared in periodicals and anthologies, particularly his signature poem

"Stupid America," which depicts the alienation suffered by young Chicanos. Clearly, his work reflects thematic versatility alongside social commitment. It offers vivid descriptions of social and economic injustices, including satirical poems that offer political insight as well as tender and sensitive poems. In expressing the people's hopes, struggles, and dreams, Delgado's creative and political work represents a significant legacy in Chicano letters.

Paulo Freire (1921–1997) is one of the most important voices in pedagogical philosophy and in developing a congruent approach to learning. His work in critical pedagogy has had an extraordinary influence on educators engaged in social change and in the struggle for equality for disenfranchised and marginalized social sectors. Delgado's poetic discourse exposes the impact of dominant cultural forces on the lives of Latinos/as as a subordinate group in the United States. Upon close analysis, one finds compatibility in political insights between Freire's work and Delgado's poetry. Their discourses cross textual, cultural, and political borders to reinforce each other's specificity.

As a critical educator and "cultural worker," Freire theoretically engages in a political practice that challenges hegemonic power. While his work emerges in theory and practice as anti-colonial and postcolonial discourse, Delgado's poetic discourse comes to light from a subaltern location within colonial hegemony. His poetry is far from being considered an entity in and of itself as his work derives from, and stands in dialectical relation to, a specific historical and cultural context in which cultural representation makes visible a reality rendered meaningless by dominant culture. It is at this point about how knowledge is produced and communicated that Delgado's poetry connects with Freire's pedagogy of liberation. This, as well as other fundamental concepts, constitutes the overlap between theories of education and Delgado's cultural representation—for example, the significance of critical awareness (conscientization) and action (praxis) in social transformation, dialogue and questioning as a method of learning, teaching by working *with* the people, education imbued with political values, the importance of lived experience and knowledge of the learner, engagement and equality in community building. Therefore, it is possible to examine how Freire explores education as cultural action and Delgado explores cultural action as education.

EDUCATION AND THE STRUGGLE FOR EQUALITY

Antonia Darder, in *Culture and Power in the Classroom* (1991), observes that rapid demographic shifts in the United States indicate that increasing numbers of students in the public educational system are bicultural. Her work offers a culturally democratic vision based on educational principles shaped by Paulo

Freire and Henry Giroux, as she affirms that the current U.S. educational system is designed to educate Euro-American students and, as such, does not meet the needs of bicultural students. This has resulted in a historical marginalization of these students from mainstream American life and in the creation of a subordinated population. Students who are disenfranchised by dominant cultural forces are a product of disenfranchised communities.

Furthermore, in *The Politics of Education* (1985), Freire asserts that an educational process that is not related to students' lives achieves two things: it functions as an obstacle to students' learning and prevents the acquisition of knowledge and specific skills, particularly in literacy. This kind of learning fails to take account of what the student knows about the world and how she or he understands his or her place in that world. Freire is critical of an educational system that disconnects the student from this kind of knowledge because it reinforces the learner's sense or perception that she or he is ignorant of and unknowledgeable about the world. This kind of learning process makes students feel inadequate and unsuccessful (Freire 1985:177), and it does not work with what they know about their world. Educational processes must be situated in the students' lived experience. Freire states that it is important to question: "to make mistakes is the element of creativity, and when this element is lost knowledge becomes bureaucratizing and anti-democratic as in the case of standardized education" (Freire and Faundez 1989:39). This kind of prescriptive learning, as opposed to an engaged learning process based on dialogue and questioning, is a way to impose conformity on students; as such, it has an insidious ideological effect. It is based on intolerance and a sense of superiority.

It is the nature of covert discrimination that whereas difference may be an acceptable social behavior in a politically correct environment, equality is not necessarily a social and an educational goal. This may explain why after so many efforts, in some respects the educational and social objectives of the Chicano Movement remain unrealized. As Darder observes, there is still a struggle for equality and social justice in the educational system as a result of advanced capitalism and postmodern culture (1995). Darder's work builds on Freire's linkage between educational theory and social justice. Freire offers a pedagogy that challenges hegemony as educators engage in a decolonizing process that builds on and recognizes the value of the knowledge of subjugated social sectors.

Through his poetry, Delgado occupies a space left by an alienating and oppressive public educational system that has historically failed to serve the needs of a great number of Chicana/o students. He presents his critique of the educational system by describing it as a "battleground where the front /

continues to swallow up chicanos ... / the blessings of accreditation / are only dispensed by an anglo pope" (1978:33). An educational model founded on White middle-class values exists at the expense of culturally divergent students. And yet there is hope in what Delgado calls "die-hard" Chicanos who "continue their dream / of diplomas con el shape de tortillas. / de no tener que comprar nuestra educación de rodillas / ni con estampillas ... / lo nuestro es sueño y es también trabajo, / siguen siendo así mientras seamos los de abajo" (continue their dream / of diplomas with the shape of tortillas / of not having to buy our education on our knees / or with food stamps ... / ours is a dream and is also effort, / that is how it is while we are the ones who continue to be at the bottom; my translation) (1978:33). In this context, Delgado's poetry communicates the need for individuals subjected to domination to carry out a struggle for emancipation through individual and community education.

While emerging from territorial conquest as a result of the Mexican-American War, or "La Invasión Norteamericana" (the North American Invasion) as the war is known in Mexico, Mexican literary expression attempted to make sense of the new power relations. In some instances the purpose of writing was conceived as a defense of the people's own belief system and a subversion of competing ideologies. From that date on, writers were to define their social and political location in relation to a geographically and culturally contested territory. Given an ideology of conquest, writers negotiated a space of forced coexistence, but their voice was often relegated to a subaltern space, to silence, or both. Given this reality, writers struggled with questions of place, identity and survival.

The Chicano Movement, in its struggle for civil rights, approached the borderline between mainstream culture and Chicana/o literary practices as an epistemological rupture resulting from radical differences in beliefs, cultures, and historical experience. One characteristic of the Chicano Movement was its political and cultural challenge to a denial of the humanity of Chicana/os by a White supremacist history that justified the morality of conquest, among other acts of oppression. During the period of the Chicana/o Movement, disenfranchised communities found a voice through creative expression in literature, music, and visual art. Specifically, Movement Poetry contained educational practices of liberation in its intent and in the way it generated its discourse. Movement Poetry developed a poetic discourse of transformation and critique, not a discourse of submission and reverence within dominant cultural practices. In this cultural and political context, Delgado's poetics were a resource for a social vision, another way of imagining the self connected to decolonizing cultural practices. The poetic discourse of Delgado, as well as that of other

Movement poets, interprets history as a way of reclaiming power and identity by creating a specific cultural space in the practice of political resistance.

Accordingly, Delgado's poetry has a pedagogic function in that it represents an effort to render a political conquest unintelligible; to create a liberating reflection of the conditions of cultural, linguistic, and economic domination. For example, in poems such as "Mexican Culture" and "Raíces Mestizas," indigenous and mestizo cultural roots are privileged as a source of strength for survival. Delgado states that "the Mexican mestizo carries / cosmic characteristics" and characterizes a people as "chameleons" in their ability to endure an oppressive history and environment (1994:11, 13). Therefore, poetry becomes an invocation of Chicano culture that was rendered inferior, if not subservient, to dominant culture as a result of conquest.

When considering Abelardo Delgado's poetics within the context of Movement Poetry, there is a discourse in which colonialism is subjected to critical analysis as cultural memory is activated by the "emergence of consciousness" and by referents in the poetry with the purpose of inscribing the historical experience of Chicana/os. Through the experience of the individual, poetry portrayed social concepts and developed greater consciousness of what it meant to be Chicano, Mexican American, Pachuco, even American. During the Chicano Movement an epistemological conceptualization appeared defined as "La Raza." Delgado recognizes the heterogeneous nature of La Raza, but in particular he identifies the indigenous as the "sacred origin," as "la goma" (the glue) "to serve as paste" to unite the various identities dispersed by history (1969:6). La Raza created a space for debate and the celebration of an individual and collective historical and political identity.

Movement Poetry represented an alternative educational practice; as such, it was a statement on formal education or mis-education, as viewed by activists in Colorado such as Delgado and Rodolfo "Corky" Gonzales. In fact, "Corky" established Escuela Tlatelolco as a community response to the cultural, political, and educational needs of the Chicana/o community. Delgado, like many Chicana/o poets during this time, utilized his poetry to appropriate an ideology that had given dominance to White cultural and political values. A negotiation of conquest and colonial difference takes place within his poetry, which also appropriates a cultural space to resist and subvert White discursive practices and filter them through a Chicana/o perspective. In "The Fence" the poetic speaker states, "now the U.S. is in the business / of fencing off the Mexican border / in order / to keep away / hunger / they themselves create ... do you suppose the same fence can be used / to keep U. S. corporations from crossing / over into Mexico" (Delgado 1979:19). In many ways his poetry presents an inversion of a supremacist discourse that viewed Chicanos as uncivilized and less than human. One only has to take a quick look at the supremacist history of the United States and its critique in Gloria Anzaldúa's theoretical and creative work (1987) and in Arturo Aldama's *Disrupting Savagism* (2001). The public presentation of Delgado's poetry resists historical, cultural, and political marginalization in that it is a performance of Chicanos' own humanity, in Freire's words, a way to become "more fully human." Thus, coupling Freire's work with that of Movement poets and Delgado's work sheds light into the porous boundaries among poetics, education, and political discourse.

EDUCATION AS POLITICAL ACT AND POETRY AS POLITICAL DISCOURSE

Freire and Antonio Faundez discuss power as separated from the role of the state in that it exists at various levels and therefore needs to be recognized, regained, or "discovered" by the people. They encourage the need for people to become aware of the importance of "gaining power first in our everyday lives, in schools, in jobs, in all the most basic aspects of life" (Freire and Faundez 1989:64). Using power to resist undemocratic systems means questioning the power that has been appropriated from the people. In Freirian terms, moving away from a banking educational process to a democratic one and from knowledge that reflects the values of the dominant culture to one that includes knowledge of the people or popular culture is an act of resistance and the democratic use of power. This includes questioning what is accepted as "national" culture, since it is the culture of the dominant social and economic sector.

In *Learning to Question* and other works, Freire asserts the fallacy that educational processes are value-neutral. Quite the contrary, education is a political act, although a kind of teaching takes place as if disconnected from an axiological system in which knowledge is presented as a universal truth. Educators must be aware of the political dimension of their actions. Delgado would agree with Freire in that his concept of poetry is connected to a specific historical and cultural context that generates poetic discourse. Writing, like teaching practices, takes place within a given set of social and ideological constructs that inform education as well as literary creation. Just as Freire conceptualizes education as a political act, Delgado conceives poetry as creative political discourse. However, at the same time he maintains a critical perspective in demanding justice and denouncing the U.S. historical role of domination. In *Here Lies Lalo*, Delgado critiques the U.S. bicentennial celebration by referencing a history of violence and oppression:

> make a historical flashback
> to the time a white man
> first fired upon a native american
> and killed him.
> he liked it so much he institutionalized the sport.
> the calvin mandate . . . manifest destiny . . . christ's cohort . . .
> can it be the war with mexico
> we so gloriously engaged upon
> or the extra million pounds of napalm
> we did not know what to do with
> so we decided to drop 'em
> on a peasant woman from cambodia
> and her two month old child . . .
> strategic error . . . of course.
> what about the time we panicked
> or were so blind with rage
> that we collected slant eyed butterflies
> called japs and placed them
> in concentration camps
> because they resembled the enemy too much.
> we could not find
> the germans or italians
> among the anglos
> so we did not do the same with them.
> maybe our recession is the ghost
> of two hundred klu klux klans
> burning, whipping, hanging
> tarring, raping, scarring
> a black girl twelve years old.
> the truth is that these last two hundred years
> don't balance out at all.
>
> ("IT'S BUY CENT ANAL TIME, CARNALES" 1979:14)

This poem presents a critique of white supremacy and dominant ideology that systematically destroys the potential of Chicana/o people. Thus the word becomes the site where colonialism is textualized and deconstructed, and it is in the performance of the poem, either in print or embodied, where difference is enacted.

CRITICAL AWARENESS AND ACTION

According to Freire's theory of conscientization, a discursive interactivity takes place. Awareness rendered by reflection is the result of questioning dominance and acculturation and reinforces a new social imaginary. It is through conscientization that a human being becomes critically aware of her or his social and historical positioning and how action becomes part of a process to transform reality (Freire 1985:169). However, conscientization is an evolving process connected to critical reflection coupled with action. Praxis is informed action derived from conscientization, a dialectical movement from thought to action that takes place as individuals build and enhance their community. Freire defines praxis as "reflection and action upon the world in order to transform it." It is the way humans construct their own reality, the way they intervene in their own growth (Freire 2006:51). Therefore, consciousness coupled with action has the power to transform reality; it is the method for bringing about meaningful social change and producing new knowledge of the world.

In reinscribing history from a Chicana/o point of view, Delgado conceptualizes his poetry as a way to incorporate a collective past and to increase and build community consciousness: "We do come out of our imaginary 'hoyos' as if we were rodents. Now we look around and see each other and rejoice with each other's presence" (1978:26). He is aware that as a representation of colonized people, his poetry presents a restaging of the conquest, which indicates that the locus of ethical authority lies not with dominant culture and power structures but within the Chicana/o community embedded in his poetry.

After the conquest of a great portion of Mexico's territory, literary discourse became a contentious site in which various histories engaged with each other in asymmetrical relations of power. Literary practices intended to inscribe the beliefs and traditions of hegemonic culture became dominant as Mexicano/Chicano ways of knowing and looking at the world become subjugated and relegated to subaltern status. Delgado's poetry deals with the consequences of conquest in questioning the morality and objectives of internal domination in the form of exploitation of the migrant worker:

> the migrant is developing holes all over
> his body for sadistic growers
> and sugar companies,
> senile crewleaders,
> pimping field men . . .
> worse than whores on overtime,
> laws are being passed
> over him,
> under him, around him
> and through him.
>
> ("THE WILLING AND UNWILLING VICTIMS" 1978:37)

It is the point of the encounter of at least two worlds, a site of contact in which power relations and historical experience are enacted. As readers and audiences gain awareness rendered by the poetry, a Freirian dialectical movement between thought and action emerges. Through the exercise of a critical consciousness, the reader and the audience intervene in the production of new meaning by imagining and positioning themselves in the world. Thus meaning remains within the text until the reader mobilizes it. As Freire observes:

> The reading of a text is a transaction between the reader and the text, which mediates the encounter between the reader and writer. It is a composition between the reader and the writer in which the reader "rewrites" the text making a determined effort not to betray the author's spirit. . . . When the reader critically achieves an understanding of the object that the author talks about, the reader knows the meaning of the text and becomes coauthor of that meaning. (1998:29–31)

What about the role of the writer? According to Delgado, the poet is to create critical awareness by bearing witness to injustices committed. His intention is to subvert dominant cultural codes of communication and use them to the community's advantage. Delgado defines his role as poet when he states: "I fear so much that my words will fail to accurately paint my most profound desires to unite, to animar, to encourage, to move, to make people feel, to love, to laugh, to fight, to believe. I, in very commercial terms, sell hope" (1978:26). Both Freire and Delgado know that critical consciousness is essential for the production of new knowledge, of ways of understanding and decoding the world. Delgado becomes a poet with a social responsibility because, as Freire states, human beings have the ability to affect their own growth as individuals (1998:94).

KNOWLEDGE AND CHICANA/O CULTURAL EXPERIENCE

Connected to the importance of the learner's common reality, Freire affirms the value of popular culture, or culture of the people, in the way society is transformed. In *Learning to Question* he views the cultural experience of the people as a source of strength and a fundamental principle in developing a pedagogy of liberation. Along with questioning the idea of education as a value-neutral process, Freire also questions the notion that there is one universal truth or one "true knowledge" with a universal value. For him, knowledge is generated within the context of a dialogic situation in which the educator works *with* the people and not *for* the people. Therefore, in an educational setting, cognition and awareness arise from asking questions to understand culturally divergent knowledge. Similarly, in Delgado's poetry the image of "el barrio," the migrant worker, the Virgen de Guadalupe, the figure of La Llorona, the tradition of Día de los Muertos, names of political activists, and other cultural referents connect with learners because they bring with them the language, experience, knowledge, and dreams of the community. His is an effort of imagining a better way, another means of shaping a future by becoming subjects rather than objects of their own history.

However, "[T]eaching cannot be a process of transference of knowledge from the one teaching to the learner. . . . Learning is a process where knowledge is presented to us, then shaped through understanding, discussion and reflection" (Freire 1998:31). When the educational process is such that the student realizes that she or he is a subject, not just an object of history and culture, there is a claim to agency. When the educational process is engaging, it creates a space in which it is possible for students to deconstruct the reality of their lives and at the same time participate in the reconstruction of the world: "To study is not to consume ideas, but to create and re-create them" (Freire 1985:4). As Freire asserts, praxis is the other side of conscientization as critical thought and action form an organic whole in a process in which the individual and a community will become agents of social change. In claiming agency the individual becomes a participant in his or her world, in understanding and decoding the historical context that shapes it and the way he or she is socially positioned in an emancipatory process.

In Delgado's poetry, Chicana/os become subjects of their particular historical moment as relations between dominant and marginalized or subaltern communities are altered. He does not expect dominant culture to authorize him, since he authorizes himself to create a voice that gives meaning to the representative function of the word. It is evident when we read "tiembla ciudad del paso / que hoy hablan tus chicanos / tiembla nación de América / que ya se llaman hermanos . . . hoy es desafío lo que antes era un ruego" (tremble city of el paso / today your chicanos speak / tremble America / they call each other brothers . . . today it is resistance / challenge what used to be a plea; my translation) (1969:30). Furthermore, in the same poem Delgado enumerates the names of political leaders who were to gather in El Paso, Texas, for the La Raza Unida convention. Delgado states the meeting's purpose: "van a enseñarle a los gringos lo que es ser de deveras" (they are going to teach the gringos what it really means to be; my translation) (1969:30). The text creates a space in which subaltern or colonized people possess agency.

In *The Practice of Everyday Life* (1984), Michel de Certeau observes that systems of domination are not altered but rather are modified by the tactical appropriation of discourse of power. Such appropriation constitutes a subversive and transgressive act as subaltern cultures struggle to achieve representation of their own reality. Manipulating and appropriating the dominant semiotic system represents a symbolic struggle for power. Thus subaltern peoples possess agency in the way they represent their own culture. The text then becomes the "contact zone," as defined by Mary Louise Pratt in *Imperial Eyes*. It is "the space in which peoples geographically and historically separated come into contact with each other and establish ongoing relations, usually involving conditions of coercion, radical inequality, and intractable conflict" (Pratt 1992:6). In this sense, Delgado's text becomes the locus or site of moral authority, as well as a site of negotiation and resistance. Even the fact that Delgado became his own publisher represents a claim to agency. Barrio Publications, where he published much of his work, became an appropriation of the communicative medium of dominant culture that had generally ignored Chicana/o literary production. By appropriating a mode of literary production, Delgado was able to utilize multiple signifiers through his use of Spanish, English, and mixed form. He connects with Freire's thinking on language and power when the latter states that "the rediscovery of power should also be directed toward the rediscovery of language away from the language of the ruler to the creation of a Nationalist Populist Culture" (Freire and Faundez 1989:82). Thus Freire makes a case for bilingualism as validation of people's knowledge and the way the subject experiences, expresses, and constructs the world through language: "The problems of language always involve ideological questions and, along with them, questions of power" (1998:74).

The bilingual nature of many of Delgado's poems through his use of Spanish and English independently or in mixed form reinforces the Freirian concept that language and thought are inseparable from action. Consciousness is affected by language in relation to reality in a continuous dialectical movement between action and reflection, and so on. It is through language that marginalized and oppressed groups claim agency and participate in a shared reality. They participate in expanding their understanding of the world, claiming a place in history, and creating the possibility to change the collective reality. Language provides a means for individuals to see themselves outside of their own selves and to understand their place in the world. Language provides Delgado with the ability to resist dominant views, beliefs, and cultural practices while taking ownership of cultural representation and community building.

THE DIALOGIC SITUATION AND COMMUNITY

As the poet claims agency, a dialogic situation takes place in two directions. One is engaging in dialogue with power as an act of subversion and resistance. The other is a transformational act in a creative and political educational process through dialogue within the Chicana/o community. For both Freire and Delgado, dialogue is the point of encounter. There is a connection between Freire and Delgado in that a truly communicative act becomes a shared cultural and political project. For Freire, dialogue is the site of liberation, whether in print or embodied. Similarly, Delgado's poetry achieves a pedagogical purpose by connecting the word to its own history. While for Delgado the word is the site of cultural and ideological encounter, for Freire teaching means engaging in dialogue, which is essential to the emergence of consciousness coupled by praxis leading to transformative social change (Freire 2006:87–124). In a dialogical relationship between teacher and learner, critical consciousness emerges and teachers and learners become self-educators and self-learners (Freire 1985:105). To engage in dialogue means working with each other, teaching and learning from each other, not one entity acting on the other: "We can learn a great deal from the very students we teach. For this to happen it is necessary that we transcend the monotonous, arrogant and elitist traditionalism where the teacher knows all and the student does not know anything" (1985:177). From the educator's perspective, meaningful exchange involves content that is relevant to the learner's reality. Freire calls it "generative themes" culled from the people's "thematic universe." Generative themes are found in "the thought-language in which men and women refer to reality, the levels at which they perceive that reality, and their view of the world" (2006:97). Such content inaugurates the "dialogue of education as the practice of freedom" (2006:96). In fact, Freire argues that "there is no true word that is not at the same time a praxis" (2006:87).

Therefore, individuals and society have the power to dominate or liberate the human spirit through language and, in Delgado's case, through poetry. In the poem "La causa," discourse is directed to a collective listener. It is an urgent call to action for the "faceless chicano" to regain dignity through the cause of La Raza, described as "an anthill upon your chest" (1969:12). Delgado's poetry is praxis in the Freirian sense, which means recovering "the people's stolen humanity" (Freire 2006:95). This perspective culminates in one of Delgado's most anthologized poems, "Stupid America," in which the poet challenges the social and cultural structures utilized to create and maintain conditions of exploitation and stereotypical images of Chicana/os. The poem is constructed on the basis of dialogical interaction and a symbolic act of oral communication:

> stupid America, see that chicano
> with a big knife
> on his steady hand
> he doesn't want to knife you
> he wants to carve christfigures
> but you won't let him . . .
> stupid America, remember that chicano
> flunking math and english
> he is the Picasso
> of your western states
> but he will die
> with a thousand masterpieces
> hanging from his mind.
> (1969:32)

In *Learning to Question,* Freire and Faundez agree that intellectuals have the responsibility to create and shape a new vision of the future, again, *with* the people, not *for* the people. This presupposes an interactive situation that takes into account possibilities for social transformation present in the specific historical and social reality and in relation to the Chicana/o community in the context of Delgado's poetry. Community, as a descriptive category, is composed of various elements, such as a given physical space in which people find commonality. For example, Delgado personifies the barrio in a 1978 essay: "the barrio develops a philosophy of life. . . . It must manufacture its own pride out of the raw materials there. The barrio knows the skin of the streets and alleys trap people within . . . but also keeps those from without" (1978:77). But community can also be attained by individuals who share a common interest. In this case, the group constructs a symbolic space on the basis of shared identity, as evidenced by Delgado's further definition of el barrio:

> I am that piece of land
> which is always getting out of hand,
> the one la ciudad
> is trying to hide.
> I house gente to whom
> the American dream has lied . . .
> yo soy el barrio, the slum, the ghetto,
> progress' sore thumb . . .
> soy a casa for all
> who suffer, thirst and hunger.
> (1994:16)

Community is central to a people's sense of belonging to a place and to each other as family, friends, and neighbors individually and within social institutions and organizations. Delgado focuses on everyday reality, since that is the locus of invisibility, of reification of the individual. This cultural space justifies social struggle and presents a recognizable reality defined by socio-economic forces. As social beings, humans construct community by creating and connecting with social networks of shared relations. For Delgado, the poet is embedded in the community where several dialogic situations develop and are implicitly and explicitly staged within the text itself and through public readings. His poetry addresses this collectivity, simultaneously challenging the underlying white supremacy of the dominant culture. Ethnic and cultural negotiations between dominant and subordinate cultures are articulated and enacted within this physical and symbolic space. As the poet becomes an interlocutor with the audience, primarily Chicanos, he engages in dialogical interaction that activates the pedagogical function and power of language in a process of social change. It is a question of using language and community in the appropriation of dominant spaces through performance and orality within a dialogic situation.

ORALITY AND PERFORMANCE OF POETRY

By reading his poetry on the steps of the Colorado State Capitol building in Denver in front of a multitude of marchers, Delgado links this iconic space to relations of power and power structures. He creates a space of resistance. In some respects, his sense of performance connects with the embodiment of social and political constructs enacted by El Teatro Campesino. Like the works performed by this renowned theater company, which emerged from working hand in hand with the economic and political struggles of César Chávez and the United Farm Workers Union, Delgado never lets the reader or audience forget the connection between the text and its own historicity. There are poems that present the experience of the farm worker or undocumented worker with the intent to serve as an explicit critical testimony:

> Hunger is the modus operandus.
> exploitation is de facto . . .
> if the honorable chairman of these hearings
> yields the floor to a chicano for a minute
> I will elaborate on what appears to me
> to be a well plotted cons-pi-ra-cy:
> cheap labor to maximize the margin of profits.
> ("THE I.A.," 1978:32)

Orality in Delgado's poetry is most evident when one considers that much of his poetry was written to be read aloud in public places, among the community gathered to protest inequalities and show commitment to social justice. Delgado takes advantage of the declamatory style of rhetorical traditions that became popular during Mexico's nation-building stage, particularly in the mid-nineteenth century, and that embed orality and civic pride in the text. However, the tradition of oratory poetry dates back to pre-Colombian times. In the indigenous tradition, Nahua elders used a formal oratory style called "Huehuehtlahtolli." Furthermore, after gaining its independence from Spain in 1821, during the period 1829–1836 Mexico had to contend with Texas's drive for independence followed by the U.S. invasion of Mexico, in which it lost half its territory in 1848 under the pretext of Manifest Destiny. In 1863 Mexico suffered an invasion by France known as the French Intervention and an occupation that lasted until 1872. It is no wonder that during the period of romanticism in Mexico and as a result of such great social, economic, and political instability, writers such as Ignacio Manuel Altamirano (1834–1893) aimed to produce a literature of "national character." Following the Romantic period in literary history, Ramón López Velarde (1888–1921) became a civic poet. His renowned poem "La suave patria" (The Gentle Homeland) is imbued with nationalism, connecting López Velarde with predecessors such as Altamirano and Justo Sierra (1849–1912), who as minister of education lent significant support to civic culture. The rhetorical tradition in Mexico developed along the lines of a public concept of poetry by designated poets who used a formal oratory and declamatory style as part of official government ceremonies and other social and civic events often organized by the upper sectors of society.

However, while Delgado continues the rhetorical Mexican tradition of civic poetry, he disrupts it by changing the location of the generative subject, the intended "message," and the type of public. His working-class perspective places the subject at the center of political and cultural agency in an ideological struggle against domination and colonialism. Thus Delgado unsettles the paradigm of civic poetry and the political practices that keep privilege and oppression as operational forces. He achieves this unsettling by problematizing the subject of Anglo and Eurocentric traditions while providing other forms of self-representation and collective knowledge. His work represents a kind of counter-discourse in which a cultural critique is articulated. For example, it is worth analyzing the concept of nation present in all of Delgado's work but most specifically in two poems. In one of these poems, Delgado expresses a bittersweet affection in regard to the United States:

> U.S.A., my country, my sweet oppressing adversary . . .
> We must acknowledge our historical sins,
> Errors, premeditated genocides,

> Robberies, broken treaties, double talk,
> Abuses, oppression, imperialistic deeds,
> Snobby attitudes, acts of arrogance, racism,
> Laws written to steal and with fraudulent intentions,
> Our selfish imposition, intervention,
> And profit chasing madness.
> ("HAPPY 200TH ANNIVERSARY," 1978:5)

Given the underlying textual orality of his work, Delgado embodies his poetry through performance, establishing a connection within a dialogic situation with his community. Delgado often reclaimed public spaces with poetry readings at the Colorado State Capitol building—a seat of power—but also in marches, political rallies, and community events in schools, public programs, and political meetings. In this, Delgado comes closer to oral indigenous tradition in that poetry during the colonial period was presented in church squares built on the sites of the people's own destroyed temples, buildings, and plazas. There is a similar spatial multilayering in the case of Delgado, where public readings at political meetings, marches, protests, and public and cultural events take place on Mexican soil invaded and conquered by the United States.

Furthermore, he uses a declamatory style as a strategy of self- and community empowerment, since oral expression supports direct discourse and a communicative situation based on familiarity. Poetic discourse is in several instances spontaneous, with emotional overtones, a kind of informal writing inspired by the lived moment that includes thoughts expressed in a prosaic form in which one observes easily recognizable images. Delgado utilizes rhyme and repetition to facilitate understanding and memorization. This results in a poetry that seems more oral than written discourse, more of an auditory experience than a visual one. It was designed to stir emotions, to connect with repressed historical experiences of a conquered people, and to allow the audience to identify with the outrage of conquest and the violence perpetuated. Consequently, the conversational tone of Delgado's poetry creates a dialogic situation with the audience in a shared emancipatory process. Such connectedness intends to question white supremacy and the validity of a dominant position by denouncing injustice.

Thus the Mexican rhetorical tradition of civic poetry was used to resist White ideologies and oppressive cultural norms. Because for Delgado this was the primary function of poetry, even in written form, at times his poetry sounds like a public speech intended to educate a community, to produce awareness (conscientization) in the Freirian sense, and to inspire the struggle (praxis) for social and economic justice.

Those who participated in the struggle for civil rights and heard "Lalo" cannot forget the performative quality of his poetry. To perform is to present, to bring forth or through. In the context of the Chicano Movement and its cultural expression, the performativity of literary works involves creating dialogical interactions in the construction of group and individual identities. Whether in print or in embodied performance, it is the site where a liberating ideology of self-affirmation and resistance is enacted, where unequal relations of power are revealed and disputed, and where normative values of the dominant society are questioned and challenged.

SOCIAL TRANSFORMATION AND HOPE

Freire defines culture as the way a person lives life every day. In this context it is possible that "[e]ducation as an exercise of domination . . . indoctrinates students to adapt to the world of oppression" (2006:78). As a response to such conditioning, Freire asserts that individuals and societies hold the power to engage in educational and social practices that transform the world by "denouncing the process of dehumanization and announcing the dream of a new society" (2001:74). In his introduction to Freire's *The Politics of Education*, Henry Giroux describes his work as an amalgamation of "hope, critical reflection, and collective struggle" (1985:xviii).

To a critique of denouncing and announcing as a utopian concept, Freire responds that "to be utopian is not to be merely idealistic or impractical but to engage in denunciation and annunciation" (1985:57). Denunciation is rooted in Freire's concept of praxis in a critical reading of oppression as part of the educational process. A commitment to social change rises from a belief in hope that powers a plan of action as the basis of annunciation. Thus utopia is investing in the belief that social change is possible through a transformative educational process at the heart of the way societies construct knowledge on a basis of equality and justice. In this sense, education and cultural representation fulfill an important emancipatory role. Freire's central message is the value of becoming more human as a result of critical reflection, action, and hope.

Delgado's vision and social critique are also rooted in hope because he shares with Freire an activist concept of the word. While Freire conceptualizes dialogue as the site of liberation, Delgado views poetry as the site of cultural and ideological encounter. Delgado's tone is passionate and consistently unrelenting in his outrage at the domination of white supremacy and the marginalization of Chicana/os. In relation to a dominant discourse that pretends to be universal in an educational setting or in cultural representation,

Delgado's poetry and Freire's theoretical formation of a pedagogy of liberation constitute a space of instruction (critical awareness) and empowerment in a political call for action re-inscribing in history the hopes and dreams of an oppressed people.

REFERENCES

Aldama, Arturo. *Disrupting Savagism*. Durham, NC: Duke University Press, 2001.

Anzaldúa, Gloria. *Borderlands/La Frontera: The New Mestiza*. San Francisco: Aunt Lute, 1987.

Darder, Antonia. *Culture and Difference: Critical Perspective on the Bicultural Experience in the United States*. Westport, CT: Bergin and Garvey, 1995.

———. *Culture and Power in the Classroom: A Critical Foundation for Bicultural Education*. New York: Bergin and Garvey, 1991.

De Certeau, Michel. *The Practice of Everyday Life*. Trans. Stephen Rendall. Berkeley: University of California Press, 1984.

Delgado, Abelardo B. *An Autobiographical Sketch of Abelardo*. Arvada, CO: Barrio, 1992.

———. *A Day Is Coming: Thirty-Two Days of Abelardo*. Arvada, CO: Barrio, 1994.

———. *Here Lies Lalo*, 2nd ed. Denver: Barrio, 1979.

———. *Under the Skirt of Lady Justice: Forty-Three Skirts of Abelardo*. Denver: Barrio, 1978.

Freire, Paulo. *Pedagogy of Freedom: Ethics, Democracy, and Civic Courage*. Lanham, MD: Rowman and Littlefield, 2001.

———. *Pedagogy of the Oppressed*. Trans. Myra Bergman Ramos. 30th anniversary ed. New York: Continuum, 2006.

———. *The Politics of Education: Culture, Power and Liberation*. Trans. Donaldo Macedo. Westport, CT: Bergin and Garvey, 1985.

———. *Teachers as Cultural Workers: Letters to Those Who Dare to Teach*. Trans. Donaldo Macedo, Dale Loike, and Alexandre Oliveira. Boulder: Westview, 1998.

Freire, Paulo, and Antonio Faundez. *Learning to Question: A Pedagogy of Liberation*. New York: Continuum, 1989.

Pratt, Mary Louise. *Imperial Eyes: Travel Writing and Transculturation*. London: Routledge, 1992.

ADDITIONAL (UNCITED) DELGADO BIBLIOGRAPHY

———. *Bajo el sol de Aztlán: Twenty-Five Soles de Abelardo*. El Paso: Barrio, 1973.

———. *Chicano: 25 Pieces of a Chicano Mind*. Denver: Barrio, 1969.

———. *The Chicano Movement: Some Not Too Subjective Observations*. Denver: Colorado Migrant Council, 1971.

———. "Due Process of Law." In *Aztlan and Viet Nam: Chicano and Chicana Experiences of the War*, George Mariscal, ed. Berkeley: University of California Press, 1999, 269–270.

———. *It's Cold: Fifty-Two Cold Thought Poems of Abelardo*. Salt Lake City: Barrio, 1974.

———. *La Llorona: 25 Lloronas of Abelardo*. Arvada, CO: Barrio, 1992.

———. *Mortal Sin Kit*. Arvada, CO: Barrio, 1973.
———. *A Quilt of Words: Twenty-Five Quilts of Abelardo*. Denver: Barrio, 1974.
———. *Reflexiones: Sixteen Reflections of Abelardo*. Salt Lake City: Barrio, 1976.
———. *Siete de Abelardo*. Denver: Barrio, 1979.
———. *A Thermos Bottle Full of Self-Pity: Twenty-Five Bottles of Abelardo*. Denver: Barrio, 1975.
———. *Totoncaxihuitl, a Laxative: Twenty-Five Laxatives of Abelardo*. Arvada, CO: Barrio, 1981.
———. *Unos perros con metralla: Twenty-Five Pieces of Abelardo*. Arvada, CO: Barrio, 1982.

Elisa Facio

(Re)constructing Chicana Movimiento Narratives at CU Boulder, 1968-1974

INTRODUCTION: PEDAGOGY AND MOVIMIENTO POLITICS

The project described in this chapter began during the 2000 spring semester in a class titled Chicana Feminist Thought. As a teacher, I was primarily concerned with deploying pedagogical practices and interrogating epistemological perspectives from a critical Chicana standpoint. I was not particularly interested in educational research per se but rather in using radical educational approaches to understand the noteworthy and significant herstory of Chicanas who attended the University of Colorado (CU) at Boulder from 1968–2000.

As put forth by Alejandra Elenes, I attempted to teach and engage the class as an "activist insurgent educator who interrogates social theory and reproduction to create political and cultural projects to transform existing social inequalities and injustices. These spaces are referred to as pedagogies" (2001a:105). Adriana Hernandez speaks of "teaching and learning as a political practice intended to enhance personal and social possibilities while also interrogating social practices and forms of hierarchies-power within a political and economic context" (1997):13. This perspective resonates with Regina Austin, who names woman-ist instincts, sensibilities, and politics as "sources of inspiration for teaching and learning to resist (both personally and collectively) the racism, sexism, homophobia, and exploitation in the different spheres of our lives" (1995:427). In this project, I also recognize and honor the everyday spaces of learning and teaching. Ruth Trinidad proposes that pedagogical formations are tied to women's ways of knowing and their everyday ways of being in the world (2001). To expand the understandings and workings of pedagogy, it is necessary to theorize "where" feminist pedagogies might take place, such as the kitchen table, church steps, local stores, and other locations.

In my efforts to radically transform the classroom, I developed a collaborative class project focusing on the herstory of Chicanas at CU Boulder, which was nearly unknown to the students. Thus began a collective research effort to (re)construct the educational narratives of Chicana students who attended CU Boulder during the years 1968–2000.[1] To date, we have identified our research intentions as threefold. First, in line with the works of Gloria Anzaldua (1999) and Dolores Delgado Bernal (2000), this project deconstructs the Chicano master narrative of Chicana student activity, protest, and power movements. Second, an obvious intention is to disclose, describe, and critically understand the educational experiences of Chicana students who attended CU Boulder during the 1968–2000 period. More specifically, the negotiation of Chicana subjectivity(s) and agency in relationship to the university is illuminated. Finally, our third objective is that the documentation of this research serve as a tool for the recruitment and retention of all Chicana/Latina and Chicano/Latino students at CU Boulder and throughout the state of Colorado.

This project is principally concerned with (re)constructing Chicana educational narratives by locating the historical presence and voices of Chicana undergraduate students, or the *sitios y lenguas* (spaces and languages) set forth by Emma Perez (1998). Perez argues for "marginalized lesbians and women of color to continue framing their decolonized spaces and languages, *sitios y lenguas*. These women have done so within designated, colonial spaces. They seek decolonized spaces beyond the third world spaces of White women's kitchens and White men's cotton fields where some Chicanas can be found today" (1998:91–92). We are also interested in recognizing the vital contributions made by these women in the establishment of Chicana and Chicano studies and the recruitment and retention of Chicana and Chicano students. In illuminating Chicanas' silenced herstory, we intend to critically understand the implications of their negotiations of resistance, identity, and feminist consciousness for themselves as students at an elite university and for radical social change in the pursuit of educational justice and democracy.

Interestingly but not surprisingly, students enrolled in the 2000 spring class Chicana Feminist Thought, many of whom were Chicanas and Chicanos, literally had no knowledge of CU Boulder's arduous struggle to develop a program of Chicana and Chicano studies and to recruit Chicana and Chicano students. Even more disheartening was the lack of noteworthy political and educational information regarding Los Seis de Boulder, the six student activists killed during the pinnacle of CU Boulder's Chicano Student Movement.[2] This period has been described as one of the bloodiest Chicano movements in any North American university. On May 27, 1974, Neva Romero (twenty-one) and Una Jaakola (twenty-four), two student activists who shared an off-campus house, and attorney Reyes Martinez (twenty-six) were killed in a car bomb in Chautauqua Park in Boulder. Forty-eight hours later Chicano activists Francisco Dougherty (twenty-two), Florencio "Freddie" Granados (thirty-two), and Heriberto Terán (twenty-four) died in a station wagon parked near 30th and Canyon. Antonio Alcantar, twenty-three, was entering the car as it exploded. He was seriously injured and burned and was disabled for life. The deaths of Los Seis de Boulder, as they came to be known, shocked the state, and the news reverberated throughout the Southwest and Mexico. To this day, mystery surrounds one of the most wretched and appalling events of the Chicano Student Movement. No official explanation has ever been provided by the Boulder Police Department, the CU Police, or the FBI, saying only that they believed the victims were arming the bombs, thus leading to their accidental deaths. A federal grand jury was convened, but its findings were not made public and no person(s) was indicted.

Given the university's erasure and omission of critical historical educational memory, the students expressed a profound desire to construct their own historicity as Chicana and Chicano students at CU Boulder. In addition, they seized the opportunity to recognize students before them by drawing on the legacy of previous generations of student activists who demanded, struggled, and in some cases died for educational rights. This chapter focuses on the educational journeys of Chicanas who attended CU Boulder during the years 1968–1974.[3]

RECLAIMING CHICANA HERSTORY

As extensively documented, throughout the Southwest, people of Mexican descent have found themselves engaged in various social movements ranging from land rights to education and civil demands to cultural preservation. Influenced by the Black national movement and the Mexican American community's historical legacy of agency against discrimination and structural inequality in North American society, a generation of Mexican Americans channeled its collective energies into a militant civil rights and ethnic nationalist movement in the late 1960s and 1970s. Surrounded by a radical climate of national political protests and insurgency, such as the Black Power Movement, the anti–Vietnam War Movement, and the second wave of the Women's Movement, El Movimiento focused on social, political, and economic self-determination and autonomy for Mexican American communities throughout the United States. The focus simultaneously manifested a paradoxical agenda of civil rights and equal opportunity demands, on the one hand, and a more separatist ethnic nationalist rebellion on the other (Garcia 1997). This paradox did not reveal a monolithic political base but instead a Chicano movement that evolved from various struggles with specific leaders, agendas, and organizational strategies and tactics.[4]

Drafted into the military in large numbers and in greater proportions than their population in the country, Chicanos organized their own significant antiwar movement. This protest reached its zenith when over 20,000 demonstrators, mostly Chicano, protested the war at the National Chicano Anti-War Moratorium in East Los Angeles on August 29, 1970. Culturally, the movement released a new energy of artistic and literary expression in what constituted a "Chicano Renaissance." Poets, writers, playwrights, and artists mobilized art as a political weapon for "La Causa," the Chicano Movement. The movement was not the first time Mexican Americans had protested their second-class status. Indeed, a strong historical legacy of protest existed, but the movement was the largest and most widespread expression of Mexican American discontent (Garcia 1997).

It is important to contextualize and highlight the social struggles that took place in Colorado because they had a momentous influence on the Chicano Student Movement at CU Boulder. One such political effort was the Alianza Federal de Mercedes, initiated in the 1960s to protect the land rights of Hispanic New Mexicans. The group was led by Reyes López Tijerina and was headquartered in New Mexico and Colorado.[5] The Alianza fought for the rights of dispossessed Hispanos, as those from New Mexico called themselves, whose lands had been lost as a result of the war, or illegal confiscation, between the United States and Mexico (1846–1848).

In April 1966, Rodolfo "Corky" Gonzales began his public fight in Colorado by creating one of the most influence programs of the Chicano Movement, the Crusade for Justice. The urban-based Crusade for Justice mobilized Mexican American communities around the issues of self-determination and community autonomy. The Crusade for Justice attempted to create a model of urban reform by eliminating police brutality and poverty within the Chicana/Chicano community.[6]

Sharing ideological roots with Black cultural nationalism, Chicano cultural nationalism, known as Chicanismo, advocated an ideology and spirit of active resistance within Mexican American communities throughout the United States.[7] Chicanismo served as a dynamically effective tool capable of mobilizing divergent struggles within the Chicano Movement. By the late 1960s, cultural nationalism was serving a dual political purpose. Chicanismo provided a unifying worldview for El Movimiento while simultaneously providing the ideological link that cut across such groups as La Raza Unida, the United Farm Workers (UFW), the Crusade for Justice, and the Chicana/ Chicano Student Movement.

CHICANAS AND THE COLORADO CHICANO MOVEMENT

Drawing from archival research, interviews, and documentaries, Priscilla Falcón, Florencia (Flo) Hernandez, Ester Acosta, and Cleo Estrada—considered prominent leaders as both students and community activists—have noted that the Colorado Chicano Movement was a civil rights movement dedicated to Chicano cultural preservation. Falcón stated, "[W]e were busy surviving, so we lived our theory" (Rocky Mountain PBS 2005). Chicanas were active in and influenced by three interdependent movements in Colorado—the Crusade for Justice, the United Farm Workers Movement, and the high school student movements—all of which had implications for Chicana student activity at CU Boulder.

Women associated more closely with the Crusade for Justice included Nita Gonzales, the eldest daughter of Corky Gonzales; Deborah Mora-Espinosa, who worked primarily in Pueblo; Gloria Velasquez, and Enriqueta Vasquez. In general, these women were greatly concerned about threats of acculturation, primarily through the loss of the Spanish language. In addition to a lifetime of political activity, Vasquez wrote for *El Grito del Norte* from 1968 to 1972. Historians Lorena Oropeza and D. Espinoza described Vasquez's writings: "Unwavering in her conviction that change was both possible and necessary, on the pages of *El Grito del Norte* Vasquez crafted a unique pedagogy of hope" (2006:xxi).

Juanita Herrera along with her husband, Alfred, were UFW organizers in Colorado. On weekends, Herrera spearheaded the boycott against grapes by picketing Safeway stores. Herrera also successfully organized boycotts of Coors and Taco Bell. Juanita Herrera's efforts are recognized more as part of the larger working-class struggle at that time than as part of El Movimiento. Nonetheless, Herrera's efforts were instrumental in the successful grape boycott in Colorado and are recognized as part of the state's Chicano Movement. In addition to the boycotts, Herrera demanded better working conditions for farmworkers, such as access to bathrooms. Orlinda de Vargas organized lettuce and vegetable workers under the program titled "Dicho y Hecho." Under de Vargas's political guidance, workers marched from Pueblo to the State Capitol in Denver. This effort is noted as setting the stage for the nationwide lettuce boycott.

In 1968 Denver West High School students took to the streets protesting the hostile racial campus environment and demanding Chicano studies classes. When West High administrators failed to meet the students' demands, students joined the Crusade for Justice to advance their political efforts. Other high schools, including North High and Lincoln, joined in solidarity marches throughout Denver. A number of events shed light on the social and political context of the time. Students at the University of Rome held demonstrations in protest of the country's university system; San Francisco teachers, with community support, walked out in protest of poor schools and low pay; the president's National Commission on Civil Disorders released the Kerner Commission Report in 1967, finding the basic cause of racial violence to be White racism; conservative California governor Ronald Reagan was one of the few governors to disagree with the Kerner Commission Report; and César Chávez continued his twenty-plus days of fasting in protest of farmworkers' living and working conditions.

The Denver High School walkouts culminated in Chicano Youth Liberation Conferences held in 1969, 1970, and 1971, which were attended by approximately 1,500 people in 1969 and 3,000 in 1970. Corky Gonzales's poem "Yo Soy Joaquin" was adopted as the Movimiento anthem. Women's workshops were sponsored at all three conferences. Enriqueta Vasquez's *testimonio* regarding her attendance at the 1969 Chicano Youth Liberation Conference reveals an interesting Chicana perspective. She notes that "when the time came for the women to report to the full conference, the only thing that the workshop representative had to say was this: 'It was the consensus of the group that the Chicana woman does not want to be liberated'" (Vasquez 1972:66). Vasquez states that she felt this action was a tremendous blow and she could have cried. Vasquez explains this statement as a reaction to the entrenchment of "machismo," or patriarchy, and the strong cultural nationalist ideology that guided Denver Movimiento politics.

Feminists such as Vasquez who raised their voices in collective protest proved contentious in the political struggle. Their efforts to redefine themselves as equal participants transformed them into an oppositional group in relation to their male and female counterparts who supported the view that feminism was a divisive force within the Chicano Movement. Throughout the 1970s, this initial generation of self-proclaimed Chicana feminists viewed the struggle against sexism within the Chicano Movement and the struggle against racism in the larger society as central ideological components of their feminist thought.

CHICANAS AND THE CHICANO STUDENT MOVEMENT AT CU BOULDER

In 1968 people witnessed a worldwide rise in student movements in countries such as France, Italy, Mexico, and the United States. In March of that year, more than 10,000 students walked out of the mostly Chicana/Chicano schools in East Los Angeles to protest the inferior quality of their education. Scholars have studied this event from the perspective of protest politics (Puckett 1971), a spontaneous mass protest (Negrete 1972), internal colonialism (Muñoz 1973), the Chicano Student Movement (Gomez-Quinones 1978), and a socio-political development of the wider Chicano Movement (Rosen 1973).

As Carlos Muñoz (1989) points out, the 1960s were unique because they marked the first time youth played such a central role in shaping oppositional movements aimed at those in power. Street politics and mass protests marked the period, and student movements that helped shape larger struggles for social and political equality emerged from the youth protest. However, Muñoz fails to include a serious analysis of gender in his examination of the Chicano Movement. Likewise, Juan Gomez-Quinones (1978) fails to address adequately the participation of women in his identification of several factors and individuals who contributed to the rise of the Chicano Student Movement. First, he identifies the influence of social unrest external to the Chicana/Chicano community. Abroad, national liberation movements were taking place in Mexico, Latin America, and Vietnam. Domestically, the influence of civil rights and the radical Black and antiwar movements were important. Second, as a result of the civil rights struggle, there were somewhat more working-class students and students of color on college campuses to form a critical political mass. Many Chicana and Chicano college students experienced a sense of alienation and recognized the contrast between the privileged university and their own communities. Finally, Gomez-Quinones points to the immediate organizational and ideological influence and relevance of the wider Chicano Movement. The influence of the UFW, the Crusade for Justice, and the Alianza of New Mexico affected available economic, political, and cultural issues and positions (Delgado Bernal 2000).

Historical accounts of the Chicano Movement in general and the participation of women in particular in the Crusade for Justice and CU Boulder's student movement have either ignored women or dealt with them only marginally and have adhered to the dominant definition of leadership that equates leaders with public spokespersons or elected officials. In fact, a significant error in understanding the Chicano Movement has been an adherence to this domination notion of leadership, or the "great man" approach to history. Consequently, women's key leadership roles have been overlooked and ignored. Indeed, women played different roles in these movements and engaged in different dimensions of leadership.

Chicana student activity at CU revolved around the establishment of UMAS (United Mexican American Students) and demands for financial aid, culminating in the takeover of Temporary Building #1 in 1974 (discussed later). The radicalization and politicization of the Denver High School student movement served as a model for college protests at CU Boulder. Student activists such as Priscilla Falcón and Rita Montero were instrumental in establishing UMAS at the university. UMAS engaged in demands for bilingual education, participated in the lettuce boycotts, and protested the Vietnam War not only as politically unjust but as racially unjust as well, given the number of men and women of color drafted from Colorado. Thus statewide antiwar protests occurred on Colorado campuses.

In August 1968 the University of Colorado chapter of UMAS applied for recognition as an official student group at the university. The CU Boulder chapter had an initial membership of fifty students, representing about one-third of the Chicano students on campus. The purpose of UMAS, as articulated by Pete Reyes, the group's first president on the Boulder campus, was "to formulate a philosophy for our people and provide hope for future generations of Mexican-Americans" (*El Diario*, 1:2). UMAS activism centered on social, political, and especially educational goals. One of the group's primary concerns was to increase the number of Chicanas and Chicanos attending major universities across the country. As Reyes pointed out, during 1967–1968 CU had enrolled only twenty-eight full-time Mexican American students, even though at the time Mexican Americans made up about 11 percent of the state's population.[8]

Chicana/Chicano students were aware of the plight of their people and the poverty and social degradation they suffered. They believed the institutions that comprised the establishment in U.S. society were responsible for the social alienation of Mexican American people. Thus they came to the university with the awareness that the institution was part of the establishment that perpetuated prejudice. As part of the La Raza initiative, the national struggle of Chicanas and Chicanos for identity and racial pride in the face of racism,

Chicana and Chicano students planned to attend the university yet remain apart from it.

In 1969, after considerable student and community pressure, the University of Colorado established the Chicano Studies Program in Boulder. The program was initially loosely structured under the direction of various Chicano professors from the Spanish department, pending the search for a permanent director. A series of directors followed without permanency or stability during the years 1970–1978 as the administration refused to grant resources, a budget, and permanent full-time faculty to the program.

In the summer of 1972, UMAS-EOP (Equal Opportunity Program) recruited 950 Chicanas and Chicanos to CU. Instead of commending the UMAS-EOP directors for their accomplishment, the university fired them and appointed two new directors, with the motive of undermining and subsequently dismantling UMAS. Consequently, Chicana/Chicano student enrollment dropped by 33 percent in one year, exactly what the administration wanted or intended. In the fall of 1973 UMAS students requested that the newly appointed directors resign, but they were ignored.[9]

In time, Chicanismo gave rise to a parallel movement of ideological opposition that began to gain momentum. Many Chicanas, active in every sector of the movement, raised their voices in a collective feminist challenge to the sexism and male domination they were experiencing within El Movimiento. Developing first as cultural nationalists, these Chicanas began to see and experience some of the contradictions of Chicanismo, specifically as it applied to women. From their nationalist base, the Chicana activists also began to evolve as feminists. Chicanas participated actively during this entire period of social protest and community mobilization. Their work within each of the strands of the movement undermined long-standing stereotypes of Mexican American women. Chicanas struggled for social equality during this period, as had past generations of Mexican women in the United States.[10]

The political struggles of Chicana feminists during the late 1960s and early 1970s reflected a continuation of women's activism that paralleled the experiences of other women of color in the United States. A Chicana feminist movement, such as that of African American women, originated within the context of a nationalist movement. As Chicanas assessed their role within the Chicano Movement, their ideological debates shifted from a focus on racial oppression to one that would form the basis for an emergent Chicana feminism discourse: gender oppression. Like other feminist women of color, Chicanas recognized that their feminist movement involved a confrontation with both sexism and racism. As a result, feminism, as articulated by women of color, represented an ideological and a political movement to end patriarchal oppression within the structure of a cultural nationalist movement. Thus a Chicana feminist movement represented a struggle that was both nationalist and feminist.

Although many issues influenced the development of Chicana feminist thought, the ideological critique of sexism, or machismo, contributed significantly to the formation of Chicana feminism. Chicana feminists challenged the portrait of the so-called Ideal Chicana drawn by Chicano cultural nationalists. This portrayal was inspired by a cultural nationalism that indiscriminately equated Chicano cultural survival with the glorification of traditional gender roles for Chicanas. Thus Chicano cultural nationalism praised the "Ideal Woman" of El Movimiento for representing strong, long-suffering women who endured social injustice, maintained the family as a safe haven in a heartless world for their families, and, as a result, assured the survival of Chicano culture.

Like many Chicana student activists throughout the country, Chicana students at CU Boulder were subjected to callous acts of sexual terrorism intended to manipulate their political consciousness and control their political activity. Chicano activists who engaged in sexual terrorism thereby facilitated the construction of a Chicana political performance that sustained the interests of Chicanos—namely, the political and sexual control and exploitation of Chicanas. Hence, sexual terrorism is a system by which men frighten and, by doing so, control and intimidate women through nonviolent sexual intimidation and the threat of violence, as well as overt sexual violence. A number of women interviewed for this project noted that they were threatened, physically and verbally abused, and coerced into sexual relations (known today as date rape) because of their Chicana feminist or woman-ist standpoint. The dynamics that underscore all manifestations of sexual terrorism are patriarchy and misogyny, or the hatred of women. Violence against women is a power expressed sexually. Sexual terrorism is violence erotized.

Chicana feminists came under further attack for their explicit critique of Chicano cultural nationalism. Some were criticized as followers of White feminists or as lesbians. Their opponents labeled their feminist concern about patriarchal oppression as secondary in importance to the more salient issues of racial and class oppression. Chicana feminist discourse responded directly to such feminist-baiting attacks by stressing the universal aspect of sexism. Chicana feminist lesbians contributed to the further development of Chicana feminist discourse and, as such, precipitated more virulent feminist baiting. As a result of the oppressive climate, Chicana feminist lesbian voices were generally silenced. Participants in this study noted that there was an unspoken knowledge about lesbian and gay communities, but Chicana lesbians did not openly identify themselves as such. Chicana lesbians participated in Chicana feminist activities, but it was not until the late 1970s that they made their protests significantly vocal.

Given the limitation of space, this chapter briefly notes the work of Dolores Delgado Bernal (2001) in understanding how Chicana students negotiated various forms of domination while trying to put forth a revolutionary agenda. Delgado Bernal proposes that "pedagogies of the home extend the existing discourses on critical pedagogy by putting cultural knowledge at the forefront to better understand lessons from the home space and local communities" (2001:623). She argues that the teaching and learning of the home allow Chicana college students to draw from their own culture to resist multiple axes of domination. Because they come from the home space and the community, Chicana feminist pedagogies are partially shaped by community memory and the experience taught in legends, *corridos* (ballads), storytelling, and behavior. The crucial importance of these pedagogies is that they are transmitted from generation to generation as everyday survival skills.

Despite Chicana struggles with Chicano cultural nationalism fueled by sexual terrorism, students' educational rights continued to be threatened. Chicanas therefore had to turn their attention to "academic colonialism," or educational oppression, as argued by Teresa Cordova (1998:18). Cleo Estrada recalls that students had not yet been provided with their entitled financial aid and thus were unable to purchase books during the 1973 fall semester. In the spring of 1974, students continued to attend classes without textbooks (Estrada, interview with the author, October 2009). UMAS students decided to take action to ensure that their demands were met. Hence, students occupied Temporary Building #1 (TB 1) demanding financial aid to purchase books. They also demanded the resignations of Joe Franco and Paul Acosta, the newly appointed directors of UMAS-EOP. During the eighteen-day occupation of TB 1, the Crusade for Justice supported the students' efforts by bringing food, clothing, and other necessities to sustain them. University officials failed to negotiate with the students and the larger Chicana/Chicano community. It was during the occupation of TB 1 that Los Seis de Boulder were killed. According to the women interviewed for this study, the students experienced a range of emotions, from utter shock to betrayal to being marked as racial political targets who feared for their lives. The deaths of Los Seis within a forty-eight-hour time span nearly annihilated the students spiritually. In that same year Ricardo Falcón, a CU Boulder alumnus, was murdered on his way to a La Raza Unida convention in Texas. The deaths of Los Seis and Richard Falcón were deemed an attack on the student community, leaving the students emotionally and spiritually devastated. We have yet to determine the numbers of students who left CU, those who opted to attend other universities, and, as mentioned by some of the women, those who completely disassociated themselves publicly and physically from student movement activities.

Our preliminary research findings on Chicana educational experiences at CU Boulder are categorized within three major historical periods. The first period, 1968–1974, and the focus of this chapter, was extremely turbulent and was marked with the deaths of Los Seis de Boulder. This unfortunate historical event has not been recorded as a prominent part of the university's history. Consequently, the second period, 1975–1983, was inundated with right-wing discourse, leaving Chicana and Chicano students without historical memory of the previous decade, which was instrumental in the creation of UMAS and the Chicano Studies Program and in the recruitment of the largest numbers of Chicanas and Chicanos to CU Boulder to that date.

Interestingly, however, it was during this time period that a notable presence of Chicana leadership and voices took hold in questioning the master narrative of Chicano nationalism, the guiding ideology of the Chicano Movement during the 1960s and 1970s. Chicanas expanded the Chicana/Chicano Movement's agenda by giving attention to international issues, namely in El Salvador and Nicaragua. In addition, Chicana lesbian discourse and political activity were placed at the forefront of Chicana/Chicano studies and community activism. With the dismantling of the former Soviet Union in the 1990s and the supposed end of the Cold War, globalization and its impact and influence on Chicana/Chicano communities became a major academic focus and impetus for political activity, with a particular interest in Mexican women and immigration.

At the turn of the twenty-first century, Chicana/Chicano students have continued to question the implications of nationalism as they relate to the decolonial project. In addition, the decolonial project critically engages globalization, trans-nationalism, feminist discourse, queer feminist discourse, Chicana indigeneity, and spirituality. This project intends to explore the idea of a Chicana generational feminism, a feminism that points out continuities and discontinues in Chicana feminist consciousness, identity, subjectivity, and activism from a Chicana-indigenous perspective. Such ambitions will entail deconstructing how Chicana feminism(s) has been cyclically framed at CU Boulder during the past forty years (Perez 1999:xiii).

CONCLUSION

The historical knowledge and memory provided by this discussion can offer a reference point from which to examine past and present similarities and differences and can be helpful in shaping Chicana educational experiences at CU Boulder. Our readings and data from initial interviews of Chicana activism, both in the larger Denver-Boulder community and on the CU Boulder campus, reveal a complex and enthralling political imagery.

In general, ancestral wisdom is necessary for the survival of Chicanas. Chicanas learn through action and use resistance as an act of liberation. Chicanas are aware of the social inequalities present in everyday life and are thus increasingly motivated by their emancipatory interests. They engage in acts of everyday resistance and employ multiple strategies within the context of the intersection of the realities of oppression. The political consciousness Chicanas maintain is born out of oppression. Their consciousness is an active struggle against all forms of oppression and exploitation. Decolonization has a fundamentally pedagogical dimension—an imperative to understand, reflect upon, and transform relations of objectification and dehumanization and to pass this knowledge along to future generations. Therefore struggle is inherently a decolonial project.

In sum, during the turbulent time period 1968–1974, a generation of Chicana feminists raised their voices in opposition to the gender tensions and conflict they were experiencing as women within the Chicano social protest movement. Although the Chicano Movement—an insurgent uprising among a new political generation of Mexican Americans—challenged persistent patterns of societal inequality in the United States, it ignited a political debate between Chicanas and Chicanos based on the internal gender contradictions prevalent within El Movimiento. Chicana feminists produced an ideological critique of the Chicano cultural nationalist movement, which struggled against social injustice yet maintained patriarchal structures of domination. Chicana feminist thought reflected a historical struggle by women to overcome sexist oppression but still affirm a militant ethnic consciousness. As they forged a feminist consciousness, Chicana feminists searched for the elusive "room of their own" within the socio-historical and political context of the Chicano Movement. Women may not have been the visible leaders of and orators within the Chicano Movement during this time period, but, more important, they were the pivotal leaders who articulated a revolutionary Chicana and Chicano agenda.

NOTES

1. Subsequent courses continued to engage students in the aforementioned research project until the 2002 spring semester, then resumed in the fall of 2007. Hence, the project's current focus covers a forty-year period, 1968–2008. While interrogat-

ing the subject matter of Movimiento politics, I remained intrigued with practices of pedagogy and issues of epistemology. I acknowledged pedagogies that recognize knowledge, power, and politics as central to all teaching and learning. Guided by the works of Delgado Bernal (2001), Elenes (2001a, 2001b), F. Gonzalez (2001), and Villenas (2006), I sought to rethink traditional notions of educational spaces where teaching and learning take place. Hence, teaching the course on Chicana Feminist Thought presented an opportunity to reconstruct the classroom using feminist pedagogy and to place Chicana experiences at the forefront of our discussions.

2. Los Seis exemplified the leadership of the Chicana/Chicano Movement. For example, Neva Romero, a UMAS leader, was a CU student senator; Terán, a former UMAS student, was an accomplished poet and artist; Granados, a former UMAS president, had been a La Raza Unida candidate for CU regent and published *El Escritor del Pueblo*, a Denver community newspaper; and Dougherty, active in theater, had organized voters in Texas. Martinez, a well-known attorney, worked among the poor, traveling the state representing clients in court cases while working out of his car. He believed in focusing his professional abilities on helping Chicana/Chicano activists. Una Jaakola, his partner, worked with youth in Denver. Los Seis are regarded as martyrs of the Chicana/Chicano Movement and are commemorated annually in communities throughout Colorado. A memorial stone for Reyes Martinez was dedicated in a park named in his honor in his hometown, Alamosa.

3. The methodology used for questioning and challenging the historical myth surrounding the educational experiences of Chicanas involved archival research using the President's files, UMAS/MEChA (Movimiento Estudantil Chicano de Aztlan) files, and issues of *El Diario* (Chicana/o student newspaper)—all in the CU Archives Library. Qualitative methods were also employed by conducting informal interviews among ten women who attended CU Boulder during the years 1968–1974 and were considered instrumental in promoting Chicana and Chicano studies and university policies conducive to the recruitment and retention of Chicana students. In addition, detailed content analyses of secondary sources, such as the campus newspaper, *The Colorado Daily*, and local media, namely *The Denver Post* and *The Rocky Mountain News*, were conducted for this time period.

4. In 1962, for example, César Chávez, Dolores Huerta, Phillip Vera Cruz, and Larry Itliong organized the National Farm Workers Association, which led the Delano Grape Strike from September 8, 1965, through 1970. In 1965 El Teatro Campesino was founded as a theatrical troupe and cultural arm of the UFW. The actors were farmworkers who wanted to inspire other workers by using their own lived experiences as the events enacted in the performances. The initial performances took place on the backs of trucks in the middle of fields. The founder, Luis Valdez, a student at San Jose State University, later gained recognition for his play *Zoot Suit*, produced on Broadway, and as the director of the movie *La Bamba*. By 1967, as a result of its success, the troupe was able to raise funds for striking farmworkers and expanded its performances by focusing on Chicano culture, education, the Vietnam War, indigenous heritage, and racism.

5. On June 5, 1967, in Tierra Amarilla, members of the Alianza attempted to arrest the county's district attorney and put him on trial. In the process, shots were fired and

two men were wounded. The Alianza held the courthouse for two hours before realizing that the district attorney was out of town. The governor of New Mexico called in the National Guard to put an end to the situation. The gunmen fled, but many of their family members were held as prisoners. This incident, which became known as the Tierra Amarilla Incident, garnered the group national attention.

6. In 1967 Corky Gonzales's poem "I Am Joaquin" reverberated "a triumphant vision, a teary lamentation, and affirmation of Chicano people. Written in fire, shouted in song and whispered in pain" (2001:2). Gonzales was instrumental in creating La Raza Unida in 1970, a third political party for Chicanos. In 1973 he also founded Escuela Tlatelolco, a private school focused on building students' self-esteem by using culturally relevant materials.

7. Chicanismo emphasized cultural pride as a source of political unity and strength capable of mobilizing Chicanos and Chicanas into an oppositional political group within the dominant U.S. political landscape. As an ideology, Chicanismo crystallized the essence of a nationalist ideology: a collective ethnic consciousness (Muñoz 1989). Chicano cultural nationalism placed the socio-historical experiences of Mexican Americans within a theoretical model of internal colonialism. Chicano communities represented ethnic "nations" or "internal colonies" under the domination and exploitation of the United States.

8. In 1968 there were nine Chicana/Chicanos at CU Boulder. In the summer of 1968, the founders of UMAS recruited twenty-three Chicanas/Chicanos to CU. The enrollment of not only Chicanas/Chicanos but of all students of color exceeded the administration's goals. Through the UMAS-EOP, Chicana and Chicano students were recruited across class and geographical boundaries. More specifically, the Migrant Action Program (MAP) recruited students from migrant farm families. The MACHO program recruited ex-convicts from Colorado prisons. These programs marked the beginning of challenging the university's ethnocentricity.

9. During this time period the Crusade for Justice was growing and gaining momentum. In 1970, 3,000 people attended the Second National Liberation Conference in Denver, at which La Raza Unida was created. In 1973 the crusade supported the American Indian Movement's (AIM) efforts at Wounded Knee. In March of that year, Denver police killed Luis Martinez Jr. because of his involvement with the crusade and AIM. In western Colorado, Shirley Otero Romero created the Land Rights Council in 1977, granting Chicana/Chicano and indigenous people the rights to mountain grazing and to gather wood. Maria Mondragon-Valdez also focused on land issues in the San Luis Valley.

10. For one of the first anthologies on Chicanas, see Mora and del Castillo (1980); Ruiz (1987).

REFERENCES

Anzaldua, Gloria. *Borderlands/La Fontera,* 2nd ed. San Francisco: Aunt Lute, 1999.
Austin, Regina. "Sapphire Bound!" In K. Crenshaw, N. Gotana, G. Peller, and K. Thomas, eds. *Critical Race Theory: The Key Writings that Form the Movement.* New York: New Press, 1995, 426–437.

Barry, Naomi. "Women's Participation in the Chicano Movement." *Latino Studies Journal* 8 (1997): 47–52.

Cordova, Teresa. "Power and Knowledge: Colonialism in the Academy." In *Living Chicana Theory*, Carla Trujillo, ed. Berkeley: Third Woman Press, 1998, 17–45.

de Baca, Vincent C. *Hispano History and Life in Colorado*. Denver: Colorado Historical Society, 1998.

Delgado Bernal, Dolores. "Chicana/o Education from the Civil Rights Era to the Present." In *The Elusive Quest for Equality: 150 Years of Chicano/Chicano Education*, J. F. Moreno, ed. Cambridge: Harvard Educational Publishing Group, 2000, 77–108.

Delgado Bernal, D., Elenes, C.A., Godinez, F., and Villenas, S., eds. *Chicana/Latina education in every day life: Feminista perspectives on pedagogy and epistemology*. Albany: State University of New York Press, 2006.

———. "Learning and Living Pedagogies of the Home: The Mestiza Consciousness of Chicana Students." *International Journal of Qualitative Studies in Education* 14, 5 (2001): 623–639.

Elenes, Alejandra. "Chicana Feminist Narrative and the Politics of Self." *Frontiers: A Journal of Women Studies* 21, 3 (2001a): 105–124.

———. "Introduction: Chicana/Mexicana Feminist Pedagogies: Consejos, Respeto, y Educacion in Everyday Life." *International Journal of Qualitative Studies in Education* 14, 5 (2001b): 595–602.

Garcia, Alma. *Chicana Feminist Thought: The Basic Historical Writings*. New York: Routledge, 1997.

Gomez-Quinones, Juan. *Mexican Students por La Raza: The Chicano Student Movement in Southern California 1967–1977*. Santa Barbara, CA: Editorial La Causa, 1978.

Gonzalez, Francisca E. "Haciendo que hacer—Cultivating a Mestiza Worldview and Academic Achievement: Braiding Cultural Knowledge into Educational Research, Policy, Practice." *International Journal of Qualitative Studies in Education* 14, 5 (2001): 641–656.

Gonzalez, Rodolfo "Corky." *Message to Aztlan: Selected Writings of Rodolfo "Corky" Gonzales*. Houston: Arte Publico, 2001.

Hernandez, Ariana. *Pedagogy, Democracy, and Feminism: Rethinking the Public Sphere*. New York: SUNY Press, 1997.

Mora, Magdalena, and Adelaida R. del Castillo (eds.). *Mexican Women in the United States: Struggles Past and Present*. Los Angeles: UCLA Chicano Studies Research Center, 1980.

Muñoz, Carlos, Jr. "The Politics of Chicano Urban Protest: A Model Political Analysis." Unpublished PhD diss., Claremont Graduate School, Claremont, CA, 1973.

———. *Youth, Identity, Power: The Chicano Movement*. New York: Verso, 1989.

Oropeza, Lorena, and D. Espinoza. *Enriqueta Vasquez and the Chicano Movement: Writings from El Grito del Norte*. Houston: Arte Publico, 2006.

Negrete, C., Jr. "Culture Clash: The Utility of Mass Protest as a Political Response." *Journal of Comparative Cultures* 1, 1 (1972): 25–36.

Perez, Emma. *The Decolonial Imaginary: Writing Chicanas into History*. Bloomington: Indiana University Press, 1999.

———. "Irigaray's Female Symbolic in the Making of Chicana Lesbian *Sitios y Lenguas* (Sites and Discourses)." In *Living Chicana Theory*, Carla Trujillo, ed. Berkeley: Third Woman Press, 1998, 87–101.

Puckett, M. "Protest Politics in Education: A Case Study in the Los Angeles Unified School District." Unpublished PhD diss., Claremont Graduate School, Claremont, CA, 1971.

Revilla, A. "Muxerista Pedagogy: Raza Womyn Teaching Social Justice through Student Activism." *High School Journal* 87, 4 (2004): 80–94.

Rocky Mountain PBS. *La Raza de Colorado: El Movimiento*. DVD. Denver: Rocky Mountain PBS, 2005.

Rosen, G. "The Development of the Chicano Movement in Los Angeles from 1967–1969." *Aztlán* 4, 1 (1973): 155–183.

Ruiz, Vicki L. *Cannery Women/Cannery Lives: Mexican Women, Unionization, and the California Food Processing Industry, 1930–1950*. Albuquerque: University of New Mexico Press, 1980.

Trinidad, Ruth. "Portraits of Mujeres Desjuiciadas: Woman Galvan Pedagogies of the Everyday, the Mundane, and the Ordinary." *International Journal of Qualitative Studies in Education* 14, 5 (2001): 603–621.

Vasquez, Enriqueta. "The Women of La Raza." *Magazin* 1, 4 (1972): 66–68.

Vigil, Ernesto. *The Crusade for Justice*. Madison: University of Wisconsin Press, 1999.

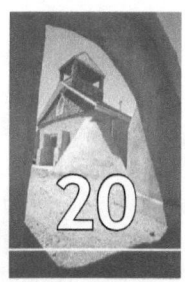

Adriana Nieto

Running the Gauntlet: Francisco "Kiko" Martínez and the Colorado Martyrs

> This case is one of the most frightening examples of the government's expansive power to use the criminal laws to torment a citizen for purely political and racist reasons.
> —ANTONIO D. BUSTAMANTE, TUCSON ATTORNEY

> Mr. Martínez has endured a decade-long agony, in which he has successfully resisted the most scandalous and ill-motivated government misconduct that has ever disgraced the American judicial system.
> —MICHAEL E. TIGAR, ATTORNEY FOR FRANCISCO E. MARTÍNEZ

Francisco "Kiko" Eugenio Martínez, armed with his knowledge of the legal system and of the complex social, political, and economic conditions of Chicano and Mexicano communities, committed his professional and personal life to a struggle for justice for the community from which he came. Kiko's political convictions would result in a battle to defend his beliefs, his family, and ultimately his life. The 1960s and 1970s were turbulent years in the United States. Historically marginalized peoples were mobilizing massive political and social movements. The Chicana/o, American Indian, and Black Liberation movements were increasingly frustrated by failed attempts at peaceful negotiation with the state and its various institutions; indeed, "they were violent times."[1]

School dropout rates were at record highs among communities of color in the United States. Incarceration rates were rising, as were incidents of police brutality. Representation of these historically marginalized peoples' interests was virtually nonexistent in the courtrooms and universities and in local institutions such as city councils and school boards. Civil unrest was prevalent, both throughout the country and internationally. These social movements were gaining widespread participation by all people who held the ideals of social justice, equality, and accountability. Confrontations between institutions and movement activists included demonstrations, sit-ins, walkouts, and boycotts. In was in this social, political, and historical context that Kiko Martínez's story takes place.

The history of Kiko Martínez and events surrounding his family and friends is made up of amazing stories that represent the experiences of thousands of Chicana/os and Mexicanas/os. Many of the historical events in this collection include major occurrences of violence, many of which resulted in the loss of lives and are mostly unknown to scholars of the times.[2] Kiko's story is not commonly referred to as a significant aspect of the Chicano Movement; many published overviews of the movement tend to overlook these events as side notes. The manuscript collection is crucial to add to the literature of the time to create a fuller and deeper understanding of Chicano Movement politics, individual activists, and community responses to state repression. In addition, this chapter seeks to provide a glimpse into the complex nature of the Colorado Chicano Movement by viewing Kiko and his struggles as symbolic of the experiences of large sectors of the Chicana/o and Mexicano/a communities.

Kiko was born to José and Pauline López de Martínez on November 26, 1946, in Alamosa, Colorado. He graduated from Alamosa High School in 1964 and received degrees in business administration, anthropology, and sociology from Adams State College in 1968. As an attorney, Kiko combined his activist commitment with an acute knowledge of the legal system. He not only believed in social protest and civil disobedience, as was common during those years, but he also utilized his role as an attorney to fight for justice inside the walls of institutions.

Early in his career Kiko served as counsel for victims of police brutality, including political cases such as defending Francisco Luevano against charges of disturbing the peace, made by the University of Colorado (CU) at Boulder. Luevano had participated in a demonstration at a speaking engagement by Henry González of Texas. Members of the student organization UMAS (United Mexican American Students) protested Gonzalez's presence because of his support for a Chicano administrator who authored documents that eliminated funding for Chicano programs at CU. Luevano was named an agitator by the CU police, the Boulder Police Department, and the Federal Bureau of Investigation (FBI).[3]

Kiko's decision to represent such politically volatile issues contributed to the ammunition the major news media used in portraying him as a "crusading attorney" and a "zealot."[4] Further fueling Kiko's media image was his role in assisting inmates at the Colorado State Penitentiary. He filed the first in a series of lawsuits against the state prison for failure to grant civil and human rights to inmates in March 1972. The director of the institution filed a grievance against Kiko with the Colorado Bar Association, which was dismissed for lack of merit. Kiko described the prison system as "one of the greatest crimes of our time" and considered the prison population as among the most vulnerable class of people—including people of color, the economically poor, women, and youth. He once said that prison inmates are subjected to sensory deprivation and are enduring conditions no less than "hellish."[5] As a result of Kiko's commitment to confront the state's constant attempts to intimidate, infiltrate, and delegitimize the Chicano Movement and its various sectors, he became known in the public eye as a militant Chicano lawyer and was considered an enemy of the state.[6]

Active in various social justice campaigns, Kiko earned a reputation for standing behind his convictions. For example, he was almost denied admission to the Colorado Bar after protesting inflammatory and derogatory statements about American Indians that were in the bar exam, but he was admitted in October 1971. Kiko served as an attorney in various cases involving highly racialized and politicized issues early in his legal career. In addition to representing the interests of prison inmates and student activists, Kiko played a particularly visible role in the events following the murder of Ricardo Falcón. Falcón was a young Chicano leader in Colorado and a La Raza Unida candidate in various local elections in his hometown of Fort Lupton, Colorado.[7] Local electoral victories had occurred in Texas, Colorado, New Mexico, and California, but little success had been made at the state and national levels. The first Raza Unida National Convention was scheduled for Wednesday, August 30, 1972, in El Paso, Texas. Falcón was one of the Colorado delegates and was also a candidate in a local election in Fort Lupton. Falcón never reached the historic convention, however.

Falcón was traveling to the convention with five other people, including Florencio Granado, in a 1961 Chevrolet. They needed to add water to the car's radiator every fifty miles, and Oro Grande, New Mexico, would be Falcón's last pit stop. The party stopped at a Chevron station owned by Perry Brunson. Witnesses' accounts varied in small details, but the consensus was that words were exchanged between Falcón and Brunson because Brunson refused to allow the group to use his water for the radiator. Falcón and Brunson were inside the gas station when the rest of the party heard four shots fired: "Granado ran to Falcón's side and turned him over. He then yelled for someone to call an ambulance. Since Brunson was still in the station, Falcón's companions ran to nearby businesses and asked for the use of the telephone; they were refused. During this time Brunson called the police, reloaded his revolver and ran next door to his home."[8] Kiko, Kenneth Padilla, and Julius Martínez made up the investigative team sent by the Mexican American Legal Defense and Education Fund (MALDEF). As a result of its findings, MALDEF recommended that Brunson be tried for first-degree murder.

Also revealed during the investigation was the fact that Perry Brunson was a well-known organizer for the American Independent Party. He had a petition posted outside his Chevron station door seeking to have the party placed on the local ballot. The American Independent Party was known for "extreme right-wing and racist policies."[9] Among the names on the petition were those of Brunson; his wife; Charlotte Cunningham, the wife of the investigating officer; and Jerry Hamilton, an officer with the New Mexico State Police. MALDEF attorneys recommended to the court that Brunson be tried for first-degree murdered based on his affiliation with a racist political party. Citing the fact that Brunson had called Falcón a "Chicano motherfucker," Ricardo's widow Priscilla, along with the MALDEF team, sought to prove the murder was racially motivated. Instead, Brunson was released on his own recognizance the night of the shooting. Otero County district attorney Norman Bloom filed manslaughter charges just two hours after the incident, before police reports or written statements were submitted. Bloom, a friend of Brunson's, apparently saw no need to wait for the usual proceedings to occur before releasing Brunson.

A group of Falcón's family, friends, and sympathizers traveled from northern Colorado to Oro Grande and marched to Alamogordo. The march was intended both to commemorate Falcón's life and death and to inform local authorities that they were waiting for a fair and lawful trial for Brunson. Kiko's request to serve as co-counsel with Bloom had been denied, but he watched the proceedings carefully, taking note of the all-Anglo jury. He also played a key role in organizing and advising the marchers to avoid violent confrontations between Falcón supporters and police or local citizens. The march proceeded without incident. Perry Brunson was found not guilty in

December 1972. Ricardo Falcón would be remembered as a "martyr" of the Chicano Movement, and to this day commemorations continue in Denver, Fort Lupton, and Greeley.

Although Kiko's participation in the Falcón death investigation and the subsequent march to Alamogordo was not the first time he had played a key role in controversial cases, his name was brought up as a "pester" to the judge when the not-guilty verdict was read.[10] Kiko and his MALDEF colleague Kenneth Padilla were protesting the fact that none of the delegates from MALDEF and none of the marchers were allowed entrance to any of the trial proceedings. The jury was undoubtedly intimidated by the police presence on the roof of the courthouse to secure its safety from the radical Chicanos outside.

Kiko attended a Chicano Indian Unity Conference in Scottsbluff, Nebraska, in January 1973. Along with several other Chicanos, Kiko's car was stopped and searched by Scottsbluff police. The police justified the search based on suspicions that Kiko possessed a Molotov cocktail. Everyone in the vehicle was arrested, fingerprinted, and held overnight. All charges against Kiko were eventually dropped because the arrest was based on an illegal search and seizure. This time the law was on Kiko's side, but his luck soon ended.

Kiko frequently donated his time and services to the Crusade for Justice (the Crusade) and its members. He defended many youth who were victims of police brutality. The tension between Mexicans and Chicana/os in Denver came to a head on March 17, 1973, when police surrounded the Crusade building while a meeting was taking place inside. Descriptions of this event vary depending on whose records are examined. According to police reports, they were responding to a call about a disturbance at the apartment building adjacent to the building owned by the Crusade. When they arrived at the scene, they entered the Crusade's building and alleged to have found explosives. Why they entered the Crusade building if they were responding to a call at the apartment building was not addressed in the police report.

Members of the Crusade recalled that the police performed a paramilitary raid and entered the Crusade building illegally. Dynamite and hand grenades were launched into the building, and a shootout ensued between police and Crusade members. Dozens of Crusade members were arrested, a large part of Escuela Tlatelolco was blown up, and Luis Junior Martínez was fatally shot by officer Stephen Snyder. Martínez (no relation to Kiko) was a dance instructor at the Crusade and joined Ricardo Falcón on the list of those who gave their lives in the name of El Movimiento.

Many in the Denver remember the police raid at the Crusade as fueling the rage felt toward police departments around the country. The violence experienced daily in these communities was rooted in the impunity police enjoyed when applying order. Antonio Cordova, Rito Canales, and Tammy Valles of Albuquerque; Mario Barrera in Blythe, California; Santos Rodriguez of Dallas; Jack Rodriguez of Yakima, Washington; and Roy Gallegos of Santa Fe, New Mexico, were shot and killed between 1968 and Luis Junior's death in 1973.[11]

Kiko's involvement in the events mentioned thus far is representative of the activism that was part of the times. What distinguished his role from that of others, however, was his knowledge of the law and its institutions and the power that knowledge gave him and those he represented. Without his professional background, would he have grasped the irregularities in the Falcón case? Regardless of whether he possessed a Molotov cocktail in Nebraska, would he have been convicted of the charges if he had not known search and seizure was illegal? The documents point to the conclusion that he was more lethal and better armed in his critique of overarching state power and the unfair treatment of racial minorities in the United States with a law degree. He could give concrete examples of where the laws say one thing but are applied differently in cases involving people of color, specifically Chicanos and Mexicanos. Did Kiko's legal knowledge make him more of a threat in the eyes of a reactionary, paranoid government? Logic points to the answer as no. If he had invested the time, energy, and money to acquire a law degree, could it not be assumed that he believed in working within the system as opposed to outside it through protests, marches, and bombs?

The sequence of events that followed the Martínez killing suggests that the state was more threatened by Kiko's willingness to engage in a struggle both within and outside the system. These events, as revealed in the manuscript collection, also prove that the state was willing to go to great lengths to discredit him, his career, and his politics.

After the Crusade for Justice shootout, Denver policed alleged to have found a "series of bombs" throughout the city within a week-long period. Media reports linked the alleged bombs with some sort of retaliation against the police for the murder of Martínez in March. The original indictment, returned on November 9, 1973, contained seven counts. The allegation was that Frank or Francisco "Kiko" Martínez had sent three bombs through the mail. The first was to Officer Carol Hogue, the second to city councilman Robert Crider, and the third to the Two-Wheeler Motorcycle Shop in north Denver on West 38th Avenue. Hogue was an officer involved in the March 17 shootout at the Crusade for Justice. Crider was a city councilman from a predominantly Chicana/o district who was notorious for reactionary, racist views. The motorcycle shop was located across the street from La Raza Park/ Columbus Park, and the owners and managers were rumored to have aided the police in the surveillance of Chicana/o activities at the park.

An area drugstore cashier claimed to have sold five pocket watches to a man matching Kiko's description. She said she remembered the transaction because the man became hostile when she asked about the purchase. The transaction allegedly occurred approximately three weeks prior to the discovery of the bombs. Other evidence linking Kiko to the charges was based on single fingerprints found on the interiors of the envelopes encasing each of the alleged bombs. Kiko's fingerprints had been obtained from the Nebraska police and sent to Denver to make a match. Recall that those prints from Nebraska were obtained in an illegal search and seizure when Kiko and his companions were stopped in Scottsbluff.

On or about October 27, 1973, three explosive devices were alleged to have been placed in U.S. Postal Service mailboxes for delivery in the Denver area. On October 30, 1973, a warrant was issued for the arrest of Frank Eugenio Martínez in connection with the crimes. *The Denver Post* and the U.S. Postal Service offered $2,500 rewards for information leading to Kiko's capture. After hearing of the warrants and a "shoot on sight" order given to area police, Kiko left Denver. He went into self-imposed exile and was not seen again in public until 1980. After he returned to the country in 1980, eight years of litigation commenced, discussed in more detail later in the chapter. However, while Kiko was in exile, more attacks were made against his community and his family members.[12]

A grand jury was convened in November 1973 to investigate the Chicano community in an attempt to locate Kiko. During the grand jury investigation several people were subpoenaed, including Kiko's family, members of the Crusade for Justice, Kiko's family's neighbors, and others. The collection includes two boxes of documents obtained from the FBI through the Freedom of Information and Privacy Act. Most of the written statements by those subpoenaed are in the files, but virtually all of them have significant portions blacked out in ink. Information regarding the investigation of Los Seis de Boulder, however, contains a substantial amount of information on surveillance within the Chicano Movement.

Six months after Kiko left the country, on May 27, 1974, his brother Reyes was killed in a car bomb in Boulder, Colorado, along with Neva Romero and Una Jaakola. A second car bomb exploded just two days later, on May 29, killing Florencio Granado, Francisco Dougherty, and Heriberto Terán and leaving a fourth person, Antonio Alcantar, missing a leg. These victims became known as Los Seis de Boulder and were remembered as martyrs, along with Ricardo Falcón and Luis Junior Martínez.

The bombs were reported to have exploded prematurely, and reports in area newspapers implied that they went off because dynamite was handled carelessly by the militants, who were on their way to bomb something. Allegations have been made in various sectors of the area's Chicano community that the government or at least "right-wing" elements were involved in the explosions.[13] Full investigations by forensics teams were never conducted. According to FBI documents released, both explosions were the result of the mishandling of explosives by the occupants of the vehicles.

Boulder police reports and FBI documents regarding the May 27 explosion, released ten years later, indicated that a passenger in the car, who they ascertained was Neva Romero, was assembling the bomb. The official conclusion was that since the victims themselves were responsible for the explosions, no charges could be filed; therefore, the case was dropped. The FBI files revealed that Romero was also suspected in the alleged bombing of a dormitory at the University of Northern Colorado in Greeley. These reports contained statements by anonymous witnesses. All five of those cited in the report denied being able to positively identify Romero as the woman they saw coming out of the dorm a month before her death. Interviews with witnesses who implicated Romero in the Greeley bombing were conducted after her death. The FBI based its decision to blame the victims for the Boulder explosions in part on its conclusion that Romero had placed explosives in the Greeley dorm. The FBI's decision to try to convict a dead woman ended with the destruction of the physical evidence collected from the May 27 explosion at Chautauqua Park and the May 29 explosion in front of a Burger King just a few blocks away. It appears that correspondence found in Freedom of Information and Privacy Act documents convinced the FBI to close the case and destroy the evidence.

The second explosion on May 29, as mentioned, killed Heriberto Terán, Francisco Dougherty, and Florencio Granado. Granado had been present when Ricardo Falcón was shot and killed two years earlier. Granado is referred to in FBI files by a file number established for him prior to his death. A fair amount of information had been gathered on Granado, including reports on his vocal role in UMAS and his Raza Unida candidacy for the University of Colorado's board of regents in 1972. He was also implicated in the case of alleged explosives found in Greeley and was referred to as a "militant" who collaborated with Neva Romero.

Disturbing details of the events leading up to the explosion were revealed in the FBI report. An unnamed (which simply means the names were blacked out in ink in the files the FBI handed over) security guard at the Boulder Public School administration building noted the car and its license plate number approximately fifteen minutes before the explosion. The other unnamed witnesses interviewed immediately following the explosion testified that Granado went into the liquor store next door to the Burger King to get matches. When he returned to the driver's seat, the car exploded.

The only survivor, Antonio Alcantar, was severely burned and lost one leg as a result of his injuries. The FBI wanted to press charges against him, but he was unconscious at the time of the hearing, and they left him alone. The FBI documents also mentioned that Alcantar had a brother who had been killed in Texas in a similar explosion, but all further references made in the files were inked out in black.

Obviously, questions about both incidents remain. In the May 29 explosion, why did the security guard feel the need to note the license plate before anything happened? In both cases, if the victims were assembling explosives, why would they choose such public places as the parking lot of a Burger King during daylight and a parking place under a street lamp at Chautauqua Park? At a press conference held on May 31, it was suggested that the deaths might be "part of the nation wide conspiracy documented by the recently released COINTELPRO [Counter Intelligence Program] documents."[14] Denver area community leaders demanded an independent investigation: "The police and FBI must be forced to reveal all their secret plans to harass, intimidate, and otherwise disrupt the struggle of Chicanos, Blacks, Socialists and others fighting for social justice."[15] The FBI, however, was already conducting its own investigation, as revealed in the files it released, mentioned earlier. By the time Los Seis were buried, almost all of the evidence had been destroyed.

The Chicano community was warned to avoid talking to any "fed" or "pig," and rumors spread that a grand jury investigation was being conducted, although not to find the culprit(s) in the car bombings. It was felt that the investigation was using the bombings as fronts for further invasion into activists' lives and was considered to be only for intelligence gathering. Because of the confidential nature of the grand jury proceedings, findings were never released.

The FBI searched at least four residences of individuals suspected of being connected to the bombing victims. Items such as masking tape, wire cutters, 9-volt batteries, and wristwatches were found in the home of one of the victims of the second explosion. The presence of these common household items justified charging the victims as those responsible for their own deaths.

Plain-clothes officers were present at the funeral of Kiko's brother Reyes. Perhaps they hoped Reyes's death would lure Kiko out into the public, but he was not at the funeral. Nor did he attend his mother's funeral in Alamosa. Reports of Kiko's whereabouts surfaced occasionally between 1973 and 1980. Allegations of his involvement in the assassination of a Union City, California, police chief were printed in various media. A Pueblo, Colorado, paper reported that Kiko was in Cuba. Kiko's father's and sister's post office boxes were constantly monitored for suspicious correspondence.

The media attention and the inability of the police to find Kiko earned him a hero's reputation. He became a symbol of resistance for the communities so deeply affected by him and those close to him. Kiko's name and photograph were included in flyers and leaflets scattered throughout various neighborhoods in Boulder, Denver, Alamosa, and Pueblo. Some of the flyers included images of Los Seis, Ricardo Falcón, and Luis Junior Martínez with captions such as "Revolucionarios del Movimiento Chicano Mexicano Contra el Imperialismo" (Revolutionaries of the Chicano Mexicano Movement against Imperialism); above the images of the blown-up cars in Boulder was a drawing of Kiko with the caption "Upon These Ruins We Will Build a Movement Ten Thousand Times Stronger."[16] The legend of Kiko soon ended, however.

Kiko was arrested at the Nogales, Arizona, Port of Entry on September 3, 1980, marking the beginning of the legal battles that would consume the next eight years of his life. He told customs inspectors that he was a citizen of the United States, that his name was José Reynoso-Diaz, that he lived in Des Moines, Iowa, and that he worked at the John Deere plant putting ball bearings into power takeoff units. Kiko made a customs declaration of one blanket and some toy airplanes. The inspector admitted Kiko as a citizen and commenced a search of his luggage. When the inspector pulled a manicure kit from a backpack and opened it, she discovered a Mexican passport with the name Reynoso-Diaz. At that point Kiko bolted out of the room, ran north into the United States, and was apprehended after a brief struggle. Once the Immigration and Naturalization Service verified that he was actually Frank Martínez, he was extradited to Denver. In Colorado bail was set for $1 million—an unprecedented amount for charges that did not involve a death (the three letter bombs he sent [discussed earlier in the chapter] never detonated, and no one had been injured).

The setting of the million-dollar bail marked the beginning of a mass mobilization of community support for Kiko. He was facing eleven state and seven federal mail bomb charges. Neighbors, relatives, and concerned community members posted their houses as bond, exemplifying the faith the Colorado Chicano and Mexicano communities had in Kiko. The Francisco E.

Martínez Defense Committee was formed at this point and would play an invaluable role in Kiko's defense during the trials and hearings that followed.

The original eighteen counts were reduced to three federal and three state counts. Chief U.S. district court judge Fred M. Winner presided over the federal cases.[17] The defense team included Kiko and Kenneth Padilla, who seven years earlier had served on the MALDEF team investigating the Falcón murder. Padilla lost major motions to dismiss the charges based on unfair publicity from 1973 up until Kiko's apprehension at the U.S. border in 1980. The motions were denied, and Kiko went to trial on January 26, 1981, on one count of conspiracy. The other two counts were possession of explosives and mailing explosives to Officer Carol Hogue.

Widespread support was evident by the large numbers of people wearing "Free Kiko" T-shirts inside and outside the courtroom. On the evening of the third day of the trial, January 29, the trial judge held a secret meeting with the prosecutors, court personnel, and several government witnesses in his hotel room. Neither the defendant nor his counsel was notified of the meeting. Judge Winner stated that he believed an atmosphere of intimidation existed in the courtroom, caused by some spectators sympathetic to the defendant. He wanted hidden cameras installed to record the intimidation. Judge Winner informed the prosecutors that he would grant a motion for a mistrial but advised them not to make such a motion until after the cameras had been installed and the defense had presented its case. The defense had requested a mistrial the day before the meeting, but the motion was denied. The reason the judge gave for not inviting the defendant's counsel to the meeting was the court's suspicion (unverified in the record) that one of the defendant's lawyers might be involved in a conspiracy to intimidate the jury. Thus was born the term "Winnergate."[18]

Before the secret meeting had been discovered, however, the mistrial was declared, and a second federal trial was scheduled for July the same year. Evidence of the secret meeting was leaked to the press and subsequently verified by U.S. marshals' testimonies. The new federal judge dismissed the three counts against Kiko on the grounds of double jeopardy and improper judicial conduct.

One year later, in February 1981, one count of possession of explosives and one count of mailing those explosives to the Two-Wheeler Motorcycle Shop were brought before another federal jury. The jury found Kiko not guilty on both counts. There were still two remaining charges relating to the bombs allegedly mailed to city council member Robert Crider. The defense moved to dismiss those charges. By this time it was widely accepted, based on testimony and much media coverage, that the Denver Police Department had lost the bomb used to indict Kiko back in 1973. Prosecutors pressed on regardless, basing the case on photographs of a partial palm print suspected to be Kiko's. Judge Frank G. Theis dismissed the charges for lack of evidence.

By January 1985 Kiko and his defense team had presented his case before state and federal courts in Pueblo and Denver, appeals courts in Kansas City and St. Louis, and the U.S. Supreme Court in Washington, DC. He was exonerated of all charges of possession of explosives, mailing explosives, and intent to commit murder. Kiko's ultimate triumph was seen as a triumph for all those in Chicana/o and Mexicano/a communities who were struggling for equality in an unequal system: "By helping free Kiko each of us gains a slice of our liberation as individuals, as a nation and as a class."[19]

Just when he thought his life could return to normal, police conducted a paramilitary raid of Kiko's house in Alamosa. Kiko faced charges of giving false statements to federal officers while posing as José Reynoso-Diaz in 1980. The trial judge dismissed the charges, citing the appearance of vindictive prosecution. On appeal in San Francisco, the government won the right to go to trial again. Kiko was convicted of giving false statements and sentenced to five years in prison. The judge suspended the entire sentence except for ninety days in jail and four and a half years of probation.

The defense committee was with Kiko during every proceeding. They printed materials that translated the legal jargon into understandable terms. The committee organized support rallies outside courthouses. There were letters of support, protests, and requests for donations of time, money, and other resources.

The legacy of Kiko's struggle is immeasurable. Kiko incorporated the ideals of the liberation movements of the 1960s and 1970s while defending himself against criminal charges. Yet he always acknowledged the role Los Seis, Ricardo Falcón, and Luis Junior Martínez played in building the movements. This chapter presents only part of the information that can be gleaned from the manuscript collection housed at the Center for Southwest Research in Albuquerque. Further research in the areas of critical race theory, community organizing, and the history of the Colorado Chicano Movement is needed. This chapter is merely an attempt to tell the stories of Kiko and the movement to which he was and remains committed and to describe where we all fit into those histories.

NOTES

1. Francisco E. Martínez, talk given at a reception announcing the donation and processing of his manuscript collection, Albuquerque, NM, November 11, 1999.

2. The Francisco E. Martínez Papers are housed in the Grassroots Activism Collection, Center for Southwest Research, Zimmermann Library, University of New Mexico, Albuquerque (hereafter referred to as FEM Papers). I was one of four archival assistants who worked on "processing" the collection between 1997 and 2000. Today, as an instructor in Chicana/o studies, I rely on my personal knowledge of the collection to draw from for my teaching. To my knowledge, this is the first published piece on Kiko, Los Seis, and Ricardo Falcón. Credit should also be given to the student group Los Heredores de Esperanza y Cambio at Metropolitan State College in Denver for self-publishing "Symbols of Resistance," for which they conducted oral histories in an attempt to document the stories of those affected by the events this chapter covers.

3. United State Federal Bureau of Investigation, obtained through the Freedom of Information and Privacy Act, date blacked out on documents. Box 24, folder 26, FEM Papers.

4. *The Denver Post* and *The Boulder Daily*, box 20, folder 23, FEM Papers.

5. Speech cited in note 1.

6. "FEM Defense Committee Statement," box 19, folder 24, FEM Papers.

7. La Raza Unida was formed as a result of the Plan Espiritual de Aztlán, which called for the "creation of an independent local, regional and national political party" to meet the needs of the community that were unmet by the two-party system. Among La Raza Unida's concerns were implementing security for bilingual education programs, retaining and recruiting Chicana/o faculty and administrators, and working on community-centered issues such as community centers, public parks, and facilities.

8. "Statements by Chicano Witnesses," collected by MALDEF, box 22, folder 2, FEM Papers.

9. "MALDEF Report," box 21, folder 30, FEM Papers.

10. Richard Williams, "Verdict Is in—Brunson 'Not Guilty' in Slaying," *The Albuquerque Journal*, December 6, 1972, box 21, folder 27, FEM Papers.

11. In Elizabeth Martínez, *500 Years of Chicano History* (Albuquerque: Southwest Organizing Project, 1991), 140–144.

12. These reports are from the FEM Papers. Many are from the folders containing defense committee documents, and several come directly from the court transcripts of the legal proceedings that began after 1980. See box 19, folders 4–24; box 20; box 21, folders 1–24, FEM Papers.

13. See Ernesto Vigil, *The Crusade for Justice: Chicano Militancy and the Government's War on Dissent* (Madison: University of Wisconsin Press, 1999); also box 24, folders 22–27; box 25, folders 1–6, FEM Papers.

14. Peter Seidmen, "Colorado Chicanos Demand Investigation of Bombings," no date, box 24, folder 27, FEM Papers.

15. Ibid.

16. Defense committee boxes and Los Seis boxes, FEM Papers.

17. I acknowledge Arturo B. Nieto for the sections relating to the legal aspects of Kiko's complicated battles. Arturo worked on processing the legal documents in the FEM Papers and provided me with the interpretation of those documents for a history paper.

18. U.S. Attorney Joseph Dolan, signed affidavit of secret meeting, February 1981, box 14, folder 33, FEM Papers.

19. FEMDC pamphlet asking for contributions to the defense fund, April 1981, box 19, folders 20–24; box 20, folders 1–10, FEM Papers.

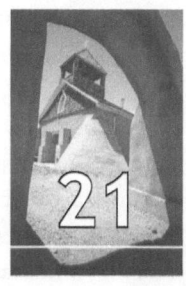

Reiland Rabaka

Toward a Critical Theory of the African American West

Black Studies/African American Studies/Africana Studies was born with the express purpose of *decolonizing the minds of people, especially black people.* Although writing histories and social scientific studies can produce much knowledge, no amount of information could get very far in the absence of minds unable to see or understand it. Important as empirical work has been and continues to be, without interpretation, even at the level of the methods used for organizing the research and gathering data, such work would be meaningless. The power of interpretation is such, however, that it, too, is embedded in a special type of interpretation or hermeneutic without which it, as well, would be meaningless. And that interpretation we call *theory*.[1]

When one thinks of Colorado, African Americans and other folks of African descent are usually not the first cultural group to come to mind. African Americans constitute less than 5 percent of Colorado's total population and only about 10 percent of the population of Denver, Colorado's state capital and largest city. However, one would be remiss to overlook African Americans, not simply in Colorado but in the North American West in general.[2] African Americans, in fact, have made countless seminal contributions to the history and culture of the North American West and to Colorado and the Denver metropolitan area in particular. A short list of respective research topics includes

Black Indians, Black cowboys, buffalo soldiers, the twin-city Black settlements of Chapelton and Dearfield, Colorado, Denver's Five Points neighborhood, and Colorado's contributions to the Black Women's Club Movement, the National Association for the Advancement of Colored People (NAACP), Marcus Garvey's Universal Negro Improvement Association (UNIA), the Urban League, the Civil Rights Movement, and the Black Power Movement, especially the Black Panther Party.[3] Major Colorado African American personalities who have made their mark on African American and, truth be told, American history and culture include Bill Pickett, James Beckwourth, Nat Love, Cathy Williams, Henry Parker, Madame C. J. Walker, Oliver T. Jackson, Dr. Justina Ford, Dr. Ruth Flowers, George Morrison Sr., Hattie McDaniel, Leroy Smith, Burnis McCloud, Paul Stewart, Omar Blair, Elvin Caldwell, Don Cheadle, Philip Bailey (of Earth, Wind, and Fire fame), Dianne Reeves, and India.Arie, among others.[4]

The fact that African Americans have historically made, and continue to make, pivotal and pioneering contributions to the North American West, and to the state of Colorado specifically, can hardly be denied. However, locating African American historical and cultural contributions to the North American West is not nearly as difficult as identifying and, if need be, developing critical theories and research methods suitable to the task of answering the crucial questions of *how*, *what*, and *why* African Americans, among other folks of African descent, contributed to the North American West. Colorado, as quiet as it is kept, has been and remains a major research site for the study of African American contributions to the North American West. For example, the Denver metropolitan area boasts both the Black American West Museum and Heritage Center and the Blair-Caldwell African American Research Library. The latter is especially distinguished, considering that it is "the only library of its kind between Detroit and Oakland." It represents and concretely demonstrates the social responsibility and community outreach emphasis of African American studies insofar as its basic mission is to "serve as an educational and cultural resource for the people of Denver, Colorado, and the world, focusing on the history, literature, art, music, religion, and politics of African Americans in Colorado and throughout the Rocky Mountain West."[5]

African American (and more recently Africana) studies in Colorado and the wider Rocky Mountain region has been well under way for close to four decades. As is fairly well-known, one of its earliest incarnations was established at the University of Colorado at Boulder in the form of a Black Studies Program in 1968.[6] A Black Studies Program was launched at the University of Northern Colorado in 1969, and programs or concentrations in Black studies were initiated at Metropolitan State College of Denver, Colorado State University, and Colorado College soon thereafter. Currently, the University of Northern Colorado houses a Department of Africana Studies and Metropolitan State College boasts a Department of African and African American Studies, both offering bachelor's degrees; Colorado College, Colorado State University, and the University of Colorado at Boulder offer bachelor's degrees with concentrations in African American studies under various headings: American studies, American cultural studies, American ethnic studies, cultural studies, ethnic studies, comparative ethnic studies, and interdisciplinary studies.

Colorado has more African American studies concentrations and degree-granting programs and departments than any other state in the Rocky Mountain region, the Southwest, and the West in general, with only California offering more degrees in African American studies. Idaho, Utah, and Wyoming colleges and universities offer no major or minor in African American studies; in Arizona, only Arizona State University and the University of Arizona grant degrees in African American studies. Montana, Nebraska, Nevada, and New Mexico each have one college or university that offers concentrations in African American studies; Kansas and Oklahoma each have two colleges or universities that offer undergraduate degrees in African American studies; Oregon and Washington each have three colleges or universities that confer bachelor's degrees with concentrations in African American studies; and Texas has four colleges or universities that offer specialized degrees in Africana American studies. Second only to California, then, Colorado can be considered a major African American studies research site in the North American West.

Considering the pivotal position and historical development of African American studies in Colorado, it would seem that the time is ripe to initiate a discussion of the particularities and, if you will, the peculiarities of (re)developing and doing Africana studies in Colorado and the wider North American West. The work I propose to do here has more to do with conceptual generation, critical theoretical development, and research methodology than with highlighting this or that important historical, cultural, social, or political African American issue, event, or individual. Part of my task in the remainder of this chapter, consequently, entails elaborating on a distinct conception of critical theory that speaks to the special needs of Africana studies scholars and students conducting research on or within the North American West and in Colorado in particular. This conception of critical theory, Africana critical theory, is grounded in and grows out of Africana studies, specifically the discourses of Africana philosophy, Africana social and political theory, and Africana intellectual history. Contrary to the plethora of polemics, simplifications, mystifications, and misinterpretations of African Americans in the North American West, their thought and practices have made and continue to make several significant contributions to the discourses of Africana studies and contemporary critical theory. In an effort to emphasize these contributions, I will discuss the unique history of Africana thought, the role and tasks of theory in Africana studies, critical social theory in general, and, ultimately, my conception of Africana critical theory.

By analyzing and criticizing African American thought in the North American West and the politico-economic and socio-cultural situations to which it responds, the ideas and actions of Black folks in the West can be accessed and assessed for their contribution to (1) contemporary Africana studies and critical social theory; (2) modern mass movements calling for radical social transformation, from the Civil Rights and Black Power movements to the brewing antiwar and peace movements at the dawn of the twenty-first century; and (3) future multicultural and trans-ethnic social thought and practices. In what follows I first engage the discourse and development of Africana studies. Then I discuss the nature and nuances of philosophy and critical theory in Africana studies discourse. Finally, I introduce my conception of Africana critical theory and briefly explicate ways it can be applied to Africana studies in the North American West.

(INTER)DISCIPLINARY DEVELOPMENTS AND NEW DISCURSIVE DIRECTIONS IN AFRICANA STUDIES

Africana studies blurs the lines between disciplines and offers interdisciplinarity in the interest of continental and diasporan Africans. Drawing from and contributing to the natural and social sciences and the arts and humanities, Africana studies is a broadly construed interdisciplinary discipline that critically interprets and analyzes classical and contemporary continental and diasporan African thought and practice. The agnomen *Africana* has come to represent many things to many different people, not all of them of African descent. It has a long and discontinuous history of use, from W.E.B. Du Bois's 1909 contraction of the term for a proposed encyclopedia "covering the chief points in the history and condition of the Negro race," with contributions by a board of 100 "Negro American, African and West Indian" intellectuals; to James Turner's assertion that "the concept *Africana* is derived from the 'African continuum and African consociation' which posits fundamental interconnections in the global Black experience"; to Lucius Outlaw's utilization of the term as a "gathering" and "umbrella" notion "under which to situate the articulations (writings, speeches, etc.)" of continental and diasporan Africans "collectively ... which are to be regarded as philosophy"; to Emmanuel Eze's employment of the heading to emphasize, in a "serious sense," the historical and cultural range and diversity of continental and diasporan African thought in consequence of *"the single most important factor that drives the field and the contemporary practice of African/a Philosophy ... the brutal encounter of the African world with European modernity"*; to Lewis Gordon's recent adoption of the term to refer to "an area of thought that focuses on theoretical questions raised by struggles over ideas in African cultures and their hybrid and creolized forms in Europe, North America, Central and South America, and the Caribbean."[7] Whether "thought," "philosophy," or "studies" accompanies Africana, the term and its varying conceptual meanings have indeed traversed a great deal of social, political, historical, cultural, philosophical, and physical terrain. However, if there is one constant concerning the appellation "Africana," it is the simple fact that for nearly a century intellectuals and activists of African origin and descent have employed the term to indicate and include the lifeworlds and lived experiences of both continental and diasporan Africans.

Disciplinary development is predicated on discursive formations to which Africana studies—that is, African, African American, Afro-Asian, Afro-European, Afro-Latino, Afro–Native American, Black, Caribbean, and pan-African studies—is not immune.[8] Discursive formations, meaning essentially knowledge production and dissemination—what we would call in Africana studies epistemologies or theories of knowledge—provide the theoretical thrusts that help guide and establish interdisciplinary arenas while simultaneously exploding traditional disciplinary boundaries. As a consequence of the overemphasis on experience and emotion in the study of continental and diasporan African life, there has been a critical turn toward Africana thought or, more properly, Africana philosophy.[9]

After 500 years of the Europeanization of human consciousness, it is not simply European imperial thought and texts that stand in need of Africana critical analysis. Africana theorists, taking a long and critical look at Africana history and culture, argue that consequent to holocaust, enslavement, and—as Frantz Fanon and Ngũgĩ wa Thiong'o note—physical and psychological colonization, Africana people have been systematically socialized and ideologically educated to view and value the world and to think and act employing a Eurocentric or, more directly, a European imperial modus operandi.[10] This means, then, that many Africana people, many of W.E.B. Du Bois's most beloved "black folk," in the modern moment have internalized not simply imperial thought and practices but, to put it plainly, *anti-African* thought and practices.

Internalized anti-African thought and practices have problematicized and plagued Africana studies almost since its inception. This has led to a specific species of intellectual reductionism that turns on an often clandestine credo which warrants that Black people ante up experience and emotion whereas White people contribute theory and philosophy. The internalization of this thought expressed itself most notably in the work of Negritude poet and theorist Léopold Sedar Senghor, who infamously asserted that reason is Europe's great contribution to human culture and civilization while rhythm is Africa's eternal offering. In Senghor's ironic infamous words: "'I think therefore I am,' wrote Descartes, who was the European *par excellence*. The African could say, 'I feel, I dance the Other, I am.'"[11]

The implication, and what I wish to emphasize here, is not that there is no place for discussions of the experiential aspects of Black life in Africana studies but rather that this experiential/emotional approach has become, in many scholars' and students' minds, the primary and most privileged way of doing Africana studies. On the one hand, one of the positives of the experiential/emotional approach to Black life obviously revolves around the historical fact that people of African descent have long been denied an inner life and the time and space to explore and discover their deep (social, political, and spiritual, among other) desires, what Black feminist theorist bell hooks has referred to as "radical black subjectivity."[12] Even the very thought, let alone serious consideration, of an Africana point of view would be an admission of consciousness, which in turn would call for the dynamism and dialecticism of reciprocal recognition and some form of (we hope critical) reflection. On the other hand, one of the many negatives of privileging the experiential/emotional approach is that we end up with a multiplicity of narratives and biographies of Blacks' experience of the world but no theoretical tools (developed or developing) with which to critically interpret these distinctly Black experiences. In some senses this situation forces Africana studies scholars and students to turn to the theoretical breakthroughs and analytical advances of other (read: "traditional," White/Eurocentric) disciplines to interpret Black life-worlds and lived experiences. Thus this reproduces intellectually what Africana men, women, and children have long been fighting against physically and psychologically: a dependency and a colonial complex.[13]

A disciplinary dependency complex collapses and compartmentalizes the entirety of Black existence into the areas of experience, emotion, intuition, and creative expression and advances White theory, White philosophy, White science, and White concepts of culture and civilization as the normal and neutral sites and sources of intellectual acumen and cutting-edge criticism.

This conundrum takes us right back to Du Bois's contention in *The Souls of Black Folk* that Black people not be confused with the problems they have historically confronted and continue to confront.[14] "Africanity," or Blackness, to put it bluntly, has so much more to offer the human and social sciences than merely its experiential/emotional aspects.[15] Without conscious and conscientious conceptual generation, Africana studies will be nothing more than an academic ghetto. By "academic ghetto" I mean a place where Africana intellectuals exist in intellectual poverty, on the fringes of the White academy, and eagerly accept the dominant White intellectuals' interpretations of reality.

If, indeed, Africana studies seeks to seriously engage continental and diasporan African thought and practice, it cannot do so with the experiential/emotional approach alone, which almost by default emphasizes Africana practice and privileges it over Africana thought. The experiential/emotional approach in Africana studies has a tendency to employ White/Eurocentric theoretical frameworks to interpret and explore Africana practice(s), meaning essentially that it uses White theory to engage Black behavior, thereby negating Black thought on, and Black critical conceptual frameworks created for the interpretation of, Black behavior. What is more, the experiential/emotional approach, by focusing on Black actions and emotions and relying on White theory to interpret these actions and emotions, handicaps and hinders the development of Africana studies because disciplines cannot and do not develop without some form of conceptual generation that is internal and endemic to their distinct disciplinary matrices and ongoing academic agendas. This disciplinary dependency complex on White theory, instead of aiding in the development of Africana studies as an independent interdisciplinary discipline, unwittingly helps to confirm the age-old anti-African myth that thought and philosophy should be left to Whites and that Blacks should stick to the arts, entertainment, and athletics. The negation or, at the least, the neglect of thought or philosophy in the systematic and scientific study of continental and diasporan Africans' experience and thoughtful or thought-filled engagement of the world has led to several counter-discursive formulations and formations, two of the more recent being Africana philosophy and what I have humbly chronicled and called Africana critical theory.

AFRICANA PHILOSOPHY AND CRITICAL THEORY OF/IN AFRICANA STUDIES

To theorize Blackness—and some might even argue to practice Blackness, which is to say, to actually and fully live our Africanity—some type of thought or, more to the point, some form of philosophy will be required. "Days are gone," the Nigerian philosopher Emmanuel Eze asserts, "when one people, epoch, or tradition could arrogantly claim to have either singularly invented philosophy, or to have a monopoly over the specific yet diverse processes of search for knowledge typical to the discipline of philosophy."[16] I think it is important for us to extend this critical caveat further to encompass, in specific, the work of contemporary Western European–trained philosophers of African descent in relation to the discursive formations of Africana philosophy. Being biologically Black, or of African origin or descent, and having received training in Western European philosophy does not necessarily make one and one's thought and texts Africana philosophy. A critical distinction, then, is made at this juncture between philosophers of African origin and descent and Africana philosophers. The former group has more to do with biology, phenotype, and academic training than with any distinct philosophical focus that would warrant an appellation of a "school" or "tradition." The latter group is consciously concerned with discursive formations and practices geared toward the development of thought and thought-traditions that seek solutions to problems plaguing people of African origin and descent. The latter group also, like Africana critical theory, does not adhere to the protocols and practices of racialism(s) and traditional disciplinary development but harbors an epistemic openness to the contributions of a wide range of thinkers (and doers) from trans-ethnic, multiracial, and multicultural backgrounds, various academic disciplines, and assorted activist traditions.[17]

All of this brings us to the questions recently raised by the discursive formation of Africana critical theory of contemporary society. Africana critical theory is theory critical of domination and discrimination in classical and contemporary, continental and diasporan African life-worlds and lived experiences. It is a style of critical theorizing, inextricably linked to progressive political practice(s), that highlights and accents Africana radicals' and revolutionaries' answers to the key questions posed by the major forms and forces of domination and discrimination that have historically and continue to shape and mold our modern/postmodern and neocolonial/postcolonial world.

Africana critical theory involves not only the critique of domination and discrimination but also a deep commitment to human liberation and radical social transformation. Similar to other traditions of critical social theory, Africana critical theory is concerned with thoroughly analyzing contemporary society "in light of its used and unused or abused capabilities for improving the human [and deteriorating environmental] condition."[18] What distinguishes and helps to define Africana critical theory is its emphasis on the often overlooked continental and diasporan African contributions to critical theory. It draws from critical thought and philosophical traditions rooted in the realities of continental and diasporan African history, culture, and struggle. In other words, Africana critical theory inherently employs a methodological orientation that highlights and accents Africana theories and philosophies "born of struggle."[19] If it need be said at this point, Africana struggle is simultaneously national and international, transgender and trans-generational and therefore requires multidimensional and multi-perspectival theory in which to interpret and explain the various diverse phenomena, philosophical motifs, and social and political movements characteristic of—to use Fanon's famous phrase—*l'expérience vécue du Noir* (the lived experience of the Black), that is, the reality of constantly wrestling simultaneously with racism, sexism, colonialism, and capitalism, among other forms of imperialism.[20]

One may ask, why focus on Africana radicals' and revolutionaries' theories of social change? An initial answer to this question takes us directly to Du Bois's dictum, in the "Conservation of Races" (1897), that people of African origin and descent "have a contribution to make to civilization and humanity" that their historical experiences of holocaust, enslavement, colonization, and segregation have long throttled and thwarted.[21] He maintained that "[t]he methods which we evolved for opposing slavery and fighting prejudice are not to be forgotten, but learned for our own and others' instruction."[22] Hence, Du Bois is suggesting that Africana liberation struggle(s)—that is, the combined continental and diasporan African fight(s) for freedom—may have much to contribute to critical theory, and his comments here also hit at the heart of one of the core concepts of critical theory: the critique of domination and discrimination.[23]

From a methodological point of view, critical theory seeks to simultaneously (1) comprehend the established society, (2) criticize its contradictions and conflicts, and (3) create egalitarian (most often revolutionary or radical democratic socialist) alternatives.[24] The ultimate emphasis on the creation and offering of alternatives brings to the fore another core concept of critical theory: its theory of liberation and social transformation.[25] The paradigms and points of departure for critical theorists vary depending on the theorists' race, class, gender, sexual orientation, religious affiliation, nationality, intellectual interests, and political persuasions. For instance, many European critical theorists turn to Hegel, Marx, Freud, Gramsci, Sartre, and the Frankfurt School (Adorno, Benjamin, Fromm, Habermas, Horkheimer, and Marcuse), among others, because they understand these thinkers' thoughts and texts to speak in special ways to modern and "postmodern" life-worlds and lived experiences.[26]

My work, Africana critical theory, utilizes the thought and texts of Africana intellectual ancestors as critical theoretical paradigms and points of departure because so much of their thought is not simply problem posing but solution providing where the specific life struggles of persons of African descent (or "black people") are concerned—human life struggles without hyperbole and high-sounding words, which European critical theorists (who are usually Eurocentric and, often unwittingly, white supremacist) have woefully neglected in their classical and contemporary critical theoretical discourse. This discourse, ironically, has consistently congratulated itself on the universality of its interests, all the while—for the most part—side-stepping the centrality of racism and colonialism both within its own discursive communities and out in the wider world.[27] Moreover, my conception of critical theory is critically preoccupied with classical Africana thought traditions, not only because of the long unlearned lessons they have to teach contemporary critical theorists about the dialectics of being simultaneously radically humanist and morally committed agents of a specific nation or cultural group's liberation and social(ist) transformation but also because the ideas and ideals of continental and diasporan African intellectual-activists of the past indisputably prefigure and provide a foundation for contemporary Africana studies and Africana philosophy specifically. In fact, in many ways Africana critical theory, besides being grounded in and growing out of the discourse of Africana studies, can be said to be an offshoot of Africana philosophy, which according to the acclaimed African American philosopher Lucius Outlaw is

> a "gathering" notion under which to situate the articulations (writings, speeches, etc.), and traditions of the same, of Africans and peoples of African descent collectively, as well as the sub-discipline or field-forming, tradition-defining, tradition-organizing reconstructive efforts which are (to be) regarded as philosophy. However, "Africana philosophy" is to include, as well, the work of those persons who are neither African nor of African descent but who recognize the legitimacy and importance of the issues and endeavors that constitute the disciplinary activities of African or [African Caribbean or] African American philosophy and contribute to the efforts—persons whose work justifies their being called "Africanists." Use of the qualifier "Africana" is consistent with the practice of naming intellectual traditions and practices in terms of the national, geographic, cultural, racial, and/or ethnic descriptor or identity of the persons who initiated and were/are the primary practitioners—and/or are the subjects and objects—of the practices and traditions in question (e.g., "American," "British," "French," "German," or "continental" philosophy).[28]

Africana critical theory is distinguished from Africana philosophy by the fact that critical theory cannot be situated within the world of conventional academic disciplines and divisions of labor. It transverses and transgresses boundaries between traditional disciplines and accents the interconnections and intersections of philosophy, history, politics, economics, the arts, psychology, and sociology, among other disciplines. Critical theory is contrasted with mainstream mono-disciplinary social theory through its multidisciplinary methodology and its efforts to develop a comprehensive dialectical theory of domination and liberation specific to the special needs of contemporary society.[29] Africana philosophy has a very different agenda, one that seems to me more meta-philosophical than philosophical at this point because it entails theorizing-on-tradition and tradition construction more than tradition extension and expansion through the production of normative theory and critical pedagogical praxis aimed at application (i.e., immediate self- and social transformation).[30]

The primary purpose of critical theory is to relate radical thought to revolutionary practice, which is to say that its focus—philosophical, social, and political—is always and ever the search for ethical alternatives and viable moral solutions to the most pressing problems of our present age. Critical theory is not about, or rather should not be about, allegiance to intellectual ancestors and ancient schools of thought but is about using all (without regard to race, gender, class, sexual orientation, and religious affiliation) accumulated radical thought and revolutionary practices in the interest of liberation and social(ist) transformation. With this in mind, Cornel West's contentions concerning "Afro-American critical thought" offer an outline for the type of theorizing Africana critical theory endeavors:

> The object of inquiry for Afro-American critical thought is the past and present, the doings and the sufferings of African people in the United States. Rather than a new scientific discipline or field of study, it is a genre of writing, a textuality, a mode of discourse that interprets, describes, and evaluates Afro-American life in order comprehensively to understand and effectively to transform it. It is not concerned with "foundations" or transcendental "grounds" but with how to build its language in such a way that the configuration of sentences and the constellation of paragraphs themselves create a textuality and distinctive discourse which are a material force for Afro-American freedom.[31]

Although Africana critical theory encompasses and is concerned with much more than the life-worlds and lived experiences of "African people in the United States," West's comments are helpful because they give us a glimpse at the kind of connections critical theorists make in terms of their ideas having an impact and a significant influence on society. Africana critical theory is not thought-for-thought's sake (as it often seems is the case with so much contemporary philosophy—Africana philosophy notwithstanding); on the contrary, Africana critical theory is thought-for-life-and-liberation's sake. It is not only a style of writing that focuses on radicalism and revolution but a new way of thinking and doing revolution that is based and constantly being built on the radicalisms and revolutions of the past.

From West's frame of reference, "Afro-American philosophy expresses the particular American variation of European modernity that Afro-Americans helped shape in this country and must contend with in the future. While it might be possible to articulate a competing Afro-American philosophy based principally on African norms and notions, it is likely that the result would be theoretically thin."[32] Contrary to West's comments, Africana critical theory represents and registers as that "possible articulat[ion] of a competing [Africana] philosophy based principally on African norms and notions," and although he thinks the results will be "theoretically thin," Africana critical theory—following Fanon[33]—understands this risk to be part of the price the oppressed ("the wretched of the earth") must be willing to pay for their (intellectual, political, and physical) freedom. Intellectually audacious, especially considering the widespread Eurocentricism and white supremacism of contemporary conceptual generation, Africana critical theory does not acquiesce or give priority and special privilege to European history, culture, or thought. It turns to the long overlooked thought and texts of women and men of African descent who have developed and contributed radical thought and revolutionary practices that could possibly aid us in our endeavors to continually create a theory critical of domination and discrimination in contemporary culture and society.

Above and beyond all of the aforementioned, Africana critical theory is about offering alternatives to what is (domination and discrimination) by projecting possibilities of what ought to be and what could be (human liberation and revolutionary social transformation). It is not afraid, to put it as plainly as possible, to critically engage and dialogue deeply with European and other cultural groups' thought traditions. In fact, it often finds critical cross-cultural dialogue necessary considering the historical conundrums and current shared conditions and crises of the modern, almost completely trans-ethnic and multicultural world.[34] Africana critical theory, quite simply, does not privilege or give priority to European or other cultural groups' thought traditions since its philosophical foci and primary purpose revolve around the search for solutions to the most pressing social and political problems in continental and diasporan African life-worlds and lived experiences in the present age.

NEW CRITICAL THEORY, CRITICAL MULTICULTURALISM, AND COLORADO'S CONTRIBUTIONS

Keeping all of this in mind, what is important here is to critically engage the essays, not simply in this section but in this volume as a whole, as long overdue contributions to the reconstruction of critical social theory, making it more multicultural, trans-ethnic, transgendered, and trans-generational. Surely critical theory has developed to the point where it can search for solutions to the social and political problems of specific regional and cultural groups, especially if those groups have been long locked out of the purview of the dominant forms of critical theory, that is, Eurocentric, Marxist, patriarchal, and heterosexist critical theory.[35] If critical theory purports to be a theory of social change, if critical theory claims to be in the best interest of the most downtrodden in contemporary society, and if, indeed, critical theory is ever to really and truly live up to and earnestly embrace its lofty ideals (ideals I continue to be critically, although compassionately and completely, committed to), then it cannot and must not continue to disregard the contributions people of color, women, homosexuals, and folks with a wide range of religious affiliations have made and continue to make.

The people of color of Colorado and, even more, of the Rocky Mountain region, the American West, and the Southwest offer new critical theory, new paradigms and points of departure. There are cultural, social, and political problems to which they have long sought (and in many instances found) solutions that have seminal significance not only for local communities but also possibly for national and international communities and cultures. Considering the multiracial, multicultural, multilingual, trans-ethnic, transgender, and trans-generational nature of the various communities of color in the American West, and in Colorado in particular, and considering the wide range of religious affiliations, political persuasions, sexual orientations, access to education and income, and relationships with state and federal government, it would seem that new critical theorists have before them an ideal opportunity to simultaneously reconstruct critical social theory and contemporary U.S. culture and society. We are reminded here of something Du Bois wrote more than a century ago in reference specifically to African Americans and African American studies but that has enormous implications for American, cultural, and ethnic studies and, more directly, our current discussion of the nature and tasks of new critical theory and theorists. Du Bois declared:

> [T]here lies before the sociologist of the United States a peculiar opportunity. We have here going on before our eyes the evolution of a vast group of men from simpler primitive conditions to higher more complex civilization.

> I think it may safely be asserted that never in the history of the modern world has there been presented to men of a great nation so rare an opportunity to observe and measure and study the evolution of a great branch of the human race as is given to Americans in the study of the American Negro.[36]

Du Bois's extremely patriarchal, Eurocentric, ethnocentric, and anthropological language aside (language I have taken to task on numerous occasions),[37] what is most telling here is that he helps emphasize the "peculiar opportunity" the critical theorists of the twenty-first century have at hand. Indeed, we, critical theorists of Colorado and the North American West, are presented with a "rare . . . opportunity to observe and measure and study the evolution of a great branch of the human race," that branch which has long labored in the American West and which has been routinely rendered invisible and left out of the histories of not simply the American West but of the United States in general. American Indians, African Americans, Asian Americans, and Chicana/os have each made indelible contributions to the history and culture of Colorado and the wider North American West, and Du Bois's words will continue to haunt the intellectual and cultural workers of the West (and the United States) so long as the "peculiar opportunity" before us is overlooked.

Clearly, a new conception of critical theory is needed, one that moves beyond radical rhetoric concerning its commitment to revolutionary humanism and one that is epistemically open to the radical thought and revolutionary praxis of people from diverse races, ethnicities, and cultures. In terms of reconstructing a critical theory of contemporary society applicable to the United States, an increasingly multicultural and trans-ethnic society, critical theorists must consider and incorporate the contributions of non-Europeans and non–European Americans or continue developing "bad faith" critical theory—theory that really isn't so "critical" after all since it is one-dimensional, mono-cultural, Eurocentric, and subtly white supremacist. People of color, and, as this section highlights, African Americans in particular, have bequeathed much to Colorado and U.S. history and culture; therefore, it may very well be here in these hidden histories, enduring legacies, and long-muted voices that a truly trans-ethnic critical theory of the United States, and Colorado specifically, is finally brought into being.

ACKNOWLEDGMENTS

I am indelibly indebted to several intellectual-activists who have contributed (either directly or indirectly) to this book chapter and my ongoing intellectual and political development. A humble and heartfelt *asante sana* (a thousand thanks) to Marilyn Giles, Lucius Outlaw, Rhonda Tankerson, Lewis Gordon, Martell Teasley, Patrick De Walt, Lamya Al-Kharusi, William King, and my colleagues in the Department of Ethnic Studies and the Center for Studies of Ethnicity and Race in America (CSERA) at the University of Colorado at Boulder.

NOTES

1. Lewis Gordon and Jane Anna Gordon, eds., *Not Only the Master's Tools: African American Studies in Theory and Practice* (Boulder: Paradigm, 2006), x; emphasis in original.

2. To begin, for example, see Ollie Solomon Barefield, *Negro Pioneers in Colorado* (Greeley: Colorado State College, 1966); Monroe Lee Billington, *New Mexico's Buffalo Soldiers, 1866–1900* (Niwot: University Press of Colorado, 1991); Monroe Lee Billington and Roger D. Hardaway, eds., *African Americans on the Western Frontier* (Niwot: University Press of Colorado, 1998); Thomas Merritt Carhart III, "African American West Pointers during the Nineteenth Century" (PhD diss., Princeton University, 1998); Arnoldo De León, *Racial Frontiers: Africans, Chinese, and Mexicans in Western America, 1848–1890* (Albuquerque: University of New Mexico Press, 2002); James Rose Harvey, "Negroes in Colorado" (MA thesis, University of Denver, 1941) and "Negroes in Colorado," *Colorado Magazine* 26, 3 (1949): 165–176; John Stokes Holley, *The Invisible People of the Pikes Peak Region: An Afro-American Chronicle* (Colorado Springs: Friends of the Pikes Peak Library/Friends of the Pioneer Museum, 1990); Elizabeth Jameson and Susan Armitage, eds., *Writing the Range: Race, Class, and Culture in the Women's West* (Norman: University of Oklahoma Press, 1997); William Loren Katz, *The Black West*, 3rd ed. rev. (Seattle: Open Hand, 1987); Polly E. McLean, ed., *A Legacy of Missing Pieces: The Voices of Black Women of Boulder County* (Boulder: Center for Studies of Ethnicity and Race in America, 2002); Doug McNair and Wallace Yvonne McNair, *Colorado Black Leadership Profiles* (Denver: Western Images, 1989); Harmon Mothershead, "Negro Rights in Colorado Territory, 1859–1867," *Colorado Magazine* 60, 3 (1963): 212–236; Clementine Washington Pigford, *They Came to Colorado . . . with the Dust of Slavery on Their Backs: Information about Zion Baptist Church, Its Members and Societal Affiliations* (Denver: Zion Baptist Church, 2000); Kenneth Wiggins Porter, *The Negro on the American Frontier* (New York: Arno, 1971); John W. Ravage, *Black Pioneers: Images of the Black Experience on the North American Frontier* (Salt Lake City: University of Utah Press, 1997); Isetta Crawford Rawls, *The Negro in Early Colorado* (Denver: Colorado Historical Society, 1968); Ira De Augustine Reid, *The Negro Population of Denver, Colorado: A Survey of Its Economic and Social Status* (Denver: Lincoln, 1929); W. Sherman Savage, *Blacks in the West* (Westport, CT: Greenwood Books, 1976); Lillian Schlissel, *Black Frontiers: A History of African American Heroes in the Old West* (New York: Simon and Schuster, 1995); Dorothy Bass Spann, *Black Pioneers: A History of a Pioneer Family in Colorado Springs* (Colorado Springs: Little London, 1978); Quintard Taylor, *In Search of the Racial Frontier: African Americans in the American West, 1528–1990* (New York: Norton, 1998); Quintard Taylor and Shirley Ann Wilson Moore, eds., *African American Women Confront the West, 1600–2000* (Norman: University of Oklahoma Press, 2003).

3. See, for example, Wilbur Ball, *Black Pioneers of the Prairie* (Eaton, OH: W. P. Ball, 1988); Ann Batey, *A Study of Black Organizations of Pueblo, Colorado* (Pueblo: Pueblo Regional Planning Commission, 1975); James F. Brooks, ed., *Confounding the Color Line: The Indian-Black Experience in North America* (Lincoln: University of Nebraska Press, 2002); Lynda Faye Dickson, "The Early Club Movement among Black Women in Denver, 1890–1925" (PhD diss., University of Colorado at Boulder, 1982) and "Lifting as We Climb: African American Women's Clubs in Denver, 1880–1925," *Essays in Colorado History* 13 (1992): 69–98; Philip Durham and Everett L. Jones, *The Negro Cowboy* (New York: Dodd-Mead, 1966) and *The Adventures of the Negro Cowboys* (New York: Bantam, 1969); John P. Langellier, *Men A-Marching: The African American Soldier in the West, 1866–1896* (Springfield, IL: Wright, 1995); Lionel Dean Lyles, "An Historical-Urban Geographical Analysis of Black Neighborhood Development in Denver, 1860–1970" (PhD diss., University of Colorado at Boulder, 1977); Laura M. Mauck, *The Five Points Neighborhood of Denver* (Chicago: Arcadia, 2001); Melvin Edward Norris Jr., "Dearfield, Colorado: The Evolution of a Rural Black Settlement: An Historical Geography of Black Colonization on the Great Plains" (PhD diss., University of Colorado at Boulder, 1980); Margaret Picher, "Dearfield, Colorado: A Story from the Black West" (MA thesis, University of Denver, 1976); Shelley Rhym, *Through My Eyes: The Denver Negro Community, March 1934–January 1968* (Denver: Core City Ministries, 1968); Keith Schrum, "Of Myth and Men: The Trail of the Black Cowboy," *Colorado Heritage* (Autumn 1998): 2–17; Paul Stewart and Yvonne Ponce Wallace, *Black Cowboys* (Denver: Black American West Museum and Heritage Center, 1986); James Pleasant Thogmorton, "The Urban League of Denver: A Study in Techniques of Accommodation" (MA thesis, University of Denver, 1951); George H. Wayne, "Negro Migration and Colonization in Colorado, 1870–1920," *Journal of the West* 15, 1 (January 1976): 102–120.

4. For further discussion, see James de T. Abajian, *Blacks and Their Contributions to the American West: A Bibliography and Union List of Library Holdings through 1970* (San Francisco: San Francisco Public Library, 1970); Susan Armitage, "'The Mountains Were Free and We Loved Them': Dr. Ruth Flowers of Boulder, Colorado," in *African American Women Confront the West: 1600–2000*, Quintard Taylor and Shirley Ann Wilson Moore, eds. (Norman: University of Oklahoma Press, 2003), 165–177; James Pierson Beckwourth, *The Life and Adventures of James P. Beckwourth as Told to Thomas D. Bonner* (Lincoln: University of Nebraska Press, 1972); A'Lelia Bundles, *On Her Own Ground: The Life and Times of Madame C. J. Walker* (New York: Scribner, 2001); Harold W. Felton, *Edward Rose: Negro Trail Blazer* (New York: Dodd-Mead, 1967) and *Jim Beckwourth, Negro Mountain Man* (New York: Dodd-Mead, 1966); Nat Love, *The Life and Adventures of Nat Love, Better Known in the Cattle Country as "Deadwood Dick," by Himself* (Lincoln: University of Nebraska Press, 1995); Beverly Lowry, *Her Dream of Dreams: The Rise and Triumph of Madam C. J. Walker* (New York: Alfred A. Knopf, 2003); Joan Reese, "Two Gentlemen of Note: George Morrison, Paul Whiteman, and Their Jazz," *Colorado Heritage* 2 (1986): 2–13; Jessie Carney Smith, "Justina L. Ford," in *Notable Black American Women, Book II*, Jessie Carney Smith, ed. (New York: Gale Research, 1996), 229–231; Phillip Thomas Tucker, *Cathy Williams: From Slave to Female Buffalo Soldier* (Mechanicsburg, PA: Stackpole Books, 2002); Elinor Wilson, *James Beckwourth: Black Mountain Man and War Chief of the Crows* (Norman: University of Oklahoma Press, 1972).

5. Available at the Denver Public Library Online, http://aarl.denverlibrary.org/.

6. For further discussion, see Glenn Ray Smith, "The Black Studies Program at the University of Colorado, 1968–1973: Development, Change and Assessments" (PhD diss., University of Colorado at Boulder, 1974).

7. W.E.B. Du Bois, *The Correspondence of W.E.B. Du Bois: Volume III—Selections, 1944–1963*, Herbert Aptheker, ed. (Amherst: University of Massachusetts Press, 1997), 146; James Turner, ed., *The Next Decade: Theoretical and Research Issues in Africana Studies* (Ithaca, NY: Africana Studies and Research Center, Cornell University, 1984), viii; Lucius Outlaw, "African, African American, Africana Philosophy," in *African American Perspectives and Philosophical Traditions*, John P. Pittman, ed. (New York: Routledge, 1997), 64; Emmanuel Eze, ed., *(Post)Colonial African Philosophy: A Critical Reader* (Malden, MA: Blackwell, 1997), 4, emphasis in original; Lewis Gordon, *Existentia Africana: Understanding Africana Existential Thought* (New York: Routledge, 2000), 1.

8. The literature on Africana studies—which, to reiterate, encompasses African, African American, Afro-Asian, Afro-European, Afro-Latino, Afro–Native American, Black, Caribbean, and pan-African studies—is multicultural, trans-ethnic, transgendered, trans-generational, and extensive. The most noteworthy overviews and analyses are Delores Aldridge and Carlene Young, eds., *Out of the Revolution: An Africana Studies Anthology* (Lanham, MD: Lexington, 2000); Talmadge Anderson, ed., *Black Studies: Theory, Method and Cultural Perspective* (Pullman: Washington State University Press, 1990); Molefi Asante and Maulana Karenga, eds., *The Handbook of Black Studies* (Thousand Oaks, CA: Sage, 2006); Mario Azevedo, ed., *Africana Studies: A Survey of Africa and the African Diaspora* (Durham, NC: Carolina Academic Press, 1993); Nikongo Ba Nikongo, ed., *Leading Issues in African American Studies* (Durham, NC: Carolina Academic Press, 1997); Jacqueline Bobo and Claudine Michel, eds., *Black Studies: Current Issues, Enduring Questions* (Dubuque, IA: Kendall/Hunt, 2000); Jacqueline Bobo, Cynthia Hudley, and Claudine Michel, eds., *The Black Studies Reader* (New York: Routledge, 2004); James L. Conyers, ed., *Africana Studies: A Disciplinary Quest for Both Theory and Method* (Jefferson, NC: McFarland, 1997); Lewis Gordon and Jane Anna Gordon, eds., *A Companion to African American Studies* (Malden, MA: Blackwell, 2006) and *Not Only the Master's Tools: African American Studies in Theory and Practice* (Boulder: Paradigm, 2006); Manning Marable, ed., *Dispatches from the Ebony Towers: Intellectuals Confront the African American Experience* (New York: Columbia University Press, 2000) and *The New Black Renaissance: The Souls Anthology of Critical African American Studies* (Boulder: Paradigm, 2005); Nathaniel Norment Jr., ed., *The African American Studies Reader* (Durham, NC: Carolina Academic Press, 2007).

9. My interpretation of Africana philosophy is grounded in and grows out of the thought and texts of several classical and contemporary continental and diasporan African theorists whose works lend themselves to a critical theoretical framework or discursive formations regarding the history, nature, and tasks of Africana thought traditions and how these thought traditions can be used in the interest of human liberation and radical social transformation. For further discussion, see Reiland Rabaka, *Africana Critical Theory: Reconstructing the Black Radical Tradition, from W.E.B. Du Bois and C.L.R. James to Frantz Fanon and Amilcar Cabral* (Lanham, MD: Lexington Books, 2009).

10. Frantz Fanon, *A Dying Colonialism* (New York: Grove, 1965), *Black Skin, White Masks* (New York: Grove, 1967), *The Wretched of the Earth* (New York: Grove, 1968), and *Toward the African Revolution* (New York: Grove, 1969); Ngũgí wa Thiong'o, *Decolonizing the Mind: The Politics of Language in African Literature* (Portsmouth, NH: James Currey/Heinemann, 1986), *Moving the Center: The Struggle for Cultural Freedoms* (Portsmouth, NH: James Currey/Heinemann, 1993), and *Writers in Politics: A Re-Engagement with Issues of Literature and Society* (Portsmouth, NH: James Currey/EAEP/Heinemann, 1997). For further discussion, see Rabaka Reiland, *Forms of Fanonism: Frantz Fanon's Critical Theory and the Dialectics of Decolonization* (Lanham, MD: Lexington Books, 2010).

11. Léopold Senghor, "On Negrohood: Psychology of the African Negro," in *African Philosophy: Selected Readings*, Albert Mosley, ed. (Englewood Cliffs, NJ: Prentice-Hall, 1995), 120. My criticism of Senghor here does not negate my critical appreciation of some aspects of his conception(s) of "African Socialism." For further discussion, see Rabaka, *Africana Critical Theory*, chapter 3, "Aimé Césaire and Léopold Senghor: Revolutionary Negritude and Radical New Negroes," where I critically discuss Senghor's, as well as Aimé Césaire's, advances and retreats with regard to the development of Africana philosophy and Africana critical theory.

12. bell hooks, *Yearning: Race, Gender, and Cultural Politics* (Boston: South End, 1990) and *Killing Rage: Ending Racism* (New York: Henry Holt, 1995).

13. My analysis here smacks of Black existentialism or Africana philosophy of existence, which afforded me the theoretical tools to tease out the issues involved in the experiential/emotional approach in Africana studies. Interpreting experience, that is, investigating any lived reality, almost inherently entails a confrontation with existential and ontological questions and claims. These questions and claims, as quiet as it is kept, differ for each human group because each human group's historical horizon and cultural contexts, which were created either by it or some other human group, are wide and varied and always vacillating between human homogeneity and heterogeneity, often ultimately giving way in our postmodern moment to hybridity. For further discussion of Africana philosophy of existence or Black existentialism, see Lewis Gordon's groundbreaking volumes, *Existence in Black: An Anthology of Black Existential Philosophy* (New York: Routledge, 1997) and *Existentia Africana: Understanding Africana Existential Thought* (New York: Routledge, 2000). For the best brief overview of Black existentialism, see Lewis Gordon, "African American Philosophy of Existence," in *A Companion to African American Philosophy*, Tommy L. Lott and John P. Pittman, eds. (Malden, MA: Blackwell, 2003), 33–47.

14. W.E.B. Du Bois, *Du Bois: Writings*, Nathan Irvin Huggins, ed. (New York: Library of America Press, 1986), 363–371. Also see Elijah Anderson and Tukufu Zuberi, eds., *The Study of African American Problems: W.E.B. Du Bois's Agenda, Then and Now* (Thousand Oaks, CA: Sage, 2000).

15. The conception of "Africanity" that I invoke and employ here involves a combination of African identity and African personality theory and is drawn primarily from the work of the Eritrean philosopher Tsenay Serequeberhan in his article "Africanity at the End of the Twentieth Century," *African Philosophy* 11, 1 (1998): 13–21. Senghor theorized and helped popularize this term in Africana philosophical discourse with

The Foundations of "Africanité" or "Negritude" and "Arabite" (Paris: Presence Africaine, 1971), which more or less uses European thought and culture as a paradigm to develop a racially reactionary, and therefore extremely essentialist, African identity. I critique Senghor's essentialism, assimilationism, quasi-cultural nationalism, and African socialism in my books *Africana Critical Theory* and *Forms of Fanonism*.

16. Emmanuel Eze, ed., *African Philosophy: An Anthology* (Malden, MA: Blackwell, 1997), ix.

17. With regard to my conception of a "philosopher," I follow Lewis Gordon's lead in making a critical distinction between "philosophers" and "scholars of or on philosophy." In his words: "'Philosopher' here means something more than a person with a doctorate in philosophy. I regard many individuals with that title to be scholars of or on philosophy instead of philosophers. Philosophers are individuals who make original contributions to the development of philosophical thought, to the world of ideas. Such thinkers are people whom the former study. It is no accident that philosophers in this sense are few in number and many of them did not [and do not] have doctorates in philosophy, for example, René Descartes, David Hume, Søren Kierkegaard, William James, Edmund Husserl, Karl Jaspers, Jean-Paul Sartre, Simone de Beauvoir, and Alfred Schutz" (Gordon, *Her Majesty's Other Children: Sketches of Racism from a Neocolonial Age* [Lanham, MD: Rowman and Littlefield, 1997], 48–49). This distinction between "philosophers" and "scholars of or on philosophy" is also in line with Lucius Outlaw's articulation of Africana philosophy and Africana philosophers. Within the world of this discursive formation, "persons past and present, who were and are without formal training or degrees in philosophy[,] are being worked into developing canons as providing instances of reflections, on various matters, that are appropriately characterized as philosophical" (Outlaw, "African, African American, Africana Philosophy," 63). Outlaw's timely tome, *On Race and Philosophy* (New York: Routledge, 1996), also offers critical insights on the academic tasks and some of the social and political challenges confronting Africana philosophers, as well as philosophers of African descent, as they increasingly transgress the boundaries of the "traditional" White philosophy discipline/department and their training in Western European and European American philosophy.

18. Herbert Marcuse, *One-Dimensional Man: Studies in the Ideology of Advanced Industrial Society* (Boston: Beacon, 1964), xlii.

19. Leonard Harris, ed., *Philosophy Born of Struggle: An Anthology of Afro-American Philosophy from 1917* (Dubuque, IA: Kendall/Hunt, 1983).

20. Frantz Fanon, "The Lived Experience of the Black," in *Race*, Robert Bernasconi, ed. (Malden, MA: Blackwell, 2001), 184–202. Also see Lewis Gordon, T. Denean Sharley-Whiting, and Renee T. White, eds., *Fanon: A Critical Reader* (Cambridge: Blackwell, 1996); Ato Sekyi-Otu, *Fanon's Dialectic of Experience* (Cambridge: Harvard University Press, 1996); Jeremy Weate, "Fanon, Merleau-Ponty and the Difference of Phenomenology," in *Race*, Bernasconi, ed., 169–183; Rabaka, *Forms of Fanonism*.

21. Du Bois, *Du Bois*, 825.

22. W.E.B. Du Bois, *The Education of Black People: Ten Critiques, 1906–1960*, Herbert Aptheker, ed. (New York: Monthly Review Press, 1973), 144.

23. Ben Agger, *The Discourse of Domination: From the Frankfurt School to Postmodernism* (Evanston, IL: Northwestern University Press, 1992); John O'Neill, ed., *On Critical*

Theory (New York: Seabury, 1976); David M. Rasmussen and James Swindal, eds., *Critical Theory*, 4 vols. (Thousand Oaks, CA: Sage, 2004).

24. Raymond A. Morrow, with David D. Brown, *Critical Theory and Methodology* (Thousand Oaks, CA: Sage, 1994).

25. Herbert Marcuse, *Negations: Essays in Critical Theory* (Boston: Beacon, 1968) and *An Essay on Liberation* (Boston: Beacon, 1969); James L. Marsh, *Critique, Action, and Liberation* (Albany: SUNY Press, 1995) and *Process, Praxis, and Transcendence* (Albany: SUNY Press, 1999); Larry Ray, *Rethinking Critical Theory: Emancipation in the Age of Global Social Movements* (Thousand Oaks, CA: Sage, 1993).

26. See, for example, David Held, *Introduction to Critical Theory: Horkheimer to Habermas* (Berkeley: University of California Press, 1980); Martin Jay, *The Dialectical Imagination: A History of the Frankfurt School and the Institute of Social Research, 1923–1950* (Berkeley: University of California Press, 1996); Douglas Kellner, *Critical Theory, Marxism, and Modernity* (Baltimore: Johns Hopkins University Press, 1989); and Rolf Wiggerhaus's magisterial *The Frankfurt School: Its History, Theories, and Political Significance* (Cambridge: MIT Press, 1995).

27. For further discussion, see my books *W.E.B. Du Bois and the Problems of the Twenty-First Century* (Lanham, MD: Lexington Books, 2007), *Du Bois's Dialectics: Black Radical Politics and the Reconstruction of Critical Social Theory* (Lanham, MD: Lexington Books, 2008), *Africana Critical Theory, Forms of Fanonism*, and *Against Epistemic Apartheid: W.E.B. Du Bois and the Disciplinary Decadence of Sociology* (Lanham, MD: Lexington Books, 2010).

28. Outlaw, "African, African American, Africana Philosophy," 64.

29. Jürgen Habermas, *Theory of Communicative Action*, vol. 1 (Boston: Beacon, 1984), *Theory of Communicative Action*, vol. 2 (Boston: Beacon, 1987), *On the Logic of the Social Sciences* (Cambridge: MIT Press, 1988), and *On Society and Politics: A Reader*, Steven Seidman, ed. (Boston: Beacon, 1989); William S. Wilkerson and Jeffrey Paris, eds., *New Critical Theory: Essays on Liberation* (Lanham, MD: Rowman and Littlefield, 2001).

30. Part of Africana philosophy's current meta-philosophical character has to do with both its critical and uncritical appropriation of several Western European philosophical concepts and categories. As more philosophers of African origin and descent receive training in and dialogue with Africana studies theory and methodology, the basic notions and nature of Africana philosophy will undoubtedly change. Needless to say, Africana philosophy has an intellectual arena and engages issues often distinctly different from the phenomena that preoccupy and have long plagued Western European and European American philosophy. I am not criticizing the meta-philosophical motivations in the discourse of contemporary Africana philosophy as much as I am pleading with workers in the field to develop a "division of labor"—à la Du Bois's classic caveat(s) to continental and diasporan Africans in the face of white supremacy. A move should be made away from "philosophizing on Africana philosophy" (i.e., metaphilosophy), and more Africana philosophical attention should be directed toward the cultural crises and social and political problems of the present age. To do this, Africana philosophers will have to turn to the advances of Africana studies scholars working in history, cultural criticism, economics, politics, and social theory, among other areas.

For further discussion, see W.E.B. Du Bois, *Du Bois on Education*, Eugene F. Provenzo Jr., ed. (Walnut Creek, CA: Altamira, 2002); and note 8 in this chapter.

31. Cornel West, *Prophesy Deliverance! An Afro-American Revolutionary Christianity* (Philadelphia: Westminster, 1982), 15.

32. Ibid., 24.

33. Fanon, *The Wretched of the Earth* and *Toward the African Revolution*. See also Rabaka, *Africana Critical Theory* and *Forms of Fanonism*.

34. David Theo Goldberg, ed., *Multiculturalism: A Critical Reader* (Cambridge: Blackwell, 1994); David Theo Goldberg and John Solomos, eds., *A Companion to Racial and Ethnic Studies* (Malden, MA: Blackwell, 2002).

35. Several works that would fall under the rubric of what is currently called "new critical theory" are already taking up the challenge of making critical theory speak to more than merely European, European American, patriarchal, and heterosexual crises, cultures, and socio-political problems. See, for example, Yoko Arisaka's excellent "Women Carrying Water: At the Crossroads of Technology and Critical Theory," in *New Critical Theory: Essays on Liberation*, William S. Wilkerson and Jeffrey Paris, eds. (Lanham, MD: Rowman and Littlefield, 2001), 155–174; Michael Hames-Garcia, "Can Queer Theory Be Critical Theory?" in *New Critical Theory: Essays on Liberation*, Wilkerson and Paris, eds., 201–222; Patricia Huntington, "Challenging the Colonial Contract: The Zapatistas' Insurgent Imagination," in *New Critical Theory: Essays on Liberation*, Wilkerson and Paris, eds., 105–134; Naqi Husain Jafri, *Critical Theory: Perspectives from Asia* (New Delhi: Jamia Millia Islamia University Press, 2004); Eduardo Mendieta, *Global Fragments: Critical Theory, Latin America, and Globalization* (Albany: SUNY Press, 2006); Lucius Outlaw, *Critical Social Theory in the Interest of Black Folk* (Lanham, MD: Rowman and Littlefield, 2005); Rabaka, *W.E.B. Du Bois and the Problems of the Twenty-First Century*, *Du Bois's Dialectics*, *Africana Critical Theory*, and *Forms of Fanonism*; Lorenzo C. Simpson, "Critical Theory, Aesthetics, and Black Modernity," in *A Companion to African American Philosophy*, Tommy L. Lott and John P. Pitman, eds. (Malden, MA: Blackwell, 2003), 386–398; Cynthia Willet, "The Mother Wit of Justice: Eros and Hubris in the African American Context," in *New Critical Theory: Essays on Liberation*, Wilkerson and Paris, eds., 223–248.

36. W.E.B. Du Bois, "The Atlanta Conferences," in *W.E.B. Du Bois on Sociology and the Black Community*, Dan S. Green and Edwin D. Driver, eds. (Chicago: University of Chicago Press, 1978), 54. This classic essay was originally published in *Voice of the Negro* 1 (March 1904): 85–89. This essay lucidly demonstrates my claims that Du Bois was indeed a major, if not "the," architect of what we are currently calling "African American" and "Africana" studies and that African American/Africana studies has been well under way for more than a century, especially when Du Bois's intellectual and political life and legacy are critically considered from an Africana studies frame of reference. For further discussion, see Reiland Rabaka, "The Souls of Black Radical Folk: W.E.B. Du Bois, Critical Social Theory, and the State of Africana Studies," *Journal of Black Studies* 36, 5 (2006): 732–763 and *Against Epistemic Apartheid*.

37. See, for example, Reiland Rabaka, "W.E.B. Du Bois and 'The Damnation of Women': An Essay on Africana Anti-Sexist Critical Social Theory," *Journal of African American Studies* 7, 2 (2003): 39–62, "The Souls of Black Female Folk: W.E.B. Du Bois

and Africana Anti-Sexist Critical Social Theory," *Africalogical Perspectives* 1, 2 (2004): 100–141, "The Souls of White Folk: W.E.B. Du Bois's Critique of White Supremacy and Contributions to Critical White Studies," *Journal of African American Studies* 11, 2 (2007): 117–131, *W.E.B. Du Bois and the Problems of the Twenty-First Century, Du Bois Dialectics,* and *Against Epistemic Apartheid.*

Contributors

Arturo J. Aldama earned his Ph.D. in ethnic studies from the University of California–Berkeley. He serves as the associate chair of ethnic studies at University of Colorado at Boulder. His research focuses on Chicana/o cultural studies. His publications include *Disrupting Savagism: Intersecting Chicana/o, Mexican Immigrant and Native American Struggles for Representation* (Durham, NC: Duke University Press, 2002); ed., *Decolonial Voices: Chicana and Chicano Cultural Studies in the 21st Century* (Bloomington: Indiana University Press, 2002); *Violence and the Body: Race, Gender and the State* (Bloomington: Indiana University Press, 2003); and *Performing the US Latina and Latino Borderlands* (Bloomington: Indiana University Press, in press).

Osita Afoaku serves as clinical professor in the School of Public and Environmental Affairs at Indiana University. His research focuses on human rights, sustainable development, and democratization and state reconstruction in Africa. He is the author of *Explaining the Failure of Democracy in the Democratic Republic of Congo: Autocracy and Dissent in an Ambivalent World* (Lewiston, NY: Edwin Mellen Press, 2005), among other book publications.

Rhonda R. Corman is a lecturer / regional economist at the University of Northern Colorado. Her research focuses on sustainable development and environmental impact; emergence, chaos, and complexity modeling; and behavioral and experimental economics.

Miriam Bornstein-Gómez earned her Ph.D from the University of Arizona. She is an associate professor in the Department of Languages and Literatures at the University of Denver. Her research interests are in Latina/o and Latin American poetry. She is the author of two poetry collections, *Bajo Cubierta* (Sacramento: Spanish Press, 1993) and *Donde Empieza la Historia* (Tucson: Scorpion Press, 1976), and has published poetry in several anthologies.

Ramon Del Castillo earned his Ph.D. in public administration from the Graduate School of Public Affairs at the University of Colorado at Denver. He is an associate professor and chair of the Chicana/o Studies Department at Metropolitan State College of Denver. His areas of research include public policy issues in Chicana/o communities.

Robert J. Durán earned his Ph.D. in sociology from the University of Colorado. He is an assistant professor of criminal justice at New Mexico State University, and his areas of research include race, crime and justice, social control, and deviance through the lens of ethnography. His book on gangs in the Southwest is under contract with Columbia University Press.

Elisa Facio earned her Ph.D. in sociology from the University of California at Berkeley. She is an associate professor in the Department of Ethnic Studies at University of Colorado at Boulder and former CSERA director. She teaches courses on Chicana feminism and Anzaldúan theory. Select publications include "The Queering of Chicana Studies: Philosophy, Text, and Image," in *Reversing the Lens, Ethnicity, Race, Gender, and Sexuality through Film*, ed. Jun Xing and Lane R. Hirabayashi (University Press of Colorado, 2003). She is working on several book projects related to Chicana activism and spirituality and on post-Soviet Cuba.

Bernadette Garcia Galvez earned her M.A. in education. At University of Colorado at Boulder, she serves as the associate director of the Colorado Space Grant Consortium in the College of Engineering and Applied Sciences. Her works in print include "Poem, This World Is My Place," in *This Bridge We Call Home—Enacting the Visions of Radical Women of Color*, ed. Gloria Anzaldua and AnaLouise Keating (New York: Routledge, 2002), and "A History of Western

Music," *The High School Journal: Special Issue—Chicana/o Activism in Education*, ed. Luis Urrieta Jr. (2004).

Phillip Gallegos earned his Ph.D. in architecture from the University of Hawaii at Manoa, his Master of Architecture in urban design from the University of Colorado at Denver, and his Bachelor of Architecture from the University of Notre Dame. His publications include a chapter in *Moving beyond Borders: Julian Samora and the Establishment of Latino Studies*, ed. Alberto López Pulido, Barbara Driscoll de Alvarado, and Carmen Samora (University of Illinois Press, 2009). He is a licensed architect in Colorado and New Mexico

Peter J. García is an assistant professor of Chicana/o studies at Cal State Northridge and completed his Ph.D. in Latin American ethnomusicology at the University of Texas at Austin in 2001. Research areas include Southwest borderlands music cultures. His monograph *Decolonizing Enchantment: Lyricism, Ritual, and Echoes of Nuevo Mexicano Popular Music* is forthcoming from the University of New Mexico Press.

Helen Girón received her MA from University of Colorado at Boulder. She is an affiliate professor at Metropolitan State College of Denver in the Chicana/o Studies Department and a doctoral student at Iliff School of Theology. Her areas of interest include spiritual activism (faith in motion), equity in education, and gender equality.

David M. Hays received his B.A. in history from the University of Idaho and his M.A. in U.S. history from University of Colorado at Boulder. He is an archivist at the University of Colorado at Boulder.

Matthew Jenkins is a visiting assistant professor of digital art at Metropolitan State College of Denver. He has a B.A. in art from Adams State College, an M.A. in American studies from the University of New Mexico, and an MFA in electronic media art and design from the University of Denver.

George H. Junne Jr. received his Ph.D. in higher and adult continuing education from the University of Michigan. He is professor and chair of Africana studies at the University of Northern Colorado. He is the author of *History of Blacks in Canada: A Selectively Annotated Bibliography* (Westport, CT: Greenwood Press, 2003); *Blacks in the American West and Beyond—America, Canada, and Mexico: A Selectively Annotated Bibliography* (Westport, CT: Greenwood Press, 2000); and *Afroamerican History: A Chronicle of People of African Descent in the United States* (Dubuque, IA: Kendall/Hunt, 1996).

CONTRIBUTORS

William M. King received his Ph.D. from the Maxwell Graduate School of Citizenship and Public Affairs at Syracuse University. He is professor of Afroamerican studies at the University of Colorado at Boulder, and his research areas include Afroamerican studies, citizenship and public affairs, education, and social justice.

Enrique R. Lamadrid received his Ph.D. from University of Southern California. He is professor of Spanish and chair of the Department of Spanish and Portuguese at the University of New Mexico. His research focuses on literary folklore, cultural history, ethnopoetics, and folk music. His books include *La Acequia de Juan del Oso* (University of New Mexico Press), *Hermanitos Comanchitos: Indo-Hispano Rituals of Captivity and Redemption* (University of New Mexico Press), *Nuevo México Profundo* (Museum of New Mexico Press), *Tesoros del Espíritu* (Academia / El Norte Publications).

Suzanne MacAulay is an art historian and folklorist and she chairs the Department of Visual and Performing Arts at the University of Colorado at Colorado Springs. Her research interests focus on material culture and address themes of cultural politics, arts revitalization, memory, diaspora, and the sensate experience of objects and creative expressiveness.

Daryl Maeda is an associate professor in the Department of Ethnic Studies at the University of Colorado at Boulder, where he teaches Asian American studies and comparative ethnic studies. He is the author of *Chains of Babylon: The Rise of Asian America* (Minneapolis: University of Minnesota Press, 2009), a cultural history of the Asian American movement of the late 1960s and early 1970s.

Jessica Natsuko Arntson received her dual M.A. from the University of Colorado at Boulder in history and Japanese language and literature. Research areas include the internment of Japanese Americans during World War II, the life of Nisei artist Isamu Noguchi, and early pre-war Japanese language pedagogy pioneered by Noe Naganuma.

Adriana P. Nieto received her Ph.D. from the University of Denver and Iliff School of Theology, Religious, and Theological Studies. She serves as an assistant professor of Chicana/Chicano studies at the Metropolitan State College of Denver. Her areas of teaching and research include Chicana/Latina religious histories and Chicana and women of color feminist theories and praxis.

Reiland Rabaka is an associate professor of Africana studies in the Department of Ethnic Studies at the University of Colorado at Boulder. Professor Rabaka is the author of several books: *W.E.B. Du Bois and the Problems of the Twenty-First Century: An Essay on Africana Critical Theory* (Lanham, MD: Lexington Books, 2007), *Du Bois's Dialectics: Black Radical Politics and the Reconstruction of Critical Social Theory* (Lanham, MD: Lexington Books, 2008), and, most recently, *Forms of Fanonism: Frantz Fanon's Critical Theory and the Dialectics of Decolonization* (Lanham, MD: Lexington Books, 2010).

Robert J. Reinsvold received his Ph.D. at Purdue University, and serves as assistant professor in the School of Biological Sciences at University of Northern Colorado. Books in print include *Laboratory Manual for Applied Botany*, coauthored with Estelle Levetin and Karen McMahon (New York: McGraw Hill, 2002).

David A. Sandoval is a professor of history at Colorado State University, Pueblo. He is a Colorado borderlands scholar with publications focused on Santa Fe Trail and Chicano history.

Ronald J. Stephens received his Ph.D. at Temple University. He is an associate professor and chair of African American studies at Ohio University. His books in print include *Idlewild: The Black Eden of Michigan* (Charleston, SC: Arcadia, 2001) and *African Americans of Denver* (Charleston, SC: Arcadia, 2008).

Lorenzo A. Trujillo received his Ed.D. from the University of San Francisco and his J.D. from the University of Colorado Law School, where he also served as assistant dean and professor (now retired). He is an attorney at Sherman and Howard LLC in Denver, Colorado. His areas of research include law, education, and the arts, specifically traditional Southwest music and dance.

William Wei received his Ph.D. from the University of Michigan, Ann Arbor. He is a professor of history at the University of Colorado at Boulder. Research areas are modern China and Asian America. His books in print include *Counterrevolution in China: The Nationalists in Jiangxi during the Soviet Period* (Ann Arbor: University of Michigan Press, 1985) and *The Asian American Movement* (Philadelphia: Temple University Press, 1993).

Index

Abiquiu, 91, 93, 94
Acacio, San, founding miracle of, 35, 38–39, 41, 42, 44–45
Acoma Pueblo, miracle of, 35, 36, 37–38
Acosta, Esther, 351
Acosta, Paul, 357
Acuña, Rodolfo, 242, 287(n38)
Adams, Billy, 243
Adams State College: Chicana/o and Native students at, 318–19, 320–23; "Indian" mascot at, 15, 309–10, 311, 312–17, 323–24, 324–25(n16)
African Americans, 1–2, 3, 4, 7, 8–10, 212(n5), 213(nn15, 36); in Boulder, 105–6, 112–13, 162–63, 165–66; in Colorado, 101–4, 141, 379–80; in Colorado Springs, 142–43; in Denver, 143–45, 201, 202–4, 216(n39); discrimination against, 122–23, 164, 205–6; Garveyism, 139, 140, 146–51; segregation, 104–5, 161–62; University of Colorado, 166–67; during World War II, 196, 199, 200, 207–12, 217(n55)

African American studies, in Colorado, 379, 380–81
Africana studies, 381, 395(n9), 396–97(nn13, 15, 17), 398–99(nn30, 36); anti-African thought and, 383–84; critical theory, 386–90; definition of, 382–83; disciplinary dependency, 384–85
African Methodist Episcopal (A.M.E.) Congregation, 143, 145
Agricultural colonies, 104, 106. *See also* Dearfield; Greeley
Agriculture, 5, 104; African Americans in, 141, 142; Girón family in, 280, 288(n49); Hispanic work in, 221, 222; Mexican American labor in, 239, 245, 351–52; Weld County, 111–12
Aguilar, Frank, 248
Aguirre, Natividad Vallejos, 222, 223, 224, 226, 227, 229, 231
Ah Fee, 72, 73, 76
AIM. *See* American Indian Movement
Alcantar, Antonio, 349, 371, 373

407

Alianza (New Mexico), 63, 353, 360–61(n5)
Alianza Federal de Mercedes, 350
Alianza Hispano America, 243
"All Ute Removal" plan, 42
Altamirano, Ignacio Manuel, 341
Altman, Robert, *McCabe & Mrs. Miller,* 74–75
Alvarado, Ernesto, 292; on curanderismo and mental health, 293–94, 302–5
American Citizens of Spanish Descent, 244, 246, 248
American Independent Party, 368
American Indian Movement (AIM), 4, 284, 361(n9)
American Legion, anti-discrimination resolution, 169
American Student Union (ASU), 159, 162, 163, 168, 169, 172(n11)
ANGF. *See* Asociación Nacional de Grupos Folklóricos
Anti-African thought, and Africana studies, 383–84
Anti-discrimination campaign. *See* Civil rights
Anti-Semitism, 163, 173(n22)
Antiwar movement, 350
Anzaldúa, Gloria, 266; *Borderlands/La Frontera: The New Mestiza,* 262–63
Apache Kid, 276–77, 286–87(nn25, 27, 29)
Apaches, 13–14, 36, 281, 286(n16), 287(n36); histories, 278–79, 284–85(n1); identity as, 273, 274–75, 285(nn8, 9), 286(n23), 288(n56); resistance, 275–77, 286(nn15, 17, 19), 287(n35)
Arabs, influence of, 51–52
Arase, David, 189
Arase, Noboru, 189
Architecture, 12; religious, 87, 90, 91, 93–94
Archuleta, Damián, 61
Arkansas Valley, 5, 48(n2)
Artists, colcha, 24, 25–33
Arvada Center for the Arts and Humanities, 2
Asian Americans, 3, 4–5, 6–7. *See also* Japanese Americans
Asociación Nacional de Grupos Folklóricos (ANGF), 65
Assimilation, 243; Native American, 13, 276, 285(n6), 286(n24)
ASU. *See* American Student Union
ASUC, 164, 168, 169

Baca land grant, 10
Bailey, Frank, 202–3
Ballad of Little Jo, The (film), 81–82
Barrera, Mario, 370
Barrio, as community, 339–40
Barrio Publications, 327, 337
Barrio Warriors, 280–81
Bassett, Lonnie C., 151, 158(n58)
BAWM. *See* Black American West Museum
Bean, Luther E., 40, 41–42
Bear Dances, in San Luis Valley, 46
Beaubien Deed, 27
Beckham, J. B., 106
Bernard, W. S., 162
"Bésame Mucho" (Velázquez), 269
Bicentennial celebration, critique of, 332–33
Bilingualism, 261–62, 337
Black, Hugo, 203
Black American West Museum (BAWM) and Heritage Center, 380; and Dearfield, 114–15
Blackness, theorizing, 385–86
Black Star Line Steamship Company, 147, 148
Black Studies. *See* African American Studies
Blair-Caldwell African American Research Library, 380
Bloom, Norman, 368
Bombings and bomb plots: in Boulder, 349, 357, 358, 360(n2), 372–73; Kiko Martínez and, 370–71, 373–76
Booker, Z. M., 142
Boothroyd, Donald E., 163, 168, 169, 170
Borderlands, 1, 2–3, 11
Borderlands/La Frontera: The New Mestiza (Anzaldúa), 262–63
Boston Tea Party, 311
Boulder: African American community in, 105–6, 112–13; civil rights campaign in, 7–8, 162–63, 168; Japanese Americans in, 179, 180, 181, 183–87, 189–90, 192(nn51, 52); Navy Japanese Language School in, 175–76, 192(n52); segregation in, 160, 161–62, 165–66
Boulder-Colorado Sanitarium, 166
Boulder Public Schools, 168, 174(n31)
Boycotts, agricultural, 351–52
Boyd, David, *A History: Greeley and the Union Colony of Colorado,* 105

Boyer, S. J., 181–82
Bracero Program, 241, 252; music, 65–67
Brandeis, Louis D., 205
Briones, Rogelio, 315
Brockman, Squire, 115
Brooks, James D., 147, 157(n41)
Brown, Clara, 102
Brown, Harold, 162
Brown Scare, 241
Brunson, Perry, murder of Ricardo Falcón, 368–69
Bureau of Immigration, 102–3
Burke, James T., 129
Businesses, Black-owned, 142–43, 144–45
Byers, William N., 103

Calderwood, Stanford, 170
Canales, Rito, 370
Cantar de Mio Cid, El, 52, 54, 57, 59
Capillas, 87, 90, 92(fig.), 98–99; Conejos area, 94–96, 97; San Luis Valley, 93–94
Capulin (Conejos County), 93
Cárdenas, Lazaro, 244
Cárdenas, Victor, 61
Carey, Samuel E., 198
Carillo, Alvaro, "Sabor a Mi," 269
Carlota, 60, 62
Carlson, Harry, 166
Carpio, "Frank," 248
Carr, Ralph L., on Japanese Americans, 5–6, 181, 182
Carter, Ethel, 114
Carter brothers, 143
Cashion, Susan, 65
Castillo, Phil, 313, 315, 319, 320–21
Catholic Church, 90; education, 221, 222, 223; and Ku Klux Klan, 107, 122; social justice, 259–60
Catholic Workers Protective Alliance, 123
"Causa, La" (Delgado), 338
Cazares, Leonel, 268
Central City, African Americans in, 102
Centro de las Familias, 298, 307; curanderismo at, 291–92, 293–97, 302–5, 306; professional legitimacy of, 299–300
Certeau, Michel de, *The Practice of Everyday Life*, 336–37
Chapman, Walter, 107

Chávez, César, 352, 360(n4)
Chavez, Jack, 131
Chicana/os, 1, 3, 10, 11, 67(n1), 240, 253(n6), 262, 285(n10), 287(n36), 288(n44), 365; activism of, 14, 242–43, 251–52; and Adams State mascot, 314–17; civil rights, 366–67; at CU-Boulder, 354–55, 359, 361(n8); feminism, 347–49, 352–53, 355–56; Governor Johnson's actions against, 244–48; identity, 248–49; indigenous identity of, 13–14; murders, 283–84, 289(n64), 349, 357, 358, 367–70, 371–72; music, 257–58, 259; nativism and, 243–44; New Hispano Party, 249–50
Chicana/o Movement, 65, 280–81, 282, 289(nn65, 66), 329, 350, 365; at Adams State College, 315–17; bombings and bomb plots, 370–74; at CU-Boulder, 353–58, 366–67; development of, 242–43; feminism and, 352–53; poetry of, 330–31; United Farm Workers and, 351–52; violence and, 283–84, 289(n64), 349, 367–69
Chicanismo, 351, 355, 361(n7)
Chicano Movement Poetry, 15, 327–28; discourse of, 330–31; educational critique in, 329–30, 331–32. *See also* Delgado, Abelardo Barrientos "Lalo"
Chicano Renaissance, 350
Chicano studies, 352; at University of Colorado, 355, 358
Chicano Youth Liberation Conferences, 352
Chinatown (film), 78–79
Chinatowns: Denver's, 72–73; perceptions of, 78–79
Chinese, 2, 3, 7, 84(n23); early immigrants, 4–5; exclusion of, 79–80; Hop Alley riot, 77–78, 85(n30); prostitution, 72–74, 75–77, 83–84(nn5, 13, 15, 21); representations of, 69–71, 74–75, 81–82
Chinese Exclusion Act, 79
"Chinese Romance, A," 69–70, 71, 72–74, 76
Chotis (schottische), 62
Chumpo, 37
Churches, 87, 90, 91, 147; African American, 143, 145; San Luis Valley, 88, 93–98
Cid, El, 52, 54
City across the River (film), 130
Civil rights, 4, 205; Chicano, 242–43, 264, 349–50; Kiko Martínez defenses of, 366–67;

postwar planning and, 210–12; University of Colorado campaign, 7–8, 159, 162–63, 166–70, 173(n28)
Civil Rights Movement, 159, 281; Chicana/o, 10, 14, 251, 282
Class, and education, 223–24
Clover, school in, 222
Coal industry, 278–79, 288(nn42, 43, 45)
Coalition for the Respect of Indigenous Peoples, 310, 317; on "Indian" mascot, 314–15, 318–20, 321, 322–24
Coca, Cora Martinez, 222, 224, 228, 231–32
Codina Fernández, Génaro, "Marcha de Zacatecas," 55
Cohen, Joseph, 164
Colcha embroidery, 24; memory narratives in, 25–33
Colonialism, 331, 348, 383; and history, 219–20, 234(n4), 284–85(n1)
Colorado Chautauqua, segregation at, 165–66
Colorado College, Black studies at, 381
Colorado Springs, 153, 264; African Americans in, 9, 102, 141, 142–43; Marcus Garvey in, 149–51; Garveyism in, 139, 140; UNIA-ACL in, 147, 148–49, 152, 154–55(nn3,4), 158(n58)
Colorado Springs Sun (newspaper), 142
Colorado State Constitution, 102, 160, 210
Colorado State Division of Mental Health, curanderismo, 296
Colorado State Federation of Labor, 5
Colorado State Legislature, 198, 215(n36)
Colorado State Penitentiary, civil rights at, 367
Colorado Statesman, The (newspaper), 144, 154–55(n4), 195–96, 198, 199
Colorado State Supreme Court, 204
Colorado State Teachers College, and Dearfield, 107
Colorado State University, Black studies at, 381
Columbus Day, Indigenous peoples' objections to, 315–16
Columbus Day Parade, 4
Committee for Public Relations (CU), 186
Communities: Hispanic, 226–27, 232; planned all-Black, 101, 105
Community, 357; Delgado on, 339–40; poetic performance and, 340–41
Conejos, capillas in, 93–94

Conejos County, 88, 97–98; capillas in, 93–94, 95(table); Spanish settlement of, 91–93
Conejos Land Grant, 10, 92–93, 97
Congress on Racial Equality (CORE), 170
Conquistadora, La, 36
Con Sabor a Latino America (Lobato), 268
Conscientization, 333–34
Coors family, Adolph, political support from, 198
Cordova, Antonio, 370
CORE. *See* Congress on Racial Equality
Corps of Topographical Engineers, African Americans in, 102
Corridos, 62–63
Cortez, Jaime, 259
Cosmopolitan (Cosmo) Club, anti-discrimination committee, 162, 169
Costilla County, 24–25, 88, 91
Criados (Indian servants), Ute, 44–45
Crider, Robert, 370–71, 375
Crime, 122; Mexicans and, 123–25
Critical theory: Africana, 386–90; new, 391–92
Crusade for Justice, 4, 14, 250, 251, 264, 283–84, 350, 351, 352, 353–54, 357, 361(n9); activism of, 369–71
Culebra Peak, 31
Cultural competency, in mental health care, 296–97, 306–7
Culture and Power in the Classroom (Darder), 328, 329
Culture(s), 343; subaltern, 336–37
Cuna, La, 62
Cunningham, Charlotte, 368
Curanderas, 14; training of, 292–93
Curanderismo: in mental health system, 291, 293–97, 298–99, 301–5; training in, 292–93

Dances, 51, 59, 63; European influences on, 60–62; Moorish and Arab influences on, 52, 53(fig.)
Darder, Antonia, *Culture and Power in the Classroom*, 328, 329
Davis, Edward C., 147
Davis, George W., 199, 216(n41)
DCHR. *See* Denver Commission on Human Relations
Dearfield, 9, 101, 104, 105, 117(n48); decline of, 112–14; development of, 108–11; founding

of, 107–8; political and economic support for, 106–7; preservation plans for, 114–15
Delgado, Abelardo Barrientos "Lalo," 335, 337; Chicano Movement Poetry of, 327–28, 336; on community, 339–40; educational critique, 329–30, 331–32; *Here Lies Lalo*, 332–33; poetry as performance, 340–43; poetic discourse of, 330–31, 338; "The Willing and Unwilling Victims," 334
Delgado Bernal, Dolores, 357
Delinquency, of Mexican youth, 123–26, 133–34
Deloria, Phillip, *Playing Indian*, 311–12
Democracy, morality of, 207
Democratic Party, 77, 106–7, 212(n5), 249, 250
Demonstrations: on Falcón murder trial, 368, 369; at CU-Boulder, 366–67
Denver, 4, 135(n4), 352; African Americans in, 8, 102, 103–4, 106, 141, 142, 143–45, 197, 198, 199, 200–201, 202–4, 216(n39), 379, 380; Chinese in, 5, 69, 72–73, 75, 76, 77–78, 85(n30); Crusade for Justice in, 369–71; Marcus Garvey in, 151, 152; Garveyism in, 139, 140, 147, 148; Latino gangs in, 121–22, 124–28, 130–34, 136(n6); Ku Klux Klan in, 13, 107, 145–46; mental health center in, 293–97; Mexican Americans in, 123–24, 128–29
Denver Commission on Human Relations (DCHR), on discrimination, 129–30
Denver County Public Welfare Bureau, 203
Denver Doers Club, 107
Denver Riot (1880), 5, 7, 77–78, 85(n30)
Denver Star, The (newspaper), 144
Denver West High School, 352
Denver Youth Leadership Conference, 14, 264
Deportations, during Great Depression, 241
Desert Land Act, 108
Detentions, of Hispanics, 246, 247
Dialogue, poetry as, 338–40
Diaspora, Mexican, 278
Diaz, Manuel, 249
Díaz, Porfirio, 239–40
"Dicho y Hecho," 352
Dilchthe, 275–76
Discrimination, 329; in Denver, 129–30, 200–201; and education, 225–26; against Latinos, 122–23, 128, 134, 224; Mann's columns on, 199–200, 202–7, 216–17(n46); postwar planning and, 210–12; University of Colorado campaign against, 161–64, 168–69; during World War II, 207–10
Dobson, James, 264
Dodson, Jacob, 102
Dominguez, Francisco Atanacio, 98
Don Quixote, 59
Dorsey, E. V., 199
Dougherty, Francisco, 349, 360(n2), 371, 372
Downs, Lila, 67
Drought, 112
Du Bois, W.E.B., 383, 387, 391–92, 399(n36); *The Souls of Black Folk*, 385
Duncan, W. H., 142
Dust Bowl, 112

Eckhardt, Carl, 159, 163–64, 166, 167, 168, 169, 170
Economic boycott, Tingley's proposal of, 247–48
Education, 211, 357; bicultural students and, 328–29; bilingual, 261–62; Delgado's critique of, 329–30, 331–32; and family, 226–227; importance of, 230–31, 288(n51); of mestizas, 13, 219, 220, 221–26, 235(n7); politics and, 332–33; process of, 335–36; for Spanish speakers, 227–30
El Rito (N.M.), 91, 93
Embroidery, colcha, 24, 25–33
Empire Ditch Company and Reservoir, 109
Enterprise, The (newspaper), 142
Entriega de los Novios, La, 52; language in, 57–59; music of, 54–57
Escuela Tlatelolco, 331, 361(n6)
Estrada, Cleo, 351, 357
Estrada, Noel, "En mi Viejo San Juan," 269
Estudiantes Unidos, 315, 316
Ethnicity, 24, 235(n8); education, 223, 224
Ethno-psychiatry, 294
Evangelical Christian movement, 264
Evans, John, 103
Executive Order 9066, 175, 176
Exoduster movement, 104
Eze, Emmanuel, 386

Fachs, Donald, 115
Fair Employment Practices Act, 198

INDEX **411**

Falcón, Priscilla, 351, 354, 368
Falcón, Ricardo, murder of, 357, 367–69, 372
Family, 295; Hispanics and, 226–27
Fandangos, 61–62
Farisita, 219, 221
Farmer, James, 170
Farm Security Administration, 42
Farmworkers, 360(n4); better conditions, 351–52
Faundez, Antonio, *Learning to Question*, 332, 335–36, 339
FBI, bombing investigations, 372–73
Feminism, Chicana, 347–49, 352–53, 355–57
"Fence, The" (Delgado), 331
Fenner, Katie, 152
Fiestas, 24, 36; dance, 61–62
Films, Western, 74–75
Five Points (Denver): African Americans in, 139, 143–45, 152, 200; zoot suiters in, 125–26
Flaubert, Gustave, 71, 83(n8)
Focus on the Family, 264
Folktales, in colcha embroidery, 26–27
Fong Lea, 71, 72–73
Ford, Barney, 104
Fort Garland (Fort Massachusetts), 42
Fort Lupton, Japanese agriculture in, 5
Franco, Joe, 357
Fraternal organizations, Hispanic, 240–41
Freire, Paulo, 327, 328, 332, 337, 338; on conscientization, 333–34; *Learning to Question*, 335, 339; *The Politics of Education*, 329, 343
Frémont, John C., 102
Fresques, James, 129
Fujii, Kozo, 179–80
Fulkerson, William M., Jr., 314, 322

Gallegos, J., 97
Gallegos, Joe, 32
Gallegos, Roy, 370
Gangs, 13; girls in, 133–34; Latino, 121, 124–28, 130–33, 136(nn5, 6)
Gardner, 219, 221, 222, 223, 229
Garfield, James R., 77
Garvey, Amy Jacques, 139, 146, 154(n3); activism of, 140, 151–52; in Colorado Springs, 149–50; UNIA-ACL leadership, 152–53
Garvey, Marcus, 9, 139, 140, 146–47, 152, 154(n3), 157(n54); in Colorado Springs, 149–51
Garvey Movement, Garveyism, 9, 139, 140, 146, 147
Gender, 223, 273, 353; and gang activities, 133–34; and protection, 224–25
General Allotment Act, 281
Genizaros, 60
Geronimo, 276, 277, 286(nn20, 23), 287(n31)
G.I. Forum, 251
Gilliam, Judge, 132–33
Gilmore, James, 310
Girón, Elicia Martinez, 279, 280(fig.), 281(fig.)
Girón, Francisco "Frank," 280, 282(fig.)–83, 289(n61)
Girón, Jose Dolores "Lolo," 280
Girón, Tiburcio, 279–80, 288(n47)
Girón family, 278–79, 287(nn35, 39)
Globeville, Latino gangs in, 132
Gold rushes, 2, 102
"Golondrina, La" (Seradell Sevilla), 268
González, Henry, 366–67
Gonzalez, Nita, 351
Gonzalez, Rodolfo "Corky," 4, 14, 249, 331; Crusade for Justice, 250, 251, 350; "Yo Soy Joaquin," 352, 361(n6)
Goss-Grove neighborhood (Boulder), 105, 169
Granados, Florencio "Freddie," 349, 360(n2), 367, 371, 372, 373
Grant, R. S., 142
Grape boycott, 351, 360(n4)
Grazing rights, communal, 28, 31
Great Depression, 241, 280, 288(n48); anti-Mexican actions during, 244–48
Great Western Sugar Company, 245
Greeley, 5, 104, 116(n19)
Greeley, Horace, 103
Greenwald, Maggie, *The Ballad of Little Jo*, 81–82
Grey, Tomasina, 319, 320, 321, 323
Griego, Roberto, 258, 270(n1)
Groves, Harry, 169, 170, 174(n31)
Guadalupe (Conejos County), 93, 97
Guangdong Province, prostitutes from, 76
Gunnell, John T., 201

Hackley, Edwin H., 195
Haggard, Ted, 264

Hamilton, Jerry, 368
Hancock, Winfield S., 77
Hanem, Kuchuk, 71
Hardin, William Jefferson, 103–4
Heart Mountain Relocation Center, 182
Henderson, Margaret, 186
Here Lies Lalo (Delgado), 332–33
Hernández, Benjamin, 65
Hernandez, Florencia "Flo," 351
Herrera, Alfred, 351–52
Herrera, Juanita, 351–52
Hicks, Paul, 199
Hill (Boulder), anti-discrimination campaign, 162–63, 168, 170
Hilos Culturales, 65
"Himno a la Nacioncita de la Sangre de Cristo" (Vigil), 46–47
Hirabayashi, Martin, 185
Hispanics, 7, 164
Hispana/os, 1, 67(n1), 88, 262, 264; education, 13, 220–27; identity as, 248–49; land grants, 3–4, 10–11; music and dance of, 53, 59–67; in San Luis Valley, 12, 24–25, 42, 46, 90; wedding customs of, 54–59
Historia de la Nueva México (Pérez), 37
Histories, 332, 334; Apache, 278–79; in colcha embroidery, 25–33; of colonized, 219–20, 234(n4); regional, 232–33
History: Greeley and the Union Colony of Colorado, A (Boyd), 105
Hitler, Adolf, Mann on, 206, 208
Hogue, Carol, 370, 375
Hok Yop Tea and Coolie Importing Company, 72, 73
Holmes, C. W., 143
Holmes, Lorrie, 114
Homemakers, women as, 273–74
Hop Alley riot, 77–78, 85(n28)
Hostetler, Marilyn Medina, 221
Housing: discrimination in, 172–73(n15); segregated, 161–62, 165, 166; University of Colorado, 167–68, 169, 170
Huerfano County, 13, 233(n2); family and community in, 226–27, 232; mestiza education in, 219–31, 235(n7); school enrollment in, 220, 234(n5)
Hughes, S. Leon, 149

Identities, 1, 330; American, 273, 285(n2); Apache, 274–76, 281, 285(nn8, 9), 286(n23), 288(n56); Chicano/Hispano, 248–49; cultural, 24, 235(n8); Indian in American national, 311–14; Indigenous, 13–14; racial, 122–23; Spanish American, 240, 241, 243, 246
Iglesia de Nuestra Señora de Guadalupe (Conejos), 93
Imai, Martha, 185
Immigration, 242; African American, 102–3; Chinese, 75, 79, 82–83; Mexican, 240, 241, 279
Immigration Act, 191(n22); Japanese and, 179–80
Immigration laws: and Chinese, 71, 83; and Japanese, 179–80
Immigration Reforms (1965), 6
Imperial Eyes (Pratt), 337
Inabu, Ruth, 162
Indianness, in American national identity, 311–14
Indita, 60, 61(fig.)
Indo-Hispanas/os, 262, 271(n8)
Industrialization, European workers, 242
Industrial Workers of the World (IWW), 240
Innovation, in mental health system, 291–92, 293–97, 302–6
Internment camps, Japanese, 176, 178, 191(n11)
Irish, Donald, 170
Irrigation, 104, 109
Ishizaki, Takako, 179
Isidro, San, 45
Isleta Pueblo, 36
IWW. *See* Industrial Workers of the World

Jaakola, Una, 349, 360(n2)
Jacales, at Guadalupe, 97
Jackson, Jennie, 113–14
Jackson, Minerva J. Matlock, 106
Jackson, Oliver Toussaint, 105, 107–8, 109, 112, 113
Jackson, Robert F., 108
Jackson, Sarah "Sadie," 105
JACL. *See* Japanese American Citizens League
Jacques, Amy. *See* Garvey, Amy Jacques
Jacques (Jaquez), Jose María, 93, 97

Japanese, 5, 191(nn11, 22); discrimination against, 122–23, 162, 172(n11), 198, 208
Japanese American Citizens League (JACL), 162, 178–79
Japanese Americans, 2, 3, 4, 7, 10; in Boulder, 183–87, 191(n11), 192(nn51, 52); discrimination against, 164, 165, 217(n59); loyalist, 178–79; at Navy Japanese Language School, 175–77, 179–80, 192(n51); during World War II, 5–6, 181–83, 190(n2)
Japanese and Korean Exclusion League, 5
Japanese studies programs, 176
Jáquez, Dolores "Lula," on El Milagro de San Acacio, 40–41, 42, 48(nn3, 4)
Jáquez (Jacques), Miguel, 39, 40, 48(n3)
Jáquez family, 30
"Jarabe Tapatío," 63, 68(n23)
Jencks, Clinton, 169
Jews, 107, 122, 163, 164, 165, 173(n22)
JLS. *See* Navy Japanese Language School
"John Chinaman," 5
Johnson, Edwin, 212(n1); anti-Mexican actions of, 123, 243, 244–48
Jones, Mother, 279, 288(n42)
José, San, 36
Juglares, 54, 64

Kane, J. H., 249
Keene, Donald, 188, 189
Kerner Commission Report, 352
Kimball, Neil W., 246
King Yok, 71; and prostitution, 72–74, 76
King Yow, 71; and prostitution, 72–74, 76
Kinship, historical memory, 26–27, 30
Knowledge, 29, 302; culturally divergent, 335–36
Korean War, Girón family in, 280
Ku Klux Klan, 9, 13, 107, 140; in Denver, 122, 129, 134, 145–46

Labor, 5, 288(n49), 334; African Americans as, 103, 106; farm, 280, 351–52; Japanese Americans as, 177, 181–82; Mexican, 239, 241, 245, 246, 248
Labor organization, 240; coal miners, 279, 288(nn42, 43, 45)
La Capilla de San Acacio, 93–94
La Garita, 243

Lamy, John Baptist, and Conejos settlements, 93, 97
Land grants, Hispano, 3–4, 10–11, 27–28, 30–32, 97
Land rights, 24, 361(n9); New Mexico, 350, 360–61(n5)
La Raza Cósmica, 240
La Raza Unida, 251, 351, 361(nn6, 9), 367, 377(n7)
Las Golondrinas Ranch (N.M.), fandangos at, 62
Las Mesitas (Conejos County), 93
Latina/os, Catholic Church and, 259–60. *See also* Chicana/os; Hispana/os; Mexican Americans
Learning to Question (Freire and Faundez), 332, 335–36, 339
Legends: Milagro de Acoma, 37–38; El Milagro de San Acacio, 26–27, 29–30, 39–42
Leone, Alejandro, 97
Lesbians, Chicana feminism and, 356–57
Lester, O. C., 164
Lettuce boycott, 352
Liberian Construction Loan, 147
Librada, Santa, 39
Lincoln High School (Denver), 352
Lincoln Sanatorium for Colored People, 142–43
Literary discourse, 334, 335
Literature: Chicana/o, 262–63; Mexican, 341
"Little Tokyo," 5
Lobato, Gene, 31
Lobato, Josephine, 24, 25; *El Milagro de San Acacio*, 26–27, 29–30; *La Sierra*, 27–28, 30–33
Lobato, Michelle, 15, 257, 259–60; on bilingualism, 261–62; as Coloradoan, 269–70; musical development of, 267–69; on musical ministry, 264–65; as new mestiza, 265–66
Lobato v. Taylor, 30, 33(n4)
LoDo: African Americans in, 143; Chinese settlement in, 77–78
Logging, protests against, 30
Look Young, 77
Loo Quong, 71, 72–73
Loper, Frank J., 141, 143, 156(n11)
López, Alejandro, 40

López Tijerina, Reyes, 63, 350
López Velarde, Ramón, "La suava patria," 341
Los Angeles, zoot suiters and, 125, 126
Los Pinos chapel, 97
Los Rincones, 93, 97
Los Sauces (Conejos County), 93
Lovato, Pabla Cruz, 221, 223, 229, 231
Lowry, 201, 206, 215(n33)
Loyalty, of African Americans, 205
Ludlow Massacre, 279, 288(n44)
Luevano, Francisco, 366–67
Lusky, Sam, 130, 136(n5)
Lynchings, Hop Alley riot, 77

McCabe & Mrs. Miller, anti-Chinese stereotypes in, 74–75
Machebeuf, Joseph, 97–98
McCullough, Helen Craig, 188
McCollough, Odessa, 110
McCottery, James, 142
McNichols, William, 249
Madrid, Rocky, 31
Maes Creek school, 222
Mal de ojo, 294–95
"Mananitas, Las," 266
Mann, Earl W., 9–10, 213(nn15, 18, 19), 215–16(nn38, 41); childhood and career of, 197–98; on discrimination and bigotry, 202–7, 216–17(n46); on moral character, 201–2; World War II columns of, 195–97, 199–200, 207–12, 217(n55)
Mann, Grace Wills, 198
"Marcha de Zacatecas" (Codina), 55
Mariachi, 62, 65
Mariachi Tigre, El, 260
Marriages, 84(n21); Chinese-White, 79–81; of El Cid's daughters, 52, 54; interracial, 79–81
Marro, Jose, 97
Martial law, Governor Johnson's, 123, 243, 244–48
Martinez, Antonio, 97
Martínez, Francisco "Kiko," 14, 365; arrest and trials of, 374–76; bomb plot accusations, 370–71, 373; legal activism of, 366–67, 368, 369
Martinez, Herman, 65

Martínez, José, 366
Martínez, Julius, 368
Martinez, Levi, 250
Martínez, Lorenzo, 259, 267–68
Martinez, Luis "Junior," murder of, 283–84, 289(n64), 361(n9), 369
Martínez, Maclovio, El Milagro de San Acacio narrative, 43–45
Martinez, Patsy, 65
Martínez, Pauline López de, 366
Martínez, Roberto, 63, 259
Martinez, Reyes, 349, 360(n2), 371, 373
Martínez Defense Committee, Francisco E., 374–75
Marwick, Arthur, 196
Mascots: Adams State College Indian, 15, 309–10, 314–17, 319–24; Indians as, 311–14, 324–25(n16)
Ma-si, 276, 286(n22)
Mata, Delfino J., 250
Matachines, 36
Maw, Herbert B., 181
Maximilian, Archduke, 60, 62
Memory, pictorial narratives of, 25–33
Mental health system: cultural competency in, 296–97, 306–7; cultural specialty services, 298–99; curanderismo in, 291, 293–96, 302–5; innovation in, 305–6
Merced, La, 30, 32, 33
Mershon, Nellie, 80
Mestiza/os, 233(n1); education of, 13, 219, 221–26, 235(n7); family, 226–27; higher education, 230–31; new, 262–63, 265–66
Mestizaje, 12, 325(n24), 331; at Adams State College, 315, 316, 317; in San Luis Valley, 46–47
Metropolitan State College, Black studies at, 381
Mexican American Legal Defense Fund (MALDEF), 368, 369
Mexican Americans (Latinos), 239, 241; Chicana/o movement, 349–50; discrimination against, 128–30; in Denver, 124, 135(fig.); gangs, 121, 125–28, 130–34, 136(n6); Governor Johnson's actions against, 244–48; racial status of, 122–23. *See also* Chicana/os
Mexican Revolution, 55, 240, 241

Mexicans, 1, 239, 278, 279, 287(n36); Governor Johnson's actions against, 245–48; immigration by, 240, 241; racism, 13, 122–24, 244–45
Mexico, 244, 341; land grants, 3–4
Meyer, S. A., 78
Migration: African American, 102–3, 141–42; Chicano and Mexican, 240, 241
Milagro de San Acacio, El (Lobato), 26–27, 29–30, 32
Military, 206, 215(n33); African Americans in, 196, 197, 198, 200, 201, 210, 217(n55); Japanese Americans in, 177, 178
Military Intelligence Service (MIS), 177
Miller, Roy Andrew, 189
Mining, 5; coal, 278–79
Mining camps, 102, 279
Minorities, at University of Colorado, 164–65
Minority rights: universities, 159–60; University of Colorado, 161–62, 164–65, 166–70
Mio Cid. See *Cantar de Mio Cid, El*
Miracles, foundational, 36–42
MIS. *See* Military Intelligence Service
Miscegenation: Chinese-White, 79–81; laws against, 71, 79
"Mi Viejo San Juan, En" (Estrada), 269
Mondragon, Ruth Martinez, 222, 223, 224, 225, 231–32, 235(n9)
Montano, Fr., 97
Montero, Rita, 354
Montour, Eddie, 280
Moon, Jim, 78
Moore, Isaac Edward, 142–43
Moors, influence of, 51–52
Mora-Espinosa, Deborah, 351
Moral character, morality: Mann on, 201–2, 207; postwar actions and, 211–12
Morely, Clarence, 146
Mountain Tract, 30, 31
Movimiento, El. *See* Chicana/o Movement
Murders, of Chicana/os, 283–84, 289(n64), 349, 357, 358, 361(n9), 367–69, 370
Music, 15, 270(nn3, 5); Chicana, 257–58, 259–60; corridos and rancheras, 62–63; European court influences, 60–61; Hispana/o, 264–66, 270(n4); La Entriega de los Novios, 54–59; Michelle Lobato's, 265–69; mariachi, 63–64; Native American, 59–60; new use of transitional styles, 65–67; Rio Grande Chicano/Hispano, 12, 51; traditional and folk, 261, 270–71(nn4, 6, 7, 10)
Musical instruments, 54, 59–60, 61, 63, 64(fig.)
Musso, Jewel "Jay" Medina, 221
Mutualistas (Sociedades Mutualistas), 13, 240–41, 243

NAACP, 200, 212(n1)
Narratives, pictorial, 25–33
Nash, Gerald D., 196
Nation, Delgado's concept of, 341–42
National Association of Folkloric Groups (ANGF), 65
National Chicano Anti-War Moratorium, 350
National Commission on Civil Disorders, 352
National Guard, Colorado border deployment of, 244–47
Nationalism, 240, 358; Chicano cultural, 356, 361(n7)
National Socialism, 196
Native Americans, 281, 288(n56); assimilation, 13, 276, 285(n6), 286(n24); and "Indian" mascots, 312–14, 320–21; music and dance, 59–60; in San Luis Valley, 92–93
Native Unity, 315, 316
Nativism, 123, 241, 243–44, 245
Navy Japanese Language School (JLS), 7, 175–76, 185, 191(n10); impacts of, 187–89; instructors in, 179–80, 181; public response to, 183–84; recruitment to, 177, 178, 192(n51)
Nazi Germany, persecution of Jews in, 163
Nebrija, Antonio de, 58
Negro Townsite and Land Company, 106
Negro World, The (newspaper), 154–55(n4)
Neighborhood Improvement Associations, 146
New Hispano Party, 243, 249–51
New Mexico, 98, 258; and Johnson's anti-Mexican stance, 246, 247–48; land rights, 350, 360–61(n5); Spanish settlement of, 90–91
Newsom, A. S., 106
Newspapers, Black-owned, 142–43, 144
Newton, James Quigg, 129

Nieto, Adriana, on Adams State mascot, 315, 316–17, 319, 322
Nisei: and JACL, 178–79; in U.S. military, 177, 190(n2)
Nolds, Mr. and Mrs. Harry E., 113
Noller, Ted, 113–14
Norlin, George, 161, 162, 163, 168, 170
Norris, Eunice, 112
North High School (Denver), 352
Nuánez, Eva, 57, 61
Nuevo Casas Grandes, Apaches in, 275

Oakley, Ronald, 115
Oil industry, 244
Okamoto, Allen, 187
Okamoto, Kathleen Kazuko, 180, 185
Okamoto, Takeo, 180
Operation Wetback, 252
Opium, 75, 76–77
Orality, of poetry, 340–43
Orden de Hijos de America, 243
Order of the Wolf, 126
Orientalism, representations of Chinese and, 70, 71, 74
Orientalism (Said), 71, 83(n8)
Oro Grande (N.M.), Ricardo Falcón murder at, 367–69
Otagiri, Chiyoko, 179, 185
Otagiri, James, 179, 180
Otagiri, Katherine, 179
Other, the, 70, 71, 74
Outlaw, Lucius, 382, 388

Padilla, Kenneth, 368, 369, 375
Page Act, 79
Pai, Lou, 32
Paisaje (San Rafael), 93; church at, 95(fig.), 96
Patriotism, 122, 207
Payne Chapel A.M.E. Church, 143
Pedagogy, 328, 331, 357; womanist/feminist, 347–48
Peoples Methodist Episcopal Church (Colorado Springs), 139, 143, 152, 154(n3)
Peoples' Methodist Presbyterian Church, James D. Brooks at, 147, 157(n41)
Pérez de Villagra, Gaspar, *Historia de la Nueva México*, 37
Persone, Salvadore, 97

Petriken, William L., 245
Philosophy, Africana, 383, 395(n9), 396–97(nn13, 15, 17), 398–99(n30)
Phyllis Wheatley (ship), 148
Pino, Tom, 249, 250
Place: knowledge of, 29–30; sense of, 24, 28–29, 32
Placitas, 87, 91, 98–99
Playing Indian (Deloria), 311–12
Poema. *See Cantar de Mio Cid, El*
Poetry, 15, 52, 331, 337; Chicano Movement, 327–28; as dialogue, 338–40; educational critique in, 329–30; public performance of, 340–43
Poets, role of, 335
Polak, Paul, 292; management style of, 300–302, 306; and Southwest Denver Community Health Center, 297–99
Polanski, Roman, *Chinatown*, 78–79
Police: and Chicano Movement, 369–70; and mail bomb investigation, 375–76
Politics, 77, 85(n30), 212(n1); African Americans and, 106–7, 198, 201, 204, 212(n5), 213(n15), 215(n36); Chicano, 249–51, 252, 253(n6); education and, 332–33; Mexican American, 239–40; poetry, 340–43
Politics of Education, The (Freire), 329, 343
Polk, Harry E., 162
Polkas, polkita, 62
Populations, minority, 7, 8, 11–12
Power relations, 332, 335, 340
Pratt, Mary Louise, *Imperial Eyes*, 337
Preston, Lizzie, 78
Princes of Carrión, 52, 54
Printz, William T., 80
Prison system, 123, 367
Propaganda, World War II, 208–9
Protests, against National Guard deployment, 247
Postwar planning, social equality and, 210–12
Practice of Everyday Life, The (Certeau), 336–37
Prostitution, Chinese, 7, 69–70, 71, 72–74, 75–77, 83–84(nn5, 13, 15, 21)
Psychiatry, and curanderismo, 295–96, 297
Pueblo: African Americans in, 8, 102; Chicanos in, 244, 262, 264; mestiza education in, 221, 222
Pueblo Revolt, 36, 38

INDEX

Race, 196, 224, 242, 317–18; stratification of, 13, 122–23
Racialization, 13, 16, 20(n34), 70; of Mexican Americans, 122–23
Racism, 5, 162, 279, 285(n2); against African Americans, 8, 140, 165–66, 206; against Chicanos, 244, 245; against Chinese, 5, 70, 75; crime and, 123–24; in Denver, 129–30, 132; Indian mascots, 309, 317, 318, 324–25(n16); against Japanese Americans, 176, 182, 185–86; against Latinos, 132, 224; at University of Colorado, 168–69; Vietnam War and, 282–83
Rancheras, 62–63
Ranchos de Taos, 91
Reagan, Ronald, 188, 352
Regis College, Spanish-American conference, 128
Relocation: of Japanese Americans, 6, 175–77, 180–81, 217(n59); of Mexicans, 278
Repatriation, 241, 243–44
Republican Party, 122, 250; African Americans and, 106, 204, 212(n5)
Resistance, 13, 16, 285(n10), 289(n60); Apache, 275–77; land rights, 32–33
Restaurants, segregated, 161, 170, 185, 200
Rio Grande, 91
Rivers, Joseph D. D., 195, 198, 199, 213(n19, 20), 216(n41)
Rivers, Richie Smith, 199
Rockefeller, John D., 279
Rodriguez, Jack, 370
Rodriguez, Santos, 370
Rogers, Joe, 114
Rolly, Miguel, 97
Romero, Neva, 349, 360(n2), 372
Roosevelt, Franklin D., 176, 178
Rosaldo, Renato, 263
Roybal, Walter, 316, 319, 322–23
Ruiz, Roman, 247
Rushing, Ben, 115

"Sabor a Mi" (Carillo), 269
Sadler brothers, 143
Said, Edward, *Orientalism*, 71, 83(n8)
Saints: assistance of, 36, 38–42, 45–46; crucified, 38–39; as mediators, 45–46
Salazar, Miquela Valdez, 221, 222, 228, 231, 232

Sam Sing Company, 72, 73, 74
San Acacio, 12; capilla in, 93–94; miracle of, 26–27, 29–30, 35–36, 38–42, 43–45, 46, 48(n4)
San Antonio (N.M.), 36
Sand Creek, 312
Sanderlin, Edward, 104
San Francisco (Conejos County), 93
Sangre de Cristo land grant, 10
San Luis, 23, 42, 62; Hispanos in, 11, 24–25; land grant, 30–32; pictorial narratives in, 25–33
San Luis Valley, 5, 15, 361(n9); Adams State College in, 309–10; churches in, 88, 93–98; Hispana/os in, 11, 12, 90, 261; settlements in, 46–47. *See also* San Acacio; San Luis
San Margarita (Conejos County), 93
Sano, Joe, 175, 189–90
Sano, Miya, 175, 180, 189–90; as nurse's aide, 185, 186
San Rafael (Paisaje), 93; church at, 95(fig.), 96
Santana and Santiago fiesta, 24
Santiago, visions of, 12, 35, 37, 38, 45
Santo Tomas church (Abiquiu), 94
Sawyers, G. Sterling, 148–49
Sayer, Judge, 73
Scarves, dance of, 59
Scholarship, borderlands, 2–3
Schools, 102, 143; Chicano, 331, 361(n6); mestizas in, 220, 221–22, 234(n5), 235(n7); Spanish speakers in, 227–30
Scott Methodist Church, 145
Segregation, 104–5, 242; in Boulder, 160, 161–62, 163, 165–66, 168–69; in Denver, 143, 145, 146, 200–201; U.S. military, 196, 215(n33)
Seidensticker, Edward, 188
Seis de Boulder, Los, 349, 357, 358, 360(n2), 372
Sense of place, 24; pictorial narratives of, 28–29
Seradell Sevilla, Narciso, "La Golondrina," 268
Servants, Utes as, 44–45
Settlements, 97; capillas in, 93–94; establishment of, 98–99; Spanish, 90–93
Sexuality, 7, 85(n25); Chinese, 69, 70, 76–77, 82, 84(n23)

Sexual terrorism, 356
Seymour, Robert, 103
Shafroth, John F., 106
Shorter A.M.E. Church, 145, 198, 199
Sieber, Al, 277, 287(n27)
Sierra, Justo, 341
Sierra, La (Lobato), 27–28; themes in, 30–33
Simmons, William Joseph, 107
Simpson, P. S., 142
Sing, Leo Latt, 80–81
Singers (trovadores), 257–58; Chicano, 259–60
"Si Tu Quisieras Amarme" (Lobato), 268
Smith, Thomas C., 189
Snyder, Stephen, 369
Social class, and education, 223–24
Social equality, 204, 208
Social justice, 329; Catholic Church, 259–60
Sociedades Mutualistas, 13, 240–41, 243
Sociedad Protección Mutualista de Trabajadores Unidos, 243
So Frane, 76
Soldiers, and zoot suiters, 126
Sones, 63, 68(n23)
Songs, 52, 68(n11); Bracero, 66–67; of La Entriega de los Novios, 55–59; Michelle Lobato's, 265–69
Sopris, John, 103
Souls of Black Folk, The (Du Bois), 385
Southwest Denver Community Mental Health Center, 14, 291, 292; and Centro de las Familias, 299–300, 302–5; management, 305–6; Polak as director of, 298–99, 300–302
Spain, Moorish and Arab influence, 51–52
Spanish, settlements, 90–91
Spanish American Alliance, 244
Spanish Americans, 246; cultural identity as, 240, 241, 243
Spanish caste system, 240
Spanish Land Grant (San Luis), use of, 27, 30–31
Spanish language, 264, 351; archaic, 57–58, 68(n26); in schools, 223, 227–30, 261–62
Stapleton, Benjamin, 129, 146
State Agricultural College (CSU), and Dearfield, 107
Stearns, Robert L., 164, 169, 170, 183, 186; community war work, 184–85

Stereotypes, anti-Chinese, 74–75, 81–82
Stories, memory, 25–33
Strikes, coal mine, 279
Stuart, Joseph H., 201
Students: bicultural, 328–29; Chicana/o Movement and, 350, 352, 353–58, 366–67
"Stupid America" (Delgado), 328, 338–39
"Suava patria, La" (López Velarde), 341
Suburbs, 285(nn3, 4); women's isolation in, 273–74
Sugar beet industry: Japanese labor on, 5; Mexican American labor, 122, 245, 246
Suzuki, Koshi, 179, 184
Suzuki, Mikio, 184
Swisher, Earl, 164, 169, 172(n15)

Talpa, 221, 229
Tanforan Assembly Center, 180
Taos, 62, 91
Taos Valley, 88; religious architecture in, 90, 91
Taylor, Jack, 28, 30, 31, 32
Taylor Ranch, 31, 32
Terán, Heriberto, 349, 360(n2), 371, 372
Termination Act, 274, 285(n7)
Tesoro Foundation Spanish Market, 62
Texans, at Colorado Chautauqua, 165–66
Theis, Frank G., 376
Thomas, J. M., 108
Thorpe, Charles, 80
Tiempo, El (newspaper), 249
Tierra Amarilla courthouse, 63, 360–61(n5)
Tingley, Clyde, 246, 247–48
Toler, Jerry, 115
Topaz Relocation Center, 179
Treaty of Guadalupe Hidalgo, 11
Trincheras Land Grant, 91
Trinidad, 243, 245, 279
Trovadores, 257–58
Trujillo, Lorenzo, 65, 271(n10)
Trujillo family, 93
Tularosa, 36
Turkey Creek (Trujillo Creek), 219, 221, 222, 229, 233(n3)
Turner, James, 382
Two-Wheeler Motorcycle Shop, mail bomb plot, 370–71, 375

INDEX

UFW. *See* United Farm Workers
UMAS. *See* United Mexican American Students
Underwood, Anna, 153
UNIA-ACL. *See* Universal Negro Improvement Association and African Communities League
Union Colony, 104
Unions, 5, 288(n46); coal mining, 279, 288(nn42, 43, 45)
United Farm Workers (UFW), 284, 351–52, 353
United Mexican American Students (UMAS), 354, 355, 357, 360(n2), 361(n8), 366–67
U.S. Naval Intelligence Service, Japanese Language School and, 177
U.S. Supreme Court, and Spanish Land Grant, 28, 30–31
Universal Negro Improvement Association (UNIA), 200–201
Universal Negro Improvement Association and African Communities League (UNIA-ACL), 139, 154–55(nn3, 4), 158(n58); leadership of, 152–53; Marcus Garvey and, 149–51; membership and activism in, 140, 146–49; promotion of, 151–52
University of Colorado, 380; Chicana/o activism in, 14, 366–37; Chicana/os at, 348–49, 359, 361(n8); Chicano Student Movement at, 350, 353–58; civil rights campaign, 7–8, 159, 160, 162–64, 166–70, 173(n28); desegregation at, 166–67; discrimination at, 161–62, 173(n22); Japanese Americans at, 179, 181; minorities at, 164–65; Navy Japanese Language School, 7, 175–76, 183–84, 187–88, 189, 190
University of Northern Colorado, 372; Black Studies Program, 380, 381
Urban sector: African Americans in, 8–9; Asian Americans in, 6–7; Native Americans in, 13–14
U.S.O., de facto segregation in, 201
Ussel, P. Gabriel, 97
Utah, Japanese Americans in, 181–82
Utes, Muache, 48(n2); attack on San Acacio, 26, 29–30, 35–36, 38, 39–41, 48(n4); and Hispanos, 12, 42, 46; as servants, 44–45
Ute wars, 42, 48(n2)

Vagrancy laws, 127
Valdes, Daniel T., 248–49
Valdez, Celedon, 97
Valdez, Crescencio, 93
Valdez, Julia, 28–29
Valdez, Magdalena Valdez, 222, 224
Valenzuela, Ismael, 65
Valles, Tammy, 370
Valley of Land Rights Council, 31, 32
Vargas, Orlinda de, 352
Valse de los Paños, 59
Vaquero, El (El Vaquerito), 62
Vasconcelos, José, 240
Vasquez, Enriqueta, 351, 352
Veatch, James, 78
Velasquez, Gloria, 351
Velazquez, Cecilio, 292
Velázquez, Consuelo, "Bésame Mucho," 269
Velazquez, Diana, 14; at Centro de las Familias, 298, 301–2, 303–4; as curandera, 292–97
Velazquez, Herman "Chito," 292–93
Vietnam War, 350; deaths in, 282–83
Vigil, Cleofes, 46, 48(n6); "Himno a la Nacioncita de la Sangre de Cristo," 46–47
Vigil, Ernesto, 131–32
Vigil, Joe, 320, 321
Vigil, Jose Miguel, 97
Vigil, Juan, 39, 40, 48(n3)
Vigil land grant, 10
Villa, Francisco "Pancho," 55
Violence: Chicana/o movement, 283–84, 356, 366; against Chinese, 5, 7; Latino gangs, 130, 131; police, 369–70; zoot-suit, 125–27
Violinists, 60, 61, 68(n20)
Virgen del Rosario, 36, 37, 38
Viva Kennedy clubs, 252
Voting rights, African American, 204
Voz del Nuevo Hispano, La (newspapers), 249

Wagoner, Henry O., 103
Wah Kee, 72
Walker, Richard, 148
Waller, John A., 162
Walsenburg, 223, 233(n2), 234(n5), 243
Waltzes (valses), 62, 68(n15)

Wang, Lingoh, 166
Ward, A. M., 106
Ward, M. D., 145
War propaganda, 208–9
War Relocation Authorities (WRA), 176–77, 178, 180
War work, Japanese American, 184–85
Water rights, Dearfield, 109
Watson, Hewetson, UNIA-ACL, 147, 148
Weddings, 52; La Entriega de los Novios in, 54–59
Weld County, 101, 107–8; agriculture in, 110–12. *See also* Dearfield
West, Cornel, 389
Westbrook, Joseph H. P., 108
West High School (Denver), 352
Western Federation of Miners, 240
Westerns, Chinese in, 74–75, 81–82, 84(n15)
Wheat production, Weld County, 112
White, George, 108, 113
Whittier, Judge, 73
"Willing and Unwilling Victims, The" (Delgado), 334
Willis, Lillian, 149
Wilson, Charles H., 188
Winner, Fred M., 375
Women, 71, 355; Chinese immigrant, 69–70, 75–76, 79, 82, 84(nn18, 21); Hispanic, 224–25; opportunities for, 273–74
Women's Rights Movement, 281–82
Woodward, Ralph, 264–65

Works Progress Administration, writing projects, 42
World War I: African Americans in, 197, 198, 212(n12); agricultural demand, 111–12; Tiburcio Girón in, 280, 288(n47)
World War II, 188, 251, 280; African Americans in, 9, 217(n55); and Dearfield, 112–13; Japanese Americans during, 5–6, 7, 176–80, 181–87, 190(n2); Mann's columns on, 195–97, 199–200, 207–12; Mexican Americans during, 124–28
World Youth Day, 260
WRA. *See* War Relocation Authorities
Wright, James G., 108
Writers, 330, 335

Yamada, Edwin, 180–81
Yamada, Ernest Kenichi, 180
Yaquis, curanderismo, 292–93
"Year of Indigenous People, The," 315–16
Yearwood, J. B., 148–49
"Yo Soy Joaquin" (Gonzales), 352, 361(n6)
Youth, 13, 148; in Latino gangs, 131–34; Mexican/Mexican American, 123–27
Youth Survey Committee (YSC), on delinquency, 123–24
Yumoto, Vickie, 180, 185

Zaldivar, Vicente de, 35, 37
Zampty, Charles, 149 157(n51), 158(n59)
Zoot-suiters, 125; in Denver, 126–28, 134
Zoot Suit Riots (L.A.), 125, 134

www.ingramcontent.com/pod-product-compliance
Lightning Source LLC
Chambersburg PA
CBHW020348080526
44584CB00014B/938